Politics in the Developing World

Politics in the Developing World

Second Edition

Edited by Peter Burnell and Vicky Randall

OXFORD

UNIVERSITY PRESS

OXFORD
UNIVERSITY PRESS

Great Clarendon Street, Oxford OX2 6DP

Oxford University Press is a department of the University of Oxford.
It furthers the University's objective of excellence in research, scholarship,
and education by publishing worldwide in

Oxford New York

Auckland Cape Town Dar es Salaam Hong Kong Karachi
Kuala Lumpur Madrid Melbourne Mexico City Nairobi
New Delhi Shanghai Taipei Toronto

With offices in

Argentina Austria Brazil Chile Czech Republic France Greece
Guatemala Hungary Italy Japan Poland Portugal Singapore
South Korea Switzerland Thailand Turkey Ukraine Vietnam

Oxford is a registered trade mark of Oxford University Press
in the UK and in certain other countries

Published in the United States
by Oxford University Press Inc., New York

First published 2005

This edition 2008

British Library Cataloguing in Publication Data

Data available

Library of Congress Cataloging in Publication Data

Politics in the developing world / edited by Peter Burnell and Vicky
Randall. — [2nd ed.]
     p. cm.
   ISBN-13: 978-0-19-929608-8
   1. Developing countries — Politics and government.   I. Burnell, Peter
J. II. Randall, Vicky.
   JF60.P675 2008
   320.9172′4 — dc22
                                                            2007033609

Typeset by Laserwords Private Limited, Chennai, India
Printed in Italy on acid-free paper by
L.E.G.O. S.p.A., Lavis (TN)

ISBN 978-0-19-929608-8

10 9 8 7 6 5 4 3

Preface

The editors were gratified by the general response to the first edition published in 2005, which gave encouragement to Oxford University Press to invite them to prepare a second edition. OUP organized substantial feedback on the first edition and the editors wish to thank all who took the trouble to offer comments. The revisions and improvements to the second edition reflect their suggestions to a not inconsiderable extent.

This revised and expanded second edition includes several newly commissioned chapters, ranging over the post-colonial legacy and how colonialism still exerts an influence today; 'politics from below' including such phenomena known as 'people power' and the 'alternative' politics of development; the securitization of politics and contemporary security issues in the developing world; and governance. The editors thank reviewers of the first edition for suggesting these and other additions. All the chapters from the first edition have been revised and include, among other things, fresh new and topical illustrative material and brand new pedagogic content too, extending to the sample questions and guides to further reading. Overall, increased prominence has been given to major themes whose importance has become increasingly apparent only in the last few years. These include new methodological approaches to studying politics in developing countries; the political effects of globalization; the wide-ranging consequences of the invasion of Iraq and the 'war on terror'; the significance of China's emergence as an economic superpower; and the turn towards more poverty-focused policies in development and international development cooperation. The selection of case studies offered in this second edition is also more compact than before, the accounts are brought right up to date and the most recently available data are cited in a fuller set of appendices. The grounds for choosing these cases in particular are clearly laid out.

Source Acknowledgements

The authors and publisher would like to thank the following for permission to reproduce copyright material:

Box 14.6 is an abbreviated version of 'The Democracy Template', reprinted by permission of the publisher from *Aiding Democracy Abroad: The Learning Curve*, Thomas Carothers (Washington DC, Carnegie Endowment for International Peace, 1999), www.ceip.org.

Chapter 13 by Martin Doornbos is a substantially rewritten version of his article which first appeared in *Development and Change* (Vol. 33, No. 5, Blackwell Publishing).

The following figure is reproduced by kind permission of World Bank: from *World Development Indicators 2003:* Figure 16.3, Inequality in selected countries.

The authors and publisher would also like to thank UNCTAD for data presented in Tables 3.1, 3.2, and 3.3; the World Bank for data presented in Tables 16.1, 16.2, 23b.1, 23b.2, and Box 20a.2; and the Indonesian Bureau of Statistics for data in Box 20a.2.

Guided Tour of the Textbook Features

This text is enriched with a range of learning tools to help you navigate the text material and reinforce your knowledge of politics in the developing world. This guided tour shows you how to get the most out of your textbook package.

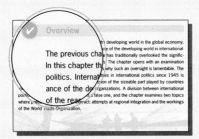

Overviews

Overviews at the beginning of every chapter set the scene for upcoming themes and issues to be discussed, and indicate the scope of coverage within each chapter topic.

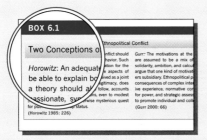

Boxes

A number of topics benefit from further explanation or exploration in a way that does not disrupt the flow of the main text. Throughout the book boxes provide you with extra information on particular topics to complement your understanding of the main chapter text.

Key Points

Each main chapter section ends with a set of Key Points that summarize the most important arguments developed within each chapter topic.

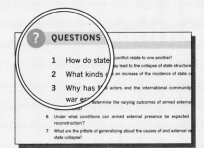

Questions

A set of carefully devised questions has been provided to help you assess your comprehension of core themes and may also be used as the basis of seminar discussion and coursework.

Further Reading

To take your learning further, reading lists have been provided as a guide to find out more about the issues raised within each chapter topic and to help you locate the key academic literature in the field.

Web Links

At the end of each chapter you will find an annotated summary of useful websites that will be instrumental in further research.

Glossary Terms

Key terms appear in colour in the text and are defined in a glossary at the end of the text, to aid you in exam revision.

Guided Tour of the Online Resource Centre

 www.oxfordtextbooks.co.uk/orc/burnell2e/

The Online Resource Centre that accompanies this book provides students with ready-to-use additional learning materials.

Peter Burnell

OVERVIEW
Zambia as a Case Study illustrates many themes showing how the politics of development interacts with developmental issues concerning the economy and society. Zambia, independent since 1964 when Britain relinquished power in Northern Rhodesia, is one of the world's least developed countries, situated at the confluence of central and southern Africa. Since 1991 the country has undergone political and economic change as a consequence of abandoning the one-party state of the Second Republic and introducing reforms to liberalize the economy. The results so far have been disappointing to many

Case Studies

Additional case studies have been included so that you can undertake more involved analyses of different scenarios.

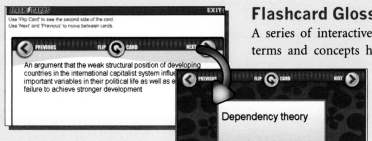

An argument that the weak structural position of developing countries in the international capitalist system influe important variables in their political life as well as e failure to achieve stronger development

Dependency theory

Flashcard Glossary

A series of interactive flashcards containing key terms and concepts have been provided to test your understanding of terminology.

Burnell & Randall: Politics in the Developing World 2e

Chapter 17

1. How effectively has a balance between environment and development been achieved on the internatio policy agenda?

2. How useful and practicable a concept is sustainable development?

3. What factors explain the different priorities that developing countries have attached to environmental is

Study Questions

A suite of study questions has been provided to encourage class debate and reinforce understanding of key chapter themes.

Chapter 11

www.transparency.org/
Website of Transparency International, offering important and interesting information on global corruption plus the annual Corruption Perception Index for all countries. You can use this site to navigate to the Global Corruption Report, annual

www.idd.bham.ac.uk/grc/index.htm
Website of the Governance Resource Centre at the University of Birmingham. It offers access to many papers, publications, and guidance concerning institutional aspects of states and governance in the developing world

www.foreignpolicy.com/story/cms.php?story=6264+2969
Website of the Foreign Policy journal's failed state index, with quantitative measures for state strength and weakness. Funded and published by the Carnegie Endowment for International Peace.

www.crisisstates.com/
Many publications and research projects on crisis states in the developing and transitional world, based at the London School of Economics and Political Science.

www.lse.ac.uk/depts/

Web Links

Additional annotated web links organized by chapter.

Brief Contents

Detailed Contents

List of Maps

List of Boxes

List of Tables

List of Acronyms and Abbreviations

ACP	Africa-Caribbean-Pacific states
AIDS	acquired immune deficiency syndrome
AKP	Justice and Development Party (Turkey)
ANC	African National Congress (South Africa)
AOSIS	Alliance of Small Island States
APRM	African Peer Review Mechanism
ARPCT	Alliance for the Restoration of Peace and Counter-Terrorism (Somalia)
ASEAN	Association of South-East Asian Nations
AU	African Union
BJP	Bharatiya Janata Party (India)
BSPP	Burma Socialist Programme Party
CACIF	Comité de Asociaciones Agrícolas, Comerciales, Industriales y Financieras (Guatemala)
CBO	community-based organization
CEDAW	Convention on the Elimination of All Forms of Discrimination against Women
CFCs	chlorofluorocarbons
CIS	Commonwealth of Independent States
CODESA	Convention for a Democratic South Africa
COSATU	Congress of Trade Unions (South Africa)
CTAs	clandestine transnational activities
DAC	Development Assistance Committee (of the Organisation for Economic Co-operation and Development)
DPKO	Department of Peacekeeping Operations (UN)
DPRK	Democratic People's Republic of Korea
DRC	Democratic Republic of the Congo (formerly Zaire)
DS	Development Studies (the discipline)
ECOSOC	Economic and Social Council (United Nations)
ECOWAS	Economic Community of West African States
ELN	National Liberation Army (Colombia)
EPB	Economic Planning Board (South Korea)
EZLN	Zapatista Army of National Liberation (Mexico)
FARC	Revolutionary Armed Forces of Colombia
FDI	foreign direct investment
FRETILIN	Revolutionary Front for the Independence of East Timor

FRG	Frente Republicano Guatemalteco (Guatemala)
FSC	Forestry Stewardship Council
G77	Group of 77 least developed countries
GAM	Aceh Freedom Movement (Indonesia)
GATT	General Agreement on Tariffs and Trade
GDP	Gross Domestic Product
GEF	Global Environment Facility
GMOs	genetically modified organisms
GNI	Gross National Income
GNP	Grand National Party (South Korea)
GNU	Government of National Unity (South Africa)
H5N1	avian influenza virus
HCI	heavy and chemical industries
HIP(I)C	Heavily Indebted Poor Countries (Initiative)
HIV	human immunodeficiency virus
IDEA	International Institute for Democracy and Electoral Assistance
IFE	Federal Electoral Institute (Mexico)
IFP	Inkatha Freedom Party (South Africa)
IMF	International Monetary Fund
IOC	international organized crime
IPU	Inter-Parliamentary Union
IR	International Relations (the discipline)
ISI	import-substituting industrialization
ISO	International Organization for Standardization
LFO	Legal Framework Order (Pakistan)
MAD	mutually assured destruction
MCA	Millennium Challenge Account (US government)
MDGs	Millennium Development Goals (of the United Nations)
MDP	Millennium Development Party (South Korea)
MERCOSUR	Southern Common Market (Latin America)
MINUGUA	Misión de las Naciones Unidas en Guatemala
MKSS	Mazdoor Kisan Shakti Sangathan (India)
MNCs	multinational corporations
MST	Movimento dos Trabalhadores Rurais Sem Terra (Landless Rural Workers, Movement) (Brazil)
NAFTA	North American Free Trade Agreement
NAM	Non-Aligned Movement
NATO	North Atlantic Treaty Organization
NDA	National Democratic Alliance (India)
NEPAD	New Economic Partnership for Africa's Development
NGO	non-governmental organization

NICs	newly industrialized countries (mainly East Asia)
NIE	new institutional economics
NLD	National League for Democracy (Myanmar)
NSSD	National Strategy for Sustainable Development
OAS	Organization of American States
OBCs	Other Backward Classes (India)
OECD	Organisation for Economic Co-operation and Development
OPEC	Organization of the Petroleum Exporting Countries
PAC	Pan Africanist Congress (South Africa)
PAN	National Action Party (Mexico)
PDP	People's Democratic Party (Nigeria)
PFN	Pentecostal Fellowship of Nigeria
POPs	persistent organic compounds
PPC	People's Plan Campaign (India)
PPP	Pakistan People's Party
PRD	Party of the Democratic Revolution (Mexico)
PRI	Institutional Revolutionary Party (Mexico)
PRN	National Revolutionary Party (Mexico)
PRSP	Poverty Reduction Strategy Process
ROK	Republic of Korea (South Korea)
RSS	Rashtriya Swayamsevak Sangh (India)
SACP	South African Communist Party
SALs	structural adjustment loans
SARS	Severe Acute Respiratory Syndrome
SAVAK	Organization for Intelligence and National Security (Iran)
SCO	Shanghai Co-operation Organization
SLORC	State Law and Order Restoration Committee (Myanmar)
TEPJF	Electoral Tribunal of the Judicial Power of the Federation (Mexico)
TERI	Energy and Resources Institute
TFG	Transitional Federal Government (Somalia)
TNCs	transnational corporations
TRC	Truth and Reconciliation Commission (South Africa)
UDF	United Democratic Front (South Africa)
UIC	Union of Islamic Courts (Somalia)
UN	United Nations
UNAIDS	Joint United Nations Programme on HIV/AIDS
UNCTAD	United Nations Conference on Trade and Development
UNDP	United Nations Development Programme
UNEP	United Nations Environment Programme
UNHCR	United Nations High Commissioner for Refugees
UNICEF	United Nations Children's Fund
UNIDO	United National Democratic Opposition (Philippines)

UNITA	National Union for Total Independence of Angola
UNMIT	United Nations Integrated Mission in Timor-Leste
UNMOGIP	United Nations Military Observer Group
UNTAET	United Nations Transitional Authority in East Timor
UP	Uttar Pradesh (India)
URNG	Unidad Revolucionaria Nacional Guatemalteca (Guatemala)
WGA	World Governance Assessment
WHO	World Health Organization
WMD	weapons of mass destruction
WSF	World Social Forum
WSSD	World Summit on Sustainable Development (2002)
WTO	World Trade Organization
WWF	World Wide Fund for Nature

About the Contributors

Tony Addison is Professor of Development Studies and Executive Director of the Brooks World Poverty Institute and Associate Director, Chronic Poverty Research Centre, University of Manchester, UK.

Edward Aspinall is a Fellow in the Department of Political and Social Change and the Research School of Pacific and Asian Studies, Australian National University, Canberra, Australia.

Peter Burnell is a Professor in the Department of Politics and International Studies, University of Warwick, UK.

James Chiriyankandath is a Principal Lecturer in the Department of Law, Governance, and International Relations, London Metropolitan University, UK.

Martin Doornbos is Emeritus Professor of Political Science at the Institute of Social Studies, The Hague, the Netherlands.

Peter Ferdinand is a Reader in the Department of Politics and International Studies, University of Warwick, UK.

Michael Freeman is a Research Professor in the Department of Government and was formerly Deputy Director of the Human Rights Centre, University of Essex, UK.

Jeff Haynes is a Professor in the Department of Law, Governance and International Relations, London Metropolitan University, UK.

Stephen Hobden is a Senior Lecturer in International Politics in the School of Social Sciences, Media and Cultural Studies, University of East London, UK.

Nicole Jackson is Associate Professor in the School for International Studies, Simon Fraser University, Vancouver, Canada.

Rob Jenkins is Professor of Political Science, Birkbeck College, University of London, UK.

Adrian Leftwich is a Senior Lecturer in the Department of Politics, University of York, UK.

Peter Newell is a Professor in the School of Development Studies, University of East Anglia, UK.

Marina Ottaway is Senior Associate in the Democracy and Rule of Law Project, of the Carnegie Endowment for International Peace, Washington DC, USA.

Jenny Pearce is Professor of Latin American Politics in the Department of Peace Studies, University of Bradford, UK.

David Pool is formerly a Lecturer in the Department of Government, University of Manchester, UK.

Vicky Randall is a Professor in the Department of Government, University of Essex, UK.

James R. Scarritt is Emeritus Professor in the Department of Political Science and Faculty Research Associate in the Institute of Behavioral Science at the University of Colorado at Boulder, USA.

Andreas Schedler is Professor of Political Science at the Department of Political Studies, Centro de Investigacion y Docencia Economicas (CIDE), Mexico City, Mexico.

Kurt Schock is Associate Professor of Sociology in the Department of Sociology and Anthropology, Rutgers University, Newark, USA.

Robert A. Schrire is a Professor and Chair of the Political Studies Department, University of Cape Town, South Africa.

Rachel Sieder is a Senior Lecturer in Latin American Politics, Institute of Latin American Studies, School of Advanced Studies, University of London, UK.

Brian Smith is Emeritus Professor of Politics, University of Dundee, and Visiting Professor of Politics, University of Exeter, UK.

Kathleen Staudt is Professor of Political Science, the University of Texas at El Paso, USA.

David Taylor is Vice Provost, Aga Khan University, Karachi, Pakistan.

Stephen Wright is Professor of Political Science, Northern Arizona University, Flagstaff, USA.

Introduction

PETER BURNELL AND VICKY RANDALL

→ **Chapter Contents**

- From Third World to Developing World
- Politics as Independent or Dependent Variable?
- Global Trends
- Organization of the Book

The aim of this book is to explore the changing nature of **politics** in the **developing world** in the early years of the twenty-first century. Both 'politics' and the 'developing world' are concepts which require further elaboration and which are discussed more fully below. By politics, we mean broadly activities associated with the process and institutions of government, or the state, but in the context of wider power relations and struggles. By the developing world, we are primarily referring to those regions which were formerly colonized by Western powers, have been late to industrialize, and sustain high levels of poverty: Africa, Asia, the Middle East, and Latin America including the Caribbean.

In our analysis of politics in the developing world, the complex and changing nexus between state and society has centre stage. This is because it is the reciprocal interaction of state and society and the influence that each one exerts on the other that most accounts for the distinctive character of developing countries' politics. Needless to say that influence varies in both degree and kind, over time, as between individual states and inside states. The book does not set out to present a case for saying the state is now marginal for the political analysis of developing countries. Nor does it argue that we must 'bring the state back in'. On the contrary, it recognizes that issues concerning the state have been, are, and will remain central to the political analysis, notwithstanding important developments—political, financial, economic, technological, and so on—at the sub-state, regional, and especially global levels that are reshaping the nature, size, role, and performance of individual states.

A book about politics in the developing world is not the same thing as a book about development per se, or development studies. Indeed, the book does not have as its main objective to give emphasis to the politics *of* development where that means the political economy of economic growth or of socio-economic change. Certainly there has been a trend in the study of development to comprehend development in an increasingly holistic sense—one that emphasizes its multifaceted nature and the interconnectedness of the various parts, of which politics provides one very important element. And key relationships between politics and society and between politics and the economy are both explored in the chapters in the book, but without any mission to demonstrate that politics is in some sense the 'master science' which unlocks all other subjects. Instead the consequences that development can have for politics in the developing countries are every bit as much a part of the analysis in this book as the implications that the politics have for development. So, although the book's primary focus is politics rather than development, we hope that its contents will also be of interest to anyone who is involved in development studies more generally.

A word is also needed explaining the geographical coverage of the book. As related below, the boundaries of the developing world are neither uncontentious nor unchanging. We have already suggested which regions have tended historically to be associated with it. However, this book's coverage, and especially the case studies, does not include all the possible candidates, primarily for pragmatic reasons. Thus countries like Cuba, Vietnam, and the rest that at one time claimed to be socialist, even Marxist–Leninist, are just as much part of the developing world as are countries that now defer to capitalism and have a form of political pluralism. They are, however, very much a dwindling band and new recruits now seem unlikely in the post-Soviet, post-cold war world, where the forces of globalization appear so hostile. They can hardly be considered very representative, and so do not feature among the case study chapters, where in any case one of the criteria governing the selection must be parsimony.

On the other hand, we have deferred to the conventional view that China, for all its developing world characteristics, is best left out of the analysis. We know this is not uncontroversial. But China is unique in many notable respects. Unlike so much of the developing world, China is not a straightforward 'post-colony'. As the accounts of developing world politics in Chapters 2 and 11 show, this point is highly significant to how we make sense of these countries' politics today. For the same reason, the developing country imperatives of state-building explored in Chapter 12 have not resonated as strongly or in the same way in China, although the Chinese state's transformation from the feudal era through the Maoist revolutionary years to its present-day configuration has of course been dramatic. And we should not forget there was an interruption of close on 50 years as Japanese occupation succeeded growing political fragmentation. Nevertheless, China is sufficiently large, complex, and important to warrant studying on its own. It offers a full dish. It would be foolish to pretend that enough space could be given to China here. That said, the new Online Resource Centre to the second edition of this book includes a case study of China, to help readers form their own opinions on these matters and offer guidance on further reading.

There are other parts of the world, beyond the regions traditionally included, that might now be considered to fall into this developing world category. Although no express reference is made in the book to those elements of the post-communist world, a handful of the new European and mostly Central Asian states that formerly belonged to the 'Second World' have certain characteristics long associated with the developing world. Some of them have come to acquire developing country status, as the Organisation for Economic Co-operation and Development's (OECD) Development Assistance Committee (DAC) has made countries like Albania, Bosnia-Herzegovina, Armenia, and Turkmenistan eligible for official development assistance. By comparison, the DAC styles the post-communist world's more advanced members 'countries in transition', entitled to compete only for a separate, much smaller category of support, called 'official aid'. However, as in the case of China, readers are free to apply the concepts and propositions in this book to an examination of all these other countries if they wish, just as area specialists seeking insights into those countries will find material here that has relevance for their own subject. After all, the growing interdependence of states and rise of trans-territorial and supranational issues, such as many of those that are embraced by what might be called the new security agenda, certainly do not respect national borders. The illicit trafficking in harmful narcotics is an example. The geopolitical unit of analysis that is most relevant to understanding the issues and possible solutions, then, can easily straddle different states only some of which have well-established developing country status. The regional constellation that brings together actors in former Soviet Central Asia and Afghanistan in the growing of opium for consumption within the region as well as much further afield is illustrative. Similarly there are specific regions and localities inside the more developed countries of the rich world that share certain 'southern' or 'Third World' characteristics, such as a significant degree of relative economic backwardness and associated deficiencies of social welfare or physical quality of life. In some cases, southern Italy for example, they show a seeming inability over many years to 'catch up', which again is reminiscent of parts of the developing world.

From Third World to Developing World

The developing world has been variously referred to as the Third World, the South, and the less developed countries, among other titles. The question of the meaningfulness of the Third World as an organizing concept has long been the subject of dispute no less than the term's precise definition or true origins. Successive rationales for marking out a distinct Third World associated this world with a stance of non-alignment towards the capitalist and communist superpowers; with post-colonial status; with dependence on Western capitalism; and with poverty and economic 'backwardness'. All together this was a confusing mélange of external as well as internal economic and political descriptors. Following the collapse of Soviet power, the disappearance of the 'Second World' served to hasten the decline of the 'Third World' as a category name. Here is not the place to revisit the history of the debates about a term, which by and large have now been brought to a conclusion. An abundant literature exists (Wolf-Phillips 1979; Berger 1994; Randall 2004). In keeping with the general trend, then, we have preferred to use the term 'developing world' for this book. But whatever term is favoured, there has also been a growing appreciation of the very considerable diversity to be found among and within those countries traditionally seen to come under its umbrella.

Notwithstanding what in many instances has been a shared colonial past, some of the differences have always been there, like the enormous range in demographic and territorial size. Just at the lower end of the scale, the distinction between 'small' and 'micro' states is an ongoing topic for debate. The total lies anywhere between 80 and 140 states, or at minimum around 40 per cent of all developing countries and territories. In contrast, in a regional context some of the larger developing countries now appear to be approaching almost superpower-like status, even while remaining vulnerable to major external shocks. Thus a state like India, a nuclear power with a population that exceeds one billion people, has very strong claims to be admitted to the permanent membership of the United Nations Security Council. Some people champion Nigeria's claims to be similarly represented, although compared to India Nigeria has been much less politically stable and its fortunes remain highly dependent on the international traded price of just one commodity, oil.

Similarly the developing world has always been noted for its considerable differences in terms of economic dynamism and technological progress, and recent decades have served only to make these contrasts more pronounced. Just as average incomes were in decline in many parts of Africa in the latter years of the twentieth century, so some of the so-called tiger economies in East Asia have become developed countries in all but name. Singapore, for instance, has one of the highest average incomes per head of any country in the world. It is no longer eligible for official development assistance by the DAC. Furthermore, in many parts of the developing world there are massive inequalities, including in some of the larger states such as South Africa and Brazil. The lifestyles enjoyed by growing numbers of an increasingly prosperous elite in developing countries such as India and in China too now compare favourably with average living standards in the more developed world. Inequality is explored further in Chapter 5.

Until the 1980s, despite the disparities in size and economic performance, it was possible to argue that most countries in the developing world had in common certain political traits. These included a tendency towards authoritarian rule, whether based on the military or a single ruling party, or severe instability and internal conflict, and endemic corruption. More recently political differences that were already there have become much more apparent. We are increasingly aware of the wide disparities in state strength and efficacy, or what the fashionable contemporary jargon calls governance. To a considerable extent this recognition owes to the growing incidence of state failure and

in the more extreme cases state collapse, of the kind discussed in Chapter 13. There are a much larger number of cases where simply the capabilities of the state appear to be weak or ineffective or are severely constrained. Corruption is widely prevalent. Doubts about the quality of governance right across the developing world, albeit with some notable exceptions, continue to suggest there are some marked political similarities among a substantial number of states. Likewise, in recent years the politics of ethnic and religious identity have been increasingly in evidence, as demonstrated in Chapters 6 and 7. Perceptions of these issues have been sharpened, perhaps, by our interest in the possible implications for regional and wider international security concerns, and by the connections with terrorist activities, international terrorism especially. But as the evidence shows, the problems have been much more visible in some developing regions or countries than others. In Latin America, in particular, ethnonationalism and religious conflict constitute only minor themes, although even there one of the more fascinating developments in recent years has been the growing and largely peaceful political mobilization of ethnic minorities and indigenous groups (Van Cott 2005). The politics of nonviolent action by social movements and 'people power' movements has gained attention in a number of Latin American countries, but as Chapter 10 discusses, can be found in other developing areas too.

In sum, we are increasingly conscious of the complexity and diversity of the developing world. Some common features among developing countries such as the colonial experience are now receding into history, which makes former practical manifestations of 'Third World solidarity' such as the Non-Aligned Movement harder to keep alive in their original form. What this means, however, is that the numerous differences within the developing world now appear in sharper relief, even as new ways of constructing shared interests vis-à-vis the rich 'developed' countries and new links forged by transnational networking across developing country societies proceed apace.

Politics as Independent or Dependent Variable?

Most people, still more so politics students, will have some idea of what is intended by the term 'politics'. Generally political scientists understand politics to refer to activities surrounding the process and institutions of government or the state and that is a focus we share in this book. However, there is another tradition, that some describe as 'sociological' that tends to identify politics with power relationships and structures, including but by no means confined to the state: they include, for instance, relationships between socio-economic classes or other kinds of social groups and between genders. When studying politics in the developing world, we believe it is particularly important to locate analysis of political processes in their narrower sense within the wider context of social relationships and conflicts. One of the themes and puzzles that pervades in this field is the relationship between the more formal aspects of political processes and institutions that may have been to some degree imposed or modelled on Western prototypes, and their 'informal' aspects. The latter can be very resilient, and may even be regarded as more authentic. For instance, to understand how political parties really work we need to consider not only formal organizational characteristics—rules, authorized decision-making bodies, membership, and so on—but informal hierarchies of power, such as those between patrons and clients, that operate within them. While this may have some relevance almost anywhere, it applies particularly strongly to political competition and party politics in much of Africa for instance.

Despite our insistence on the need to understand politics in this wider power context, this does not mean that we deny what is sometimes referred to as the autonomy of the political. That means the ability of politics to have independent and significant effects of its own. Thus any account of politics in the developing world that goes beyond the merely descriptive can have one or both of two objectives:

to make sense of the politics; to disclose what else the politics itself helps us to understand better. Succinctly, politics can be treated as *explanandum* or *explanans*, and possibly as both.

For some decades there was a large movement in political science to view politics as the dependent variable. Analysts sought to advance our understanding of politics and gain some predictive potential in regard to future political developments by rooting it in some 'more fundamental' aspects of the human condition, sometimes called structural 'conditions'. This was nowhere more evident than in the tendency to argue that the kind of political regime—namely the relationship between rulers and ruled, conventionally depicted somewhere along the continuum from a highly authoritarian to a more liberal democratic polity—is a product largely of economic circumstance. The level of economic achievement, the nature and pace of economic change, and the social consequences were all considered highly important. It was not only Marxists who subscribed to broadly this kind of view. But there were also others who sought to explain politics, especially in some parts of the developing world, more as an outcome of certain cultural conditions. This invoked a matrix of social divisions much richer and potentially more confusing than a simple class-based analysis would allow. These and other inclinations that view politics as contingent are still very much in evidence in contemporary theorizing about politics in the developing world, as several of the chapters in Parts One and Two of the book will show.

However, over recent decades in political science the larger study of comparative politics and area studies too have increased the weight given to the idea of politics as an independent variable, claiming in principle that politics matters: not only is it affected, but it too can have effects. Mair (1996) has characterized this as a shift from an emphasis on questioning what causes political systems to emerge, take shape, and possibly persist to questions about what outputs and outcomes result from the political processes and how well various political institutions perform. Making sense of the politics now goes beyond just explaining it. It extends also to an investigation of the impact of politics and its consequences. That includes the way current politics is affected by the political history of a country, for reasons that are explored in Chapter 2. It also means that such features as governance or public policy can be influenced, directly or indirectly, by yet other variables that are themselves intrinsically political even where they arise in society outside the formal embrace of the state. For instance, in an increasing number of places, including at the local or community-based level, various kind of non-state actors are coming to play a significant political role. Chapters 9 and 10 provide more detail.

This move to view politics as at least being semi-autonomous and not just the dependent variable coincides with the rise of new institutionalism in political studies. New institutionalism has been described in a seminal article by March and Olsen (1984: 747) as neither a theory nor a coherent critique of one but instead 'simply an argument that the organisation of political life makes a difference'.

The new institutionalism directs us to the study of political process and political design but not simply as outcomes or in terms of their contextual 'conditions'. This is not a completely new mood. As March and Olsen rightly say, historically, political science has emphasized the ways in which political behaviour is embedded in an institutional structure of norms, rules, expectations, and traditions that constrain the free play of individual will. The implications of this approach, as well as the idea that to comprehend politics at its fullest we should trace the meaning political forms and political choices have for a much larger set of issues of public concern, are explored in Parts Three and Four of the book especially. In doing so, the chapters provide a bridge to studying the larger phenomenon of human development. Here we take our cue from the United Nations Development Programme where it says its *Human Development Report 2002* is 'first and foremost about the idea that politics is as important to successful development as economics' (UNDP 2002: v). The UNDP's understanding is that human development, an idea that has grown in acceptance across a broad spectrum of development studies, aims to promote not simply higher material consumption but the freedom, well-being, and dignity of people everywhere.

Global Trends

Notwithstanding the increasing differentiation within the developing world, it is a fact that over the last twenty years or so there has also been a growing convergence. This is due to the presence of a number of major interconnected trends, political and economic, domestic and international. But these trends, far from reconfirming the more old-fashioned notions of the Third World, are instead ensuring that some of the most striking similarities emerging in the developing world today have a very

different character from the Third World of old. This point is well worth illustrating before moving on.

One such trend has comprised pressures from within and without the societies to adopt the so-called Washington consensus of the Bretton Woods institutions—the International Monetary Fund and World Bank—on economic policy and national economic management. These developments, which are first introduced here in Chapter 4, can be held responsible in part for a near universal movement in the direction of neo-liberalism and marketization. There is an ongoing shift from public ownership and the direct control of economic life by the state towards acceptance and encouragement of the idea of for-profit enterprise and a growing role for non-governmental development organizations. Although proceeding at a different pace in different places and experiencing widely varying degrees of success, the implications of such changes for politics generally and the state specifically are profound. Ultimately the same might be true of the more recent 'post-Washington consensus', which appears to give more priority than in previous decades to tackling poverty. However, it would be premature to conclude that the dominant thinking has changed radically—a proposition that not all commentators on development would endorse, anyway—and too early to judge the impact on what governments actually do, let alone assess the consequences. These matters are explored further in Chapters 15 and 16.

If *economic* liberalization is one prong of a growing convergence among developing countries then pressures towards *political* liberalization and democratization have been a second and, according to some accounts, symbiotically related development. Again, we should not exaggerate the amount of substantive change that has actually taken place. Indeed, after a time in the early 1990s when the third wave of democratization seemed to have unstoppable momentum and some observers talked about the 'end of history', far more cautious claims are now much in evidence. The reality is more confused and complex: authoritarian persistence in some places sits alongside evidence of democratic reversal in yet others. Many of the 'new democracies' are of questionable quality. Chapter 14 elaborates on these distinctions. Yet irrespective of how democratic or how well governed most developing countries really are, and how many countries possess genuine market economies, the pressure to engage with and struggles to adapt (or alternatively resist) economic liberalization and the goals of 'good' and democratic governance are ubiquitous. Such agendas are driven strongly by developed world institutions,

and as they came to be among the prime moving principles of the collective drama of countries from the 1980s on, the developing world began to look a very different place from the way the Third World was understood in previous decades.

But underpinning these and many other contemporary developments—such as the campaigns for gender equity (Chapter 8), the growing salience of 'new security' issues, the environmental concerns (Chapter 17), and international monitoring of human rights (Chapter 18)—there is the growing significance ascribed to globalization. Here globalization is understood at a minimum as 'the process of increasing interconnectedness between societies such that events in one part of the world more and more have effects on peoples and societies far away' (Baylis and Smith 2001: 7). Of course, the developing countries are touched unevenly and in different ways. This is made clear in Chapters 3, 4, and 15. But there is a good case for arguing that many of the so-called 'dependent countries' of the Third World now see their fortunes influenced increasingly by the forces of globalization. The influence may be direct, and positive or negative, or both. It can also work indirectly. Thus whereas Chapter 3 introduces the emergence of a global economy and its economic consequences for developing countries—which in turn can have political implications—Chapter 15 especially notes some of the more political, social, and cultural aspects of globalization that impinge directly on the state.

In purely economic terms, some countries are largely bystanders. They may share few of globalization's claimed benefits. Yet they still incur some 'collateral damage' in the shape of accidental and unintended costs, such as loss of world market share for their export products. Theorists of globalization tell us the sites of power are becoming more dispersed, and according to many, although not all, analysts power is leaking away from the state (see Chapter 15). Hardly any country seems immune from this tendency for its borders to be breached, as extra-national forces and outside institutions increasingly make close connections with domestic actors and influence events at levels of society below the central government and beyond the state. Yet there is compelling evidence to suggest that it is centres of power based in or run from North America, Western Europe, and Japan that remain dominant. In so far as state autonomy from external or supranational forces is vulnerable, the threats seem more real to countries in the developing world. That is an unwritten assumption in much of the international political economy literature on globalization, which on its own admission exhibits a bias towards studying the economically more developed parts of the world (see, for instance, Phillips 2005). This provides yet another ground for believing that treating the developing world as a distinct but not separate entity continues to make sense.

Thus while the old order summed up by First, Second, and Third Worlds has disappeared and the international system appears to be edging closer to a more diffuse, somewhat fragmented form of multi-level governance, developing world countries are different from their counterparts in the more affluent and powerful North. A contrasting claim is that in the post-communist era the world system of states has moved from bipolarity to unipolarity, given the United States' military hegemony, resurgent unilateralism, and, post-September 11, its far-reaching foreign political ambitions. This is highly significant for developing countries. If unipolarity *is* an accurate description of the new status quo, then it hardly offers an elevated reading of the developing world's own standing. China could be the one exception here, in as much as

it is increasingly being portrayed as well on the way to acquiring superpower status, by virtue of its demographic and territorial size, nuclear capability, permanent seat on the UN Security Council, and, now, enormous economic importance. Moreover, if there is some truth in claims that US foreign policy especially after 9/11 has caused widespread resentment, this has kindled a unifying anti-imperialist sentiment in parts of Asia, Latin America, and the Middle East. This reminds us once again of the more 'developed' world's role in constructing both image and reality of the 'developing' world. Clearly we should at all times remain self-aware and continue to question how we arrive at our understandings of these different societies, while at the same time being conscious of the influence that external perceptions and actions may exert upon them. That is but a modern sequel to the deep legacies that persist as a result of the historical experience of colonial rule. Moreover, these words of caution extend also to analytical frameworks, the explanatory theories, and, most especially, any normative propositions that we choose to employ. This conviction must be our starting point. As much is made clear in Chapter 1, on 'Analytical approaches'. We should be continually challenging ourselves to distinguish between, on the one side, what, how, and how far changes are taking place in politics in the developing world, and on the other side, any changing understandings that owe most to the lens through which outside observers view the developing countries, and the burning contemporary issues in and for the West and changing intellectual fashions there.

Organization of the Book

The book comprises five parts. Each part is introduced by its own brief survey of contents: short introductions can be read alongside this opening chapter. Part One on analytical approaches and

the global context should be read first. The aim of this part is to provide an introduction to general theoretical approaches, offering alternative ways of making sense of the politics in the developing world.

These simplifying devices enable us to bring some order to a great mass of facts. They are useful both for directing our inquiries and because they provide a lens or set of lenses through which to interpret the empirical information. They suggest explanations for what we find there. Ultimately, the point of theorizing is not simply to explain but to provide a gateway to prediction. And however tenuous are social science's claims to be able to predict with any confidence matters political, the book aims both to assess the present of developing countries in the light of the past and to identify the major political uncertainties facing them in the foreseeable future.

So it is entirely appropriate that immediately following the analytical overview there is a chapter on colonialism and post-coloniality, themes which still resonate in so many different ways. Then special attention is given to the international context. The glib conviction that now more than ever all of humanity resides in 'one world' betokens a very real fact of growing interconnectedness and interdependence, albeit highly asymmetric. There is increasing global economic integration at its core, but important political and other expressions of globalization should not be ignored. The different analytical approaches these chapters offer should not be viewed as entirely mutually exclusive. Each can quite plausibly have something valuable to offer at one and the same time, even though with shifting emphases when applied to the various country situations and different historical epochs. Readers must form their own judgements about which particular theoretical propositions offer most insight into particular issues and problems or the more general conditions of the politics of developing countries. It is not the book's aim to be prescriptive in this regard.

Parts Two and Three set out to illuminate the changing nature, role, and situation of the state in relation to key social variables within developing countries. The two parts are a mirror image of one another. Together they explore both how the politics reflects or is affected by social context, and how states specifically have responded to the challenges posed by society, and the social effects. Particular attention is given to what this means in terms of the changing use and distribution of political power among state institutions and other actors. Thus Part Two introduces the themes of inequality, ethnopolitics, and nationalism, religion, women and gender, civil society, and 'people power' movements, in that order. Part Three proceeds to theorize the state and examine processes of state-building and state collapse, before moving to democratization and the relevance of conditionality-based lending and globalization for the very contemporary issue of governance.

Part Four identifies major policy issues that confront to greater or lesser degree all developing countries. In general terms, the issues are not peculiar to the developing world but they do have a special resonance and their own character there. And although the issues also belong to the larger discourse on development per se, the chapters in Part Four aim to uncover why and how they become expressly political and to compare different political responses and their consequences both for politics and development. The issues range from economic development and the environment to human rights and security. Some of these could just as well have been introduced in earlier chapters of the book. This is because the presentations in Part Four do not concentrate purely on the *details* of policy, but rather out of necessity seek to locate the policies within the context of the policy *issues* as such. However, the more policy-oriented chapters are grouped together here because they are representative of major challenges for society and for government. Of course, where readers prefer to relate material from a chapter in Part Four more closely to the material that comes earlier in the book then there is no need to follow the chapters in strict numerical order.

Part Five aims to illustrate in some depth, or by what is sometimes called 'thick description', principal themes raised in the earlier parts, so complementing the use there of examples drawn from around the developing world. Each chapter in Part Five combines countries chosen both for their intrinsic value and for the contrasts they provide in relation to a larger theme. Attention has been given not simply to illustrating developing country problems and weaknesses but also to highlighting cases that offer a more positive experience. A deliberate aim of the book is to show the developing world as a place of hope, not a region of despair. All the main geographical regions are represented in Part Five. The particular selection of countries and the themes they illustrate is explained in more detail in the introduction to Part Five. Readers could usefully consult that introduction now. In total the country studies once again highlight the great diversity of experience in the developing world; they also demonstrate the benefit to be gained from a detailed historical knowledge of the individual cases. But although the cases differ not least in respect of their relative success or failure regarding development in the widest sense and politics specifically, none of them offers a simple or straightforward picture. The case studies should be read in conjunction with the appropriate chapter or chapters from the earlier parts, and are not intended to be read in isolation.

The editors' view is that a final chapter headed 'Conclusions' is not appropriate, in any case unmanageable, and probably undesirable. The chapters each contain their own summaries; such a large collected body of material is not easily reduced without making some arbitrary decisions; and, most importantly, readers should be encouraged to form their own conclusions. It is almost inevitable that readers will differ in terms of the themes, issues, and even the countries or regions they will most want to form conclusions about. And it is in the nature of the subject that there is no single right set of answers that the editors can distil. On the contrary, studying politics in the developing world is so fascinating precisely because it is such a rich field of inquiry and always has given rise to new rounds of ever more challenging questions.

So we finish here by posing some big overarching questions that you might want to keep in mind as you read the chapters. They can be used to help structure the sort of general debate that often takes place towards the end of a course or study programme similar to the ones for which this book is intended. In principle, the subject of each and every one of the chapters and all the case studies merit study as individual items. But for courses occupying a more limited number of weeks, one possibility is for lectures or presentations by tutors to concentrate on material drawn from Parts One, Two, Three, and Four, and for the allotted student reading preparatory to each week to include relevant case study material as well.

- Is politics in the developing world so very different from elsewhere that understanding it requires a distinct theoretical framework?

- Is there a theoretical framework adequate for the purpose of comprehending politics in all countries of the developing world, or should we call on some combination of different frameworks?

- Are the main political trends experienced by the developing world in recent decades summed up best by increasing diversity or, alternatively, growing convergence, and are these trends likely to continue in the future?

- In what political respects is the developing world truly developing, and in what respects are significant parts of it not developing or, even, travelling in the opposite direction?

- What grounds are there for being optimistic, or alternatively pessimistic, about the ability of states to resolve conflict and manage change peacefully in the developing world?

- Are the role of the state and nature of the public policy process fundamentally changing in the developing world, and if so, in what respects?

- What are the principal forces, domestic or global, creating incentives and pressures for change in state behaviour and the substance of public policy in the developing world?

- What lessons most relevant to other societies can be learned by studying politics in the developing world, and to which countries or groups of countries are they most relevant?

- Drawing on what you understand about politics in the developing world, does it make sense to include China in the countries that are studied as part of the developing world?

 WEB LINKS

● **www.id21.org** Information for Development in the 21st Century—a searchable online collection of short digests of the latest social and economic research studies across thirty key topics.

● **http://blds.ids.ac.uk** The British Library for Development Studies, claims to be Europe's largest research collection on social and economic change in developing countries.

● **www.eldis.org** Thousands of online documents, organizations, and messages containing development information.

● **www.gdnet.org** The site of the Global Development Network, a worldwide network of research and policy institutes aiming to generate research at the local level in developing countries and provide alternative perspectives to those originating in the more developed world.

PART 1

Approaches and Global Context

Politics in the developing world offers an enormously rich and fascinating canvas of material for investigation. If we are to make sense of what we find we must approach the subject in a structured and orderly way, with a clear sense of purpose. That means having an adequate framework, or frameworks, of analysis comprising appropriate concepts lucidly defined together with a set of coherent organizing propositions. Propositions are advanced to explain the political phenomena in terms of their relationship with one another and their relations with other variables—both the influencing factors and the factors that are themselves influenced by, and demonstrate the importance of, politics. This part of the book introduces analytical approaches to the study of politics in the developing world. It sets out to situate that politics within both an historical and an international and increasingly globalizing environment, as befits the increase of interdependence ('one world') and supraterritoriality that appear so distinctive of modern times.

This part has two aims: *first* to identify whether the 'developing world' is a sufficiently distinct entity to warrant its own theory, as we seek to comprehend its politics in the light of both the past and the present. It compares the main broad-gauge theoretical frameworks that at different times have been offered for just this very purpose. Have the theoretical approaches that were pioneered in the early years of decolonization and post-colonial rule now been overtaken and made redundant by the more recent critical perspectives offered by post-modern and post-structuralist thinking, Orientalism, and the like? Do some individual theories work better for some cases than for others?

The *second* aim is to show why and in what ways it is becoming increasingly difficult to understand or even just describe politics within developing countries without taking into account factors in the contemporary international system, as well as the influence of any precolonial and colonial legacies. These are the inter-state and supra-state influences that originate in economic, financial, diplomatic, cultural, and other forums. Many of these influences can penetrate state borders without having either express consent or tacit approval from government. They collaborate and collide with a variety of intra- and non-state actors, reaching far down to the sub-state and sub-national levels. At the same time developing countries also participate in and seek to influence regional networks and wider international organization, with varying degrees of success (Appendix 3 provides an illustrative list of regional inter-governmental organizations). Thus the place of 'south–south' relations should be compared with 'north–south' relations before and since the end of the cold war. This part helps us to consider the developing world's place within the global system as a whole: such questions as how far are developing country politics conditioned by powerful constraints and pressures originating outside? Are those pressures and constraints and their impact in any sense comparable to 'neo-colonialism' or, indeed, the imperialism of old? Is power in the developing world now being ceded not so much to governments in the rich world as to a more diffuse and less controllable multi-layered set of global commercial, financial, and economic forces and institutions? Or does their possession of a valuable resource like oil enable at least some countries such as Saudi Arabia or Venezuela to assert increasing political autonomy? Do they have certain distinguishing qualities as a result, compared with the more commonly experienced political trends and seemingly universalizing forces in the developing world? Readers are encouraged to read the introduction to Part Five and consult relevant case studies alongside the chapters in Part One.

1

Analytical Approaches to the Study of Politics in the Developing World

VICKY RANDALL

  Chapter Contents

- Introduction
- 'Politics' and the 'Developing World'
- Dominant Theoretical Approaches
- Current Approaches
- Strategies and Methods of Analysis
- Critical Perspectives
- Conclusion

  Overview

Two contrasting broad approaches long dominated political analysis of developing countries. One was a politics of **modernization** that gave rise to **political development** theory, then to revised versions of that approach which stressed the continuing if changing role of tradition, and the need for strong government, respectively. Second was a Marxist-inspired approach that gave rise to **dependency theory** and subsequently to neo-Marxist analysis that focused on the relative autonomy of the state. By the 1980s both approaches were running out of steam but were partially subsumed in **globalization theory** that emphasized the ongoing process, accelerated by developments in communications and the end of the cold war, of global economic integration and its cultural and political ramifications. Nowadays it is difficult to identify one distinct underlying approach to politics in the **developing world** as opposed to middle-range theories and a particular focus on the role of institutions more widely evident in contemporary political studies. In its absence certain key themes and agendas provide some degree of coherence. Similarly there is no distinctive set of methodological approaches but rather the application of approaches more generally available in the social sciences. Finally, whilst it is not possible to point to a systematic critique of prevailing or mainstream approaches, elements of a potential critique can be garnered from the literatures on orientalism and post-coloniality, and on post-development, and more generally from a post-structural perspective.

Introduction

This chapter provides an introduction to the main broad analytical approaches or frameworks of interpretation that have been employed in studying politics in the developing world. The 'developing world' is clearly a vast field, covering a great number of highly diverse political systems. To varying degrees those seeking to make sense of this field have felt a need for theories or frameworks of analysis to provide them with appropriate concepts or containers of information, and allow comparison and generalization across countries or regions. Some frameworks have been relatively modest or 'middle-range', but others have been much more ambitious in scope and claims. Moreover, despite aspirations to scientific objectivity and rigour, they have inevitably reflected the circumstances in which they were formulated—for instance political scientists' underlying values, domestic political pressures, and funding inducements, as well as perceived changes in the developing countries themselves. We all need to be aware of these approaches, and the surrounding debates, if we are to read the literature critically and form our own views.

We begin with what can be called the politics of modernization, emerging in the United States in the 1950s. This approach, including political development theory and its various 'revisions', operated from a mainstream, liberal, or, to its left critics, pro-capitalist perspective. The second and opposed approach, stemming from a critical, Marxist-inspired perspective, has taken the form first of dependency theory and then of a more state-focused Marxist approach. More recently the dominant, though by no means unchallenged, paradigm has been globalization theory, to some degree incorporating elements of both developmentalist and dependency perspectives. Globalization theory, however, has also served to problematize politics in the developing world as a coherent field, partly because it tends to undermine the premise of a distinct developing world. For this and other reasons, some have suggested that the field is currently in crisis. The latter part of this chapter considers how far a distinctive and coherent approach to politics in the developing world is still discernible in the present day, and also asks whether such an approach would be desirable.

'Politics' and the 'Developing World'

Before considering the three main approaches themselves, we need briefly to revisit the notions of 'developing world' on the one hand and 'politics' on the other. This is because to understand and assess the approaches we need some idea of what it is that such analysis is supposed to make intelligible or explain. As noted in the introduction, the term 'developing world' has conventionally referred to the predominantly post-colonial regions of Africa, Asia, Latin America and the Caribbean, and the Middle East, perceived to be poorer, less economically advanced, and less 'modern' than the developed world. 'Developing world' is preferred to 'Third World', because that latter term carries some particular historical connotations that make it especially problematic.

But even when we use the less problematic 'developing world', there have always been questions about what makes such a concept meaningful. What exactly are the defining features that these countries have in common and that distinguish them from the 'developed world', both generally and in terms of their politics? Are such common features more important than their differences? These questions, becoming more pressing as the differences have grown, have clear implications for both the need and the possibility for some kind of general approach to understanding and analysing them. More basically, some will want to question the assumptions underlying the notion of 'development'. From what to what are such countries supposed to be developing, and from whose perspective?

Similarly, 'politics' is a highly contested notion. Politics on one understanding is a kind of activity associated with the process of government, and in modern settings also linked with the 'public' sphere. On another understanding it is about 'power' relations and struggles, not necessarily confined to the process of government or restricted to the public domain. This volume takes the view that neither perspective on its own is sufficient, in general but particularly in a developing world context. Our preferred focus is on state–society relations and seeks to investigate both central governmental processes and power relations within society, and how they interact. One question to be asked about the various

approaches to studying politics in developing countries, surveyed below, is how far they enable us to do this.

A further important question concerns the autonomy of politics: how far is politics as a level or sphere of social life determined by economic and/or social/cultural dimensions of society and how far does it independently impact on those dimensions? Is the autonomy of politics itself variable? The different approaches to be considered all address this question, more or less explicitly, but arrive at very different conclusions.

> **KEY POINTS**
>
> - Awareness of the main analytical approaches enables students to be more critical.
>
> - The expression 'developing world' is preferable to 'Third World' but the diversity of countries included still makes generalization problematic.
>
> - Studying politics in developing countries means investigating both central government processes and power relations in society, and their interaction.
>
> - A further important question concerns the relative autonomy of politics.

Dominant Theoretical Approaches

It must be stressed that approaches to the study of politics in this vast swathe of the world's countries have in practice been extremely diverse. As discussed further below, most of the analytic and methodological toolkit of political science has been applied at one time or another. This includes statistical analysis, rational choice theory, and discourse theory. On the other hand, many country-based studies have not been explicitly theoretical at all.

Nonetheless it is possible to argue that most studies of politics in developing countries have been informed to some degree by one or other of three main dominant approaches—modernization theory, Marxism-inspired theory, and globalization theory. These approaches or theoretical frameworks themselves have not necessarily been directly or centrally concerned with politics; however, both modernization theory and dependency theory have helped at least to generate more specifically political approaches.

The politics of modernization

The emergence of the 'politics of modernization' approach reflected both changing international political circumstances and developments within social science and specifically within political science. Out of the Second World War a new world was born in which first two superpowers, the United States and the Soviet Union, confronted one another and, secondly, a process of decolonization was set in train leaving a succession of constitutionally independent states. Soon the two powers were vying for influence in these states. Within the United States, social scientists, and increasingly political scientists, were encouraged to study them.

For this, the field of comparative politics at that time was ill-equipped. It was (i) highly parochial—focused on a narrow range of Western countries, (ii) typically concerned with the legal and historical development of governing institutions, and (iii) not systematically comparative at all. Responding to this new challenge, comparative politics drew on two developments in the social sciences. First, the 'behavioural revolution' encouraged a more 'scientific' approach that sought to build general social theories and test them empirically. Second, especially in sociology but also in economics, interest was growing in tracing and modelling processes of 'modernization'. Sociology has from its inception been concerned with the impact of industrialization on pre-industrial society, and modernization theory was able to draw on the insights of its founding fathers, such as Max Weber (1864–1920). Whilst modernization theory took different forms, its underlying assumption was that the process of modernization experienced in the West provided a valuable guide to what to expect in the developing world.

Political development theory

In this context interest grew in elaborating a specific concept and theory of political development. The Committee of Comparative Politics, set up in 1954 by the American Research Council and chaired by Gabriel Almond, and the funds at its disposal, strongly influenced the emerging field of study. Whilst no one framework of analysis dominated, the one initially proposed and subsequently developed by Almond himself was both influential and highly representative.

Almond developed a structural-functional approach to compare politics in different countries and as a basis for his concept of political development. Drawing on Easton's (1965) systems theory and the 'structural-functionalism' of sociologist Talcott Parsons (1960), Almond's model distinguished a series of political functions and then examined their relationship with particular structures or institutions (see Box 1.1). There were four 'input' functions—political socialization (instilling attitudes towards the political system), political recruitment, and the 'articulation' and 'aggregation' of interests (demands). On the 'output' side three functions were identified—rule-making, rule implementation, and rule adjudication—and there was a more pervasive function of political communication.

Almond originally suggested that political development could be understood as the process through which these functions were increasingly associated with specialized structures—parties for interest aggregation, legislatures for rule-making, and so on—and with the emergence of modern styles of politics (achievement-based versus ascriptive and so forth). Later (1960) he identified five political system 'capabilities' (extractive, regulative, distributive, symbolic, and responsive), which were expected to grow as structures became more specialized and political styles more modern. These capabilities in turn would help the system to

BOX 1.1

Almond's Framework for Comparative Analysis

Political system

INPUT FUNCTIONS
and typical associated
structures

OUTPUT FUNCTIONS
and typical associated
structures

Political socialization
(family, schools,
religious bodies,
parties etc.)

Rule-making
(legislatures)

Political recruitment
(parties)

Rule implementation
(bureaucracies)

Interest articulation
(interest groups)

Rule adjudication
(judicial system)

Interest aggregation
(parties)

Political communication

Political systems develop *five capabilities*:

- extractive (drawing material and human resources
  from environment)

- regulative (exercising control over individual and
  group behaviour)

- distributive (allocation of different kinds of 'good' to
  social groups)

- symbolic (flow of effective symbols, e.g. flags,
  statues, ceremony)

- responsive (responsiveness of inputs to outputs)

These help them to face *four kinds of problem*:

- state-building (need to build structures to penetrate
  society)

- nation-building (need to build culture of loyalty and
  commitment)

- participation (pressure from groups to participate
  in decision-making)

- distribution (pressure for redistribution or welfare)

(Almond and Powell 1966)

deal with four main problems (some writers later referred to these as 'crises')—of state-building (with the focus on state structures), nation-building (focusing on cultural integration), participation, and distribution.

Almond's approach has been extensively and justly criticized, although it must be said that political scientists continue to use many of the concepts he developed, for instance state-building (see Chapter 12) and nation-building. It was argued that his political functions drew too heavily from American political experience, that his scheme was unilinear (assuming one general direction of change), teleological (holding out the goal of a modern, most of the time a liberal-democratic, polity), and ethnocentric. Similar criticisms were made of other attempts to conceptualize political development, with the added observation that they were excessively diverse, demonstrating a lack of consensus on what political development actually was (Pye 1966).

Political development theory, in this form, was in decline by the late 1960s, not least because supporting funding was drying up. But it has not entirely disappeared, and indeed one can argue that many of its characteristic themes have been taken up in the literature emerging from the 1980s concerning democratization and governance. Before leaving political development theory, though, two further developments should be noted.

Modernization revisionism

One strand of criticism of political development theory—modernization revisionism—centred on its oversimplified notions of tradition, modernity, and their interrelationship. Taking up arguments voiced by social anthropologists against modernization theory, some political scientists questioned what they perceived as an assumption that political modernization would eliminate 'traditional' elements of politics such as caste and ethnicity (the topic of religion was largely ignored until the 1980s—see Chapter 7). Instead they suggested that aspects of political modernization could positively invigorate these traditional elements, albeit in a changed form, and also that these elements would invariably influence in some measure the form and pace of political change.

This perspective also drew attention to the role of patron–client relationships. In their 'traditional' form, local notables, typically landowners, acted as patrons to their dependent clients, typically peasants, in relationships that were personalized, clearly unequal but framed in terms of reciprocity and affection. With greater 'modernization' and extension of state and market into the 'periphery', a modified kind of relationship emerged between peasant/clients and local 'brokers' who could mediate their dealings with the centre. But at the centre, emerging, seemingly modern political institutions—political parties and bureaucracies—also often operated on the basis of informal but powerful patron–client relationships, which moreover often linked into those at the periphery. This insight into the realities of patronage and clientelism was extremely valuable and has continuing relevance (see Box 1.2). Indeed, with the more recent emphasis on the role of political institutions, discussed further below, there has been renewed interest in these relationships, as part of the wider question of the relationship between formal and informal processes within institutions. Despite further criticisms that have been made of modernization revisionism in its turn, this perspective has greatly enhanced our understanding of political processes in the developing world.

BOX 1.2

Patron–Client Relations (Selected Quotations)

An anthropological account of a traditional patron–client relationship between landlord and sharecropper:

A peasant might approach the landlord to ask a favour, perhaps a loan of money or help in some trouble with the law, or the landlord might offer his aid knowing of a problem. If the favour were granted or accepted, further favours were likely to be asked or offered at some later time. The peasant would reciprocate—at a time and in a context different from that of the acceptance of the favour in order to de-emphasize the material self-interest of the reciprocative action—by bringing the landlord especially choice offerings from the farm produce or by sending some members of the peasant family to perform services in the landlord's home, or refraining from cheating the landlord, or merely by speaking well of him in public and professing devotion to him.

(Silverman 1977: 296)

Patron–client relationships in Mexican party politics:

Given PRI monopolization of public office, for much of the post-revolutionary period the most important actors in the competition for elected and appointed positions have been political *camarillas* within the ruling elite. Camarillas are vertical groupings of patron–client relationships, linked at the top of the pyramid to the incumbent president. These networks are assembled by individual politicians and bureaucrats over a long period of time and reflect the alliance-building skill and family connections of the patron at the apex.

(Craig and Cornelius 1995: 259–60)

Neopatrimonialism in Africa:

The institutional hallmark of politics in the ancient regimes of postcolonial Africa was neopatrimonialism...Neopatrimonial strongmen all relied on the award of personal favours. Within the state, these favours typically took the form of public sector jobs; within society, the distribution of public resources through licences, contracts and projects. In return for material rewards, clients mobilized political support and referred all decisions upward in mark of loyalty to patrons. This happened at every level; at the top, the ruler's faithful political aristocracy was rewarded with prebendal control of public offices, monopoly rents, and the possibility of creating its own clientelist networks.

(Bratton and Van de Walle 1997: 61, 65–6)

Politics of order

There is some disagreement as to how far the second development, referred to here as the politics of order thesis, was essentially part of the political development approach or represented a break with it. On the one hand, critics on the left have seen it as informed by the same underlying concern to promote forms of politics compatible with capitalist interests: in Cammack's words (1997: 13) 'the project at the heart of political development theory was the establishment across the developing world of stable capitalist regimes'. Even Almond himself has retrospectively argued for continuity (1987), claiming that much of the scepticism and pessimism to be found in the strong government perspective existed within political development theory from the start. On the other, its leading exponent, Samuel Huntington, launched a scathing attack on political development theory (1971) for its unrealistic optimism, suggesting that rather than political development it might be more relevant to talk about political decay.

Huntington criticized what he saw as a mistaken assumption in political development theory that in developing societies, economic growth would lead to social change (greater social pluralism, higher literacy rates, and so on) supportive of liberal democracy. Instead, rapid economic growth from low initial levels could be profoundly destabilizing, generating social dislocation and frustration that could convert into excessive pressures on fragile political institutions. In this context he maintained that what mattered was not what form of government existed (whether democratic or communist) but the degree of government. Huntington's search for the sources of strong government in developing societies led him to reassess the political role of the military, arguing that military rule could provide stability and direction in countries at an early stage of development, although he saw strong ruling political parties, whether in one-party or multi-party systems, as the best means of providing legitimacy and coherence for government.

Critics charged Huntington and others preoccupied with the politics of order and strong government with being apologists for authoritarian rule and inherently conservative, and for projecting domestic US concerns about increasing political instability (student and black protest; opposition to the Vietnam War). But it must also be said that this perspective injected a welcome dose of realism into the discussion; political development on Almond-type lines was just not happening. Secondly, it drew attention to the ability of political institutions not just to reflect economic and social development but themselves to make an active difference, that is, to the 'relative autonomy of the political'.

Marxist-inspired approaches

The second main category of approaches to be examined stems from a broadly Marxist perspective. As such, it has opposed the politics of modernization school which it sees as driven by bourgeois or capitalist interests, and has stressed the determining role of processes of economic production and/or exchange and the social class relationships embedded in them. In fact, dependency theory, which emerged in the late 1960s, was primarily concerned to refute models of economic development and also modernization theory; its implications for politics, at least in the narrower governmental sense, were almost incidental, although it had considerable impact on the study of politics in the developing world.

One main reason was that it drew attention to a serious shortcoming of all forms of political development theory: their near total neglect of the international context and implied assumption that politics in developing countries was shaped by purely domestic forces. Dependency theory originated in South America and reflected that continent's experience but was quickly applied to other parts of the developing world. It has taken numerous forms but will be briefly illustrated here through the arguments of a leading exponent, Gunder Frank (see also Chapters 2 and 4).

Frank (1969) maintained that the developing world had been increasingly incorporated into the capitalist world economy from the sixteenth century onwards. In fact, development of the developed world (known as the metropolis or core) was premised upon 'underdevelopment' of the developing world (known as satellite economies or the periphery); development and underdevelopment were two sides of the same coin. Despite formal political independence, former colonies remained essentially dependent because the metropolis was able to extract most of their economic surplus through different kinds of monopoly. Even when such economies appeared to be developing, this was only dependent and distorted development. Frank argued that the only way a satellite economy could end this dependence was to drastically reduce ties with the metropolis; later he recognized that even this was not really an option.

Whilst for a time dependency theory was extremely influential, it was also increasingly and justly criticized for the crude generalization and determinism of its economic analysis. Not all versions were quite as deterministic as Frank's. Wallerstein recognized a 'semi-periphery' of countries like the East Asian 'tigers' which over time had been able to improve their position within the overall 'world system', and by their example offered others on the periphery the hope of doing so too (Wallerstein 1979). Cardoso (1973) used the case of Brazil to argue that there could be meaningful 'associated dependent development'. By the 1980s, because of its weakness as economic theory but also because of the growing ascendancy of neo-liberal economic doctrine and developments in the world economy that appeared to contradict it, dependency theory was losing currency, although ironically the emerging 'debt crisis' of that same decade and imposition of structural adjustment requirements has seemed one of its best illustrations.

What did dependency theory have to say about politics in developing countries? Frank tended to minimize the independent effects of politics. He argued that both the state and the national political elite in such countries were identified with the 'comprador' economic class which served as the local agent of metropolitan capital and

consequently had a vested interest in the status quo. The only real possibility of change would be a revolution of those at the end of the chain of exploitation—the peasantry and urban poor—who had nothing to lose. Short of that, the different forms of politics, contests between political parties and so forth, had little significance. Again there were some variations in this position. Wallerstein had more to say about politics and a less reductionist view of the state but still ultimately saw strong states as a feature of the developed world and reinforcing capitalist interests. Even more exceptional were Cardoso and Faletto (1979), who used a comparison of Argentina and Brazil, two countries where 'associated dependent development' had been possible, to develop a complex political analysis. This showed two things. First, politics was not simply about external processes of domination but also involved national processes of reconciling and incorporating newly mobilized social groups. Second, the actual content of domestic politics differed from one developing country to another, reflecting differing resource bases and levels of foreign intervention.

With the possible exception of Cardoso and Faletto, dependency theory shed little direct light on the political process as such within developing countries (Smith 1979). Its real contributions were to insist on the intimate link between politics and economics, which had been largely neglected in the politics of modernization literature, and to demonstrate that the domestic politics of developing countries was incomprehensible without reference to their position within the world capitalist system.

Neo-Marxism rediscovers politics

Despite its Marxist associations, dependency theory had many neo-Marxist critics. In an argument paralleling modernization revisionists' criticism of modernization theory, they rejected its assumption that capitalism wiped out pre-capitalist forms. This view, they argued, was based on falsely equating capitalism with the market, rather than seeing it as a system of production. In fact capitalism as a dominant 'mode of production' could interact or 'articulate' with pre-capitalist modes. This further implied that different 'social formations' or countries on the periphery could have very different social systems (see Foster-Carter 1978).

At a more directly political level, neo-Marxist interest in developing societies was also stimulated by hopes that the socialist revolution that had failed to materialize in the West would begin there instead. Such hopes were raised by a 'third wave' of revolutionary developments (following a first wave centred on China, and a second wave from the late 1950s including Cuba and Algeria). The third wave from the late 1960s included communist victories in Vietnam, Cambodia, and Laos, revolution in Ethiopia, overthrow of Portuguese regimes in Africa, and revolution in Nicaragua (Cammack 1997). For these reasons neo-Marxists engaged in a much more detailed and rigorous analysis of social structure which was in some sense aimed at assessing the eligibility of different social categories—peasants, the lumpenproletariat (the urban poor who were not regular wage-earners), and so on—to inherit the role of revolutionary vanguard originally attributed to the industrial working class. As with 'modernization revisionism' this generated much valuable, careful research into what developing societies were actually like, although the appropriateness of the Marxist categories of social analysis imposed on them was often questionable.

As a corollary of this less determinist view of politics, there was a new interest in what Marxists typically referred to as the 'post-colonial state'. Marx himself generally depicted the state as a simple instrument of class domination—in the famous words of the *Communist Manifesto* (1872) 'The executive of the modern state is but a committee for managing the common affairs of the whole bourgeoisie.' But his writings sometimes alluded to a second possibility, as in France during the second empire under Louis Napoleon, when the weakness or divisions of the bourgeoisie allowed an authoritarian state to emerge which was 'relatively autonomous' from any particular social class. This notion was taken further by neo-Marxists

such as Gramsci (1891–1937) and more recently Poulantzas (1936–1979) analysing capitalist states in the West, but was also subsequently seized on to explore the relationship between the state and social classes in post-colonial societies. Alavi (1979), for instance, argued with particular reference to Pakistan, that the post-colonial state enjoyed a high degree of autonomy. This was first because it had to mediate between no fewer than three ruling classes but second because it had inherited a colonial state apparatus that was 'overdeveloped' in relation to society because its original role was holding down a subject people (others later questioned whether the post-colonial state in Africa could be described as overdeveloped, however). With reference to some African countries, there were also debates about whether the state itself could give rise to a new ruling class.

Globalization theory

By the early 1980s, and despite their diametrically opposed starting points, it is possible to argue that the lines of thought evolving out of early political development theory, on the one hand, and dependency theory, on the other, were converging around a reappreciation of the independent importance of 'the political' and an interest in strong government and/or the state. But both these lines of thought were also tending to run out of steam. Although strong government arguments gave the politics of modernization perspective a seeming new lease of life and, Higgott (1983) suggests, such arguments persisted into the 1980s in the guise of a spate of public policy studies, this whole approach remained vulnerable to the charge of insufficient attention to the economic and international context. The Marxist-inspired approach never in any case enjoyed levels of research funding comparable with the more mainstream modernization approach; and if dependency theory was increasingly challenged by the experience of oil-producing states in the Gulf, newly industrializing countries (NICs), and so forth, by the mid-1980s the neo-Marxist focus on socialist revolution in turn appeared increasingly anachronistic.

Reflecting these changes in the global environment, by the 1990s a new 'macro' approach was emerging, globalization theory, that tended both to absorb and displace the previous two (for a valuable overview see McGrew 1992). Globalization theory (see Chapters 3 and 15) should more properly be referred to as globalization theories, since it takes many different forms. As with the previous two approaches, it can also often seem closer to an ideology or policy strategy than a theoretical framework. Globalization theory focuses on a process of accelerated communication and economic integration which transcends national boundaries and increasingly incorporates all parts of the world into a single social system. Although this process is often seen as originating in the distant past, there is general agreement that it accelerated in particular from the 1970s, spurred by developments in transport and communications and subsequently by the collapse of the Soviet bloc and end of the cold war.

Probably the most important dimension of this process is economic, with particular attention paid to developments in global trade, foreign direct investment, and finance (see Chapter 3). Associated with these economic trends, however, has been a significant cultural dimension of globalization that is increasing cultural awareness and interaction across national boundaries. Central to this process has been the remarkable development and expansion of information technology and the new electronic mass media, enormously extending the scope and immediacy of communication. The consequences of this process are undoubtedly complex and contentious. Despite the emergence of powerful media industries in a number of developing countries such as India, Brazil, and Mexico, it is questionable just how truly 'global', in the sense of multi-directional, cultural communications have yet become. For writers like Sklair (1991: 41) the predominance of US-based media conglomerates has meant the diffusion of images and lifestyles that promote the 'culture-ideology of consumerism'. By the same token, however, the perceived threat

of cultural globalization has prompted complex counter-trends, including reassertion of local and national cultural identities (on religious identity see Chapter 7).

Different forms of globalization theory emphasize different aspects—economic, cultural, and so on. They differ in what they understand to be the prime moving mechanism of the globalization process: some see it as driven by the underlying logic of unfolding capitalism, others as primarily a consequence of developments in communications, others as a combination of factors. Some accounts, echoing modernization theory, are essentially optimistic: they stress, for instance, the extent to which a globalizing economy, in which capital is increasingly mobile, hugely extends opportunities for investment and employment for those who are enterprising and adaptable. Others, echoing the mistrust and many of the arguments of dependency theory, are pessimistic; they depict an increasingly unfettered global capitalism, ruthlessly exploiting people and resources (such themes have of course been taken up by the so-called 'anti-globalization' movement).

Although the voluminous literature on globalization has relatively little directly to say about politics in the developing world, its implications are far-reaching. First, it suggests changes in the character of politics as a whole. While it would be premature to talk about a process of political globalization comparable with what is claimed in the economic and cultural spheres, one can point to a series of developments that incline that way, including the increasing perceived urgency of a number of issues—such as global warming, refugee flows, terrorism—whose origin and solution transcend national borders; the proliferation of international regulatory organizations, and non-governmental organizations; and the growth of transnational social movements.

At the same time, globalization theory emphasizes ways in which the nation-state is losing autonomy. It is increasingly difficult for the individual state to control the flow of information across its borders or to protect its people from global security threats. Likewise, globalizing trends have greatly reduced its economic options, for instance, its ability to fend off the consequences of economic upheaval elsewhere, such as the 1997 East Asia financial crisis, or to successfully promote 'Keynesian' economic policies, to enhance welfare and protect employment, when these run counter to the logic of the global economy. With reduced autonomy comes reduction in the state's perceived competence and accordingly in its legitimacy. It comes under increasing pressure from within, as well as without, contributing to a process of 'hollowing out' the state. Critics of the globalization thesis have argued that this greatly overstates the threat posed to the nation-state, pointing out, for example, that many states, including the East Asian NICs, have actively promoted and benefited from the process of economic globalization, and suggesting that states may be able to invoke or harness nationalist reaction to globalizing pressures as an alternative source of legitimacy, as in India. However, these objections seem less relevant for many of the poorer, smaller developing countries. Clapham (2002: 785) suggests that in such countries 'the logic of incorporation into the modern global system . . . has undermined the state's coercive capabilities, weakened its legitimacy and subverted its capacity to manage the inevitable engagement with the global economy'.

But globalization theory also creates difficulties for the notion of a distinct developing world. Even if we talk about a developing world rather than a Third World and are careful about which countries we include or exclude, this still implies a distinct geographic entity. However, globalization theorists like Berger argue that if we want to retain the idea of a third or developing world, this should be conceived of in sociological rather than geographic terms. The ongoing process of economic globalization means that economically based social classes are increasingly transnational or global in span. So, on this analysis, dominant

classes in the developing world are more oriented, economically and culturally, to Western capitalist centres, where 'they have their bank accounts, maintain business links, own homes and send their children to school', than to their own countries (Berger 1994: 268). On the other hand, countries in the developed world, not least the United States, each have their own underclass (or 'Third' or developing world), even if there are few signs that such underclasses are coming together at a global level.

Overall, it is difficult to assess the globalization perspective as a framework for understanding politics in the developing world, because it takes such a variety of forms and reflects such a range of ideological positions, extending from a messianic optimism that echoes the crassest forms of modernization theory to doom-laden warnings that come close to the claustrophobic determinism of unmodified dependency theory. However, arguably even the left-wing version of globalization theory goes much further than dependency theory in recognizing the *inter*-dependence of developed and developing economies. Globalization theory is much more open-ended than dependency theory; ultimately it envisages an integrated global economy but in the shorter term acknowledges developments are unpredictable and could include increasing differentiation between beneficiaries and losers. Perhaps the theory's most valuable contribution to understanding politics in the developing world is that, like dependency theory, it emphasizes the impact of global processes. But in other ways it poses problems for this field of study. First, it calls into question the concept of the 'developing world' as a geographically distinct entity. Second, whilst it does not discount the political level, it tends to depict economic and/or technological change as driving cultural and political change and thereby to downplay the importance of the independent effects or autonomy of the 'political' and certainly of the state.

Current Approaches

It is more difficult to characterize the study of politics in the developing world today. The main emerging trends will become clearer in retrospect but some preliminary comments are in order.

A state of 'disarray'?

Both modernization-based approaches and Marxist-inspired approaches were found increasingly wanting by the 1980s. Although globalization theory incorporates significant elements of both, it too tends to undermine the rationale for studying politics in the developing world as a distinct field. Moreover, globalization theory reflects changes in the real world, including increasing differentiation amongst countries of the 'developing world', which pose further problems for meaningful generalization.

These developments within the field have coincided with a wider disillusionment with attempts at grand theory-building in the social sciences. (Globalization theory may well seem an obvious exception to this aversion, but it has been attacked precisely for its sweeping generalizations and also it nonetheless contrives to be extraordinarily open-ended and flexible.) One general school of thinking, originating in linguistics and philosophy, that has contributed to and helped to articulate such misgivings has been post-structuralism. The approach adopted by post-structuralists, discussed further below, questions the epistemological basis and claims of all the great theoretical approaches or 'meta-narratives' such as liberalism, Marxism, or indeed 'modernization'.

There has also been a steady growth of information about politics in different developing countries since the first attempts at generalization in the 1950s. Western governments, above all the US government, have funded research and teaching, some of it under the rubric of 'area studies'. Professional associations of area specialists, conferences, and journals have proliferated. At the same time, political science expertise—concerning both the country in question and politics in developing countries more broadly—is expanding in a growing number of developing countries: not just in India where authors like Rajni Kothari have been challenging received thinking over many decades, but for instance in Mexico, Chile, Argentina,

Brazil, Thailand, South Korea, Taiwan, and South Africa (although there is also often a tendency for such country experts to gravitate to the relative comfort and security of American universities). Examples include Guillermo O'Donnell, from Argentina, who devised the influential concept of 'delegative democracy' (see Chapter 14); Arturo Escobar from Colombia (see below); Claude Ake, from Nigeria, who has written on democracy and the political consequences of globalization in Africa (Ake 2000); and Doh Chull Shin from South Korea who has written on democracy with special reference to that country's experience (see Chapter 23b). All of this has heightened awareness of the complexity and diversity of politics across this great tranche of the world's countries. Surveying all these developments, one might well conclude that politics in the developing world no longer even has pretensions to being a coherent field of study; rather, to quote Manor (1991: 1), it is 'in disarray'.

Themes and agendas

But a consideration of the general character of publication and research in the broad field of politics in the developing world over the last few years suggests that this is an exaggeration. Even though one of the logical implications of globalization theories may be to call the need for this distinct field into question, the frequent presence in such work of ideas about globalization does provide one significant element of theoretical common ground. Moreover, against this globalization background, three, partly overlapping, themes or research issues tend to predominate and shape lines of current comparative inquiry.

One is democratization (see Chapter 14). When the **third wave of democracy** broke in the mid-1970s, spreading through South America in the 1980s and much of tropical Africa in the 1990s, it served to confound the expectations of a generation of political scientists who had come to see political authoritarianism or decay as an intrinsic political feature of the developing world. Nonetheless, the global reach of democratization was extended not

only as a consequence of pressures within developing countries, or of the collapse of the Soviet bloc and end of the cold war, but by more deliberate interventions of Western governments and intergovernmental organizations. As Chapter 14 describes, these included attaching political conditions to forms of economic assistance but also more direct international **democracy promotion** through financial and other forms of support to democracy projects. Linked to this drive, Western government and research foundation funding has helped to generate a huge literature apparently covering every aspect of democratic transition.

The second theme is the relationship between politics and economic development or growth. This overlaps with the theme of democratization since an influential strand of thinking now sees good governance and even democracy as a prerequisite of economic growth. As noted by Leftwich (1993), this represents an inversion of the early political development literature where economic growth was generally assumed to be a condition of democracy. The concern with the politics of growth has also led to a reassessment of the importance of the state by bodies like the World Bank, which opened its 1997 report, *The State in a Changing World*, by declaring that the state is central to economic and social development, not so much as a direct provider of growth but rather as a partner, catalyst, and facilitator. It has also led to an interest in the economic role played by civil society organizations and **social capital**. This theme, again, lacks a fully elaborated theoretical context but owes something to the strong government variant of the politics of modernization. But again, like the democratization theme, it is clearly partly driven by concerns of Western governments and intergovernmental organizations.

A third, increasingly prominent, theme concerns peace, stability, and security versus conflict and risk. Again this overlaps with the two previous themes: domestic conflict inhibits the emergence of political conditions conducive to economic growth, for instance, whilst many champions of democratization believe that democratic values and institutions provide the best guarantee both of domestic and of international security and order. The growing focus on causes and consequences of conflict and instability within developing countries is also, however, due to the perception that such conflict has been on the increase since the end of the cold war. An additional impetus has been the perceived need to combat international terrorism, heightened in the wake of September 11. In this context there has been particular interest, on the one hand, in the pathology of 'failing' and 'failed' or collapsed states and, on the other, in the 'politics of identity', especially ethnic and religious identity, in developing countries (see Chapters 6, 7, and 13).

These three themes do not amount to, or derive from, one coherent analytic framework, although they echo and incorporate elements of the earlier dominant paradigms as well as globalization ideas. But they do overlap in the sense that democratization, economic performance, and the presence or absence of internal conflict either do, or are seen to, significantly affect one another. These themes also clearly relate to observable trends in the developing world and resonate strongly with important constituencies there. At the same time, however, they reflect the concerns, interests, and research-funding priorities of international agencies, Western governments, and to a lesser extent non-governmental organizations (NGOs).

In pursuing these agendas of inquiry, then, political analysts have tended to eschew 'macro' political frameworks or narratives but, in keeping with trends in political science as a whole, have been more inclined to work with more modest 'middle-range' theories. These focus on particular issues or subsets of political structures or processes, for instance electoral systems, party systems, neo-patrimonial regimes, democratic developmental states, and corruption. And in many cases they involve applying or developing concepts and propositions that derive from reflection on experience in the developed world.

One further feature of much recent analysis of politics in developing countries, already alluded to in this volume's Introduction, is the importance attached to political institutions. This is again part of a broader trend in contemporary political science from the 1980s. It been described, for instance, by Goodin and Klingemann (2000: 11) who suggest, perhaps over-optimistically, that the rise of the 'new institutionalism' has helped to usher in an era of 'rapprochement' within the discipline, following the aggressive proselytizing of first behavioural and then rational-choice 'revolutionaries'. The new institutionalism is only partly new of course, in that it is rearticulating what has been a longstanding concern in political science. But traditional institutional analysis placed greater emphasis on formal, legal, and constitutional aspects of institutions, whereas the new version has tended to adopt a very broad understanding of institutions as sets of rules that constrain individual behaviour, and there is an emphasis on informal as well as formal rules. Political institutions are seen as potentially exerting an influence over individual behaviour either through affecting (rational) decisions by a combination of incentives and disincentives or through instilling (cultural) values (for an excellent overview, see Lowndes 2002).

KEY POINTS

- Decline of modernization- and Marxist-based approaches and ascendancy of globalization theory have coincided with questioning of the need for grand theory in political studies.

- Expanding scholarship has increased awareness of the empirical complexity of the field.

- However, some coherence is provided by key themes of democratization, politics and economic development, and conflict.

- Recent scholarship is marked by a preference for middle-range theory, with an emphasis on the role of political institutions, broadly understood.

Strategies and Methods of Analysis

As noted earlier, the tendency when analysing the politics of developing countries has been to use the strategies and more specific methods of analysis that have been developed within 'mainstream' and Western political science. This was always to an extent the case but is even more noticeable now that the notion of a distinct 'developing world' is increasingly problematized. The politics of individual developing countries is studied in the context of area or regional studies (for instance centred on Latin America, the Caribbean, or South Asia), or as part of cross-national and regional thematic inquiries (for instance into executive–legislative relations or corruption). There has also latterly been some tendency to emphasize the international or global dimension of politics, for example the increasing salience of the religious dimension of politics (see Chapter 7), in individual developing countries, especially those in sub-Saharan Africa. The implicit argument is that in such countries external determinants are so powerful that apparently domestic political processes are best understood through the prism of international political economy and international relations approaches.

Most commonly, studies of developing country politics fall into the broad category of comparative politics. Accordingly we find a range of comparative 'strategies' deployed. First is the case study approach, where the politics of a single country is explored in some depth. In theory at least, such exploration should be informed by a research agenda reflecting a wider body of comparative research and should aim to test or generate propositions relating to that research. Case studies that simply celebrate the 'exceptionalism' of the country in question would not be considered proper social science, although of course even the idea of an 'exception' implies a broader pattern which is being deviated from. More middle-range comparative studies focus on particular questions. They may use

a subset of cases (such as countries, local governments, parties) selected to illuminate the matter in question. In a methodological distinction going back to J. S. Mill (1888), cases in a 'most similar' design will be similar in a number of key respects whilst differing in regard to the variable being explored. In a 'most different' design they will differ in many key respects but not as regards that variable. In-depth qualitative analysis, often involving a historical perspective, will aim to identify particular factors associated with the variable under review. A good example of such an approach is Bratton and Van de Walle's study of *Democratic Experiments in Africa* (1997). Alternatively studies take a 'large N' of cases and use statistical methods to manipulate comparative data (for instance, elections data, or databases like those constructed by Freedom House and Transparency International). Such an approach, increasingly favoured within mainstream political science and international relations, can yield valuable and counter-intuitive findings, but is of course heavily dependent on the availability of reliable, valid, and appropriate data (for an excellent account of these issues, see Landman 2003).

In arriving at propositions to be explored, or even tested statistically, studies draw on existing studies and middle-range theorizing. Some, however, establish their own central propositions more systematically and deductively, building on the precepts of rational choice theory. This is an approach that takes as its primary unit of analysis the individual actor who is presumed to make rational choices on the basis of self-interest. Within the framework of the 'new institutionalism' the focus is on the way that institutional incentives and opportunities influence the individual's strategic calculations. An early pioneer of this approach in the context of developing countries was Robert Bates. In his work on agricultural policy in Africa, he stressed the rationality of farmers given the choices they were presented with and later pointed to the rational actor origins of political institutions (Rakner 1995). Rational choice approaches have more recently been very evident in work on constitutional and electoral systems design in new democracies.

The dominant assumption in the 'mainstream' comparative strategies and methods of analysis explored so far is that it is appropriate to apply them in contexts differing from those in which they first evolved. This is in many ways an attractive argument that emphasizes what is common and continuous in human experience—in contrast to those which point to possibly unbridgeable cultural differences, as is said to be the case in forms of 'Orientalism' discussed below. Nonetheless, there is a danger unless these approaches are used sensitively that aspects of politics in developing countries will be wrongly assumed or misinterpreted. For a long time comparative political analysts have been warned to beware of concept-stretching and to ensure that the concepts they use actually do 'travel'. We have seen the dangers of inadvertently projecting assumptions from a Western to a developing country setting in the elaboration of Almond's structural-functional model. More recently, doubts have been raised about the relevance of rational choice theory, for instance in contexts where cultural values weigh heavily; indeed, the notion of rational choice itself could be seen as the product of a specific US social science culture.

Here we can consider the contribution of alternative approaches that focus more centrally on issues of meaning and thus potentially suffer less from problems of cultural imposition or misinterpretation—constructivism and discourse theory. Constructivism or the application of constructivist epistemology—the idea that central concepts like 'power' or 'ethnicity' through which we organize our understanding are themselves 'socially constructed'—has been at the heart of a major challenge to traditional thinking in the field of

International Relations. Within comparative politics it is less a case of explicit confrontation and more one of reasonably amicable coexistence and a de facto division of labour. Thus constructivism is used particularly in analyses of the construction of political identities, for instance ethno-political identity (see Chapter 6).

Post-structural or 'discourse' approaches go much further than constructivism, in questioning the very epistemological foundations of knowledge, including political science. Within the study of politics, the ideas of Foucault (1926–1984) have been especially influential. He understood political processes, institutions, and indeed 'subjects' (actors) to be constructed through dominant 'discourses', understood not simply as language and ideas but also as the practices embodying them. A central concern of discourse theorists then has been to trace the governing rules (archaeology) and originating historical practices (genealogy) of such discourses. Whilst rigorous applications of this approach can be found for instance in Norval's (1996) analysis of apartheid ideology in South Africa, more typically its concepts and arguments have been drawn on selectively (as in some of the chapters in Manor (ed.) 1991). As with constructivism, in practice within political studies, discourse-related approaches tend to be applied to particular issues, notably the constitution of political identities, including social movements, the articulation of hegemonic ideologies, and the construction of social or political antagonisms.

KEY POINTS

- Politics in developing countries is generally studied using 'mainstream' political science comparative strategies and methods, although these may not always be appropriate or sensitively applied.

- Constructivist and post-structural approaches run less risk of misrepresentation but have a limited range of applications.

Critical Perspectives

As the field of developing country politics has become more fragmented and complex, with no clearly dominant narrative in the way that the 'modernization' narrative dominated before, so it has become more difficult to identify a main line of critique. Within the broad compass of globalization theory, the debates between the liberal-modernizers and radical-socialists certainly persist, as we can see for instance in disagreements over the criteria for democratic consolidation or deepening (see Chapter 14), or for good governance (Chapter 15). At the same time alternative critical perspectives have emerged, although these are directed less at politics as commonly understood and more at social science understandings of development and non-'Western' societies. I shall consider here two in particular, both of which have tended to be associated, though by no means inevitably so, with post-structural modes of argument. Neither, it must be emphasized, originates within political studies or has had a major impact on the way that politics in the developing world is studied. But each raises serious issues for those engaged in this field.

First is the critique associated with the notion of Orientalism. In his influential book, published in 1978, Edward Said wrote about the lens of 'Orientalism' through which many Western scholars have interpreted Asian and Middle Eastern societies, in imperial times. This discourse, which tended to 'essentialize' such societies, rendering them as exotic and 'Other', could also be seen as instrumental to the political aims of the imperialist powers (though it was not confined to them, as demonstrated in Marx's account of the 'Asiatic' mode of production). Although Said was primarily writing from a historical and cultural viewpoint, subsequently he argued that Orientalist discourse was being revived in the post-cold war context, and especially after September 11, to help to justify US policy in the Middle East. Huntington's (1996a) clash of civilizations thesis (see Chapter 7) could seem to bear out this perception.

Said's work is said to have inspired a broader movement of 'post-colonial studies'. Specifically in India it stimulated the emergence of 'subaltern studies' whose original rationale was to rewrite India's colonial history from the standpoint of the oppressed, subaltern classes (for a fuller discussion of these developments see Chapter 2). At the same time it generated much criticism. Halliday (1993), for instance, claims first that Said insufficiently acknowledged earlier formulators of this critique, and second that the notion of Orientalism has itself been too static, and over-generalized.

Second is the critique that has emerged in different forms of the assumptions of development theory and the development 'industry', referred to as post-development theory. This entails a criticism of development as discourse. One influential exponent, Arturo Escobar (1995), who incidentally acknowledges a debt to Said, suggests that whatever kind of development is advocated, whether capitalist or 'alternative', there is still the assumption that developing countries have to be made to change, which helps to rationalize continuing intervention of outside interests, experts, perspectives, and so forth. Ferguson (1997) has also written about external intervention in Lesotho, drawing a contrast between the repeated 'failure' of development projects and the significance of their apparently unintentional political side-effects (see Box 1.3). Again such arguments have generated much counter criticism (see, for instance, Pieterse 2000), not least that 'development' is not just an elite preoccupation but an almost universal aspiration.

Both these kinds of critique—of Orientalist thinking and of developmentalism—have implications for the way we think about politics in developing countries. It is probably fair to say they are stronger on pointing out problematic assumptions in mainstream literature than in offering satisfactory alternative approaches. Nonetheless, considering these potential critiques have been around for well over ten years, their impact in this field has so far been quite limited.

BOX 1.3

The Development Industry in Lesotho

Lesotho is a small landlocked country in southern Africa with a population of around 1.3 m. Ferguson (1997) lists 72 international agencies and non- and quasi-governmental organizations operating in Lesotho, and notes that in 1979 it received some $64 m in official development assistance.

❝ What is this massive internationalist intervention, aimed at a country that surely does not appear to be of especially great economic or strategic importance? . . . Again and again development projects in Lesotho are launched, and again and again they fail: but no matter how many times this happens there always seems to be someone ready to try again with yet another project. In the pages that follow, I will try to show . . . how outcomes that at first appear as mere "side-effects" of an unsuccessful attempt to engineer an economic transformation become legible in another perspective as unintended yet instrumental elements in a resultant constellation that has the effect of expanding the exercise of a particular sort of state power while simultaneously exerting a powerful depoliticizing effect. ❞

(Ferguson 1997: 7–21 passim)

KEY POINTS

• In addition to continuing arguments between liberal and socialist-inspired camps, new critiques of conventional forms of social science have emerged drawing on discourse theory.

• In particular, the critique of Orientalism and post-development arguments are relevant for studying politics in developing countries, though their impact has been limited.

Conclusion

The dominant paradigms in the past, associated with modernization theory and dependency theory, were valuable to the extent that by suggesting the importance of particular factors or relationships, they helped to generate debate; also, they encouraged political analysis and generalization beyond the particularities of individual country case studies. But at the same time, they were overgeneralized, excessively influenced by Western ideological assumptions and agendas, whether 'bourgeois' or 'radical', and Western historical experience and based on inadequate knowledge and understanding of the developing world itself. They created, as Cammack *et al.* (1993: 3) phrased it, 'a problem of premature and excessive theorization'.

Over time our knowledge of the developing world has grown and with it inevitably our awareness of its diversity and complexity. Moreover, that developing world itself has become increasingly differentiated. Especially in the context of globalization theory, this greater recognition of diversity has called into question the coherence of the developing world as a geographic—and political—category. These developments have coincided with a tendency for political science to rein in its theoretical aspirations, focusing on 'middle range' rather than grand theory. Post-structural thinking has also diminished the appeal of grand interpretative narratives.

Presently, then, whilst globalization theory continues to provide an implicit backdrop to much political analysis, the field of politics in the developing world has become less obviously coherent. However, it is possible to perceive an implicit agenda of inquiry, focusing around democracy or governance, development and conflict and—still—strongly influenced by Western interests and perspectives. At the same time radical, critical perspectives persist. In addition to a continuing Marxist-inspired materialist critique can be found alternative critiques that seek to problematize the whole enterprise of 'Western' attempts to understand and influence politics in developing countries. For many of us, this may be a step too far but we should by now recognize the need to proceed with all caution and humility.

? QUESTIONS

1 What were the main shortcomings of political development theory as a way of understanding politics in the developing world?

2 In what ways does globalization theory draw on modernization theory and dependency theory?

3 What are the implications of globalization theory both for the character of politics in the developing world and the way in which it should be studied?

4 Which theoretical approaches to politics in the developing world shed most light on the relative autonomy of politics and the state?

5 Is the study of politics in the developing world currently in 'disarray'?

6 Do we need a distinct theoretical framework for analysing politics in the developing world?

7 In what ways is Said's critique of 'Orientalism' relevant to the understanding of politics in developing countries?

8 To what extent do mainstream approaches to the analysis of politics in 'developing countries' embody or impose an ideology of development?

9 With particular reference to the developing world, what should we understand as 'politics'?

 ## GUIDE TO FURTHER READING

■ Berger, M. (ed.) (2004), 'After the Third World?', special issue of *Third World Quarterly*, 25/1. Collection of articles that reflect upon the historical significance and contemporary relevance of the notion of a 'third world'.

■ Cammack, P. (1997), *Capitalism and Democracy in the Third World: The Doctrine for Political Development* (Leicester: Leicester University Press). Well-argued, critical reflection, from a left-wing perspective, upon 'mainstream' accounts of the political development literature.

VICKY RANDALL

■ Hagopian, F. (2000), 'Political Development Revisited', *Comparative Political Studies*, 33/6 and 7: 880- 911. Retrospective overview of political development thinking.

■ Higgott, R. A. (1983), *Political Development Theory* (London and Canberra: Croom-Helm). Account of the development and persistence of political development thinking.

■ Manor, J. (ed.) (1991), *Rethinking Third World Politics* (London: Longman). Collection of essays, some using post-structuralist concepts or approaches, seeking to go beyond old theoretical perspectives.

■ Moore, M. (2000), 'Political Underdevelopment', paper presented to 10th Anniversary of the Institute of Development Studies Conference, 7–8 September. See also at www.ids.ac.uk/ids/govern. Attempt to rework the notion of political development, focusing on state legitimacy.

■ Randall, V., and Theobald, R. (1998), *Political Change and Underdevelopment: A Critical Introduction to Third World Politics*, 2nd edn. (London: Macmillan). Provides an account of theories and debates concerning politics in the developing world, from political development to globalization.

■ Said, E. (1995, originally published in 1978), *Orientalism* (Harmondsworth: Penguin). Influential critique of 'orientalist' approaches to history and culture.

■ Smith, B. C. (2003), *Understanding Third World Politics*, 2nd edn. (Basingstoke: Palgrave). Useful, recently updated, overview of themes in the study of the politics of the developing world.

 WEB LINKS

● http://faculty.hope.edu/toppen/pol242/ Hope College course website providing materials on the scope and methods of political science.

● www.multitude.org/wiki/ Collaborative site allowing users a further opportunity to explore post-structuralist ideas.

 ONLINE RESOURCE CENTRE

For additional material and resources, see the Online Resource Centre at:
www.oxfordtextbooks.co.uk/orc/burnell2e/

2 Colonialism and Post-Colonial Development

JAMES CHIRIYANKANDATH

 Chapter Contents

- Introduction: The Post-Colonial World
- Pre-Colonial States and Societies
- Colonial Patterns
- Post-Colonial Development
- Conclusion: The Colonial Legacy

 Overview

The variety of states and societies found in the developing two-thirds of the world is reflected in their political diversity. The contemporary polities of the Global South bear the imprint of the legacy of colonialism but are also marked both by their pre-colonial heritage and their different post-colonial experiences. This chapter traces these ingredients in the making of politics in the developing world. It argues that while the historically proximate experience of colonialism has had a significant impact on post-colonial political development, attention to the *longue durée*, and to political agency after independence, produce a more rounded and nuanced perspective on the varied politics found across the developing world. The different ways in which post-independence politicians adapted to—and were constrained by—the past legacies and present situations of their countries helped determine the shape of the new polities.

JAMES CHIRIYANKANDATH

Introduction: The Post-Colonial World

From the vantage point of the early twenty-first century it is hard to imagine how just sixty years ago the world was dominated by mainly European empires. In 1921, 84 per cent of the surface of the earth had been colonized since the sixteenth century, and following the establishment of League of Nations mandates over formerly Ottoman and German territories in Africa, the Middle East, and the Pacific, there were as many as 168 colonies—(Go 2003: 17). Though by the mid-1960s most colonies were, at least formally, independent, the experience of subsequent decades showed how much the ghost of colonization still loomed over the post-colonial world. While the varied history of **post-colonial states** illustrates the importance of their pre-colonial past, as well as of factors such as geography, geopolitics, and political agency, Hall (1996: 246, 253) points out that the fact that countries are not 'post-colonial' in the same way does not mean that they are not 'post-colonial' in any way—colonization 'refigured the terrain' everywhere. At the very least, the concept of the post-colonial offers a point of entry for studying the differences between formerly colonial societies (Hoogvelt 1997: xv).

Whatever the varied reality of their present condition, their colonial background is still used to identify the contemporary states of the developing world with a pre-modern, traditional, backward past—the antithesis of the 'modern' post-imperial West (Slater 2006: 61–2). In this way, a colonial cast of mind persists, one that geopolitical power relations (North–South, West–non-West) make it very hard to shake off. One important result is the remarkable resilience of racialized discourse in the West when it comes to discussing issues such as migration and development, albeit one that shifted from being expressed in biological terms during the heyday of colonialism to being voiced

in a socio-cultural idiom in the wake of decolonization (Duffield 2006; see also Wallerstein 2003: 124–48).

It is this reality that the rise of post-colonial theory, especially in the field of cultural studies, sought to draw attention to. Influenced by post-modernist and **post-structuralist** perceptions, it was born out of disillusionment with the failure of the Third World to, in Frantz Fanon's words, start a new history and 'set afoot a new man' (1967: 255). To many it seemed that colonialism was the obvious place to start in explaining why political independence had not resulted in the emancipation that people like Fanon, a black psychiatrist from the French Caribbean who devoted himself to the Algerian struggle for independence, yearned for. The problem appeared to be that the emancipatory project, belying the hope expressed by Fanon, had been fatally undermined by its 'imperial genealogy' (Cooper 2005: 25). However, while a number of political scientists, historians, and anthropologists (Crawford Young, Mahmood Mamdani, Bernard Cohn, and Nicholas Dirks among them) sought to analyse the lasting impact of colonialism on the colonized, much post-colonial theory has followed Edward Said's seminal work on **Orientalism** (1978, 1993) in focusing attention more on imperial intent than colonial consequence (e.g. Viswanathan 1990). (Few, at least in the developing world, sought to suggest that colonialism may not necessarily be to blame for the problems of governance afflicting post-colonial societies.)

That the colonial past might be of great significance in determining the future of post-colonial states was recognized even as decolonization proceeded, though then it was adherents of what they saw as the imperial mission who were more inclined to do so. Margery Perham, colonial historian of British Africa, remarked in 1961:

" our vanishing empire has left behind it a large heritage of history which is loaded with bequests good, bad and indifferent. This neither they [the critics of colonialism] nor we can easily discard. "

(1963: 18)

Thirty years later, the interest aroused by post-colonial theorists served to refocus attention on the nature of the colonial legacy. Mayall and Payne, dealing with the 'Commonwealth Third World', suggested that the more durable legacies of the British Empire may have been its military and statist characteristics rather than ideologies such as **liberalism** and nationalism (1991: 3–5). Birmingham, writing of post-colonial Africa, while echoing this view, also highlighted lasting geographical, financial, and cultural legacies: the remarkable persistence of colonial borders, trade and currency links (especially in the ex-French colonies), and the way in which 'the minds of many Africans continued to work on colonial assumptions' (1995: 6–8). That the impact of colonialism has been transformative rather than transitory is now widely accepted. Half a century or more after their independence, developing countries still live with colonialism (Sharkey 2003: 141; Dirks 2004: 1).

Despite the differences in formation and practice between the European colonial powers, it is argued that the phenomenon of colonialism is united to a large extent by its legacies (Dirks 2004: 2). Yet differences in the trajectories of post-colonial development matter and require explanation. One way of attempting to do so that has been gaining currency is **path dependence**, an idea borrowed from economics. This emphasizes the importance of history—of choices made and those not—for the future and the difficulties of changing a course once set (see Box 2.1). Yet, as we shall see, other factors also matter—geopolitical and strategic considerations and political agency.

BOX 2.1

Colonizing the Mind

How to come to terms with the survival of not just institutional forms (administrative, legal, educational, military, religious) and languages (English, French, Portuguese, Spanish, Dutch) but the mentality bequeathed in part by the colonial heritage has been a preoccupation of Third World intellectuals. Some, like the Kenyan writer Ngũgĩ wa Thiong'o, sought a resolution to the dilemma by abandoning the colonial language (English) to write in their native tongue, in Ngũgĩ's case Gĩkũyũ (Ngũgĩ 1986). However, mentality is shaped by much more than just the language used, and Partha Chatterjee and Ramachandra Guha have noted nationalism's role in embedding colonialist historiography into Indian understandings of India (Chatterjee 1986; Guha 1989), European history serving as a kind of *metahistory* (Chakrabarty 2003) that relegated the people of the developing world to being 'perpetual consumers of modernity' (Chatterjee 1993: 5). When it came to defining state forms and political structures, Indian nationalist and post-independence leaders, 'coloured by the ideas and institutions of Western colonialism' (Jalal 1995: 11), largely ignored what were seen as the idiosyncratic views of Mahatma Gandhi, the revered father figure of the Indian independence movement. They preferred the familiar structures of the British Raj. Though no African or Asian state went to the extent of the founders of the Brazilian republic, who in 1889 adapted the motto of Auguste Comte, the nineteenth-century French Positivist philosopher, in adding the words 'order and progress' to their flag, the post-Christian myth of modernity (Gray 2003: 103) certainly found many devotees across the developing world.

KEY POINTS

- Politics in developing countries are influenced by their pre-colonial heritage and colonial and post-colonial experiences.

- Virtually all developing countries are in some sense post-colonial, though not necessarily in the same ways. Post-colonial theory seeks to examine the continuing impact that colonialism has on post-colonial development.

- The impact of colonialism was transformative rather than transitory. As well as reshaping economic and political forms, it also changed the way people, especially the educated, came to see the world.

- Path dependence is a concept borrowed from economics that emphasizes the importance of history in shaping choices for states and societies.

Pre-Colonial States and Societies

It is plausibly argued that one of the best predictors of the resilience of post-colonial states is whether the societies they contain possess a significant pre-colonial experience of statehood (Clapham 2000: 9). From this perspective, it is instructive to consider the political map of the pre-colonial world. Eighteenth-century Asia, the most populous continent, was dominated by states that included some of the world's largest empires (Ottoman Turkey, Safavid Iran, Mughal India, and Manchu China) with only sparsely populated Central Asia and the interior of the Arabian peninsula occupied by nomadic pastoral societies. In contrast, prior to the sixteenth-century Spanish and Portuguese conquest, the Americas were largely inhabited by dispersed hunter-gatherer, fishing, and farming communities. The important exceptions were the Inca empire on the western seaboard of South America and in Central America the Aztec empire, a number of smaller kingdoms, and Mayan city-states. Before being overwhelmed in the nineteenth-century European scramble for Africa, more than two-thirds of the African continent was also occupied by non-state societies with kingdoms and other state formations found only along its Arabized Mediterranean coast and scattered across

more densely populated pockets in the west (Asante, Segu, Benin, Bornu, and, earlier, Mali, Songhai, Oyo, the Hausa states, and Wadai), east (Ethiopia, Zanzibar, and, earlier, Darfur, Funj, and Oromo), centre (Congo and, earlier, Lunda and Luba) and south (the Zulu and Swazi kingdoms, Basutoland, Lozi, and Ndebele).

In the Americas colonization by European settlers resulted in the creation of some twenty independent settler states in the century following the US Declaration of Independence in 1776. In the 1900s Australia and New Zealand also became self-governing British dominions. The post-colonial experience of the USA, Canada, Australia, and New Zealand is thus quite distinct from that of Asian and African states, while Latin American states are distinguished by the varying admixture of European and indigenous native American elements in their social makeup. In recent years Latin American political leaders, especially those of, at least partly, non-European descent, such as Hugo Chávez in Venezuela (president from 1999) and Evo Morales in Bolivia (president from 2006), have sought to emphasize the latter, still visible in syncretic political, religious, and social practice. In Africa and Asia, European settlement was not a

BOX 2.2

Africa's Geography and the Concept of Extraversion

The history of Africa has been profoundly influenced by its geography. Clapham describes the bases for states in pre-colonial sub-Saharan Africa as 'peculiarly feeble' with the few relatively densely populated pockets creating a very discontinuous pattern of state formation across the vast continent (2000: 5). It is this historical geography that the French political scientist Jean-François Bayart has in mind when elaborating the concept of extraversion to explain the politics of post-colonial Africa. He argues that the relatively weak development of its productive forces and its internal

social struggles have, through history, combined to make political actors in Africa disposed to mobilize resources from their relationship with the external environment (1993: 21–2). The collaboration of African rulers in the transatlantic slave trade that resulted in the transportation of perhaps eleven million Africans to the Americas between the sixteenth and nineteenth centuries was the most notorious aspect of this. Afterwards, colonialism and its legacy only served to emphasize the operation of the logic of extraversion.

significant feature of colonization except for isolated instances such as French Algeria, the 'white' highlands of Kenya, and, most importantly, South Africa, where the white supremacist **apartheid** state was only displaced in 1994 (Chapter 20b). The focus of the rest of this section is, therefore, on Africa and Asia, particularly India (on Latin America see Chapter 11).

Pre-colonial Africa featured a variety of polities, among which were the city-states (e.g. Kano) and empire-states (e.g. Songhai, Ghana, Mali, Asante) of the west (Mazrui 1986: 272–3), as well as conquest states, such as that of the Zulus in the south, emerging in the period preceding European colonial rule. African scholars (e.g. Mazrui 1986: 273; Mamdani 1996: 40) have stressed the discontinuity between the pre- and post-colonial state, Mahmood Mamdani blaming, in particular, the deliberate colonial generalization of the conquest state and the administrative chieftainship as the basic modes of African rulership that were to serve as the template for their practice of **indirect rule** (see next section). In doing so, the colonial rulers disregarded differences between societies and the restraints sometimes placed by tradition upon rulers. For instance, among the Akan of southern Ghana the king (Asantehene) was chosen by a group of 'kingmakers' from among a number of candidates from a royal matrilineage and could be removed if

deemed to have breached his oaths of office (Crook 2005: 1). In contrast, societies in northern Ghana had kings who ruled in a much more authoritarian manner, or had chiefs imposed by the British of a kind that did not previously exist. (See Box 2.2.)

Basil Davidson, in contrasting the achievements of Meiji Japan with the Asante state, argues that colonialism prevented the potential for the natural maturing of pre-colonial African institutions (1992), but this is unconvincing given the continent's relative economic backwardness and the deeply rooted historical factors that gave rise to the logic of **extraversion**. Reinforced by its relative isolation, nineteenth-century Japan was a nation-state in being—'Meiji political nationalism [creating] the modern Japanese nation on the basis of aristocratic (*samurai*) culture and its ethnic state' (Smith 1991: 105). There were hardly any pre-colonial nation-states in sub-Saharan Africa (though there might be a case for suggesting that Buganda in East Africa, what is now southern Uganda, was one (Green 2005)).

Pre-colonial Asia represented a considerable contrast to sub-Saharan Africa. Whether we refer to the Ottoman Middle East, the Indian subcontinent, Burma, Malaya, Indochina, or the Indonesian archipelago, these areas were all dominated by states, albeit diverse in size, depth, and durability. Indeed, the Mughal empire that flourished in north and central India between the sixteenth and eighteenth centuries dwarfed its European counterparts in extent, population, and wealth, as did the Ming and, subsequently, Manchu, empires in China and the Ottoman and Safavid empires to the west. Only in the Philippines did the establishment of Spanish dominion in the sixteenth century largely succeed in erasing the pre-colonial past from history (the country has the dubious distinction of being the only post-colonial state that bears the name of a colonial ruler, Philip II of Spain). In terms of pre-colonial state tradition there is no gainsaying the antiquity of those in the rest of Asia. Yet, at first glance, the lineage of the post-colonial states of Asia seems to owe far more to their immediate colonial predecessors than their historic traditions.

There are a number of reasons for this. Perhaps most important are the obvious institutional, and more subtly influential ideological, legacies of colonialism, both of which appear more tangible despite the efforts to trace a pre-colonial ideological lineage, not least by nationalist leaders like India's Jawaharlal Nehru (1961). Typically, descriptions of post-colonial institutions *begin* with the colonial past. For instance, an account of the Indian parliament by its then Secretary-General (chief administrative officer) devoted barely two unconvincing pages to the pre-colonial period, almost wholly focused on ancient India—the two millennia prior to the advent of British rule were thought to merit less than a sentence (Kashyap 1989: 1–3)! While between one and two centuries of British dominion over the subcontinent may have left only a slight imprint on aspects of the everyday lives of many people, especially in the more rural and remote areas, it was long enough, and the nature of the contrast stark enough, to alter the context of government and politics fundamentally.

Anthropologists have been better at capturing this alteration than political historians or political scientists (Cohn 1996; Dirks 2001). Bernard Cohn notes that while 'Europeans of the seventeenth century lived in a world of signs and correspondences, . . . Indians lived in a world of substances' (1996: 18). His phrase captures a profound shift in how people first constituted and then transmitted, perceived, and interpreted authority and social relations. In the mentality of government, the malleability and pliability afforded by 'substance' gave way to the unyielding notional rigour of scientific classification—the intention being to set rigid boundaries so as to control variety and difference. As Cohn put it, the 'command of language' was paired with the 'language of command' (1996: 16). While this did not erase the legacy of the pre-colonial, it certainly transformed it. How it did so is what we shall now consider in examining patterns of colonial rule.

KEY POINTS

- The pattern of state formation in pre-colonial Africa, Asia, the Americas, and Australasia varied. This influenced both the kind of colonization they experienced and post-colonial development.

- The post-colonial experience of areas that were the focus of European settlement is quite distinct from that of Asia and Africa. However, in Latin America indigenous American influences are still perceptible.

- It has been argued that the geography and demography of Africa has had a significant influence in the persistent weakness of states. Bayart's theory of extraversion approaches contemporary African politics from this perspective.

- However, even in Asia, where the pre-colonial era was one dominated by state societies, the colonial state appears to have had a profound effect on the development of politics and government.

Colonial Patterns

The era of European colonialism overseas was proclaimed in 1493, a year after Christopher Columbus's 'discovery' of America, when Pope Alexander VI apportioned newly discovered non-Christian lands between the two main Catholic maritime powers of the day, Spain and Portugal. Over the next four and a half centuries, the scope of European settlement and dominion expanded to cover the whole of the Americas and much of South and Southeast Asia, Oceania (including Australia and New Zealand), Africa, and the Arab Middle East. Typically beginning with small coastal, generally commercial enclaves (examples are St Louis, Luanda, Benguela, Cape Town, and Mozambique in Africa; Surat, Bombay, Goa, Cochin, Pondicherry, and Calcutta in India), they subsequently expanded to cover the hinterland as conquest followed trade. The different periods in which regions were colonized by a number of European states (Spain and Portugal being followed by Holland, England, and France in the course of the sixteenth and seventeenth centuries, and by Belgium, Germany, and Italy in the nineteenth century) gave rise to a varied pattern of colonialism. The emergence of the United States (Hawaii, Cuba, Puerto Rico, Guam, and the Philippines) and Japan (Taiwan, Korea, Manchuria) as overseas colonial powers in the late nineteenth and early twentieth centuries added to the variety.

Although their respective colonialisms expressed their distinctive experience of statehood, colonial powers also borrowed and learned from each other, by the early twentieth century perceiving themselves as being engaged in a common progressive endeavour of developing 'scientific colonialism' (Young 1998: 105). While the pattern varied, it is therefore possible to discern certain common features across the colonial world. Referring to Michel Foucault's characterization of power as 'capillary', the African historian Frederick Cooper argues that power in most colonial contexts was actually 'arterial'—'strong near the nodal points of colonial authority, less able to impose its discursive grid elsewhere' (2005: 49). This was, in part, because, as a number of writers put it, the colonial intent was to 'rule on the cheap' (Sharkey 2003: 122; Cooper 2005: 157). On the eve of its transfer from the brutally exploitative personal rule of King Leopold II to the Belgian state in 1908, the Congo Free State had only 1,238 European military and civilian officers covering over 900,000 square miles (Young 1994: 107). In British India, the centrepiece of Britain's colonial empire, the entire European population in 1921 amounted to just 156,500 (or 0.06 per cent) out of a total of over 250 million (Brown 1985: 95). The colonial state was therefore coercive and extractive, yet thin, with local collaborators, especially those recognized as 'traditional' rulers, forming an indispensable element. Such a state also made the exercise of symbolic, as well as punitive, power very important. The routine British use of aircraft to both awe and bomb into submission rebellious Arab tribes in Iraq in the 1920s was an innovative case in point.

Until relatively late in their history, colonial states had a poor record of investment with barely a tenth of total British overseas investment in the Victorian era going to the non-white colonies (Chibber 2005). Davis (2001: 311) damningly notes that India recorded no increase in its per capita income in 190 years of British rule, with the colonial regime operating a policy of deliberate neglect when it came to development (Tomlinson 1993: 217). Lord Lugard, the Indian-born first governor-general of Nigeria credited with introducing the policy of indirect rule to British Africa, admitted that 'European brains, capital, and energy have not been, and never will be, expended in developing the resources of Africa from motives of pure philanthropy' (1965: 617). The fact was that the philanthropic element was not readily evident. The widespread consequence of cheap colonialism was uneven development and wide disparities between small, more or less Westernized elites and the rest (Dirks 2004: 15). In addition, the movement of labour between colonies to work in the plantation sector in particular introduced new social and economic divisions. In the course of the nineteenth and early twentieth centuries, hundreds of thousands of Indians, mainly indentured labourers, were transported to British colonies in the Caribbean, as well as to Burma, Ceylon, Malaya, Fiji, South Africa, Kenya, and Mauritius—a factor that contributed to ethnic political tensions in all these territories after they became independent.

Leftwich (see Chapter 11) reviews the chief characteristics of the colonial state. The focus below is more upon the cultural and ideological impact that it had. For colonial powers such as Britain and France, a central paradox of their rule was that its survival depended on *failing* to fulfil the universal promise of their liberal state ideology. For instance, the rule of law in British India was necessarily despotic in that the rulers could not be held to account by those they governed but only by their imperial masters in London. In the French colonies the concept of assimilation (i.e. to ultimately make colonial subjects French) was never officially jettisoned, though by the 1920s it was obvious that the language of assimilation was merely the 'rhetoric of colonial benevolence' (Dirks 2004: 14). Under such circumstances it was logical that the post-eighteenth-century European Enlightenment discourse of rights should become translated into the language of liberation for the Western-educated colonized elite (Young 1994: 228).

A feature of colonial rule that was to have far-reaching consequences for the post-colonial world was what Nicholas Dirks has described as a 'cultural project of control', one that 'objectified' the colonized and reconstructed and transformed their cultural forms through the development of a colonial system of knowledge that outlived decolonization (foreword to Cohn 1996: ix–xv; also Dirks 2004: 1). It was an approach that reified social, cultural, and linguistic differences, causing the colonial state to be described as an 'ethnographic state' (Dirks 2001).

Yet while imperial anthropologists such as Herbert Risley, census commissioner and later Home Secretary in British India in the 1900s, helped furnish 'a library of ethnicity, its shelves lined with tribal monographs' (Young 1994: 233), what colonial regimes generally did was adapt and develop difference rather than create it where none previously existed.

In India the British rulers certainly learned from the practices of their Mughal, Hindu, and Sikh predecessors in categorizing their Indian subjects, the novelty lying in their systematic method, modern 'scientific' techniques, and the scale on which they sought to enumerate and classify castes, tribes, and religions (Bayly 1999). The effect was to make consciousness of such group identities far more pervasive and politically potent. The creation of separate representation and electorates in the representative and elected bodies that were introduced from the 1900s on (Chiriyankandath 1992) also served to institutionalize these identities, making them less fluid than they had been. While such categorization may have initially had as its primary purpose making intelligible, and encompassing, an alien public sphere (Gilmartin 2003), it also proved useful in deploying divide-and-rule tactics against emergent anti-colonial nationalism. In the Indian case, the eventual outcome was the partition of the subcontinent in 1947 with the creation of Muslim Pakistan, and a post-independence politics in which such group identities remain of central significance (see Chapter 22a).

The colonial investment in emphasizing the traditional character of the colonized 'others' produced another of the peculiar paradoxes of colonialism—the civilizing colonizer's preference for, in the words of the British imperial writer Rudyard Kipling, 'the real native—not the hybrid, University-trained mule—[who] is as timid as a colt' (1987: 183). On the one hand, deprecating the 'inauthentic' hybrid did not prevent colonial regimes from often favouring politically useful pre-colonial elites in imparting Western education, thereby creating a monocultural elite that created a nationalism in their own image. In more extreme cases such as Pakistan and Sudan, this proved impossible to sustain in the multicultural context of the post-colonial state (Alavi 1988; Sharkey 2003). On the other hand, internalizing the colonial representation of them as the 'other' caused Asians and Africans to stress their 'dedicated' non-Western identities (Sen 2006: 102), ironically making the identities shaped under colonialism the force for decolonization (Dirks 2004: 30). Anti-colonial nationalists sought to distinguish between a material 'outer' domain of economy, statecraft, science and technology in which they acknowledged the superiority of Western modernity, and a spiritual and cultural 'inner' domain of language, religion, and family—the 'private essences of identity' (Young 1994: 275)—the distinctness of which had to be preserved (Chatterjee 1993: 6–9).

Despite overarching commonalities, there were important differences between colonies (see Box 2.3). While the British colonial state left behind an entrenched legacy of autocratic government in both India and Africa, in India this was tempered by nearly three decades of a widening measure of partly representative quasi-constitutional self-government at the provincial level, as well as a superior administration (the Indian Civil Service) that was nearly half Indian when independence came (Chandra *et al.* 1999: 18). Although anti-democratic tendencies persisted in post-independence India (and, for reasons considered later, much more obviously in Pakistan) (Jalal 1995), the contrast with the rapid breakdown of post-colonial constitutional government in Britain's erstwhile African colonies was striking.

From the outset of the establishment of colonial rule, the weak demographics that underpinned what Bayart calls the politics of extraversion meant that the primary focus of colonial extraction in Africa was labour rather than land revenue as in the much more densely populated Indian subcontinent (Young 1994: 273). From their relatively late inception, mainly in the late nineteenth century, the European colonial states in Africa relied heavily on the institution of various forms of forced and tributary labour. Although its most brutal manifestations, as in King Leopold II's Congo Free State, largely disappeared after the First World War, the practice survived well into the first half of the twentieth century. The colonial economics of sub-Saharan Africa resulted in the development of a much weaker indigenous capitalist class, with Africans effectively excluded from all but petty trade in most regions (Tordoff 1997: 42). European companies and immigrant Asian merchants dominated larger-scale economic activity with African integration in the global economy mainly taking the form of cash crop farming, especially in French and British West Africa, and labouring in diamond, gold, copper, bauxite, and other mines, particularly in central and southern Africa. These features, together with the relatively brief span (sixty to eighty years) of colonial rule across much of the continent, had the consequence that both the colonial state in Africa and indigenous political and economic forces were more weakly developed than in India.

Colonies have been described as 'underfunded and overextended laboratories of modernity' (Prakash 1999: 13). They were laboratories within which the subjects of the experiments proved unwilling to live. Through specific ideologies such as Gandhian nationalism in India, Negritude, Pan-Africanism and African socialism in sub-Saharan Africa, Arabism in the Arab Middle East, and varieties of nationalism influenced by pre-colonial Muslim identity across the Islamic world and Buddhism in Southeast Asia, the anti-colonial nationalism of the Western-educated elite succeeded in mobilizing a mass following. Yet while this evocation of what Chatterjee termed the 'inner domain' proved effective as an anti-colonial tool, colonialism left a more material legacy in the institutions of state (bureaucratic, judicial, and educational systems, police and military) and entrenched patterns of trade and exchange (e.g. the French franc zone and the British sterling area in Africa). It also bequeathed ideologies exported from the West—nationalism itself, liberalism, and socialism—as well as global languages of power (English, French, and, to a lesser extent, Spanish and Portuguese). The rest of this chapter describes how this polyglot legacy has served post-colonial states and societies.

BOX 2.3

Colonial Mutations of the Modern State

Colonialism in Africa created mutations of the modern state. Among the ways in which this has been theorized is in terms of a 'gatekeeper' (Cooper 2002) or, from a different perspective, 'bifurcated' (Mamdani 1996) state. Unlike the night-watchman state favoured by libertarians (Nozick 1974), the role of the colonial gatekeeper state was not to serve its inhabitants but to control the intersection of the colony and the outside world, collecting and distributing the resources that that control brought. However, while such a state was conceived as weak in terms of its social and cultural penetration, the same could not be said of the bifurcated colonial state. Seen as the prototype for the apartheid regime in South Africa (1996: 29), Mamdani describes it as the outcome of the simultaneous operation of two different modes of dominion: a racially discriminatory direct rule, based on the exclusion of most, if not all, natives from civil rights, in urban centres; and a method of indirect rule resting upon the institution of customary tribal authority that produced a system of 'decentralized despotism' in the rural hinterland. The latter generally involved the conflation of a variety of forms of pre-colonial authority into one essentially monarchical, patriarchal, and authoritarian model (1996: 39) that was also territorially demarcated (see Samatar 1999: 45 for the Botswana example). Elements of this model could be discerned in colonial practices outside Africa, most notably in the colonial search for—or creation of—a more authentically native, aristocracy to enlist as subordinate collaborators. A case in point was the transformation of the role of the tribal *shaikh* and the institution of a dual (tribal and civil) legal system in Iraq under the British mandate in the 1920s.

KEY POINTS

- The era of European colonialism stretched over five centuries. Over this period different colonial powers emerged and patterns of colonialism changed.

- The colonial state was, typically, extractive in intent and autocratic and coercive in form. A thin, cheap state, it relied on local collaborators to maintain its authority.

- Colonialism developed a system of knowledge that 'objectified' the colonized. An important consequence was to harden and make ethnic and religious distinctions salient.

- The way in which patterns of colonial rule varied had important repercussions for post-colonial development. While there was not much of a prelude to decolonization in Africa, in India the introduction of representative institutions and Indianization of the civil service went much further.

- Colonialism created mutations of the modern state. In Africa, this has been described variously in terms of a 'gatekeeper' or 'bifurcated' state.

Post-Colonial Development

In contrast to the drawn-out history of colonization, the tide of decolonization came in fast across Asia, the Middle East, Africa, the Caribbean, and the Pacific. Beginning in Asia, the Middle East, and North Africa in the decade after the Second World War, it covered most of sub-Saharan Africa within a few years of Ghana (formerly the British Gold Coast) becoming the first independent black African state in 1957, and by 1980 had taken in much of the rest of the erstwhile European colonial empire in the Caribbean, the Persian Gulf and South Arabia, and the Pacific. This rapid transformation was in part the outcome of geopolitical factors: the perceptible weakening of European power following the two world wars, and the emergence of the United States and the Soviet Union, each competing to win over anti-colonial nationalists to their respective camps in the cold war, as the pivots of the post-war bipolar world. However, it was increasing pressure from anti-colonial nationalism, inspired in part by Indian independence in 1947, that forced the pace of change.

But how much change did decolonization bring? The passionate desire of anti-colonial idealists such as Fanon not to imitate Europe (1967: 252) starkly contrasted with the imperial paternalism of colonial officials such as Phillip Mitchell, the British Governor of Kenya, who could say as late as 1945 that faced with 'the choice of remaining a savage or of adapting our civilisation, culture, religion and language, [the African] is doing the latter as fast as he can' (quoted in Cooper 2002: 73). The post-colonial reality belied both Mitchell's belief and Fanon's hope. Colonialism, by globalizing the European template of an international system constituted of sovereign nation-states (based on the Peace of Westphalia in 1648), determined that the primary object of anti-colonial nationalism would be the transformation of colonies into independent nation-states. Despite seeking to assert their political and cultural autonomy, anti-colonialists demanding independence found they had little choice but to operate within this system, since it was the only one that was also imaginable to their rulers (Cooper 2003: 67). This was the dynamic that helped ensure that while, for instance, pan-African and pan-Arab dreams remained unrealized, Muslim insecurities in British India resulted in partition and the creation of Pakistan as a separate 'Muslim' nation-state.

The new states faced the unprecedented challenge of fashioning 'a peculiarly *modern* form of statehood', modelled not on earlier, more basic, forms of the state but on the elaborate modern Western state that had been developed over centuries (Clapham 2000: 6–7). They were also inhibited by the fact that the conditions in which power was generally transferred were far from optimal. Even though in the majority of cases, independence was not accompanied or preceded by war or violence, it was marred by the hurried transfer of administrative responsibilities, belated and unsustainable political compromises, economic dependence, and largely untested legislatures and governments. In noting how colonialism fatefully structured political choices along regional and ethnic lines in Britain's most populous African territory, Nigeria, Sam Nolutshungu observed that the political systems of post-colonial societies 'carried . . . in their genes—the heritage of the colonialism that designed them, authoritarian in its day, but also, invariably, in its retreat, a champion of elitist and paternalist notions of democracy' (1991: 100). In Nigeria, the system quickly, and tragically, gave way—successive military coups in 1966, six years after independence, being followed by a three-year civil war that claimed between one and three million lives.

Whether states achieved independence via a negotiated constitutional transition or a war of liberation did not appear to make much difference to the lasting influence of the colonial legacy. Certainly in Africa the trajectory of development of the minority of post-colonial states that were the outcome of armed struggle (Algeria, the ex-Portuguese colonies of Guinea-Bissau, Angola, and Mozambique, as well as Zimbabwe, Namibia, and Eritrea) showed much in common with that of their neighbours (Young 1998: 107). Although peaceful transfers of power may have assisted what Crawford Young calls the inertial forces favouring the retention of colonial legal and bureaucratic legacies (2004: 29), the troubled post-independence histories of the liberated colonies demonstrates that it was not possible to remove the long shadow cast by the colonial past through struggle. In fact, the bitterness of the struggle itself seems to have, in some cases (Algeria, Angola, Mozambique), contributed to subsequent civil war.

Being accepted as legitimate by its population was a major preoccupation for post-colonial states. Their colonial predecessors had demanded obedience, not consent, and been content with commanding fear rather than affection. This presented a formidable challenge, given the generally multi-ethnic and multi-religious character of most post-colonial states, and often, especially in Africa and the Middle East, the absence of a pre-colonial state tradition. While the legacy of anti-colonial nationalism was helpful, especially where, as in India, it encompassed decades of struggle and mass engagement, this plural context meant that the concept of development was particularly attractive to post-colonial leaders pursuing popular acclaim. Even in India, one of the main nationalist criticisms of British rule was that, having brought the gift of science, they were stunting India's growth and arresting her progress (Nehru 1942: 433–49; and 1961: 508). A developmental ideology thus became central to the self-definition of the post-colonial

state (Chatterjee 1993: 203)—in 1945, Jawaharlal Nehru, soon to become independent India's first prime minister, felt that 'planned development under a free national government would completely change the face of India within a few years' (1961: 504).

In Africa, the predilection on the part of post-colonial leaders to embrace the cause of development was strongly influenced by the late British and French colonial interest in ushering in a **developmental state**. A belated attempt to justify colonialism as it found itself under challenge in the wake of the two world wars and the spread of nationalism and communism, the shift from a primarily exploitative and preservationist colonialism to one that claimed to actively champion and invest in progress and development did not save the colonial state (see Box 2.4). Indeed, Cooper (2002: 66) suggests that in Africa it was the lead the British and French took in this shift that ensured that it was their empires that first started giving way as the changes introduced stimulated growing demands for self-government. The developmentalist authoritarianism subsequently pursued by their post-colonial successors also failed to secure their

---

BOX 2.4

Ingredients for Post-Colonial Success: East Asia and Botswana

Despite lingering until the 1990s, developmentalist authoritarianism in Africa proved a dead end. Whereas in East Asian states like South Korea and Taiwan, both Japanese colonies in the first half of the twentieth century, it was credited with producing an economic miracle, post-colonial Africa was very different. It lacked the societal cohesion, state tradition, and cold war geopolitical significance of the East Asian states, as well as the peculiar legacy of state-led capitalist development left by a colonial power that was close both geographically and culturally. In this connection, it is noteworthy that Botswana, despite inheriting a 'colonial state not worth the name' and long serving as a labour reserve for the South African mining industry (Samatar 1999: 95), represented a rare African success story, recording average

annual growth of over 6 per cent even in 1985–95, a decade in which most other African states recorded negative growth (World Bank 1997: 214–15). While very different in other respects, Botswana benefited, like Korea and Taiwan, from an ethnically homogenous society with a cohesive dominant class and a purposeful leadership under the country's first president, Seretse Khama, also the hereditary chief of the Ngwato, the biggest *morafe* (nation) in the country. Khama's administration built public development institutions that operated effectively on a commercial basis (the Botswana Meat Commission and the Botswana Development Corporation), avoiding the rampant corruption and autocratic tendencies that disfigured post-colonial Africa.

regimes. The successful military coup in Ghana in 1966 against President Kwame Nkrumah epitomized this failure (inheriting the economically interventionist and centralizing late colonial state in the Gold Coast, Nkrumah had assumed dictatorial powers and pursued a succession of wasteful and ill-planned projects aimed at transforming Ghana into an industrialized state).

In most of Africa, the patterns of post-colonial government that developed in the 1960s and 1970s traced their lineage to colonial forms. However, there were important differences that rendered the post-colonial variants more vulnerable. Mamdani's 'bifurcated' colonial state mutated into two types. In the majority of cases, conservative post-colonial decentralized despotisms were not really transformed by the reintroduction of multiparty systems in many countries in the 1990s (for example, Kenya under President Daniel Arap Moi in the 1990s). A minority turned into radical centralized despotisms in which local authority was dismantled without central government being democratized (for example, Uganda in the first decade after Yoweri Museveni's National Resistance Movement took control in 1985).

Alternatively, Cooper's **gatekeeper state** in its post-colonial form, lacking its predecessors' external coercive capacity or financial resources, was left dependent on either the former colonial power or one of the main protagonists in the cold war—the USA, the USSR, or, in a few cases, Communist China. This was perhaps most obvious in the Francophone states in West and Central Africa, most of which belonged to the *Communauté française d'Afrique* (French Community of Africa) and had their currencies pegged to the French franc (and, after 1999, the Euro). Into the early twenty-first century, France continued to be an important source of economic aid. Often maintaining a longstanding military presence, she intervened militarily to prop up post-colonial rulers in several ex-French colonies (as in Djibouti, Chad, the Central African Republic, Ivory Coast). To a lesser extent, Britain played a similar role in countries such as Sierra Leone, intervening to put an end

to the civil war there in 2000–2. Political independence, by placing the resources of the 'gate' in local hands rather than involving a change in the nature of the state, simply intensified the struggle for the gate, making the beleaguered new gatekeepers, usually ethnically defined, dependent on external agencies for international recognition and aid (Cooper 2002: 200).

These trajectories of dependent political development can be interpreted in different ways. Some see it as basically an adaptation of the inherited Western colonial template of **modernization** as Eurocentric development and progress, albeit inflected locally through a continuing process of hybridization (Ahluwalia 2001: 67–71). Others, a minority, reject the extraneous nature of the post-colonial state. Bayart, for instance, suggests that what is negatively described in terms of 'tribalism' or 'instability' in Africa reflects the local appropriation of alien institutions (1993: 265). He evokes the image of a rhizome—a continuously growing underground stem constantly generating both shoots and roots—to explain the dynamic linkage of African societies to institutions of the post-colonial state (1993: 220–1).

Bayart's notion has the value of conceiving of the post-colonial as part of a historical continuum (the *longue durée*), but in doing so it risks underplaying the impact of colonialism. Bayart's rhizome concept avoids the link between political regimes in post-colonial states and the **globalization** of capitalism that European colonialism did so much to bring about. From a Marxist perspective, there was no gainsaying that 'two-thirds of the world's people do not have liberal states because of the structure of the capitalist world-economy, which makes it impossible for them to have such regimes' (Wallerstein 2003: 164).

The European export of the idea of the monocultural nation-state left most post-colonial states with the dilemma of how to reconcile this with ethnically and religiously plural societies. Chatterjee identifies this 'surrender to the old forms of the modern state' as the source of 'post-colonial misery' (1993: 11). In some countries, such as Iraq, created under a British League of Nations mandate in 1921 and formally independent by 1932, the shallow foundations of colonial rule necessitated recourse to particularly high levels of violence, setting a pattern for post-colonial government that has persisted (Dodge 2003: 157–71).

As in Africa, colonialism in South Asia left in its wake visions of society and polity that were distorted—that did not match. Some outside observers have suggested that India owes its comparatively stable post-independence political and economic development to its 'relative immunity from western ideologies' (Gray 2003: 18), but this is an argument that is hard to sustain. More to the point perhaps are three kinds of ingredients that were more evident in the post-colonial Indian mix than, say, in Africa. First, in the realm of cultural politics there ran a deep vein of the non- (if not pre-) modern. Gandhi tapped into this in developing the 'saintly' idiom of Indian politics (Morris-Jones 1987: 60), and the metaphor of the sanctified and patriarchal extended family has been described as one of the most important elements in the culture of Indian nationalism (Chakrabarty 2003: 71). Second, the phenomenon of caste associated with Hinduism, while rendered less fluid, more regulated, and institutionalized under colonialism, gave to India a particularly encompassing yet supple resource in adapting colonial institutions (Rudolph and Rudolph 1967). Thirdly, there was the important role played by political agency, in this case the Congress Party that had spearheaded the campaign for independence. Already over sixty years old at independence, the oldest anti-colonial nationalist organization in the world, Congress under the leadership of Nehru reinforced India's liberal democratic institutional framework by accommodating not only the dominant classes but a variety of caste, religious, linguistic, and regional identities, both through the party and in the structures of government (Adeney and Wyatt 2004: 9–11).

In contrast, lacking in these ingredients, India's subcontinental neighbours, Pakistan and Sri Lanka, proved far less successful, both in sustaining stable constitutional government and preventing civil war. While India experienced localized civil wars, these outbreaks were insulated and, ultimately, defused (in this respect, Kashmir, a bone of contention between India and Pakistan since independence, remains the exception). However, as the 'formal' democracy of the British Dominion of Ceylon (as it was until 1972) was progressively displaced by the more brash and intolerant 'social' democracy of the Republic of Sri Lanka (Wickramasinghe 2006: 160), the island state witnessed a descent into decades of civil war between the Sinhala Buddhist majority and the minority Tamils. In contrast, although the 'democratization' of Indian democracy, through the politicization of previously oppressed and marginalized lower castes and other peripheral groups (Yadav 1996), has confronted the state in India with formidable challenges, its post-colonial institutions coped. The partition of the subcontinent, by removing roughly two-thirds of the Muslim population, might have made the issue of state and national identity in India less problematic. Even so it is because the post-colonial state in India transcended, in some measure, the colonial logic of divide and rule that it has been better at digesting ethnic and religious plurality. Despite the recent political salience of Hindu chauvinism, it is still possible to conceive of Indian culture as 'constructed around the proliferation of differences' (Ghosh 2002: 250).

KEY POINTS

- In contrast to colonization, decolonization occurred apace. Within quarter of a century of the end of the Second World War in 1945, much of the European colonial empire had been dismantled.

- Colonialism shaped the form independence would take in the developing world. Colonies became nation-states despite the form being ill-suited to most post-colonial societies.

- Development was prominent as a legitimizing motif for late colonialism. It also became central to the self-definition of its post-colonial successors, albeit often degenerating into unsuccessful developmentalist authoritarianism.

- While the development record of many post-colonial states was disillusioning, a few (South Korea, Taiwan, Botswana, India) registered conspicuous success. The reasons for this emphasized the crucial importance of history, geopolitical situation, and political agency.

Conclusion: The Colonial Legacy

In 2007, India and Pakistan commemorated sixty years of independence, while Ghana marked half a century as the first black African colony to win political freedom. As the tide of decolonization was reaching its peak, both the departing colonizers and the anti-colonial nationalists anticipating freedom were disposed to strike a positive note. The colonial historian Margery Perham held, in 1961, that 'Britain on the whole was the most humane and considerate of modern colonial nations and did most to prepare her subjects for self-government' (1963: 99). As power was handed over by the last British Governor of the Gold Coast, Kwame Nkrumah, Ghana's first leader, declared confidently, 'We have won independence and founded a modern state' (James 1977: 153). Yet less than a decade later, on the eve of losing power, Nkrumah's summed up his misgivings about the reality of independence in a book entitled *Neo-Colonialism*: 'The essence of neo-colonialism is that the State which is subject to it is, in theory, independent and has all the outward trappings of international sovereignty. In reality its economic system and thus its political policy is directed from outside' (Nkrumah 1965: ix). A quarter of a century later, one international

relations theorist coined the phrase 'quasi-states' to describe the majority of post-colonial states (Jackson 1990).

More recently, there has been a resurgence of interest in the West in the idea of a **liberal imperialism**, if not the actual restoration of formal empire, as a solution to the continuing political and economic crisis that many post-colonial states, especially in Africa and the Middle East, appear to face (Ferguson 2004; Cooper 2004; Lal 2004). Echoing earlier justifications for colonial rule, these adherents of a revival of paternalist imperialism share a sense of civilizational superiority, and a common blind spot for the logic of domination and **exploitation** that underpinned European colonialism. This logic had also been apparent in the behaviour of the United States, the first post-colonial imperial power, towards native, African, and Hispanic Americans in extending its domain across North America in the course of the nineteenth century, and then in the Philippines, Latin America, and the Caribbean in the years following the Spanish-American War of 1898 (Slater 2006: 15, 44–53). Attributable to a 'geopolitical amnesia' engendered by imperial—and post-imperial—culture in the west (Slater 2006: 148), the renewed fascination with liberal imperialism is more a reflection of post-cold war Anglo-American hubris than a legacy of the historical experience of colonialism.

While virtually the entire developing world experienced colonialism, the experience differed from place to place, and this is reflected in the varied legacy. To begin with the settler and slave societies of post-colonial Latin America and the Caribbean present a contrast to Africa and Asia. For example, in the Caribbean the private hierarchies of exploitation that underpinned slavery, and the subsequent drawn-out history of slave emancipation and struggle for political rights, helped the state structures, closely modelled on the British parliamentary system, gain acceptance as autochthonous (Sutton 1991: 110).

In the African case, the patchiness of pre-colonial state traditions, and the relative brevity and 'thinness' of colonial rule, generally resulted in post-colonial states incapable of achieving the ambitions of nationalist leaders and the expectations of their peoples. By the end of the twentieth century, a large part of the colonial state legacy in many African countries had been effaced by institutional decay (Young 1998: 116), eroding 'the explanatory power of the post-colonial label' (Young 2004: 49). However, this does not negate the continuing historical significance of the colonial and, indeed, pre-colonial past. For instance, contrasting the former Belgian Congo with regions that possessed effective states before colonialism, such as the south of Uganda (Buganda) and Ghana (Asante) and northern Ethiopia, the latter have proved better able to survive phases of bad government (Clapham 2000: 9).

Although the model of the nation-state has proven a burdensome legacy for contemporary Africa, the consequences of state collapse in Somalia, Liberia, Sierra Leone, and Congo in the 1990s and 2000s showed the high human cost exacted by its absence. The lesson seemed to be that in a world of states vulnerable regions and their inhabitants are left dangerously exposed by state collapse, even if the post-colonial state concerned is nothing but a gatekeeper state. Though some (Clapham 2000) argue that societies might conceivably be able to function without states, it is difficult to foresee them being tolerated for long in the globalized world of states, and the unresolved question for many African countries remains how to fashion a sustainable state (Cooper 2002: 186).

Historical differences reflected in institutional weakness may have compounded the crisis faced by the post-colonial state in Africa, but in Asia too the colonial legacy presented post-colonial states with their greatest challenges, especially in grappling with issues of political identity. The problem in countries such as Sri Lanka was that the concept of multiculturalism introduced by the British colonial rulers stressed the fragmentary nature of society (Wickramasinghe 2006: 13). By doing so, it left the post-colonial state with its composite identity particularly vulnerable to being torn apart by incompatible visions of the nation.

The colonial legacy has been likened to a poisoned pill (Chibber 2005: 11). Reviewing the mixed record of post-colonial development, it is hard not to agree, the health of the poisoned post-colonial state being determined by its condition (history and geopolitical situation) and the skill of the doctor (the role played by political agency).

? QUESTIONS

1 Of what use is the post-colonial category in analysing the politics of the developing world?

2 How important is pre-colonial history in explaining post-colonial development?

3 What impact did colonialism have on how people in both the 'South' and 'North' saw the world and their place in it?

4   How did diverging patterns of colonial rule influence post-colonial development?

5   What does the idea of 'gatekeeper' state contribute to our understanding of politics in developing countries?

6   Why did development loom so large in the discourse of both the late colonial and post-colonial state?

7   What is the relative importance of history, geopolitical situation, and political agency in shaping post-colonial development?

 ## GUIDE TO FURTHER READING

■ **Bayart, J. F. (1993),** *The State in Africa. The Politics of the Belly* **(London: Longman).** A leading French political scientist provides a different perspective on the politics of post-colonial Africa through introducing the concept of 'extraversion'.

■ **Chatterjee, P. (1993),** *The Nation and Its Fragments. Colonial and Postcolonial Histories* **(Princeton: Princeton University Press).** An insightful examination of the impact of colonialism on the nationalist imagination in Asia and Africa by a leading Indian political theorist.

■ **Chiriyankandath, J. (1992), '"Democracy" Under the Raj: Elections and Separate Representation in British India',** *Journal of Commonwealth and Comparative Politics,* **30/1: 39–63.** Shows how the British introduction of communal forms of political representation helped shape the post-colonial politics of the Indian subcontinent.

■ **Cooper, F. (2002),** *Africa since 1940. The Past of the Present* **(Cambridge: Cambridge University Press).** Considers the post-colonial development of Africa from an historical perspective with particular reference to the concept of the 'gatekeeper' state.

■ **Hall, S. (1996), 'When Was "The Post-Colonial"? Thinking at the Limit', in I. Chambers and L. Carti (eds.),** *The Post-Colonial Question. Common Skies, Divided Horizons* **(London: Routledge), 242–60.** A thoughtful exploration of the term 'post-colonial'.

■ **Slater, D. (2006),** *Geopolitics and the Post-Colonial. Rethinking North-South Relations* **(Oxford: Blackwell).** A political geographer's perspective on the post-colonial world that devotes special attention to Latin America.

■ **Young, C. (1994),** *The African Colonial State in Comparative Perspective* **(New Haven, CT: Yale University Press).** Wide-ranging comparative study of the colonial state by a political scientist.

■ **——(2004), 'The End of the Post-Colonial State in Africa? Reflections on Changing African Political Dynamics',** *African Affairs,* **103: 23–49.** Young's reconsideration of the condition of the post-colonial African state.

 ## WEB LINKS

● **http://bostonreview.net/BR30.1/chibber.html** Chibber, V. (2005), 'The Good Empire. Should We Pick Up Where the British Left Off?', *Boston Review,* 30/1. An Indian political scientist's damning critique of Niall Ferguson's (2004) *Colossus: The Rise and Fall of the American Empire* (London: Allen Lane), and of the poor scholarship that lies behind the early twenty-first-century idea of a new liberal imperialism.

JAMES CHIRIYANKANDATH

● **http://hdr.undp.org/publications/papers.cfm** Nicholas Dirks (2004), 'Colonial and Postcolonial Histories: Comparative Reflections on the Legacies of Empire', Global Background Paper for United Nations Development Programme, Human Development Report, *Cultural Liberty in Today's Diverse World.* A historical anthropologist, specializing in South Asia, considers the colonial legacy.

 ONLINE RESOURCE CENTRE

For additional material and resources, see the Online Resource Centre at:
www.oxfordtextbooks.co.uk/orc/burnell2e/

3 The Developing World in the Global Economy

STEPHEN HOBDEN

→ **Chapter Contents**

- Introduction: The Emergence of a Global Economy
- Trade
- Foreign Direct Investment
- Financial Flows
- China in the Global Economy
- Conclusion

✔ **Overview**

This chapter and the following inter-linked one provide an overview of the international context in which politics in the developing world operates. In this chapter the focus is on the global economy. Over the past fifty years there has been a general increase in global economic integration, often described as **globalization**. The chapter focuses on three key features of the global economy—trade, foreign direct investment, and financial flows—discussing their significance for the developing world. At the start of the twenty-first century, the character of the global economy is changing, particularly with the emergence of China as an economic superpower. The conclusion to the chapter discusses the significance of these developments.

STEPHEN HOBDEN

Introduction: The Emergence of a Global Economy

For the purposes of this chapter, the term 'global economy' is understood as all international economic transactions which occur across national borders: trade, financial flows, and foreign direct investment (commonly known by its initials as FDI). Many observers claim to see evidence of increasing global economic integration, a feature usually associated with globalization. However, the meaning of the concept of globalization is a subject of much debate, and, in particular, there is considerable disagreement over the precise implications for economic well-being in the developing world of increased economic integration (see Box 3.1).

A major component of the emergence of a global economy has been the growth in the value of trade. For many writers, the economic growth of the West is largely explained by its involvement in an international trading system, leading to the view that 'free trade' is inherently beneficial. Yet, despite the developing world's increasing inclusion in the global economy, the benefits from trade do not appear to have reached the large proportion of the globe's population who live in absolute poverty. Indeed,

---

BOX 3.1

Globalization

Globalization is a term much used in contemporary social sciences. Some suggest that it 'might justifiably be claimed to be the defining feature of human society at the start of the twenty-first century' (Beynon and Dunkerley 2000: 3). However, it is a deeply problematic term because there is no accepted definition, nor little agreement about how to measure the process or even whether the term provides a useful way of assessing contemporary global developments (Hirst and Thompson 1999).

O'Brien and Williams define globalization as 'an uneven process whereby the barriers of time and space are reduced, new social relations between distant people are fostered and new centres of authority are created' (2004: 132).

When we turn to the developing world the key argument is about whether globalization increases or decreases levels of poverty. As with the discussion over definition and measurement, there is little agreement over the impact. Here are two rather divergent views:

" Globalization has been a force for higher growth and prosperity for most, especially for those in the bottom half of the world's population. "

(Bhalla 2002: 11)

" Globalization speeds up the economy magnifying the chasm between [rich and poor]. Both at home and abroad, the extremes of wealth and deprivation have become so great that the stability of the global system is threatened. "

(Isaak 2005: xxi)

How are such divergent views possible? One reason is that that there is no agreement as to what constitutes poverty. Should poverty be measured in absolute or relative terms? The most widely used absolute measure of poverty is the World Bank's figure for the number of people living on less than a dollar a day. Measures of relative poverty compare the proportion of global wealth enjoyed by the richest people in the world compared to the poorest. Although the figures are disputed, most absolute measures suggest that poverty is declining (there are fewer people living on less than a dollar a day), whilst relative measures suggest that poverty is increasing (the gap between the richest and poorest is getting wider). Attitudes towards globalization may depend on the way in which poverty is measured. The picture is complicated when the situation within countries is also considered. The population of China living on the country's eastern edge has benefited much more from the country's recent rapid growth compared to the large rural population living on the western side.

Globalization is best understood as a multifaceted process which affects different countries and different social groups within countries differently. Most observers would agree that levels of inequality have increased, both nationally and internationally, while levels of absolute poverty, when examined globally, have decreased.

although the developing world increased its share of world manufacturing output from a mere 5 per cent in the early 1950s to close to 25 per cent by the end of the century, much of this was accounted for by only a handful of countries that includes China, Brazil, South Korea, and Taiwan (Dicken 2003: 37). The same is true of the increase in merchandise exports, where again China and Hong Kong dwarf the other exporting countries such as Mexico, Singapore, and Taiwan. The arguments that lead many to suggest that there are enormous benefits to be gained from joining the world economy need to be balanced against a consideration of the reasons why developing countries are not always able to exploit the potential gains from trade. A country's role in the global economy could determine the ability to derive the benefits.

There is evidence of trade between different social groups for as long as written records have existed, and it has provided much of the motivation for people to explore the globe. By the end of the nineteenth century, much of Asia and Africa had been included in the European empires, and trade between the colonial powers and their subject states provided the bulk of trade between what came to be called 'First' and 'Third' worlds. The colonies provided guaranteed sources of essential raw materials, and also markets for manufactured goods from the metropolitan centres. One historian of empire notes that 'Britain prospered ... by manufacturing articles for sale abroad, which her customers paid for in raw materials and food' (Porter 1996: 4). An international division of labour developed in which European powers exported manufactured goods to the colonies and imported the materials needed to make these goods (McMichael 2000: 8–13). One way of imagining this process is to think of the international trading system as a number of segments, each segment comprising the colonial power and its colonies. A considerable amount of trade took place within the segment, and to have an empire was seen as essential for the economic well-being of the core.

Standing outside this segmented economic system was the United States, which in the early twentieth century was becoming a significant source of global production. Successive US administrations sought a larger role in the international economy, which would require the breaking up of the European imperial systems of trade. At the outbreak of the Second World War, planners in the United States started to think about what the postwar economic and political order might look like. The fruits of this planning emerged in a document known as the Atlantic Charter signed by President Roosevelt and Britain's Prime Minister Churchill in 1941. At the core of the charter was a commitment to the end of empire and the creation of an open world economy.

Despite the resistance of the European powers, decolonization gradually occurred following the end of the Second World War. However, as a result of the cold war, a world economy segmented by the European colonies was replaced by a world economy divided between, on the one hand, the USA, its allies and client states, and, on the other, the Soviet Union, its allies and client states. These systems resembled in many ways the imperial systems which had preceded them, in the sense that the cores provided manufactured goods whilst developing countries were major sources of raw materials.

One major attempt to overcome this reliance on the export of raw materials was the development of a policy of import-substituting industrialization (ISI). The promotion of local manufacturing was seen to have several advantages. It would employ local labour and thereby reduce unemployment, and allow production of manufactured goods at prices lower than available on international markets. Producing locally would reduce imports, potentially allow some of the production to be exported, and promote the introduction of new technology. To allow local industries to develop without competition, tariffs were imposed on imports.

ISI is generally regarded as having been a failure for the developing world. In general, it did not promote the stated objectives, but resulted in rather inefficient government-owned industries that were unable to compete internationally. The reason for this is generally cited as being a reluctance to move towards reducing the tariff walls so that the industries are forced to compete internationally. Particularly in Latin America, pressure was put on governments to maintain subsidies and high levels of protection underpinning the industries. A further problem was that in many developing countries the market was not large enough to reap economies of large-scale production. Finally, ISI did not even break the reliance on imports: instead of relying on imported manufactured goods, the countries became reliant on the import of machine tools, spare parts, and specialized knowledge. Although ISI is normally now depicted in negative terms, it should be remembered that much of European and US industrialization occurred behind tariff walls, and that the success of the newly industrializing countries of East Asia depended to varying degrees on this approach (see Box 3.2).

BOX 3.2

The Newly Industrializing Countries of South-East Asia and Export-Led Industrialization

The so-called NICs include Taiwan, South Korea, Hong Kong, and Singapore, with perhaps a second wave including Malaysia, Indonesia, and the whole of the People's Republic of China. The NICs have seen a remarkable turnaround in their economic fortunes, developing from being very poor, largely agricultural economies in the wake of the Second World War to industrialized countries, some with average incomes comparable to the developed world. On some measurements, for example, Singapore is now among the top ten countries in average income per capita. Free trade advocates have cited the NICs with varying justification as models for how to develop an economy.

The economic success of the NICs has many possible explanations, for example, their exceptionally favourable geopolitical location during the cold war period and even the cultural attributes of the people. But to most economists a major reason is their adoption of policies of export-led industrialization. This can be contrasted with the policies of import substitution industrialization. The policy of the NICs has been to direct industrialization to fulfil the demands of world markets, and gradually to expose their industries to world competition through lowering tariff barriers. They have been prepared to switch production in order to maintain their position of comparative advantage—starting with textiles, then moving into mass-production items such as toys, and then into more high-tech goods. The NICs in particular have been successful in specializing in areas of production that have become unprofitable in the more developed world.

Economists who wish to promote free trade have seen the NICs as a good model because of their willingness to trade in the global economy, and their readiness to reduce tariff barriers over time. Furthermore, the NICs have succeeded in exploiting their comparative advantage. However, the position is more complicated. It is true that the NICs have reduced tariffs over time so that their industries are now more exposed to international competition. But they have been prepared to use tariffs to protect their industries in the early stages while they were becoming established. This is known as infant industry protection, and was used as an argument for the protection of industry in Europe during the nineteenth and early twentieth centuries. A further point that is often overlooked is the important role the state played in developing industry in the NICs (see Chapter 23b on the example of South Korea). The state maintained subsidies and investment as a way of developing parts of the economy that were perceived to have the greatest potential or were strategic in some sense.

As with the use of infant industry protection, this suggests that the history of the NICs is more complicated and perhaps more difficult to replicate than is suggested by free market proponents.

Despite an increasing level of contact between the capitalist and communist systems, it was not until the collapse of Communist Party rule in the Soviet Union that it is possible to start talking of a global economy—one, exclusively capitalist, system.

While trade has been a feature of human societies dating back thousands of years, there are two other features of economic activity, also associated with the term 'globalization', but which have gained greater significance over recent decades. The first of these is foreign direct investment. This refers to the practice of firms, usually described as transnational corporations (TNCs) locating production and marketing facilities in other countries. The level of this foreign direct investment has increased massively over recent years, and concerns have been raised about whether the activities of TNCs have assisted or undermined economic development. A further recent development has been the enormous financial flows occurring in the global economy. While foreign direct investment can be seen as a relatively long-term form of investment, financial flows are primarily short term. They refer to the buying and selling of currencies and stocks and shares in local economies. While FDI refers to investments like buildings and machinery, and therefore takes some time to create, vast amounts of money in the

financial system can be moved by the pressing of a computer button. Concerns have therefore been raised as to whether rapid financial movements can be de-stabilizing to developing world economies—though it should also be noted that economies in the developed world are not immune to the turbulence caused by rapid and speculative financial flows.

KEY POINTS

- The global economy can be considered as comprising three main activities which occur across national borders: trade, investment, and financial movements. There is a long history of trade between different societies, though large-scale FDI and financial flows are a relatively more recent feature of global economic activity.

- During the period of European colonialism, the major pattern of trade was for the colonies to export raw materials, while the metropolitan cores exported manufactured goods. These structures of trade have persisted into the post-colonial period.

- Following the end of the cold war, it is possible to talk about the emergence of a global economy—a single, capitalist system.

Trade

Patterns of global trade

During the second half of the twentieth century, the rate of growth of trade far outstripped that

of production. Between 1950 and the close of the twentieth century, world trade increased almost twenty times while production increased only sixfold (Dicken 2003: 35). Yet this growth has not been at a constant rate, and has been subject to considerable fluctuation. During the 1950s, levels of trade grew extremely rapidly as the world, and in particular Western Europe, recovered from the Second World War. In contrast, the rate of growth was much slower during the 1970s as the international economy contracted in the wake of large oil price rises.

World trade is relatively concentrated. Table 3.1 shows the breakdown between different regions of the world and their contributions to merchandise and trade in services. The developed world is responsible for the vast bulk of exports in merchandise and services, though the rapidly increasing contribution of China to merchandise exports suggests that the character of the global economy is undergoing a profound transformation. Manufactured goods make up approximately 75 per cent of merchandise trade, and one of the striking developments is the increasing amount of manufactured goods flowing from the developing world. Despite the large increases in the proportion of manufactured goods coming from some countries in the developing world, many maintain their traditional role of providing raw materials and agricultural products. Many countries in sub-Saharan African rely on just one primary product for over 50 per cent of their exports (Harrison 2004: 219).

The promotion of free trade

The relative prosperity of the developed world during the latter half of the twentieth century is linked by many economists to the rapid rise of global trade. In other words, prosperity can be increased by increasing a country's involvement in the global trading system. The view that free trade works in the interests of all participants now holds a predominant position in economic thinking. The idea that unimpeded trade will lead to a material benefit to developing countries is a core idea of the neo-liberal agenda, and is expressed in what became known as the Washington consensus. The neo-liberal agenda derives from classical liberal economics. The 'consensus' denotes the primacy of related ideas in the World Bank and the International Monetary Fund (IMF), both based in Washington (see the next chapter). These ideas have proved to be very

Table 3.1 Relative Shares in Global Exports by Region and for Selected Countries

	Merchandise (%)		Services (%)	
Developed world	63		75	
Germany		*10*		*6*
USA		*9*		*15*
Japan		*6*		*5*
CIS & SE Europe	4		3	
Developing world	33		23	
Africa		2.5		2
S. Africa		*0.5*		*0.3*
Asia		26		17
China		*6*		*2.5 (2003)*
Latin America (incl. Caribbean)		5		3
Brazil		*1*		*0.5*

Note: CIS refers to Commonwealth of Independent States
Source: United Nations Conference on Trade and Development (UNCTAD) 2005a: Tables 1.1A and 5.1

powerful. Policies based on the theory of comparative advantage, implemented by international organizations, have dramatically affected the lives of millions of people around the globe (for a clear discussion of the theory of comparative advantage, see Dunn and Mutti 2004: chapter 2).

The package of measures associated with the neo-liberal agenda comprises both national and international elements. At the national level, free trade policies fall into two main areas: the promotion of a more efficient use of labour, and the reduction of the role of the state in the economy. The first requires the labour force to be flexible, which can often require the power of trade unions to be curbed. The second is premised on the assumption that the state acts as a drag on the free operation of the markets, and that its role should be reduced to providing a minimal set of public goods such as national defence and overseeing the legal system. At the international level, policies are advocated which aim to remove hindrances to trade and to promote the inflow of FDI. Tariffs on imports or exports are seen as a major impediment to trade. Tariffs are a form of taxation that are levied on the value of goods which are entering or leaving a country. They can be both a form of revenue and a way of protecting domestic industries. For free trade advocates, tariffs are seen as acting to undermine the potential gains to be derived from comparative advantage. Therefore it is argued that removal or reduction of trade tariffs will promote trade and lead to a more efficient use of resources, as domestic industries are exposed to international competition. Free traders have also argued in favour of allowing currencies to float freely rather than being managed by governments. In the past currencies have frequently been overvalued, making imports cheaper and exports more expensive. As part of free trade regimes countries have been persuaded to allow their currencies to float freely. This often means devaluation of the currency, making domestic production more competitive internationally, while increasing the cost of imports. Many developing countries also placed considerable restrictions on the permitted levels and forms of international investment in their economy. Restrictions on the parts of the economy in which foreign investment is allowed, higher levels of taxation for international firms, and limits on the expropriation of capital have all been typical in the past, especially before the 1980s. However, free market policies argue that there should be no discrimination against foreign capital wishing to invest in the country, and that any barriers to investment should be removed. Box 3.2 discusses the newly (or new) industrialized (or industrializing) countries (NICs) of South-East Asia, often seen as examples of the successful implementation of free trade policies.

Limits on comparative advantage for developing countries

The examples of the Asian NICs suggest that in certain circumstances free market policies can contribute to rapid economic growth. Why have other developing countries not been able to replicate this success? Why has the enormous growth in international trade not resulted in a wider distribution of the fruits of that trade, as the theory of comparative advantage would suggest? And why have some parts of the developing world barely participated at all in the growth of world merchandise trade—Africa's share of such trade is now less than half its contribution of over 5 per cent in 1980, and the developing countries of the Americas have remained static at just under 6 per cent (UNCTAD 2003: 3)? Critics of the neo-liberal agenda suggest that in some ways the developing world is in a disadvantaged position in the global economy compared to more developed countries.

Following decolonization the same basic pattern whereby the developing areas under colonialism were primarily providers of raw materials and markets for manufactured goods has largely persisted, with some notable exceptions (see Weiss 2002). For many non-Asian developing countries, over 70 per cent of exports still comprise primary products. For many sub-Saharan African countries, the figure is over 80 per cent (World Bank 1999). This can be a problem for developing countries because of the failure of the prices of primary commodities to keep pace with manufactured goods (known as the declining terms of trade). Also primary commodities have historically been liable to confront very large fluctuations in prices, coffee being a particular example (see Box 3.3).

Between 1997 and 2001, the UNCTAD combined price index of all commodities in US$ fell by 53 per cent in real terms; that is, primary commodities lost

---

BOX 3.3

Coffee

Coffee is a commodity that illustrates clearly the problems that can confront the producer of raw materials, especially agricultural products. With the exception of oil, it is the commodity that earns the most for developing countries. An estimated 125 million people in the developing world depend on coffee production for their livelihoods. Yet it is an item whose price fluctuates wildly, and in recent years has shown a dramatic fall in price.

Coffee basics: there are two main types of coffee beans—*Robusta*, grown in lowland areas in, for example, Brazil and West Africa, and the main source of instant coffee; and *Arabica*, grown in highland areas such as Kenya and Colombia, which is the main source of expressos and filter coffees. Most coffee is grown on small independent farms, in contrast to, for example, bananas, which are frequently grown on large plantations. It takes three years from planting a coffee bush until it produces the first beans.

Coffee prices: over the past twenty-five years, international coffee prices declined rapidly. After frost destroyed much of the coffee harvest in Brazil in March 1977, coffee reached a peak price of £3,000 a tonne, from £500 per tonne in 1975). Since then it has declined rapidly to a price of around £350 per tonne.

Coffee problems: three main problems confront the producers:

- *Price fluctuations*: the price hike of 1977 demonstrates what can happen when a harvest fails. The fall in output (or even a fear of a fall in output) from one region can send the price rocketing. For a short while the production of the commodity can be extremely profitable, and this of course can prompt new producers to switch to growing the product, in the (mistaken) belief that the price will remain high.

- *Oversupply*: the price of coffee on the international market has fallen dramatically because too much was being grown. Global overproduction has been exacerbated by a World Bank programme to introduce coffee production into Vietnam, which has risen rapidly to account for 10 per cent of global production.

- *Structure of the industry*: although the large fluctuations in price and the oversupply of raw commodities are not unique to coffee, the industry's structure adds special problems. The millions of small farmers, with very limited power, face a very small number of producers with enormous power to dominate the final retailing of the product. In between there are numerous levels of wholesalers and other intermediaries. Coffee beans can change hands more than 150 times between farmer and supermarket shelf, and each time they change hands a smaller proportion of the final price reaches the grower. Thus while the coffee growers earned $10–$12 billion of the $30 billion global retail market for coffee in the early 1990s, by 2004 they were forecast to earn just $5.5 billion from a market now worth $70 billion.

Can fair trade provide an answer? Much has been made of the increasing share of the coffee market that sells under the label of Fair Trade. Fair trade coffee aims to benefit growers by dealing directly with farmers, eliminating layers in the supply chain. Farmers are guaranteed a floor price that at least covers the costs of production. Additionally, a bonus is always paid above international prices should they rise above the floor. The premium is earmarked for development projects agreed with the producers. Clearly fair trade is advantageous for those producers fortunate to be included. However, although fairly traded coffee as a proportion of the total is increasing, the figure is still very low, benefiting only thousands of farmers out of the millions involved in coffee production.

(UNCTAD 2003: 24–5)

more than half their purchasing power relative to manufactures (UNCTAD 2003: 19). Movements like this make it harder to predict what revenues will be derived from exports in any particular year. Agricultural products are particularly prone to large price fluctuations. Years when there is a glut in production can lead to price falls, while crop failures can lead to massive price increases. Agricultural production can also be hit by changes in fashion in the developed world. One exception to

this pattern for primary commodities has been oil (Box 3.4).

Many developing countries have also been hampered in their attempts to participate more fully in the global economy by a continuing and chronic shortage of capital. Investment is significant for trade, particularly in the modern world economy, because it is only possible to compete in the most profitable areas with the most up-to-date equipment. Where equipment is outmoded, or the

---

BOX 3.4

Organization of the Petroleum Exporting Countries (OPEC)

In terms of commodity exports, oil represents a special case. Nevertheless, it highlights further the difficulties that commodity exporters face.

Oil basics: amongst oil's many uses are: as a source of energy for domestic and industrial electricity; to power transportation systems; as a lubricant; as the raw material for plastics. It has become central to the way of life of the developed world, but ultimately is a limited resource.

OPEC was founded in 1960 by a number of oil-producing countries in the developing world in an attempt to increase export revenues. In the 1950s, world oil consumption was growing rapidly. But oil prices fell throughout the decade. However, between 1970 and 1973 OPEC succeeded in doubling oil prices, through negotiation with Northern governments. Then, between October 1973 and January 1974, OPEC was able to further quadruple oil prices, by reaching an agreement between the members to restrict supply. In the 1970s, OPEC's success in increasing oil prices seemed to be a signal to developing countries that others too could get a better price for their commodity exports. But was oil a special case?

Accounting for OPEC's success: OPEC is an example of an export quota commodity agreement. Its members have been able to manipulate the price by regulating the supply. But this is not easy.

On the supply side, export quota commodity agreements tend to be fragile because there is always a temptation for producers to defect. When prices rise through joint action to limit supply, there is always a risk that some member(s) will exploit the situation by increasing their supply to take advantage of the higher price. At times this has been a problem for OPEC and

would be a much bigger issue where the number of producers is larger, like millions of coffee growers. Moreover, oil is not perishable, and to leave it in the ground does not affect its quality, unlike agricultural goods, which cannot be stored indefinitely.

On the demand side, there are ways of reducing its use (seeking other non-OPEC-controlled sources, using increased insulation, using coal or synthetic substitutes, or reducing energy use generally), but these take time to introduce. Oil is still an essential item. And although oil as a proportion of total energy use has declined since the 1970s (in 1973 oil supplied 45.1 per cent of the world's energy requirements, compared to 35 per cent in 2001), this decline has to be seen in the light of an overall increase in demand for oil, particularly from rapidly growing economies such as China and India.

Since 2003 oil prices have been rising rapidly, reaching a peak in the summer of 2006. This has been the result partially of events in Afghanistan and Iraq, and partially of an increased demand for oil. For many developing countries this has resulted in a worsening in their economic position. Compared to developed countries, developing countries use more than twice as much oil to produce one unit of economic output. However, for oil-producing countries the increased oil price has provided a large increase in export earnings. Some argue that this allows authoritarian governments in oil-producing countries to entrench their positions, contrary to a global shift towards democracy (Friedman 2006).

(BP 2003, 2006; International Energy Agency 2003, 2004)

technology outdated, it becomes harder to manufacture goods, or even to extract raw materials or grow crops that can compete on the global market. Patterns of direct foreign investment are discussed in the next section.

A further problem that developing countries confront is that of protectionism. Perhaps the simplest is the implementation of a trade tariff, the application of a tax on imports. A large element of the Common Agricultural Policy of the European Union involves the use of tariffs to protect farmers from certain agricultural products from outside Europe. One effect of these tariffs is that countries within the European Union produce more than 45 per cent of the world's agricultural exports (WTO 2005: Table III.32). Another form of protectionism is the use of subsidies; so, for example, cotton farmers in the USA receive large subsidies on their production. Furthermore, there are non-tariff barriers, such as quotas, whereby only specified quantities of a product can be imported, and other restrictions such as safety requirements, environmental, or labour standards that must be adhered to and which might be judged unreasonable (see Chapter 17). This whole area has been described as the **new protectionism** because governments have sought to defend domestic industries, while at the same time honouring commitments to lower trade tariffs as part of international agreements.

According to Oxfam (2001) developing countries are losing US$100 billion each year from protectionist measures in industrialized countries. Tariff barriers are far higher in developed countries than in the rest of the world. At the same time, the richest countries in the world have increased their subsidies to their agricultural industries, making it harder for developing countries to compete.

KEY POINTS

- Since 1945 there have been massive increases in the levels of international trade.

- Although there are some exceptions, many countries in the developing world do not appear to have benefited greatly, and the proportion of the world's exports provided by Africa and Latin America has declined.

- Although the theory of comparative advantage suggests that all countries would benefit from participation in trading, the 'gains from trade' are not shared equally for various reasons.

Foreign Direct Investment

The theory of comparative advantage suggests that a country should specialize in those goods which it can produce relatively more cheaply. One area where the developing world has a distinct economic advantage is in labour costs. Throughout the developing world it is cheaper to employ workers than in developed economies. It would therefore seem logical for companies from the developed world to relocate production from those economies where labour costs are high to those where such costs are lower. With improvements in transportation and communications associated with globalization it has become easier for companies to set up production facilities in different parts of the world. O'Brien and Williams define FDI as 'investment made outside the home country of the investing company in which control over the resources transferred remains with the investor' (2004: 168–9). In other words, a key feature of FDI is that production will be directed by (and presumably organized to benefit) a corporation from outside the territory in which the investment is made. One of the aims of much recent policy promoted by the World Bank and IMF has been to encourage governments in the developing world to promote FDI—for example, by reducing taxation levels, and removing controls on capital flows. However, there has been much debate about the extent to which investment by TNCs benefits the host economies, with accusations that they use their size to extract inordinate benefits (see Box 3.5). This is an area of much controversy, and it is better to look at the actions of individual TNCs in different countries rather than necessarily drawing general conclusions.

There is a considerable amount of data on the levels of FDI, and one of the features of this activity is that it fluctuates on a year by year basis. Levels of FDI dropped off quite considerably following the terrorist attacks on the World Trade Center in New York in 2001, though they now appear to be increasing again. Tables 3.2 and 3.3 present data taken from statistics compiled by the United Nations Conference on Trade and Development. From these tables a few general observations can be derived.

BOX 3.5

Advantages and Disadvantages of Foreign Direct Investment

Advocates of FDI argue that TNCs

- *Introduce additional resources.* In particular they bring capital, a resource that many developing countries are particularly short of. Furthermore, they bring technology, financial resources, managerial expertise, and access to foreign markets.

- *Increase tax revenues.* TNCs will contribute to government revenues by paying local taxes.

- *Increase efficiency.* By providing links to the global economy, TNCs introduce competition into the local economy, thus encouraging more efficient local production.

- *Improve the balance of payments.* TNCs improve the balance of payments by producing local goods which previously had been imported, and producing goods for export.

While critics suggest that TNCs

- *Bring little in the way of new technology.* Most of the activities carried out by TNCs primarily involve assembly of parts produced elsewhere, and involve very little in the way of high technology.

- *Contribute little to the local economy.* TNCs, through a process known as 'transfer pricing', are able to ensure that they pay their taxes on profits in countries with low tax regimes (usually in the developed world). Furthermore, critics argue, TNCs drive local firms out of business using unfair competitive practices.

- *Worsen the balance of payments.* TNCs can have a negative impact on the balance of payments through the need to import machinery, spare parts, and payments to the parent company.

- *Adversely affect the local culture.* By introducing global brands, TNCs can undermine the market for locally produced goods and tastes.

- *Have a negative effect on the political system.* As TNCs are so large and powerful, and have a large impact on a small economy, they are able to extract concessions from governments by threatening to withdraw their facilities, or through bribery and corruption.

Table 3.2 Foreign Direct Investment Inflows by Region, 2000 (US$ Billion)

Region	1989–1994		2000		2004	
	annual average	% of total	Total	% of total	Total	% of total
World	200.2		1,270.8		648.1	
Developed world	137.1	68	1,005.2	79	380.0	59
Developing world	59.6	30	240.2	19	233.2	36
Central and Eastern Europe	3.4	2	25.4	2	34.9	5
Africa	3.9	2	8.2	0.6	18.1	3
Latin America and the Caribbean	17.5	9	86.2	7	67.5	10
Asia	37.7	19	143.8	11	147.6	22

Source: United Nations Conference on Trade and Development (UNCTAD) 2001: Table B1, 291–5, and 2005b: Table B1, 303–7

Table 3.3 Top Ten Recipients of Foreign Direct Investment in the Developing World, 2000 and 2004

	2000			2004	
Country	US$ billions	% of developing world total	Country	US$ billions	% of developing world total
Hong Kong, China	64.5	27	China	60.6	26
China	40.8	17	Hong Kong, China	34	15
Brazil	33.5	14	Brazil	18.2	8
Mexico	13.2	6	Mexico	16.6	7
Argentina	11.2	5	Singapore	16.1	7
South Korea	10.2	4	South Korea	7.7	3
Bermuda	6.6	3	Chile	7.6	3
Singapore	6.4	3	India	5.3	2
Malaysia	5.5	2	Malaysia	4.6	2
Taiwan	4.9	2	Argentina	4.3	2

Source: United Nations Conference on Trade and Development (UNCTAD) 2001: Table B1, 291–5, and (2005b): Table B1, 303–7

- Levels of FDI have risen considerably since the early 1990s. In the year 2000, levels of FDI were five times higher than the average for 1989–2004. This figure has declined since then, leading some commentators to suggest that the process of globalization is now stalling.

- The bulk of FDI is made by companies from the developed world investing in other developed countries (for example, Japanese car plants in Britain). However, the figures for 2004 suggest that the proportion of investment flowing to the developing world is increasing. It should also be noted that developing world TNCs have now started to emerge as some of the largest companies in the world.

- Although the proportion of FDI flowing to the developing world is increasing, it is very concentrated. Just ten countries absorb 75 per cent of

FDI directed to the developing world. In 2004, China was the largest recipient, and if the figures for China and Hong Kong are taken together, they account for over 40 per cent of developing world FDI. The whole of Africa receives just 8 per cent.

KEY POINTS

- FDI is a major component of global financial flows.

- Although the bulk of investment occurs in developed countries, a number of developing countries receive a significant, and increasing, proportion of the global total.

- There is considerable debate over the costs and benefits of FDI for developing countries.

Financial Flows

Trade and FDI are the more visible aspects of the global economy, yet in numerical terms they are dwarfed by the movements of money through the world's foreign exchanges. World trade amounts to approximately US$ 11 trillion per year (WTO 2005: 3). This is the equivalent of approximately six days' trading on the world's money markets (BIS 2005: 5). The sheer size of these financial flows compared to the volume of global production suggests that a large component of these transactions is speculative (see Scholte 2005: 166). The operation of financial markets, and the rapid flows of what is described as 'hot' money, is often perceived as having an adverse effect on local economies, especially those in the developing world, and has been the subject of considerable criticism (see Box 3.6).

These financial flows comprise two main elements. First, quite simply the buying and selling of money. Some of these transactions are related to trade and investment. For example, a company in Britain that wanted to purchase goods from Ghana would first need to purchase Ghanaian *cedi* in order to pay the supplier. However, much of the activity on the global currency markets could be more closely equated to gambling. Since the 1980s, many of world's major currencies have been free-floating.

BOX 3.6

Susan Strange on the Irrationality of Financial Markets

> Mad...is exactly how financial markets have behaved in recent years. They have been erratically manic at one moment, unreasonably depressive at others. The crises that have hit them have been unpredicted and, to most observers surprising. Their behaviour has very seriously damaged others. Their condition calls urgently for treatment of some kind.

(Strange 1998: 2)

In other words, governments have allowed the value of the currency to be largely dictated by the sentiments of the market. Some investors have made, and continue to make, large fortunes simply based on the buying of currencies which they anticipate will go up in value and selling those that they expect will become worth less. These financial movements can have implications for even the largest of economies: in 1992 Britain was forced out of the European

Exchange Rate Mechanism following large-scale selling of sterling.

A second feature of global financial flows is investment in the stock markets of other countries, usually described as 'portfolio investment', or indirect foreign investment. FDI usually involves the construction of factories and offices and the purchase of machinery. If the owner wishes to move production to another country these need to be disposed of or transferred, possibly a time-consuming activity. Holders of portfolio investment do not have a direct link to the bricks and mortar of the company concerned. They can sell their holdings of shares in overseas territories at the press of a computer button. This buying and selling of shares can take the pattern of a herd instinct. Certain countries or regions become very popular, meaning that large numbers of shares are bought, leading to stock market booms. At other times the same regions suddenly become unpopular—large numbers of shares are sold, leading to stock market crashes. These sudden changes of sentiment often have very little to do with the underlying economic stability or potential of the countries concerned. However, as with the buying and selling of currencies, for the insightful (or lucky) investor there are fortunes to be made by 'buying cheap and selling dear'. Furthermore, the rapid movements of money into and out of economies can be extremely destabilizing to the domestic economy.

During the late 1980s and early 1990s, many countries in the developing world were encouraged to open their economies to these kinds of financial flows. Financial liberalization involved removing restrictions on the buying and selling of the country's currency, and on the movements of capital in and out of the country. Such policies were adopted by many countries in Latin America, East Asia, and the former Soviet Union. For many analysts it is not a coincidence that these regions were afflicted

be severe financial disruption during the 1990s. Examples are the Mexican *peso* crisis of 1994–5, the Brazilian crisis, and Russia's *rouble* crisis of 1998, and a crisis in Argentina dating from 2000.

Perhaps the most famous of the financial crises of the 1990s was the one that swept through East Asia in 1997. There is much debate about the causes, and no simple explanation. However, one factor might be that these countries were simply the victims of their own success. As discussed in Box 3.2, the countries of East Asia have been very successful at following export-led models of development. They also were enjoying very high levels of domestic saving and low inflation—a perfect conjunction for continued growth. However, following financial liberalization, the perceived profitability of the region led to a vast inflow of speculative investment that the countries' domestic financial institutions were not able to manage. A speculative boom was followed by a crash. Bankruptcies in South Korea and Thailand led to a rapid withdrawal of funds from the entire region. The *Financial Times* described the events as follows: 'Investors piled into East Asia at the start of the decade with scant regard for the risk. When the mood changed, investors betted in the opposite direction with equally scant regard for the economic fundamentals. Small economies can be overwhelmed when large financial institutions make fractional adjustments to their global portfolios' (quoted in Valdez 2003: 354). The outcome was reductions in the rate of growth and in GDP per head, the second taking several years to recover. Analyses by the World Bank and IMF now suggest that the pace of financial liberalization was the problem. It is also worth pointing out that India and China, two of the fastest-growing economies in the world, have not implemented equivalent levels of financial liberalization, and were only indirectly affected by the crisis that swept through the region.

KEY POINTS

- A major component of the global economy is the movements of money involved in the buying and selling of currencies and stocks and shares in local economies.

- The rapid movement of capital associated with these markets can be extremely disruptive to local economies.

- In the 1990s, a number of countries in the developing world adopted financial liberalization policies, removing restrictions on the flows of international capital into and out of their economies. Many of these countries were affected by subsequent financial crises.

China in the Global Economy

Napoleon Bonaparte is alleged to have said that 'China is a sleeping giant. Let her sleep, for when she awakes she will astound the world.' A close examination of the information contained in Tables 3.1 to 3.3 and any other global economic statistics can only lead to one conclusion—China is awakening from a slumber that has lasted half a millennium. Less than a generation ago, China was a marginal economic actor, virtually an autarkic state, having little interaction with the global economy. However, a series of economic reforms, embarked on in the late 1970s, have brought about major, indeed startling, changes in the country's fortunes which have global implications. Not only does China's increased economic prominence have enormous implications for the entire global economy, its rise means that the whole economic textbook will have to be rewritten.

The statistics are staggering. Since economic reforms were introduced in 1978, China's economy has grown at an average of 9.5 per cent per year. It now consumes approximately a quarter of the world's steel production, a third of the world's rice, and nearly a half of the world's cotton and cement. Although on a per head basis China uses a twelfth of the oil consumption of the United States, its total oil usage exceeds that of Japan or Germany (all figures from Flavin and Gardner 2006). If China continues to grow at the same rate, its economy will undoubtedly become larger than that of the United States, although few agree about when this might occur.

China's rapid rise, however, poses a direct challenge to the economic developmental policies advocated for over two decades. Its economic system in no way conforms to that advocated by the Washington consensus. Economic development has occurred under a government that is not democratically elected. A measure of capitalist competition has been introduced into the society, and the non-state economy probably now accounts for more than half of total output, and yet public authorities, including especially the local governments, still exercise considerable control. Exports and imports are subject to restriction as are the activities of TNCs that invest in the country. The exchange rate is controlled, as well as the movements of capital both in and out of the country. As noted above, China and India, both countries that retained considerable controls over the movement of capital, were two countries that avoided the direct impacts of the East Asian financial crisis. In short, China has been a country which has pursued some policies that are contrary to those advocated by global financial institutions—and seems to have done extremely well.

Two important questions emerge from China's remarkable economic transformation. First, is the current rate of economic growth sustainable? The standard answer to this question is a distinct 'yes', and that China is emerging on the global scene as a significant economic and political actor, that will indeed 'astound' the world (see, for example, Kynge 2006). But some writers suggest a more cautious judgement. China's rapid economic expansion started from a very low base, and it will become increasingly difficult to maintain the momentum. They point to high levels of corruption and high levels of inefficiency in government-owned sectors, plus an inefficient banking and credit system. Furthermore, questions have to be raised about the ability of the political system to oversee the changes that are occurring in the economy and the high levels of inequality that are being created (see Waldron 2005: 717–21).

Second, does China's experience provide a model that is replicable by other developing countries? The development model being followed is not unique. There are considerable similarities to the export-oriented industrialization policies that have been utilized to great effect in other parts of South-East Asia (see Box 3.2). Where China is different is with regard to its size—the application of export-oriented approaches in a country that has a fifth of the world's population truly is world-shaking—and has prompted protectionist measures elsewhere (for

example, restrictions by the European Union on clothing imports). Furthermore, it is possible to argue that China has benefited from its position as relatively detached from the global economy during much of the second half of the twentieth century. As a result it has been able to avoid pressure to pursue policies which may have hampered and limited its economic growth. A further feature of this model is its association with authoritarian government. Industrialization in much of South-East Asia has been accompanied, at least in its early stages, by the absence of democratically elected government. It is unlikely that the level of sacrifices required in the pursuit of this model would be possible in a liberal democracy, though it should be noted that much of South-East Asia has now undergone a transition to democracy. China's population has also benefited from comparatively high levels of education, which date back to the revolution in 1949. High levels of investment in this area are finally paying off by providing a well-skilled workforce, who, for the time being, are prepared to work for comparatively low wages (for more discussion of China and its relevance to the developing world, visit the Online Resource Centre for this book).

KEY POINTS

- In the past twenty-five years, China has been transformed from a minor contributor to the global economy to an economic power house.

- China is experiencing a period of consistently high levels of economic growth, and is becoming a major consumer of raw materials.

- This has been achieved through the pursuit of policies at odds with the 'Washington consensus'.

Conclusion

Since 1945, the global economy has seen not only massive increases in the levels of world trade, but also an enormous growth in the prosperity of the developed world. With the emergence of a single global economy since 1990, these processes have accelerated. For most analysts these two features are closely linked. Yet the benefits of greater engagement in the global economy do not appear to have been obtained by the poorest countries. Why, in an era of a global economy and neo-liberal policies, are some countries poorer than they were a decade or even much longer ago?

A free market analysis would suggest that there are still too many blockages to the free movement of investment and goods. Poorer countries have undermined their own prospects of development by working against the market. A second position maintains that greater engagement is potentially beneficial, but because developing countries are behind the developed world in terms of industrialization, reforms to the global economy are required. A more radical position would argue that the global economic system entrenches inequality between the richest parts of the world and the poorest. For the past twenty years, the free market philosophy has dominated development policy (see Chapter 16). But although many developing countries have followed neo-liberal prescriptions, they still face protectionist measures imposed by governments in the developed world. This makes it more difficult to persuade them to proceed faster or in a more comprehensive fashion. Protectionist measures in the developed world have become a major

cause of divisions in the World Trade Organization (see Chapter 4).

The reasons for the disparity of wealth in the global economy will be disputed indefinitely. For the foreseeable future developing countries will have to make their way within a global capitalist environment. The operation of global markets has the potential to generate enormous wealth as well as the capability to exploit the most vulnerable. The governments of developing countries have the awesome task of trying to minimize the negative impacts of global capitalism, while attracting the potential benefits for their populations. China's rise displays the possibilities for developing countries in a global economy. Indeed, its rapid economic expansion is a contributory factor in decreases in global absolute poverty. Yet China has not played, so far, by the globalization 'handbook'—its participation in the global economy is by its own rules, and thus far, this seems to have been to its benefit. Meanwhile, governments of the developed world also confront a challenge: to resolve the contradiction of promoting free trade as a solution for the developing world while maintaining protectionism at home. While they fail to resolve this it would appear that the global economy operates largely in the interests of the rich and powerful and against some of the poorest and least influential parts of the world.

? QUESTIONS

1   Does globalization increase or decrease poverty in the developing world?

2   What are the 'gains from trade', and who benefits?

3   Assess the arguments for and against encouraging direct foreign investment in developing countries.

4   To what extent does financial liberalization lead to financial crisis?

5   What are the implications for the developing world of China's emergence as an economic superpower?

STEPHEN HOBDEN

GUIDE TO FURTHER READING

■ **Dicken, P. (2003),** *Global Shift: Reshaping the Global Economic Map in the 21st Century* **(London: Sage).** Clear overview of the emergence of a global economy, with good sections on the newly industrializing countries.

■ **Mandel, J. R. (2003),** *Globalization and the Poor* **(Cambridge: Cambridge University Press).** A good overview of arguments for and against economic globalization.

■ **O'Brien, R., and Williams, M. (2004),** *Global Political Economy: Evolution and Dynamics* **(Basingstoke: Palgrave Macmillan).** Clear discussion of the development of the global economy and key contemporary issues in international political economy.

■ **Scholte, J. A. (2005),** *Globalization: A Critical Introduction* **(Basingstoke: Palgrave).** A superb discussion of the subject and associated literature.

■ **Todaro, M., and Smith, S. (2003),** *Economic Development*, **8th edn. (Boston, Mass.: Addison Wesley).** Regularly revised and updated, contains excellent chapters on the role of developing countries in the global economy and on theories of trade.

■ **Valdez, S. (2003),** *An Introduction to Global Financial Markets*, **4th edn. (Basingstoke: Palgrave).** Effective introduction to the murky world of global finance.

■ **Van Marrewijk, C. (2002),** *International Trade and the World Economy* **(Oxford: Oxford University Press).** Excellent introduction to theories of trade and investment in the global economy.

WEB LINKS

● **www.freetrade.org** The site of the Center for Trade Policy Studies, Washington DC, whose 'mission' is to increase public understanding of the benefits of free trade and costs of protectionism.

● **www.twnside.org.sg/trade.htm** Third World Network page on trade issues, provides research critical of current global economic policies.

● **www.unctad.org** United Nations Conference on Trade and Development, containing voluminous data on trade and investment, and reports on the latest developments in the global economy.

● **www.oxfam.org** The site of the non-governmental organization Oxfam (UK), containing many of its reports on trade and protectionism.

● **www.undp.org** United Nations Development Programme—the United Nations body that focuses on development issues and produces annually a human development report.

ONLINE RESOURCE CENTRE

For additional material and resources, see the Online Resource Centre at:
www.oxfordtextbooks.co.uk/orc/burnell2e/

4

The Developing World in International Politics

STEPHEN HOBDEN

Chapter Contents

- Introduction: International Relations and the Developing World
- North–South Relations since 1945
- The Developing World in International Organizations
- The World Trade Organization
- Regional Integration
- Conclusion

Overview

The previous chapter examined the role of the developing world in the global economy. In this chapter the emphasis changes to the role of the developing world in international politics. International Relations as a discipline has traditionally overlooked the significance of the developing world in global politics. The chapter opens with an examination of the reasons for this and goes on to discuss why such an oversight is lamentable. The significant role played by developing countries in international politics since 1945 is demonstrated. This is followed by a discussion of the sizeable part played by countries of the developing world in international organizations. A division between international politics and international economics is a false one, and the chapter examines two topics where politics and economics interact: attempts at regional integration and the workings of the World Trade Organization.

STEPHEN HOBDEN

Introduction: International Relations and the Developing World

The developing world has been 'on the periphery' of the study or discipline of international relations (IR) (Thomas and Wilkin 2004). The discipline has primarily been concerned with relations between the great (or super) powers. Although perhaps understandable, this concentration is deeply problematic. It has meant that at least four-fifths of the global population was excluded as a subject of study. This has reflected a North American and European perspective on the world. It fails to acknowledge that while, during the cold war, there was a 'long peace' in Europe, many parts of the developing world were deeply mired in violent conflict, in which the superpowers were frequently involved. The rivalry between the superpowers was played out in a way that was far from 'cold', fuelling **proxy wars**, for instance in southern Africa and Central America. It also overlooks perhaps the most fundamental change to the international system during the twentieth century: the dissolution of the European empires. Finally, the opening years of the twenty-first century appear to be characterized by increasing conflict between parts of the developed and developing worlds, most notably in Iraq, but also including issues such as terrorism and migration (see Chapter 19).

The focus on the superpowers may reflect a deeper problem with the discipline. That is quite simply that traditional IR theory does not have the tools to understand the developing world. The traditional worldview of IR is one where the state is the key actor, and is the guarantor of the 'good life' for its citizens. States operate in a situation of 'anarchy', where they all have equal sovereignty, and must all in the final instance be liable for their own self-defence. Within the confines of the state there is order and hierarchy, while outside of the state is characterized by unregulated disorder. From the developing world this worldview may make little

sense. The state, rather than being the guarantor of the 'good life', has frequently been a major threat to the well-being of the individual. Many developing countries have been governed at some time or another by military regimes, which have targeted sections of the society for repression. The states of Latin America have, by and large, lived at peace with each other since the 1930s, but regimes in virtually every country in the region have committed major human rights violations. The anarchy has been on the inside rather than the outside. Furthermore, the state, rather than being the key actor, has had to compete with numerous other powerful actors, such as **warlords**, guerrilla groups, and drug cartels, which in some places appear to threaten its very existence. More recently, when developing countries acquiesced in **structural adjustment programmes**, external actors have had more power over the running of the society than the state itself. At the same time that domestic politics in the developing world perspective can be viewed as disordered, the external world appears to be more hierarchical, with the most powerful states determining the fates of the less powerful. Sovereignty, the right of states to govern within their own territory without external interference, a fundamental tenet of the charter of the United Nations, has been breached many times since 1945 (see Dickson 1997: chapter 1; Neuman 1998: 2–12).

While traditional approaches have tended to focus on those states with the most power, there have always been perspectives that attempted to incorporate an analysis of the developing world. Marxist approaches, in particular dependency and world-systems schools, have stressed the importance of a global economic system where the developing world has played a key role as the supplier of cheap labour and raw materials, and as a market for surplus production. More recently, post-colonial theorists (heavily influenced by post-structuralist approaches) have focused on questions of identity during and after the colonial period (see Chapter 2).

This chapter stresses the importance of the developing world in the cold war and post-cold war periods. It begins by considering the situation of developing countries during the cold war, followed by the implications of the collapse of the Soviet Union and the emergence of the United States as the dominant global power. It also examines the role of developing countries in international organizations, particularly the United Nations. A final section considers how the politics of North–South relations cannot be separated from the developing

countries' economic position, by discussing the significance of attempts at regional integration, and the workings of the World Trade Organization.

> **KEY POINTS**
>
> - The discipline of international relations has tended to focus on the role of the great (or super) powers.
>
> - This focus has ignored the vast proportion of the global population, and the key role that the developing world has played in the global politics of the cold war and post-cold war periods.

North–South Relations since 1945

The cold war

The now obsolete notion of a 'Third World' is closely linked to the period of the cold war, and is derived from a perceived tripartite division of the world:

- a 'First World', the United States, and its allies;

- a 'Second World', the Soviet Union, and Eastern Europe;

- a 'Third World' comprising the rest—the newly decolonized countries of Asia and Africa, and the countries of Latin America, most of which had gained their independence at the start of the nineteenth century.

This was a ridiculous oversimplification, though the ideological and strategic conflict played out between the superpowers certainly had a major impact felt by most countries of the Third World. This conflict took a variety of forms. There were cases of direct military intervention by the superpowers, such as the USA in Vietnam, and the Soviet Union in Afghanistan. There were many examples

of indirect intervention using either the carrot of aid policy, or the stick of sanctions, or the threat of the withdrawal of aid. There was also the use of proxy fighting forces to avoid direct intervention. Examples here include the funding by the USA of the Mujahidin to challenge the Soviet Union in Afghanistan, and the use of the Cuban army in southern Africa.

Once both superpowers had access to nuclear weapons, any direct confrontation would have been, in the terminology of the time, MAD—mutually assured destruction. A range of interests underpinned the superpowers' policies towards the developing world. For both there were security issues, both had trading concerns, and for both there were ideological issues that related to their views of themselves as nations. These different interests played out in different ways at different times.

In the beginning of the cold war, the US government's main interest in the developing areas was in supporting the calls for decolonization, in line with its worldview that a decolonized world would be more in its own interests. This was coupled, however, with a concern that newly independent countries should not fall under Soviet influence. Therefore there was a tension between the USA's support for decolonization, and its wish to maintain international stability. Additionally, with the triumph of Mao's revolutionary army in China, and North Korea's invasion of the south of the country, there was fear that communist influence was spreading in East Asia. The Soviet Union was barely engaged at this time. Stalin, now in physical decline, did not try to exploit Lenin's theory that the developing world was a weak link for the capitalist system, and had done little to support the Communist Party in China.

From the late 1950s and through the 1960s, both superpowers increased their activities in the developing world. The USA was particularly active in its own 'back yard', supporting the overthrow of democratically elected President Arbenz in Guatemala (1954), and attempting to overthrow Castro in Cuba (1961 onwards). Through this period it also became increasingly involved in the war between North and South Vietnam. Following the death of Stalin, the Soviet Union gave more attention to the newly independent countries, seeking to draw them under its influence. However, it lacked the power projection to protect potential satellite states. For example, in 1960 Prime Minister Lumumba of the Congo sought military aid to counter secessionists in his newly independent country, but the Soviet Union was not able to respond and the country soon came under the rule of Joseph Mobutu, who looked to the West. The Soviet Union ultimately did not offer protection to Cuba when its missiles were found on the island in the autumn of 1962.

As the USA became increasingly drawn into the Vietnam quagmire, confidence about its role in the world declined, and anti-US sentiment grew. The Soviet Union was now getting closer to strategic parity with the USA and was able to project its power with greater confidence. It gave direct support to revolutionary movements in Vietnam, Ethiopia, and Angola, and as a result gained strategic bases in Africa and Asia. It also supported revolutionary movements in Central America, giving it influence

very close to the United States. This growing confidence led it to launch a major military intervention in Afghanistan in late 1979 to support a friendly regime on its southern border.

The global situation changed dramatically in the following decade. It was now the Soviet Union that was mired in a foreign war, and the USA under President Reagan exploited the situation. The USA sought 'rollback'—reversing Soviet gains of the 1970s, and under the 'Reagan doctrine' support was given to anti-communist guerrillas. In Afghanistan the USA supported the Mujahidin, in Nicaragua the 'Contras', and in Angola UNITA (National Union for Total Independence of Angola). As the decade drew on, the cold war moved to a close. Mikhail Gorbachev's 'new thinking' in the Soviet Union sought a new relationship with the West and a Soviet withdrawal from Afghanistan. The impact of the Afghan war on the Soviet Union was at least comparable to that of the Vietnam War on the USA. Although not the sole cause of the collapse of the Soviet Union, within two years of the withdrawal from Afghanistan, Communist Party rule had ended. At the same time, material support for former satellite states, even Cuba, also ended.

The cold war was a time of great upheaval for the developing world. In the period immediately after the Second World War, most of it was still under colonial control. By the end of the cold war it was mostly independent. This wave of decolonization was accompanied by an international conflict between the two superpowers, fought over and in developing countries. For their governments it meant making a choice to align with one superpower or the other. This pressure provoked the creation of the Non-Aligned Movement in 1961—a collection of states that claimed to reject both superpowers, although in reality most states, Cuba for example, were aligned with one or other superpower.

The existence of two competing superpowers did mean that a choice existed for developing countries. Many countries were courted by both sides, with rival offers of financial and economic aid. For some the possibility existed to switch allegiances (or at least to threaten to switch). Egypt in the early 1970s changed its alignment from the Soviet Union to the United States, becoming one of the largest recipients of aid. The cold war provided these countries with at least an option between two superpowers with two ideologies concerning the operation of social and economic systems and the goals and modalities of development (see Allison and Williams 1990; Halliday 1989; Merrill 1994; and Westad 2005).

The post-cold war period

The end of the cold war in the late 1980s was greeted with optimism. In a 1991 speech, US President George H.W. Bush spoke of a New World Order which would be 'an historic period of cooperation . . . an era in which the nations of the world, East and West, North and South, can prosper and live in harmony' (quoted in Acharya 1999: 84). In the early 1990s, there was a sense that a new form of global cooperation could result in solving many of the world's problems. For many in the developed world this sense of peace and well-being was enhanced by a prolonged economic boom through much of the 1990s.

For developing countries too there were reasons to be optimistic. The cold war had been a cause of instability, and its end promised greater peace and stability. Accompanying the end of the forty-year superpower conflict a number of regional conflicts were also resolved—particularly in southern Africa (Mozambique, Namibia, and, temporarily,

in Angola) and Central America (Nicaragua and El Salvador). A new spirit of cooperation in the United Nations Security Council enabled that organization to become more active in conflict resolution. The UN achieved notable successes in Namibia, El Salvador, and Cambodia. It authorized an international military response to Iraq's invasion of Kuwait in 1990. Furthermore, a number of corrupt regimes which had been supported by one side or the other were replaced by democratic governments. There was much talk of a 'peace dividend' and considerable reductions in arms spending which could be funnelled towards development projects. At the Millennial UN General Assembly ambitious commitments were made by the member states to reverse global poverty. Also, the prospect of a truly global economy appeared to promise more extensive trading links with the hope of generating greater wealth.

Such developments did indeed suggest that the world had reached the 'end of history' as claimed by Francis Fukuyama. There were indications, however, that this view might be optimistic. A UN sponsored intervention in Somalia resulted in a humiliating withdrawal following the killing of eighteen US soldiers. In 1994, the global community looked the other way while genocide occurred in Rwanda. A more sombre account of post-cold war international relations was provided by Samuel Huntington's view that the cold war would be replaced by a clash of civilizations (see Box 4.1). For many the terrorist attacks

---

BOX 4.1

'End of History' or 'Clash of Civilizations'?

With the end of the cold war, and the emergence of the United States as the dominant world power, two accounts of international politics made a cross-over from the academic arena to the wider policy and media arenas. Both had implications for North–South relations. In 1989 Francis Fukuyama published a much-discussed article in which he speculated whether, with the demise of the Soviet Union as an ideological and

military threat to the United States, the human race had reached the end of history.

The triumph of the West, of the Western idea is evident first of all in the total exhaustion of viable systematic alternatives to Western liberalism. What we might be witnessing is not just the end of the Cold War, or the passing of a particular period of post-war history, but the end of history as such: that is the end of mankind's ideological evolution and the universalisation of Western liberal democracy as the final form of human government. The vast bulk of the Third World remains very much mired in history and will be a terrain of conflict for many years to come, but large scale conflict must involve large states still caught in the grip of history, and they are what appear to be passing from the scene. (Fukuyama 1992, first written 1989, emphasis in original)

Fukuyama's was essentially an optimistic liberal account. The global future was liberal democracy. Crucially, as conflict between democratic states was unlikely (the so-called democratic peace theory), the future prospect was for a more peaceful world.

A different view was offered by Samuel Huntington in an equally famous article, published in 1993. Rather than having reached the end of history, where conflict over the best form of social organization was over, Huntington argued that there were real differences at a civilizational level that would in the future lead to conflict:

The fundamental source of conflict in this new world will not be primarily ideological or primarily economic.

The great divisions among humankind and the dominating source of conflict will be cultural. Nation states will remain the most powerful actors in world affairs, but the principal conflicts of global politics will occur between nations and groups of different civilizations. The clash of civilizations will dominate global politics. The fault lines between civilizations will be the battle lines of the future. (Huntington 1993)

This more pessimistic, Realist-influenced view of global politics suggests that the future will be dominated by conflict between the developed and the developing world, though primarily divided by civilization. Interestingly, current US foreign policy seems to be influenced by both views. Although often denied, the notion of a clash of civilizations, seems to underlie the war on terror–controversially US President George W. Bush described the campaign as a 'crusade' in its early phases. Yet the declared aim of taking democracy to Iraq seems to be influenced by Fukuyama-like notions of liberal democracy as a universal and ultimate form of social organization.

on the USA in 2001 (9/11) appeared to confirm this gloomy prognosis, and the euphoria of the immediate post-cold war period appears to have been replaced by a 'global melancholy' (Halliday 2002: 214). The opportunities that appeared to be emerging for developing countries now look less promising. While the end of the cold war did provide greater stability in some areas, there has been greater instability in other regions. Afghanistan, for example, has been in a constant state of

upheaval, and the Democratic Republic of Congo descended into chaos, with its neighbouring countries intervening on opposing sides. There have also been concerns about how the USA will use its position as the only superpower. In the aftermath of 9/11 the US government declared its willingness to act unilaterally and pre-emptively to further its national security interests, and the invasion of Iraq in 2003 occurred without the clear support of the United Nations Security Council (see Box 4.2).

BOX 4.2

US President George W. Bush, 9/11, and the 'War on Terror'

There has been much discussion about whether the election of George W. Bush to the White House, the terrorist attacks of 11 September 2001, and the subsequent 'war on terror' mark a distinct turning-point in US foreign policy. Two aspects of the Bush administration policy appear to be particularly important. First, the US appears more prepared to act unilaterally,

and to be openly hostile to global organizations and commitments. Before 9/11 the Bush administration had signalled that it would withdraw from the Kyoto Agreement which the previous Clinton administration had been involved in negotiating. Following 9/11 the invasions of both Afghanistan and Iraq occurred without a Security Council mandate. The invasion of

Iraq occurred after an attempt to get UN authorization had been blocked in the Security Council. This leads on to a second area where a major change is claimed to have occurred–the so-called 'Bush Doctrine'. Under the Bush Doctrine, the US claims a right to intervene in other countries not only to *prevent* an imminent threat of attack on the US, but also to *pre-empt* such a threat from emerging. According to the September 2002 National Security Strategy of the USA:

For centuries, international law has recognized that nations need not suffer an attack before they can lawfully take action to defend themselves against forces that present an imminent danger of attack ... We must adapt the concept of imminent threat to the capabilities of today's adversaries ... The United States has long maintained the option of preemptive actions to counter a sufficient threat to our national security ... To forestall or prevent such hostile attacks by our adversaries, the United States will, if necessary, act preemptively. (White House 2002, emphasis added)

The presidential letter accompanying the Strategy document puts the point more directly:

As a matter of common sense and self-defense, America will act against such emerging threats before they are fully formed. (White House 2002)

These two developments would appear to be of particular concern to countries of the developing world. International organizations and international law provide some measure of protection for the weak against the strong. By distancing itself from such arrangements, the US government is indicating that it is not prepared to be constrained by international commitments. Foreign policy will primarily be directed by US interests rather than global concerns. Likewise, the claimed right to intervene in countries solely on the basis that a threat to US security *may emerge* is open to abuse.

However, has foreign policy under the Bush administration changed dramatically? Although it played a central role in the creation of much of the current international architecture, the US has always had vacillating relations with international organizations. Relations with the United Nations have been uneasy since the General Assembly became dominated by countries from the developing world following decolonization. Relations were particularly difficult during the Reagan era, when the US fell into serious financial arrears. Furthermore, the US has displayed a consistent pattern of intervention in countries of the developing world, during and after the cold war. In the immediate aftermath of the cold war, the US invaded Panama (during the presidency of George W. Bush's father)—a country that could hardly be considered a threat to US security. What, perhaps, has changed since 9/11 is that US policymakers are now more open about the rationale of foreign policy. As Slater observes:

The unilateralist dimension of US foreign policy has a long history, as does the belief that the US has the right to act above the law when its own perceived interests are imperilled. The Bush administration is not the first US administration to behave in such a way, but its lack of interest in concealing such a strategy is quite distinctive. (Slater 2004: 190)

Furthermore, the hoped-for increases in development aid have been slow to materialize; levels of aid, particularly to Africa, fell throughout the 1990s. The global total has picked up since then, but with debt relief and US aid to post-Saddam Iraq accounting for a significant share.

The global picture for developing countries is therefore mixed. Some states have benefited from a greater stability, while for many citizens the end of the cold war has meant greater instability. The post-cold war boom of the 1990s also offered increased possibilities for more countries to participate in the global economy. However, the demise of the Soviet Union has removed an option of choice. There is now one global economy, and one system—capitalism—and the costs of defaulting from this system have become higher. The option of playing one superpower off against the other no longer exists, and hence the room for manoeuvre has been reduced (see Fawcett and Sayigh 1999; Halliday 2002; Mesbahi 1994; Swatuck and Shaw 1994).

KEY POINTS

- During the cold war the superpowers intervened in the developing world in a variety of different ways.

- The superpowers were motivated by a variety of different interests: military security, trade, and ideology. The significance of these interests varied over time and location.

- The cold war was a source of instability for many countries in the developing world. However, in a

world where neutrality from the global struggle was difficult there was a choice of ideology and model of development.

- A post-cold war peace dividend has failed to appear for the developing world. Although some areas have experienced greater stability, many have not. There are also increasing fears regarding the deployment of US power.

The Developing World in International Organizations

Having considered the broader environment of international relations, the role of developing country states in international organizations merits closer attention, particularly in view of the clear majority of seats they now command in the United Nations General Assembly.

The United Nations

The United Nations system comprises six principal organs (the General Assembly, the Security Council, the Trusteeship Council, the Economic and Social Council, the Secretariat, and the International Court of Justice), plus numerous subsidiary organs, agencies, and programmes. Many of these subsidiary organizations are of direct relevance here, especially the Development Programme (UNDP), the Children's Fund (UNICEF), and the International Monetary Fund and World Bank (which are discussed below).

In theory the core of the organization is the General Assembly. All nations that are members of the United Nations have a seat in the Assembly. Its decisions are taken on the basis of sovereign equality (namely one member, one vote). The vote

of the United States carries the same weight as that of Haiti, and China (with approximately one-quarter of the world's population) has the same vote as Tonga (which has a population of 104,000). Members of the Assembly can raise any issue for discussion that falls within the range of the Charter. The call for a ' New International Economic Order', a major attempt by the developing world to restructure the global economic system was launched in the General Assembly.

Although the General Assembly appears to be at the centre it is the Security Council which has the real power. It comprises five permanent members (Britain, China, France, Russia, and the United States, usually known as the P5), plus ten non-permanent members. The non-permanent members are elected by the General Assembly and have a seat for two years. The non-permanent seats are allocated on a regional basis—five for Africa and Asia, two for Latin America, one for Eastern Europe, and two for Western Europe. The charter imbues considerable power in the Security Council. Under Article 24(1) the Council is given 'primary responsibility for the maintenance of international peace and security'. The power of the veto is a key distinction between the permanent and non-permanent members in the Security Council. This power to block action has become a major issue in the UN, particularly given that the membership of the P5 is based on the distribution of international power at the end of the Second World War. With the exception of China, there is no permanent representation from the developing world, and none from Africa, or Latin America. Reform of the Security Council is a frequent topic within the UN, with countries such as Brazil, Nigeria, South Africa, and India being suggested as possible candidates for a permanent seat. However, any proposed reform of the charter of the United Nations can be vetoed by one of the P5. To date these countries appear to have little enthusiasm for extending the privileges of permanent membership to other countries.

The Economic and Social Council (ECOSOC) is part of the UN that has particular relevance for developing countries because it has specific responsibility for overseeing development-related activities. ECOSOC comprises fifty-four members elected by the General Assembly, each serving for a period of three years. ECOSOC primarily has a coordinating role, overseeing the activities of the various UN institutions having economic and social responsibilities. For example, in theory the International Monetary Fund is a subsidiary institution of ECOSOC. In addition, ECOSOC is the key forum in the UN for the discussion of economic and social issues. It can initiate studies and organize conferences and make recommendations to the Security Council. It also has a key role in promoting human rights (see Chapter 18). Box 4.3 assesses some of the successes achieved by the UN with regard to development issues, while Box 4.4 outlines the key role played by the UN in the process of decolonization, one of the most significant developments of the second half of the twentieth century.

The International Monetary Fund, and the World Bank

The International Monetary Fund (IMF), the World Bank, and the World Trade Organization (see next

---

BOX 4.3

United Nations' Achievements in Development

The UN has been involved in development issues in a number of ways:

- As an information source, with experts in economics, agriculture, and industrial development.
- Direct assistance in emergency situations.
- The creation of regional organizations to address the particular problems of specific areas, for example the Economic Commission for Asia and the Far East.
- Specific development responsibilities of UN agencies, for example the UNDP and the UNHCR (High Commissioner for Refugees).
- Numerous resolutions in the General Assembly related to development issues.
- A series of 'development decades', intended to keep issues such as global inequality on the agenda.

The UN can point to a number of areas of success:

- Life expectancy globally has increased.
- Child mortality rates for under-5s have decreased.
- Immunization levels have improved, as has access to primary health facilities, availability of clean water, and literacy levels.
- An achievement that can be directly attributed to a UN agency is the eradication of smallpox, coordinated by the World Health Organization.

That the organization retains such goals is demonstrated by the Millennium Declaration adopted in September 2000. This pledged the member states to work towards ambitious goals including halving the proportion of the world's population living on less than $US1 a day, and ensuring that all the world's children receive a primary education (see Chapter 16).

BOX 4.4

United Nations and Decolonization

The end of the European empires is one of the most significant developments of the last century. The oversight of this process is perhaps one of the UN's greatest achievements. The notion of self-determination is at the core of the Charter, articulated in Article 1(2) and repeated in Article 55. Furthermore, a pledge to develop self-government in non-self-governing territories (a euphemism for colonies) is made in Article 73.

In the immediate aftermath of the Second World War a small number of countries became independent. For example, India gained independence from Britain in 1947. The first move of newly independent countries was to take up a seat in the UN General Assembly as a mark of sovereignty and independence. The newly independent states were critical of the continuation of empire, and the General Assembly became the main forum where calls for decolonization were voiced. By 1960, there were sufficient members to allow the passing of Resolution 1514, which condemned the continuation of colonialism. In the 1960s, several African states became independent and further resolutions were passed calling for colonialism to be eradicated.

The UN also acted in a very practical way to smooth the process of decolonization. The withdrawal of colonial powers from territories was seldom a straightforward affair, frequently leaving civil strife and disastrous levels of underdevelopment. The UN was frequently drawn into such situations, as peacekeeper and as provider of essential services. With the withdrawal of the British from India, massive unrest broke out between the Hindu and Muslim populations of India and the newly created state of Pakistan. There was massive loss of life and displacement of population. The UN Security Council voted to send an observer group to monitor the situation in the hope that an outside group might calm the situation. UNMOGIP (United Nations Military Observer Group in India and Pakistan) was created in 1949 to patrol the border area in Kashmir. It remains in place today.

Decolonization also transformed the organization itself. There were fifty-one original members in 1945, and the USA and the West in general had a built-in majority in the General Assembly. By 1960 (when Resolution 1514 was passed) the situation had changed dramatically—to a hundred members, of whom sixty-six were from the developing world, including forty-six from Africa and Asia. By this point, the General Assembly was supporting the position adapted by the United States in around half of all votes taken. By 1980, more than half of the UN consisted of non-founder members, which had not been sovereign states in 1945. Their loyalty to a US-dominated world order was low and the vast majority of the votes in the Assembly were against the US position and in support of the Soviet Union. As a result, the General Assembly became the forum for issues that were a priority for the developing world.

section) all have their origins in the conference held at Bretton Woods, USA, in July 1944. The International Monetary Fund (IMF) is primarily concerned with maintaining the operation of the global financial system. The World Bank concentrates on providing loans to developing countries. Both have had profound implications for the developing world.

The IMF

The aims of the IMF are laid out in its Articles of Agreement. They are:

- to increase monetary cooperation between member states,

- to facilitate increased trade,

- to promote foreign exchange stability,

- to help member states overcome balance of payments problems,

- and to reduce the duration of international financial disequilibria.

Unlike the UN General Assembly, voting in the IMF is not based on one country, one vote—instead voting is based on the size of the quota that each country pays into the fund. This in turn is related to the size of the country's economy. Hence the USA, with the largest economy, has the largest proportion of the vote (approximately 17 per cent), while many of the poorest countries have a mere 0.001 per cent. As a result the developed world always has a majority.

The prime activity of the IMF has always been to make short-term loans to countries undergoing balance of payments crises (when the value of imports exceeds those of exports for a prolonged period). Countries can borrow money in 'tranches', but the more they borrow, the greater the level of conditionality (see Chapter 15). These requirements frequently take the form of structural adjustment packages.

In recent years, the IMF has concentrated on four main functions. First, it has taken a surveillance role, both of member states and of the global economy. It produces a bi-annual World Economic Outlook giving information on the main economic trends. Through its publications it also seeks to promote its own preferred neo-liberal policy preferences. Secondly, it has intervened to a large extent in the economic policies of a number of countries, particularly as a result of the debt crisis. For many countries it has been essential to get an IMF 'seal of approval' in order to be able to attract finance from other sources. Thirdly, the IMF provides training for government officials, and technical assistance missions to assist governments with economic planning. Finally, the IMF has been involved in a number of global initiatives to help resolve particularly large financial crises, for example in Mexico (1994), several countries in South-East Asia (1997), and Brazil (1999).

The World Bank

The World Bank is in a sense a more complex organization than the IMF. It makes more sense to talk of the World Bank group, rather than a single organization. At the core of the group is the International Bank for Reconstruction and Development, usually known as 'The Bank'. This started off by making loans to aid the reconstruction of

Europe following the destruction wreaked by the Second World War, but now specializes in making loans to finance major projects in the developing world. In terms of its organization the World Bank group operates in a way very similar to the IMF. It has a Board of Governors, one from each member, which meets twice per year, while an Executive of twenty-four meets twice a week to oversee the normal running of the group. The mix of elected and permanent members is similar to the IMF, as is the system of weighted voting.

A contradiction lies at the heart of the World Bank in the sense that it operates in many ways similarly to a commercial bank yet has development objectives of reducing poverty and promoting economic growth. As a result, its policies have tended to change. From the 1950s to the 1970s, it promoted state-led development, seeing government very much as the agent of development, and its loans reflected this view. From the 1970s, it started to accept the neo-liberal agenda, and its loan policies reflected the view that states should now withdraw from direct intervention in many development activities. Most recently it has engaged with the notion of participatory development, which means seeking to gain wider agreement in society for development policies.

The debt crisis

The World Bank and the IMF played significant roles in the 'Third World debt crisis'. During the 1970s, Western banks became very heavily involved in lending to developing countries. This was a time when interest rates were low, and borrowing looked attractive. However, interest rates rose rapidly in the early 1980s. Much of the borrowing had been from private banks, and this had the result of increasing repayment levels dramatically. The debt situation became a 'crisis' for Western banks when in August 1982 Mexico announced that it could no longer meet its interest payments. The USA made short-term bridging loans to enable Mexico to maintain its interest payments, and by November Mexico had agreed a package of measures with the IMF that allowed the extension of further loans to the country.

A similar approach was applied to other countries throughout Latin America as they faced difficulties in making interest payments. However, the IMF on its own could not resolve the crisis. In 1985 the US Treasury Secretary, James Baker, announced a plan that would encourage the World Bank and commercial banks to increase lending to fifteen of the most indebted countries, in exchange for thoroughgoing restructuring of their economies. The 'Baker Plan' was superseded in 1989 by the 'Brady Initiative' (after Treasury Secretary Nicholas Brady). The Brady Initiative extended the Baker Plan by attempting to introduce some mechanisms by which debt could be forgiven, or at least reduced. IMF structural adjustment programmes became the standard by which a country's eligibility for relief under the Baker and Brady initiatives could be assessed. These initiatives together with a number of other piecemeal measures were sufficient to avert an international banking crisis.

The reactions of the developed world and of the IMF and World Bank to the debt crisis have had two main effects. First, the crisis has been 'managed'. Although debt remains a problem, the crisis was dealt with in such a way that the entire banking system was ultimately not threatened. Secondly, it shifted the crisis onto the poorest peoples of the developing world. Furthermore, the emphasis that structural adjustment programmes have placed on promoting exports to earn revenue so as to service debts has meant that many developing countries have increased their reliance on commodity exports, notwithstanding the economic drawbacks and negative environmental impact.

KEY POINTS

- International organizations have had a profound effect on developing countries, whilst providing them with a forum to raise development issues.

- The UN General Assembly has frequently been used to pass resolutions critical of the developed world.

- The IMF and World Bank are significant actors in global finance. Critics of these organizations argue that power over decision-making is held disproportionately by the richest countries.

- The IMF and World Bank played central roles in the management of the debt crisis.

The World Trade Organization

Like the World Bank and IMF, the World Trade Organization (WTO) is a multilateral agreement which has an enormous impact on the developing world, and has been the object of considerable criticism. The aim of the WTO is to promote trade, a central feature of economic globalization, as discussed Chapter 3. The changing character of international politics and the inseparability of the economics and politics are both born out in the World Trade Organization and its predecessor.

The idea of establishing an international trade organization was originally discussed at the Bretton Woods conference. However this ambitious project was replaced by a more limited General Agreement on Tariffs and Trade (GATT). 'General Agreement' sounds like a one-off trade agreement, but became an ongoing process of negotiation. In line with the general assumption of the immediate post-war period that the great depression of the 1930s and the move into protectionism bore heavy responsibility for the Second World War, the GATT was an attempt to promote international trade through lowering barriers to trade, and providing a method by which trade disputes could be adjudicated. The members of the GATT first met in 1947 and then proceeded, through a succession of 'rounds', or series of agreements, to extend the range of items covered by GATT agreements.

During the Uruguay Round of the GATT 1986–94, the decision was made to create the WTO as a more formal organization to oversee the working of the global trading system. The Uruguay Round ended with an 'all in one' agreement, meaning that potential members had to sign up to the whole agreement and could not opt out of particular sections. Critics argue that developing world countries were pressured into signing up to an agreement that from the outset was biased against their interests.

The WTO has three main roles. First, it provides an institutional and legal framework for the operation of world trade. Secondly, it provides the arena where international trade issues can be discussed and policies formulated. Finally, it provides a mechanism whereby trade disputes between members can be settled.

Supporters of the organization argue that it is a technical rules-based organization. They point out that all members have one vote. All decisions are based on consensus. Compared to the World Bank and the IMF, the voice of the developing world can be expressed much more forcefully. However, critics of the organization argue that the inequalities of the global system are woven into the organization. The poorest countries find participation in its proceedings costly whilst, according to critical **non-governmental organizations**, much of the real decision-making takes place 'behind the scenes' (Box 4.5). More fundamentally, even though it gives the appearance of being based on rules and equality of power, it is still possible for the richer countries to manipulate the system in their own interests and maintain the liberalization agenda where it works in their favour (see Stiglitz 2002; Thomas 2000).

Despite these criticisms, the operation of the WTO matches the changes in the global distribution of power suggested in the previous chapter. The latest, so-called 'development' round of WTO talks was launched at Doha in 2001, but ground to a halt in the summer of 2006. Although the issues and discussions are immensely complex, the key point is the failure of the United States and European Union to reduce subsidies to their agricultural producers. Countries of the developing world are no longer prepared to accept further reductions in their industrial tariffs (which would favour exports from the developed world) without the reduction of protection provided to agricultural

---

BOX 4.5

The Politics of Pressure at the World Trade Organization

Jawara and Kwa (2004) in their assessment of decision-making processes at the WTO point to several ways in which countries with most power exert influence on developing world countries.

- *Inducements*: countries are promised more aid, or preferential trade deals, in exchange for signing agreements that favour the developed world.
- *Threats*: by contrast, countries that raise issues that confront the interests of the most powerful confront the possibility of reduced aid and/or the removal of preferential trade deals.

- *Exclusion*: some countries are not invited to discussions that occur in the 'green room'. These are 'mini-ministerials' that occur before the main gatherings of the WTO.
- *Complaints against ambassadors*: in some instances, in order to gain agreement, or to eliminate proposals that are not in the interests of the most powerful, complaints are made against representatives of developing countries 'over their heads', resulting in their instructions being amended, or even their dismissal.

producers in the developed world—which has been promised since the conclusion of the Uruguay Round. Furthermore, there are now countries such as Brazil and India which, given their growing contribution to world trade, are less susceptible to pressure and more able to represent the interests of the developing world.

These issues are very difficult to resolve; domestic political pressure in the US and European Union especially make it very difficult for the governments to remove the protection given to their agricultural producers. Further agreements within the WTO may not be possible. Some critics of the WTO would welcome the dissolution of the organization; however a completely unmanaged system of international trade would probably not benefit the poorest in the world. A key influence on the future of the organization will be China. China joined the WTO in December 2001, and although reservations have been expressed since then about the policy concessions that were made to gain membership the country now relies for a good deal of its new-found prosperity on international trade. However, China was not involved in the series of talks which resulted in the suspension of the Doha Round.

KEY POINTS

- The World Trade Organization, the successor organization to the General Agreement on Trade and Tariffs, attempts to promote trade by persuading its members to reduce tariff levels.

- It also provides a mechanism by which trade disputes can be adjudicated.

- Many argue that it operates in the interests of the richest countries, who are able to apply political pressure to ensure that decisions taken prioritize their concerns.

Regional Integration

The overlap between the international economy and international politics is also found in the attempts of developing countries to pursue policies of regional integration. Regionalism emerged as a separate strategy with a first wave in the 1960s, but which had run its course by the early 1970s, and a second wave or 'new' regionalism in the 1990s. The prime aim of the first wave of regionalism was to increase the size of the market for locally produced manufactures. Regional blocks were also thought potentially to increase negotiating power in international organizations. One of the features of the first wave of regional organizations, such as the Caribbean Common Market (established 1973), was the attempt to implement a high level of political control over production, so that decisions about the siting of industrial production were supposed to be made at a regional level. The idea was that by sharing out industrial production, the benefits from economies of scale could be maximized. This proved to be both politically and economically unviable. The first wave of regionalism foundered when the required degree of political cooperation and coordination failed to materialize. The maintenance of high tariffs once again resulted in inefficient industries, unable to compete internationally. Weak transport and other infrastructural links also played a part.

By the mid-1970s, many of the first wave of regional organizations were moribund in all but name. However in the 1990s, a 'new' regionalism emerged, inspired by the European Union. These organizations adopted a much larger free market agenda, without the political baggage associated with the first wave. Some formerly dormant organizations such as the Central American Common Market have been revitalized, and other new groups have emerged, such as MERCOSUR—the common market of the Southern cone, in South America. The aim of these organizations has been to promote inter-regional trade through the lowering of internal tariffs, without ambitious attempts at controlling the economic diversification of the countries involved (see Appendix 3: Regional inter-governmental organizations in the developing world).

In some ways this can be seen as a reaction to the impacts of globalization. As a way of protecting their economies from the pressures of the global economic market, countries in different parts of the world have joined together to form regional blocks. However, in some ways, the 'new regionalism' can be viewed as a way of increasing the speed of globalization even further. The aim of the old regionalism was to erect *external* barriers to protect domestic production. The aim of the new regionalism is to *reduce* internal barriers to trade as a means of promoting trade within the region (Payne 2004: 16–17).

KEY POINTS

- There have been two main waves of regionalism in the developing world.

- In the first wave ambitious political attempts were made to develop large internal markets protected from the rest of the global economy by high tariff walls.

- A second wave, or 'new regionalism', by contrast has focused on reducing internal tariffs as a means of promoting trade locally while remaining open to the global economy.

Conclusion

The notion of a 'Third World' was primarily a construction of the cold war. As the conflict drew to an end increasing diversity between regions, based on divergent rates of economic growth and competition between countries for the supposed fruits of globalization, has eroded the perception of shared interests that underlay earlier groupings, such as the Non-Aligned Movement. It is too early to say whether this is a permanent feature, or whether durable new alliances will be forged in response to a US-dominated world order. The increasing economic power and confidence to act on a global stage displayed by countries such as India, and especially China, suggest that major changes are occurring in the international system.

A key argument of this chapter has been that countries in the developing world have, and continue to have, a major impact on international relations. Organizations such as the Non-Aligned Movement provided a voice during the cold war. The diversity of patterns of development now means that organizations claiming to represent all less-developed countries are unlikely to be effective. The new drive to regionalism offers an alternative forum and possibilities of exerting greater influence in negotiations with the developed world. The emergence of a global economy also offers immediate advantages to some. Where capital is more mobile, developing countries can exploit their advantage of lower wages. Countries where there are high educational standards are particularly likely to be able to gain from this. For example, India has been particularly successful in attracting jobs in the information technology and call centre sectors. India, Brazil, and China are all regional superpowers, able to exert their influence internationally. In due course the first two might gain more formal institutional recognition in the UN Security Council if that body is reshaped. The emergence of what has been described as a global civil society offers

STEPHEN HOBDEN

additional possibilities. Neo-liberalism is under attack from some quarters in the developed world, as the anti-globalization movement has demonstrated. There are increasing avenues for the development of transborder and supraterritorial alliances between the peoples of the North and South.

The character of the global system remains unsettled following the end of the cold war. But the situation of the majority of the world's population who reside in the developing world should become a more central area of study for those who seek to comprehend international processes.

QUESTIONS

1 Why have theorists of international relations consistently underestimated the significance of the developing world?

2 Assess the significance of the role played by the developing world in the cold war conflict between the Soviet Union and the United States.

3 Should the developing world welcome the emergence of a US-dominated world order? Give reasons for your answer.

4 Has the world reached the 'end of history', or is there a 'clash of civilizations' instead?

5 Critically assess the role of the UN in promoting development.

6 To what extent can countries from the developing world influence decision-making in the WTO?

7 How does 'new regionalism' differ from 'old regionalism'?

GUIDE TO FURTHER READING

■ **Duffield, M. (2001), *Global Governance and the New Wars: The Merging of Development and Security* (London: Zed).** Analyses the position of the developing world in the emerging world (dis?)order.

■ **Jawara, F. and Kwa, A. (2004), *Behind the Scenes at the WTO: The Real World of International Trade Negotiations* (London: Verso).** Accessible account of the WTO, detailing negotiating practices of the member states.

■ **Payne, A. (2005), *The Global Politics of Unequal Development* (Basingstoke: Palgrave).** Superb discussion of issues of development and underdevelopment from a New Political Economy perspective.

■ **Slater, D. (2004), *Geopolitics and the Postcolonial: Rethinking North-South Relations* (Oxford: Blackwell)**. Outstanding overview of approaches to thinking about North–South relations, influenced by post-colonial and post-structuralist approaches.

■ **Thomas, C. (2000), *Global Governance, Development and Human Security: The Challenge of Poverty and Inequality* (London: Pluto).** Excellent study of the role of international organizations in dealing with development and security issues.

■ **Westad, O. A. (2005), *The Global Cold War: Third World Interventions and the Making of Our Times* (Cambridge: Cambridge University Press).** Recent account of the cold war focusing on the key role played by the developing world, and the implications for contemporary international relations.

WEB LINKS

● **www.twnside.org.sg/econ_1.htm**   Third World Network reports on international organizations.

● **www.un.org**   Official site provides overview of the organization and workings of the United Nations.

● **www.imf.org**   Official site provides details of role of the International Monetary Fund.

● **www.worldbank.org**   Official site provides complete overview of the operation of the World Bank Group.

● **www.wto.org**   Overview of history, purpose, and working of the World Trade Organization.

● **www.jubileeresearch.org**   Successor organization to the Jubilee 2000 campaign against 'Third World debt', it provides a wealth of information on debt-related issues.

● **www.worldbank.org/hipc**   The World Bank Group's site for the heavily indebted poor countries initiative, containing much useful statistical and other information.

 ONLINE RESOURCE CENTRE

For additional material and resources, see the Online Resource Centre at:
www.oxfordtextbooks.co.uk/orc/burnell2e/

PART 2

Society and State

In Part Two we introduce the social and cultural aspects of developing countries within which their politics are embedded, and which are so central to understanding political behaviour.

The part has two main aims. The *first* is to indicate the great diversity of social structure found in the developing world and in countries individually; the variety in terms of religious, ethnic, and other identities; and the divisions that these features together with gender- and economically based inequalities give rise to. In contemporary social science, civil society also ranks very high as both a constituent feature and determining influence upon politics; that too can vary widely in practice. The role played by social movements and 'people power' too is gaining in recognition.

The *second* aim is to show the political significance of these complex social contexts and diverse forms of social and political organization and how problematic they can be for political management. They pose challenges as well as opportunities for the institutional arrangements centred on the state, in some cases expressly demanding political solutions outside of and alternative to the conventional mechanisms and processes of the state. The contents of this part thus set the scene for the investigation in Part Three of how developing world states have responded to the many internal and external demands on them and to their transformation in recent decades. So, for instance, societal features introduced in Part Two can help explain tendencies towards state collapse and the pressures to engage in political liberalization and democratization as well as the forces resisting those agendas.

The illustrative material included in Part Two is drawn widely from around the developing world. By comparison, case studies of individual countries selected to illustrate specific themes can be found in Part Five. For example, tendencies towards social fragmentation and political disintegration in developing countries, and conversely steps to nation-building, are revisited in Chapter 20 in relation to Indonesia and South Africa respectively. This choice of countries illustrates how easy it is to oversimplify and misjudge the likely consequences of diversity for political unity, especially when set against a background of rapid change from more authoritarian and less inclusive forms of political rule to governing arrangements that resemble more closely the model of Western-style liberal democracy. Similarly, for example, Chapter 9 on civil society is complemented in Chapter 21 by a detailed investigation of how active or passive civil society really is in two very different but nonetheless high-profile countries, namely India and Saudi Arabia. Readers are encouraged to study the introduction to Part Five and consult the relevant case studies in that section when reading the chapters in Part Two.

5 Inequality

JENNY PEARCE

Chapter Contents

- Introduction
- Charting the Conceptual Waters
- The Political Economy of Inequality in Developing Countries
- Equality Questioned; Inequality Revisited
- Equality and Diversity
- Conclusion

Overview

Inequality is at the heart of discussions on the political economy of development. Development economists have long debated whether there are trade-offs between growth and equality which will affect the rate at which poverty will be addressed. Sociologists have drawn attention to the horizontal inequalities around gender, ethnic, and other social differences which have persisted in the global South as well as the vertical inequalities around income and assets. Political geographers have emphasized the regional and spatial dimensions of inequalities in development, and the gaps between rural and urban livelihoods. Political scientists have explored the impact of gender, ethnic, and class inequalities on the nature of the state and political life in the developing world. These discussions are also influenced by assumptions about whether or not equality is a goal of human development and whether, for instance, it means equality of opportunity or equality of outcome. Following an Introduction, the first section of this chapter charts the conceptual waters of thinking about equality and illustrates this with examples of social inequalities and their impact on politics in the developing world. The second section explores the political economy of inequality in the developing world, as government responsibilities around ensuring equality of opportunity, if not equality of outcome, have become more widely accepted. The third section traces the way market liberalization of the 1980s and 1990s sidelined or excluded equality as a goal of development only to see it come back on the agenda at the beginning of the twenty-first century, as evidence mounted of growing income inequality within and between developing countries and between them and the developed world. The debate is no longer confined, however, to income inequality. The relationship between social, political, and economic inequalities has expanded and deepened. It is acknowledged even in the mainstream that entrenched social and economic inequalities can constrain the poverty reduction impact of growth. The fourth section returns to the conceptual field and contemporary discussion on inequality. The idea of the 'equality of man' as an ontological assumption has been challenged by the recognition that human beings are born with different attributes and capacities, as well as into diverse belief systems and groupings, and the resulting divergences in needs might require policies which compensate the disadvantaged, in other words unequal treatment. However, while the 'equality of man' may arguably have limitations as a basis for thinking about equality, equality of human worth, whatever the differences between people, must surely be essential to such thinking. Translating this into political institutions and economic policy is still very limited in practice, however. In the meantime, inequalities in power, status, assets, and income continue to be major sources of contentious politics in the developing world. It remains difficult to envisage progress in addressing such inequalities without energetic political participation through collective action in social movements and other forms of 'people power' (see Chapter 10), as well as formal politics, by those presently disadvantaged.

Introduction

The issue of inequality was raised by development economists soon after 'development' emerged as a field of policy and study. Harvard economist Simon Kuznets (1955) put forward his 'inverted-U hypothesis', arguing that relative income inequality increases in the early stages of economic development and does not improve until countries reach middle-income levels. If economic growth leads to increased inequality in this way, it could take many years to eradicate poverty in the so-called 'developing' countries. In the post-war years, the inequality and development debate remained framed in terms of income and wealth disparities, and the struggle for a model of development premised on economic equality was intense.

An implicit post-war consensus emerged in the industrialized world that government has a responsibility to address inequalities. This was disturbed in the 1980s when the rise of the paradigm of market liberalism posed a serious theoretical and practical challenge to redistributive theories of justice. Concern with income inequality as a goal of development policy declined. In its 1990 *World Development Report* (1990: 47) the World Bank charted the effect on poverty of economic growth in eleven countries, concluding 'in the low-income countries inequality consistently improves (contrary to the Kuznets' hypothesis), and there is no case in which the effect of growth is offset by changes in inequality . . . In short growth reduces poverty.' This signalled a major shift in mainstream thinking about the relationship between inequality, poverty, and development. Pro-poor growth rather than the impact of growth on distribution became the core goal of development.

Paradoxically, the conceptual debate on inequality remained lively. The collapse of universalizing social theory has resulted in an unprecedented uncovering of differential life experiences throughout societies all around the world, which has favoured new thinking on social stratification dynamics. The cultural dimensions of inequality were exposed, while recognition of human differences suggested that the 'equality of man' is not necessarily the best foundation for egalitarian theory. In its 2001 *World Development Report*, the World Bank acknowledged that 'high initial inequality' reduces the poverty impact of a given rate of growth, and that there may even be circumstances in which addressing asset inequality can enhance economic efficiency and benefit growth. It also recognized that gender inequalities have a particularly negative impact on economic growth as well as poverty reduction, and that interventions in the market can aid poverty eradication amongst such socially disadvantaged groups as indigenous peoples and certain castes and tribes. In 2005–6, both the World Bank and the United Nations Development Programme produced annual development reports dedicated to the themes of equity and inequality.

The building of appropriate new social, political, and economic arrangements and institutions at the global and national levels remains, however, a distant goal. Improving individual advantages through aggregative growth approaches is still considered preferable on efficiency grounds to redistributive policies aimed at reducing the inequalities in the distribution of advantages. Inequalities in income, assets, access to services, and political power continue to generate a politics of contestation, led sometimes by social movements seeking social justice and sometimes by politicians as a means of building political power. These extra-institutional challenges suggest that the inequality that has been confronted least is that of political power and its impact on all the other forms. Who, on what grounds, and through what process, is to determine the developmental goals a society and indeed all of humankind sets for itself when initial inequalities become so embedded over time that they are not recognized as such? Inequality not only impedes access to the fruits of development, it limits access to decision-making and the exercise of full citizenship. But which inequalities should be addressed first? Is political equality a precondition for economic equality or vice versa? Do we sufficiently understand how horizontal differences in terms of group identity become 'institutionalized categorical inequalities' (Tilly 1999) if we want to eliminate them from our social and political arrangements?

KEY POINTS

- Post-war development thinking was influenced by the argument that economic development may enhance income inequality and postpone poverty change.

- Post-war acceptance that governments have some responsibility to redress inequality was challenged by the rise of neo-liberalism.

- Recognition of human differences came to challenge the idea of 'equality of man'.

- Major development institutions now acknowledge that high existing inequality can retard poverty reduction.

- Inequality impacts on the exercise of citizenship and ultimately who determines the goals of development within and between nations. What, then, is the relationship between political and economic equality?

Charting the Conceptual Waters

The importance that we attach to the issue of inequality is rooted in some fundamental questions of political philosophy and shifting values and norms. Do societies think that equality is a legitimate aspiration? And if so, how is it to be achieved? Over the past two centuries or more these questions have been discussed repeatedly. During this period there was a 'steady erosion in the legitimacy accorded to social inequality . . . for students of social stratification, this . . . is perhaps the most important feature of the nineteenth and twentieth centuries' (Béteille 1969: 366). However, by the end of the twentieth century the pursuit of greater social and economic equality has become increasingly discredited; such concepts as 'social exclusion' and 'pro-poor growth' have gained ground. The poor became 'targets' of anti-poverty programmes. Traditional leftist concerns about distribution and 'exploitation' have been abandoned. At the same time, interest has grown in human diversity in terms of identity and culture and its relationship with equality—a development Fraser (1997) calls a shift from the 'politics of redistribution' to the 'politics of recognition'. Such a shift appears to imply abandonment or at least weakening of the idea of economic equality in favour of more robust mechanisms for ensuring political equality. But does equality of civil and political rights compensate for, or even work in the context of, social and economic inequalities?

Ontological equality and equality of outcome

The relative material prosperity achieved by American colonizers by the eighteenth century demonstrated that poverty was not inevitable. However, it was the French Revolution of 1789 that brought equality and the 'social question' to world attention. It showed not only that traditional social stratifications were not divinely sanctioned but that they could be challenged by the people acting collectively as citizens with equal rights. The First Article of the 1789 Declaration of the Rights of Man and Citizen states famously 'Men are born and remain free and equal in rights. Social differences, therefore, can only be based on common utility.'

The idea that men are born equal had emerged as a philosophical challenge to the prevailing assumption that social stratification was a result of natural differences of rank between individuals. The Greeks had built the *polis* on that assumption, and equality only existed in that realm; it was an attribute gained through citizenship not birth. Rousseau (*Discourse on Inequality*, 1755) began his investigation into inequality by assuming instead the equality of men in a pre-social original state of nature—an assumption of **ontological equality**. In the course of the eighteenth century, the idea that men are equal rather than unequal by nature took hold with powerful political and intellectual consequences. But it inevitably led to the question: what are the origins therefore of inequality? Rousseau's answer is usually summed up as 'private property', starting a debate that has raged ever since. Those who came to see private property as a social evil emphasized the need for society to promote **equality of outcome** despite individual human differences. Karl Marx made equality of outcome the central tenet of his vision of the good society.

For Marx, writing in 1845–6, inequality had its origins in the division of labour as well as private property. It is the former which 'implies the possibility, nay the fact that intellectual and material activity—enjoyment and labour, production and consumption—devolve on different individuals'. And with the division of labour comes the question of distribution and 'indeed the *unequal* distribution, both quantitative and qualitative, of labour and its products, hence property, the nucleus, the first form of which lies in the family, where wife and children are the slaves of the husband' (Marx 1970: 52). Capitalism is the most advanced system of labour division yet, in which the capitalist class owes its wealth to its exploitation of another class with only its labour to sell. Marx not only places this unequal relationship to the means of production at the heart of his class analysis of history, but the emphasis on exploitation indicates that such inequality between classes is unjust, and this has been a very influential argument for nationalist as well as socialist movements.

Marxist thinking tapped into deeply felt injustices at the popular level. For some, largely pre-industrial, developing societies, Marxist ideas appealed to the desire to retain some of the primitive communal forms of equality that persisted in agrarian societies and to restrain the differentiating process that comes with socio-economic change. Much Third World sociology in the post-war years was an effort to clarify its distinct forms of class composition and social inequality, and the relationship between class formation and development. A particularly vibrant debate concerned the analytical categories for exploring relationships between the developed and underdeveloped worlds. Could one nation exploit another? Gunder Frank (1971) powerfully argued that it could and traced the history of **underdevelopment** from 'core' to 'periphery'. He was criticized by others who claimed that he saw feudalism and capitalism only in terms of market exchange, not in Marx's true sense of relations to production and class exploitation. The ideas of **unequal exchange** and dependency would nevertheless provide one of the most important frameworks for understanding inequalities between countries in the North and the South in the early post-war decades.

Differentiating inequalities: class, status, and power

Max Weber, writing early in the twentieth century, provided a more differentiated categorization than Marx. He argued that social divisions and the distribution of power they convey encompass a range of non-economic as well as economic determinates. He said 'The emergence of economic power may be the consequence of power existing on other grounds', arguing:

> Man does not strive for power only in order to enrich himself economically. Power, including economic power, may be valued 'for its own sake'. Very frequently the striving for power is also conditioned by the social 'honour' it entails. Not all power, however, entails social honour ... Quite generally, 'mere economic' power and especially 'naked' money power, is by no means a recognized basis of social honour. Nor is power the only basis of social honour. Indeed, social honour, or prestige, may even be the basis of political or economic power, and very frequently has been.

(Weber 1970: 180–1)

For Weber, in addition to class stratifications that emerge out of a person's relationship to the market, there is **status**—a quality of social honour or a lack of it, which is mainly conditioned as well as expressed through a specific style of life. Social honour can adhere directly to a class situation, and for most of the time will be determined by the average class situation of the status-group members. This, however, is not necessarily always the case. Status membership, in turn, influences the class situation in that the style of life required by status groups makes them prefer special kinds of property or gainful pursuits and reject others. A status group can be closed ('status by descent') or it can be open. Weber's understanding of the distinctiveness of status groups was particularly helpful for those wishing to understand social differentiations in situations where market transactions were fairly simple and class formation limited. He also observed, however, that technological advances and economic transformation threaten stratification by status and will push the class situation further into the foreground.

In terms of the developing world, Weber was able to draw into the picture the forms of social stratification that Marxists have often found particularly difficult to explain, such as caste and tribe and the distinctions between them. Caste, Weber argued for instance, belonged to the 'closed status group', where status distinctions are guaranteed not just by conventions and laws but also by rituals, such as stigmatizing any contact between lower and higher castes through religious acts of purification. He explored the complexity of the **Hindu caste system** in India in some detail, seeking to explain its relationship to economic change and its 'elasticity' and hence survival in the face of the logic of labour demands in the modern economy.

The nature of these traditional relationships and the impact of processes of economic change are particularly significant for an understanding of social divisions in the developing world. Systems of 'inherited inequality' such as those based on descent, lineage, and kinship have persisted in many parts of the developing world. Anthropologists have long studied the lineage and kinship stratifications of indigenous populations. For example, Sahlins (in Béteille 1969: 239), who studied kinship in Polynesia in the 1950s, referred to 'a graduated series of different degrees of stratification'. He distinguished between stratified and egalitarian societies, and implied that ranking processes emerge in all human societies, but they vary a great deal in terms of ranking criteria and how far they formally sanction social inequality (see Box 5.1). This is why writers like Béteille (1969) have emphasized the values and norms that underpin social inequality or its qualitative dimensions. It has often been assumed that ranking on the basis of the hereditary principle will

disappear with the process of economic development, and that industrialization will overcome the differentials associated with traditional and agrarian societies. The persistence of caste in India, where status is determined by birth and legitimized by religio-cultural belief, questions that assumption. In modern India caste and class intersect in particularly complex ways, creating a potent and enduring source of social, economic, and political inequality (see Chapter 21a).

But across the developing world even where 'closed status group' systems such as caste do not exist, kinship and ethnic group identity have been the basis of stratified as well as segmented forms of social differentiation. Ethnic coexistences have become the source of ethnically based stratifications at various points in history. Pre-colonial conquests, colonialism, and post-colonial political mobilization have all played a critical role in privileging some ethnic groups over others and usually for some political as well as economic gain. As market economies expanded, so some ethnic groups were in a more privileged position than others to take advantage of opportunities. In this context, the debate about whether emerging stratifications are derived from market positioning, or from the logic of capital and its search for exploitable labour, or from ethnic identity per se has been particularly protracted. Thus, relationship to production is a source of inequality but not the only source of social differentiation. When class and status, economic and social power all coincide, however, one of the most powerful sources of inequality is created with capacity to perpetuate itself through the generations.

The political consequences of inequality

One means by which inequality perpetuates itself is through the political system that develops around it. Unequal societies, no matter what the source of inequality, generate differential means of influencing political processes. This is true at

---

BOX 5.1

Béteille on Inequality

Béteille (1969: 365) points out that the sanctioning of social inequality has taken place on very distinct grounds often legitimized by religious systems that paradoxically and simultaneously contain messages of equality. In the United States, commitment to the equality of man was a strong feature of cultural values and political ideals, though for many years black people were denied the vote and were evidently not treated as equals by the dominant white population. Most societies have denied, and many still deny, women formal as well as informal social, economic, and political equality.

all levels from micro to macro, and in traditional as well as more 'modern' development contexts. That means power and powerlessness emerge out of inequality and create the source for recycling it. As societies undergo transitions from more traditional to 'modern' economies, traditional power structures and ways of exercising power have often adapted to changing social conditions so that they survived more or less intact or persisted in new but recognizable forms. As the idea of political contestation (if not modern democracy) began to take root in the developing world, it frequently did so in contexts where political and economic power was already tightly meshed. The 'delivery' of the political support of a dependent rural population to particular leaders and interests quickly became the norm. Such practices were then adapted to urban contexts, where the rapid growth of cities without adequate services or employment gave brokerage power to individuals with access to elites and decision-makers. **Clientelism** and **patronage** networks emerged throughout the developing world, creating vertical links to tie the poor to political power structures through favours granted in return for support. Such networks reflect differentials in power and income and act as obstacles to independent political action and democratization, further entrenching the pre-existing structures of inequality. More than this, the relationships between dominated and dominant create internalised feelings of humiliation which have a lasting impact on generations of poor people, as Scheper-Hughes illustrates in her study of the landless squatters of the north-east of Brazil (Box 5.2).

In Latin America, where inequalities across class, gender, and ethnic lines are so deeply entrenched, it is not surprising that centuries of humiliation can only be overcome when the denigrated group gain dignity through building a positive identity around themselves. At the same time, this can serve to mobilize politically the previously dispossessed. This is clear, for instance, in the case of those indigenous people of Guatemala who towards the end of the twentieth century began to see themselves as 'Mayans' as a way of re-valuing themselves and their differences with the non-indigenous elites who have dominated and oppressed them historically (Box 5.3).

BOX 5.2

Inequality, Patrons, and Humiliation in North-East Brazil

" With respect to relations across class, between the foresters and their variously described bosses, patrons, and owners, an altogether different image of the impoverished *morador* (squatter) emerges, that of a fawning, 'humble' man or woman, hat in hand, eyes cast downward, as unctuous and dishonest and conniving as Dickens's Uriah Heep. The history of the sugar plantation, slavery, peonage, paternalism, and *coronelismo* (rule by local big bosses) can weigh heavily on the demeanor and behaviour of the rural workers, who throughout their lives put up with humiliating gestures and postures and with unequal exchanges that obligate them to people who would only take further advantage of them. The squatters behave toward their bosses in ways that end up angering and disgusting themselves, so that later and in private they rain forth invectives on the head of their bad boss or greedy patron, vowing never again to trust the man (or woman) who only hours before they had endearingly referred to as *meu branco* (my white one) or *meu careca* (my bald one). "

(Scheper-Hughes 1992: 108)

BOX 5.3

How Historically Oppressed Guatemalan Indians Find Dignity in the Word 'Maya'

" The term 'Maya' began to be used to unify identities beyond the local and linguistic groups, and for that reason also, they have called themselves 'pan Maya' (all the Mayans). To call themselves 'Maya' includes an entire shift towards a positive self-recognition. The terms 'indian' and 'indigenous' were imposed by the invaders and their descendents, and have a negative weight, of stigma, that leads to subordination. In the face of those, 'Maya' is a term chosen voluntarily by the actors themselves, who consciously refer to belonging to a distinct group with historic roots and connected to a grand and ancient civilisation. "

(Bastos and Camus 2003: 102)

Equality strategies and equality theories

The French Revolution placed equality on the political agenda, but some later argued that it succeeded only in abolishing the arbitrary privileges and restrictions imposed by the old regimes. Tawney (1952: 106) argued this powerfully, claiming that it resulted in the view that 'the inequalities of industrial society were to be esteemed, for they were the expression of individual achievement or failure to achieve'. However, he pointed out: 'Opportunities to "rise" are not a substitute for a large measure of practical equality . . . The existence of such opportunities in fact, and not merely in form, depends, not only upon an open road, but upon an equal start.'

Tawney's essay was an appeal for measures that would ensure that society actively aimed at 'eliminating such inequalities as have their source, not in individual differences, but in its own organization,

and that individual differences, which are a source of social energy, are more likely to ripen and find expression if social inequalities are, as far as practicable, diminished' (Tawney 1952: 57). He made the critical distinction between equality of capacity or attainment, and that of circumstance, institutions, and manner of life. He had in mind strategies such as progressive taxation, the strengthening of trade unionism and industrial legislation, and economic policy for the communal good.

Over the next five decades, equality as a goal was hotly debated in the advanced industrial countries, and the view that governments had some responsibility to pursue strategies of greater equality was broadly accepted. But there was little agreement on which strategies, and conservatives worried that they would limit individual freedom and choice. Nevertheless, by the 1960s social scientists on both sides of the Atlantic were challenging claims that their societies were moving towards greater equality despite the welfare state, estate duties, and higher taxation (in the UK), and the reforming impetus towards equal opportunity (USA). In doing so they raised important questions about the relationship between equality strategies and social justice theories, which John Rawls tried to clarify in his *Theory of Justice*, arguing that 'All social values—liberty and opportunity, income and wealth and the bases of self-respect—are to be distributed equally unless an unequal distribution of any, or all, of these values is to everyone's advantage. Injustice, then, is simply inequalities that are not to the benefit of all' (1971: 62). This was an influential contribution for post-war social democrats as it premised that neither social nor natural advantages of birth give a moral claim to more or better goods. However, it still allowed the possibility for inequality if it could be shown that the least advantaged gained from growth models which generated high levels of personal wealth accumulation.

The Political Economy of Inequality in Developing Countries

Moral and political arguments for an equitable model of economic development found concrete expression in a number of experiments that spanned the post-war decades, such as the model of socialism which followed the 1959 revolution in Cuba; the 1967 Arusha declaration and *Ujamaa* (*kiswahili* for community-hood) Socialism of Nyerere's government in Tanzania; and the Chilean Road to Socialism of Salvador Allende between 1970 and 1973. These experiments went further than economic egalitarianism. They were also about new forms of political participation and how to address the impact of economic inequality on political decision-making.

The inequality question in development is partly about these morally and politically based arguments, but it is also partly about the facts and how to measure them. Development economists in the Bretton Woods institutions (World Bank, International Monetary Fund) and universities were concerned with measurement and the potential trade-off between economic growth and inequality

that Kuznets had highlighted. Their objective was to understand the contribution that factors of production such as land, labour, and capital make to output, and not who gets what and why. Inequality mattered if it impacted negatively on growth and development. Quantitative surveys during these decades broadly tended to confirm Kuznets's findings but they did not show a fixed relationship in all cases. However, the argument that inequality was impeding development appeared to have been partially accepted when in the mid-1970s, the World Bank embarked on a new strategy of 'redistribution with growth'. At the same time, arguments that a New International Economic Order should address the inequalities between nations were also topical.

Income distribution measurement is by no means straightforward. Unreliable data, choices over the best unit of measurement (individuals or households), the timescale of measurement, and the definition of income itself, which given the high level of informal and unregistered earnings is particularly problematic in developing countries, all

JENNY PEARCE

Tanzania's President Julius Nyerere on Equality

Tanzania's President Julius Nyerere set out the country's broad policy on socialist development in a document called the Arusha Declaration, adopted by the ruling party in 1967. The opening proposition declared that all human beings are equal. The Arusha Resolution that accompanied the Declaration stated that every party and government leader must be either a peasant or a worker and should in no way be associated with the practices of capitalism or feudalism. Leaders were forbidden to hold shares in any company or directorships in privately owned enterprises. They should not receive two salaries or own houses that were rented out to others. Ten years later, in a review of the Arusha Declaration that he presented to the ruling party's Executive Committee, Nyerere defined three aspects to the goal of equality: in respect of differentials in personal incomes; in access to public services; in how far taxation-supported activities serve the interests of the people as a whole rather than those of a small minority.

represent significant problems. Fields (1980: 66–7) identified four approaches to measurement in 1980: relative inequality (income changes of various groups relative to others), absolute income (changes in various groups' incomes), absolute poverty (focus on changes in economic well-being of the poor ignoring the remainder of income distribution), and relative poverty (absolute income received by the poorest 40 per cent or some other defined percentage). (See Box 5.4.)

The most frequently used approaches to measurement are the Lorenz curve and the **Gini coefficient**. The Lorenz curve, named after the American statistician Lorenz, who developed it in 1905, uses a vertical axis (percentage of income earned) and horizontal axis (percentage of the population earning that income); the greater the bow of the curve, the larger the degree of inequality. The Gini coefficient, named after the Italian statistician who created it in 1912, uses areas of the Lorenz curve and is the

ratio of the area between the line of equality and the Lorenz curve, and the total area under the line of equality. It offers an aggregate measure of inequality and can vary between 0 (perfect equality) and 1 (perfect inequality). The Gini coefficient for countries with highly unequal income distribution tends to lie between 0.50 and 0.70, while for those with relatively equitable distributions it is between 0.20 and 0.35. The World Bank in addition uses a numerical format, the distribution by quintiles (20 per cent of the population) measured by household or individuals (see Figure 16.1 for inequality measured by Gini index in selected countries).

Following Kuznets's challenge, many studies in the 1960s and 1970s sought to explore and measure the impact of economic growth on income distribution and the influence of income distribution on growth. Large-scale, cross-country surveys were undertaken using improving data sets. Some confirmed the trend towards rising inequality in the less developed countries, although they varied in terms of whether the trend was weak or strong, that is whether the trend reflected a prolonged absolute impoverishment of large sections of the population in the course of development. Evidence was clearly not uniform across countries. Chenery (1974) argued that ultimately the evidence and judgements cannot be separated from 'social and ethical postulates'. In other words, the patterns of growth and distribution reflected political priorities and values in particular countries. He discussed three models: growth-oriented patterns, illustrated by Brazil and Mexico, including an equity-oriented, low-growth variant, illustrated by Sri Lanka; rapid growth with equity, illustrated by Taiwan, Republic of Korea, and Singapore; and an average pattern illustrated by India, the Philippines, Turkey, and Colombia, where patterns of growth and distribution follow the average relations of the Kuznets curve.

A great many qualitative, but empirically based studies tried to identify the causes of income inequality, and some examined its consequences. These explorations began to bring in non-economic as well as economic factors. The distribution of ownership of assets between households (the question of asset distribution *within* households was not yet on the agenda) was clearly vital, but it could be influenced by historical, institutional, and political forces as well as economic and policy ones. Some authors (Adelman and Morris 1973) concluded that economic structure, not level of income or rate of economic growth, is the primary determinant of patterns of income distribution. So-called structuralist theorists of development emphasized the impact on income inequality of such factors as historically unequal landownership patterns and social structures that excluded people on such bases as caste, race, sex, or religion. The concentration of physical and financial capital as well as land in the hands of small elites enabled them to buy access to educational opportunity and control an ever greater proportion of national product. The consequences of this unequal distribution included malnutrition, poor housing, and little or no education for the majority, resulting in low levels of productivity. In contrast the argument was made that a redistribution of income would increase production by increasing the consumption and hence the health and productivity of the poor.

Non-structuralists countered that inequality was the logical (some would say inevitable) outcome of economic growth. The apparent increase in inequality during the early stages of development is because development does not start at the same time in all parts of the economy. Growth in a poor, underdeveloped country will always raise some people's income before others, notably those where the growth is first located, for instance in urban rather than rural areas. Shifts in a country's structure of production will inevitably create inequalities between those engaged in agriculture compared to those in new, more highly remunerated industries. The non-structuralists argued that these inequalities would not necessarily result in absolute impoverishment but only a relative decline in income of the poorest. The argument that the poor would see their living standards rise through economic growth even though their relative share of income might not, would gain ground in the 1980s.

However, structuralist arguments and the prevailing climate of normative opinion against economic inequalities were still ascendant in the late 1960s and early 1970s. The early conviction that economic modernization and growth would trickle down had been gradually eroded by the evidence of persistent poverty and inequality. Radical movements called for land reform, wealth redistribution, and state economic planning to guarantee egalitarian development. Structuralists who remained committed to economic growth maintained that state intervention could ensure that such growth and economic diversification, particularly industrialization, would gradually incorporate labour into the higher wage and more productive sectors. But by the 1970s, they too were becoming sceptical. Even the President of the World Bank, Robert Mac-Namara, was forced to admit that despite a decade of unprecedented increase in the gross national product of the developing countries, the poorest segments of their population had received relatively little benefit. Policies aimed primarily at accelerating economic growth in most developing countries had benefited at most the upper 40 per cent of the population.

Thus considerable attention was given to the question of whether an egalitarian development process was possible. Much depended on whether 'egalitarian' meant equality of outcome or opportunity or condition, distinctions that were rarely made. Reforming economists put forward a range of policy measures that could combine changes in the distribution of the ownership of productive assets while maximizing the development effort and even accelerating the growth rates. Radicals pointed to the political obstacles to such measures, which came not only from the governments and ruling elites in the developing world but also from Western governments opposed to what they judged non-capitalist paths to development. Cuba and Allende's Chile faced hostility from the United States in their pursuit of more egalitarian development, while even Tanzania, one of the most heavily aided countries, found its strategy of self-reliance and equality extremely difficult to combine with growth and development.

KEY POINTS

- Egalitarian thinking influenced several experiments in egalitarian development in developing countries from the 1960s but they ran into difficulties.

- A general trend towards rising inequalities in the less developed countries was not uniform, and patterns reflected local policy priorities and choices.

- Structuralists argued that economic structures and ownership patterns largely determined inequality.

- Non-structuralists argued that economic growth inevitably entailed some inequalities, but this did not mean absolute impoverishment, only relative impoverishment for the poorest.

- From the 1970s, as agreement grew that economic modernization was not benefiting the poor, international development policies focused on raising their living standards but without radical redistribution.

Equality Questioned; Inequality Revisited

By the 1980s, support for the idea that the pursuit of inequality is a task of government eroded in the Anglo–American world especially and in the international institutions it influenced. The global economic recession which followed the 1973 oil shocks had resulted by the end of the decade in a shift from Keynesian policies of demand management and welfare-oriented state interventions, to monetarism, which cuts public expenditure on welfare and prioritizes investment and profitability. Toye (1987: 71) called this a counter-revolution in development thinking, referring specifically to the thinking of P. T. Bauer. Bauer had argued that some individuals are better off than others because of different aptitudes and personal advantages. Measures to counteract economic differences, 'the pursuit of the holy grail of economic equality', he argued, 'would exchange the promised reduction or removal of differences in income and wealth for much greater actual inequality of power between rulers and subjects. There is an underlying contradiction in egalitarianism in open societies' (Bauer 1981: 8).

Bauer attacked the political consequences of an increasingly coercive and bureaucratic state pursuing egalitarian goals. Many developing world egalitarian states had indeed shown that these

dangers were real. Even where such states had consciously sought to avoid such tendencies, for example Nyerere's Tanzania (1962–85) and the Sandinistas' Nicaragua (1979–90), they could not entirely avoid state-heavy political structures that concentrated power in new elites, such as the 'bureaucratic bourgeoisie' of the former and the party *caudillos* of the latter. Bauer also maintained that promotion of economic equality and the alleviation of poverty are distinct and often conflicting goals, and that to make the rich poorer does not make the poor richer. Others added that good government is something that promotes opulence through a policy of promoting liberty by establishing laws of justice which guarantee free exchange and peaceful competition, leaving the improvement of morality to non-governmental institutions.

These and related ideas informed the broad trend in thinking away from government regulation and intervention in markets for any purpose, including social justice. The argument against Kuznets that in any case inequality had no inevitable consequences for poverty gathered support in the 1980s, boosted by the publication of several time series studies showing that income inequality does not in any case change much over time, so economic growth must reduce poverty to some extent. The pattern of overall distribution of goods in society now seemed less important than individual well-being and freedom to pursue private interests in the marketplace. These arguments paved the way for market liberalization, which was expected to reduce poverty through growth. It was followed by emphasis on political liberalization and governance aimed at enhancing the institutional framework for growth and poverty reduction.

It was not long, however, before confidence in neo-liberal-driven development policies was under challenge. One of the grounds of the challenge was the growing evidence that market liberalism was generating increased inequality within developing countries as well as income disparities at the global level. The construction of a World Income Inequality Data Base by the United Nations University-World Institute for Development Economics Research produced more reliable time series data on income inequality and led to a research project into the relationship between income inequality and poverty reduction. On the basis of these data, Cornia and Court (2001) concluded that worsening inequality was due less to the traditional causes such as land ownership patterns and urban bias or the impact of new technologies on skilled and unskilled wages, although all these remain significant. These new causes include most notably macro-economic stabilization, labour market and financial deregulation, and excessively liberal economic policies.

Statistical evidence portrays a stark picture of the extent of income inequality today, particularly in Latin America and Africa. The Gini coefficient for sub-Saharan Africa is 72.2 and for Latin America it is 57.1, compared to 52.0 for East Asia, 42.8 for Central and Eastern Europe and Commonwealth of Independent States, 36.8 for the high-income OECD countries and 33.4 for South Asia (UNDP, 2005: 55). Countries with high income inequality require much higher rates of growth for poverty reduction than those with lower inequality (Ravaillon 2001). New questions have been raised on the relationship between poverty, growth, and distribution, such as whether inequality might actually slow growth. The distributional consequences of growth have also come under renewed scrutiny. Income transfers can improve human capital, such as nutrition levels, amongst the beneficiaries and in effect lead to forms of wealth accumulation. The moderate left-wing Brazilian government of President Lula channelled extra income to poor families on condition that their children were in education.

The renewed mainstream interest in inequality and its relationship to development is reflected in the 2005 and 2006 development reports of the UNDP and World Bank respectively, which were devoted to inequality (UNDP) and equity (World Bank). These reports explore the deep effects of income inequality on wider life chances of people in developing countries, including staying alive.

BOX 5.5

The World Bank on Inequalities of Power and the Quality of Institutions

" How do societies develop equitable non-market institutions? First, there must be sufficient political equality—equality in access to the political system and in the distribution of political power, political rights and influence. Poor institutions will emerge and persist in societies when power is concentrated in the hands of a narrow group or an elite.... Because the distribution of power, through its impact on institutions, helps to determine the distribution of income, the possibility of vicious and virtuous circles is clear. A society with greater equality of control over assets and incomes will tend to have a more equal distribution of political power. It will therefore tend to have institutions that generate equality of opportunity for the broad mass of citizens. "

(World Bank 2006b: 108)

The UNDP (2005: 57) points out that in Bolivia and Peru infant death rates are four to five times higher for the children of the poorest 20 per cent of the population than the children of the richest 20 per cent. Perhaps what is most interesting about these reports is that they go well beyond income inequality in their understanding of the relationship between inequality and development, a trend which has unfolded over the past decades, led by the discussion on gender inequality. A link is made between social and political inequalities, and economic inequalities, and between all of these and poverty and development. The World Bank even recognizes how inequality impacts on the distribution of power and the quality of institutions (see Box 5.5). Economic and political inequalities have been created around human differences and embedded over time in structured social relationships. The next section explores the way conceptual tools have evolved to help understand these links further, but suggests we are far from understanding how to address them either in institutional arrangements or social relationships.

KEY POINTS

- In the 1980s priority was given to market-driven growth and new arguments were mounted to suggest why economic growth was bound to be positive for the poor.

- Economic inequality and social justice were no longer on the mainstream political agenda.

- Increasing evidence suggested that market liberalization was a new cause for growing inequalities within and between nations, and mainstream economists began to review some of the conventional assumptions about growth, distribution, and poverty reduction.

- Inequality comes back onto the mainstream agenda and is recognized as an obstacle to poverty reduction in development.

- But, this time it is not only income inequality that is seen as the problem. Inequalities have been constructed around multiple human differences and embedded in structured social relationships over time and in the political institutions charged with making economic and social policy.

Equality and Diversity

Various egalitarian theories have identified at least three different kinds of socio-economic injustice: exploitation, **economic marginalization**, and **deprivation**. In Fraser's words (1997: 13), exploitation means 'having the fruits of one's labour appropriated for the benefit of others'; economic marginalization is 'being confined to undesirable or poorly paid work'; and deprivation is 'being denied an adequate material standard of living'. She contrasts these approaches with those that emphasize cultural or symbolic injustice, rooted in social patterns of representation, interpretation, and communication, but allows that the different forms can intersect. Economic institutions are imbued with cultural meanings and norms, while cultural practices have a political-economic dimension. The dilemma that interests Fraser is that while the claim for redistribution calls for the abolition of economic arrangements that underpin group specificity, such as the gender division of labour, recognition claims call attention to the specificity of a group and the affirmation of its value as a group. How can a society's social and political arrangements embrace both imperatives together? In the developing world, such questions have considerable salience for ethnic as well as gender stratifications. A great deal of debate is now taking place around these issues amongst scholars of multiculturalism, indigenous and minority rights, and citizenship. The debate has gained urgency as conflict and violence in the name of identity differences intensified in the developing world in the 1990s.

Progress has been made in terms of the abandonment of the single axis of difference such as woman or class, and the acknowledgement of the differences between women, for example, and the interaction among race, gender, and class identities. But how are the multiple connections between identities and social position linked to the question of equality in terms of the practical design of human social arrangements? And without some rethinking of those arrangements, are not certain people doomed to political as well as social exclusion, unable to effectively influence decision-making processes because of entrenched social and cultural hierarchies and power imbalances?

Sen, in *Inequality Re-examined* (1992) offers one of the most sophisticated efforts to address the relationship between human diversity and equality. It has been particularly influential in development studies, refocusing attention away from income as a poverty and development measure, to human capabilities—a shift that can be followed in the evolution of the United Nations Development Programme's annual *Human Development Reports* (Box 5.6). Sen is not concerned to justify equality as such, but is more interested in the question, 'equality of what?', which in itself clarifies the question 'why equality?'. His thinking is heavily influenced by Rawls here, but he has gone beyond Rawls in moving the emphasis from the *means* of freedom, that is to say primary goods in Rawls's account, to the **extents of freedom**. In Sen's terminology that means the capabilities or the freedom to achieve whatever functionings an individual happens to value.

The logic of Sen's argument is based on the assumption of human diversity. Equality claims must come to terms with this fundamental empirical fact, as there are times when equal consideration for all may demand unequal treatment in favour of the disadvantaged. Indeed, because we are diverse in our personal qualities, such as age, gender, talents, proneness to illnesses, physical abilities, as well as in our external circumstances like material assets, social backgrounds, and environmental circumstances, insistence on egalitarianism in one field may imply rejecting it in another. Disadvantage is itself diverse. Moreover, disadvantage is not just about consumption of resources; Sen recognizes the active agency in human beings that can be unleashed in other ways than the allocation or reallocation of goods. The 'focal variable' for the

---

BOX 5.6

Human Development Index

The UNDP's annual *Human Development Reports* contain a range of indices that try to take into account non-income measures of development and enable us to view the performance of a country in terms of both growth and freedoms. The best known is the Human Development Index, which incorporates data for human longevity and educational attainment as well as material living standards. Comparing countries by their place in the Human Development Index produces a very different picture to a rank that is based on the Gini coefficient alone. For example, Chile and Guatemala have a comparable level of inequality measured by the Gini coefficient that is very high. But in human development terms, Chile easily qualifies among the top fifty countries (high human development) whereas Guatemala is in the middle of the medium human development range, placed many countries below Chile. The contrast between, for instance, South Korea and Rwanda is even greater. Similar in terms of the Gini coefficient (where both appear significantly more equal than, say, the United States or United Kingdom) in human development, Rwanda features among the least developed countries anywhere while South Korea features in the top thirty countries of the world.

inequality that matters is itself internally diverse, so that for Sen the question 'equality of what?' has a plurality of potential answers. Income alone cannot be an adequate measure of inequality. Our capabilities to achieve whatever we value do not ultimately depend on income but on all the physical and social characteristics that make us what we are and which affect who we are. Substantial inequalities in well-being and freedom can, given our variable needs and disparate personal and social circumstances, result directly from an equal distribution of incomes. Sen turns our attention to the fact that some countries with higher per capita incomes enjoy lower life expectancies. The Indian state of Kerala has one of the lower real per capita incomes in India but the highest life expectancy, lower infant mortality, and higher general literacy, particularly female literacy. This is true even if the average Gross National Product is adjusted for distributional inequality; Kerala remains even with this statistical adjustment one of the poorer Indian states. The explanation lies in the history of public policy, most notably education, health services, and food distribution, which reaches the rural as well as urban population (Sen 1992: 128).

So it is now possible to appreciate the diversity of inequalities and to take a wider view of the social and political arrangements that should be aspired to. However, we are still left with some very intractable problems, such as how, given their relative powerlessness, the politically and economically marginalized can transform the social, political, and economic arrangements that marginalize them? Some market liberals may have recognized that embedded social inequalities negatively impact on development and the need for equal political representation and citizenship rights, and a very, very few have started to discuss whether a small amount of targeted income distribution might be less negative to growth than conventionally assumed.

However, the challenge of addressing inequality goes much deeper. Anne Phillips (1999), for example, argues that political inequality cannot be addressed without addressing economic inequality. Disparities between rich and poor impede

recognition of equal human worth; poverty, relative as well as absolute, is associated with lower status and not only less political power and fewer resources but debilitating self-perceptions. Political equality assumes equal worth as well as equal access to political influence: 'The problem for democracy is not just how to equalize people's political resources but how to establish their equal human worth; the problem with economic inequality is not just that it constrains the exercise of political rights but that it shapes (and damages) perceptions of fellow citizens' (Phillips 1999: 83). Economic inequality is about assets and access to health, education, and other services, but it is also about wage differentials and why we sanction often huge disparities between skilled and unskilled labour, professional and manual work, and are prepared to accept that some can live luxurious lifestyles while others live on the edge of destitution. When such disparities coincide with gender, race, and ethnic divisions they undermine any claim to equal citizenship and the equal exercise of political rights.

When in its 2001 *World Development Report*, the World Bank acknowledged that social discrimination can have economic effects that will undermine efforts at pro-poor growth, it advocated making 'public spending pro-poor', recognizing that this would encounter political resistance: 'Governments face important political issues in redistributing public spending to support asset accumulation by poor people. With finer targeting, public funds may in principle reach more poor people. But such targeting may lack political support from powerful groups that may lose out. Hence the importance of building pro-poor coalitions' (World Bank 2001: 82) (for more on the policy issues see Chapter 16). While political liberalization has opened up some new political spaces for participation, these have often been filled by self-appointed allies of the poor, such as non-governmental organizations. These organizations can at least advocate policies which might equalize the playing field politically and/or economically. Collective action remains another means by which the disadvantaged make their voice heard, and **social movements** have proliferated in the developing world (see Chapter 10). Such movements enable the discriminated against and disadvantaged to gain worth in their self-organization and agency. Social movements see struggles in terms of rights and entitlements and challenge the mainstream thinking that the poor are a 'target group' for policies which ultimately maintain the division between 'rich' and 'poor'. Political leaders can also emerge to mobilize the poor on grounds of class and ethnic exclusion, such as Hugo Chávez in Venezuela and Evo Morales in Bolivia. We may have progressed in understanding the many forms inequality takes and the need for nuanced policy responses, but the politics of inequality remains highly contentious. Inequality is a motor for political action of all kinds in the developing world, sometimes with productive outcomes, but sometimes with violent and even anti-democratic ones. Horizontal inequalities around religious and ethnic identities, particularly when they are reinforced by economic inequality, have in some contexts generated extreme violence and even civil war. This suggests that the struggle for political systems where all individuals and social groups can participate and feel represented in decision-making cannot be divorced from the struggle for egalitarian economic systems. It is the latter that

guarantees the recognition of equal human worth despite the multiple differences of belief, identity, and allegiance and ensures that political equality is meaningful.

KEY POINTS

- New awareness of social and cultural diversity has increased the complexities of the inequality issue and encouraged a focus on recognition as well as redistribution, identity as well as wealth as sources of inequality.

- Sen, taking human diversity as a starting point, argues that policies need to recognize that people are diverse in their disadvantages and advantages.

- The UNDP has introduced new measures to estimate non-income aspects of inequality.

- Inequality is a source of contentious politics in the developing world, which can be positive in the case of self-empowering social movements but can also be negative, polarizing, and potentially violent.

- The struggle for political equality could enhance the representation of excluded or marginal groups, but political equality includes recognition of equal human worth, a recognition undermined by economic inequalities.

Conclusion

The conceptual waters of the inequality debate have ebbed and flowed since the eighteenth century, with ontological equality challenged by the end of the twentieth century by the idea of equality based on human diversity. Sen has advanced on Tawney's vision of the 'largest possible measure of equality of environment', to the multiple environments that must be tailored to the capability enhancements of a diverse humanity. However, humankind

is a long way from constructing the new social, political, and economic arrangements that would enable inequalities to be addressed in the multiple 'spaces' in which they appear. Equality practice has foundered on the power at the global, national, community, and family levels that protects embedded inequalities and allows some people to exploit, marginalize, and deprive others of a full life. In turn, inequality impacts on the political system, limiting participation of poor and discriminated people and hence the possibilities of prioritizing the search for new solutions that might truly enhance the life chances of all.

The prevailing development discourse has shifted since the 1980s but still has a long way to go before inequality is given full weight in the measurement and understanding of economic development. Economic policy continues to prioritize efficiency over equity and to assume there is a tension between the two. The idea that the success of economic management should be assessed in terms of increasing social cohesion and lessening social disparities rather than growth and efficiency, has only recently begun to receive serious attention. In the meantime, according to the *Human Development Report 2002* (UNDP 2002), the level of worldwide inequality is 'grotesque'—the world's richest 1 per cent of people being reckoned to receive as much income as the poorest 57 per cent, and the combined income of the world's richest 5 per cent being fourteen times

that of the poorest 5 per cent. In turn, the way in which economic inequalities impact on recognition of equal human worth has now begun to generate debates on a new economics of egalitarianism that eliminates the 'rich–poor' divide.

Embedded, 'initial', or structural inequalities remain huge obstacles to the possibility of new egalitarian societal strategies that acknowledge human diversity, and respond appropriately to the diverse forms of inequality that arise from it. These are due to such long histories that people have often forgotten the social origins of the inequalities. Those who lose out come to assume they are less equal and that this may be so in several 'spaces of inequality' at once; those who gain have accumulated power to enforce and defend the visible and invisible boundaries between them and disadvantaged others. Political contention will arise from inequality until political arrangements and economic structures guarantee political equality in theory and practice.

? QUESTIONS

1 Why have inequalities based on hereditary principles of kinship and caste persisted in the course of economic development and political change?

2 Is inequality unjust?

3 Does it matter if the evidence shows that economic growth increases inequality but nevertheless raises absolute living standards amongst the poor?

4 To what extent should the state address the question of inequality as well as poverty in its development strategies?

5 Assess the evidence that there is a relationship between neo-liberal globalization and increasing inequality between and within nations.

6 Can embedded or structural inequality be addressed by political institutions that reflect those structures, and if not, how can it be challenged?

7 Can cultural and social inequality be tackled by addressing income inequality?

8 To what extent does Sen's approach to inequality, human diversity, and capabilities satisfy a feminist critique of social inequality?

9 Is political equality meaningful without economic equality?

GUIDE TO FURTHER READING

■ **Bauer, P. T. (1981), Equality, the *Third World and Economic Delusion* (London: Methuen).** A major source of the neo-liberal questioning of the goal of pursuing equality in development.

■ **Béteille, A. (ed.) (1969), *Social Inequality* (Harmondsworth: Penguin).** A good set of conceptual and anthropological essays on social inequalities which still merits reading.

■ **Chenery, H. *et al.* (1974), *Redistribution with Growth* (New York: Oxford University Press).** Had a major impact on World Bank and other institutions involved in development policy in the 1970s.

■ **Fraser, N. (1997), *Justice Interruptus, Critical Reflections on the 'Postsocialist' Condition* (London: Routledge).** A very useful discussion on the relationship between the redistributionist and recognitionist emphases within inequality thinking.

■ **Kuznets, S. (1955), 'Economic Growth and Income Inequality', *American Economic Review*, 45: 1–28.** An important benchmark study on the relationship between inequality and development.

■ **Phillips, A. (1999), *Which Equalities Matter?* (Cambridge: Polity Press).** A very lucid discussion of the relationship between political and economic equality.

■ **Ravallion, M. (2001), 'Growth, Inequality and Poverty: Looking Beyond Averages', *World Development*, 29/11: 1803–15.** A good discussion of the relationship between growth, distribution, and poverty.

■ **Rawls, J. (1971), A *Theory of Justice* (Oxford: Oxford University Press).** A very influential contribution to the political philosophy of inequality.

■ **Sen, A. (1992), *Inequality Re-examined* (Oxford: Oxford University Press).** Includes good discussions of both the state of welfare economics measurement and the relations between aggregative and distributional considerations and economic efficiency.

■ **Tawney, R. H. (1952), *Inequality* (London: Allen and Unwin).** A classic essay on inequality which challenges the notion that equality of opportunity is a sufficient approach to the question.

WEB LINKS

● **www.worldbank.org/poverty/inequal** The World Bank Group site on the concept of inequality and its links to poverty and to socio-economic performance, and pro-poor growth specifically.

● **www.wider.unu.edu/** Contains United Nations University–World Institute for Development Economics Research Database on world income inequality.

● **http://ucatlas.ucsc.edu** The University of California, Santa Cruz Atlas of Global Inequality, includes downloadable maps and graphics.

● **www.undp.org** Site of the United Nations Human Development Programme contains links to its annual *Human Development Report*.

 ONLINE RESOURCE CENTRE

For additional material and resources, see the Online Resource Centre at: **www.Oxfordtextbooks.Co.UK/orc/burnell2e/**

6

Ethnopolitics and Nationalism

JAMES R. SCARRITT

 Chapter Contents

- Introduction
- The Construction and Politicization of Ethnic Identities
- Varieties of Nationalism in the Developing World
- Ethnopolitics in Multi-Ethnic and Deeply Divided Societies
- The State and Nation-Building in the Developing World
- Conclusion

 Overview

This chapter stresses the significance of both: (1) differences among ethnic, ethnopolitical, and **national identities**; and (2) different types of relations among groups having these identities in countries of the developing world. **Ethnic identities** are constructed and reconstructed over time, and some but not all are politicized. Specific processes for construction and politicization and their variations across countries are discussed. National identities in the developing world, which are inherently political, vary in strength as well as the degree to which they are civic, multi-ethnic/multicultural, or ethnic, and the chapter explains these variations. Both types of identities have been strongly influenced by European colonialism. Both types interact variously with group morphology, group advantages and disadvantages, organizations, institutions, mobilization and state response histories, and international influence. Based on such interactions ethnopolitical groups engage in conflict, competition, and cooperation with one another and the state in different countries and at different points in time. Different interaction patterns are explored. Since national identities are relatively weak in many developing countries while sub-national ethnopolitical identities and groups are often stronger, developing states more or less successfully engage in a variety of **nation-building** activities; the chapter describes these activities and explains their degree of success in the current era of electoral democracy, globalization, and the **war on terror**.

Introduction

Defining ethnicity and nationalism in ways that are uncontroversial is probably an impossible task. Yet these are vitally important topics in the politics of the developing world, affecting and affected by the other social and economic cleavages and characteristics discussed in this book, the nature of the state and its degree of democratization, and policies for economic development and human rights protection. Boldly stated, a reasonably strong sense of civic or multi-ethnic nationalism and interactions among politicized ethnic groups based primarily on cooperation and institutionalized competition rather than on conflict tend to moderate economic and religious cleavages, strengthen civil society, and enhance state-building, democratization, economic development, and the provision of human rights. Although these generalizations are only tendencies rather than universal relationships, and reverse causal effects of other cleavages, civil society, state-building, democratization, economic development, and human rights on ethnopolitics and nationalism are also important, these relationships leave no doubt about the vital importance of ethnicity and nationalism.

Rather than dwell on controversies about the definition of ethnicity and nationalism, this chapter assumes that: (1) they are different and only sometimes closely related; (2) both are socially constructed identities that are subject to change in interaction with group morphology, group advantage or disadvantage, political organizations and institutional rules, mobilization histories, and international influences; and (3) ethnicity is only politicized in some cases, but nationalism has an inherent political component. The discussion thus begins with the construction and politicization of ethnic identities, or—in other words—the construction of ethnic and ethnopolitical identities, and then turns to the construction of a variety of nationalist identities. The next section deals with the conflictual, competitive, and cooperative interactions of groups based on these identities with one another and with states, while the final section before the Conclusion deals with states' efforts to mould these interactions in ways that enhance the legitimacy of state-based nations and their support from various groups.

The Construction and Politicization of Ethnic Identities

Ethnic identities are constructed when some people self-consciously distinguish themselves from others on the basis of perceived common descent (perhaps mythical), shared culture (including values, norms, goals, beliefs, and language), or—most commonly—both. There is thus a wide variety in the specific contents of these identities even within

a single country, to say nothing of across the countries of the developing world. Actual commonalities of language, a broader culture, or a common line of descent are often but not always central to ethnic identities. In spite of this wide variety in specific content, the common characteristics of these identities are sufficient to separate them clearly from other identities and to justify generalizing broadly about them (Eriksen 1993: 10–12; Gurr 2000: 3–5; Horowitz 1985: 51–64). Religious identities are the closest ones to ethnicity but, as discussed in Chapter 7, it is useful to separate them.

Many but not all ethnic identities are politicized (made politically relevant). This distinction is obviously very important for the analysis of the role of ethnicity in politics in the developing world and elsewhere. **Ethnopolitical identities** are those ethnic identities that have been politicized. This term deliberately emphasizes the interactive causal significance of the ethnic and political components of these identities in their formation, continuing mobilization, and interaction with concrete organizations, institutional rules, and international influences (Gurr 2000: 5–8; Mozaffar, Scarritt, and Galaich 2003: 382–3). There is much debate about the relative strength of each component of ethnopolitical identities, with a majority of recent analysts giving predominance to the political. But their relative strength, as well as the specific form of their interaction, may vary across ethnicities or countries and over time, so what is crucial is to emphasize their interaction and examine it empirically in different cases. Young (2001: 176) suggests that the political component is more important in Africa than in Eurasia. That ethnopolitical identities are constructed through the processes just discussed, and thus change over time, does not mean that they are not often held with deep emotional intensity. They are constructed through a variety of interactions between leaders and masses in which everyone's rational calculations are structured by their existing values, norms, and identities.

With very few exceptions, the countries of the developing world experienced European colonialism, which played a crucial role in the construction of ethnic identities and an even more crucial role in their politicization and organization into ethnopolitical groups. But the timing of colonial rule, the European powers involved, and the specific policies that affected ethnic identities varied sharply between Latin America and the Caribbean on the one hand, and Asia, the Middle East, and

North Africa, sub-Saharan Africa on the other, and to a lesser extent among and within the latter areas. The Spanish and Portuguese colonized virtually all of Latin America and much of the Caribbean from the sixteenth century until the first quarter of the nineteenth century. They brought in large numbers of settlers from their own countries and other European countries, and it was the Creoles—the American-born descendents of these settlers (Anderson 1991: 47; Young 1976: 84)—who seized power from the decaying colonial empires at the time of independence. In many of these countries they were outnumbered by indigenous Indians alone, or (as in Brazil) in combination with imported African slaves, although extensive intermarriage created intermediate groups of people, many of whom adopted Creole identities. European or Creole, mixed-race or Mestizo, Indian and African ethnopolitical identities developed over the following decades, roughly in that order. The increasing strength of Indian identities as disadvantaged minorities—more focused on individual 'tribes' than on multi-tribal Indian populations in specific countries—has been the primary change in the landscape of ethnopolitical identities in recent decades. Ethnopolitical mobilization and the globalization of information have played crucial roles in strengthening these identities, as discussed below. British and French colonialism in the Caribbean began slightly later, and the British held on to their colonies until the end of the Second World War. Descendants of former slaves from Africa are the overwhelming majority of the population in most of these countries. However, those countries with substantial East Indian populations are deeply divided in terms of ethnopolitical identities.

English, French, Dutch, and Spanish/American colonialism in South and South-East Asia occurred somewhat later, beginning as early as the sixteenth century in the Philippines and as late as the late nineteenth century in Indochina, and lasting until after the Second World War. Very few permanent European settlers were brought in, although Chinese and Indian settlers were brought into some South-East Asian countries. A core pre-colonial ethnic identity existed in many but not all Asian colonies, and was usually reinforced and given increased political significance by colonial rule. Burma is a clear example of this pattern. But minority ethnic identities within or outside the core were recognized and also politicized, especially by the British. Minority identities were strengthened in the process of resistance to the colonial reinforcement of the core identity. The two largest Asian colonies—British India and Dutch Indonesia—and a few others were amalgamations of a vast array of ethnic identities without a single dominant core. The British politicized these multiple identities more intensively and intentionally (through granting limited political autonomy to indigenous princely states) than the Dutch did, but the latter's classification of customary law zones constructed and politicized the ethnicity of their residents (Young 1994: 270), and amalgamation of groups into a common state inevitably had a politicizing effect. Post-independence politics have intensified group politicization in both countries, reinforced by international support for some disadvantaged minorities.

English, French, Belgian, and Portuguese colonialism in sub-Saharan Africa occurred much later, not really penetrating the subcontinent beyond a few coastal areas, the Portuguese-influenced Kongo Kingdom (most of which is now in Angola) and areas of European settlement in South Africa until the 1880s. Colonial rulers' reliance on local agents to cope with the dilemma of maintaining control at low cost encouraged these agents to differentiate their groups from those not so privileged by colonial authority, either by recombining and redefining existing objective markers of ethnicity or by accentuating previously minor group differences. Colonial rulers' creation of administrative units to secure additional economies in the cost of governance incorporated culturally disparate groups within single administrative units or separated culturally similar groups into separate units.

At independence, therefore, sub-Saharan African countries inherited a distinctive **ethnic morphology** (the form and structure of groups) with three defining features: (1) marked differences in group size, such that virtually no major ethnopolitical group comprises an outright majority in a country, although some comprise a large plurality; (2) considerable variety and complexity in ethnic markers combined with limited cultural differences among groups; and (3) the territorial concentration of some ethnic groups that facilitates their construction as cohesive units for collective political action. These three features have combined with the accommodation by post-colonial regimes of instrumental ('pork-barrel') ethnopolitical demands to foster *communal contention* as the typical pattern of political interactions in which ethnopolitical groups serve as cost-effective strategic resources for organizing political competition for power and resources. Communal contention discourages political entrepreneurs from exaggerating cultural differences among groups and encourages them instead to maintain strong group and coexisting sub-group identities that are strategically sustained by their ability to access the state and secure valued goods and services for their followers (Mozaffar, Scarritt, and Galaich 2003: 382–3).

In sub-Saharan Africa, construction of *ethnopolitical* groups occurred through organized group mobilization (primarily in ethnic associations or cliques of leaders within the same party, the bureaucracy, or the military), articulation of grievances by leaders claiming to speak for a group rather than a party, participation in collective action or (violent or non-violent) conflict with other groups or the state and being subjected to state violence, encapsulation within or domination of an officially designated administrative unit, occupying a disproportionate number of high positions in the bureaucracy or the military, controlling disproportionate socio-economic resources, or forming or joining an ethnic or multi-ethnic political party (Mozaffar, Scarritt, and Galaich 2003: 383).

French and British colonialism came to North Africa with the French occupation of Algeria in 1830, fifty years before neighbouring Morocco and Tunisia, and the British occupation of Aden in 1839.

The presence of numerous French settlers in Algeria who campaigned to incorporate the colony permanently into France was eventually a major force in politicizing Algerian and regional (Maghreb) Arab identity. Colonial rule by the same European powers came to the Asian Middle East the latest of all regions (the end of the First World War in which the Ottoman Empire—the former colonial power in most of this region—was defeated), and lasted less than thirty years. Ottoman rule was assimilative rather than alien, but it was more interventionist and integrative than previous localized rulers, and thus stimulated Arab nationalism within its territories, especially in its waning years. Post-independence interventionist states continued this process, as did the conflict surrounding the arrival of large numbers of European Jews in Palestine before and after the founding of Israel in 1948. Other Arab countries have had few European settlers. Thus the construction and politicization of Arab as the dominant ethnopolitical identity in the entire bi-continental region was a long process in which European colonialism played a more limited role than in other regions (Young 1976: 373–427). Apart from the Kurds of Iran, Iraq, and Turkey, whose identity was politicized primarily in the twentieth century, and Berber speakers in western North Africa, the main lines of division are religious. The Western powers have been seen as opposed to the emergence of a transnational Arab identity, and not only with respect to Palestine. This opposition has been a powerful politicizing force.

> **KEY POINTS**
>
> - Ethnic identities are constructed and then are often politicized to become ethnopolitical.
>
> - The ethnic and political components of ethnopolitical identities are both important, but their relative importance varies among groups, countries, and regions.
>
> - Most ethnopolitical (politically relevant ethnic) identities in the developing world were constructed during the colonial period, but some have been modified by post-independence politics.
>
> - Differences among regions of the developing world in the timing of colonialism, the policies of the major colonial powers, and the presence of European settlers significantly affected the construction of ethnopolitical identities.

Varieties of Nationalism in the Developing World

National identities are inherently political, emphasizing the autonomy and unity of the nation as an actual or potential political unit (Hutchinson and Smith 1994: 4–5; Smith 1995: 149). They can be broadly characterized as civic, multi-ethnic and multicultural, ethnonational, or a combination of these types (Croucher 2003: 3–5; Eriksen 1993: 118–20; Scarritt and Mozaffar 2003). Civic national identities involve unity among citizens of an autonomous state. Whatever social cleavages may divide these citizens are irrelevant; their common citizenship unites them. The only cultural uniformity that is demanded is commitment to the existence of the nation and its political institutional norms and values. Ethnonational identities define the nation in ethnic terms, attaining unity through the merger of ethnic and national identities, and demand autonomy for ethnic nations. Multi-ethnic/multicultural national identities define the nation in terms of several ethnic identities that are united by or nested within citizenship and political interaction in an autonomous state, while often excluding other ethnic identities. They differ from civic **nationalism** in accepting the legitimacy and political utility of ethnopolitical identities, as long as they do not undermine national unity. This difference is not sufficiently recognized in the literature on nationalism. Very few national identities in the developing world are purely civic, but a substantial majority of them contain civic or multi-ethnic aspects, so that they do not identify the nation with a single ethnic group. Consequently, there is an ongoing tension between the ethnic, multi-ethnic, and civic aspects of these identities in their interaction with group advantages and disadvantages, concrete organizations, institutional rules, and international influences.

Since nationalism is a constructed identity, the significant variations in the specific nature of nations in the developing world are not surprising. Colonialism played an even greater role in the construction of national identities than it did in the construction of ethnopolitical identities. The boundaries of the vast majority of developing states were determined by colonial rulers, and the varieties of nationalism are products of the interaction between the states that rule within these boundaries and the morphology of ethnopolitical identities, the tactics of ethnopolitical groups, and the presence of alternative identities within the same boundaries, which is discussed in the next section of this chapter. 'The normative model of the contemporary polity calls for the coincidence of nation and state' (Young 1976: 70). States attempt to create national identities that are coextensive with their boundaries, and the constituent ethnopolitical groups support or oppose these identities. Disadvantaged minority groups are especially likely to oppose **ethnonational identities**, and groups that are politically dominant demographic majorities are likely to oppose civic or **multi-ethnic national identities**, but other patterns of support and opposition also occur. National identities are still being constructed, and this process is more advanced in some regions of the developing world than in others. But only in a very few developing countries have national identities become banal—accepted as a matter of course and

constantly reinforced by popular culture—as these identities are in most developed countries (Billig 1995). Thus nationalism in every country—one nation in a world of nations—develops in relation to nationalism in all other countries, but especially in relation to nationalism in neighbouring countries and to the strong nationalism of the former colonial powers including the United States, which is all the more galling to the developing world because it is banal. It is impossible to specify exactly the number of nations or potential nations in the developing world, but if one includes every state and every ethnopolitical identity that engenders an ethnonationalist movement, there are probably several hundred.

Latin American states are former colonial administrative units. 'The first century of independent life saw the gradual transformation of what began primarily as the territorial heirs to colonial administrative divisions into nation-states' (Young 1976: 85). These countries officially pursue civic nationalism but until the late twentieth century this was actually a cover for Creole assimilationist ethnonationalism. Since the awakening of indigenous and/or African ethnopolitical identities in most countries, there has been a struggle by these groups to redefine national identity in more multi-ethnic/multicultural terms. Because of Creole elite resistance, the outcome of this struggle is very much in doubt. Civic and ethnic nationalism tend to merge in racially homogeneous Caribbean countries, but civic national identities are much weaker and ethnonational ones much stronger in countries such as Trinidad and Guyana with significant East Indian populations.

Nationalism in Asian countries having politicized ethnic cores has tended to be ethnonationalism focused on these cores, and thus is often rejected by members of non-core cultural groups who advocate civic or multi-ethnic nationalism or desire secession. As discussed in the next section, this can lead to violent conflict over the definition of the nation. In substantially different ways, multi-ethnic India and Indonesia constructed relatively strong multi-ethnic/multicultural national identities during the struggle for independence and the first decades of post-colonial rule. In India, the multiplicity of types of ethnic identities and the integrating force of the multi-ethnic and nationalist Congress Party facilitated the emergence of a multi-ethnic national identity, while the adoption of a lingua franca developed through trade as the national language did the same for Indonesia. These multi-ethnic national identities have weakened substantially in recent decades, as discussed in the following section and in Chapters 20 and 21. The role of religion in weakening these identities is discussed in Chapter 7.

Sub-Saharan Africa is the region in which multi-ethnic nationalism is most commonly found, although ethnonationalism is by no means absent there. The predominance of ethnopolitical cleavages, their complex multi-level morphology described above, the absence of large cultural differences in most African countries (in contrast to the multi-ethnic/multicultural societies of Asia, Latin America, and the Caribbean) except those divided by religion, and the politics of communal contention (mentioned above) combine to produce multi-ethnic national identities that most effectively integrate national and ethnopolitical identities in this context. The presence of substantial numbers of foreign Africans in the presently or formerly wealthier African countries helps to solidify the multi-ethnic national identities that exclude them but include all ethnic groups comprised primarily of citizens. It should be noted that these identities are emerging rather than fully formed, and that they mitigate rather than eliminate ethnopolitical conflict. A minority of African societies are deeply divided, and thus torn by conflicts about national identity. That small cultural differences do not always eliminate such conflict is amply illustrated by Rwanda and Burundi, which can be called culturally homogeneous because the pre-colonial Tutsi conquerors adopted the culture of the conquered Hutu, but in which colonial policies and post-independence political competition have created violent deeply divided societies.

In the Middle East and North Africa the national identities of states with colonially (Ottoman or European) created boundaries compete with the transnational Arab nationalism—the primary competitor in the middle decades of the twentieth century, transnational Islamist identities (see Chapter 7)—the primary competitor today, transnational non-Arab identities—Berber in Algeria and Morocco and Kurdish in Iran, Iraq, and Turkey, and small sub-national identities. Consequently, these national state identities are probably the weakest in the developing world.

KEY POINTS

- National identities are inherently political.

- National identities can be ethnonational, multi-ethnic/multicultural, and civic in varying degrees.

- Most national identities in the developing world were constructed during the colonial period, but some have been modified by post-independence politics.

- Differences among regions and countries of the developing world in the morphology of ethnopolitical identities, the tactics of ethnopolitical groups, the policies of the major colonial powers and post-independence states, and the presence of alternative identities significantly affected the construction of national identities.

Ethnopolitics in Multi-Ethnic and Deeply Divided Societies

Ethnopolitical morphology

The discussion of the construction of ethnopolitical and national identities in various regions of the developing world has revealed that the morphology of ethnopolitical groups varies greatly among the developing countries. Borrowing from Young (1976: 95–7), it is possible to specify five patterns of ethnopolitical morphology: (1) homogeneous societies such as Korea, Lesotho, and Haiti; (2) societies with a single clearly dominant group, numerically and socially, and minorities such as Algeria, Burma, and Nicaragua; (3) bipolar or deeply divided societies such as Burundi, Guyana, Rwanda, and Sri Lanka; (4) multi-polar societies, divided primarily on a single dimension, with no dominant groups, such as many sub-Saharan African countries; and (5) societies with a multiplicity of cultures, with more than one dimension of differentiation, such as India and Indonesia. Countries having the last two patterns and those having the second pattern in which the minorities do not cohere (a substantial majority of societies in that pattern at most points in time) can be called multi-ethnic societies.

Another approach to comparing ethnopolitical morphologies is to develop an index of fractionalization or fragmentation for each country. To do this, one must first specify all of the ethnic or ethnopolitical groups that exist in each country of the developing world because of past construction processes. Fearon (2003) has recently attempted to do this; Scarritt and Mozaffar (1999) have attempted to do it for Africa; and Gurr and his associates in the Minorities at Risk (MAR) project (1993, 2000) have attempted to specify a narrower list of groups 'at risk'. These authors have different definitions of politically relevant ethnic groups; it may be the case that different groups have been politicized for different purposes, including economic

policy-making (Fearon), electoral politics (Scarritt and Mozaffar), and political protest and rebellion (Gurr); and construction and politicization are ongoing processes. But it is nevertheless useful to examine these efforts to specify groups, as is done in Table 6.1, in order to get an idea of the very large number of them and to show that the regions are ranked in the same order in the three data sets

Table 6.1 Numbers of Ethnopolitical Groups in the Developing World

Region	Fearon	Scarritt/ Mozaffar	Gurr
Latin America–Caribbean	84		32
Asia	108		59
Sub-Saharan Africa	351	382	67
Middle East–N. Africa	70		28
Total	613		186

Table 6.2 Ethnic Fractionalization in the Developing World

Region	Average	Range	% of countries with majority group
Latin America–Caribbean	0.41	0.743–0.095	0.78
Asia	0.44	1.00–0.002	0.78
Sub-Saharan Africa	0.71	0.953–0.180	0.28
Middle East–N. Africa	0.45	0.780–0.039	0.84

in terms of the number of groups specified: sub-Saharan Africa first, Asia second, Latin America and the Caribbean third, and the Middle East and North Africa last.

Only Fearon's data allow comparison of countries and regions in terms of fractionalization, which varies in his scale between 0 (homogeneous) and 1 (totally fragmented). These data (Fearon 2003: 204, 209, 215–19), summarized in Table 6.2, show that, within the developing world, the average level of ethnic fractionalization is lowest in Latin America–Caribbean, slightly higher in Asia and the Middle East–North Africa, and much higher in sub-Saharan Africa. The range of countries in terms of fragmentation is greatest in Asia, almost as great in sub-Saharan Africa, and less in the other two regions. Finally, the percentage of countries in which the largest group comprises the majority of the population is only 28 per cent in sub-Saharan Africa and between 78 per cent and 84 per cent in the other three regions. Thirty African countries (70 per cent of the total) have fragmentation scores above 0.7, while only four Asian countries (including the two largest ones, India and Indonesia), three Middle Eastern countries, and one Latin American country have scores this high. Fearon's data thus support the conclusion that most African countries are far more fragmented than most countries in other regions.

Other relevant aspects of ethnopolitical morphology are geographic concentration, the extent of cultural differences among groups, and the presence of ethnic groups that have not been explicitly politicized as described above. Available data indicate that ethnopolitical groups in sub-Saharan Africa tend to be the most geographically concentrated and to have the smallest cultural differences, and that there are more ethnic groups that have not been politicized there than in other regions of the developing world (Fearon 2003: 211–14; Gurr 1993: 344–51; Scarritt and Mozaffar 2003: 9–10).

Collective action and interaction

These different ethnopolitical morphologies interact with group advantage or disadvantage, political organizations and institutional rules, mobilization and state response histories, and international influences in causing different types of collective action by ethnopolitical groups and different types of interaction among them or with the state. Human agents who are rational within their belief and normative frameworks carry out these processes enabled and constrained by social structures (Gurr 2000: 65–95; Mozaffar 1995; Mozaffar, Scarritt, and Galaich 2003: 380–2, 385–7; Scarritt and Mozaffar 2003: 12–16). Ethnopolitical interactions cannot be fully explained without taking all of these factors and their interactions into account; the following presentation is organized factor by factor but incorporates interactions among factors into the discussion of each one. Group advantage or disadvantage can be economic, political, or cultural, or any combination of these forms. Crucial political organizations include various civilian state agencies, the military and police, political parties, and interest associations that are not ethnically based. Some are more institutionalized than others. Institutional rules can be broadly categorized as democratic, transitional, or autocratic (Gurr 2000: 154). Rules about the formation and control of ethnopolitical associations and the conduct of elections are of special importance. Group collective action and state responses have historical patterns that have varied in violence and intensity in different countries of the developing world, although these patterns are more firmly established in some countries than in others. These patterns are of course subject to change, but they have self-perpetuating qualities that resist change unless the forces supporting it are sufficient to overcome them. Finally, although ethnopolitics is primarily internal to states, it is significantly influenced by several aspects of globalization, diffusion, and contagion among identical or similar groups across state boundaries, and external political and material support.

Interaction among groups and between them and the state can be categorized as cooperative, competitive, or conflictual. The boundaries among these three types of collective interaction are by no means perfectly clear, and a given action by a group or the state may involve any two or all three types vis-à-vis various targets. The relative importance of these interaction patterns nevertheless provides a very useful way of comparing ethnopolitics in the countries of the developing world. As illustrated in Box 6.1, the literature on ethnopolitics there (Gurr 1993, 2000; Horowitz 1985; Young 1976) emphasizes the complex causation of conflict involving some degree of violence, and to a lesser extent competition, but a greater emphasis on the latter and the inclusion of cooperation are necessary for a more balanced treatment. To highlight this point, it is useful to separate—within the discussion of each factor and its interactions with others—the explanation of cooperation, institutionalized competition, and peaceful protest from the explanation of conflict and non-institutionalized competition.

Cooperation and institutionalized competition among ethnopolitical groups and states in the developing world do not get much attention in the global media, yet they occur with great frequency and have significant consequences. They are substantially greater in frequency and consequences than conflict is in many countries, although they often coexist with conflict (involving the same or other groups). Peaceful protest attracts more media attention. It is not institutionalized but is more properly seen as competition rather than conflict, although it is easy for such protest to turn violent

and thus become conflictual through the actions of the protesters or the authorities (usually the police). This is one reason why the boundaries between cooperation and competition and between competition and conflict are often difficult to draw. On the other hand, conflict in the forms of violent protest, rebellion, and repression, as well as its almost indistinguishable cousin non-institutionalized violent competition, get a great deal of attention from global media (and scholars); they are 'newsworthy'. The consequences of such conflict can indeed be horrific, but this is not always the case, and the media's view of ethnopolitical conflict as prevalent in most developing countries is distorted.

Ethnopolitical morphology and types of ethnopolitical interaction

Cooperation, institutionalized competition, and peaceful protest, aspects of the politics of communal contention, are much more frequent and consequential in multi-ethnic than in deeply divided societies, although they are not limited to the former type. The impossibility of majority support for the regime (which is important even for autocratic regimes) in the absence of such cooperation in the former type of society and the tendency towards the mutual fears and hopes of ethnonationalist winner-takes-all politics among both groups in

---

BOX 6.1

Two Conceptions of the Causes of Ethnopolitical Conflict

Horowitz: An adequate theory of ethnic conflict should be able to explain both elite and mass behavior. Such a theory should also provide an explanation for the passionate, symbolic, and apprehensive aspects of ethnic conflict. Group entitlement, conceived as a joint function of comparative worth and legitimacy, does this—it explains why the followers follow, accounts for the intensity of group reactions, even to modest stimuli, and clarifies the otherwise mysterious quest for public signs of group status.

(Horowitz 1985: 226)

Gurr: The motivations at the heart of ethnopolitics are assumed to be a mix of grievance, sentiment, solidarity, ambition, and calculation. It is simplistic to argue that one kind of motivation is primary and others subsidiary. Ethnopolitical protest and rebellion are consequences of complex interactions among collective experience, normative commitments, contention for power, and strategic assessments about how best to promote individual and collective interests.

(Gurr 2000: 66)

the latter type of society account for this difference. Small cultural differences and the presence of non-politicized groups (impossible in deeply divided societies) facilitate cooperation, while geographic concentration (less likely in deeply divided societies) has more ambivalent effects. Conflict and non-institutionalized violent competition are more likely to occur in deeply divided than in multi-ethnic societies, although they are not limited to the former type. The reasons for this are the inverse of those for the greater significance of cooperation in the latter type of society. Organizations such as political parties and the military tend strongly to be arenas of conflict in deeply divided societies (Horowitz 1985: 291–525). But within each type of society, other factors account for substantial differences in cooperation, competition, and conflict.

Group advantages and disadvantages and types of ethnopolitical interaction

Cooperation is easier the smaller the advantages or disadvantages of different groups. Advantages or disadvantages can be economic, political, or cultural, and can be due to discrimination in either state policies or well-established social structures, or to more accidental factors such as regional differences in resource endowments. Disadvantages that are seen as caused by discrimination in state policies make cooperation especially difficult (Gurr 1993: 34–60; 2000: 105–32), but disadvantages caused by social structural discrimination and not counteracted by state policies also hinder it. Since many groups in most countries of the developing world have advantages or disadvantages caused by discrimination (as described below), ethnopolitical cooperation and the reduction of discrimination through state policies tend to go together.

Conflict is more likely to occur the greater the advantages or disadvantages of different groups, especially if these advantages or disadvantages are seen as due to discrimination in state policies. Horowitz

(1985: 32) indicates that 'virtually all ranked systems of ethnic relations [in which class and ethnicity coincide] are in a state of rapid transition or of increasing coercion by the superordinate group to avert change'. Almost 90 per cent of the 186 groups in the developing world that were included in the MAR survey in the mid-1990s because they were judged to be at risk of being involved in violent conflict experienced one or more forms of discrimination, and most of the rest were at risk because of advantages gained from such discrimination. Over two-thirds of these groups experienced economic discrimination, and 40 per cent experienced high levels of such discrimination. Within the developing world economic discrimination is greatest in Latin America and the Caribbean (where indigenous peoples are subject to severe discrimination of all types), followed by the Middle East and North Africa, Asia, and sub-Saharan Africa in that order. Political discrimination is even more prevalent in the developing world. Over 80 per cent of the 186 groups experienced political discrimination in the 1990s and over half experienced high levels of such discrimination. This form of discrimination is also greatest in Latin America and the Caribbean and least in sub-Saharan Africa, but Asia ranks a close second in this case. Finally, cultural discrimination is less frequent, with small majorities of groups experiencing it in Latin America and the Middle East, a large minority of groups in Asia (mainly 'hill tribes'), and only a few groups in sub-Saharan Africa. Unlike the other forms of discrimination, a majority of groups that experience cultural discrimination experience it at low or medium levels. These forms of discrimination were highly correlated with group disadvantages (Gurr 2000: 105–27).

Organizations, institutional rules, and types of ethnopolitical interaction

Cooperation among ethnopolitical groups occurs primarily within the political organizations listed two pages back, operating with more or less firmly institutionalized rules. Institutional differences are probably the most important factor in explaining cooperation in such organizations. Cooperation requires a relatively high degree of institutionalization of the organizations within which it occurs, although it is impossible to specify the required level exactly. Democratic institutions, particularly if they are strong (highly institutionalized), promote cooperation, are the primary basis of institutionalized competition, and allow—and in some ways encourage—relatively peaceful protest. Institutional rules providing relatively unrestricted freedom for group activities are crucial for both institutionalized competition and peaceful protest. Not surprisingly, the MAR data demonstrate the greater use of peaceful protest and less ethnopolitical conflict in democratic countries and, perhaps more surprisingly, in transitional countries in the developing world as well.

In multi-ethnic societies, political parties contesting democratic elections need multi-ethnic support to win unless one group constitutes a majority of the population or is close enough that a non-proportional electoral system can give them control of a majority of seats in the legislature (Scarritt and Mozaffar 2003: 1). But even in the latter cases, democratic institutions value inter-ethnic cooperation and thus multi-ethnic parties more than autocratic institutions do. Multi-ethnic parties predominate in sub-Saharan Africa, and are found in a number of countries in other regions of the developing world. There is considerable debate about whether proportional representation or first-past-the-post electoral institutions are more likely to promote cooperation in multi-ethnic parties. The influence of such electoral institutions is probably outweighed by other factors. Horowitz (1985: 291–440) has analysed the ways in which ethnic parties, whose support comes overwhelmingly from a single ethnopolitical group, enhance conflict in deeply divided societies by unreservedly pursuing the interests of that group and failing to form stable majority coalitions.

Conflict and non-institutionalized violent competition occur within and among the organizations in which cooperation occurs (Horowitz 1985: 291–525), but more frequently occur outside formal organizations in the forms of violent protest, armed rebellion, and state repression varying from restrictions on civil and political liberties through conventional policing to genocide. Conflict has been most violent in deeply divided societies, when groups are severely disadvantaged by multiple forms of discrimination, and under weak autocratic institutions. In the MAR data violent rebellion between 1985 and 1998 had a mean annual magnitude in autocracies that was two and a half times that in new democracies. Rebellion in transitional regimes was much closer to the level in new democracies. Partial or failed transitions in the developing world tend to increase protest but decrease rebellion (Gurr 2000: 151–63). The data show that, in part, democratization decreases conflict by decreasing discrimination (Gurr 2000: 163–77). Thus, while the institutional instability engendered by democratization can increase ethnopolitical conflict, as Snyder (2000) suggests, this is not its most common effect, at least beyond the transition period.

Mobilization, state response, and types of ethnopolitical interaction

Ethnopolitical identity construction and ethnopolitical group mobilization are closely related processes that tend to occur together over time. As discussed above, mobilization of ethnic associations is part of the politicization of ethnic identities, which then leads to ethnopolitical mobilization through political parties. Thus ethnopolitical mobilization has a history going back to the colonial period in most countries of the developing world. Since independence, such mobilization has been most intense and most violent in deeply divided societies, when groups are severely disadvantaged by multiple forms of discrimination, under weak autocratic institutions, and in the presence of international political and material support for or against mobilization. It has been least intense and most peaceful in highly multi-ethnic societies, when few or no groups are severely disadvantaged by any form of discrimination, under strong democratic institutions, and in the absence of international political and material support. The longer a specific pattern of mobilization occurs, the more likely it is to be self-perpetuating unless changed deliberately by powerful actors. It is very difficult to change a primarily conflictual pattern of collective interaction into a primarily cooperative pattern or vice versa, and somewhat difficult to institutionalize un-institutionalized competition or change violent protest into peaceful protest.

The tendency for patterns of mobilization to be self-perpetuating is reinforced by state repression of a pattern of mobilization or the absence of such repression. Not surprisingly, the more intense and violent the mobilization the more severe the repression. In the MAR data repression varies from conventional policing to **genocide** (extermination of an ethnic group) and **politicide** (extermination of political enemies). Between 1955 and 1995 extensive ethnopolitical repression occurred in all areas of the developing world. It involved the largest number of groups in Asia and sub-Saharan Africa, but was least intense in Latin America and the Caribbean during the last decade of that period. Repression was far more likely to intensify violent mobilization than to stop it. Harff (2003: 66) found that genocide or politicide is most likely to occur or to be repeated after political upheaval in autocracies based on the support of advantaged minorities with exclusionary ideologies. State response to peaceful protest, most common in democratic states, has often been to grant only a small proportion of the protesters' demands but not to engage in repression. This response has typically led to the continuation of peaceful protest.

International influences and types of ethnopolitical interaction

International influences have fostered both ethnopolitical cooperation and ethnopolitical conflict. Scholars have given some attention to the direct diffusion or indirect contagion of ethnopolitical conflicts across national borders through the presence of the same or closely related groups on both sides of the border. Much less attention has been paid to the diffusion of ethnopolitical cooperation, which is more difficult to study. But as democracy has been diffused to much of the developing world since the end of the cold war it is possible to argue that ethnopolitical cooperation and institutionalized electoral competition have often been diffused with it.

During the cold war, the superpowers and former colonial powers frequently gave material, political, and/or military support to parties to ethnopolitical conflict in the developing world. This was done to further the objectives of the powers giving aid, but it undoubtedly substantially exacerbated such conflict in a number of countries, including Afghanistan, Angola, Ethiopia, Guatemala, and Nicaragua. It is argued below that international intervention in ethnopolitical conflicts has been less self-interested since the end of the cold war, but the combination of the persistence of some degree of self-interest and lack of adequate information about the consequences of specific forms of intervention mean that political and/or material support can still have conflict-enhancing effects. French intervention in Rwanda in favour of the existing government (and thus of its followers who were bent on genocide) before and during the genocide of 1994 and increased Sunni–Shia conflict in Iraq after the Anglo–American invasion are cases in point. Regional powers within the developing world have also supported parties to ethnopolitical conflict in their regions out of self-interest, which formerly included rewards from their cold war patrons. Finally, regional and international organizations—governmental and especially non-governmental—have struggled to resolve a number of ethnopolitical conflicts with consequences that have varied from success to exacerbating the conflict, but it appears that some of them are becoming more successful.

Globalization has stimulated ethnopolitical mobilization and probably terrorism as tools in ethnopolitical conflict, but it has also strengthened

JAMES R. SCARRITT

international norms of democratization, human rights, and non-discrimination. International norms now favour ethnopolitical cooperation, institutionalized competition, and the peaceful resolution of ethnopolitical conflicts to a greater extent than ever before. However, this may be changing with terrorism and Anglo–American reactions to it, as discussed below. Economic globalization has strengthened national identities in the developing world, while also weakening the capacity of most developing states to carry out nationalist policies that challenge multinational corporations or international financial institutions. Globalization of communications has provided new tools for constructing ethnopolitical groups as well as nations. But, as Billig (1995: 128–43) argues, global culture cannot serve as the primary basis of resistance to economic globalization because it is less banal than the cultures of the developed nations, which support such globalization.

KEY POINTS

- Ethnopolitical morphology takes a variety of forms in the countries of the developing world ranging from highly multi-ethnic to deeply divided and homogeneous.

- Interaction among ethnopolitical groups and between them and states involves a mixture of cooperation, competition, and conflict.

- Cooperative interactions are most easily achieved in multi-ethnic societies that have small group advantages and disadvantages, democracy based on relatively institutionalized multi-ethnic parties, a historical pattern of non-violent ethnopolitical mobilization and minimal repression of it, and international influences that support 'managed heterogeneity' rather than one side of ethnopolitical conflicts.

- Cooperation is possible when some of these conditions are absent.

The State and Nation-Building in the Developing World

Nationalism was relatively weak in most developing states at independence, and was essentially absent in those that lacked meaningful nationalist movements and won their independence through a combination of the spillover effect of nationalist movements in neighbouring countries and the colonial powers' desire to extricate themselves from their colonies. 'The initial "nation-building" ethos [in Africa] proposed to resolve the ethnic question by confining it to the private realm' (Young 2001: 174). Civic nationalism was asserted ideologically in spite of its empirical weakness. But authoritarian 'banishment of ethnicity from political assertion merely drove it underground' (Young 2001: 176), while rulers continued to make

ethnopolitical calculations in appointments to high political positions and the placement of development projects. Many essentially similar histories of failed efforts to extinguish ethnopolitical identities and movements and either create civic nationalism by fiat or assimilate minorities into the core ethnonational identity by force are found in other regions of the developing world. Forced assimilation to ethnonationalism has had the more severe consequences; in deeply divided societies with long histories of ethnopolitical mobilization, especially those characterized by great group differences and external material and political support for one side or the other, it has usually led to extremely violent conflict.

Due in part to the desire to reduce the negative effects of economic globalization and the support received from international norms and the globalization of communications, there has been a shift in some developing states from these unsuccessful policies of trying to impose civic nationalism by fiat or majority ethnonational identities by force to accepting multi-ethnic/multicultural national identities as a viable compromise. As Sen points out (see Box 6.2), there is a substantial difference between state policies promoting rational multiculturalism and policies promoting plural monoculturalism. In the former national identity is based on a freely chosen blend of diversity and commonality among interacting ethnic groups. In the latter full diversity is enforced by isolated groups and national identity is based on a 'federation' of group identities. The shift to rational multiculturalism/multiethnicity has been easier in multi-ethnic societies than in societies with a single dominant group or deeply divided societies, but such national identities are potentially viable in all of these societies (Snyder 2000: 33). They tend to make state and nation mutually reinforcing; 'the persistence of states, however challenged or changed by globalization they may be, offers a partial explanation for the continuation of nationhood as a salient form of belonging' (Croucher 2003: 14). Immigration compels states to clarify and reinforce national boundaries; responses to terrorism have the same effect. 'Nationhood, then, continues to be a functional, familiar, and legitimate mechanism for belonging' (Croucher 2003: 16). The aspirations of stateless peoples to national states prove its value.

Similarly, Smith (1995: 154) argues that 'Only nationalism can secure the consent of the governed to the territorial units to which they have been assigned, through a sense of collective identification with historic culture-communities in their "homelands". As long as any global order is based on a balance of competing states, so long will the principle of nationality provide the only widely acceptable legitimation and focus of popular mobilization.' He cites the rarity of defections from, and the frequency of self-sacrifice for, nationalism as evidence in support of this claim. Although Smith exaggerates the significance of long-established traditions for national identities, as well as the differences between national and other identities, he is right about the functionality of nationalism in the contemporary world. He does not recognize, however, that this is a multi-ethnic/multicultural nationalism with civic overtones in the vast majority of countries of the developing world that are not homogeneous.

Gurr (2000: 195–211, 275–7) presents data, summarized in Box 6.3, to show that the number and severity of ethnopolitical conflicts have declined since the end of the cold war, reversing the upward trend of the preceding three decades. He attributes this change to the emergence of a 'regime of managed ethnic heterogeneity, shorthand for a bundle of conflict-mitigating doctrines and practices' (2000: 277–8). This regime has both domestic components—essentially those described above as promoting ethnopolitical cooperation—and international components—international norms and changes in the behaviour of outside states and transnational organizations reflecting decreased

---

BOX 6.2

Sen's Definitions of Types of Multiculturalism

Plural monoculturalism: values the diversity of existing cultures for itself and makes the nation a federation of isolated cultures.

Reason-based multiculturalism: focuses on the freedom of reasoning and decision-making, and cele-brates cultural diversity among interacting groups to the extent that it is as freely chosen as possible by the persons involved, and makes the nation truly multicultural.

(Sen 2006: 150–60)

BOX 6.3

Gurr on the Post-Cold War Decline in Ethnopolitical Conflict

A global shift from ethnic warfare to the politics of accommodation is amply documented in previous chapters. In the late 1990s the most common political strategy among the 275 ethnopolitical groups surveyed in the Minorities at Risk study was not rebellion; it was symbolic and organizational politics. Equally important, the number of groups using armed violence has been declining after decades of increase.

The eruption of ethnic warfare that seized observers' attention in the early 1990s was actually the culmination of a long-term general trend of increasing communal-based protest and rebellion that began in the 1950s and peaked immediately after the end of the cold war.

(Gurr 2000: 275–6)

self-interest and increased competence. It fosters multi-ethnic/multicultural nationalism. But Gurr (2000: 223–60) also acknowledges that some ethnopolitical groups are still at risk of being involved in future violent conflicts because they maintain the interaction patterns with other groups and states that have led to violent conflict in the past.

The United States, an important player in this international regime, has moved back to self-interest and interventionism since Gurr wrote. The consequences of this change for national identities is uncertain. As mentioned above Iraqi national identity has not been strengthened by the Anglo–American invasion as the Bush administration anticipated, and has instead been weakened, and the same can be said for national identity in Afghanistan. Terrorists tend to promote transnational identities. On the other hand, national identities have probably been strengthened in countries such as Venezuela and Bolivia where elected leaders have both reached out to indigenous groups and defied American pressures. It is far too soon to

declare the demise of ethnopolitical conflict, exclusionary ethnonationalism, or their exacerbation through foreign intervention and terrorism.

KEY POINTS

- Many states of the developing world have attempted to suppress ethnopolitical identities and conflicts by declaring civic nationalism by fiat or assimilating minorities into their core ethnonational identity by force, but more are now accepting multi-ethnic national identities as a viable compromise.

- National identities in the developing world, usually based on existing states, continue to be viable in the era of globalization, and offer a basis for resisting the negative effects of economic globalization.

- The number and severity of ethnopolitical conflicts have declined since the end of the cold war because of the emergence of a 'regime of managed ethnic heterogeneity', but some violent conflicts persist.

Conclusion

In conclusion, we can briefly summarize the major themes of this chapter. Ethnopolitical and national identities are different, although both are socially constructed and thus change over time. The pattern of ethnopolitical identities (the ethnopolitical morphology) within countries involves the number and relative size of groups, their geographic concentration and degree of cultural differences, and varies from deeply divided to highly multi-ethnic. National identities are civic, multi-ethnic, or ethnonational. Collective action by ethnopolitical groups and cooperative, competitive, and conflictual interactions among them and with states are influenced by the interaction of ethnopolitical morphology, group advantages and disadvantages, political organizations and institutional rules, mobilization and state response histories, and international influences. Cooperative interactions are most easily achieved in multi-ethnic societies that have small group advantages and disadvantages, democracy based on relatively institutionalized multi-ethnic parties, a historical pattern of non-violent ethnopolitical mobilization and minimal repression of it, and international influences that support 'managed heterogeneity' rather than one side of ethnopolitical conflicts. These interactions, in turn, tend to promote nation-building through multi-ethnic/multicultural nationalism. There is evidence of a shift in this direction in some countries of the developing world, but conflictual interactions and failures of nation-building still occur all too frequently.

QUESTIONS

1   If ethnopolitical and national identities are constructed and thus can change, why do they not change more rapidly?

2   What are the major types of national identities and how different are they?

3   How many ethnopolitical groups and nations are there in the developing world?

4   Does the nature of ethnopolitical identities determine whether democracy can be effective in the developing world?

5   If the amount of violent ethnopolitical conflict has declined in the developing world as a whole, why is such conflict still so strong in some countries?

6   What are the effects of globalization and foreign intervention on national identities in the developing world?

GUIDE TO FURTHER READING

■ **Eriksen, T. H. (1993),** *Ethnicity and Nationalism: Anthropological Perspectives* **(London: Pluto Press).** Presents an anthropological perspective on ethnicity, identity, ethnic relations, nationalism, and relations between states and ethnic minorities.

■ **Fearon, J. D. (2003), 'Ethnic Structure and Cultural Diversity around the World: A Cross-National Data Set on Ethnic Groups',** *Journal of Economic Growth,* **8: 191–218.** Describes a global data set under construction on ethnic and linguistic/cultural groups and compares it to other data sets; highlights the difficulties encountered in specifying ethnic groups cross-nationally.

■ **Gurr, T. R. (1993),** *Minorities at Risk: A Global View of Ethnopolitical Conflicts* **(Washington DC: United States Institute of Peace Press).** The first book based on the Minorities at Risk project. It identifies communal groups at risk and analyses forms of risk, group grievances, group mobilization, group protest and rebellion, and the resolution of group conflicts; it includes chapters on the Middle East and Africa.

■ Gurr, T. R. (2000), *Peoples Versus States: Minorities at Risk in the New Century* (Washington DC: United States Institute of Peace Press), is the second book from the same project. It analyses the same topics as its predecessor plus the role of democracy and the risk of future ethnic violence; it includes a number of illustrative sketches from the developing world.

■ Horowitz, D. L. (1985), *Ethnic Groups in Conflict* (Berkeley: University of California Press). Presents a definition of ethnicity and a theory of ethnic conflict among unranked groups derived primarily from social psychology; discusses the roles of political parties and the military in ethnic conflict and strategies for its resolution; emphasizes deeply divided societies in South-East and South Asia, Africa, and the Caribbean.

■ Hutchinson, J., and Smith, A. D. (eds.) (1994), *Nationalism* (Oxford: Oxford University Press). A very comprehensive reader that includes selections from classic works on the definition of nationalism, theories of nationalism, nationalism in the developing world, and the effects of trends in the international system on nationalism.

■ Scarritt, J. R., and Mozaffar, S. (1999), 'The Specification of Ethnic Cleavages and Ethnopolitical Groups for the Analysis of Democratic Competition in Contemporary Africa', *Nationalism and Ethnic Politics*, 8/1 (Spring): 82–117. Lists African ethnopolitical groups that are relevant for electoral politics and describes the methodology developed to specify them.

■ Sen, A. (2006), *Identity and Violence: The Illusion of Destiny* (New York: W. W. Norton). Argues that all people have multiple identities, and that movements that restrict relevant identities to ethnic or national ones only promote violence.

■ Young, C. (1976), *The Politics of Cultural Pluralism* (Madison: University of Wisconsin Press). Discusses cultural pluralism, identities, the state, nationalism, and cultural mobilization in Africa, the Arab world, Asia, and Latin America; includes comparative case studies from these regions.

WEB LINKS

● **http://webhost.bridgew.edu/smozaffar** The website for the Scarritt/Mozaffar data set on African ethnopolitical group fragmentation and concentration.

● **www.minoritiesatrisk.com** The website of Minorities at Risk project, covering 285 politically active ethnic groups coded on approximately 1,000 variables. Qualitative assessments of every group's risk are included.

● **www.stanford.edu/~jfearon** Go to egreousrepdata.zip for Fearon's data that is summarized in this chapter in Tables 6.1 and 6.2.

ONLINE RESOURCE CENTRE

For additional material and resources, see the Online Resource Centre at:
www.oxfordtextbooks.co.uk/orc/burnell2e/

7

Religion

JEFF HAYNES

Chapter Contents

- Introduction
- Religion and Politics
- Religious Fundamentalism
- Religious Fundamentalism and Politics in the Developing World
- Religion and the State
- Religion in International Politics after September 11
- Conclusion

Overview

Recent decades have seen widespread involvement of religion in politics, especially in parts of the developing world. This chapter, examining the relationship between religion and politics, is structured as follows. First, the concept of religion is defined and its contemporary political and social salience in many developing countries is emphasized. Second, the chapter examines the notion of religious fundamentalism, not least because it is often associated with religious competition and conflict. Third, a survey of extant religious competition and conflict in the developing world is presented, with brief examples drawn from Christianity, Islam, Hinduism, and Buddhism. Fourth, the chapter considers the extent to which, after September 11, the world has changed in terms of the political salience of religion, by examining the importance of both domestic and external factors in conflicts characterized by religious concerns in the developing world.

Introduction

Open a 'quality'—that is, a 'broadsheet'—newspaper on almost any day of the week and turn to the foreign news pages. You might be struck by the number of news items with religious and political dimensions (**religio-politics**). For example, a recurring theme is widespread Islamic militancy or 'fundamentalism', particularly in the Arab Middle East. It sometimes seems that the entire region is polarized between Jews and Muslims—both over the status of holy sites claimed by the two sides and the political and economic position of the mostly Muslim Palestinians.

However, it is not only international relations that are informed by Islamic militancy. For example, for a decade from the early 1990s Algeria endured a civil war between Islamic 'fundamentalist' (or, as I prefer, for reasons to be noted later, Islamist) rebels and the state. The roots of this conflict went back to a contested election and, more generally, highlight the often problematic political relationship between religious and secular actors in the Middle East. In December 1991, Algeria held legislative elections which most independent observers characterized as amongst the freest ever held in the Middle East. The following January, however, Algeria's armed forces seized power to prevent what was likely to be a decisive victory in the elections by an Islamist party, the Front Islamique du Salut (FIS). The assumption was that if the FIS achieved power it would then erode Algeria's newly refreshed democratic institutions. In London *The Economist* posed the question, 'What is the point of an experiment in democracy if the first people it delivers to power are intent on dismantling it?' (2 January 1992). The answer might well be: 'This is the popular will, it must be respected—whatever the outcome.' Instead, Algeria's military leaders imposed their preference. The FIS was summarily banned, thousands of its supporters were incarcerated, and, around 120,000 Algerians died in the subsequent civil war.

It is worth noting at this point that there is no obvious reason why **political Islam** cannot compete for power democratically. Political Islam refers to a political movement with often diverse characteristics that at various times has included elements of many other political movements, while simultaneously adapting the religious views of Islamic fundamentalism or Islamism. In both the Palestinian authority and Iraq in recent years, as well as in Turkey, Islamists have gained power alone (Hamas in the Palestinian authority and the Justice and Development Party or AKP in Turkey) or as part of a ruling coalition (Iraq). In none of these cases, were Islamists unwilling to play by the democratic rules of the game.

Elsewhere in the developing world, Islamists are also politically active. For example, in Africa, Nigeria is increasingly polarized politically between Muslim and Christian forces, fragmented Somalia may eventually have an Islamist government, while Sudan has also experienced a long-running civil war between Muslims and non-Muslims. In none of these cases have Islamists been particularly attracted to using the ballot box to try to achieve power, although it should be noted that in none of the three examples mentioned has that particular option been available as a result of constitutional restrictions or constraints or wider political factors.

Not only Islamists pursue political goals related to religion. In officially secular India, a growth in militant Hinduism was highlighted by, but not confined to, the Babri Masjid mosque incident at Ayodhya in 1992, instrumental in transforming the country's political landscape. This mosque, according to militant Hindus, was built on the birthplace of the Hindu god of war, Rama. As long ago as 1950, the mosque was closed down by the Indian government, for militant Hindus wanted to build

a Hindu temple there. Since then, Hindu militants or 'fundamentalists', whose primary political
organization is the Bharatiya Janata Party (BJP),
have grown to political prominence. From 1996 to
mid-2004, the BJP was the dominant party in three
ruling coalitions.

On the other hand, religion can significantly contribute to political and social stability, for example,
in the way that the Roman Catholic Church was
a leading player in the turn to democracy in Latin
America in the 1980s and 1990s.

KEY POINTS

- The last three decades have seen widespread
  involvement of religion in politics, especially in
  many countries in the developing world.

- Several religious traditions have experienced increased political involvement.

- Religion and democracy do not always seem
  compatible, although religious actors have contributed to democratization.

Religion and Politics

Before proceeding, it is necessary to define 'religion'. In this chapter, religion has two analytically
distinct, yet related meanings. In a *spiritual* sense,
religion pertains in three ways to models of social
and individual behaviour that help believers organize their everyday lives. First, it is to do with the idea
of *transcendence*, that is, it relates to supernatural
realities. Second, it is concerned with *sacredness*,
that is, a system of language and practice that organizes the world in terms of what is deemed holy.
Third, it refers to *ultimacy*: it relates people to the
ultimate conditions of existence.

In another, *material*, sense, religious beliefs can
motivate individuals and groups to act in pursuit of social or political goals. Very few—if
any—religious groups have an *absolute* lack of
concern for at least *some* social and political issues. Consequently, religion can be 'a mobiliser of
masses, a controller of mass action . . . an excuse
for repression [or] an ideological basis for dissent'
(Calvert and Calvert 2001: 140). In many countries, religion remains an important source of basic
value orientations; and this may have social and/or
political connotations.

One final point concerns the relationship
between religion and ethnicity. As Chapter 6
demonstrates, religion is a very common basis for

ethnic identity. For instance in India, Sikh ethnic
identity has been defined largely in terms of adherence to a common religion. It could seem then that
ethnicity is the overarching concept and religious
identification is one sub-type. However, there are
situations where people sharing a single religion
are divided by ethnicity, as for example in Pakistan
where people share a common Islamic faith but are
ethnically divided on the basis of region and language. Moreover appeals to religion often seek to
transcend particular local or ethnic identities in the
name of a supposedly universal ideal. It is wisest,
therefore, to see ethnicity and religion as terms
whose potential meaning and content overlap but
remain distinct.

An American commentator, George Weigel,
claims there is an 'unsecularization of the world',
that is, a global religious revitalization (quoted in
Huntington 1993: 26). This is manifested in a global
resurgence of religious ideas and social movements,
not confined to one faith or only to poor, developing countries. This unexpected development
can be explained in various ways. No simple,
clear-cut reason or single theoretical explanation
covers all the cases. Yet the widespread emergence
of religious actors with overtly social or political goals is often linked to **modernization**—that

is, the prolonged period of historically unprecedented, diverse, massive change, characterized by urbanization, industrialization, and abrupt technological developments that people around the world have experienced in recent times. Modernization is said not only to have undermined traditional value systems but also to have allocated opportunities—both within and between countries—in highly unequal ways. This has led many people to feel both disorientated and troubled and, as a result, some at least (re)turn to religion for solace and comfort. In doing so, they seek a new or renewed sense of identity, something to give their lives greater meaning and purpose.

A second, although linked, explanation for apparent religious resurgence moves away from the specific impact of modernization to point to a more generalized 'atmosphere of crisis'. A key factor is said to be widespread popular disillusion with the abilities of secular state leaders to direct their socio-economic polities so that people generally benefit. Such disappointment can then feed into perceptions that these leaders hold power illegitimately—a sense bolstered when leaders resort to political oppression. Adding to the sense of crisis is widespread popular belief that society's traditional morals and values are being seriously undermined, not least by the corrosive effects of globalization, Westernization, and **secularization**—the reduction in influence or even withdrawal of religion from the public realm. These circumstances are said to provide a fertile milieu for many people's 'return' to religion.

This suggests that the influence of religion will not be seen 'only' in relation to personal and social issues. Commentators have additionally pointed to *political* effects of the 'return of religion' where, in many developing countries, highly politicized religious groups, institutions, and movements have emerged—or adopted a higher profile—in recent years. Such actors are found in many different faiths and sects and what they have in common is a desire to change domestic, and in some cases international, arrangements, so as to (re)instate religion as a central societal and political influence. They adopt

a variety of tactics to achieve their goals. Some actors confine themselves to the realm of legitimate political protest, seeking reform or change via the ballot box; others resort to violence and terror to pursue their objectives.

Other explanations are offered for what is widely seen as a global religious revival and revitalization, but some commentators suggest that, in the developing world, there is not a religious resurgence per se; rather, political religion is simply more visible—largely as a consequence of the global communications revolution. In other words, religion is not a novel political actor, so much as a stubbornly persistent one. For Smith (1990: 34), 'what has changed in the present situation . . . is mainly the growing awareness of [global manifestations of political religion] by the Western world, and the perception that they might be related to our interests'. This makes the recent trends just the latest manifestation of *cyclical* religious activity, made more highly visible (and to many alarming) by advances in communications technology and availability. In short, globalization is a multifaceted process of change, universally affecting states, local communities, and individuals. Religions are not exempted from its influence and, as a result, like other social agents, they participate in and are affected by globalization. Academic discussions of religion and globalization often highlight trends towards cultural pluralism as a result of globalization, examining how various religions respond (Haynes 2007). Some believers react 'positively', accepting or even endorsing pluralism, including some Christian ecumenical movements. Others emphasize more inter-religious differences, sometimes confronting non-believers in attempts to preserve their particular values from being eroded by globalization. So-called fundamentalist Christian, Muslim, and Jewish movements are well-known examples.

But they are not necessarily *sui generis*. In the developing world, various religious traditions—for example, Hinduism, Buddhism, and Islam—all experienced periods of pronounced political activity in the first half of the twentieth century in what were then mostly colonized countries. In the 1920s and the 1930s, religion was frequently used in the service of anti-colonial nationalism, and was a major facet of emerging national identity in opposition to alien rule (see Haynes 1996: 55–6). For example, in various Muslim countries, such as Algeria, Egypt, and Indonesia, Islamic consciousness was the defining ideology of nationalist movements. In 1947, immediately after the Second World War, Pakistan was founded as a Muslim state, religiously and culturally distinct from India, which was 80 per cent Hindu. A decade later, Buddhism was politically important, *inter alia*, in Burma, Sri Lanka, and Vietnam. Later, in the 1960s in Latin America, both **Christian democracy**—the application of Christian precepts to politics—and **liberation theology**—a radical ideology using Christianity as the basis of a demand for greater socio-economic justice for the poor—were politically consequential. More recently and in diverse countries including Iran, the United States, and Nicaragua, religion (re)appeared as an important political actor. Religious actors became skilled at using the media to spread their political messages (Tarrow 1998: 115). In sum,

political religion is nearly always in opposition to the status quo; and in the developing world this has been the case since at least the early years of the twentieth century, a time of widespread external colonial control. Current manifestations of political religion can be located in this historical continuum and context, to stress *continuity* rather than *change*.

> **KEY POINTS**
>
> - Religion has spiritual, material, and in some cases political, aspects.
> - Religion played an important political role in many developing countries during the last years of colonialism.
> - Patchy modernization and/or a more generalized 'atmosphere of crisis' are said to underpin religious resurgence.
> - It is often claimed that there is a near-global religious revival but globalization may simply be rendering religion in politics more visible.

Religious Fundamentalism

Many religious actors with political goals are routinely labelled 'fundamentalists'. **Religious fundamentalism** has been described as a 'distinctively modern twentieth-century movement' albeit with 'historical antecedents' (Woodhead and Heelas 2000: 32). The label, 'religious fundamentalism' has been widely employed since the 1970s, especially by the mass media, to describe and account for numerous, apparently diverse, religious and political developments around the globe. The term's genesis is in a group of socially conservative evangelicals inside the mainstream Protestant denominations in the United States. There, in the early twentieth century, such people first applied the designation

'religious fundamentalist' to themselves. Now, however, as a generic term, it is widely applied to groups outside the corpus of Christianity, notably Hindu and Islamic entities.

What fundamentalist doctrines generally have in common is that their character and impact are located within a nexus of moral and social issues revolving in many cases around state–society interactions. In some cases, the initial defensiveness of beleaguered religious groups later developed into a political offensive that sought to alter the prevailing social and political realities of state–society relations. Religious fundamentalists often accused their rulers of performing inadequately and/or corruptly; with the exception of Buddhist and Hindu fundamentalists, they criticized contemporary developments in the light of religious texts, such as the Bible or the Koran.

The significance of this from a political perspective is that religious fundamentalism can, and often does, supply an already restive group with a ready-made manifesto for social change: fundamentalist activists use suitable religious texts both to challenge secular rulers and to propose a programme for radical political and social reform. Under these circumstances, it can be relatively easy for fundamentalist leaders to gain the support of people who feel particularly aggrieved that, in various important ways, society's development is not proceeding according to God's will and/or the community's interests.

Contemporary examples of religious fundamentalism are often said to be rooted in the failed promise and impact of modernization, such as apparently declining morals. To many fundamentalists the current era is one where God is in danger of being superseded by a gospel of technical progress accompanying sweeping socio-economic changes. The pace of change strongly challenges traditional habits, beliefs, and cultures. In an increasingly materialist world, individual worth often seems to be measured according to standards of wealth and status, while religion is ignored or belittled. This development is thought to lie behind the growth of religious militancy and to account in general terms for the recent rise of religious 'fundamentalism'.

But some argue that, in fact, religious fundamentalism is an empty and therefore meaningless term, erroneously and casually employed 'by western liberals to refer to a broad spectrum of religious phenomena which have little in common except for the fact that they are alarming to liberals!' (Woodhead and Heelas 2000: 32). Critics contend that the range of so-called fundamentalist groups is so wide—for example, resurgent Islam in Iran and Latin American Pentecostalism—that the term has no meaning and, moreover, is insulting to many people described as fundamentalists. Such groups actually differ markedly among themselves: some

aspire to influence or even control the public and political arena; others actively work to disengage from social and political issues. As a consequence, Hallencreutz and Westerlund (1996: 4) argue the:

> broad use of the term has become increasingly irrelevant. In sum, viewed as a derogatory concept, tied to Western stereotypes and Christian presuppositions, the casual use of the term easily causes misunderstandings and prevents the understanding of the dynamics and characteristics of different religious groups with explicit *political* objectives. (my emphasis)

In contrast, those accepting the analytical relevance of the term do so because they perceive contemporary movements of religious resurgence—albeit encompassing different religious traditions—as having features in common which denote a shared concern with fundamentalism. In general, fundamentalist doctrines share the following: (a) a strong desire to return to what are believed to be a faith's fundamentals; (b) forceful rejection of Western-style secular modernity; (c) 'an oppositional minority group-identity maintained in an exclusivist and militant manner' (Woodhead and Heelas 2000: 32); (d) rejection of secularization, and a demand to retrieve the public realm as a place of moral and religious purity; and (e) perception that patriarchal and hierarchical ordering of relations between the sexes is both morally and religiously appropriate.

Drawing on data from a large variety of fundamentalist movements, Marty and Appleby (1993: 3) define religious fundamentalism as a 'set of strategies, by which beleaguered believers attempt to preserve their distinctive identity as a people or group' in response to a real or imagined attack from those who, it appears, want to draw the religious believers into 'syncretistic, areligious, or irreligious cultural milieu[s]'. Such defensiveness may develop into a political offensive aiming to alter prevailing socio-political realities.

So far, then, it seems that what religious fundamentalists share is the fear that their religiously orientated way of life is under threat from unwelcome alien influences, especially secular-orientated governments. As a result, they often seek to reform society in accordance with what they believe are suitable religious tenets, to change laws, morality, social norms, and, if necessary, the polity. They may seek to create a traditionally orientated, less modern(ized) society, and are willing in some cases to fight governments if the latter's jurisdiction appears to be encompassing areas which the fundamentalists believe are integral to its realization—education, gender relations and employment, and social morality. Fundamentalists may also attack those they see as 'nominal' or 'backsliding' co-religionists and members of opposing religions.

Drawing on the example of contemporary Christian fundamentalists in the United States, many analysts who employ the term fundamentalism also suggest that it is only properly applicable to Christianity and other Abrahamic religions of the 'book': Islam and Judaism. This is because, like fundamentalist Christians, Muslim, and Jewish fundamentalists take as their defining dogma what is believed to be the inerrancy of God's own words set out in holy books like the Bible. In other words, in these three religions, singular scriptural revelations are central to each set of fundamentalist dogma. The inference is that,

because neither Hinduism nor Buddhism have central tenets of political, social, and moral import conveniently accessible in holy books, it is not logically possible for there to be Hindu or Buddhist fundamentalism. However, in recent years a popular fundamentalist movement within Hinduism has emerged in pursuit of demonstrably political goals. Such a group is not defined by its absolutist insistence upon the veracity of God's revealed will, but instead by a desire to recapture elements of national identity that are perceived as being lost, either by dint of cultural dilution or mixing, or by perceived deviations from the religious philosophy and/or teaching (Ram-Prasad 1993: 288).

KEY POINTS

- All major religious traditions have fundamentalist variants.

- Fundamentalist doctrines are concerned with moral, social, and sometimes political, issues.

- Fundamentalist concerns may supply an already restive group with a manifesto for social and political change.

- Fundamentalists fear their way of life is under threat from secular forces.

Religious Fundamentalism and Politics in the Developing World

This section considers four kinds of religious fundamentalism, most prominent in the developing world—Islamic, Christian, and Hindu—focusing on their main socio-political characteristics.

Islamic fundamentalism

Like Christianity, Islam is by no means monolithic but has taken many different forms, one important

distinction being between the Sunni and Shia traditions (see Box 7.1). In 2004 clashes between these two communities in Iraq and Pakistan were only the latest tragic reminder of the endurance of these divisions. Both these main branches however have given rise to fundamentalist movements.

A defining character of religious fundamentalism is that it is always socially but not necessarily politically conservative. Thus some Islamic fundamentalist

BOX 7.1

Theological Differences between Sunnis and Shi'ites

More than four-fifths of all Muslims are Sunni, the largest sect of Islam. Less than 20 per cent of Muslims are Shi'ites, although in some countries, such as Iran, they are in the majority. Differences between Sunni and Shia sects of Islam are not that extensive. Both emphasize the importance of five key beliefs—or pillars—of Islam (profession of faith in the one God and in Muhammad as his Prophet; pray five times a day, donate alms to the poor, fast during the month of Ramadan, undertake pilgrimage (*hajj*) to Mecca), read the same holy book—the Koran—and regard each other as Muslims. Differences between them centre on two issues: how each attaches meaning to the history of Muhammad's family; how each regards their religious leaders.

Sunni and Shia sects divided nearly 1,400 years ago, soon after Muhammad's death in 632. Ali, his son-in-law, received support as the figure who henceforward would lead the struggle to spread Islam. ('Shia' is an abbreviation of 'Shiat Ali', or the people of Ali.) But not all Muslims believed that Ali should play this leading role, although most did believe that he was a holy man. Shi'ites believed Ali was the first Imam, a direct descendant of Muhammad and messenger of God. Twelve Imams lived before the lineage came to an end over 1,000 years ago. Within Shia Islam, each of the 12 has sub-sects who worship them.

Sunnis do not attach any special power to the Imam, and overall have a somewhat less structured hierarchy of religious leaders, called caliphs. They are important advisers and community leaders who teach Islam; they are not infallible or chosen by God.

(Islamist) groups seek to overthrow the existing socio-economic and political order by various means, including violence or terrorism, incremental reform of existing political regimes, or winning elections through the mobilization of a political party. Islamists take as their defining dogma what are believed to be God's words written in their holy book, the Koran. In other words, singular scriptural revelations are central to Islamic fundamentalist beliefs.

Modern Islamic resurgence dates from the 1920–40 period, when growing numbers of countries in the Middle East were demanding—and in some cases receiving—national self-determination. The main point of contention was how far these predominantly Muslim states should employ the tenets of *Sharia*—that is, Muslim religious—law in their legal systems. This example of a desire to Islamicize polities had its precedents in the Muslim world in anti-imperialist and anti-pagan movements (*jihads*), periodically erupting from the late nineteenth century, especially in parts of West Africa and East Asia (see Haynes 1993). In these regions, conflict between tradition and modernization and between Islam and Christianity was often acute.

In the early stages of Islam, nearly 1,400 years ago, religious critics of the status quo periodically emerged in opposition to what they perceived as unjust rule. Contemporary Islamists are only the most recent example of such a phenomenon, often characterizing themselves as the 'just' involved in a 'holy war' against the 'unjust'. This dichotomy between just and unjust in the promotion of social change parallels the tension in the West between state and civil society: both juxtapose mutually exclusive concepts where a strengthening of one necessarily implies a weakening of the other. The implication is that the unjust inhabit the state while the just look in from the outside, aching to reform the corrupt political system. The Islamic 'just' strive to achieve their goal which is a form of direct democracy under the auspices of *Sharia* law, in which the ruler uses his wisdom to settle disputes brought before him by his loyal subjects. The Islamic concept of *shura* (consultation) by no means necessarily implies popular sovereignty, which is with God alone; 'rather it is a means of obtaining unanimity from the community of believers, which allows for no legitimate minority position' (Dorr 1993: 151–2).

The goal of the just is an Islam-based society. Currently, in many Muslim countries, Islamist groups believe themselves to be the appropriate vehicle to achieve this goal. For them, Western-style liberal democracy is fatally flawed and compromised, a concept relevant only to secular, Western(ized) societies which appear unacceptably decadent. As a young Algerian graduate of the Islamic Science Institute of Algiers averred in the early 1990s, 'The modern world is going through a major moral crisis which can be very confusing to young people. Just look at what is happening in Russia. Personally I have found many of the answers and solutions in Islam' (cited in Ibrahim 1992).

The global Muslim community, the *umma*, is a good example of a transnational civil society (the Roman Catholic Church, with its institutional support for democratization in the 1990s, is another), containing the seeds of both domination and dissent. Shared beliefs, relating especially to culture and identity link Muslims. For this reason it is unsurprising that international manifestations of Islamic resurgence appeared after the humbling defeat of Arab Muslims by Israeli Jews in the six-day war of June 1967. Since then a combination of bad government, growing unemployment, and generalized social crisis in the Muslim world has produced Islamist movements. When possible, as in the Persian Gulf, rulers have been content to live on the 'rents' accrued from their control of oil exports with little done to reduce unemployment and underemployment, develop more representative polities, or plan successfully for the future. In short, there has been a skewed modernization; urbanization and the creation of a centralized state proceeded at the same time as many people became increasingly dissatisfied with the way that their rulers rule.

Christian fundamentalism

Africa has experienced the spread of **evangelical Christianity**. Evangelical Christianity usually refers to conservative, nearly always Protestant, Christian religious practices and traditions, which emphasize evangelism, a personal experience of conversion, faith rooted in the Bible and a belief in the relevance of Christian faith to cultural issues. Some commentators suggest this spread is linked to the influence of American fundamentalist Christian churches (Gifford 2004). Sponsored by American television evangelists and their local allies, thousands of conservative, mainly foreign, Protestant evangelical crusaders have promoted American-style conservative Christianity in Africa since the 1980s.

Norms, beliefs, and morals favourable to American interests were in turn disseminated as a fundamental aspect of the religious message (Freston 2004). African converts to US conservative evangelical churches have been said to be victims of manipulation by the latest manifestation of neo-colonialism. The objective was not, however, to spirit away Africa's material resources, but rather to deflect popular political mobilization away from seeking structural change of the society and the economy, in order to serve either American strategic interests and/or financial objectives of US transnational corporations (Pieterse 1992: 10–11).

Others contend that foreign Christian proselytization in Africa resulted *not* in imposition of an alien doctrine but instead in the indigenization of Christianity (Ter Haar and Busutill 2005; Freston 2004: 1–2). During the colonial era European-style Christianity tried unsuccessfully to appropriate the richness of local people's imagination and beliefs, in order better to convert and to dominate. But the outcome was different to what was anticipated: African independent churches emerged.

Some such churches have been described as fundamentalist. Nigeria is a useful example to highlight because of the significance of this issue to the country's political and economic developments. Since the 1970s there have been growing signs of tension between Islamists and the state in Nigeria. This has paralleled increasing hostility between Muslim and Christian communities leading to the emergence of an organization representing fundamentalist

Christians whose main purpose is to comment on both religious and political issues. The Pentecostal Fellowship of Nigeria (PFN) is an influential voice in the inter-denominational Christian Association of Nigeria that claims to represent the interests of the country's Christians at both federal and national levels. The PFN was formerly an avowedly apolitical organization. It re-evaluated its traditional stance of indifference to political issues in the mid-1980s because of its fear of creeping Islamicization. Some influential figures in the PFN, including the late Benson Idahosa, founder of the international Church of God Mission, have warned of religious war in Nigeria—if tensions between Muslims and Christians are not diminished.

Somewhat ironically, religious tensions were exacerbated in northern Nigeria in the 1990s and early 2000s in part because of the aggressive proselytizing of missionaries of several of the fundamentalist churches, including Idahosa's, which led to some conversions in the predominantly Muslim north. In that region, where socio-cultural norms make Islam an integral facet of many people's lives, conversion to Christianity was facilitated by a modern variant of the colonial missionaries' 'gospel of prosperity' argument. During colonial times, Christianity was seen to bring medicine, education, and wealth to the country, so it was quite sensible for those who wished to share these benefits to follow the Christian faith. 'Muslims in power know that they have nothing to offer the country,' claimed Idahosa (Elliot 1993), alluding to the three decades of 'Muslim rule' that saw living standards of most Nigerians plummet.

In Nigeria, the Christian fundamentalist churches consider themselves involved in a three-way conflict, not only with Muslims, but also with mainstream Christians. They accuse the latter of being apostates who have abandoned the fundamentals of the Christian faith, while their leaders have set themselves up as individuals whose power challenges that of God. In short, all people of whatever religious faith outside the community of Christian fundamentalists are beyond the pale of true believers and can only be saved from hell if they convert.

The growth of fundamentalist churches in Nigeria has probably been encouraged by the country's deteriorating socio-economic conditions over the last quarter century (see Chapter 22b). The volatility of the religious environment mirrors the unpredictability of the political arena: the battle for power between various ethnic groups, and between civilian politicians and military figures, corresponds to the fight for 'theological space' between traditional and *arriviste* religions. Interlinked economic, social, and spiritual crises help to spread fears of the end of the world and an accompanying, increasingly desperate, striving for salvation. This combination of predicaments is good business for the plethora of emergent preachers who capitalize on fear and a common desire for order, stability, and community. Traditionally, politics, business, and religion have been the three areas of endeavour from which individuals may expect financial reward; politics in Nigeria has long been the domain of a homogeneous (northern-military) elite. Business success requires capital, contacts, and luck, all generally in short supply, while religious success may only require a charismatic personality with the ability to attract disciples and followers. The supporters, as a sign of their faith, are often willing to pay for the costs of running a church and the considerable expenses incurred by its leader.

With economic decline from the 1980s and increasing social disorder, the hierarchies of the mainline Christian churches conspicuously failed to speak up for ordinary people, or even to criticize the inept political system and the accompanying corruption in public life. The fundamentalist churches offered, in contrast, a sense of solidarity between co-religionists, a code of behaviour, moral values, and, above all, a sense of stability in a world profoundly disrupted. The Christian revival involved a movement away from the crassly materialist ways of the established churches and an attempt to reconstruct a new type of socially responsive organization. It stressed a fundamentalist return to the tenets of the Bible, calling on Christians to experience spiritual rebirth.

In sum, the growth of fundamentalist Christian communities in Nigeria is linked to the country's socio-economic deterioration that, in turn, follows the fortunes of the oil industry. Like fundamentalist churches elsewhere in Africa, those in Nigeria have offered their followers the possibility of joining a new Christian community—where solidarity between individuals is a function of religious belief. At the same time Nigeria's Christian fundamentalists' political concerns have been forged by the fear of a growth in Islamist groups in the country.

Hindu fundamentalism

The roots of Hindu fundamentalism are said to lie both in the desire of some Hindu nationalists in India to privilege their culture over others and in the perception that 'Hindu' India is surrounded and threatened by Islamic resurgence—notably in Pakistan (where the Kashmir issue focuses such concerns), Iran, and Afghanistan. We should note, however, that Hindu nationalism is not a new development. Mahatma Gandhi, the leading Indian nationalist and a committed Hindu, was assassinated by a Hindu extremist in 1948 for the 'crime' of appearing to condone the creation of a new homeland—Pakistan—for India's Muslims. Subsequently, Prime Minister Indira Gandhi played to such sentiments in the early 1980s, in her confrontation with Sikh militants. From that time also simmering Hindu fundamentalist suspicion of India's largest religious minority—the Muslims, comprising about 11 per cent of the population, more than 100 million people—has been reflected and fostered by a growing 'family' (parivar) of organizations embodying the Hindu chauvinist doctrine of *Hindutva*, and reached a kind of apotheosis in the violent destruction in 1992 of a historic mosque at Ayodhya in Uttar Pradesh. Since then, the BJP has grown out of this movement, becoming an important political player; by May 2004 it had led the ruling NDA (National Democratic Alliance) coalition government for six years, although ousted from power in that year's general election by the secular Congress Party, the dominant party in the subsequent ruling coalition.

KEY POINTS

- Many Islamic fundamentalists in the developing world seek to change political arrangements by a variety of methods.
- Christian fundamentalists in Nigeria fear Islamicization.
- Hindu fundamentalists feel under threat from Muslims, both within India and without.

Religion and the State

These examples of religious fundamentalisms in the developing world point more generally to the importance of state–church relations, that is, the interactions in a country between the state and the leading religious organization(s). A major difficulty in trying to survey existing church–state relations in the developing world is that the very concept of *church* reflects a somewhat parochial Anglo–American standpoint with most relevance to Western Christian traditions.

Extending the question of church–state relations to non-Christian and developing world contexts necessitates some preliminary conceptual clarifications—not least because the very idea of a prevailing state–church dichotomy is culture-bound (Box 7.2). *Church* is a Christian institution,

JEFF HAYNES ·

BOX 7.2

Religion, Nationalism, and Identity

What is the relationship between religion and nationalism? The first point is that nationalism is a source of identity for many people in the developing world. Many identities are based on shared values, beliefs, or concerns that not only include religion but can also extend to ethnicity, nationality, culture and political ideologies (Gopin 2000, 2005). This does not imply that such expressions of identity are necessarily monolithic entities—because in fact *everyone's* self-conception is a unique combination of various identities that can include, but are not limited to, community, religion, ethnicity, nationalism, gender, class, and family. Their relative importance and compatibility will differ at various times and circumstances. For example, race and religion are important sources of identity in some societies, while in others political ideologies and nationalism are judged to be of more significance. In short, both individual and collective senses of identity are socially constructed from a number of available traits and experiences, all of which are subject to interpretation. People *choose* their history and ancestry and, as a result, can *create*, as much as *discover*, differences from others (Gopin 2000; Malek 2004).

---

while the modern understanding of *state* is deeply rooted in the post-Reformation European political experience. Overloaded with Western cultural history, these two concepts cannot easily be translated into non-Christian terminologies. Some religions—for example, Hinduism—have no ecclesiastical structure at all. Consequently, there *cannot* be a clerical challenge to India's secular state comparable to that of Buddhist monks in parts of South-East Asia or of *mullahs* in Iran. However, political parties and movements energized by religious notions—such as Hinduism and Sikhism—have great political importance in contemporary India. Within the developing world, only in Latin America is it pertinent to speak of church–state relations along the lines of the European model. This is because of the historical dominance in the region of the Roman Catholic Church and the creation of European-style states in the early nineteenth century.

The differences between Christian conceptions of state and church and those of other world religions are well illustrated by reference to Islam. In the Muslim tradition, mosque is not church. The closest Islamic approximation to 'state'—*dawla*—means, conceptually, either a ruler's dynasty or his administration (only with the specific proviso of *church* as generic concept for *moral community, priest* for *custodians of the sacred law*, and *state* for *political*

community, is it appropriate to use these concepts in Islamic and other non-Christian contexts). On the theological level, the command–obedience nexus that constitutes the Islamic definition of authority is not demarcated by conceptual categories of religion and politics. Life as a physical reality is an expression of divine will and authority (*qudrah*). There is no validity in separating the matters of piety from those of the polity; both are divinely ordained. Yet, although both religious and political authorities are legitimated Islamically, they invariably constitute two independent social institutions. They do, however, regularly interact with each other. In sum, there is a variety of church–state relations in the contemporary world (see Box 7.3). Note, however, that the typology is not exhaustive but instead identifies common arrangements.

In the *confessional* church–state relationship, ecclesiastical authority is pre-eminent over secular power. A dominant religion—Islam in the countries in Box 7.3—seeks to shape the world according to its leadership's interpretations of God's plan for humankind. However, confessional states are rare in the early twenty-first century. One of the most consistent effects of secularization is to separate religious and secular power almost—but not quite—regardless of the religion or type of political system. However, as events in Saudi Arabia after the

BOX 7.3   141

A Typology of Church–State Relations

Confessional	'Generally religious'	Established faith	Liberal secular	Marxist secular
Iran, Saudi Arabia, Sudan, Afghanistan (under the Taliban, 1996–2001),	Indonesia, USA	England, Denmark, Norway	Netherlands, Turkey, India, Ghana	China, Albania (until 1991), Russia (until 1991), North Korea

country's creation in 1932, in Iran since the 1978–9 Islamic revolution, and in Sudan and Afghanistan from the 1980s indicate, several Muslim countries have sought to build confessional polities.

Because of Islam's pivotal role, the overthrow of the Shah of Iran in 1979 was one of the most spectacular political upheavals of recent times. The outcome of the revolutionary process was a clerical, authoritarian regime. The Shah's regime was not a shaky monarchy but a powerful centralized autocratic state possessing a strong and feared security service (SAVAK) and an apparently loyal and cohesive officer corps. Unlike earlier revolutions in other Muslim countries, such as Egypt, Iraq, Syria, and Libya, Iran's was not a secular, leftist revolution from above, but one with massive popular support and participation. The forces that overthrew the Shah came from all urban social classes, Iran's different nationalities and ideologically varying political parties and movements. Nevertheless an Islamic Republic was eventually declared. In these events the *ulama* or Muslim clerics, who adhere like the bulk of Iran's Muslims to the Shia tradition, played a central role. Organized in and by the Islamic Republican Party, they came to power, established an Islamic constitution and dominated the post-revolutionary institutions.

The Iranian revolution was internationally significant in a number of ways. It was the first since the anti-monarchist, anti-confessional French Revolution of 1789 in which the dominant ideology, forms of organization, leading personnel, and proclaimed goals were all religious in appearance and inspiration. The guide for the post-revolution Iranian state was the tenets of the Muslim holy book, the Koran, and the Sunnah (the traditions of the Prophet Muhammad, comprising what he said, did, and approved of). While economic and political factors played a major part in the growth of the anti-Shah movement, the leadership of that movement (the clerics) saw the revolution's goals primarily in terms of building an Islamic state that rejected Western materialism and political ideas. This in turn came to determine poor relations with the West.

The radicals within Iran's ruling post-revolution elite began to lose ground following the death of Ayatollah Khomeini, the revolution's charismatic leader, in June 1989, just months after the end of the bloody Iran–Iraq war (1980–8). As it became clear that Iran was in dire need of foreign investment and technology, the then state president, Hashemi Rafsanjani, and his political allies seemed to gain ascendancy. The lesson was that even a successful Islamic revolution could not succeed in splendid isolation. Iranians, like people everywhere, hoped for improving living standards. They were not content with increased Islamicization of state and society, which many perceived as little more than political and social repression behind a religious façade. A reformist President Khatami, in office between 1997 and 2005, found himself caught between demands of those wanting social and political liberalization—headed by radical students—and the conservatives, led by the *mullahs*. His successor, Mahmoud Ahmadinejad, elected president in July 2005, quickly established a reputation as a religious hardliner, with a focus on three main issues: Iran's interests in Iraq; relations with the Muslim world; and interaction with the United States and Europe, especially in relation to Iran's nuclear power programme—which Iran claims is for purely civilian purposes and has no military ambitions.

Ahmadinejad is not a dictator and even though Iran is not a 'standard' democracy, it is by no means a closed society. Citizens can openly discuss matters of state whether among themselves or in the pages of the country's notable vibrant press. Policy debates fill the Iranian press and there are frequent deliberations in the Iranian parliament, the Majlis, about the future direction of society. The Ministry of Foreign Affairs is a key promoter of Iran's secular state interests, while religious hardliners advocate Islamic causes and expressions of Muslim solidarity with coreligionists beyond Iran's borders, including in Iraq (Barnes and Bigham 2006).

Alongside the confessional states such as Iran there are the 'generally religious' states, like the USA and Indonesia. They are guided by religious beliefs in general, but are not tied to any specific religious tradition. Both the USA and Indonesia have a belief in God as one of the bases on which the nation should be built. In Indonesia, under General Suharto (1965–98), such a belief formed one of the five pillars of the state ideology, *Pancasila*. This position is very similar to the notion of 'civil religion' in the USA. However, whereas the generally religious policy of religion in Indonesia is an official policy, civil religion in the USA is not formally recognized.

Then there are countries that have an officially established faith but are also socially highly secular, of which the Scandinavian countries and England are examples. Over time the voices of the established churches in public policy issues have become increasing marginal. However, in England at least, the Anglican Church has recently begun once again to try to add its voice to demands on social policy issues.

Next, and frequently encountered in the modern era, is the *liberal secular* model that encapsulates the notion of secular power holding sway over religion, with distance, detachment, and separation between church and state. Here, the state strives to use religion for its own ends, to 'legitimate political rule and to sanctify economic oppression and the given system' of social stratification (Casanova 1994: 49). Secularization policies are widely pursued as a means of national integration in post-colonial multi-religious states, like India. It is worth noting, however, that the concept of secularism is not necessarily straightforward. For example, Hindu critics of India's religiously 'neutral' Constitution contend that it is not neutral but rather privileges India's religious minorities, including Muslims, Sikhs, and Christians. In the liberal-secular model, no religion is given official predominance. In fact, in vigorously modernizing countries such as India and post-Ottoman Turkey, state policies of modernization were expected to lead—inevitably—to a high degree of secularization; hence, their constitutions are neutral towards religion. But things turned out differently: in recent years, democratization and secularization have worked at cross purposes. Increasing participation in the political arena has drawn in new social forces in India, religious Hindus, Sikhs, and Muslims—who, in demanding greater formal recognition of their religions by the state, have been responsible for making religion a central issue in contemporary politics. In Turkey, the accession to power of the Islamist Welfare Party (*Refah Partisi*) in 1996—claiming to be the party of the poor and the alienated—suggests that even when secularization is pursued with great determination over a long period—in Turkey's case for eighty years—there is still no certainty that, for important constituencies, the socio-political appeal of religion will wither.

Finally, there is the category of *Marxist secular* states. Before the overthrow of communism in 1989–90, Eastern Europe contained anti-religious polities where religion was stifled by the state. Most Marxist regimes were less hardline than Enver Hoxha's Albania—where religion was 'abolished'—but religion was typically permitted to exist only as the private concern of the individual. This constituted a kind of promise that the authorities would respect the people's religious faith and practice—as long as it remained behind closed doors. Skeletal religious organizations were, however, allowed to exist—but only so the state could use them for purposes of social control. They were reduced to liturgical institutions, with no other task than the holding of divine services. Numbers of permitted places of worship were greatly reduced.

Paradoxically, however, even the most strident and prolonged Marxist anti-religion campaigns failed to secularize societies. The pivotal role of the Christian churches in the democratic openings in Eastern Europe and non-Marxist Latin America in the 1980s and 1990s, and the contemporary revival of Islam in some of the formerly communist Central Asian countries, indicate that popular religiosity has retained immense social importance.

But we should not take it for granted that Marxist, 'anti-religion' states are only of historical interest. For example, the government of China—home to more than a billion people—launched a fierce campaign in the mid-1990s to 'teach atheism to Tibetan Buddhists'. This was necessary, the Chinese government argued, to enable Tibetans to 'break free of the bewitchment' of religion.

In sum, none of the various models of church–state relations has been permanently able to resolve the tension between religion and the secular world. The chief manifestation of this tension in recent times is the desire of many religious organizations not to allow the state to sideline them as—almost everywhere—increasingly secularized states seek to intervene ever deeper into social life.

KEY POINTS

- 'Church' is a concept that derives from Christianity and may have little relevance in other religious settings.

- There are various relationships between church and state in the developing world.

- States often seek to secularize their societies, to the dismay of religious actors.

- No model of church–state relations has been permanently able to resolve tensions between the religious and the secular world.

Religion in International Politics after September 11

So far, we have been concerned primarily with the domestic interaction of religion and politics within developing countries. However, no survey of the issue can legitimately ignore the impact of the terrorist events of 11 September 2001 (9/11) on issues of religion and politics in general and those of the Muslim world and the West, in particular.

Prior to the eighteenth century and the formation and development of the international state system, religion was the key ideology that stimulated conflict between social groups. However, following the Peace of Westphalia in 1648 and the consequent development of centralized states, religion took a back seat as an organizing ideology at the international level. As already noted, it was not until the Iranian revolution of 1978–9 that religion resumed a significant political role. Ten years later in 1989, the cold war came to an end. Since then, international politics has been characterized by four significant changes:

- Change from a bipolar (USA, Soviet Union) to an arguably unipolar (USA) structure of power.

- Culture replacing ideology as a chief source of identity, leading to changes in extant affiliations and antagonisms in world affairs.

- Some commentators argue that there is a religious resurgence in countries around the world, excepting Western Europe.

- The nature of international conflict has changed, with fewer inter-state wars. Of the 110 major conflicts during the 1990s—that is, those involving more than 1,000 fatalities each—only seven were interstate wars, while 103 were civil wars. Of the latter, over 70 per cent are classified as communal wars: that is, wars among ethnic and other national groups, with religion very often playing an important part.

Western Europe, including Britain, is characterized by both religious privatization and secularization. In contrast, over half of all US citizens claim to attend regular religious, mostly Christian, services. Moreover, eight words are juxtaposed—'In God We Trust' and the 'United States of America'—on all US currency, both coins and notes.

The issue of what role religion should play there was sharpened by the arguments of the US academic, Samuel Huntington (1993; revised and expanded version, 1996a), in his now (in)famous **clash of civilizations** thesis. Huntington's key argument is that following the end of the cold war, future international conflicts are increasingly likely to be along cultural fault lines. In his view, this would replace the forty years of competition between two secular ideologies: liberal democracy/capitalism and communism. Now, he suggests, new rivalries are most important, notably between the (Christian) 'West' and the (mostly Muslim, mostly Arab) 'East'. In short, the core of Huntington's argument is that in the post-cold war era the 'Christian', democratic West is likely to find itself in conflict with radical Islam (Islamic fundamentalism), a global anti-Western political movement said to be aiming for fundamental changes to the political order. Another influential US commentator, Francis Fukuyama (1992: 236), argued that Islamic fundamentalism is the antithesis of Western liberalism, with 'more than superficial resemblance to European fascism'.

Critics of such arguments argue that although many radical Islamist movements and political parties would not classify themselves as liberal democratic, we cannot assume this necessarily implies that such actors are willing to engage in violent conduct, including terrorism, to pursue their aims. The September 11 atrocities in the USA—as well as the Bali and Kenya terrorist incidents that followed—appear to have been carried out by a shadowy transnational terrorist group—al-Qaeda. However, it is by no means clear that most 'ordinary' Muslim men and women support either its goals or the violent means it employs.

It is also important to see the struggle in the Islamic world of groups like al-Qaeda as directed against their own rulers as well as the West, especially the USA. Since the beginning of Islam in the seventh century, Muslim critics of the status quo have periodically emerged to oppose what they perceive as unjust rule. Current Islamists, including, arguably, bin Laden and al-Qaeda, are contemporary examples, who portray themselves as the 'just' involved in struggle against 'unjust', 'anti-religious' rulers and their allies. Bin Laden's key goal is said to be the creation of a pan-Islamic state to revive the glories of the Ottoman califate that collapsed after the First World War. Bin Laden and his followers certainly oppose Western interpretations of democracy, where sovereignty resides with the people, because it is seen as a system that negates God's own sovereignty. Finally, it is suggested that Western support for so-called 'un-Islamic' rulers in, for example, Algeria and Saudi Arabia, led some radical Islamist groups to target the West. For example, French support for the military junta in Algeria is said to be why Islamist terrorists detonated bombs on the streets of Paris in the mid-1990s. Similarly, US support for Saudi Arabia's allegedly unpopular rulers is said to be part of the reason why America was targeted on September 11.

But it would be wrong to see the rise of Islamist groups—now found throughout the Arab countries of North Africa and the Middle East—as the result of bin Laden's influence. Instead, we might look to the failure of state-sponsored modernization as a key explanation. The contemporary Islamist resurgence is argued to be a vehicle for popular disillusion in the Muslim world, as many governments have failed to achieve what they promised—both developmentally and politically—since independence from colonial rule. In addition, existing communitarian structures have been confronted by state power that apparently seeks to destroy and replace them with the idea of a national (increasingly secularized) citizenry. A common response has been the rise of popular (as opposed to state-controlled) Islamist groups to become in many places a major vehicle of popular political aspirations. Thus the widespread Islamic awakening can be seen in relation to its *domestic* capacity to oppose what are perceived as oppressive states: 'It is primarily in civil society that one sees Islam at work' (Coulon 1983: 49). The point is that this domestic response does not necessarily translate into a wider Muslim threat to *global* order.

KEY POINTS

- Religion now plays a central role in international politics.

- Most Islamic critics of the status quo see their own governments as the main cause of political and developmental failures.

- September 11 is sometimes said to provide evidence of an emerging 'civilizational' clash between Christianity and Islam, but most Muslims were probably appalled by these and related terrorist acts.

Conclusion

The last thirty years have seen much involvement of religion in politics. A serious new threat to world order, some claim, now emanates from Islamic fundamentalism, with September 11 as the key example. However, such fears do not appear to have very strong foundations. In the case of Islamic fundamentalism (Islamism), various domestically orientated groups threaten the incumbency of their own rulers rather than the security of the global order. In short, there is very little—if anything—in the spectre of an 'Islamic' threat per se to global order.

Globally, the recent political impact of religion falls into two—not necessarily mutually exclusive—categories. First, if the mass of the people are not especially religious—as in many Western countries—then religious actors tend to be politically marginal. However, in many developing countries, most people are already religious believers. Unsuccessful attempts by many political leaders to modernize their countries have often led to responses from various religious actors. Often, religion serves to focus and coordinate opposition, especially—but not exclusively—that of the poor and ethnic minorities. Religion is often well placed to benefit from a societal backlash against the perceived malign effects of modernization. In particular, various religious fundamentalist leaders have sought support from ordinary people by addressing certain crucial issues. These include: the perceived decline in public and private morality and the insecurities of life, the result of an undependable market where, it is argued, greed and luck appear as effective as work and rational choice.

And what of the future? If the issues and concerns that have helped stimulate what some see as 'a return to religion'—including socio-political and economic upheavals, patchy modernization, increasing encroachment of the state upon religion's terrain—continue (and there is no reason to suppose they will not), then it seems highly likely that religion's political role will continue to be significant in many parts of the developing world. This will partly reflect the onward march of secularization in many countries and regions, linked to the spread of globalization—which no doubt will be resisted by religious leaders and their followers, with varying degrees of success. This suggests that a period of religious reinterpretation will follow—spurred by changes both within individual countries and at the global level. For this reason it would be very unwise to neglect religion in analyses of contemporary politics in the developing world.

? QUESTIONS

1 What are the characteristics of religious resurgence in the developing world and how are they important politically?

2 What do religious fundamentalists have in common? Illustrate your answer with examples from *two* developing countries.

3 Is Iran a theocracy and how does your answer contribute to understanding politics in Iran?

4 Now, more than six years after September 11, is it fair to say that religious issues dominate the international relations of the developing world?

5 Are modernization and secularization the same thing?

6 Does globalization increase the significance of religio-political actors or undermine them?

≋ GUIDE TO FURTHER READING

■ **Beyer, P. (1994),** *Religion and Globalization* **(London: Sage).** Surveys transborder religious interactions in the context of globalization.

■ **Gifford, P. (2004),** *Ghana's New Christianity: Pentecostalism in a Globalising African Economy* **(London: Hurst).**

■ **Haynes, J. (1998),** *Religion in Global Politics* **(Harlow: Longman).** A survey of religio-political developments around the world.

■ **——(2007),** *Introduction to Religion and International Relations* **(Harlow: Pearson Education).** A survey of how international relations is affected by religious global resurgence.

■ **Huntington, S. P. (1996),** *The Clash of Civilizations* **(New York: Simon and Schuster).** Articulates the thesis that the world is poised to enter an era of 'civilizational clashes'.

■ **Mainuddin, R. (ed.) (2002), *Religion and Politics in the Developing World: Explosive Interactions* (Aldershot: Ashgate).** Examines a number of key religio-political interactions in the developing world.

■ **Volpi, F. (2003), *Islam and Democracy. The Failure of Dialogue in Algeria* (London: Pluto).** A well-researched account of the failure of religious and political actors to arrive at a modus vivendi.

■ **Westerlund, D. (ed.) (1996), *Questioning the Secular State. The Worldwide Resurgence of Religion in Politics* (London: Hurst).** Series of predominantly developing country, national case studies examining the attitudes of 'fundamentalist' groups to the state and state policies.

■ **Woodhead, L., and Heelas, P. (eds.) (2000), *Religion in Modern Times* (Oxford: Blackwell).** A very useful survey of the contemporary position of religion.

WEB LINKS

● **http://Godlas.myweb.uga.edu/** Islam and Islamic Studies resources.

● **www.calvin.edu/henry/** The Paul B. Henry Institute for the Study of Christianity and Politics at Calvin College, USA.

● **www.csmonitor.com/** *The Christian Science Monitor*. This is a useful source of material on many aspects of religious politics, including in the developing world. It does not have a Christian bias in its coverage.

● **www.vanderbilt.edu/csrc/politics.html** Center for the Study of Religion and Culture at Vanderbilt University, USA.

● **www2.fmg.uva.nl/assr/research/clusters/identity.html** Details of a research programme on 'Religion, Politics and Identity' at the Amsterdam School of Social Research.

● **www.archive.org/details/iraq_911** A collection of archive video footage and films relating to the 11 September 2001 terrorist attacks against the World Trade Center and Pentagon.

ONLINE RESOURCE CENTRE

For additional material and resources, see the Online Resource Centre at:
www.oxfordtextbooks.co.uk/orc/burnell2e/

8 Women and Gender

KATHLEEN STAUDT

Chapter Contents

- Introduction: Historical Perspectives
- Women's Policy Interests
- Policy Injustices
- Women's Political Activism: Movements, Non-Governmental Organizations, and Decision-Makers
- More Global Dimensions
- Conclusions

Overview

Nearly all nations in the world could be considered still 'developing' or not yet developed if judged against full democratic standards both of women's representation in decision-making positions and of responsiveness to women's policy interests. Only a few exceptions exist, most notably Scandinavian, but even these countries became more inclusive and responsive to women only in recent decades, a result of women's organized strength (including in unions), progressive public policies since the 1930s, and especially open and democratic political structures. This chapter draws attention to the widespread reality that women have little voice in established politics, and their 'interests' are muted, given the existence of overwhelming male privilege and preference in the policy-making and policy-implementation processes.

The chapter first examines key ways in which men's privileges became institutionalized in the state, political institutions, and governments during history. In so doing, it will not only incorporate the language of **gender** which leads to an examination of social structures that 'construct' male and female differently in different nations, regions, and historical eras, but also consider the political institutions that shape women's and men's lives. While the term gender is contested and does not translate well into all languages, it facilitates emphasis on the larger social structure, including relations between men and women, and away from biology as the essential determinant of behaviour. The chapter then considers women's work, paid and unpaid, and women's reproductive capabilities in order to outline typical obstacles that women face in different places and why gendered 'stakes' have been maintained or changed in the policy status quo. It moves on to examine women as voters, activists, and decision-makers in different nations and the effects of their actions on policy responsiveness. Finally, more global and local perspectives are introduced as being essential to moving towards gender-fair politics and policies.

Introduction: Historical Perspectives

In geographic spaces around which national boundaries are drawn, relatively stable institutional structures and decision-making patterns have emerged that reflect values and ideologies, including beliefs about men and women. This structure is known as the state, and it is different from the regional units of government also known as states, provinces, or districts, such as the State of Coahuila in Mexico, Western Province of Kenya, or the State of Texas in the United States. From the outset of the modern state in Europe, men, not people generally, crafted the skeletal structure of the state during an era when men spoke for most women and children in both societies and families, as fathers, husbands, and brothers, and when institutions absorbed gender assumptions and practices like these. While wealth, position, and authority concentrated power among the few, virtually all men exercised formal power and authority in 'their' households. Power is relational: the relatively more and less powerful can shift the balance through force, knowledge, and resistance, among other things, opening opportunities for women to

exercise power. Rights to hold office and to vote first benefited men, and only much later, women. These rights and opportunities themselves augmented the social construction of gender in ways that associated men with the public sphere of politics and paid labour, and women with the private sphere of family and household.

Patriarchy—the ideology and institutions of male rule, male privilege, and female subordination—exists in most societies to different degrees. It is embedded in all states, made 'normal' and routine in laws and public policies that often change only incrementally over time. By the twentieth century, state policies and laws institutionalized male privilege and transplanted the tools, ideology, and machinery of privilege from one nation to another, and throughout colonial empires in nearly global breadth. This gender baggage constructed men as family breadwinners, legally and financially responsible for land and households, and attendant policies benefited men through education, training, and employment. For Latin America and the Caribbean, colonial masters included Spain, Portugal,

BOX 8.1

Amartya Sen Asks if '100 Million are Missing'

Using demographic data for Asia, which showed highly imbalanced gender ratios for regions with strong patriarchal traditions, Sen found that 100 million women were 'missing' in existing demographic ratios. What he meant was that gender ratios, usually displaying relative balance (slightly over or under) 100:100, exhibited skews as disparate as 88 females to 100 males. In northern India and elsewhere, girl infants and children are ignored so badly that some die needlessly for lack of food, amounting to the waste of enormous numbers of female lives. Patriarchal traditions like these developed long before colonialism. Many indigenous societies vested control over economic resources and political voice in men rather than women or both. Deep patriarchal traditions, both indigenous and 'modern', are legacies that people will have difficulty shedding.

(Sen 1990)

the Netherlands, Britain, and France. For Africa, the masters included Britain, Belgium, France, Germany, Italy, Portugal, and Spain. For Asia from west to east and south, the masters included France, the United States, Britain, and the Netherlands. Nations like China and Japan, despite alternative and historically deeper indigenous patriarchal sources in their states, also exhibited male dominance in and benefit from the public sphere. Consider an example from South Africa in 2006. High-level political leader Jacob Zuma raped a young woman, used Zulu masculine culture as the justification, and was judged not guilty at the trial in 2006. The case roused people to reflect on misogyny. Organized women pushed parliament—including its large critical mass of female parliamentarians—to pass stronger sexual assault laws.

Male privilege and gender social constructions have enduring legacies for women's quality of life and opportunity. Life itself may be in question (see Box 8.1).

KEY POINTS

- Laws, public policies, and decisions about how to implement public policies are deeply and historically embedded in states, with their concentrated political authority in government that affects the whole of society.

- Men captured and controlled these political institutions in ways that disempowered women and muted their policy interests.

- In the developing world, this patriarchal state model both emerged from indigenous practices and/or was spread through colonialism.

Women's Policy Interests

Women and men have stakes in any and all public policies, from education to health, safety, and employment. Policies articulate official decisions on issues that have been perceived as public, rather than private matters; and governments raise money—through taxes, tariffs, and fees—and spend that money (documented in budgets) in ways that resemble official policies. However, policy implementation is crucial, for much policy is merely rhetoric, lacking budgetary resources, staff, and commitments to put policy decisions into practice.

From private problems to public policies

The social construction of gender has given men and women different stakes in policies, for the ways that policies are formulated, finalized, implemented, and evaluated have usually meant that women's and men's 'interests' were benefited and burdened in distinctive ways. Women's policy interests, then, refer to their shared stakes in issues over which governments exercise decision-making, spending, or withholding money for implementation. The identification of shared stakes is complex, given the differences that exist among women based on ethnicity, class, age, geography, and other factors. People contest whether policies should be neutral to gender (for example parental leave from paid employment obligations after birth, rather than just maternal leave) or take into account gender specifics, such as realities over who—men or women—care for infants after birth. That is, should they recognize gender difference, whether constructed through social norms or reduced to biological factors such as reproductive organs? And if difference is recognized, will that reinforce and sustain gender difference?

Often extraordinary efforts are required to bring issues and problems deemed part of a 'private' sphere onto the public policy agenda (Box 8.2). A key example is found in sexual assault and domestic violence, which primarily burdens women.

Weldon (2002) compared 36 countries in various regions and different levels of development with respect to factors that led to seven progressive policy responses. She examined cultures, which are notoriously difficult to generalize about, women politicians, women's offices in the bureaucracy, and social movements and non-governmental organizations (NGOs), to find that the last two are the most significant factors. Public policies to diminish violence against women are a recent innovation for most countries. Governments with better records than most on the issues include Costa Rica in the developing world and Canada.

BOX 8.2

A 'Private Problem' is Made Public

Only in the last three decades have most governments treated violence against women as a public, rather than a private, problem. Historically, in many cultures worldwide, women moved from the patriarchal control of the father to the husband, reinforced in legal systems. Control often authorized physical punishment, short of death. Assault from strangers merited more accountability than assault from intimate partners. In many countries, radical feminists spread awareness in the late 1960s to put violence against women on the public agenda, later joining forces with liberal feminists to change laws and law enforcement.

Police agencies in many countries are dominated by men who work in a militaristic organizational culture that has historically been unresponsive to women. In some countries, special women's police stations have been established, with Brazil as one of the pioneers. India is the largest country to have established staffed police stations in this way. The stations produce mixed results: more crimes are reported, but serial battering and raping persist.

Women and wage inequalities

Until the latter part of the twentieth century, it was considered to be no violation of cultural norms or laws to pay women lower wages and salaries than men. While the United Nations-affiliated International Labour Organization produced conventions that established principles (such as 'Equal Pay for Equal Work')—agreed to in tripartite negotiations among government, business, and labour—national governments enforced these principles only to the extent that internal political forces and laws supported such measures. For women who laboured for income in the informal economy, laws and regulations had no impact on earnings.

Women work in many kinds of occupations, from paid to unpaid. But, virtually everywhere, women earn less than men in paid employment. The United Nations Development Programme (UNDP) annual *Human Development Report* shows no countries without gender wage gaps, even in Scandinavia. But wage gaps range in degree, with some countries that govern by rule of law instituting laws that require equal pay for equal work or equal employment opportunity. Yet many women do not take advantage of these laws, or enforcement of the laws requires access to expensive and time-consuming legal services.

Because women generally form at least a third to a half of the labour force, the unequal pay adds up to considerable value or profit that is extracted from, but does not benefit women. Worldwide, labour unions are the collective means by which workers use the power of numbers to threaten work stoppage, strike, and/or to negotiate with generally more powerful employers, whether nationals or foreigners. Only a minority of all paid workers belong to such organizations; and genuinely independent unions, able to negotiate on national and transnational bases, are rare. Moreover, lower wages, discriminatory job entry, and/or high unemployment levels leave many women dependent upon men. (See Box 8.3.)

With the rise of the global economy, much attention has focused on the recruitment of young women into export-processing factories such as garment and electronics manufacturing. Compared with work as maids or street vendors, the factory jobs have fixed hours and pay the legally minimum (although artificially low) wages. However, the jobs are often unsafe and insecure, involving minuscule wages compared with profits earned or executives' salaries. In Mexico, workers' minimum wages are less than US$5 daily, compared with US$1 daily or less in parts of Asia (or ten to thirty times those values in many developed countries, or fifty to a hundred times those values for management executives) (Staudt and Coronado 2002; UNDP *Human Development Reports*).

Unpaid labour in households

Women also invest considerable unpaid labour in households, from food cultivation and preparation to caring for family members, especially children. In subsistence economies, which characterize many parts of the developing world in Asia and Africa, female labour time in unpaid labour to grow food, process it, cook and feed, and provide water for families usually exceeds male labour time in unpaid labour.

BOX 8.3

Latin American Wage Struggles

Labour unions have been slow to organize women workers. Historically, men organized men, viewed as the family breadwinners, to obtain 'family wages' that could support women and children. In many countries, the percentage of economically active people organized into unions diminished by the close of the twentieth century. Informal workers are rarely organized despite their labour burdens: they work outside regulations on minimum wage, social security benefits, and maximum hours.

In most Latin American countries, the most common paid job for women has been domestic labour: working as servants in other people's households. Live-in maids are notoriously exploited, with employers calling upon them for far more than a forty- or fifty-hour working week. And their pay supplements may consist of discarded clothing and left-over food. Employer–employee relationships take on feudal overtones, and women may be labelled *muchachas* (girls) well beyond the age of adulthood. Chaney and Castro (1989) document the struggles of domestic workers to organize themselves in cities like Bogotá, Colombia, and Mexico City. They show that although organized *trabajadoras domésticas* agree on wage rates and hourly commitments, organizing domestic workers is very challenging, given the competition for work and desperation that characterizes many who seek earnings.

Managing households is a time-consuming activity in most societies, considering the child-rearing and emotional care that is generally thought necessary to hold families together. Women are primarily care-givers in families. In societies lacking running water and basic technology, tasks that seem manageable in the developed world become onerous physical and time constraints. For example, carrying water from rivers, or collecting firewood from forests surrounding villages, can consume an inordinate number of hours each day. Or pounding dried grains to make flour for cooking can take hours of arduous labour. (See Box 8.4.)

Reproductive choices

State policies and local customs mean that many women lack the abilities to make decisions about their bodies and voluntary motherhood, wherein it is often not women themselves who decide on the timing and spacing of pregnancy or, even, whether to become mothers at all. Although, historically, women relied on indigenous knowledge and practices related to birth, most states until the last few decades have been pronatalist, that is, encouraging multiple births and restricting contraception and abortion. As primary care-givers,

multiple births consumed much female time and energy. As overpopulation became a global issue with United Nations conferences beginning in 1972 (Stockholm) and cheap contraception technology became widespread, more governments began to legitimate and to disseminate advice on and the means of contraceptive use. Countries like Yemen, Angola, Mali, and Niger have Total Fertility Rates (average numbers of births per woman) as high as 7 or more, in contrast to figures more like 1.2–3 per woman in developed countries (UNDP 2002: 163–5). However, the population policy agenda has often appeared to prioritize government planners' desires to slow population growth, rather than the enhancement women's choices over healthy and voluntary motherhood. Exploration of the connections between development and user-friendly women's health emerged in the United Nations International Conference on Population and Development in Cairo in 1994. Approximately half a million women die annually giving birth, yet restrictions are still in place for contraception, emergency contraception, and abortion. Women resort to informal providers, resulting also in complications and even death. A backlash against women's voluntary motherhood is occurring worldwide.

BOX 8.4

Kenyan Women Farmers

In many cultural groups, women grow food for home consumption. Occasionally they sell surplus food, or brew grains into beer to earn cash incomes. When colonial authorities attempted to 'modernize' agricultural economies, they introduced cash crops like coffee and tea to men, bypassing women, as Ester Boserup analysed in *Woman's Role in Economic Development* (1989, originally published in 1970). Colonial agricultural ministries established agricultural extension systems in colonial headquarters, focused on men delivering advice, training, and credit to men farmers. But many men disdained agricultural work, seeking wage labour in distant locales to which they migrated. After gaining independence, countries maintained the bureaucratic status quo in many instances. Kenya is an example, where large numbers of men migrate away from agricultural households, where women remain to grow food and feed their families. Studies of agricultural policy implementation showed that few extension officers visited women even when sizeable numbers, up to 40 per cent, managed farms on their own. And women rarely receive credit in many societies because they have limited opportunity to own the land and so have no collateral to offer. In Kenya women's voices have been virtually silenced in the man-made political machinery (Nzomo and Staudt 1994). Yet women continue to operate self-help groups, rotating savings among themselves, even as small numbers of women are elected and appointed to political office.

KEY POINTS

- Women may have different policy interests from men, requiring policies that recognize gender rather than being gender neutral.

- Many issues affecting women are defined as 'private' and it is a struggle to get them onto the public agenda.

- Women workers are regularly paid less than men, and the value of women's unpaid domestic and agricultural labour is insufficiently recognized.

- Women generally lack autonomy over reproductive choices.

Policy Injustices

How and why could these unequal gender patterns prevail for so long? The answers involve a confluence of education, discrimination, state inaction, economic inequalities, and women's muted political voices. The most privileged people rarely organize to dismantle privilege, so organized constituencies and political parties rarely advocated gender equality until women acquired voices, rights, economic strength, networks, and organizations to promote change. This section looks first at educational inequalities, then voting rights, and finally the expanding field of women's movements.

Mass education arrived only in the twentieth century in most countries, but usually boys had preferential access and wider opportunities for education that prepared the privileged among them for technical, management, legal, business, health, and other professional occupations. Even in the twenty-first century, girls are the majority of illiterates in South Asian and some African countries, although equal access to primary and secondary education now exists in many Latin American countries.

The UNDP *Human Development Report* collects data on gender-disaggregated adult literacy rates. In thirty-nine developing countries, there is a gender gap of fifteen points or more (UNDP 2002: 223–5). They are concentrated in the band of deep patriarchy (West Asia and North Africa) and

impoverished countries of Africa and South-East Asia. Many of those countries show not only stark gender disparities, but also the desperate poverty within many of the countries. However, poverty and opportunity are structured to produce different outcomes for men and women, the essence of a gendered approach.

Who is responsible for the massive historical disinvestment in girls' education, parents or governments? In nations without social security and state-provided welfare or poverty alleviation programmes, parents have typically relied on grown children to support them in old age. Marital and settlement customary patterns tended to result in girl children joining their future husbands' families upon marital age, but with boy children remaining near home, therefore expected to support parents. Yet, historically, governments did little to alter inequalities.

In the late twentieth century, states like Bangladesh, Pakistan, and Nepal offered incentives such as free uniforms, subsidized fees, and books to parents with girl children in school attendance. These incentives, sometimes funded through international assistance, reduce the costs of female education to parents. However, even under such conditions of equal access, girls' and boys' experiences may be quite different, for subtle but accumulating cues are communicated to both boys and girls that

BOX 8.5

Access to Credit via Women-Friendly Approaches

Women often resort to self-employment, usually as part of the informal economy, in income-generating strategies outside the state regulatory apparatus. Outside the state, women's group members save money and rotate total amounts to individuals. These are called *mabati* groups in Kenya and *tandas* in Mexico. Many NGOs model themselves on the Grameen Bank in Bangladesh, started by Mohammad Yunus. The Bank channels microcredit to small entrepreneurs, either as individuals or in groups, and peer responsibility provides the guarantee for loans. The approach has flaws, but many view the model as an advance from the male-to-male credit approach that still dominates banking throughout the world.

men are and should be the household breadwinners, leaders, and household decision-makers.

Even when girls and boys complete primary and secondary school in relatively equal proportions, gender patterns diverge in higher education, especially in coursework that results in marketable employment and political careers. In most societies, professional, business, and economic careers are not only the occupational groups from which leaders emerge, they also provide the material resources to fund political careers and organizations. Men are channelled into these occupations, thereby accumulating wealth and contacts that translate into political recruitment opportunities. 'Money talks' in many countries, despite attempts to create democratic machinery and voting rights that seemingly foster equality. (See Box 8.5.)

On voting rights, when foreign powers controlled large parts of the developing world during the eras of imperialism and colonialism, few (male) inhabitants exercised political voices except those appointed to or co-opted in the colonial state. After the Second World War and the general movement towards independence, women participated in nationalist movements, but often did so primarily as budding nationalists, not advocates of women's interests. But, as such, the voting franchise was often granted to all adults—women and men—once independence came, in countries that instituted elections. The countries in which women currently still lack the right to vote include Brunei, Kuwait, Oman, and the United Arab Emirates.

Finally there is the expansion of women's movements. The structure of the male-dominated state that preserved male privilege has consolidated after independence. Women's movements began to challenge policies only in the latter quarter of the twentieth century, legitimized with the global organizing around the United Nations-sponsored International Women's Year of 1975, which turned into an International Women's Decade, followed up with global conferences in 1980 (Copenhagen), 1985 (Nairobi), and 1995 (Beijing). These conferences fostered the development of more networking, global, regional, and local levels, and gender visibility at other UN meetings. Naturally, women's movements experienced resistance to change from those with stakes in perpetuating the status quo and the privileges they enjoyed.

Women's movements rose hand in hand with the emergence of diverse **feminist** philosophies, which at a generic level focus on inequalities and injustices between men and women, especially in the areas of income, political voice, and violence (Staudt 1998: chapter 2). Ironically, many women's movements do not use feminist labels, so as to avoid the appearance of replicating or accepting philosophies developed elsewhere rather than customizing issues within their own communities and nations. Feminist approaches are wide-ranging, preceded with adjectives that provide distinctive ways in which to problematize and address injustices: liberal, socialist, radical, black, maternal, conservative, and others. But, by the late twentieth century, some feminists were converging in their efforts to deal with typical widespread injustices like, for instance, domestic abuse and sexual violence. For example, liberal feminists who had worked within given political-economic systems to change the laws found common ground with radical feminists, who are suspicious of the state. They combine forces to demand stronger laws regarding rape, policy implementation over police training to enforce domestic violence laws, and resources for battered women's shelters and counselling for abusers.

Not everyone agrees that political power is the key to generating greater equality. Some focus on strengthening women's ability to earn and control income and other assets. If women had economic resources greater than or comparable to those of men, then they could either make individual choices to benefit themselves or organize collectively to press governments to change. After all, public policy often changes in response to constituencies with money. But it is only public policies that have the capacity to make systemic change, involving large numbers of people.

> **KEY POINTS**
>
> - In women's everyday lives, from unpaid and paid work, to reproductive activities, the political framework has devalued women's experiences and increased their dependency on men.
>
> - Gradually, once private issues within the household have entered the public policy agenda, women have made gains that increase their value and autonomy.
>
> - The explanations for past policy disadvantage are numerous, herein focused on (still lingering) educational inequalities, economic inequalities, and delays in women's exercise of their political voices. Those causes for policy disadvantage invite specific solutions: women's increasing economic and political power will enhance their ability to gain responsive and accountable government that serves their interests and needs.

Women's Political Activism: Movements, Non-Governmental Organizations, and Decision-Makers

Women's political activism has gradually increased at the local, regional, national, and international levels, both in government and non-government organizations. Still, however, the power that women exercise collectively is far less than that of men, and few countries exhibit gender-balanced decision-making. Men continue to monopolize politics, and much of that monopolization contributes to sustaining male privileges in the status quo.

In preparation for the United Nations-sponsored women's conference in Beijing in 1995, the United Nations Development Programme (UNDP)

Human Development Report produced a special publication on gender (1995). One of its chapters focused specifically on women in political decision-making positions and politics. This represents a baseline from which to examine change in women's participation, around ten years later.

Political structure matters

In the 1995 UNDP report the concept of a 'participation pyramid' was introduced and graphed. It illustrated how men's monopolization was stronger at the pinnacle of the pyramid, for chief executives, and how this steep pyramid broadened only slightly in descent from the top, to cabinet members, elected representatives of the legislature, and finally to eligible voters, the bottom of the pyramid that exhibited greater gender balance. In some parts of the world, namely western Asia, no women serve in cabinets. Often there is only a token female presence in the cabinet, serving in posts with limited resources, staff, and authority. Yet there are differences among countries, based on their political structures. Even democracies come in different forms, and questions have often been raised about which form is the more woman-friendly.

Chief executives in government consist primarily of presidents and prime ministers, illustrating two variations in democracy: presidential and parliamentary (though hybrid systems also exist). Presidential forms of government, most common in the Western hemisphere, have three separate branches (executive, legislative, judicial) that, ideally, are equal and check one another's power. The president is elected separately from legislators, members of congress in what is often a bicameral system of a lower and upper house. The president appoints cabinet members from various walks of life: interest groups, campaign supporters, loyal friends, experts, academics. These cabinet members are not elected, but are accountable to the people indirectly through the appointment process. Presidential systems, as is evident, are fragmented, consuming a great deal of time for decision-making. Their officials are elected for fixed terms, lending stability to the system but also less responsiveness. Yet presidential systems also offer many decision points at which to advocate or resist policy change, including policy that concerns women especially.

Parliamentary forms of government, most common in Europe and in former European colonies in Asia and Africa, fuse the executive and legislative in the form of a chief executive called a prime minister. The prime minister is elected to parliament, and rises to executive leadership as a result of leadership in the majority political party or party coalition. Cabinet ministers come from the majority party or

a coalition of parties, and are thus elected officials. As is evident, parliamentary systems concentrate power, thus making the decision-making process potentially more efficient. They can be more responsive to the people because new elections can be called if, on important measures before parliament, a majority vote does not prevail (that is, if there is a 'vote of no confidence').

Women in decision-making positions

Few women have risen to become a chief executive in democratic governments. In the 1995 *Human Development Report* only twenty had ever achieved this position, about equal numbers of presidents and prime ministers. In the early twenty-first century, only a handful more women have been added; the Philippines, Sri Lanka, and Bangladesh are the only countries to have elected two different women as chief executives. In 2005, parliamentarians selected Angela Merkel as the first female Chancellor of Germany. In 2006, voters elected two women presidents and set important precedents. In war-torn Liberia, Ellen Johnson Sirleaf became the new president, the first-ever female chief executive in an African country. In Chile, voters selected first-ever female president, socialist, and feminist Michelle Bachelet.

Women are beginning to be selected or appointed for cabinet positions in larger numbers than

---

BOX 8.6

Imagine Femistan!

Student exercise: a new country has emerged, after twenty years of mostly non-violent struggle amid economic chaos. Both men and women actively participated in the struggle for democracy. Fifty people will be appointed to design democratic political institutions at a Constitutional Convention. Use your knowledge and imagination to outline gender-fair political institutions that address formerly 'personal' problems that have entered the public policy agenda.

two decades past. For the 1995 report, women held 7 per cent of cabinet posts, and in two out of every five governments, men monopolized all the cabinet posts. Often, however, women's portfolios involved 'women's affairs', 'family affairs', or peripheral bureaucracies not central to core government missions and budgets. Mexico has appointed women to the Fisheries Secretariat in several administrations. Only twenty years ago, many governments had no woman in the cabinet, or a single token woman. Now, pairs or handfuls of women lead government bureaucracies, their programmes, and employees.

Moving down to legislatures, the 1995 *Report* calculated an average of 10 per cent women's participation for democratic and non-democratic countries. These figures illustrate men's near-monopolization of legislative politics. The average figures had actually decreased, from 13 per cent in the late 1980s when women's participation was slightly inflated until the demise of the former Soviet Union and authoritarian Eastern European countries, many of which installed quotas that guaranteed seats for women.

Women's representation varied by world region a decade ago. Asian, European, and Latin American figures surpassed world averages, while African, Pacific, and Arab countries were well below world averages. But the differences were not dramatic. Since 1995, women's participation in legislatures has risen slightly, to 16.6 per cent. The Inter-Parliamentary Union compiles data on parliaments for many countries. Scandinavian countries and the Netherlands have always been at the top (though recently surpassed by Rwanda—see below), exhibiting critical masses of women, at a third or more of the representatives. Of course, one-third never constitutes a majority—the proportion usually required for voting bills into laws! Updated lists are easily available for readers who wish to consult each and every country (www.ipu.org). (See Table 8.1).

The regional patterns outlined for a decade ago still persist. That is, the Latin American region retains the highest level of female participation in the legislature among developing countries, with African, Pacific, and Middle Eastern countries following in that order (IPU 2006). The highest levels in Latin America are found in Cuba (36 per cent) and Costa Rica (38.6 per cent). Post-war Rwanda sets the world record, with 48.8 per cent in its lower house. Elsewhere in Africa, the highest levels are found in Mozambique (34.8 per cent) and South Africa (32.8 per cent, 33.3 per cent upper house), while the lowest are Egypt (2 per cent, 6.8 per cent upper house). In Asia, the highest levels are in South-East Asia (Vietnam, 27.3 per cent). In several Pacific, Arab, and Middle Eastern countries, there are no women at all elected to the legislature.

Table 8.1 Women in National Parliaments

	Single or Lower House (%)	Upper House (%)	Both (%)
Nordic countries	41.6	—	41.6
Americas	20.0	19.4	19.9
Europe (excluding Nordic)	18.4	17.7	18.2
Sub-Saharan Africa	17.2	18.6	17.3
Asia	16.6	16.6	16.6
Pacific	13.1	31.8	15.3
Arab states	9.6	6.3	9.0

Source: Inter-Parliamentary Union: www.ipu.org/wmn-e/world.htm

BOX 8.7

Quota Debates

In more than forty countries quotas have been adopted to increase the number and percentage of women candidates or office-holders in legislatures or parliaments. Argentina in 1993 adopted rules that required all party candidate lists to have a minimum of 30 per cent women. Quota rules have increased the percentage of women representatives in many countries and the attention paid to women's many diverse issues, but quotas have not transformed legislative climates or outcomes. In a special section of the journal *Politics & Gender* (2005), authors evaluated quotas positively, yet with some ambivalence for the way quotas may reinforce essentialist thinking of women as beings who think and act alike due to their biology. Quotas work best in multi-party systems with proportional representation, rather than single-member districts.

Why the variation? The answers lie in political party actions and in the structure of electoral systems. Proportional representation electoral systems produce higher percentages of women in politics than do single-member constituencies.

Political parties are also crucial, and in some countries parties commit themselves to greater gender balance. Both national governments and political parties have adopted special measures like quotas to assure that critical masses of women are elected (Box 8.7). For example, in 1992, India passed a law that required women to hold one-third of all local council (*panchayats)* seats, although a similar law was not passed at the national level. This introduced nearly a million women into public decision-making positions, theoretically a stepping-stone into other political offices (Rai 2003). Yet India falls well below the international median in national representation rates for women—in the 1999–2004 parliament, there were 8.3 per cent in the lower house, 11.2 per cent in the upper.

Do women in the legislature expand the policy agenda and address gender inequalities? This is a perennial question in research on women in politics. Women often follow different pathways into the political process, such as through non-government organizations (NGOs) with possible commitments to women's policy interests. As a result, they may even bring a new way of interacting with colleagues and constituents. Once in office, women's party loyalties, ideologies, and constituencies influence their legislative behaviour.

Women in office may come from markedly different and privileged income backgrounds than the majority of (poor) people. And women may belong to political parties that operate under ideologies that ignore 'private' injustices. Conservative politicians cut public spending programmes from which poor women may benefit. Yet women have sometimes coalesced across party lines to vote for women's policy interests. This happens periodically in Mexico around anti-violence laws. And in Rwanda, with its legislature reflecting the world's greatest gender-balance in 2006, women worked to pass laws to address gender-based violence. Yet consider the South Africa rape case cited earlier. Even though women make up more than a quarter of its parliament, the passage of new laws requires a majority. Majority votes are difficult to build, given divisions around political parties, ideologies, and other issues.

Non-governmental organizations

The crucial ingredient for bringing about more gender-just policies and better accountability lies with the political engagement of NGOs and social movements with women (and men) representatives. NGOs come in many different forms, active at the local, regional, national, transnational, and international levels. Some NGOs are registered with the United Nations or with government (the latter seeking to qualify for tax-exempt status), known as non-profit organizations, or *asociaciones civiles* in parts of the Spanish-speaking world. Others are looser informal networks or coalitions, including movements that may avoid registration (particularly with undemocratic governments). In these circles consultants create organizations, but tend to operate more like a business. Just as governments need to be accountable to their citizens and residents, so must NGOs become more accountable than many of them actually are.

In many countries, NGOs work with political parties, legislatures, political executives, and bureaucracies to press for more responsive policies and resources. They push for goals like equal employment opportunities, non-sexist education, better health care, loans for micro-businesses, and laws to prevent violence against women, among many other areas. It is NGOs that give life and energy to democracies and the women (and men) who are elected and appointed to office.

Tools for policy change

Women are gradually increasing their share of power in public affairs, in NGOs, and in governments. Women's participation expands public policy agendas to include women's policy interests. What tools exist to ensure that policies are implemented?

Once public officials adopt new policies, some resistance can be expected in the policy implementation process of government bureaucracies. The last quarter-century has pioneered the use of several tools to overcome that resistance, including more academic research and the innovative policy tools associated with gender mainstreaming, such as establishing women's 'machinery' in government and introducing gendered budget-making (BRIDGE 2003).

Although policy-making is an inherently political process, in which power is brought to bear on policy adoption, the idealized policy-making process involves the application of research findings to policy deliberation and adoption (see Box 8.8). There is now a considerable body of findings concerning various

BOX 8.8

Evaluation Research as an Accountability Tool

Evaluation research typically asks: What outcomes occurred as a result of the programme intervention or policy changes? Who benefited and who was burdened? How well were programme and policy goals accomplished? What lessons can be learned for future change? Evaluation research of this type has lent itself well to addressing inequalities, whether by gender, ethnicity, class, and/or geographic regions.

developmental, educational, and health policies relevant to women and gender. This research has been spurred on by the rise of policy, programme, and project evaluation.

Other innovations have moved beyond just policy rhetoric that promises greater equality and more responsive governance, towards initiating real action in government bureaucracies as it interacts with people. The first such innovation involved the creation of what the United Nations initially referred to as women's policy machinery, or units within government such as women's bureaux, commissions of women, ministries of women, and women's desks. Within ten years, virtually all governments hosted some women's machinery, but many had minimal staff and low budgets. They tended to operate in isolation, without really influencing the core of government policies and programmes. This separate sidelining gave rise to strategies to 'mainstream' all government efforts, even those without obvious women's policy interests or those based on women's special needs (Staudt 1997; Rai 2003). However, the effectiveness of mainstreaming strategies depends on good leadership, wide receptivity, adequate resources, strong incentives for change, and strategic locations within government agencies. Moreover, the machinery was not always connected well enough to NGOs, highlighting concerns raised generally about the need for transparency and accountability in democratic governance.

Gender mainstreaming machinery has not operated with sufficient power and resources to transform government, giving rise to a more recent innovation, one that would analyse budgets in gendered ways. Budgetary decision-making is at the very heart of the political process, and some countries have pioneered methods to dissect budgets by gender and make the process more transparent in this way, and to involve more women and their organizations. The phrase 'gender audits' has also been used to analyse spending, and it resonates well with the technical accountability tools deemed necessary to exercise oversight on government.

KEY POINTS

- Women are gaining power both in official positions and in relation to government through social movements and NGOs.

- Political structure matters: democratic systems that are parliamentary, with political parties that gain seats through proportional representation that implement goals for more critical masses of women, have higher rates of women representatives than presidential systems, although fewer decisional access points.

- However, once in office, bureaucratic or elected, women decision-makers will respond to women's interests and needs only if committed to justice in a political party that does the same and where accountable to relevant NGOs.

- Tools available to nudge the more resistant bureaucracies include mainstreaming strategies, budgets, and audits.

More Global Dimensions

This chapter has focused primarily on nations, but it cannot close without noting the growing global inequalities in which nations are fixed. Even as developed countries exhibit average annual per capita incomes of many thousands of dollars, there are numerous countries in which per capita income is equivalent to only a few hundred dollars (US$1–2 per day). The *Human Development Report* (UNDP 2005: 4) estimates that the world's richest 10 per cent of people receive as much income as the poorest 54 per cent. Women in developing countries are burdened by this grave poverty.

International conferences, many of them held under the auspices of the United Nations, have provided space for women to articulate their interests. These meetings range from those that focus specifically on women, such as the women's conferences of 1975, 1985, and 1995 (mentioned earlier), and those that focus on public policies in which women have stakes, such as the environment, population, and others. Typically, official delegations meet and at the same time parallel meetings of international or national NGOs also take place. Transnational networks and bonds are formed, and resolutions are passed. While the United Nations exerts little authority over sovereign countries (save peacekeeping missions), the passage of resolutions provides leverage for local and national organizations to press their governments for accountability and change. Legal instruments such as the UN Convention on the Elimination of All Forms of Discrimination against Women (CEDAW), also provide leverage for change. War and civil conflicts take their tolls on all people, but women often bear disproportionate burdens on themselves and their children in refugee and humanitarian crises. Women face special forms of terror, such as sexual assault and torture in the southern Sudan. The Darfur Region of Sudan is an ongoing civil war without much intervention, save rhetoric, given the lack of economic incentives therein for rich countries.

International women's NGOs work on transnational bases on a variety of issues, from human rights and business to research and labour solidarity. They include the Association for Women's Rights in Development, the Solidarity Center in Mexico City (affiliated with American Federation of Labor-Congress of Industrial Organizations, the largest labour union in the United States), Women Working Worldwide (with a UK base), Women's International League for Peace and Freedom, and the International Federation of Business and Professional Women. Other national organizations have acquired international fame, such as the Self-Employed Women's Association (India) and GABRIELA (Philippines). While many of these organizations are registered with the United Nations, most operate with focused agendas and have useful websites. Yet it is important for them to be grounded in concrete personal relationships that are linked regionally, nationally, and internationally, as occurs in international border communities (see Staudt and Coronado 2002).

KEY POINTS

- Analysts must think outside the box of nation-states to understand the global politics of over-prosperous women (and men) versus desperate women (and men) struggling for basic amenities. Gender balance within the nation-state obscures those politics.

- Global and local forces structure women's everyday lives and gender relations.

- It is a challenge to organize across borders, even in crisis-laden policy areas such as violence against women.

Conclusions

Women and their policy interests have been marginalized as a result of historic state structures and political institutions that privilege men and their voices in the decision-making process. Over the last century, women have gradually increased their participation in politics as voters, decision-makers, and members of non-government organizations. Public policy agendas have widened, taking into account discrimination and gendered inequalities. Progressive policies have yet to be fully implemented, but various bureaucratic tools and NGO oversight increase the prospects for implementation and accountability. Women are gaining ground in most nation-states, thus altering power relations between men and women. The meagre pace of change in most countries, however, may mean that at best our great grandchildren will be among the first to experience a gender-balanced polity in most of the developing (and developed) nation-states.

? QUESTIONS

1   Critically examine the role of the state in the subordination of women and in facilitating gender equality for both historical and contemporary times.

2   What are the historical and institutional conditions that open political space for women's voices and issues in government?

3   Do 'private' or 'personal' issues become politicized as public policy issues? Use examples associated with violence against women.

4   Do women share identical policy interests?

5   Compare the contribution of economic and political power in facilitating gender equality.

6   What role does reproductive choice have in gender equality?

7   Will poverty-alleviation policies automatically address gender inequalities? Make reference to education and literacy in the response.

8   Discuss three features of the political structure that open or close spaces for women's voices, individually and collectively.

9   Compare parliamentary and presidential governance institutions in terms of prospects for women's participation in strategic decision-making.

10   Do women in the legislature expand the policy agenda and address gender inequalities?

11   Design a debate around the merits of quotas in a particular country.

12   Develop an evaluation plan for the education system in a particular country.
See also exercise in Box 8.6.

GUIDE TO FURTHER READING

■ **Basu, A. (ed.) (1995),** *The Challenge of Local Feminisms: Women's Movements in Global Perspective* **(Boulder, Colo.: Westview Press).** A collection of chapters on grass-roots women's movements in Asia, Africa, and Latin America, most of them authored by women from those areas.

■ **BRIDGE Development–Gender (2003),** *Gender and Budgets* **(Brighton: Institute of Development Studies, University of Sussex).** Offers valuable concepts for application to real problems in government and organizations.

■ **Goetz, A. M. (ed.) (1997),** *Getting Institutions Right for Women in Development* **(London: Zed).** About transforming and tinkering with institutional machinery to make it more accountable to women and gender equality.

■ **Jahan, R. (1995),** *The Elusive Agenda: Mainstreaming Women in Development* **(London: Zed).** A comparison of two multi-lateral organizations (World Bank and UNDP) and two relatively progressive bi-lateral technical assistance institutions (NORAD-Norway and CIDA-Canada).

■ **Jaquette, J. S. and Summerfield, G. (eds.) (2006),** *Women and Gender Equity in Development Theory and Practice: Institutions, Resources, and Mobilization* **(Durham and London: Duke University Press).** Compares recent analyses of the women in development and gender and development approaches.

■ **Jaquette, J. S., and Wolchik, S. L. (eds.) (1998),** *Women and Democracy: Latin America and Central and Eastern Europe* **(Baltimore: Johns Hopkins University Press).** About women activists and politicians in regions undergoing 'transitions to democracy', with transitions either opening or closing space to women and gender policy issues.

■ Lockwood, Bert B. (ed.) (2006), *Women's Rights: A Human Rights Quarterly Reader* (Baltimore: Johns Hopkins University Press).

■ Moghadam, V. (2006), M., *Globalizing Women: Transnational Feminist Networks* (Baltimore: Johns Hopkins University Press).

■ Pettman, J. J. (1996), *Worlding Women: A Feminist International Politics* (London: Routledge). An overview of international/global and comparative gender issues.

■ Stromquist, N. P. (ed.) (1998), *Women in the Third World: An Encyclopedia of Contemporary Issues* (New York and London: Garland Publishing). A 683-page reference work with geographic, functional, and international sections, divided into seventy plus chapters and selections.

WEB LINKS

● **www.ids.ac.uk/ids** BRIDGE Development—Gender, Institute of Development Studies, University of Sussex 'cutting edge' packs on trade, migration, citizenship, participation, and many more issues.

● **www.icrw.org** International Center for Research on Women—policy research.

● **www.wedo.org** Women's Environment and Development Organization.

● **www.wluml.org** Women Living Under Muslim Law.

● **www.awid.org** Association for Women's Rights in Development (English, Spanish, French).

● **www.whrnet.org** Women's Human Rights Net Global Fund for Women.

● **www.globalfundforwomen.org** English, Spanish, French, Portuguese, Arabic.

● **www.ipu.org** Inter-Parliamentary Union.

● **www.undp.org/unifem** United Nations Development Fund for Women (UNIFEM).

● **www.worldbank.org/gender** World Bank Gender Home Page.

● **www.undp.org/gender** United Nations Development Programme (UNDP).

● **www.un.org/womenwatch** United Nations gateway on women's advancement and empowerment

● **www.un.org/womenwatch/daw** United Nations Division for the Advancement of Women (DAW).

● **www.sewa.org** Self-Employed Women's Association (SEWA), India.

● **www.vday.org** Offers organizing ideas, including drama performances of *Vagina Monologues*, a play by Eve Ensler, performed in thousands of cities worldwide (in mid-February, 'V-Day') to raise money for activities to stop violence against women.

● **www.womensenews.org** A source of daily news about women.

● **http://libarts.wsu.edu/polisci/rngs** Research Network on Gender and the State (RNGS).

● **www.who.int/gender/en/** World Health Organization's Department of Gender, Women and Health.

- **www.womenlobby.org** European Women's Lobby, over 4,000 NGOs.

- **www.amnesty.org** Amnesty International, with a global campaign to stop violence against women.

- **www.dawncenter.or.jp** Osaka Prefecture's large anti-violence women's centre, with substantial newsletters in Japanese and English.

 ONLINE RESOURCE CENTRE

For additional material and resources, see the Online Resource Centre at:
www.oxfordtextbooks.co.uk/orc/burnell2e/

9

Civil Society

MARINA OTTAWAY

 Chapter Contents

 Overview

The expression 'civil society' has metamorphosed during the 1990s from a relatively obscure concept familiar mostly to scholars of Marxism into a mainstream term freely used by social science analysts in general and by practitioners in the international assistance field specifically. Several factors contributed to these developments. First, there was growing interest by the United States and many European countries in promoting democracy abroad during the 1990s. The demise of the Soviet Union and the Eastern European communist regimes triggered a wave of more or less successful democratic transitions further afield, where regimes formerly influenced by the Soviet model and often by the Soviet government struggled to transform themselves into something both more acceptable to their populations and less anachronistic internationally. This wave of political transformations provided an opportunity for the industrialized democracies to actively promote the spread of political systems similar to their own. As international actors devised **democracy promotion** strategies, they focused much effort on promoting citizen participation and activism—what quickly came to be known as a vibrant civil society.

Another factor was the changes taking place in the established democracies themselves. Many organizations of what used to be called broadly 'the left', inspired by socialist or social democratic ideals of socio-economic equity and justice, were replaced by newer groups whose concept of justice extended beyond the traditional concerns of socialist parties and labour movements. They embraced a broad array of causes such as environmental protection and sustainability, opposition to globalization, and protection of gay rights. The old left was rooted above all in political parties and labour unions. The new activists were organized in smaller non-governmental organizations, often loosely tied in broad networks that saw themselves as the embodiment of a mobilized civil society.

Disenchantment with the performance of state institutions was an additional factor, as political leaders made concerted efforts to narrow the functions of government and enlarge the spheres of the private and non-profit sectors. At the same time, the corruption and inefficiency of many developing countries' governments prompted international development agencies to rethink the assumption that development required state intervention. As a result, they sought ways to bypass governments and implement some development projects and programmes through non-governmental organizations.

Needless to say, the popularization of the concept of civil society has led to a blurring of its meaning. It has also led to a blurring of its political connotations: a greater role for civil society is now extolled by conservatives, liberals, and radicals alike as a crucial component of political and even economic reform. Analysts of different persuasions do not agree about which organizations should be considered part of civil society and which should not, but they all agree that civil society is a good thing.

Introduction: Defining Civil Society

Defining the meaning of civil society is difficult because the term is laden with theoretical assumptions, unsolved problems, and value judgments. According to Hegel's oft-cited but ultimately unsatisfactory definition (in his *Philosophy of Right*, 1821), civil society comprises the realm of organizations that lie between the family at one extreme and the state at the other. While superficially clear and logical the definition generates a lot of conceptual confusion and some political booby traps. The result is that very few scholars, and virtually no practitioners of democracy promotion, now accept such a broad definition in practice, even if they cite it.

Intellectual conundrums

The definition is clear on one point: civil society is not the whole society, the entire web of social institutions and relations, but only one part of it. The problem is how to define that part with any degree of precision. Citing the realm of voluntary associations between the family and the state does not provide sufficient clarification. Three problems deserve special attention: (1) distinguishing organizations that are truly voluntary from those that are not; (2) determining whether all voluntary organizations between the family and the state deserve to be considered civil; and (3) determining whether there is a conceptual difference between civil society and political society, as some argue, or whether this is a distinction with little analytical value, which has gained currency for reasons of political expediency.

The concept of voluntary association contains ambiguities, particularly when applied to the less formal organizations that constituted civil society in the past and are still important in the developing world. According to definitions that stress civil societies' voluntary character, a civil society group is a formally constituted association of which individuals become members as part of a completely free choice—a club, for example, is undoubtedly a voluntary association. The family is not, because membership in it is not chosen. But there is a grey area of groups in which membership is not formally compulsory, but is not completely a matter of free choice, either. Religious associations offer one example. Very often people are born into a church or another type of religious association by virtue of having been born in a family, and inertia explains continued membership; in other cases, membership in a religious group is a truly voluntary choice. Similarly, people are born members of a clan, tribe, or ethnic group, but membership in an organization that claims to represent that group is a political choice made voluntarily and deliberately by some but by no means all members of that particular group. South Africa provides a telling example of how membership in an ethnic group can be an accident of birth or a voluntary decision to join a group. In the early 1990s, at a time of intense fighting between the supporters of Inkatha, a political party with a Zulu nationalist agenda, and other black South Africans, ethnic Zulus who did not support the party and its agenda referred to Inkatha supporters, but not to themselves, as Zulus.

The ambiguities even extend to organizations that appear at first sight to be clearly voluntary, such as political parties. In the early twentieth century many Europeans were born as members of social democratic parties, figuratively, because of their families' allegiances, or even literally, being delivered by 'mid wives' paid by the party as a service to their members. Membership was voluntary in that anybody could stop paying dues and quit the party, but, for many, membership became part of an identity acquired at birth. A contemporary example of this phenomenon is offered by the Sudan, where major religious brotherhoods, into which people are born when families belong, have formed political parties to which adherence is equally automatic.

Another common problem in determining whether an association is voluntary arises in relation to ruling political parties and the mass organizations they control. Membership in the party or mass organization is rarely compulsory, but the absence of membership has negative consequences and many are forced to join. One of the difficult tasks faced by the United States as the occupying power in Iraq in 2003 was to distinguish between committed members of the Baath Party, who were part of the defunct regime of Saddam Hussein, and those who had joined in order to keep their jobs so as not to attract undue attention to themselves.

A second thorny problem in determining the boundaries of civil society is ideological in nature, hinging on the interpretation of the word 'civil', which can mean both 'relating to citizens or the general public' and 'civilized'. The expansive definition of civil society as comprising all voluntary associations between family and state is based on the first meaning. For many, this is an unacceptable approach because it combines in one category, for example, human rights groups and terrorist organizations. In practice, the word civil society is almost invariably used to denote organizations that share certain positive, 'civil' values. But there is no consensus on that point. During the 1980s, Scandinavian countries considered the organizations fighting apartheid in South Africa as 'civil' and provided support. The United States defined them as terrorist organizations and refused to help; Nelson Mandela, the much acclaimed first president of post-apartheid South Africa, was once considered a terrorist by the United States. Many liberals or radicals have no problem accepting labour unions as organizations of civil society, but are often reluctant to see a federation of employers in the same light.

Another controversial issue influenced by political and policy consideration is whether it is valid to draw a distinction between civil and political society. Those who defend the distinction, first made by Gramsci (in 1929–35 in *Prison Notebooks*), admit that both civil society and political society play a political role and seek to influence policy decisions. But the political role of civil society is indirect: civil society groups do not aspire to control the government and exercise power, but see their role as that of influencing policies in the public interest. Political society organizations—essentially, political parties—want to control the government. A corollary of this view is that the civil society is virtuously dedicated to giving citizens a voice, while political society is power-hungry, self-interested, and considerably less virtuous. A second corollary is that international agencies seeking to promote democracy can and should provide assistance to civil society organizations; supporting political society, which aspires to power and thus is partisan by definition, would be morally questionable and could also represent unjustifiable interference in the domestic politics of another country.

The distinction between civil and political society has theoretical justification. Its usefulness, however, is scant, because most civil society organizations are, overtly or covertly, more partisan and political than they claim to be. True, there are organizations of civil society that act purely as pressure or advocacy groups and have no intention of contesting public office. But civil society activists are often close to specific political parties, and many move freely between civil society organizations and parties. Furthermore, many political parties, including some in power, set up organizations of civil society in an attempt to capture some of the assistance that is available only to civil society organizations.

Examples of the blurring of the lines between political and civil organizations exist in most countries, though more pronounced in some than in others. Civil society organizations may be pushed into close alliance with political parties by government repression. Many non-governmental organizations (NGOs) in Zimbabwe, for example, developed during the 1990s as bona fide, non-partisan civil society organizations lobbying for improved human rights, constitutional reform, better legal services for the poor, and a variety of similar causes. As the government, when challenged by the opposition party, the Movement for Democratic Change, turned increasingly repressive, violating laws and human rights principles in order to stay in power, civil society organizations increasingly became part of the political opposition. Formally organized NGOs operating at the national level are particularly likely to become politicized when confronted by a repressive regime. But less formal, local groups, sometimes referred to as community-based organizations (CBOs), rarely become openly political. CBOs are usually concerned about local level development and welfare issues, focusing on service delivery or simply self-help.

Politics and expediency

The abstract problems of how to define civil society remain a source of debate among academics, but in the meantime, civil society is being defined in practice by the policies of bilateral and multilateral aid agencies, by the governments of countries receiving democracy assistance, and by civil society organizations themselves.

Bilateral and multilateral international aid organizations define the boundaries of civil society when they decide which organizations are eligible for assistance under democracy promotion programmes or should be consulted in the preparation of an assistance strategy. This definition is based on a mixture of political considerations and administrative requirements. The major political requirement is that such organizations focus their activities either on civic education or advocacy for democratic reform. Civic education programmes, particularly common in countries in the early stages of political transition, seek to convey the basic meaning of democracy as well as teach about the political and institutional mechanisms of democratic systems. In its more sophisticated, advanced form, civil education is also training for political activism: citizens are encouraged to scrutinize the action of politicians, to lobby them to enact reforms, and to hold them accountable by voting them out of office. Advocacy organizations that attract international support focus on human rights, women's rights, legal reform, judicial reform, and, occasionally, environmental sustainability. To be part of civil society thus means to belong to one of these types of organizations.

The aid agencies' definition of civil society is further narrowed by their administrative requirements. The groups must be organized in a formal way because donors cannot provide support for an organization that is not registered in some way, that does not have a name and address, or that cannot be audited. Informal networks or vaguely organized civic movements may play an important part in a society or a democratic transition, but they do not meet donors' needs and only some foreign funders will provide support for them on an exceptional basis. For example, during the apartheid era is South Africa a few donors, mostly Scandinavian countries, agreed to provide assistance to informal organizations affiliated to the African National Congress. Such willingness to deal with informal organizations is exceptional, however. For practical reasons, donors also prefer to deal with organizations that speak, literally and figuratively, the same language.

As a result, the donors' civil society is an entity very different either from the society at large or from civil society as the realm of voluntary organizations between the family and the state. The term civil society as used, and financed, by the international aid agencies refers to 'a very narrow set of organizations: professionalized NGOs dedicated to advocacy or civic education work on public interest issues directly relating to democratization, such as election monitoring, voter education, governmental transparency and political and civil rights in general' (Ottaway and Carothers 2000: 11).

Direct funding of civil society is not the only way in which international assistance agencies support that society. NGO influence is strengthened by the requirement under which many agencies now operate that they consult with local civil society in implementing a wide variety of development and democracy aid programmes. The World Bank has such civil society requirements and many bilateral agencies also hold wide consultations. In practice, many of the groups so contacted are the same organizations the assistance agencies helped set up or fund in the first place—the ones they know and are capable of sending representatives to meetings.

The governments of countries that are recipients of democracy assistance also try to shape the definition of civil society by imposing registration requirements, which are sometimes very strict and used to prevent the formation of antagonistic organizations. Many also try to limit the access to donor funding to only some categories of organizations or to prevent it outright. Some international agencies are willing to circumvent such regulations and provide funding covertly, others are more anxious not to antagonize the government.

Civil society activists have also played a very important part in determining which organizations are recognized as part of civil society. Transnational networks of NGOs, usually led by the better-funded groups of the industrialized countries, have been particularly influential here. For example, they successfully pressed the United Nations to accept their presence at international meetings; and the World Bank agreed to undertake re-evaluations of some of its practices, particularly lending for the construction of dams, and to consult with the NGO sector before reaching decisions on certain issues. For example oil companies in Chad are now required to pay royalties into specially controlled funds where they are administered under strict controls with the participation of civil society organizations. These examples of success are counterbalanced by more numerous examples where the militancy of transnational civil society networks has failed to earn them recognition as rightful participants.

> ### KEY POINTS
>
> - The widespread agreement about the importance of civil society is accompanied by a great deal of controversy about what civil society is, not only among theorists but also among practitioners.
>
> - The term has been given a concrete meaning by the policies of international assistance agencies and to a lesser extent by the efforts of civil society organizations.

Traditional and Modern Civil Society

It is common for donors to bemoan the weakness, or even the absence, of civil society in countries where they try to promote democracy. This concern has spurred governments of industrialized countries, as well as international NGOs and private foundations, to launch an array of civil society assistance programmes to strengthen what is invariably referred to as a 'fledgling' civil society. In many instances, even after years of effort, donors express concern about the slow progress of civil society development and its continuing need for support (see Box 9.1). Paradoxically, in the countries where civil society is deemed at its weakest, for example in war-torn African countries, the population relies for survival on civil society networks that go well beyond the family and reveal a high degree of sophistication and organization. One of the problems faced by countries undergoing political upheaval is that some civil society networks quickly establish themselves in major fields of economic activity and even within parts of the government. The criminalization of the state that has been witnessed in failing states in West and Central Africa is the result of the disparity between the power of civil society organizations and that of a duly constituted government and administrative structure.

These considerations point to the need to put the discussion of civil society in a broader perspective.

Following the current use of the term, the discussion so far has dwelt on 'modern' civil society, that is, the part of civil society organized into formal, professionalized NGOs typical of the late twentieth century. But in all countries including the industrialized ones there is another civil society—'traditional society'. This society is organized more informally, often through networks rather than formally structured organizations, and often following patterns that existed in earlier times.

Traditional forms of civil society exist in most countries today, but particularly so in countries where the state is weak. Organizations that are traditional in form do not necessarily perform only traditional roles. On the contrary, they grow in new directions in response to contemporary needs and requirements. West African Sufi organizations such as the Mourides are ancient, but when they establish control over the wholesale rice trade in Senegal, or set up mechanisms to help members of the brotherhood emigrate to the United States and find jobs there they are performing definitely non-traditional functions in response to new challenges.

Modern and traditional civil society stand in inverse relation to each other. In countries where the state is strong, traditional civil society is weak and modern civil society is strong. If the state is weak, so is modern civil society but traditional civil society

---

BOX 9.1

Poppy Growers and the Afghan State

Poppy cultivation for heroin production has become the most important economic activity in Afghanistan since the overthrow of the Taliban in 2001. In 2006, an estimated 2.9 million farmers, or 12.6 per cent of the population grew poppies. During this time, poppy growers could obtain production loans from illegal organizations controlling the illicit trade, but farmers growing legal crops could not obtain loans through government banks or extension services. Poppy cultivation generated over US$3 billion in revenue in 2006 while the government could only generate about $300 million in custom and tax revenue, and foreign assistance only brought the country's total budget to $600 million.

is strong (Migdal 1988b). This explains the paradox outlined above: in countries in the throes of a difficult, state-weakening transition, citizens rely on civil society networks in many aspects of their lives even as donors bemoan the weakness of civil society.

Traditional civil society

Organizations of civil society have taken a great variety of forms traditionally, from the very informal to the highly structured. Loosely structured but culturally sanctioned mechanisms for swapping labour and joining efforts in the performance of large collective tasks exist in all societies, as do more structured mechanisms—for example, the rotating credit associations that exist, under different names, almost everywhere (Box 9.2). Compared to modern ones, traditional civil society organizations were less specialized and formal.

They were extremely unlikely to have full-time organizers and certainly not offices. Even in industrial countries, the professionalization of civil society, hence its separation from the society at large, is a recent phenomenon. When Alexis de Tocqueville visited the United States in the first half of the nineteenth century and wrote *Democracy in America* (published in two volumes, in 1835 and 1840) he was struck by the American propensity to form intermediate associations in the pursuit of a wide range of interests and projects; he was looking at loosely structured, ad hoc groups, not at formal organizations with professional staffs.

Modern civil society, defined as a set of NGOs, has clear boundaries that separate it from the family and indeed from the rest of society as well as from the state. The expression 'members of civil society' refers to a rather small number of people who belong, and very often work for, such NGOs, not to all citizens. Traditional civil society has no such clear boundaries, but fades into the larger society at one extreme and non-state forms of political authority on the other. In non-state societies, governance was an extension of the overall social organization, not the activity of specialized institutions.

The blurring of the lines between the society at large, more organized associations within it, and political authority is not completely a thing of the past, but can reappear in extreme situations of state collapse, as in Somalia (see Box 9.3).

Traditional civil society performed important economic activities that today are considered to be the responsibility of state authority. For example, long-distance trade was once organized and carried out through private, civil society networks that extended over long distances. States took over much

---

BOX 9.2

From Rotating Credit Associations to Microcredit

Rotating credit associations exist in all countries and provide loans, usually small, to people who do not have access to or do not trust banks. Members of such associations pay a small fee to the association every week, and every week one of the members, in turn, receives the entire amount. Women use such credit association to capitalize small businesses, pay school fees, or finance a celebration. Shoeshine boys in Addis Ababa use the system to cover the costs of a can of polish or a new brush.

The modern, formal variant of the rotating credit association is microcredit. The Grameen Bank in Bangladesh pioneered the idea. The bank grants small loans to clients, predominantly women who cannot offer collateral and thus cannot obtain loans from a normal commercial bank. Repayment of the loan is ensured by a group of guarantors, who are not entitled to receive loans themselves until the original borrower has repaid his or her loan. The idea has been replicated widely across the world. The founder of the Grameen Bank, Muhammad Yunus, was awarded the Nobel Peace Prize in 2006 for his pioneering work on microcredit.

BOX 9.3

Islamic Courts in Somalia

In the power vacuum created by the Somali state's collapse and the failure of the United States and the United Nations to secure an agreement among warring clans and warlords, clan elders and ad hoc organizations tried to provide order and structure. Among these organizations were the Islamic courts, which sought to impose order and administer justice on the basis of a strict interpretation of *sharia*. First appearing in the early 1990s, these courts slowly organized into a Union of Islamic Courts. By 2006, the Islamic Courts were well armed and competing with an official but powerless government, which had emerged from negotiations backed by the international community, for control over the country.

of the responsibility for protecting trade routes and otherwise making large-scale economic activity more feasible. In places where the state has collapsed or is severely weakened, civil society is taking on again some of those functions. This has been the case in the Democratic Republic of the Congo (formerly Zaire) since at least the 1980s, for example.

Traditional civil society and the state in the contemporary world

Some traditional forms of civil society exist even in the industrialized countries and they pose no problem. On the contrary, they contribute to the reservoir of what Putnam (1993) calls social capital. When traditional forms of civil society grow very strong as a result of the weakness or total collapse of the state, however, they can become highly problematic. Traditional civil society in the contemporary world is both indispensable and dangerous. Where the state is incapable, it can help people survive and maintain a semblance of normal life under very difficult conditions. But in the absence of a strong state, civil society networks can also turn into a source of power and domination for an oligarchy, become estranged from the broader society, and thus prevent the rebuilding of the state and the introduction of democratic forms of governance (Migdal 1988b: 24–41).

The benign side of the reappearance of traditional civil society is apparent every day in countries where government is unable to perform functions expected of a modern state. The government cannot fund schools for all children, and civil society responds by setting up alternative schools. (This also happens in some industrialized countries: the Charter School movement in the United States is a civil society response to the failure of many urban public school systems.) State collapse forces banks to close, and civil society responds by setting up informal systems that may not be officially recognized or formally registered. Noteworthy particularly in the Arab world (the *hawala* system), they move money rapidly and efficiently across continents and into remote villages. The formal economy cannot provide jobs for everybody, and civil society develops an informal sector that provides the livelihood of the majority of the population.

Another traditional civil society mechanism that becomes more prominent in weak states is clientelism. Instead of coming together in an organization to solve the problem they face collectively, people who cannot get what they need through formal state institutions, be it medical care and schooling, or justice through a corrupt court system, may turn to a powerful and rich individual for help. This person, the patron, will help them get their children into school, obtain the ration card necessary to receive subsidized food, make sure their unlicensed small business will not be closed down by the police. The recipient of this largesse, the client, will repay the patron by giving his or her allegiance, voting for the patron if elections are held, or otherwise providing political support. Patron–client relations provide poor, powerless people with a useful form of access to power. However, they do so to the detriment of the development of modern institutions and forms of collective action that may lead to a long-term power redistribution (Nelson 1979).

There is also a much more malignant side to the reappearance of traditional civil society, because it can further undermine the failed state institutions for which it is trying to compensate. During the transition from apartheid in South Africa, a weakened government lost its capacity to enforce the laws that kept peddlers away from the business district of Johannesburg. Informal sector businesses took over the sidewalks, to the benefit of the people who were trying to make a living by selling vegetables and braiding hair on the street. But the informal marketplace also became the territory of criminal gangs, legitimate businesses were driven out, and the once thriving business district became a 'no-go' area.

And parts of the civil society that flourish because of the absence of the state may be hostile to efforts to revive it. The trading networks that form in war-ravaged countries respond to a need, but they can also become profitable organizations that resist the efforts of the new, stronger government to revive institutions. Vigilante groups, such as those that operate in many parts of Nigeria, are a civil society response to insecurity. But they tend to turn into criminal organizations that end up by preying on those they were supposed to defend. In extreme cases, the re-emergence of traditional civil society is a threat to the continued existence of the state or can challenge its reconstruction, as in Somalia today where the clans, warlords, and Islamic courts resist any transfer of power to the state.

The tension between traditional civil society and the state is also evident in the cultural domain. Traditionally, civil society has always been a major vehicle through which culture has been transmitted. In many countries public education has deliberately sought to create a new culture, different from that transmitted by civil society and in many ways alien to it. A central part of the new public education was the effort to create a new national identity, different and often hostile to the local identities transmitted by traditional civil society. Public education historically was part of a struggle between state and traditional civil society. Thus in Turkey under Kemal Ataturk the state tried to impose secular values on a traditional society that upheld Islamic ones. This cultural conflict between states and traditional civil society continues today even in the most industrialized, democratic societies—it is evident for instance in the disputes in France over the right of Muslim girls to wear a headscarf in school. In societies where the state is weaker, or less determined to influence the culture, the battle is often won by civil society—the re-Islamization of culture in Egypt after decades of secular public education is a striking example (Wickham 2002).

KEY POINTS

- Traditional forms of civil society exist in all countries, but they do not necessarily perform traditional functions.

- When the state is weak, traditional civil society tends to be strong.

- Traditional forms of civil society help alleviate certain problems created by the weakness of the state, but they can also prevent the strengthening of the state.

The Modern State and Civil Society as a Specialized Entity

The rise of civil society as an entity separate from the broader society and from the state is part of an overall process of specialization that has affected all social and political institutions, particularly in the later part of the twentieth century. This specialization of functions has been accompanied by a formalization of the organizations that discharge those functions.

The phenomenon of specialization and formalization is visible everywhere. Governments are spawning increasing numbers of agencies and bureaux in order to perform a growing number of intricate functions. Although more evident in industrialized than in developing countries, a trend towards specialization exists in the developing countries too, driven in part by similar factors: economic change and urbanization. The multiplication of government functions is made necessary by the increasing complexity of the economy and the requirements of more urban societies. The change in lifestyles resulting from industrialization creates the need for new social institutions while reducing the importance of others. In developing countries these trends are also driven by the example of the industrialized countries and by the direct pressure exercised by international development agencies that seek to reproduce familiar forms of organization.

Such pressure is entirely understandable and probably useful in some cases, but it can also create distortions. For example, the insistence by international financial institutions such as the International Monetary Fund and the World Bank that aid recipient countries set up special anti-corruption agencies could prove beneficial, at least if the agencies were to work efficiently. However, the creation of specialized organizations in this way can lead to development of a civil society sector that is poorly suited to the prevailing conditions and financially unsustainable. It may undermine forms of civil society organizations that are more in line with the resources and needs of the developing countries (Ottaway and Chung 1999).

Contemporary civil society: myths and realities

In order to address the problem of whether the emergence of a specialized civil society in developing countries is a positive phenomenon or a distortion created by international development agencies, it is necessary to consider the main functions that civil society organizations perform in the contemporary world. This section focuses on three major functions of civil society and asks whether the new, specialized, and professionalized civil society can perform them in developing countries. The first and vaguest of these functions is the generation of social capital; the second, somewhat more specific, function is the representation of the interests and demands of the population; and the third, quite concrete, function is the provision of goods and, above all, services for the population. The specialization of civil society alters the way in which civil society performs these functions in all countries, but raises particularly serious problems in developing countries.

Take first the widely held view that civil society organizations generate social capital, a concept first set forth by Putnam (1993) in a study of regional government in Italy, as an explanation of why the same institutions functioned differently in the north and south of the country. He observed that the inhabitants of the northern region shared a civic culture rooted in earlier experiences with self-government and sustained over the centuries by a rich associational life. These attitudes constituted the social capital that determined the way people viewed government and related to its institutions. This social capital was scarce in the southern regions, which had both a different historical experience and a dearth of associational life.

It is open to question to what extent the more specialized civil society organizations of today, with their professional staffs and narrow focuses, generate social capital. Professional, specialized organizations tend to have small or even non-existent membership and thus they do not reach many people. Even if they do, they engage them only on very specific issues. They probably do not inculcate in their members the attitudes of trust and cooperation that constitute social capital. Putnam argues that professional NGOs, even if devoted to democratic causes, contribute less to the social capital that supports democracy than seemingly irrelevant associations such as bowling leagues or the charitable and social clubs once widespread in American towns. He even sees in the decreasing popularity of these organizations a harbinger of the decline of American democracy.

Putnam's concern about the capacity of specialized and professionalized NGOs to generate social capital may be exaggerated in the case of the United States. There, many types of voluntary associations thrive and NGOs are numerous, extremely varied in their ideological and policy positions, and draw support widely, thereby contributing to pluralism. But in developing countries, many NGOs have small memberships, focus on a narrow range of issues and are highly dependent on foreign governments or international NGOs. Their contribution to social capital is highly questionable, particularly

when compared to the social capital generated by more traditional social institutions (Box 9.4). Such traditional institutions also teach values and attitudes, but not necessarily those extolled by Putnam as necessary for democracy. They may include, for example, extremely negative views of other ethnic or religious groups, deep distrust of all strangers, or demeaning attitudes towards women. The fact that the content of this social capital is different and may be contrary to democratic values does not alter the fact that it is deeply embedded in social relations and not easily erased, particularly by professional NGOs with weak social roots.

The second of the three functions attributed to civil society—the representational function—raises the question whether or how far such groups can actually represent the society vis-à-vis the government. The simple answer is that specialized civil society organizations do not represent society as a whole in any country. But in developing countries and within non-democratic international institutions, however, civil society organizations do broaden the range of interests that are expressed. Yet they do so in a lopsided way that favours groups with the capacity to organize and to access resources, even if their ideas are not widely held.

In well-established democracies, the problem of representation is solved by the existence of elected officials, freely chosen by the voters to represent their interests. Organizations of civil society are simply one among many types of organized interest group that put pressure on the elected officials to adopt the policies they favour. Professional NGOs

---

BOX 9.4

The Conundrum of Islamic Charities

Since alms-giving (*zakat*) is one of the five pillars of Islam, Muslim countries have extensive webs of Islamic charitable organizations. Islamist movements and political parties have built on this charitable tradition to reach out to the population, providing educational and health services while spreading their religious and political message. Islamist movements, in other words, build on the social capital of Muslim societies. This creates a conundrum for liberal democracy advocates in Muslim countries and their Western supporters: social capital favours Islamist organizations while liberal organizations struggle to put down roots outside intellectual circles.

are numerous and hold a variety of conflicting positions, as already stated, and compete for influence with a lot of other groups including paid lobbies; thus, they cannot advance a credible claim to represent the interests and the will of the entire population.

But in many developing countries representative institutions are often weak and elections fall short of being free and fair; as a result, civil society organizations may more credibly claim to represent voiceless citizens. Civil society organizations also have a degree of credibility when they claim to speak for unrepresented constituencies in international institutions, which are designed to represent states, but provide no formal channels through which popular demands can be expressed. Because lack of popular representation is a real problem in many developing countries and in international organizations, NGOs' claims that they voice the voiceless have won a degree of acceptance in recent years, and even gained them a place at the table in many policy discussions.

The issue whether NGOs should be consulted despite their lack of representativity remains highly controversial, and unlikely to be resolved soon. As long as countries do not have truly democratic institutions, the voice of NGOs adds an element of pluralism to the political system, and the distortions created by this imperfect form of representation may be an acceptable price for such a broadening of the political process. On the other hand, there is an element of risk in mandatory consultations with organizations that are not representative and above all not accountable to the people in whose name they claim to speak.

The third function performed by modern, professional civil society organizations is the provision of goods and services to the population. Many voluntary organizations provide a wide range of assistance—from the very basic, survival-oriented food distribution or provision of emergency shelter to the funding of research on rare diseases or the formation of support groups for people facing an almost infinite variety of problems. In this field, too, there are considerable differences between the importance of this civil society in industrial and less developed countries, as well as in the issues raised by the existence of these organizations. On the one hand, these civil society organizations are much more numerous, better organized, and more capable in the industrialized countries. In developing countries they are usually highly dependent on external funding and very often find themselves in a subordinate position to the more affluent international NGOs that can access with greater ease money from rich countries and international organizations.

On the other hand, professional NGOs delivering goods and services often have a more important role in developing countries compared to richer counterparts in the industrialized West. In the poorest countries, for example, the assistance provided by NGOs is the main form of assistance available to the population, while in the richer countries NGOs supplement rather than replace the safety net provided by the government.

BOX 9.5

The Danger of International Civil Society

" The policy of donors funding two civil services—the government bureaucracy at an average wage of $50 per month; and a parallel bureaucracy of their own at $500 per month—draws talented people out of government in the short term and fundamentally undermines the creation of a sustainable state in the medium to long term. "

(Ashraf Ghani, Governor of the Bank for the Islamic State of Afghanistan, speaking to World Bank Governors, 3 October 2004)

This gives the foreign organizations that provide the funding for activities in developing countries a role that is often more important than that of the government. In extreme cases, the imbalance between the capacity of a developing country's government and that of the foreign and domestic NGOs operating there becomes dramatic and can hollow out the role of the government. To illustrate, in Afghanistan between January 2002 and March 2003, foreign donors channelled US$296 million in assistance through the Afghan government and US$446 million through international NGOs. (See Box 9.5.)

KEY POINTS

- Professionalized and specialized civil society organizations generate little social capital.

- Specialized civil society organizations are not truly representative, but they broaden the range of interests expressed in the political process.

- Professional organizations can play a crucial role in the provision of services.

Civil Society and the State in the Developing World

Relations between state and civil society, both in its traditional and modern forms, are quite complex in the developing world, more so than in industrial countries. Political systems are undergoing change in many countries, some states are still consolidating or conversely are on the verge of failure, modern civil society is a recent construct, and traditional forms of civil society are still making adaptations to a changed social and political environment. As a result, relations between state and civil society are in flux. In consolidated democracies, the relationship is more stable and thus more predictable.

Civil society organizations relate to state institutions and officials in one of three different ways: they ignore them and try to avoid their control; they oppose them and work for their replacement; or they seek to influence their policies. The pattern of avoidance is most often found in countries where the state is incapable of delivering services or other public goods. Civil society organizations give up on the state and seek to provide essential public goods on their own. Some of these activities are benign, for example the organization of

alternative self-help schools for children neglected by the public system. Others are quite problematic; for example, in countries where the police force is incapable of ensuring a minimum of security for citizens, vigilante groups sometimes degenerate into protection rackets or become predatory. The organizations of civil society that flourish in the space left by a failing state are unregistered and unlicensed, often illegal. In terms of structures, they thus fall into the category of traditional civil society, although the functions they perform are a response to contemporary problems created by state collapse and/or political repression.

When the state is capable of performing its functions, but the government is repressive and unresponsive, civil society organizations are more likely to take an antagonistic position. Some civil society organizations that take on an opposition role are simply fronts for political parties, deliberately set up to circumvent donors' rules against funding political organizations. As mentioned earlier, in some countries civil society organizations have strong party links. In others, civil society organizations turn into opposition groups after trying to influence the government and discovering they cannot do so. The example from Zimbabwe cited at p.169 illustrates this point very well. Organizations that see themselves as guardians of universal principles—human rights organizations for example—are particularly likely to turn antagonistic when the government continues to violate those principles. Civil society groups that oppose the government can be organized as professional NGOs or along less formal lines as broad social movements or loosely structured networks. Such a broad, loosely structured alliance of hundreds of small local organizations or 'civics' formed in South Africa during the 1980s. The existence of this many-headed and elusive hydra was crucial in convincing the apartheid regime that peace could not be restored by repressive measures and that a political solution was necessary.

Finally, the relationship of civil society to state and government can be a cooperative one. This is the ideal promoted by democratization programmes. There are various forms of cooperation. Civil society organizations, which possess a degree of expertise in their specialized area, lobby the government to promote specific policy reforms and even provide the government with the expertise to implement the reforms, like helping to write legislation. Women's organizations, which are not usually seen as particularly threatening by governments although they may antagonize conservative social forces, are adept at this advocacy role. For example, they helped craft legislation in Uganda that expanded landownership rights for women, as well as a new divorce law more favourable to women in Egypt.

Another form of cooperation between government and civil society is found when the government contracts out the delivery of services to non-profit non-governmental organizations. This is rarer in developing countries than in Europe because it requires strong governments, capable of establishing a regulatory framework and providing supervision, and strong civil society organizations capable of delivering complex services. The existence of a weak government on one side and strong international NGOs, often backed by large amounts of foreign money, gives rise to the common complaint that in such conditions international NGOs de facto make policy, further weakening the government and undermining its capacity.

The relationship between state and civil society in developing countries is rarely an easy one. This explains why many governments see civil society organizations as dangerous enemies to be tightly controlled. In democratic countries, setting up and registering an NGO is an easy process and regulations aim above all at preventing abuse of tax-exempt status or the misuse of donations. By contrast, in many developing countries NGOs are subject to complicated regulations aimed at suppressing groups that aspire to an advocacy role, instead of merely dispensing charity. An important issue that emerged in the 1990s in some countries is whether organizations of civil society should be allowed to receive foreign funding. Most governments welcome foreign funding of charitable organizations—for example, groups that provide assistance to AIDS orphans in Africa. Foreign funding of advocacy organizations, on the other hand, is very controversial.

KEY POINTS

- When the state is repressive, civil society organizations are usually antagonistic to it.

- When the state is weak and incapable of delivering services, civil society organizations seek to ignore the state and avoid its control, rather than press for reforms.

- When the state is strong and civil society organizations are well developed, relations tend to be cooperative and constructive.

MARINA OTTAWAY

Civil Society and Democratization

The rapid transformation of the term civil society from an obscure concept known to a few scholars to one that finds its place in all discussions of political transformation is due to the rapid spread of democracy assistance initiatives that followed the end of the cold war. However, by the end of the 1990s it was clear that many so-called democratic transitions had led at best to the formation of semi-authoritarian regimes rather than democratic ones (Ottaway 2003). Furthermore, the reform process was losing momentum almost everywhere (Diamond 1996). Nevertheless, democracy promotion abroad remains on the political agenda of most industrial democracies. And leaders in the developing world, including many with no democratic credentials and no visible intention of acquiring them, embraced the rhetoric of democracy.

The concept of civil society became an important part of all discussions of democratization for reasons grounded to some extent in theory—as discussed earlier—and to a larger extent in pragmatism. In order to provide democracy assistance, aid agencies had to break down the abstract idea of democracy into concrete component parts that could be supported with limited amounts of aid. Civil society was such a component, and a particularly attractive one. Developing civil society

meant promoting government by the people and for the people. And when civil society was defined as a narrow set of professional NGOs, it was also an entity to which assistance could be easily provided. (See Box 9.6.)

NGOs are easy to organize and cheap to fund; small grants go a long way. Professional NGOs were also a new type of association in many countries. Without roots in the traditional civil society and the culture of their countries and highly dependent on outside funding, professional NGOs were easy to train and influence to conform to the funders' concept of what civil society should do. With donor support, NGOs multiplied rapidly in all regions of the world, displaying remarkably similar characteristics. This made the aid agencies' job of supporting civil society easier. It also raised the question whether these organizations were truly addressing the specific challenges of democratization in their countries.

Many studies of the donor-assisted civil society have reached the conclusion that pro-democracy NGOs tend to be quite isolated from the society at large. For instance this was a nearly unanimous conclusion of the contributors to *Funding Virtue* (Ottaway and Carothers 2000), with the only exception being two experts on the Philippines,

BOX 9.6

Civil Society in the Philippines

In the Philippines, the NGO community has long played a significant political role—helping bring down the Marcos regime, challenging and helping define the national political agendas under presidents Aquino, Ramos and Estrada, and taking sides in the 1998 presidential elections to support Estrada over Ramos ... a reason for the unusual strength of civil society is that the focus of most NGOs in the Philippines is not the promotion of a formal democratic system but

the participation of citizens in promoting economic development and tackling the social problems that affect them directly. Democratic participation is thus not an abstraction but a means to an end that is directly important to the lives of people. Democratic participation becomes an extension of such efforts to improve one's life chances.
(Ottaway and Carothers 2000: 297; 302)

where the growth of civil society was an indigenous process that owed much less to foreign assistance. This suggests that donor support is an important contributor to the isolation of civil society organizations. Many professional NGOs have small or no membership. They are often exclusively urban organizations with little reach in the countryside—only the best organized are able to extend their reach through networks of less formal community-based organizations (CBOs). Exchanges (often called 'networking') among the NGOs from different countries provide an opportunity for organizations to discuss their problems and learn from each other, but they also contribute to creating a special international NGO world whose inhabitants talk to each other more easily than they do to their compatriots. These observations do not call into question the genuine commitment of many NGO leaders to democracy, human rights, or other causes. They do call into question, however, the capacity of these so-called organizations of civil society to influence their societies.

Democracy NGOs have other problems worth mentioning briefly. One is the opportunism that exists in the NGO world alongside genuine commitment—when assistance is available, setting up an NGO can simply be a way of making a living. Corruption also exists in the NGO world, which is unsurprising in view of its very rapid growth. And many, as mentioned earlier, become partisan organizations affiliated with political parties. These

problems are tangible, but also inevitable to some extent and not particularly worrisome unless they are extremely widespread. They are simply part of the inevitable imperfection of the real world.

What is more worrisome is whether the growth of a small professional civil society actually contributes to democratization and whether the attention lavished on these organizations has led to the neglect of organizational forms that might have greater popular appeal and greater outreach within the population. Democracy promoters recognize the weakness of the NGOs they support and they equate it with the weakness of civil society. And yet, in many of the countries where the organizations officially designated as civil society are weakest, for example in many war-torn African countries, informal civil society organizations have proven very resilient in trying to address the most severe difficulties created by state collapse (see Box 9.7). In their search for a society that is civil by their definition and assistable in terms of its formal characteristics, aid providers may have marginalized groups with a proven record of effectiveness.

Arab countries, with their contrast between a vast Islamic civil society and their struggling official civil society, illustrate the problem particularly well. In Egypt the world of Islamic civil society is large and multifaceted. It includes charitable groups, organizations that provide free of charge medical services the state has stopped delivering, organizations that offer some educational opportunities for students

BOX 9.7

Policy and Advocacy NGOs Only a Part of Civil Society

The case studies make clear the assumption of NGOs' centrality is questionable. Other kinds of civil society groups frequently drive political change, eclipsing what is often the circumscribed role of policy or advocacy NGOs. In South Africa a social movement brought down apartheid. In Egypt, traditional professional associations are major players in the struggles over political liberalization. In Latin America, the profound struggles of the 1980s against dictatorship and repression were conducted by many social and political forces very different from the technocratic advocacy NGO donors would favour in the 1990s. And in the Philippines, Bangladesh, and elsewhere in Asia, citizens' groups focused on socio-economic issues are having major effects on long-term processes of societal change.

(Adapted from Ottaway and Carothers 2000: 295)

under-served by failing public schools, and groups that provide textbooks for university students who cannot afford them. It also includes organizations with political goals that do not satisfy the principles of liberal democracy, and terrorist groups that can only be defined as uncivil.

This Islamic civil society is well rooted in the society at large. Even organizations that are by no means traditional, but represent a contemporary and, from a religious point of view, aberrant response to contemporary problems, can cast themselves as part of a well-established tradition. They are certainly better rooted in the society than the modern, professional, pro-democracy NGOs favoured by donors. But the new, donors' civil society espouses the values of liberal democracy, while the more traditional Islamic civil society is at best ambiguous on this point. In the end, neither an isolated **modern civil society** nor a well-rooted Islamic one are good vehicles for democratic transformation.

KEY POINTS

- The difference between traditional organizations well rooted in the society, relatively close to the population, but not necessarily democratic or official and the civil society recognized by international democracy promoters may be starker in the Muslim world than elsewhere at this time, but is found in all parts of the developing world.

- Democracy requires a large, active, democratically oriented civil society, but what is found in most countries is a bifurcated situation: an official civil society—small, democratic but essentially elitist; and a less formal, traditional civil society—large, popular, well-rooted but of dubious democratic credentials.

- How to combine the democratic commitment of the former to the popular roots and outreach of the other is a major conundrum for democratization.

Conclusions

The chapter started with an acknowledgement of the ambiguity of the concept of civil society and of its lack of definitional clarity. It ends on the same note, but with a normative addendum. Not only is the concept of civil society an imprecise, ambiguous one, but it must be accepted as such. The more strictly the concept is defined, the less it helps understand how people come together voluntarily to address problems that they cannot solve as individuals and that the state cannot or does not want to help solve for them.

It is of course possible to narrow down the definition closely. This is what the international development agencies do all the time when they pick the organizations to support on the basis of the civility of their goals and the adequacy of their organizational structures. But what is gained in terms of clarity is lost in terms of the understanding of the society. First, the narrow definition loses sight of the many ways in which people in any society organize themselves to pursue their interests and satisfy their needs. It may reduce the effectiveness of any outside intervention, by focusing attention on groups that may be quite marginal to the society but happen to appear all-important to aid agencies. Second, a definition that separates a democratic, virtuous civil society acting in the public interest from a non-democratic, uncivil one, selfishly promoting narrow interests is more normative than analytical. The idea of the common good and the public interest obfuscate the reality that all societies are made up of groups with different and often conflicting interests, and that all groups are equally part of the society, whether their goals conform to a specific idea of civility or not.

In conclusion, despite the caveat expressed at the outset, from an analytical point of view we need to accept that we cannot do better than accept that civil society comprises the entire realm of voluntary associations between the family and the state. It is a vast and complex realm. Voluntary associations take many different forms, ranging from small, informal self-help groups and ad hoc committees with narrow goals to large, professional, and bureaucratic organizations with large budgets. In developing countries, civil society organizations perform a wide range of functions. At one extreme, there are narrowly focused groups that seek, for example, to provide support for AIDS orphans in a community or raise money to improve the track that connects a village to the nearest highway. At the other, there are organizations tied into transnational networks with goals such as changing the World Bank's outlook on the construction of dams or delivering humanitarian assistance to populations in need. Many voluntary associations in developing countries try to provide services the state is unable to deliver. Others form to help citizens resist pressure from predatory governments. Organizations citizens develop voluntarily are not always 'civil' in the normative sense of the word. The realm of civil society comprises organizations that promote human rights and vigilante groups that prey on the people they are supposed to protect. While it is tempting to narrow the definition of civil society to organizations with commendable goals, this is not helpful. If we want to understand how people come together to defend their interests or pursue their goals, we need to accept the diversity, the complexity, and in many cases the flaws of the associational realm that has become known as civil society.

 QUESTIONS

1   How useful is Hegel's definition of civil society? Which definition is more useful, and why?

2   Where does the boundary between civil society and political society lie?

3   Do traditional forms of civil society persist in modern states? If so, do they still perform a useful role?

4   What are the potential negative repercussions of an empowered civil society for a weak state?

5   To what extent do civil society organizations represent the population?

6   Is the establishment of a modern civil society sector a precondition for democratization?

7   How can Western NGOs strengthen modern civil society groups in the developing world without putting their legitimacy at risk?

 GUIDE TO FURTHER READING

■ Florini, Ann M. (ed.) (2000), *The Third Force: The Rise of Transnational Civil Society* (Washington DC: Carnegie Endowment for International Peace). Case studies of the role of transnational networks of civil society including the global anti-corruption movement, human rights movement, organizations for democracy, and against dam-building, and for environmental sustainability.

■ Hann, Chris, and Dunn, Elisabeth (eds.) (1996), *Civil Society: Challenging Western Models* (New York: Routledge). A critical account.

■ **Kasfir, Nelson (ed.) (1998),** *Civil Society and Democracy in Africa* **(London: Frank Cass).** A critical view of conventional Western attitudes towards civil society in Africa.

■ **Nelson, Joan (1979),** *Access to Power: Politics and the Urban Poor in Developing Nations* **(Princeton, NJ: Princeton University Press).**

■ **Ottaway, Marina, and Carothers, Thomas (eds.) (2000),** *Funding Virtue: Civil Society Aid and Democracy Promotion* **(Washington DC: Carnegie Endowment for International Peace).** A critical examination of civil society aid drawing on cases in Africa, Asia, the Middle East, and Latin America.

■ ——**and Chung, Theresa (1999),** **'Debating Democracy Assistance: Toward a New Paradigm',** *Journal of Democracy,* **10/4: 99–113.** A cautious view of international 'democracy assistance' to civil society and to elections and parties too.

■ **Putnam, Robert (1993),** *Making Democracy Work: Civic Traditions in Modern Italy* **(Princeton, NJ: Princeton University Press).** A seminal work on social capital.

■ **Wickham, Carrie Rosefsky (2002),** *Mobilizing Islam: Religion, Activism, and Political Change in Egypt* **(New York: Columbia University Press).** A highly acclaimed analysis of the role of cultural identity, political economy, mobilization, and organization in political Islam in Egypt.

 ## WEB LINKS

● **www.ids.ac.uk/ids/** The site of the civil society and governance research project at the Institute of Development Studies, University of Sussex, which examines the interplay of civil society and governments in twenty-two countries. Funded by the Ford Foundation.

● **www.carnegieendowment.org/publications/index.cfm** *Middle Eastern Democracy. Is Civil Society the Answer?* by Amy Hawthorne. A critical examination of the question.

● **www.civilsoc.org** Civil Society International aims to help civil society organizations worldwide through publicity, networking, and educational initiatives.

● **www.un.org/partners** Links to the ways the United Nations system works 'in partnership' with civil society on issues of global concern.

● **www.un.org/issues/civilsociety** The United Nations and Civil Society site explains the different ways in which the United Nations interacts with and promotes the development of civil society.

● **www.civilsocietyinstitute.org** The Civil Society Institute is an advocacy group 'committed to improving society with breakthrough thinking and creative action'.

● **www.lse.ac.uk/collections/CCS** The Centre for Civil Society at the London School of Economics is 'a leading, international organisation for research, analysis, debate and learning about civil society'.

● **www.imf.org/external/np/exr/cs/eng/index.asp** The International Monetary Fund's Civil Society Newsletter provides regularly updated information on the IMF's collaborative efforts with civil society groups around the world.

● **www.grameen-info.org** The website of Grameen Bank Organization, including articles about microcredit by its founder Muhammad Yunus.

● CIVIL SOCIETY

 ONLINE RESOURCE CENTRE

For additional material and resources, see the Online Resource Centre at:
www.oxfordtextbooks.co.uk/orc/burnell2e/

10 People Power and Alternative Politics

KURT SCHOCK

Chapter Contents

- Introduction
- Social Movements and People Power
- People Power Movements and Democratization
- People Power Movements and Development
- Politics of Alternative Development
- Conclusion

Overview

In the last two decades of the twentieth century and into the twenty-first a number of 'people power' movements challenged the 'authoritarian logic' of non-democracies to promote democratization. Similarly, people power movements have emerged to challenge the dominant 'development logic' in the post-colonial era as well as the more recent 'neo-liberal logic' of development advanced by the governments of the most developed countries, transnational corporations, and international economic institutions. The chapter looks at people power movements that challenged political authoritarianism in the Philippines and Myanmar, and people power movements that challenge development policies in India, Thailand, and Brazil. It explains how these social movements mobilize people and generate pressure for social change. For pragmatic or principled reasons, people power movements tend to incorporate methods of nonviolent action in their struggles against governments, landowners, and corporations. Drawing on human rights (see Chapter 18) and sustainable development (see Chapter 17) discourses, they promote alternative visions of politics and development. This chapter discusses how, increasingly, these movements are becoming connected through transnational networks and are part of an emerging global justice movement.

Introduction[1]

In many parts of the developing world, grass-roots movements have emerged as a political force to be reckoned with. People excluded from politics and decision-making are increasingly engaging in collective action and participating in social movements to defend their livelihoods, promote a more equitable distribution of land and resources, challenge state and corporate-driven development policies, and advance democratization.

Marginalized peoples suffering from the negative consequences of the 'development project' and the globalization project of neo-liberalism (McMichael 2004) are engaging in struggles against deforestation, over-fishing, industrial and export-oriented agriculture, increasing land inequality, and large dam projects. Furthermore, resistance is being mobilized against neo-liberal economic policies and the 'new enclosures' (Harvey 2003; Shiva 2005), such as the privatization of public utilities and resources, and an intellectual property rights regime that contributes to the privatization and commodification of the knowledge and resources of peasants and indigenous peoples.

Much of the resistance has taken the form of people power movements that attempt to transform the politics, economics, and social relations of developing countries. Traditional strategies such as participating in institutional politics through political parties, or capturing state power through violence are increasingly being discarded for a social movements approach that mobilizes people through loose networks, incorporates nonviolent direct actions, and promotes grass-roots democracy and sustainable development (see Box 10.1).

Significantly, these diverse movements are part of a broader global justice movement that is emerging to contest the development agendas of states and corporations. New transnational solidarities and organizational networks have emerged and an increasingly globalized discourse of environmentalism, human rights, and sustainable development has provided new ways of expressing and legitimizing their claims.

BOX 10.1

Ten Principles of Sustainable Societies

New democracy—democracy not limited to periodic elections; officials are held accountable and there is greater popular participation in decision-making.

Subsidiarity—the authority of more distant levels of administration is subordinate to the authority of more local levels; whatever decisions and activities that can be undertaken locally should be.

Ecological sustainability—rates of resource exploitation do not exceed rates of regeneration; rates of resource consumption do not exceed the rates of renewable replacement; rates of pollution do not exceed the rates of harmless absorption.

Common heritage—prohibition on the privatization and commodification of common heritage resources,

---

[1] This chapter draws upon the author's research that was partially funded by a grant from the United States Institute of Peace. The opinions, findings, and conclusions are those of the author and do not necessarily reflect the views of the United States Institute of Peace. The section 'People Power Movements and Development' draws on Schock (2006a). The sub-section on India is based on Ramagundam (2001) and the author's field research in India in 2004 and 2005. The sub-section on Thailand is based on Baker (2003) and Missingham (2003). The sub-section on Brazil is based on Branford and Rocha (2002), Wright and Wolford (2003), and the author's field research in Brazil in 2004.

such as water, land, air, forests, fisheries, culture and knowledge, and basic public services.

Diversity—resistance to homogenization and the promotion of diversity in the cultural, economic, and biological spheres.

Human rights—assurance of economic, social, and cultural rights, as well as civil and political rights.

Jobs, livelihood, employment—assurance of the right to work, free choice of employment, just and favorable working conditions, protection against unemployment, and the right to form and join labor unions.

Food security and safety—local self-reliance in food production and the assurance of healthy and safe foods.

Equity—greater equality between developed and developing countries, between the rich and the poor within countries, and between men and women.

The precautionary principle—if an action, policy, product, or technology might cause severe or irreversible harm to the public or the environment, in the absence of a scientific consensus that harm would not ensue, the burden of proof falls on those who would introduce it.

(Cavanaugh and Mander 2004: 77–104)

Social Movements and People Power

Social movements are organized, collective, and sustained attempts to promote social change that occur partially or entirely outside conventional politics. They incorporate extra-institutional methods of political action to promote change because government officials may be corrupt or unaccountable and institutional political channels may be blocked or ineffective. Social movement participants are often drawn from marginalized segments of society that are excluded from decision-making processes altogether.

The extra-institutional methods used by social movements may be either violent, nonviolent, or a combination of the two. Violent methods involve the use of violence or the threat of physical violence against living beings. These include actions such as armed attacks, bombings, terrorism, kidnapping, imprisonment, and torture. Methods of nonviolent action, obviously, do not involve violence or the threat of violence against living beings. Instead, they involve an active process of bringing political, economic, social, emotional, or moral pressure to bear in the wielding of power in contentious interactions between collective actors.

Examples of nonviolent action include methods of protest and persuasion, such as protest demonstrations, political rallies, and marches; methods of social, economic, or political noncooperation, such as strikes, boycotts, and civil disobedience; methods of disruptive nonviolent intervention, such as sit-ins, land occupations, and obstructions; and methods of creative nonviolent intervention, such as creating alternative money schemes or parallel political institutions (see Box 10.2).

Although the twentieth century was characterized by extreme violence—world wars, civil wars, genocides, the use of chemical and nuclear weapons, violent revolutionary movements, and state and non-state terrorism—methods of nonviolent action were increasingly used in struggles against oppression and injustice throughout the world. Over the course of the twentieth century, methods of nonviolent action became a deliberate tool for social change, being transformed from a largely ad hoc strategy based on either moral or religious principles, or a lack of violent alternatives, to a conscious, deliberate, and reflective method of struggle. There was a shift from informal and

BOX 10.2

Examples of Methods of Nonviolent Action

Protest and persuasion	*Social noncooperation*	*Disruptive intervention*
protest demonstrations	offering sanctuary	land occupations
marches	general strikes	encampments
political rallies	social boycotts	sit-ins
public speeches	social ostracism	pickets
declarations	student strikes	nonviolent obstructions
displaying symbols		paralyzing transportation
vigils		nonviolent sabotage
Creative intervention	*Economic noncooperation*	*Political noncooperation*
alternative money schemes	economic boycotts	civil disobedience
parallel institutions	labour strikes	publication of banned newspapers
constructive programmes	labour slowdowns	refusal to participate in the military
alternative markets	refusal to pay debts or taxes	refusal to obey government orders

unorganized nonviolent struggle to formal and organized nonviolent struggle as expressed through social movements. By the end of the twentieth century nonviolent action had become a modular and global method for challenging oppression and injustice.

Generally, people power movements rely on methods of nonviolent action, rather than violent or institutional methods of political action in their struggles against oppression and injustice. They are composed of diverse networks of people united by an oppositional consciousness and characterized by democratic organizational structures and a diffuse leadership. By contrast, traditional forms of resistance have been characterized by hierarchical organizational structures with a distinct leadership and ideology. The power of people power movements inheres in their ability to mobilize large numbers of people to participate in various forms of protest, noncooperation, and disruption, as well as to implement constructive programmes that are autonomous from state-dominated political relations or corporate-dominated market relations (Schock 2006b).

KEY POINTS

- People suffering from the negative consequences of authoritarianism and development policies are increasingly engaging in collective action and participating in social movements to defend their livelihoods, promote a more equitable distribution of land and resources, challenge state and corporate-driven development policies, and promote democratization.

- Methods of nonviolent action have been increasingly used to challenge the political violence of authoritarianism and the structural violence of development policies.

- People power movements represent an alternative strategy for promoting social change that differs from conventional politics and violent politics.

- By the end of the twentieth century, methods of nonviolent action had become a global and modular method for resisting oppression and injustice.

People Power Movements and Democratization

During the last two decades of the twentieth century and into the twenty-first, a wave of people power movements promoted democratization throughout the world. These movements were primarily urban-based and implemented mass protest demonstrations, strikes, boycotts, civil disobedience, and other methods of nonviolent action to promote democratization. They were nonviolent struggles against the political repression and violence of the 'authoritarian logic' (Schock 2005).

Many of the successful people power movements contributed to democratization in the developing world, including in South America (Bolivia, Brazil, Uruguay, Chile, and Peru), the Caribbean (Haiti), Africa (Sudan, Benin, South Africa, Mali, Madagascar, and Nigeria), Asia (the Philippines, South Korea, Taiwan, Bangladesh, Nepal, Thailand, Mongolia, and Indonesia), the Middle East (Lebanon), and the former Soviet Union (Georgia, Ukraine, and Kyrgyzstan) (see Table 10.1) (some of these countries subsequently experienced de-democratization). More recently, people power movements have been mobilized to force corrupt officials from office. For example, in the Philippines President Joseph Estrada was forced from office in January 2001, and a people power movement contributed to the eventual removal of Prime Minister Thaksin Shinawatra in Thailand in 2006.

While all of the people power movements listed in Table 10.1 contributed to democratization, comparable movements in other places did not. People power movements in El Salvador, Niger, Palestine, Pakistan, Myanmar, Tibet, and China were brutally crushed in the 1980s, and people power movements elsewhere failed to promote substantial democratization. Below, two pro-democracy people power movements are discussed: a successful one in the Philippines, which culminated in the toppling of the Marcos dictatorship in 1986, and an unsuccessful one in Myanmar that was suppressed by the military regime in 1988.

Table 10.1 Countries in the Developing World where People Power Movements Contributed to Democratization, 1982–2005

Country	Transition year(s)
Bolivia	1982
Brazil	1984–85
Uruguay	1984–85
Haiti	1985
Sudan	1985
Philippines	1986
South Korea	1987
Taiwan	1987
Chile	1988
Bangladesh	1989–90
Mongolia	1990
Nepal	1990
Benin	1990–91
South Africa	1990–92
Mali	1991
Thailand	1991–92
Madagascar	1991–93
Indonesia	1998
Nigeria	1998–99
Peru	2000–01
Georgia	2003
Ukraine	2004
Kyrgyzstan	2005
Lebanon	2005

The Philippines: the people power movement of 1986

The declaration of martial law by President Ferdinand Marcos in 1972 marked the end of democratic politics and the beginning of a personalistic dictatorship. Marcos claimed that martial law was necessary to counter threats of communist insurgency and to implement land reform, but in reality he wanted to eliminate political opposition, consolidate his control over the state, and enrich his personal wealth.

Although the ultimate basis of Marcos's power was the military, he relied on legalistic arguments, and incorporated referenda and plebiscites as mechanisms for building regime legitimacy. These techniques were characterized by intimidation and fraud and they ultimately failed to provide legitimacy. Large segments of society became alienated by his plundering of the national wealth and his repression of political opponents.

The emergence of the people power movement in the Philippines can be traced back to the assassination of Benigno Aquino in 1983. Aquino, a long-time political opponent of Marcos, was assassinated upon his return to the Philippines from exile in the United States. More than two million people gathered for Aquino's funeral procession which was transformed into an anti-Marcos demonstration. After the Aquino assassination much of the public shifted from passive acceptance of the Marcos regime to active political opposition. Social movement organizations mobilized increasing protest demonstrations, strikes, and campaigns of civil disobedience. By 1985 it was apparent that Marcos had lost legitimacy.

In response to the rising protests, Marcos called for snap elections to be held on 7 February 1986. Confident in his ability to hold fraudulent elections and intimidate the seemingly unorganized opposition, Marcos fully expected to remain in power. He was opposed by a loose coalition of pro-democracy groups headed by Benigno Aquino's widow, Corazon Aquino, which had little in common beside their desire to oust Marcos.

Shortly after the snap elections 35 government election workers responsible for the computerized tabulation of votes walked off their jobs in protest against the election fraud being committed. On 16 February 1986 Corazon Aquino, responding to the obviously fraudulent declaration of an electoral victory for Marcos by the national assembly, led a rally of over two million people, proclaiming victory for her and 'the people', condemning Marcos, and launching a campaign of civil disobedience. On 22 February, Defence Minister Juan Ponce Enrile led two battalions of soldiers in a mutiny, barricading two major military camps just outside Manila in Quezon City. He was joined by General Fidel Ramos and they announced their support for Aquino. Shortly thereafter, Manila Archbishop Jamie Cardinal Sin condemned the election as fraudulent, declared that the regime had lost its moral authority to govern, and urged people to nonviolently resist the Marcos dictatorship. He made an appeal over the radio for people to show their support for the mutiny. In response, hundreds of thousands of pro-democracy sympathizers assembled at the military camps. Marcos ordered two battalions to the military camps to put down the rebellion, but as the tanks approached, civilians formed a human barrier between the tanks and the rebels in the camp. The troops sent by Marcos retreated in the face of a mass of unarmed civilians led by priests and nuns. These dramatic events sparked a nationwide defection of soldiers and officers. On 26 February, Corazon Aquino was sworn in as president and Marcos was escorted out of the country to Honolulu by the US military. The people power movement succeeded. It prevented a violent clash between the divided segments of the armed forces, forced Marcos from office, and ushered in a democratic transition.

Myanmar: the 8–8–88 pro-democracy movement

Myanmar has been ruled by a military dictatorship since 1962, when General Ne Win assumed dictatorial power in a coup against the democratic regime of U Nu. The alleged justification for the military takeover included a perceived turning away from the state's founding socialist principles, U Nu's policy of establishing Buddhism as the state religion, and U Nu's negotiations with leaders of two of the non-Burman states in the union for greater autonomy with the possibility that they would attempt to exercise their constitutional right to secede. Upon the declaration of martial law Ne Win expanded the role of the military in politics, bureaucratic administration, and the economy. The Burma Socialist Programme Party (BSPP) was formed as a means of mass mobilization and political indoctrination, and all other political parties were banned. All potential political rivals of the state were eliminated. The result of the military-run economy was gross inefficiency, rampant corruption, and economic decline.

Overt protest against the regime during the 1980s was minimal until 1988. In March 1988, students at the Rangoon Institute of Technology protested against the killing of university students by the police. They were soon joined by students from Rangoon University in daily protests, which took an explicit anti-government and pro-democracy stance. The state responded with force, killing scores of students and arresting more than 1,000. Hundreds of students marched from the university campuses to downtown Rangoon. As they gathered supporters along the way the protest grew into the thousands by the time it reached downtown. The demonstrators were again met with violence by the police and army. Scores of protestors and bystanders were killed and thousands were arrested. The government shut down the universities and the movement temporarily collapsed.

However, when the universities re-opened a few months later, students began organizing a mass movement. By mid-June students once again took to the streets, joined by Buddhist monks, workers from nearby factories, and unemployed urban residents. Once again they were met by violence and around 80–100 dissidents were killed. A new curfew was imposed and the universities were closed again.

In response to the spreading protests, the government announced that the BSPP would hold an extraordinary congress in late July. At the extraordinary party congress, Ne Win announced that he would step down from his position of president and chairman of the BSPP. He also suggested

that a referendum take place to gauge the public's support for a multiparty system. The proposal for the referendum, however, was rejected by the BSPP congress. The rejection of the proposal and the appointment of Sein Lwin, the universally despised commander of the riot police, to the posts of president and BSPP chairman led to a new and intensified round of anti-regime protests.

Protests once again erupted and a nationwide general strike was planned for 8 August 1988 (8–8–88). The demonstrations in Rangoon leading up to the general strike attracted huge numbers of people. On 8 August, the general strike began. The centre of Rangoon was filled with tens of thousands of peaceful pro-democracy protestors drawn from all segments of society and ethnic groups. Demonstrations erupted in cities and towns throughout the country. The festive atmosphere in Rangoon was broken that night when the military opened fire with machine guns. The massacre left an estimated one to three thousand dead in Rangoon. The demonstrations outside Rangoon were brutally suppressed as well. Smaller demonstrations in Rangoon and throughout the country continued sporadically for a few more days. Finally, on 12 August it was announced that Sein Lwin had resigned. Despite the carnage, the people power movement forced Sein Lwin from office. On 19 August, the government announced that his successor would be Dr Maung Maung, the highest ranking civilian in the party and a 'moderate' in the military regime. The next day demonstrations resumed as tens of thousands of people rejected Dr Maung Maung's nomination and demanded an end to one-party rule and the formation of a new interim government. On 22 August, a nationwide general strike was once again proclaimed. Strike centres were established in towns and cities across the country and pro-democracy demonstrations occurred on a daily basis.

Martial law was unexpectedly lifted and the military withdrew from the cities. On 23 and 24 August 1988, an estimated one million people participated in the protest demonstrations in Rangoon. On 26 August, crowds estimated to be at least

500,000 people gathered to hear Aung San Suu Kyi, the daughter of one of Myanmar's independence heroes, General Aung San, give her first public speech. She emerged as the leading voice of the pro-democracy opposition. The general strike crippled the regime and it seemed as if the pro-democracy movement would succeed. However, in early September the Philippine-style people power movement was brutally suppressed by the military government. *Agents provocateurs* from the military, along with criminals who had been released from prison, engaged in arson, looting, violence, and other destabilizing activities apparently in an effort to legitimize the military's restoration of order and return to power. Then, on 18 September, a group of generals organized by Ne Win and led by General Saw Maung announced the formation of the State Law and Order Restoration Committee (SLORC) and re-took power. Once again martial law was imposed and the army returned to the cities and brutally repressed all opposition. By 20 September the demonstrations ended and once again several thousand unarmed civilians were killed and the regime arrested and executed alleged dissident organizers. SLORC ordered people to return to work and threatened those who did not with dismissal and arrest. In need of food and money, the workers complied and almost eight-weeks of general strikes collapsed. The movement failed as sustained collective action ceased and the regime reorganized and remained in power.

Similar to Marcos' tactics in the Philippines, SLORC scheduled elections in an effort to increase its legitimacy. Elections for the national assembly were subsequently held in May 1990. The regime fully expected to win the elections having imposed severe restrictions on organizing and having arrested opposition party leaders in the months leading up to the elections. To its surprise, the most outspoken opposition to the military regime, the National League for Democracy (NLD), won 60 per cent of the vote. The goal of the NLD, led by Aung San Suu Kyi, was to form a federalist democratic system with full respect for human rights.

However, SLORC refused to honour the elections and remained in power. Thus, after more than two years, the people power movement, though successful in forcing the government to hold multiparty elections, was ultimately unsuccessful in toppling the military regime.

Divergent outcomes

What accounts for the divergent outcomes of the two pro-democracy people power movements? Characteristics of the social movements themselves as well as the political context each played a role (Schock 1999, 2005). In the Philippines, two broad-based organizations emerged to coordinate the unarmed struggle against Marcos, namely Bayan (*Bagong Alyansang Makabayan*) and the United Democratic Opposition (UNIDO). Bayan acted as an umbrella organization, coordinating the activities of a diverse array of progressive organizations promoting the interests of women, peasants, and workers. UNIDO, which represented the interests of the traditional political elite opposition and their middle-class followers, acted as both a political party and a social movement organization, engaging in nonviolent action as well as electoral activity. Both strands of the anti-Marcos challenge implemented a range of nonviolent actions and responded innovatively to government repression. General strikes, the implementation of civil disobedience, and the rejection of the official election results undermined the state's ability to control the political situation. These actions, along with the growing armed communist insurgency in the countryside, promoted capital flight, contributed to regime defection, and led to the diplomatic intervention of the United States government which severed its ties to Marcos and threw its weight behind Corazon Aquino.

In Myanmar, during the short but intense period of organizing and protest prior to the military crackdown in September 1988, protest demonstrations and general strikes implemented by the pro-democracy movement directly undermined the regime to the point where it was on the verge of collapse. However, no umbrella organization emerged that was capable of coordinating the diverse strands of resistance or organizing a parallel government. The NLD, a broad-based opposition organization, emerged only after the state had suppressed the people power movement and channelled opposition activity into tightly controlled electoral campaigning leading up to the 1990 elections. In contrast to the people power movement in the Philippines, which continued to implement methods of noncooperation in addition to participation in electoral activity, the challenge in Myanmar, which had implemented a wide range of tactics of nonviolent action before the military crackdown was primarily limited to electoral campaigning after the crackdown. Unlike the Philippines, where the movement could challenge the regime's refusal to honour the election results, the de-mobilization of the Burmese mass movement foreclosed this option. Moreover, the leverage generated by the challenge in Myanmar was also constrained by Myanmar's international isolation.

Due to the regime's isolation, no foreign government was in a position to effectively pressure the Burmese government to step aside as occurred in the Philippines.

KEY POINTS

- From the 1980s onward, a wave of people power movements contributed to democratization throughout the developing world.

- The people power movement in the Philippines in 1986 ousted Ferdinand Marcos from office and contributed to democratization.

- The 8–8–88 people power movement in Myanmar was suppressed by the military regime and failed to contribute democratization.

- Variations in the outcomes of pro-democracy movements are a function of characteristics of the movement (such as its organization and ability to implement a range of nonviolent actions) and the broader political context (such as the coherency of the military and the political elite).

People Power Movements and Development

While the people power movements in Table 10.1 were largely urban-based and aimed at toppling a regime, increasingly, throughout the developing world, rural-based people power movements have arisen to struggle against the structural violence of the 'development logic'. Mobilizing segments of society most adversely affected by 'development policies' such as indigenous peoples, small farmers, landless rural workers, and urban slum-dwellers alienated from the hinterland, they challenge the social structures and economic relations advanced by capitalist modernization that end up killing some people slowly by preventing them from meeting their basic needs. These movements are concerned

with a host of interrelated issues. Table 10.2 lists seven development issues over which social movements have arisen to promote social change and provides examples of each. These social movements involve marginalized or excluded people that are promoting redistributive agendas, grass-roots democracy, and sustainable forms of development. As discussed below, they can be considered part of an emerging grass-roots global justice movement that is challenging the dominant development paradigm and promoting an alternative politics of development.

In this section three people power movements are discussed that use various methods of nonviolent

Table 10.2 People Power Movements and the Contestation of Development in the Developing World

Issue	Examples
Opposition to large centralized development projects (e.g., dams)	Save Narmada Movement (India) Assembly of the Poor (Thailand)
Movements to protect the environment (e.g., forests)	Chipko Movement (India) Greenbelt Movement (Kenya)
Indigenous people's movements	*Coordenação das Organizações Indigenas da Amazônia Brasileira* (Brazil) *Ekta Parishad* (India)
Land reform movements	Landless Rural Workers Movement, MST (Brazil) Landless People's Movement (South Africa)
Opposition to agricultural policies of the World Bank and the WTO	Karnataka State Farmers Association, KRRS (India) Federation of Indonesian Peasant Unions, FSPI (Indonesia)
Opposition to the privatization of utilities	Protests against the privatization of electricity (India) Coalition in Defense of Water & Life (Bolivia)
Opposition to patents on nature and indigenous knowledge	Coordinating Body of Indigenous Organizations of the Amazon Basin (in nine Amazonian countries) Navdanya Movement (India)

Note: Some social movement organizations address more than one issue.

action to promote grass-roots democracy and sustainable development. The section includes a discussion of (1) Ekta Parishad, a Gandhian organization in India that promotes the access of marginalized people to livelihood resources, (2) the Assembly of the Poor, a grass-roots movement in Thailand that opposes large dam projects and promotes community control over land and resources, and (3) the Landless Rural Workers Movement (MST), an agrarian reform movement in Brazil that promotes the redistribution of agricultural land and food sovereignty.

India: Ekta Parishad

There are a variety of social movements in India addressing issues related to the control over and access to land and natural resources, including movements concerned with biopiracy, deforestation, dam building, indigenous people's rights, land reform, and agricultural policies. One social movement organization, founded in 1990, is Ekta Parishad (United Forum), a Gandhian land rights organization that struggles to prevent land alienation and to promote the access of marginalized people to livelihood resources, such as land, water, and forests. Its members are drawn from the most disadvantaged segments of society, such as lower-caste farmers and rural workers and *adivasis*. *Adivasis* are indigenous tribal peoples in India who inhabit forest land.

Ekta Parishad is concerned with a number of land- and resource-related problems in India. One problem is that although various land reform acts have been enacted at the state-level, such as land ceiling acts that limit the amount of land that an individual can own, in many cases these acts have never been properly implemented, thus land inequality remains high. Another problem is that although many large landowners donated land to the government for redistribution to the landless during the Bhoodan movement—a movement led by the Gandhian Vinoba Bhave in the 1950s whereby large landowners donated land to Bhave to be redistributed to the landless—much of the land was never redistributed due to the corruption of government officials. A third problem concerns the neo-liberal agricultural policies implemented by the government over the last decade which have driven small farmers into debt and increased land alienation. Fourth, many small farmers have never received official land titles from the government, even though they, or their families, have been working on the land for years or even for generations. Without land titles, they are easily evicted by more powerful landowners or government officials. A fifth problem is that *adivasis* are being evicted from the forests. This is occurring for a variety of reasons, such as timber extraction, mining operations, the setting up of eucalyptus plantations, and the creation of tiger reserves. Generally speaking, more powerful individuals, groups, and corporations, use a combination of cunning, corruption, and violence to alienate people from the land.

Ekta Parishad attempts to organize, mobilize, and build solidarity among marginalized groups, generate public awareness about land-related problems, and put pressure on the government to address these problems. A major method used by Ekta Parishad is the *yatra*. A *yatra* is an extended journey

through the countryside that may last in duration from a few weeks to many months. It draws on the Hindu tradition of spiritual pilgrimages, and is used as a political tool to draw attention to injustices and to generate pressure against the government. Well-known *yatras* include Mohandas Gandhi's Salt March to Dandi in 1930, as part of a campaign of civil disobedience that challenged British rule, and Vinoba Bhave's travels throughout the countryside during the Bhoodan movement for land reform in the 1950s.

While Ekta Parishad implements multiple methods of nonviolent action, such as sit-ins in front of government offices and reoccupations of forest land, the *yatra* is its major method. Since 1999, Ekta Parishad has undertaken six major state-wide *yatras*: three in the state of Madhya Pradesh, and one each in the states of Bihar, Chhattisgarh, and Orissa. It has also implemented numerous smaller *yatras* focused on a few districts within a particular state. Prior to commencing a *yatra*, Ekta Parishad releases a 'Declaration of Satyagraha' that proclaims the intent and purpose of the campaign. The declaration highlights the problems that exist concerning land- and resource-related issues, and states that repeated appeals to government officials to address these issues have failed to bring any action. Since conventional politics has been ineffective, it is proclaimed, it is necessary to engage in large-scale mobilizations and acts of civil disobedience that the government cannot ignore.

Each *yatra* occurs in a particular state and begins with a large political rally in a major city that draws thousands of people. Speeches are made by members of Ekta Parishad and others who are sympathetic to their movement. Following the rally, the *yatra* commences, with a core of activists and supporters travelling by foot and jeep throughout the countryside. In each village where the activists stop, a public hearing is held in which villagers are encouraged to openly state their grievances. Villagers submit petitions and Ekta Parishad activists write up petitions based on the grievances aired by the villagers. By the end of the *yatra*, thousands of petitions are collected and submitted to government officials. Ekta Parishad activists also prepare a case study for each village, documenting and summarizing the problems concerning access to land and resources, corruption, and violence. Ekta Parishad activists encourage people to overcome their fear, fight evictions, and resist land alienation.

During the *yatra* campaigns, press releases are made and the media is encouraged to cover the events. Campaigns typically involve some acts of civil disobedience, such as blocking a highway with a march. The *yatra* ends in the same way as it begins, with a mass rally in a major city. Depending on the length of the journey, the marchers may pass through hundreds of villages. A six-month long *yatra* carried out in the state of Madhya Pradesh in 1999 and 2000, for example, passed through approximately 1,500 villages.

The successes of the campaigns have varied by state. They have been most successful in Madhya Pradesh, the state where Ekta Parishad was founded and where it is the strongest. The Madhya Pradesh *yatra* in 1999 and 2000 resulted in the distribution of over 150,000 land plots to landless rural workers, numerous land titles were given to people who had been working on their land for years, and the eviction of tribal people from the forests was stopped, at least temporarily. Ekta Parishad has had only mixed success in other states where they are still in the process of building their organizational strength.

Ekta Parishad is significant, because it is organizing, empowering, and promoting the rights and citizenship of people who have been the most marginalized in Indian society. It is also significant because it is part of a larger movement in India to revitalize the radical Gandhian tradition. Gandhi's tradition, to a certain degree, has been co-opted by the government. Ekta Parishad, along with other Indian social movement organizations, draws on Gandhi's tradition of openly defiant acts against injustice, the implementation of constructive programmes, and Gandhi's vision of revolutionary social change in an effort to transform Indian society.

Thailand: the Assembly of the Poor

The Assembly of the Poor (*Samatcha khon chon*) is composed of various groups adversely affected by development policies implemented by the Thai state to promote industrialization, export-oriented agriculture, and commercial forestry. A substantial portion of the members of the Assembly come from the hundreds of thousands of rural and forest dwelling people who have been adversely affected by the construction of large-scale dams over the past twenty years. Dam construction has resulted in the loss of fisheries and the flooding of land upon which people depend for their livelihoods. The government has failed to adequately compensate displaced people for their losses.

The Assembly of the Poor, which was officially founded in 1995, grew out of pre-existing small farmer and villagers' organizations. Urban slum-dwellers, many of which have been forced off the land in the countryside, also participate. The Assembly is not a centralized organization, but rather a horizontal network of grass-roots organizations and supporting non-governmental organizations (NGOs) which retain their autonomy and independence. The Assembly was established to enable villagers' organizations from around the country to come together in a forum to exchange information and resources, and to increase their bargaining power for their own campaigns by being part of a broader network.

The Assembly of the Poor initially attempted to redress the grievances of its members through conventional politics, but their efforts were ignored or stonewalled by the government. After exhausting institutional political channels, the movement turned to methods of nonviolent action such as marches, rallies, protest demonstrations, and civil disobedience. They realized that mass protest was the only way to create the bargaining power they needed to bring decision-makers to the negotiating table on a more equal footing.

The most powerful method of resistance developed by the Assembly of the Poor is the encampment. In an encampment, a make-shift 'rural village' is set up in the streets of Bangkok within which activists live for the duration of the protest campaign. The encampment is located in the heart of the centre of power, near the Government House, which houses the offices of the prime minister and other government officials. During the course of the encampment, political rallies and meetings are held on a daily basis, and marches through the streets are sometimes undertaken. Dramatic events depicting the plight of the poor are organized which receive considerable coverage in the mass media.

The first major encampment occurred in March and April 1996, where up to 12,000 activists participated in the month-long campaign. As a result of the encampment, the Assembly of the Poor obtained agreements in principle from the government to compensate their members for the expropriation of their land and the loss of livelihood. The Assembly was vigilant in following up the implementation stages with committees and government agencies, demanding that the government honour its promises. When the government refused, the Assembly of the Poor organized a second larger encampment to pressure the government to honour the promises it made as a result of the first encampment.

The second major encampment took place from 24 January to 2 May 1997 outside the Government House in Bangkok. The Assembly of the Poor mobilized up to 25,000 people from thirty-five provinces, and demanded that the government adhere to its promises and take action on their grievances. The Assembly put pressure on the government to compensate people for their losses, promote more sustainable forms of development, and democratize the policy-making process.

The second encampment was the most sustained and well-organized mass protest ever mounted in Bangkok. The success of the encampment depended on the protestors' ability to maintain nonviolent discipline. In doing so, it mobilized pressure against the government without raising the anxiety of the public beyond a critical threshold or justifying a violent response by the government. Due to the size and duration of the second encampment, along with the intense media coverage and the support of NGOs and segments of the middle classes, the government was pressured to negotiate with the Assembly and to implement the agreements that it had previously made.

The Assembly won unprecedented concessions from the government, including compensation to almost 7,000 families for loss of land and livelihood due to dam construction, the cancellation of one dam project and the review of five others, three resolutions ending summary evictions of villagers from forest land, and the admission in principle that long-settled groups should be allowed to remain on forest land. Moreover, a bill was initiated in parliament that would recognize community rights to forest management.

The government of Prime Minister Chavalit Yongchaiyudh had given a guarantee to address all of the grievances in the Assembly's petition. However, when the government of Prime Minister Chuan Leekpai took over from the Chavalit government in November 1997, the gains were lost as the new government refused to honour previous agreements with the Assembly of the Poor. During the more authoritarian rule of Chuan, the Assembly adopted the strategy of coordinated but geographically scattered protests at strategic sites of conflict throughout the country, rather than staging major political events in Bangkok. However, once the hard-line Chuan was replaced by Thaksin Shinawatra as prime minister in February 2001, the Assembly again pressed the national government for reform through concentrated large-scale mobilizations.

The Assembly of the Poor is significant because it represents the first major reassertion of the rural political voice in Thailand since the suppression of the Peasant's Federation in the 1980s. The Assembly differs from earlier rural political groups, due to its decentralized network style of organization, its diffuse leadership, and its ability to address local and national issues. Moreover, the movement avoids co-optation by not seeking links to political parties or seeking to gain state power.

While its success has varied depending on the political context, the Assembly has been successful in putting the issue of sustainable development on the national agenda and it is continually working to transform social relations of power to enable local communities the freedom to manage local resources and to compel the state to guarantee local community rights over the use of land and resources.

Brazil: the Landless Rural Workers' Movement (MST)

Brazil has one of the highest levels of land inequality in the world, which is a legacy of Portuguese colonization and the continued influence of the land-owning elite in Brazilian politics. Even though the 1964 Land Statute Act and the 1988 Brazilian Constitution specify that the government has the responsibility to redistribute land that is not being productively used, Brazil has never implemented a serious land reform programme. In fact, one of the reasons for the military coup that was backed by the US government in 1964 was to topple a progressive government that was considering land reform.

From the 1970s onward, the number of landless and unemployed rural workers increased due to the building of several giant hydroelectric dams, the expulsion of people from land to make way for large industrial farms for export agriculture, and the implementation of policies that favoured large-scale farming and contributed to the indebtedness of small farmers. Increasing landlessness and disillusionment with the government's failure to implement land reform resulted in peasants taking over unproductively used land through unarmed land occupations. Further land occupations were subsequently organized by the Landless Rural Workers' Movement, or the MST (*Movimento dos Trabalhadores Rurais Sem Terra*), a social movement organization that was officially founded in 1984. The MST originated in Brazil's three southern-most states, Rio Grande do Sul, Santa Catarina, and Paraná, growing out of a network of progressive members of the Catholic Church who practiced liberation theology and Marxist activists

concerned with rural violence and the highly skewed distribution of land in the countryside.

The land occupation became the major weapon for putting pressure on the government to implement land reform. It is a highly organized and disciplined method of nonviolent direct action involving substantial planning and preparation. Before a land occupation occurs, MST activists identify parcels of land that fulfill two characteristics; the land must be classified as not in productive use and therefore eligible for redistribution, and the land must be suitable for sustaining a community—that is, there must be access to water and the land must be cultivable.

Once such land is identified, the MST mobilizes landless people who are interested in obtaining land. Ideally, the mobilization is facilitated by a member of the local community who is sympathetic to the MST, such as a priest or a union leader. If no such person exists, MST activists go door-to-door attempting to recruit people. Meetings occur in churches or schoolrooms where discussions are held about agrarian reform. MST activists explain what the movement is about, why it struggles for land, and how land can be won through land occupations. People who attend the meetings are requested to invite additional people to the next meeting. Four or five meetings are carried out in parallel in different communities. When there is a critical mass interested in participating in a land occupation, a regional meeting is held and a date is set for the occupation.

An occupation occurs when a group of families, perhaps anywhere from 30 to 300, depending on the size of the land to be occupied, occupy a piece of land. Typically the land that is occupied is privately owned, but sometimes occupations occur on unused government land. While the date of the land occupation is announced in advance, the location of the land to be occupied is kept secret, known only to a few activists. This prevents the authorities or landowners from taking actions to inhibit the occupation. Entire families participate in the land occupations. The families are transported to the site of the occupation in a manner that is not intended to attract the attention of authorities. Typically, bus loads of people leave in the middle of the night from different places and at staggered times converging on the site of the occupation. Everything that is needed to live on the land is taken, such as materials to construct tents, cooking equipment, and a supply of food staples. Once the land is occupied, the families must be self-sufficient since the police sometimes set up roadblocks to prevent additional people or supplies from reaching the site of the occupation.

Once on the land, the MST flag is displayed in prominent places, a ceremony is held, and the families begin working to construct more permanent housing and to prepare the land for cultivation. The MST then commences lengthy legal proceedings in order to have the land officially expropriated by the government. Sometimes the land occupations are met with violence by the landowners or the police. If this occurs, the MST retreats and organizes another land occupation to be carried out at a different location.

The MST employs nonviolent action as a pragmatic means for promoting agrarian reform. Given the monopoly on violence held by landowners and the state, it would be suicidal for the movement to respond with violence. Moreover, if they employed violence, they would lose support from the general public and the more progressive segments of the Catholic Church, which is important for their success.

Over the past twenty years, the MST has carried out over 230,000 land occupations. Through this method, it has succeeded in putting the issue of agrarian reform on the national agenda, and it has resulted in the redistribution of 20 million acres of agricultural land to over 350,000 families.

In addition to land occupations, the movement attempts to generate pressure on the government through other methods, such as the occupation of government offices, and long marches which generate media coverage. For example, in May 2005, approximately 12,000 people marched for seventeen days from Goiânia to Brasília to raise awareness about the plight of the landless and to keep pressure on the government to proceed with land reform. Nevertheless, the land occupation is the MST's signature method and the one that has proved the most powerful in promoting land reform.

Not only has the movement been successful in promoting land redistribution, but it is also in the process of transforming Brazil's agricultural sector. Brazilian agriculture is oriented towards growing cash crops for export, such as sugar, tobacco, and soybeans, rather than producing food for local markets. This has two negative consequences. First, it contributes to hunger in Brazil since productive land is not being used to grow food staples. Second, industrial methods of mono-culture farming contribute to environmental degradation due to the use of chemical fertilizers and pesticides and the depletion of groundwater. In contrast, the MST encourages families to work the land cooperatively, engage in organic farming, and produce goods for local markets.

The MST is also concerned with environmentalism and biodiversity. The MST encourages those who obtain land to designate 20 per cent of the land as an ecological reserve. Moreover, the MST does not engage in occupations of land in the Amazon rainforest. Thus, the struggle to obtain land is viewed as part of a larger struggle to achieve a more ecologically sound and sustainable society.

The MST is significant because is has forged a strategy of land redistribution and agrarian reform that does not depend on violence. Moreover it has been able to successfully challenge the entrenched power of the land-owning elite in Brazil and has promoted the rights and citizenship of landless people who have historically been marginalized in Brazilian society.

KEY POINTS

- Examples of people power movements that challenge development policies and promote grass-roots democracy and sustainable development include Ekta Parishad in India, the Assembly of the Poor in Thailand, and the Landless Rural Workers Movement (MST) in Brazil.

- People power movements organize and give a political voice to the most marginalized segments of society.

- Although each social movement has experienced violent repression from large landowners or the government, the movements have continued to fight oppression and injustice with methods of nonviolent action.

- The nonviolent action implemented by the movements ranges from principled nonviolence of Ekta Parishad to pragmatic nonviolence of the MST.

Politics of Alternative Development

The development policies implemented by many governments of developing countries over the past three decades have prioritized constructing large dams, promoting industrial farming and export-oriented agriculture, and extracting timber and minerals. These policies have contributed to the displacement of people, the privatization of communal land and resources, increasing levels of land inequality, and environmental degradation, and they have threatened the material bases of small farmers, landless rural workers, and indigenous peoples. In response, social movements have been mobilized with strong critiques of the dominant models of development and have pursued goals consistent with environmentalism, grass-roots democracy, and sustainable development. Social movement organizations, such as those described in the preceding section, have organized, mobilized, and promoted solidarity among groups that have been the most adversely affected by development policies.

In addition, social movements like these not only resist destructive development policies but also challenge entrenched systems of inequality and traditional rural social relations such as authoritarianism, violence, and patriarchy. For example, traditional caste relations are challenged in India by Ekta Parishad, and traditional patron–client ties are challenged by the Assembly of the Poor in Thailand and the MST in Brazil. All three organizations promote gender equality and empower people to take a stand against corruption, violence, and traditional deference to authority.

These social movement organizations, and others like them, have adopted organizational forms and politics that represent a distinct break from the past. They have broken from old ideological camps and have deliberately eschewed the usual political party and lobby group format for a networked social movement approach to politics. They reject the notions of becoming political parties or capturing state power. Instead they attempt to transcend institutional political channels by emphasizing grass-roots participatory democracy, decentralization, and organizational autonomy from political parties and the state. They organize marginalized people to increase their power to influence the state through extra-institutional methods of protest, and just as importantly they stress the empowerment of poor people and their collective capacity to address the problems they experience. In doing so, they attempt to create grass-roots democracy and implement practices of sustainable development.

Moreover, the three social movement organizations in India, Thailand, and Brazil, and others like them throughout the developing world, have deliberately adopted methods of nonviolent action to challenge elites and the state. Nonviolent strategies provide a sharp contrast to guerilla insurgencies and traditional anti-imperialist movements that relied on violence to capture state power. Nonviolent strategies also provide a sharp contrast to the violence that has characterized enclosures, colonization, the expropriation of land and resources by states and corporations, and the violent repression used against those who protest against national development and neo-liberal globalization.

In order to break vicious cycles of violence, these struggles have responded creatively with nonviolent methods. Methods of nonviolent action have been used to mobilize people, draw attention to significant social problems, and generate pressure against their opponents. Direct actions have been taken to rectify problems that governments have not addressed. Rather than challenging the state on its own terms, that is through methods of violence, challenges are being waged using methods in which the people have a comparative advantage—through methods of nonviolent action.

Significantly, there is an increasing tendency toward using methods of nonviolent action in struggles over land, resources, and development policies across the globe. While violence may be justified, for pragmatic or principled reasons, many social movements have eschewed the methods of violence used by their opponents. Even struggles that were originally violent, such as the Zapatista rebellion which broke out in the Chiapas state of Mexico, have increasingly turned to methods of nonviolent action. The Zapatista Army of National Liberation (*Ejército Zapatista de Liberación Nacional*, EZLN) emerged in 1994 in opposition to the North American Free Trade Agreement (NAFTA) that opened the Mexican economy to North American enterprises. While originally violent—they engaged in armed clashes with state agents from 1 to 12 January 1994—the Zapatistas have since turned to methods of nonviolent action to promote their cause, although, paradoxically, they continue to be armed. Their struggle is framed as an indigenous struggle

against imperialism. They promote the autonomy of the indigenous people in Chiapas, their right to use and benefit from the resources in their region, and their right to exercise communal control of land, something that was outlawed by the NAFTA agreement.

Nonviolent action may be the most promising method for addressing problems associated with enclosures, commodification, and privatization, and for transforming the dominant development model. Strategies based on violence or which rely on state power have been largely unsuccessful in creating democratic polities or sustainable forms of development. Violent movements for national liberation, for example, typically resulted in authoritarian regimes throughout Africa and Asia that used state powers to exploit resources and labour.

In contrast nonviolent strategies have a number of strengths: (1) their means are consistent with their ends, (2) they allow maximum popular participation in their struggles, (3) they are more likely to win over opponents and third parties, (4) they lead to more lasting change, because they mobilize a larger portion of the population in a participatory fashion than violence or official channels, and (5) their struggles usually result in fewer casualties (Martin 2001, 2006).

Nevertheless, despite these strengths, there are potential weaknesses in people power approaches to social change. A problem with pro-democracy movements in particular, is that while they unite a diverse opposition to challenge the authoritarian regime, once a transition occurs there tends to be conflict and fragmentation among the previously united opposition. In the Philippines, for example, after the successful people power movement, members of the traditional elite regained political prominence while the more progressive segments of the movement were marginalized. Moreover, the process of democratization may be deflected into moves to establish limited democracy and a neo-liberal economy, under the influence of the US government and international financial institutions seeking to prevent popular democracy from taking root (Robinson 1996). Other problems with promoting social change through social movements include the difficulty of aggregating diverse groups into a coordinated movement, maintaining social mobilization and the capacity to disrupt over extended periods, the co-option of movement leaders or a segment of the movement by the ruling group, the formal institutionalization of the movement and consequent loss of vitality, and, of course, the vulnerability of challenges to state repression.

The global justice movement

While people power movements that challenge the dominant development paradigm are part of a long tradition of resistance against colonization and 'national development', they also differ from earlier struggles. In the current era of globalization, these struggles, which in previous times would have been isolated from each other, are part of emerging transnational networks that oppose the dominant development model. These networks draw on discourses of sustainable development, environmentalism, human and community rights, and grass-roots democracy. Highly organized social movements have arisen, that while struggling at the local level, are also networked with similar struggles in other places through transnational ties. Box 10.3 provides examples of non-governmental organizations that are part of a growing transnational network of resistance against neo-liberal economic policies.

BOX 10.3

NGOs and the Globalization of Networks of Resistance to Neo-Liberal Development Policies

Focus on the Global South—'aims to consciously and consistently articulate, link and develop greater coherence between local community-based and national, regional and global paradigms of change...strives to create a distinct and cogent link between development at the grassroots and the "macro" levels.' (Founded in 1995)

FoodFirst Information & Action Network—'an international human rights organisation that campaigns for the realisation of the right to adequate food, a human right contained in the International Covenant on Economic, Social and Cultural Rights.' (Founded in 1986)

Global Exchange—'an international human rights organization dedicated to promoting social, economic and environmental justice around the world.' (Founded in 1988)

Genetic Resources Action International—'promotes the sustainable management and use of agricultural biodiversity based on people's control over genetic resources and local knowledge.' (Founded in 1990)

Indigenous Peoples Council on Biocolonialism—'organized to assist indigenous peoples in the protection of their genetic resources, indigenous knowledge, cultural and human rights from the negative effects of biotechnology.' (Founded in the 1990s)

International Rivers Network—'protects rivers and defends the rights of communities that depend on them ... opposes destructive dams and the development model they advance, and encourages better ways of meeting people's needs for water, energy and protection from damaging floods.' (Founded in 1985)

People's Global Action—'very clearly rejects capitalism, imperialism and feudalism; and all trade agreements, institutions and governments that promote destructive globalisation.' (Founded in 1998)

Project Underground—'a vehicle for the environmental, human rights and indigenous rights movements to carry out focused campaigns against abusive extractive resource activity.' (Founded in 1996)

Third World Network—'an international network of organizations and individuals involved in issues relating to environment, development and the Third World and North-South issues.' (Founded in the 1990s)

Via Campesina—'an international movement which coordinates peasant organizations of small and medium-sized producers, agricultural workers, rural women, and indigenous communities.' (Founded in 1992)

Note: Quotations are from respective websites.

KURT SCHOCK

The World Social Forum

The World Social Forum (WSF) is an annual meeting held by members of the global justice movement to elaborate their ideas, share and refine strategies, and inform each other about struggles around the world. The WSF usually meets every January in counterposition to the World Economic Forum held in Davos, Switzerland. The WSF has inspired the organization of many regional social forums, such as the Asian Social Forum and the Latin American Social Forum.

Date and location of World Social Forums:

- 2001—Porto Alegre, Brazil

- 2002—Porto Alegre, Brazil
- 2003—Porto Alegre, Brazil
- 2004—Mumbai, India
- 2005—Porto Alegre, Brazil
- 2006—polycentric forums in Caracas, Venezuela, Bamako, Mali, and Karachi, Pakistan
- 2007—Nairobi, Kenya

(See www.forumsocialmundial.org.br)

Transnational NGOs as well as the social forums that have emerged over the past decade, most notably the World Social Forum as well as regional social forums, provide mechanisms for activists and concerned citizens from many countries to attempt to define their commonalities, share their experiences and analyses, and build their collective strength (see Box 10.4). In the past, the isolation of struggles for land and resources from those in other countries, and their isolation from concerned citizens in developed countries have contributed to their defeat. These constraints are beginning to be overcome due to a fusion between local and global activism and the emergence of a global civil society. The barriers of time and space which have formerly been effective in separating the mass of people from each other are increasingly less formidable. The social mobilization of marginalized groups and their connection with other like-minded people in other parts of the world is increasing.

People negatively affected by the policies of international economic institutions such as the World Bank, the International Monetary Fund, and World Trade Organization are increasingly mobilizing to influence the structure and policies of the institutions. As a result of this pressure, World Bank projects, for example, now include environmental assessments, attention to gender issues in development, and considerations of core labour standards

(O'Brien *et al.* 2000). Nevertheless, while the global justice movement may be united by the goals of social justice, environmentalism, and gender equity, serious differences divide broad segments of the movement. While some segments are simply trying to reform the most serious abuses of development policies others reject conventional ideas of the development project altogether and are searching for an alternative form of development.

KEY POINTS

- In addition to development policies, many people power movements address problems concerning patriarchy, corruption, violence, and traditional deference to authority.

- Increasingly local social movement organizations concerned with development issues are networked into a transnational global justice movement.

- Methods of nonviolent action have shown to be effective in promoting beneficial social change.

- Problems with a social movements approach to social change include the difficulty of aggregating diverse groups into a coordinated movement, maintaining mobilization over extended periods, the co-option of parts of the movement, the institutionalization of the movement, and the vulnerability of challenges to state repression.

Conclusion

From the 1980s onward, a wave of pro-democracy people power movements challenged authoritarian regimes throughout the developing world. Many of these movements contributed to democratization. Less dramatically, but perhaps more importantly, people power movements have also emerged throughout the developing world to challenge the dominant development logic and neo-liberal economic policies. Drawing on human rights, environmentalism, and sustainable development discourses these movements are increasingly becoming linked through transnational networks.

One way of looking at people power movements that challenge the dominant model of development is that they are simply part of a long, but ultimately futile resistance to the development logic. That is, they can be viewed as anachronistic movements against the inevitable process of capitalist modernization. However, there are reasons to believe that the dominant development logic, which has transformed the world, has inherent contradictions that humanity will have to confront sooner rather than later. What is novel about the current global situation is that there are ever fewer isolated areas for those alienated from the land to migrate to, many cities are no longer able to absorb any more people

evicted from land in the countryside, and environmental degradation has become a major global social problem. In an increasingly populous world with environmental limits to economic growth, humanity confronts a trade-off between expanding material consumption of the wealthy and meeting the basic needs of all.

So, another way of looking at struggles like these is that they are the crucibles in which alternative forms of development that are more sustainable and more democratic are being nurtured, forged, or re-created. Rather than being futile actions against the inexorable march to development, they are seed beds for the emergence of alternative development paradigms. Such alternatives emphasize the use of land and resources to promote the welfare of local communities rather than for the profit of corporations or government officials, and put a premium on using land and resources in a sustainable manner. Significantly, rather than engaging in conventional politics or taking up arms against the state, people power movements have tended to adopt methods of nonviolent action in their struggles, which have been shown to be effective in promoting beneficial social change.

? QUESTIONS

1   What are social movements and what do you understand by 'people power', and how do these differ from other forms of political organization?

2   Why have aggrieved groups turned away from both conventional politics and violent politics to the 'alternative' politics of social movement networks and nonviolent action to promote social change?

3   What methods of nonviolent action have been implemented by social movement organizations to promote democratization, land reform, and sustainable development?

4   How do the models of development envisioned by people power movements differ from those promoted by states, corporations, and international economic institutions?

5 Are the encampments in Bangkok organized by the Assembly of the Poor justified? Are MST activists in Brazil justified in trespassing and occupying privately owned land?

6 What opportunities and constraints does globalization pose for social movements and transnational activism?

GUIDE TO FURTHER READING

■ **Bryant, R. L., and Bailey, S. (1997),** *Third World Political Ecology* **(New York and London: Routledge).** Explains how unequal power relations are central to the environmental problems of the developing world.

■ *Ecologist, The* **(1993), 'Whose Common Future? Reclaiming the Commons' (Philadelphia: New Society Publishers).** A critical overview of the history of enclosures. Provides justifications and discusses strategies for reclaiming the commons.

■ **Harvey, D. (2003),** *The New Imperialism* **(Oxford: Oxford University Press).** Examines the current mode of capitalist expropriation—accumulation by dispossession, and discusses potential strategies of resistance.

■ **Khagram, S. (2004),** *Dams and Development: Transnational Struggles for Water and Power* **(Ithaca, NY: Cornell University Press).** Examines resistance to large dam projects and challenges to the dominant conceptions of development.

■ **Martin, B. (2001),** *Nonviolence versus Capitalism* **(London: War Resisters' International).** Discusses and assesses social movements that implement methods of nonviolent action to challenge capitalist economic relations and to develop alternatives.

■ **McMichael, P. (2004),** *Development and Social Change: A Global Perspective*, **3rd edn. (Thousand Oaks, Calif.: Pine Forge Press).** Explains how development came to be institutionalized as an international project in the post-colonial era and how the project of development is being revised by neo-liberal globalization and contested by social movements.

■ **Rossett, P. M., Patel, R., and Courville, M. (eds.) (2006),** *Promised Land: Competing Visions of Agrarian Reform* **(Oakland: Food First Books).** A critique of market-led agrarian reform. Examines current popular struggles for agrarian reform and food sovereignty.

■ **Schock, K. (2005),** *Unarmed Insurrections: People Power Movements in Nondemocracies* **(Minneapolis and London: University of Minnesota Press).** Examines several people power movements that mobilized to promote democratization in authoritarian regimes in the late twentieth century.

■ **Shiva, V. (1997),** *Biopiracy: The Plunder of Nature and Society* **(Cambridge, Mass.: South End Press).** A critical examination of the commercialization of science and the commodification of life and nature.

■ ——**(2005),** *Earth Democracy: Justice, Sustainability, and Peace* **(Cambridge, Mass.: South End Press).** Examines the history of the enclosure of the commons, and discusses alternative ways of organizing the economy and society.

WEB LINKS

● **www.ektaparishad.org** (*Ekta Parishad*, Bhopal, India) Contains information about the history and activities of Ekta Parishad (United Forum), a Gandhian land rights movement in India.

● **www.mst.org.br** (*Movimento dos Trabalhadores Rurais Sem Terra*, São Paulo, Brazil) Contains information about the history and activities of the MST, the Landless Rural Workers movement that promotes land reform and food sovereignty in Brazil.

● **www.irn.org** (International Rivers Network, Berkeley, United States) This organization opposes destructive dams and the model of development they advance. Works with environmental and human rights movements around the world.

● **www.forumsocialmundial.org.br** (*Fórum Social Mundial*, São Paulo, Brazil) Website for the World Social Forum, an annual event in which members of social movements and NGOs meet to discuss alternative forms of politics and development and strategies for attaining them. Provides information on the World Social Forum and other social forums held in different regions of the world.

● **www.focusweb.org** (Focus on the Global South, Bangkok, Thailand) An NGO that engages in policy research, advocacy, activism, and grass-roots capacity-building in an effort to promote alternative models of development. Contains research reports and position papers on development issues.

ONLINE RESOURCE CENTRE

For additional material and resources, see the Online Resource Centre at:
www.oxfordtextbooks.co.uk/orc/burnell2e/

PART 3

State and Society

The heading of Part Three reverses the order of the two terms contained in the previous part to signify that Part Three focuses chiefly on the institutions of state and their importance to society. In politics, institutions matter. The state is not merely one among many political institutions but historically has been the pre-eminent focus of attention. In the modern world, under the impact of rapid social, economic, technological, and other changes taking place at the global, regional, and sub-state levels the exact nature, role, and significance of the state are continually evolving. For sure the term 'governance' has taken a hold in recent development discourse and in globalization theory too, to convey a wider set of governing arrangements than those that are controlled by states either individually or collectively. Nevertheless it would be no less foolish to suggest the end of the state is nigh and to dissolve its analysis into a soup of exogenous actors and currents—domestic or international—than it is to ignore how those actors and currents set limits on and provide options for what government can do.

This part has two main aims. The *first* is to explore what the state means in a developing world context and how it differs from the state in more developed countries. Can one framework accommodate all the varieties of state formation including the special manifestations such as state failure?

The *second* aim is to show how the governance capabilities of states and even more so the kind of political regime—the relationship between the institutions of government and society—have become a major focus for political inquiry. In many parts of the world there have been significant changes especially in the last two decades or so. This part is essential for enabling us to address important questions about how far the state in the developing world should be held responsible for dealing with fundamental developmental issues. And for determining whether it is equipped to resolve pressing issues such as those affecting the economy, welfare, the environment, and human rights. For instance what is the relationship between democracy or democratization and development? Is there a specific sequence in which these must arise, or is the situation more like that of chicken and egg? And how are such themes as governance and policy convergence connected to globalization?

While Part Three ranges over these issues, the more detailed policy matters that are bound up with them will comprise the substance of Part Four—which is best consulted after and alongside the material in Part Three. The illustrations in Part Three are widely drawn from around the developing world. By comparison case studies of countries selected to illustrate specific issues and themes can be found in Part Five. For example Chapter 22 investigates Pakistan, Nigeria, and Mexico to offer contrasting types and trajectory of political regime and processes of regime transformation. Readers are encouraged to read the introduction to Part Five and consult the relevant case studies alongside the chapters in Part Three. In addition, for more extended discussion of the contribution that party politics specifically makes to politics in developing countries, readers should turn to the Online Resource Centre where there is a specially written comparative examination of the role of political parties by Vicky Randall.

11 Theorizing the State

ADRIAN LEFTWICH

Chapter Contents

- Introduction: Institutions, Politics, and the State
- The Modern State
- The State in the Developing World: Provenance and Forms
- The State in the Developing World: Characteristics, Features, and Types
- The State in the Developing World: Facing the Challenges
- Conclusion

Overview

Explanation of successful and failed states in the developing world requires an understanding of the provenance, characteristics, and functions of the modern state as it evolved in what is now the developed world. This chapter first explores the nature of institutions and, in particular, the modern state as a set of political institutions of rule, geared to the organization and continuous management of economic development. Second, it analyses the emergence and features of the state in what is now the developed world; and, third, it investigates the transportation of the modern state to the now developing world and the consequences of that. The central argument is that the characteristics of any state, anywhere, are largely defined by its relations with the economy and society which it reflects and both represents and dominates, in its historical, regional, and international context. The chapter argues that political processes in many developing countries are moving towards the establishment of state institutions of rule that may provide more stability and effectiveness for economic development and greater participation for citizens in decision-making processes. But the process is very difficult, slow, and uneven.

Introduction: Institutions, Politics, and the State

Institutions

Human societies cannot endure, prosper, or—especially—develop without broadly agreed and appropriate rules and conventions governing the conduct of social, economic, and political affairs, and about how human and other resources are to be used and distributed. Such sets of rules are what political scientists mean by institutions. In essence, institutions are collections of (broadly) agreed norms, rules, procedures, and routines—whether they are formally established and written down (in law or by decree), as with constitutions, or whether they are informal understandings embedded in the culture (March and Olsen 1989: 21–6). Essentially, institutions direct and constrain human interaction. All societies have them; they must. The different institutional spheres often overlap (and sometimes conflict to produce undesired outcomes), and include social institutions (governing social interaction and behaviour), economic institutions (the customs, rules, and procedures governing economic behaviour, ranging from silent barter to rules governing stock-market behaviour)—and political institutions (governing relations of power).

Political institutions and the modern state

Political scientists take a special interest in the last of these institutional spheres: that of politics and power, the sphere in which the *processes and practices of rule*, of *governing*, or of a particular form of *institutionalized domination*, emerged. The *forms of rule* expressed in different political systems, or *polities*, have varied widely. For instance, some polities initially involved only very basic forms of localized village headship or leadership; others, perhaps starting with such local and limited forms of rule and power, subsequently evolved at different speeds into steeper and more extensive hierarchies of centralized control and power over an increasing territorial space. The emergence of centralized polities (which some theorists refer to as early states) sometimes expanded over wide areas to encompass other societies so that they came to constitute what have been called 'centralized bureaucratic empires'.

However, the immense range of historical political systems which gave expression to the different forms and distributions of power has shrunk dramatically since the sixteenth century when one type of polity emerged in Europe and came to be the dominant political form of the recent and contemporary world: *the state* or, more accurately, the *modern state*. Though it varies in its forms, the characteristics of the modern state need to be distinguished from earlier polities, or 'non-modern' states, such as ancient city-states, feudal states, pre-modern, early modern, or absolutist states or even 'princely states'.

The emergence of the modern state in Europe was a largely endogenous process, occurring within the geography and history of particular regions in the course of conflict, competition, and, especially, consolidation among them. To illustrate, in late fifteenth-century Europe there were some 500 independent political units, but by 1900 this had shrunk to about twenty-five. Such states, in turn, came to shape the histories and geographies of the emerging countries which they both represented and dominated. And from within this history of European state formation, there developed, from the fifteenth century, outward thrusts of discovery, conquest, and control, loosely called imperialism and colonialism. These imperial processes carved out new 'countries' (in most cases which had not existed beforehand), they established new institutions of rule in the form of the colonial state (which either suppressed or used and sometimes transformed existing institutions of rulership), and drew such countries (or parts of them) into different kinds of largely subordinate economic relations with the metropolitan countries of the increasingly dominant 'West'.

KEY POINTS

- All human societies require institutions to govern and promote their collective affairs.

- Institutions, which may be informal or formal, are best understood as collections of rules, procedures, practices, and routines as well as norms and conventions.

- The emergence of specialist political institutions represents the differentiation of political systems or polities.

- The most recent and dominant form has been the modern state whose origins were primarily European.

- This form was carried outwards by European imperialism and colonialism, and imposed on diverse societies, or adopted and adapted by them. The external provenance of the state in many developing countries has been a critical factor in shaping and influencing their particular forms and the politics associated with them.

The Modern State

Traditional polities

The modern state was the product of slow evolution from prior political systems, or polities, but by the nineteenth century its central features were clear. The German sociologist Max Weber (1964) theorized those features of the 'modern' state which distinguished it from prior 'traditional' institutions of rule, or systems of authority. These earlier forms, he suggested, like the 'patrimonial' form of authority as he called it, were characterized by two overriding features.

First, there is the absence of any sharp distinction between the *rulers* and the *institutions of rule*. This was typical of the absolutist rule of some European monarchs well into the eighteenth century as well as elsewhere in East Asia and Middle America. For instance, Louis XIV, the king of France in the mid-seventeenth century, made the point with great effect when he is alleged to have said to the *parlement* of Paris in April 1655, '*L'État c'est moi*' (I am the state).

The second defining feature of traditional forms of rule was the relative absence of open, meritocratic entry, autonomy, independence, and security of tenure for the officials who surrounded the rulers. Unlike officials in the ideal-typical bureaucracy of the modern state, they were essentially the personal staff of the ruler, often paid by him or her, and with the more or less explicit requirement of personal loyalty to him or her rather than to the state or its constitution.

Defining the modern state

Many characteristics and functions distinguish the modern state. But it was the development of institutions of rule and governing which were formally separated from not just the rulers but the officials who ran them, on the one hand, and the citizenry, on the other hand, that was central in the shift from what Weber called 'traditional' forms of rule and authority, including patrimonial polities, to the modern state. Held, McGrew, Goldblatt, and Perraton (1999: 45) claim the modern state is a set of 'political apparatuses, distinct from both ruler and ruled, with supreme jurisdiction over a demarcated area, backed by a claim to a monopoly of coercive power, and enjoying legitimacy as a result of a minimum level of support or loyalty from their citizens'. Within this compact definition can be found all the essential elements of the complex set of institutions that make up the modern state:

Public institutions: the institutions of the modern state are all 'public' institutions and include 'the government' and legislature, the courts, civil service, army and police, plus any state-owned agencies. All of these are formally differentiated from other institutions (especially private and non-state institutions) and individuals, and also from the incumbents of the offices and the citizens or subjects over whom they exercise authority.

Sovereignty and hegemony: the institutions of the modern state and its laws have authority over a particular demarcated geographical area and apply in theory to everyone within its territory.

Formal monopoly of violence: the modern state has a monopoly of the legitimate use of violence and it is, or should be, the dominant agency of rule and law, whether democratic or not, in principle superordinate over all others. In practice, in the course of their history, most modern states have struggled at times to achieve that dominance (Bates 2001). And some, till very recently, have continued to do so. An example is the Peruvian state's battle to subdue the *Sendero Luminoso* guerrilla movement which exercised considerable power over parts of the country in the 1970s and 1980s.

Impartial bureaucracy: the bureaucracy is (theoretically) impersonal, impartial, and neutral and does not make law. But in practice, policy-making is much more complex, and, increasingly, specialist bureaucratic input into policy-making is the norm. Nonetheless, the central characteristic that distinguishes the modern state from prior forms of rule is the principle, at least, of *relative* independence and autonomy of the public service from both the elected political elites and parties and also from the public. Moreover, the offices of state officials, whether constitutional monarchs, presidents, ministers, legislators, judges, police, or civil servants belong to the state, not to them personally. It is a fundamental assumption of the modern state that these public offices and powers should not be used for *private* gain by the incumbents of such offices (what would normally be called corruption). Occupancy of such offices should entail no powers of private patronage nor be used for the support of any particular private client base (clientelism), whether personal, regional, ethnic, or economic.

These characteristics are of course ideal-typical. No state in the modern world has been, or can be, found which fulfils them to perfection. And while many theorists may agree on this limited set of characteristics of the modern state, the most contentious issues of debate and interpretation in political science revolve around other central issues such as: is the modern state 'neutral'? Can it be? Do classes dominate its policy output and, if so, which ones? Does the state have its own interests? What should its role in economy and society be? How far should the state intervene in the 'private' life of its subjects or should it be limited or constrained in what it does by constitutionally defined bills of rights?

Modern states differ with respect to many other variables, for example their *historical traditions* (some have longer continuous traditions of centralized rule than others, as in England, Russia, or Japan); their *structural properties* (for example whether unitary or, as in India and Nigeria, federal, and hence how state power is distributed regionally); whether they are formally *democratic or not* and for how long; their *electoral systems* and/or *consultative patterns* (and how these influence state power and policy-making); and the nature and extent of their *legitimacy* in the perception of their subjects.

The modern state: imperatives, functions, and challenges

As the modern state consolidated and proliferated through the nineteenth and twentieth centuries, more countries began to adopt its broad template as their system of rule. For example, many Latin American countries adopted and adapted from France and (to a lesser extent) the United States in shaping their constitutions (rules of the political game) as they gained independence from Spain and Portugal between 1811 and 1900.

But the really central point is that the modern state emerged in the course of the 'great transformation' from agrarian to industrial societies (mainly in Europe) and in the consequential requirements for appropriate institutional and regulatory frameworks and functions to facilitate and extend this. It was both product and agent of that transformation. Indeed it is essential to understand that the fundamental defining role and function of the modern state has been to promote, organize, protect, and sustain this economic and social transformation to industrialism—and beyond into the 'post-industrial' era. In the nineteenth and twentieth century the histories of the now industrial powers, and more recent modern history of the contemporary developing world, shows that successful and effective modern states and successful economies go hand in hand. This process of state formation was of course intensified through the competitive economic, military, and other forms of nationalism that it promoted, and by the turbulent socio-political changes associated with the economic transformation. And by the early twentieth century four critical issues had come to confront the modern state. These were: defence against external attack and internal security, the promotion and protection of the economy, democratization, and the associated demand for state provision of welfare. The manner in which each state dealt with them acted to define its character and its relations with the society it claimed both to represent and to manage.

First, with regard to defence, the period 1850–1939 saw an intensification of what has been called despotic power, that is the power to control and suppress, as opposed to infrastructural power, the power to penetrate and transform society (Mann 1986: 169–70; Weiss and Hobson 1995; Scott 1998). But, second, as indicated above, national economic development also was central to the emergence and defence of the modern state, and was closely associated with the competitive nationalisms of the nineteenth century. Thus successful modern economic growth and successful modern states with influence that extends beyond their borders have been inextricably linked. And there is nothing that sums this up better than the slogan 'National Wealth, Military Strength' (often translated as 'rich country, strong army') adopted by the new post-Meiji elites in Japan after 1870.

In pursuit of these goals, most of today's leading industrial economies used state-directed industrial, trade, and technological policies (Chang 2002: 58 and *passim*) to get ahead, to stay ahead (as in the case of Britain), or to catch up as Germany, Japan, and the United States began to do in the nineteenth century. Three broad strategies, or models, were used (though each contained a variety of distinctive forms). The first was the Anglo–American and Western European model which involved the state ensuring four prime conditions for the promotion of private, market-driven growth, as argued by Douglas S North (1990): securing property rights, establishing a fair and efficient judicial system, setting out an open and understood system of rules and regulations, and facilitating market entry and functioning, although at times state action has gone much further than this as in the depression years in the USA and in post-war reconstruction in Europe. The second model has been the Soviet model, of forced-march top-down industrialization, pioneered from the 1920s and involving pervasive state ownership, control, and management of the economy, and the mobilization by the state, not the market, of resources (including human ones) in pursuit of transformative objectives. The third model is essentially the East Asian model of the developmental state, pioneered in Japan after 1870, and especially after the 1920s, which has been replicated in some other countries like Korea and Taiwan (Leftwich 1995). This involved a much closer symbiosis between state and private sector (see Chapter 23b below) and has sometimes been called 'managed capitalism' or 'governing the market'.

Modern states in the developing world have sought to adopt modified versions of the three different strategies outlined above in their pursuit of economic growth through industrialization. Crucially, however, successful intervention along any of the strategic paths has only occurred when the appropriate political coalitions and distributions of power underpinning the state have allowed rather than hindered growth-promoting institutions and strategies. This has been one of the key differences between the older 'modern states' and the new 'modern states' of the developing world.

Finally, with regard to the challenges of democratization and redistribution, Huntington (1991) identified three great 'waves' of democratization (between 1828 and 1926, between 1943 and 1962, and from 1974 to the present). In each, dominant state elites responded to democratic pressures in different ways, hence shaping the character of the polity, depending on whether and to what extent they saw their interests being threatened by such demands. Where democratic progress occurred, the associated deepening and extension of civil society had the effect of redistributing some political power through the institutional forms of electoral, bargaining, and consultative processes. Moreover, the growth of powerful and increasingly well-organized labour movements in particular meant that few states in the developed world could ignore the demand for redistributionist programmes, for example through taxation policy, welfare provision (health, old age, and education for instance), and wage-level agreements. In consequence, those societies managed effectively by modern states are mainly characterized by levels of income inequality far less extreme than in many parts of the developing world (see Chapter 5).

KEY POINTS

- Modern states are the political institutions of rule which are in principle differentiated and distinct from both the rulers and the ruled.

- The modern state emerged, evolved, consolidated, and was borrowed as the set of centralized and organizing institutions of rule whose central function was to manage national transitions from agrarian to industrial society, and to sustain economic growth.

- Historically, the modern state has been characterized typically by its public institutions, its sovereignty and hegemony, its formal monopoly of legitimate coercion (violence), and its theoretically impartial bureaucracy.

- Though different states adopted different strategies, successful economic growth and successful states have without exception been inextricably linked.

- In promoting economic growth and development, modern states have had to provide defence and ensure law and order, respond to demands for a wider set of civic and democratic rights and manage some redistribution of resources through tax and welfare arrangements.

- The broad strategy adopted in the pursuit of economic growth has depended crucially on the character of the political forces and coalitions underpinning state power, which in turn has influenced the achievement of developmental goals.

The State in the Developing World: Provenance and Forms

Introduction

Most of the conditions and capabilities associated with the state's emergence in the now developed world have been largely absent in the developing world. In short, the formation of modern states in colonial and post-colonial contexts was not geared to the development of institutions of rule directed at promoting economic growth or transformative development, as occurred in Europe and elsewhere, whether on a capitalist, socialist, or mixed economy basis. Moreover, most of the challenges that those earlier states had to meet—especially those of democratic pressures and redistributive demands—have thus far exceeded the capability of many of the newer states. And, crucially, apart from some very important exceptions, this is explained by the quite diverse political forces and coalitions formed during or after the colonial era and which set up, inherited, adapted, or battled for control of the institutions of the modern state. Simply stated, these political forces, representing varying kinds of socio-economic elites and interests, seldom had the interest, the will, or the power to establish or encourage growth-promoting institutions in accordance with any of the three models sketched above. This is why so many states in the contemporary developing world have been associated with weak or uneven developmental performances. But before proceeding further, two important introductory points should be made.

First, the problems facing these states are, in principle, no different from those which faced states and societies in the developed world, though they may differ in timing and context. These problems have been (and remain) essentially those of how to establish and sustain the institutions of rule which promote economic development, within or outside democratic polities, whether state-led or market-led, in the face of increasing pressures for democratization and redistribution, in a globalizing political economy.

Second, the kinds of modern state institution in post-colonial developing countries varied widely and were everywhere shaped by the interaction of four main factors: the nature of the pre-colonial polities; the economic purposes of colonial rule; the characteristics of the colonial state institutions and the socio-political groups which dominated them; and the manner of incorporation of pre-colonial political processes and institutions in the systems of colonial and post-colonial rule. Accordingly, the contemporary developing world is at least as diverse as were those societies in which the modern state emerged. Nevertheless there are some major, common underlying themes too.

The modern state in the developing world: provenance

While the modern state in the now developed world grew largely through complex *internal* political processes in the course of the great transformations from agrarian to industrial societies, most states in the developing world owe their existence (and indeed their very borders) to the geographical definitions and institutional impositions of the colonial era. With few exceptions, the provenance of states in the developing world has largely been *external*, and few of them developed endogenously from prior local polities and systems of rule. In Asia, the exceptions include Korea, Indonesia, and Thailand where some continuity can be traced back to prior local (absolutist, monarchical, and imperial) systems and institutions of centralized rule, as in Egypt and Ethiopia in the case of Africa. In Latin America, the main pre-colonial political institutions, especially the great centralized tribute-extracting empires of the Aztecs (Mexico) and the Incas (Peru), were extinguished by the Spanish conquest from the early sixteenth century, though cultural legacies remain even today.

Although the patterns of colonial state institutions varied widely across time and space (Young 1994: 244–81), they everywhere left very important influences on the politics and state structures after independence. Everywhere, and almost without exception, the project of colonial rule and control was undertaken initially for the benefit of the metropolitan countries or their particular interests.

Colonial states: imposed borders and the institutional patterns of rule

External design and imposition of 'national' boundaries

Perhaps the most far-reaching influence and impact has been the external shaping of geographical boundaries and institutional structures, the most dramatic illustration being the scramble for Africa, which produced the national boundaries of Africa today. (See Box 11.1.) Of course there were no 'countries' with formally defined 'national' boundaries before this in Africa: political boundaries were often vague and porous. What there were, however, was a wide range of 'multiple, overlapping and alternative collective identities' (Berman 1998: 310) expressed in an equally wide range of institutional political arrangements. Such was the artificiality of the new, imposed boundaries that some 44 per cent of those still existing today are straight lines (Herbst 2000: 75), representing lines drawn cartographically on open maps. There was almost no indigenous definition of geographical boundaries, nor were any major 'national' movements, or 'nationalist' sentiments, involved in establishing the boundaries of modern African nation-states. The Latin American experience was not much

different, where the new states were carved from the huge Vice Royalties of the colonial system of rule in the course of the struggles for independence in the nineteenth century. Led largely by the conservative *criollos* (colonial born Spaniards) the new states in consequence expressed political and socio-economic relations which even today reflect deep and profound inequalities between a small (and very rich) elite and a large (and very poor) mass, illustrated particularly well by Brazil (a former Portuguese possession), now one of the most unequal societies in the world.

In Asia, a similar pattern occurred and the Indian subcontinent provides the best example, where British rule brought diverse ethnic and religious communities, often tense with communal rivalries, not to mention over 500 Princely States, together in colonial India. But at independence, the country

---

BOX 11.1

The Colonial Impact in Africa

In Africa, large tracts of land were claimed by European powers as their possessions, either as colonies or protectorates or as in the case of King Leopold of Belgium, as private property in the form of the Congo Free State. The distribution arising out of the powers' scramble for Africa was formally recognized by their representatives at the Congress of Berlin, 1884–5. In all of this Britain, France, Germany, and Portugal paid no regard to the enormous differences among the different African societies that ranged from small-scale self-governing hunting and gathering bands to large, hierarchical political systems as in the empires of Mali, Ghana, and Songhay in West Africa. Peoples with diverse cultures, religions, languages, and political systems who had previously lived alongside one another, sometimes peacefully and sometimes in violent conflict, but without formal boundaries, were now pulled together into entirely artificially created 'nation' states.

was divided between India and Pakistan, with East Pakistan (later to become independent as Bangladesh) being separated by a great chunk of India from West Pakistan. Indonesia emerged from Dutch rule as an improbable 'nation-state' of about 13,000 islands stretching for about 3,500 miles from west to east, containing diverse linguistic, cultural, and religious communities (see map on page 400 in Chapter 20a). Cambodia, Korea, Thailand, Myanmar, and, to some extent, Malaysia have been notable exceptions to this pattern, each reflecting closer lineages with some historical polity.

Extractive rather than developmental purposes of rule

The purpose of imperial control or rule was not developmental in the manner of the emerging modern states of Europe. On the contrary, all the major colonial powers (and often the early private companies that acted for them) saw the extraction of riches, raw materials, and taxes as their primary objective.

External design and imposition of the institutions of rule

In trying to understand the problems and failures of many states in the developing world it is fundamental to recognize that these extractive purposes shaped the kind of institutions of rule, which in turn formed the foundations for the states after independence. In so far as the institutions of colonial rule can be termed 'colonial *states*' (Young 1994), they were essentially states of extraction, and not aimed at promoting, and organizing national economic development. With the exception of Japanese rule in Korea (Kohli 2004), no colonial institutions of rule bore any resemblance to any of the three models sketched above. In short, throughout the colonial world, and until well into the twentieth century, the institutions of colonial rule and control were authoritarian, elitist, and geared to maintaining high levels of extraction for the benefit of the metropolitan powers (Box 11.2).

BOX 11.2

The Extractive Nature of Imperial Rule

The Spanish conquistador and conqueror of Mexico, Hernando Cortés, in the sixteenth century, is reputed to have said 'I came to get gold, not to till the soil, like a peasant'. In the Caribbean, plantations exploiting unfree labour (first, indentured servants and then almost entirely slaves) were established for the production and export of cotton, tobacco, and especially sugar. In Indonesia, the 'culture system' of the Dutch, first under the Dutch East India Company and then through formal colonial rule, required Indonesians to deliver set amounts of spices to the authorities. Likewise, the ruthless requirements of King Leopold's Free State in the Congo demanded that rubber and ivory be collected, on pain of often cruel punishment (amputation of hands was not unknown) by villagers. Elsewhere, throughout colonial Africa raw materials such as palm oil, beeswax, wild rubber, cocoa, and, later, tea, plus diamonds, gold, and copper flowed back to Europe.

Intensities and paradoxes of colonial institutions

The institutions of colonial rule displayed something of a paradox. At the centre, power was generally held very firmly, 'despotic' power that is: the capacity to deploy force and coercion (Mann 1986: 169–70) in order to suppress and control. Challenges to colonial rule were usually put down with sometimes spectacular brutality, commonly with the assistance of locally recruited indigenous police and soldiers. The real locus of despotic power was largely confined to areas of economic or strategic importance—such as the cities, mines, plantations, or ports.

Yet there was seldom much infrastructural power (Mann 1986: 169–70)—the capacity of the colonial institutions of rule to penetrate, administratively, the length and breadth of the country and to use

BOX 11.3

The Authoritarianism of Colonial Rule

Throughout the colonial world until well into the twentieth century the institutions of rule were authoritarian, in some places harsher than others. In Latin America, for example, Viceroys and their officials answerable to the King of Spain and his Council of the Indies ruled over vast areas. But it was the institutions of control in the silver mines and, especially, the *latifundio* or *hacienda*—the great estates of largely coerced labour—that ruled by force at the local level. In the British Caribbean, governors, appointed from London, ruled over systems of slave labour. Long after the abolition of slavery and the slave trade, the descendants of slaves had little effective say in the institutions of rule, until well into the twentieth century. Similar patterns could be found in all of colonial sub-Saharan Africa, where governors, responsible to London, Paris, or Brussels, with executive councils made up mainly of officials, ran vast territories. British rule in India, French rule in Indochina, and Dutch rule in Indonesia was little different in this concentration of power in the hands of colonial officials, until the early twentieth century when consultative and elementary electoral processes began to be introduced at local or provincial levels.

that capacity to facilitate programmes of economic change and development (Migdal 1988b: 4). For example, large areas of non-urban Latin America, in the Amazon and the Andes and especially in the huge rural hinterlands of countries like Mexico, Brazil, and Argentina, though formally under Spanish or Portuguese colonial rule, remained far beyond effective control of the centre and were run in effect by the *patrons* and *hacendados* of the great estates and the emerging *caudillos*, the local strongmen (see *caudillismo*). The same was true for much of sub-Saharan Africa and large parts of South-East Asia. This lack of infrastructural power should not be at all surprising, given that the central purpose of European colonial rule was extractive, not developmental or transformative, and much of colonial rule was done on a very limited

budget and a minimal administrative presence. But this dearth of infrastructural power of the colonial state created a legacy that characterizes many new, modern states in the post-colonial world, while despotic power—protecting the new elites which took over after independence—remained pronounced in urban centres. (See Box 11.3.)

Because of weak infrastructural power, all colonial regimes came to depend on local-level 'bosses', 'big men', brokers, or oligarchs, some of whom derived their power originally from their traditional positions (such as the *caciques* of Latin America and—the sometimes artificially created—'headmen' or 'chiefs' in colonial Africa). The net overall effect of this was generally to constrain the emergence of effective modern states capable of establishing national institutions of rule for the promotion of national economic development. Indeed, the weakness of its infrastructural penetration required the central institutions of the state always to bargain and deal with the local brokers—often later institutionalized in federal political systems after independence, as in India and Nigeria and Brazil—thereby establishing complex, reciprocal networks of political influence and patronage in and around the institutions of the state, and hence imposing serious constraints on their capacity and autonomy (Barton 1997: 49; Kohli, 2004). The pattern could not be better expressed than in Parry's description of this political process in Latin America, in his account of the legacy of colonial rule there:

> This is *caudillismo* or *caciquismo*: the organisation of political life by local 'bosses' whose power and influence derives from personal ascendancy, family or regional association. In most countries the concentration of formal authority at the centre, the weakness of lawfully constituted provincial and local authority, leave wide scope for the activities of such people. The real effectiveness of central government may depend upon the nature of the bargain which it can strike with those who wield local influence and power; while the prestige of the *cacique* (local boss) may be enhanced by the 'pull' which he can exert in the capital.

(Parry 1966: 371–2)

Patron–client relations and the politics of the new states

This particular 'organization of political life' was the context within which patterns of patronage and patron–client relations became so pervasive in the post-colonial world, frustrating the emergence and consolidation of the institutions of the modern state. Patron–client relations have typified human polities, before the modern state, almost everywhere. The basic characteristic of the institution of patron–client relations is of an unequal power relation between patrons ('big men' in African terminology) who are powerful, rich, and high in status, on the one hand, and clients ('small boys' in African terminology) who lack power, wealth, or status, on the other hand. The patron–client relationship is reciprocal but uneven in that the patron has control of, or access to, resources and opportunities which he (it is usually a male) can provide for the client in return for deference, support, loyalty, and (in the context of post-independence electoral politics) votes. Patrons have an interest in maintaining their client base by being good 'big men', that is by delivering the goods, while clients (depending on the particular pattern of the relationship) may have some freedom to move from one patron to another from whom they might expect a better deal.

Clearly the rules defining the institution of patronage are entirely at odds with the rules underpinning the modern state, and bear a striking resemblance to the pre-state European institutions of patrimonial rule, discussed by Weber. But as societies in the colonial world achieved independence from metropolitan powers, and as attempts were made to build modern states, the principles and practices of patronage quickly established themselves in the interstices of the new institutions of rule, from top to bottom, thereby weakening state capacity and undermining its autonomy. Thus in Latin America, even under the 'bureaucratic-authoritarian regimes' of the 1960s and 1970s, whether on the left or the right politically, the regimes were constrained by the immense regional and local power of the old bosses, oligarchies, and political elites, in country and town, who could contain if not derail reform even under the toughest of military regimes, as in Brazil after 1965. And in Africa, where patrimonialism pre-dated the colonial impact and where, at independence, the commercial, capitalist, or landed classes were small and weak, it was almost inevitable that the resources of the state would be the target that competing groups would seek to capture after independence, to feed and fuel their patronage links to 'friends and followers', whether of a regional, kin, or ethnic character. It was little different in much of south and South-East Asia during and after the colonial period.

Only in those few cases where revolutionary political movements seized state power and largely crushed prior elites and dominant classes, as in Cuba and (North) Vietnam, has the power of patronage been contained, though it has sometimes reappeared. Other exceptional cases, where electorally or militarily dominant elites have taken over and pursued national economic growth for purposes of national defence—the classic recipe for state formation and consolidation—include the developmental states of South Korea, Taiwan, and Singapore (see below).

KEY POINTS

- Most contemporary states in the developing world had their borders and main institutions imposed from without.

- The purpose and point of colonial rule and hence colonial institutions of state were extractive rather than developmental.

- The institutions of rule of the colonial state reflected these purposes, being characterized by generally authoritarian patterns, designed to promote extraction and the control of labour.

- Most colonial states were marked by the paradox of having strong 'despotic' (coercive) power and weak 'infrastructural' or transformative capacities.

- Many countries in the developing world achieved independence in circumstances where powerful economic and political forces in society exerted considerable regional and local influence and hence constrained dramatically the emergence of centralized, autonomous, and effective modern states.

- Colonial rule commonly built on, extended, and institutionalized patron–client relations, from top to bottom.

- In the post-colonial era, these institutions of patronage merged with the formal institutions of the modern state, commonly transforming it so that it has been unable to perform the central function of the modern state, namely the encouragement, promotion, and maintenance of economic growth.

- Many of the characteristics of pre-modern politics and 'patrimonial' polities were entrenched within the institutions of the modern state, leading to their characterization as neo-patrimonial states.

The State in the Developing World: Characteristics, Features, and Types

Introduction

It is now possible to assess the distinguishing structural characteristics of the modern state in the developing world. As before, there are two important qualifications: all states are different and generalization is difficult; and second, notwithstanding that observation, there are enough common pattern to warrant the following general points.

State characteristics in the developing world

Public institutions

One of the central characteristics of the modern state is that its institutions of rule are, or should be, essentially 'public', not owned or treated as their private domain by their incumbents. But one of the greatest problems in establishing modern states in the developing world has been to liberate public institutions from the private control of political leaders or from their 'capture' by special interests (Hellman, Jones, and Kaufmann 2000). The combined effects of patrimonial rule and patronage have been to erode the independence of public institutions—whether they be policy-making bodies,

courts, bureaucracies, armies, or other state-owned agencies—and the net effect has often been the informal privatization of public institutions in so far as they have been used to advance the private interests and clients of (usually) long-standing civilian or military leaders who have become heads of state. Essentially, this private use of public office and resources is the core definition of corruption. Certain heads of state, for instance Presidents Marcos and Suharto in the Philippines and Indonesia, Presidents Mobuto and Kenyatta of Zaire and Kenya; and Presidents Batista, Duvalier, and Somoza of Cuba, Haiti, and Nicaragua might quite easily have repeated the view of Louis XIV that 'L'État c'est moi' (I am the state). One of the key institutional instruments of the modern state in the developed world for protecting the public institutions (such as the civil service) has been the establishment of bodies such as independent civil service commissions, responsible for appointing, managing, and disciplining civil servants, thereby establishing clear differentiation from the political leadership and protecting bureaucrats from political interference. It has been profoundly difficult to establish and sustain the independence of such bodies in many developing countries.

Sovereignty, hegemony, and the monopoly of violence

Many states in the developing world have had great difficulty in establishing their hegemony and maintaining sovereignty within their borders. This is not only because of the power of local, private, or regional 'bosses' or 'influentials', but because the legitimacy of the state has been commonly challenged by various groups (ethnic, religious, cultural, or regional) which do not wish to be part of it, or by political opponents who refuse (for good or bad reasons) to accept the incumbent regime. Also, secessionist, irredentist, and civil wars have plagued the modern states of the developing world from Peru to the Philippines and from Angola to Afghanistan.

The earlier generation of modern states also faced these nation-building challenges; for instance state education policy in nineteenth-century France had as one of its prime concerns the building of a sense of national identity and unity. Indeed such issues persist to this day, as demonstrated in Basque separatism in Spain and Quebecois nationalism in Canada. However such challenges have arguably been much more severe in the developing world. While the present chapter has not identified nation-building as itself one of the core imperatives of the modern state, it must nonetheless be recognized that failure to achieve some degree of national, or multinational, integration, and cohesion will jeopardize the state-building project. In effect it is in Africa that the greatest incidence of conflicts of this kind and the adverse consequences are to be found. But there are many examples from elsewhere, such as Sri Lanka's long-running conflict between the Ceylonese majority in the south and Tamil minority in the north. Moreover, Indonesia struggled for many years to hold on to East Timor. Guerrilla movements, both urban and rural, have challenged the hegemony and legitimacy of a number of Latin American states since the 1960s. Many states in the developing world cannot claim a formal monopoly of violence, a characteristic which marks them off sharply from most states in the developed world

although not all of those have in recent years been free from all violent internal conflict, as Northern Ireland and Spain illustrate. In some societies, the collapse of the centre and the proliferation of non-state sources of violence and hence civil conflict have produced a series of failed or collapsed states (Rotberg 2004), as in Somalia, Afghanistan, and Cambodia at various points in their recent history (see Chapter 13).

Elsewhere, there are states characterized by what scholars such as Ross (1999) referred to as the 'resource curse'. This refers to states sometimes described as rentier states (Saudi Arabia is an example, described in Chapter 21b) where a major part of state revenues are derived from such sources as taxes (hence rents) on companies involved in the extraction of some valuable natural resource, such as oil (classically) or diamonds or copper. It is argued that at least two consequences can flow from this dependence on resource revenues. First, it undermines democracy or democratization by reducing the state's need to be accountable to its citizens. Secondly, as occurred in Sierra Leone, the presence of such resources (diamonds) can fuel intense conflict between groups determined to control the trade or the state in order to capture the rents, which further weakens and sometimes simply destroys the central power and authority of an already weak post-colonial state.

Thus, weakened from within by internal conflict and held down by low rates of economic growth, many states in the developing world have found it difficult to maintain sovereignty. Poor countries, especially, find it harder to maintain their sovereign independence in the international arena than rich countries. Economic strength not only provides for defensive (or offensive) military capacity but also reduces dependency and increases bargaining capacity in relations with public institutions like the World Bank, the International Monetary Fund, foreign governments, and with sources of private investment and finance. In particular, where foreign aid inflows form a significant part of government expenditure, de facto sovereignty is seriously reduced as aid donors come to apply increasingly stringent conditions. As a percentage of central government expenditures (World Bank 2002: 360–2), aid contributions have been very high in such countries as Kenya (16 per cent), Bangladesh (21 per cent), Burundi (40 per cent), Cameroon (31 per cent), Haiti (54 per cent), Madagascar (48 per cent), Nepal (46 per cent), Nicaragua (56 per cent), and Uganda (77 per cent). In other countries, with lower aid-dependency ratios, the figure has not been so high, such as Brazil (0.2 per cent), India (1.9 per cent), Morocco (6 per cent), Pakistan (5 per cent), and the Philippines (4 per cent). The second group have been better able to maintain a grip on their own policy-making, though this has not meant that they have escaped high levels of debt (see Chapter 3), another element that impacts on sovereignty.

Impartial bureaucracies

The pervasive legacy of patron–client relations, the culture of patrimonialism within the state, the absence of democratic accountability (even in its limited electoral form), low levels of economic growth, the power—and wealth—of special private interests through 'state capture', limited and often aid-dependent state budgets, low pay, high levels of state involvement in the economy, and hence much opportunity for discretionary bureaucratic decisions, have all contributed to the undermining of bureaucratic impartiality in many developing countries. Moreover, bureaucratic continuity in much of Latin America has been constrained by the politics of the appointive bureaucracy, a system whereby incoming governments are able to dismiss (often many thousands of) bureaucrats (especially senior ones) and appoint their 'own' men and women (Schneider 1999: 292–4). Corruption too erodes state capacity to pursue coherent and consistent policies of economic growth, undermines development, and institutionalizes unfairness. By discouraging political elites from taking the tough decisions that development requires and by disabling the bureaucratic institutions of the state from carrying out effective implementation, the consequences for development can be severe. The difficulties in achieving appropriate forms of land reform in many developing countries offer a prime example, of which President Bhutto's failed attempts at land reform in Pakistan in the 1970s provides an excellent case study (Herring 1979).

Effective and developmental states

Despite this generally bleak picture of state characteristics in the developing world there has also been a small group of *effective states* which must be mentioned. Chile for instance is generally perceived as having enjoyed an effective state for long periods of its history. Such states—whether democratic or not, and pursuing a wide range of economic policies—have usually been successful in promoting growth, reducing poverty, and enhancing overall welfare, even where their civil and human rights has not necessarily been good (though in some, like Chile today compared to President Pinochet's rule, it has improved greatly in the last decade with deepening democratization). Described more generally as 'developmental states' (Woo-Cumings 1999; Leftwich 2000), these states have taken both democratic and non-democratic forms, as well as pursuing both formally socialist and non-socialist paths. While most examples have been concentrated in East or South East Asia (such as South Korea, Taiwan, Singapore, Malaysia, China, and Vietnam), there are non-Asian examples

---

BOX 11.4

Types of State in the Developing World

In addition to the conventional classifications of states as democratic or authoritarian, federal or unitary, presidential or parliamentary, it is useful to think in terms of an additional and qualifying list of categories into which states in the developing world may be classified at different periods of their history: bureaucratic authoritarian states; patrimonial states; developmental states; rentier states; weak, failed and collapsed states. None of these display the characteristics of the ideal-typical 'Weberian' state of the West, though with the third wave of democratization (see Chapter 14) things have begun to change.

including Botswana, Mauritius, and Cuba. But in all cases, whether officially capitalist or socialist, democratic or non-democratic, the effectiveness of these states has been driven by political dynamics that have concentrated sufficient power, autonomy, capacity, and—sometimes—accountability at the centre to ensure the successful achievement of their developmental goals.

KEY POINTS

- States in developing countries vary greatly (see Box 11.4) but, in many, institutional and political legacies blur the boundaries between public institutions and private interests.

- Establishing institutions to monitor and control these boundaries have been difficult where there is no political will or capacity to do so.

- Many states in the developing world have found it difficult to maintain hegemony within their own territory, to protect their sovereignty and achieve a monopoly of violence.

- Impartial bureaucracies are less common in the developing than in the developed world.

- Patrimonialism and patronage, low levels of pay, and pervasive opportunities for discretionary behaviour all contribute to varying but sometimes intense patterns of corruption, thereby subverting the central purpose of the modern state: the promotion of economic growth and welfare.

- Both high levels of aid and rents from major extractive industries may undermine democratic processes.

The State in the Developing World: Facing the Challenges

Introduction

The central function of the modern state has been to establish the institutional framework for the promotion, management, and maintenance of economic transformation and growth, and especially the shift from agrarian to industrial society, and all the social and political complexities which that has entailed. The effective elimination of patronage, the de-institutionalization of corruption, the clear differentiation of private and public interests and institutions, and the establishment of relatively impartial bureaucracies have always and everywhere been both condition and consequence of national economic growth, managed directly or supervised indirectly by the institutions of the state. In the course of its evolution, the modern state has also had to respond to the challenges of democratization and the associated demands for redistribution of welfare, and has done so more or less successfully in the more developed economies in the course of the twentieth century.

The same cannot be said of many parts of the developing world where many states have not yet been able to organize or manage economic transitions on any of the three main models outlined earlier. Instead, where attempted, industrial capitalisms have been distorted by excessive state regulation, corruption, and the sorts of general weakness where social and economic classes would normally be expected to demand change. Elsewhere, revolutionary socialist, 'forced march', state-led, economic transformations and the state institutions of rule and management they have required of the kind that occurred first in the Soviet Union after 1917 and then in China after 1949, where the political forces that backed it were strong, have generally failed too. And the extraordinary symbiotic marriage of state and market typified by various forms of the developmental state that have promoted economic progress in countries as different as South Korea, Taiwan, Singapore, Malaysia, Thailand, Mauritius, and Botswana (Leftwich 1995) has simply been impossible to replicate elsewhere. It is the particular constellation of social, economic, and political forces that explains these states' success, and not whether they happen to be democracies or not. In all cases they illustrate the axiom that successful and effective modern states and successful economies go hand in hand.

Until the 1980s, few states in the developing world qualified as consolidated democracies. There were important exceptions—India, Jamaica, Venezuela, Costa Rica, Mauritius, and Botswana are but some, though many would question whether they all counted as *liberal* democracies (Burnell and Calvert 1999). This is because in much of the developing world, conflicts—of class, regional, religious, or ethnic groups—have been so sharp that consensus about rules of the political game has proved to be impossible. Different groups tend to prefer rules that would protect or advance their own particular interests and limit or reduce the interests of others. Secondly, many though not all the conflicts have been about distributional issues: land, jobs, income, welfare support. Where economic growth has been slow or negative, it has simply proved impossible (even if desired) to meet such demands.

Elsewhere, especially in Africa, cycles of military coup and counter-coup have been symptomatic of rival factions—ethnic, political, religious, or regional—seeking to gain control of the state and hence its resources and opportunities, in order to feed their clientelistic chains. This again illustrates a central theme of the chapter. The modern state in the developed world has been compatible with democratic (at least electoral) politics only where it has ensured that economic growth could subsidize a steady (if slow and sometimes intermittent) increase in the broad welfare of the majority. The more the state has been able to do that, the more robust has been its legitimacy and the more consolidated has its democracy become.

KEY POINTS

- Most states in the developing world have experienced great difficulty in overcoming the challenges of economic growth, democratic claims, and re-distributional demands.

- Many states in the developing world have been unable to establish the institutions of rule that would permit economic growth according to capitalist, socialist, or developmental state models.

- In the absence of economic growth and in the presence of profound inequalities, states in the developing world have found it impossible to absorb and institutionalize democratic demands.

- Many states in the developing world have found it impossible to deliver improved human welfare through re-distributional means.

Conclusion

Strong and effective states are inconceivable without strong economies. And strong economies are inconceivable without the institutions of state and

without the institutional framework established by the state to enhance growth and welfare, whether capitalist or socialist. All examples of sustained economic growth and development have required effective states to make (and adjust and adapt) appropriate institutions of rule and to facilitate the coordination of the public with the private institutions. Market-oriented models would have not been successful in the West without pervasive state support in the form of investment in human and infrastructural capital, the raising of taxes, the regulation of commerce, the establishment of judicial and legal systems, and welfare provision—and much more. Top-down, state-led, Soviet-style, post-revolutionary industrialization, likewise, has also required appropriate institutions for success, as have the complex developmental states of East Asia. But in each and every case, behind the state and the institutions of development it has created or facilitated, has been a coalition of political and social forces willing and able to establish, maintain, and adapt those institutions. The problem however in many developing countries has been that the politics underpinning states in many developing countries have made them inept, disjointed, and divided agencies of economic growth and hence have done little to promote human welfare or the reduction in poverty.

With the collapse of the bipolar world, the processes of globalization have accelerated. If such processes do indeed stimulate capitalist growth, then political forces will also gather momentum and help to build modern states on the template of their European precursors. Instead of being the agents and beneficiaries of patronage and corruption, such forces will become the agents of their destruction and of the creation of both the public and private institutions of rule that promote economic growth. In short, they will become much more like the states of the developed world. For sure, this will not happen everywhere. Nor will it happen quickly or simultaneously. Nonetheless, such developments will bring into politics other popular social forces—sometimes based on the classical co-ordinates of class, sometimes ethnicity, sometimes religion. They will use the new democratic space to demand social and welfare reforms that will constitute new challenges for the state and, in the process, transform it. How each will respond and adapt remains uncertain and will depend on the shifting coalitions of power and resistance which such politics will create. But what is certain is that the political science of the modern state in the developing world, and elsewhere, has not by any stretch of the imagination reached its terminus.

? QUESTIONS

1 What are institutions and why are they central to our understanding of politics and the state?

2 How and why do formal and informal institutions differ?

3 Why are the institutions of the state so important for development?

4 In what ways, if any, has the largely external origin of many states in the developing world influenced their form and function?

5 Did the different colonial economic institutions influence the character and capacity of the colonial and post-colonial states?

6 How would you distinguish between the rules which govern institutions of patronage and institutions of bureaucracy?

7 Good governance presupposes effective states. But can either be achieved without the political will and political processes to keep them in place?

8 Does globalization undermine the autonomy of states in the developing world?

9   What is the case for developmental states in an era of globalization?

10   Identify some of the different types of state found in the developing world, compare their distinguishing characteristics and illustrate with examples.

GUIDE TO FURTHER READING

■ **Bates, R. H. (2001),** *Prosperity and Violence. The Political Economy of Development* **(New York: W. W. Norton).** This short book is a brilliant and wide-ranging analysis of the kinds of political arrangements that have enhanced or hindered economic development.

■ **Chang, H.-J. (2002),** *Kicking Away the Ladder* **(London: Anthem Press).** A masterly account of how, from the eighteenth century on, the state in many now developed countries played an active role in the promotion of development.

■ **Kohli, A. (2004),** *State-Directed Development. Political Power and Industrialization in the Global Periphery*, **(Cambridge: Cambridge University Press).** An excellent comparative account of states and development in South Korea, Brazil, India, and Nigeria.

■ **Leftwich, A. (1995), 'Bringing Politics Back In: Towards a Model of the Developmental State',** *Journal of Development Studies*, **31/3: 400–27.** Outlines a model of the developmental state.

■ **——(ed.) (1996),** *Democracy and Development* **(Cambridge: Polity Press).** Essays exploring the relationship in theory and practice between democratic practices and developmental outomes in a number of different countries.

■ **Migdal, J. S., Kohli, A., and Shue, V. (eds.) (1994),** *State Power and Social Forces* **(Cambridge: Cambridge University Press).** Explores the relations between social and political forces and state power and capacity in a number of developing countries.

■ **Woo-Cumings, M. (ed.) (1999),** *The Developmental State* **(Ithaca, NY: Cornell University Press).** Explores the conditions and characteristics of developmental states.

■ **Young, C. (1994),** *The African Colonial State in Comparative Perspective* **(New Haven, CT: Yale University Press).** One of the finest accounts of the colonial state and its legacy, with insightful comparative observations.

WEB LINKS

● **www.transparency.org/**   Website of Transparency International, offering important and interesting information on global corruption plus the annual Corruption Perception Index for all countries. You can use this site to navigate to the Global Corruption Report, annual.

● **www.idd.bham.ac.uk/gsdrc/index_gsdrc.htm**   Website of the Governance Resource Centre at the University of Birmingham. It offers access to many papers, publications, and guidance concerning institutional aspects of states and governance in the developing world.

● **www.foreignpolicy.com/story/cms.php?story_id=3098**   Website of the *Foreign Policy* journal's failed state index, with quantitative measures for state strength and weakness. Funded and published by the Carnegie Endowment for International Peace.

- **www.crisisstates.com/** Many publications and research projects on crisis states in the developing and transitional world, based at the London School of Economics and Political Science.

- **www.ids.ac.uk/gdr/cfs/** Work and publications of the Centre for the Future State, at the Institute of Development Studies, University of Sussex, which promotes research on how public authority can be strengthened and reconstituted to meet the challenges of the twenty-first century.

 ONLINE RESOURCE CENTRE

For additional material and resources, see the Online Resource Centre at:
www.oxfordtextbooks.co.uk/orc/burnell2e/

12 State-Building

BRIAN SMITH

Chapter Contents

- Introduction: Varieties of State-Building
- Failures in State-Building
- Building Political Order
- Building a Developmental State
- Building Institutions
- Building Policy Capacity
- Conclusion: State-Building and Democracy

Overview

This chapter explores the concept of state-building by means of categories which reflect concerns about state failure in the developing world and the consequences of **weak states** lacking developmental, institutional, and policy-making capacity. First, different forms of state building are identified and explained. Then the economic and social consequences of state incapacity are set out. Following this, attempts to understand state incapacity and the need for state-building are examined systematically, typifying the aims of state-building as political order, developmental capacity, institution-building, and policy capacity.

Introduction: Varieties of State-Building

State-building has been a recurring theme in comparative politics and in the policy prescriptions of multilateral and bilateral aid agencies. Four themes or dimensions can be distinguished.

Political order

First, there is the concept of state-building as political order, reflecting concern about the inability of some post-colonial states to provide political stability or maintain social control. Some weak states have been unable to achieve territorial integration, or control over the whole area under their jurisdiction.

By the 1980s concepts such as soft state, 'negative sovereignty', 'juridical artefacts', and 'nominal', 'collapsed', or 'quasi' states had been devised to characterize states without a capacity for effective civil government. Within such states de facto power does not rest exclusively with the *de jure* government. In Afghanistan, for example, power

outside Kabul is in the hands of regional warlords and local commanders (Lister and Wilder 2005). In Somalia (Box 12.1 and see also Chapter 13) not even the capital is controlled by a constitutional government. In collapsed states, central government ceases to function, and is unable to protect its citizens against crime and violence let alone provide for their welfare (with education and health care) or maintain the country's physical infrastructure. The loss of population through death or migration is severe (Carment 2003).

In other cases, and despite governments being endowed with extensive constitutional powers, elaborate national plans, large bureaucracies, and an ability to 'penetrate' society, some are still unable to enforce their own legislation, achieve their objectives, and bring about social development. Even where the state has appeared strong, as under Latin American authoritarianism, for example, and able to exercise effective power against subordinate classes and organized opposition, it could

---

BOX 12.1

Somalia: A Case of Political Disorder

When the military regime of Mohamed Siyad Barre collapsed in 1991 with the withdrawal of foreign support, the Somali state totally lacked legitimacy. It was associated with the repressive personal rule of a dictator, militarism, and clan-based patronage. The Somali bourgeoisie had been systematically destroyed, state terror had been unleashed against political opposition, and clan conflict had been deliberately intensified as 'loyal' clans were encouraged to wage war on 'rebel' clans, leaving a civil society in violent turmoil. State institutions 'were thrown into gridlock, jealousy, confusion and anarchy'.

Civil society was too divided to support state authority and political order, and unable to provide national leadership. Power was monopolised by clan warlords supported by heavily-armed militias who

controlled society by extortion and violence, especially sexual violence against women. The warlords competed for control of the capital in a civil war which destroyed all institutions 'and records of central government'. Somalia reverted to the nineteenth century, with 'no internationally recognized polity; no national administration exercising real authority; no formal legal system; no banking and insurance services; no telephone and postal system; no public service; no educational and reliable health system; no police and public security services; no electricity or piped water systems; weak officials serving on a voluntary basis surrounded by disruptive, violent bands of armed youths'.

(Adam 1995: 72–78).

still demonstrate ineptness and impotence, as in Mexico in the 1980s. While the complete disintegration of governance is rare, an increasing number of states are failing to provide security, public order, welfare, and a framework of laws and institutions through which economic activity can be carried on (Milliken and Krause 2002).

The fact that many weak or failed states differ so much in respect of the qualities of statehood which they lack has prompted the idea that state failure can be arranged along a spectrum according to how many of the criteria associated with successful statehood are met. At one extreme would be cases of the total disintegration of the state, and at the other, an inability to enforce policy decisions or mobilize resources, deficiencies which make failed states 'nearly indistinguishable from the states of many, if not most, poor countries' (Brinkerhoff 2005: 4). This over-extension of the concept appears in the OECD's definition of 'fragile' states as 'those countries where the government cannot or will not deliver core functions to the majority of its people, including the poor', a definition which brings 35 countries into the category of fragile states.

An influential attempt to provide a theory explaining why some states have been unable to establish political order was made by Joel Migdal. In developing countries there are many social organizations exercising social control, apart from the state: families, tribes, traditional political authorities, churches, castes, clans, and enterprises. These come into conflict with the state over who has the right to make rules in particular areas of social and economic life. Whether the state can strengthen its capabilities and ensure that social and economic behaviour changes in the direction indicated by law and public policy depends on interactions between the state and a 'mélange' of social organizations. Political conflict arises from attempts by the state to displace alternative sources of social control (Migdal 1988b, 1994, 1996).

However, this interpretation of the relationship between state and society raises the question of whether it blurs the distinction between weak and strong states. An interdependence between state and society can empower the state, as well as generate conflict which obstructs it in its mission. State and society everywhere consist of actors in complementary as well as conflicting relationships. States are capable of shaping societies—for instance, by restructuring the political culture, or activating some group identities but not others—as well as being shaped by them. The power game between state and society is not zero-sum.

Furthermore, states may be weak in some policy areas—transforming the economy or improving human welfare—but strong in others—repression or the exploitation of natural resources (Evans 1995: 45). A capacity to implement policies is affected by the availability of human and financial resources, the ability to control the state's territory, and the quality of state organizations. Such variables are not necessarily spread evenly across policy areas.

Developmental capacity

While some states have failed, others have successfully built developmental capacity and achieved impressive records of industrialization, economic growth, and human development (though not necessarily by democratic means). For example, starting from the same level in the 1960s, by the mid-1990s incomes in East Asia were more than five times those in Africa, creating an ever-growing gap in the quality of life. Throughout the 1970s Singapore's annual growth rate in GNP per capita averaged over 7 per cent, higher than many southern European countries. By 1990 life expectancy in Taiwan was within one year of that in Germany and the USA.

The contrasting experiences of developing countries prompted attempts to explain a capacity for development on the part of some states. In the 1960s and 1970s the debate was mainly between those who believed that new states needed direct state intervention and ownership in order to achieve 'late' development and those who, faced with the ineffectiveness of national planning, widespread corruption, and disappointing economic and social achievements, advocated a more minimal state.

A third view is that a certain kind of state—a developmental state (see also Chapter 11)—can bring about successful industrialization.

Institutional viability

A parallel interest in post-colonial state-building originated in the importance attached by economic historians to institutional viability. The need for political leaders to strengthen institutional capacity as a foundation for economic and social development was also recognized within functionalist comparative politics. In the 1970s and 1980s a set of ideas known as new institutional economics (NIE) challenged the emphasis in mainstream neo-classical economics on individual preferences, technological opportunities, physical and human capital, and market opportunities as the main prerequisites of economic development. It was claimed that the quality of a country's social, political, and economic institutions is more important. In the 1990s interest in the role of institutions in development was encouraged by the perceived need to strengthen the operation of economic markets and democratic politics. The institutions most relevant to the social order which is necessary for economic and human development are property rights, bureaucracy, and the rule of law.

Policy capacity

State-building as an interest within comparative politics in the 1960s also included the need to build policy capacity. It was predicted that the modernization of society would enable new states to develop a problem-solving capacity for policy-making and an administrative capacity for effective and efficient implementation. The 1970s saw the emergence of development administration to provide an understanding of administrative performance in the specific economic and cultural contexts of poor, non-Western societies. Since 1980 public management has been seen as central to state-building in the sense of creating a strong central capacity for formulating and coordinating policy, efficient and effective delivery systems, and motivated and capable staff.

KEY POINTS

- Many developing countries have had states too weak to maintain political order and enforce their authority.

- Interdependence between state and society is as much a feature of strong as of weak states.

- Some states have impressive records of development, prompting debate about the economic polices and political conditions required for such achievements.

- Institutions are important for both economic development and human welfare, especially property rights, bureaucracy, and the rule of law.

- Efforts to promote policy capacity have proceeded against a background of debates about the role of the state in development.

Failures in State-Building

The social, political, and economic costs of failure to build state capacity in its different forms are high. Failure of the state to organize its apparatus of power effectively and so create *political order* has produced uncertain political authority, ineffective public administration, and corruption. Laws are not passed, order is not preserved, social cohesion decays, security (especially for the poor) is lost, and legitimacy evaporates. The officials of the 'soft' state also practise widespread disobedience of the law and collude with groups whose activities they are meant to regulate. Policy becomes distorted by the time it is implemented so that behaviour is not changed and benefits fail to reach the intended beneficiaries. Weak law enforcement and the distortion of public policies bias political, legal, and administrative systems heavily against the poor. State failure can jeopardize efforts to democratize if the system of government is not recognized as legitimate by all sections of society, if the electoral process is too disorganized to prevent fraud, if rebel militias have not been demobilized, and if the courts are too politicized to arbitrate independently (as in the Democratic Republic of the Congo in 2006). Such weaknesses also undermine economic development.

Too often, especially in Africa, the alternative to a developmental state has been a predatory state led by 'rapacious officialdom'. At the extreme, the state becomes a kleptocracy: less an agency for providing law, order, security, justice, and welfare, and more a device for endowing the political elite with power, wealth, and privilege. Government is neo-patrimonial, combining authority derived from traditional obligations with arbitrary rule. Political legitimacy is weak, so power has to be secured by the exploitation of ethnic loyalties, patronage, coercion, and repression of political opposition. The predatory state preys on the majority of its citizens, providing little or no collective goods in return. Bureaucracy, in the sense of an institution providing predictable, honest, efficient, and rule-governed administrative behaviour, is absent. Investment is discouraged, economic growth is severely restricted, and the country's public utilities and infrastructure—physical and social—disintegrate.

Lack of *institutional viability* is also detrimental for political, economic, and social development. Without effective property rights markets cannot develop, investor uncertainty increases, and productivity declines, for example from land that is not secured by registered titles. Poor returns are achieved from development projects. Without the rule of law, arbitrary government action disrupts business activity and threatens human rights. Economic policies can change without change in the law. Property can be expropriated and entrepreneurial minorities harassed (as in Idi Amin's Uganda). Political interference in the judicial process forces firms and individual citizens to find other ways to monitor contracts and enforce dispute resolution, for example by calling on social obligations based on personal connections, family networks or ethnic loyalties. The security and rights of the poor become particularly vulnerable.

The absence of proper bureaucracy also allows corruption to flourish, eroding the state's legitimacy. Trust and confidence in the state evaporate as corruption provides political and judicial protection to organized crime and destroys administrative efficiency. Officials respond to incentives to create scarcity, delay, and red tape, scarce public resources are misallocated, revenue is lost, and public service morale in undermined. Economically, corruption inflates business costs, distorts demand for the allocation of resources, and raises the cost of public provision when less efficient firms secure contracts with bribes. Transaction costs increase as access to officials and information has to be bought. Corruption also distorts incentives, diverts funds from productive activities (for example, in development projects), reduces tax revenues, and lowers the quality of government services. Socially, corruption strengthens inequality and has a disproportionate impact on the poor.

Weak *policy capacity* has further undermined the ability of governments with good policy objectives to bring about social and economic development. Failures in policy-making have meant that policies often contain incoherent proposals and unclear objectives with no proper plans for implementation. Coordination between departments and with finance ministries has often been poor. Important information has been unavailable, for example on public sector debt. Consequently plans are not realized. For example, in Zambia 75 per cent of cabinet decisions taken between 1991 and 1993 (the first two years of a new government) were not implemented (Garnett *et al.* 1997: 79–81).

Budgets are set without much idea of what a policy and its outcomes will cost, and often rest on unrealistic assumptions. For example, in the mid-1990s in Tanzania there was on average a 50 per cent difference between planned and actual recurrent expenditure. Plans often lack a reliable budgetary base since revenues, limited by a narrow tax base, fall short of expenditure targets. Little emphasis is placed on getting value for money.

Delivery of public services has been marred by poor quality, high cost, waste, fraud, and corruption. Public assets are neglected as central decision-makers concentrate on planning new projects rather than budgeting for the completion and maintenance of existing ones. Frequently other institutions have to compensate for inadequate state provision of essential public services; for example, in East Africa non-governmental organizations (NGOs), community associations, and the private sector provide half the education, water, and health services (Brautigam 1996: 81).

Some 14 per cent of the world's population (870 million people) live in what the OECD calls 'fragile' states, the majority of whom 'have no access to health services, education, economic resources, social security or political representation' (Klemp 2006: 209). Faulty institutions, governance, and policies reduce the annual economic growth rate in fragile states by 2.3 percentage points. People who

live in fragile states contain a third of the world's population living on less than US$1 a day, half of all children dying before the age of five, over a third of maternal deaths, a third of those without safe drinking water, and over a third of those with HIV/AIDS—an incidence four times higher than in the rest of the developing world. Profiles of the worst cases are given in Table 12.1 (though by definition statistics are hard to come by in failed states). The consequences of state failure spill over national boundaries, reducing economic growth by 1.6 per cent on average in neighbouring countries, and 'exporting' political instability and violence. There can be global implications when failed states are deemed to be havens for terrorists (Brinkerhoff 2005: 3).

KEY POINTS

- Failure of the state to create political order produces uncertain political authority and legitimacy, ineffective public policies, and insecurity, especially for the poor.

- The alternative to a developmental state has too often been a predatory state.

- A lack of institutional viability stifles economic growth, encourages corruption and increases inequality.

- Weak policy capacity has produced ill-conceived public policies, poor quality public services, and deviation from the government's policy objectives.

Building Political Order

The failure of states to provide political order is partly a consequence of failed governance, and partly of external interventions. Both types of intervention need to be revised before political order can be restored or created. A basis of security has to

be formed and some elements of good government organized, especially free and fair elections for parliaments and presidents. There must be a credible prospect of some economic prosperity. New institutions have to be established (especially the

Table 12.1 Failed States: Profiles[1]

	Per capita income (US$) 2004	% population below US$1 a day	Life expectancy (M/F) 2003	Adult% literacy)% (1998–2004) %	Infant mortality (under-five, per 1,000)	Corruption (score)[2]	Corruption (ranking)	Human Development Index value 2003[3]	Human poverty index (2003)[4]
Afghanistan	na	na	na	na	na	2.5	= 117	na	na
Cen. Af. Rep.	310	na	41/42	49	193	na	na	0.355	47.8
DRC	120	na	50/54	65	205	2.1	= 144	0.385	41.4
Guinea-Bissau	160	na	44/47	na	203	na	na	0.348	48.2
Haiti	390	67.0 (2001)	50/54	52	117	1.8	= 155	0.475	38.0
Liberia	110	na	46/48	56	235	2.2	= 137	na	na
Somalia	na	na	46/49	na	225	2.1	= 144	na	na
Sudan	530	na	57/60	59	91	2.1	= 144	0.512	32.4
Zimbabwe	620	56.1 (1996)	39/38	90	129	2.6	= 107	0.505	45.9
Low income countries	510		57/59	64				0.593	

1 These states receive high rankings from both the World Bank and Fund for Peace, in their indices of 'low income countries under stress' and 'failed states' (World Bank 2002; Fund for Peace 2006).

2 The lower the score (out of 10), the worse the corruption. The worse the corruption, the lower in the ranking of 253 countries.

3 The United Nations Development Programme's Human Development Index (HDI) is derived from scores given for life expectancy at birth, adult literacy levels, average years of schooling, and real GDP per capita (to indicate purchasing power). The two educational variables are combined but with different weightings and growth in the human development value of increases in income is assumed to fall after a certain level is reached. The three indicators are averaged to provide each country with a score from 0 to 1.

4 UNDP's Human Poverty Index is a measure which combines scores of 103 countries for deprivation in health (probability at birth of not surviving to 40); knowledge deprivation (adult literacy rate) and standard of living (combining percentage of population without access to clean water, and percentage of children under weight for age). The result indicates the proportion of the population in poverty (UNDP 2005: 342).

na = not available; M/F = male/female;

Sources: World Bank (2002), *World Bank Group Work in Low Income Countries Under Stress: A Task Force Report,* Washington DC, and *Development Report 2006,* Tables A1, 1 and 5; Transparency International, *Corruption Perceptions Index 2005,* www.transparency.org; UNDP, *Human Development Report, 2005,* Table 3, pp. 227–9; Fund for Peace, 2006.

rule of law), and civil society rejuvenated so that social capital can be revived (Rotberg 2004). Political order requires peaceful management of social conflict and an end to bad governance (see Chapters 13 and 15).

It is thus not surprising that state-building in collapsed states usually requires the support of international organizations and foreign governments such as the UN and bilateral aid agencies (as in East Timor in 2000 and Sierra Leone in 2002) (Rondinelli and Montgomery 2005). Nevertheless, aid to fragile states (almost US$10 billion in 2004) is not keeping up with aid to other low-income countries (which received twice as much).

Foreign interventions have also been responsible for state failure. The international community has legitimized self-determination and so exacerbated ethnic conflict and secession. The withdrawal of foreign support following the end of the cold war rendered some client states unviable. Armed intervention has caused disruption and conflict, as in Iraq. Foreign and domestic crises can combine when civil war invites foreign incursions, as in the Congo from 1998 to 2003, and Somalia in 2006 when Ethiopia sent troops to support the interim government against the militia of the Union of Islamic Courts that had taken control of the capital, Mogadishu. State-building in collapsed states is likely to be dependent on a revised stance among foreign powers, a development which does not seem immediately likely (see also Chapter 13).

When thinking about rebuilding 'failed' states it should not necessarily be assumed that any form of political order is preferable to the failure of state to use its monopoly of coercion effectively. The stability of South Africa under apartheid is a case in point. Not all states are benign, and resistance to the state's effective monopoly of coercive power may reflect a regime's lack of legitimacy.

The analysis of states that have failed also raises an important question about the implicit comparisons that are being made with 'strong' states. To label a state as 'failed' often seems to entail measuring state capabilities with criteria derived from Western states and their institutional capabilities. There is then a risk that the analysis of the failed state will be abstracted from its historical context (Bilgin and Morton 2002). This should not, however, lead to a relativist position where Westernized versions of democracy, the rule of law, and effective public administration are rejected as culturally specific.

KEY POINTS

- Bad governance is a major cause of state failure.

- Foreign intervention can destroy political order.

- The national and international policies contributing to state collapse need to be revised.

- The analysis of state failure risks being ethnocentric.

Building a Developmental State

The exceptional economic achievements of some East Asian countries point to the effectiveness of highly interventionist states controlling markets in favour of internationally competitive sectors selected by state technocrats. Here the state determined the scale and direction of economic growth to

a greater extent than free markets, engaging in rational planning through incentives (e.g. credit and price controls), legislation (e.g. on investment, imports, and taxation), and expenditure (e.g. on research and development) to ensure the development of manufacturing, high-technology production, and selected industrial sectors. Development thus requires not less, but better, state intervention and structures (Leftwich 2000: 169). Attempts to identify the key features of the developmental state have focused on three main factors: political institutions; the relationship between state and society; and the nature of the regime, authoritarian or democratic.

The political qualities of developmental states

A crucial requirement for a developmental state is a unified and competent bureaucracy, based on merit recruitment and offering stable and rewarding careers relatively free from political interference by sectional interests, such as traditional agrarian oligarchies, that might compromise the pursuit of economic growth. An example is South Korea.

Developmental states have also been characterized by a 'determined' set of nationalistic political and bureaucratic elites, relating to each other in shifting coalitions but all committed to developmental objectives. They have been motivated by various factors, including external threats to national security (e.g. Taiwan), shortages of raw materials (e.g. Singapore), relative material equality in the post-1945 period resulting from land reforms, and financial and technical assistance from the USA. State elites have imposed nationalistic aims on civil society, partly through repression, but also by improving living standards, reducing inequality and raising levels of educational achievement and health. Political elites have also enjoyed credibility in their commitments to development, convincing the private sector, foreign and domestic, that it could risk investment.

State–society relations

Relations between the developmental state and society have entailed embedded autonomy. This refers to the way in which the developmental state orchestrates the activities of economic bodies, offering sources of capital and other inducements in return for cooperation in the implementation of industrial policy. The concept of 'autonomy' here refers to the ability of the developmental state to transcend the interests of classes and other social forces when necessary (Chapter 23b describes how this worked in South Korea). The state consciously promotes the development of a capitalist class by providing the infrastructure needed by private enterprise, constraining working-class power, mediating between different capitalist interests (industrial, financial, and ethnic), and legislating in support of capital accumulation.

There is a 'governed interdependence' between state and industry, though the state has the power to choose which socio-economic interests to cooperate with. Linkages and collaboration between state agencies and leading private manufacturing firms, conglomerates, banks, and trading companies are established, and members of the political elite circulate between the bureaucracy, political executive, and business. The integration of state and private sector (including foreign investors and multinationals) is facilitated by joint ventures, state-owned enterprises, and networks of government personnel and business interests, sometimes bound by a common ethnicity, as in Malaysia.

A democratic developmental state?

Since most developmental states have been authoritarian rather than democratic during the decades of rapid economic growth and social development, it has sometimes been assumed that authoritarianism is a necessary condition of development. This is not necessarily the case; indeed, it has been argued that development can equally well be achieved under a democratic regime, with the added bonus of political freedoms and civil liberties (Przeworski *et al.* 2000).

Such a democratic developmental state would, however, require a number of contradictions to be resolved: between autonomous and accountable political leadership; economic growth and the redistribution of wealth; political consensus and the social inclusion of diverse ethnic groups; the concentration of power in state and business elites and public participation. These are 'fundamental contradictions which are difficult to resolve in the real world of politics'. The institutional context would also have to be receptive: accountable bureaucracy, legal stability, a strong knowledge base, and public–private cooperation, most of which are long-term projects and underline the importance of institution-building and the development of administrative capacity (White 1998: 44).

Replicating the developmental state

The question of how far the characteristics of a developmental state might be replicated elsewhere is central to any state-building project. The answer can only be conjecture, partly because of the variability of developmental states. Though common traits can be identified, there is no single model. For example, South Korea and Taiwan had stronger states than Malaysia, Indonesia, or Thailand during their respective periods of economic growth. 'Modes of involvement' in social and economic processes have ranged from the 'parametric'—providing the parameters for private economic activity—to the 'pervasive', with more direct state involvement in investment and production through state-owned enterprises, the control of labour, the political repression of classes opposed to industrialization, and the development

and control of industrial associations and cartels (White 1984: 100–1). Developmental states have varied in political structures and policy strategies, as well as undergoing great changes since the 1950s, recently in the direction of democratization. There have been variations in the style of executive leadership, relations between political and bureaucratic elites, and linkages between government agencies and social interests. Levels of state autonomy have varied over time and across economic sectors. This makes it difficult to identify a clear link between economic success and a single type of developmental state.

KEY POINTS

- Development needs better, not less, state intervention.

- All developmental states have competent bureaucracies and determined nationalistic elites.

- Relations between the developmental state and society have been conceptualized as embedded autonomy.

- Developmental states have been characterized by authoritarianism.

- A democratic developmental state would need to be 'inclusive', raising fundamental political contradictions.

- The variability of developmental states makes it difficult to replicate their characteristics elsewhere.

Building Institutions

It is now widely accepted among theorists that economic, social, and political development is dependent on the quality of institutions. Institutions are more than organizations, though they may depend on organizations for their effectiveness. For example, the rule of law depends on an impartial

judiciary. The regulation of markets needs regulatory agencies. Institutions may be likened to the rules of a game. They are humanly devised constraints on social interactions. For example, property rights over possessions are acquired within an institutional framework of legal rules, organizational forms, sanctions, and norms of behaviour. The institutions regarded as essential for development are property rights, the rule of law, and the principles of rational bureaucracy. State-building must thus include the development of strong institutions.

For the economy, institutions that protect property rights—rules establishing ownership, enforcing contracts and governing markets, administrative probity and efficiency, and the rule of law—are crucial to the scale and efficiency of investments. Institutional quality affects the level of incomes, and the rate and volatility of economic growth (see Box 12.2). In order to create market mechanisms, institutions have to protect private property against corruption and unpredictable judiciaries.

Institutions create incentives for innovation and accumulation. They reduce transaction costs and uncertainty for economic decision-makers. They encourage investment in machinery, equipment, education, and the development of the financial sector. Institutions determine whether fiscal deficits cause high inflation (greater in Latin America than South Asia), whether credit programmes will be successful (as they have been in Sri Lanka but not Bangladesh), whether state-owned enterprises will be efficient (as they are in Singapore and Taiwan but not in Argentina, Bolivia, or Nigeria), and whether rural development programmes enhance productivity (as they have done in parts of South Asia to a greater extent than in Africa and Latin America).

BOX 12.2

Institutions and Economic Development

In 2002 the International Monetary Fund commissioned research to assess the impact of institutions on three macro-economic outcomes for a sample of 94 economies, 25 advanced and 69 developing:

- *incomes*, measured by percentage change in per capita real GDP in 1995
- *economic growth*, measured by annual average growth in per capita real GDP, 1960–98
- *volatility of growth*, measured by the standard deviation of the growth rate of per capita GDP, 1960–98.

Institutional strength was measured by the average of six scores for the quality of governance, giving an aggregate governance index (see Chapter 15).

The study used a simple econometric framework to estimate:

- the empirical strength of the relationship between institutions and economic variables
- the effect that improvements in institutions could have on incomes and growth in the different regions from which the sample of countries was drawn.

Findings:

- *Institutions and income levels*: improvement in the quality of institutions substantially increases the level of per capita GDP. For example, an improvement in sub-Saharan Africa's institutions from their current average quality to that of developing countries in Asia would increase per capita incomes by 80 per cent (from about $800 to over $1,400).

- *Institutions and growth*: institutional quality is strongly and significantly related to growth. For example, annual growth in per capita GDP in sub-Saharan Africa would increase by 1.7 percentage points if African countries had institutions as good as the average for the whole sample.

- *Institutions and volatility*: an increase of one standard deviation in the aggregate governance index would cut volatility by 25 per cent, so the better the institutions, the lower the volatility of economic growth. For example, if institutions in sub-Saharan Africa were brought up to the average for the sample, African countries would experience a 16 per cent reduction in economic volatility.

The empirical results took into account the possibility of reverse causation, i.e. that since good institutions require time and resources to develop, stronger economic performance is likely to improve institutions, explaining why richer countries are more likely to enjoy good institutions.
(Edison 2003)

Socially, growth in incomes is dependent on a combination of good policies and strong institutional capacity. Social development, especially poverty alleviation, generally requires strong institutions, particularly efficient bureaucracy and the rule of law. Powerful classes are willing and able to obstruct reforms, and it is always difficult for the urban and rural poor to assert their rights. They need the protection of an independent and accessible judiciary and honest administration (Edison 2003: 35).

Politically, institutional development forms a mutually supportive relationship with democratization. Historically there is a strong correlation between the institutions of representative government and the rights of property and contract. The securing of property rights and contracts creates vested interests supportive of democracy. Democratic political institutions such as the rule of law and professional bureaucracy are more favourable to property rights than authoritarian regimes. Other characteristics supportive of democracy are also supportive of property rights and therefore economic growth: responsiveness to economic interests, impartial adjudication of disputes, and equality before the law. Bureaucracy and the rule of law also support the democratic principles of equality and justice (for example, treating like cases alike in decision-making about entitlements created by government policies; and subjecting the actions of state officials to tests of legality). Democracy enables trust in rules and institutions to grow, encouraging behaviour according to them rather than avoidance of them.

Claims that there is a positive relationship between development and institutions, though backed by quantitative comparisons, are nevertheless controversial for at least three reasons. First, there are potentially contradictory outcomes of institution-building. For example, the accumulation of wealth that is a consequence of private property rights may lead to a concentration of political power in classes tempted to subvert institutions that protect the rights of others. There may even be groups seeking to use political power to weaken property rights, so that they can benefit from the problems this causes others and from the savings (to them as taxpayers) of non-enforcement. Institutional development is a political process, differentially affecting entrenched sectional interests.

Secondly, it is unlikely that institution-building can respond to urgent needs for economic and political reform, since it takes time for new rules, practices, and values to become established. Institutional change requires cultural change and is inevitably slow and incremental. Thirdly, there is a danger that all economic achievements or problems will be ascribed to institutions, to the neglect of other factors, especially natural resources, geography, and geo-politics.

KEY POINTS

- There is a strong correlation between states with guaranteed property rights and economic growth.
- Social development is also dependent on institutional capacity,
- Institutional development and democratization are mutually supportive.
- Institution-building can have conflicting outcomes if it ignores inequalities of power.
- Institutional change requires cultural change, and is likely to be a slow and incremental process.
- Not all economic achievements can be ascribed to institutions.

Building Policy Capacity

Policy capacity includes both policy-making and implementation, since the latter exerts a strong influence on policy outcomes, sometimes leading to unintended consequences. Currently, reform efforts focus on both dimensions. The quality of the organizations supporting the institutional prerequisites of economic growth and human welfare is seen as critical for all types of development. Current efforts to build a capable public sector focus on three essentials: a strong central capacity for formulating and coordinating public policy; effective and efficient service delivery mechanisms; and staff who are motivated and competent.

To build *policy-making* capacity requires mechanisms which provide political executives with the costs and benefits of competing proposals, adequate technical and political information, a coordinated policy debate between the political heads of agencies, feedback from external 'stakeholders', and professional monitoring and evaluation of implementation. The types of mechanisms vary: secretariats for presidents, prime ministers, or cabinets; inter-ministerial coordinating councils; economic planning boards; consultations with front-line civil servants and user groups; and special policy units serving the cabinet. Whatever the arrangement, the common need is for executive agencies and deliberative councils with high professional and technical standards.

To provide more *effective and efficient implementation*, current administrative orthodoxy recommends that governments contract out service delivery to competing private firms or NGOs, for example in the management of schools and water supplies; or provide funds to NGOs, community groups, and private firms administering social services or public works projects, such as Bolivia's Emergency Social Fund (Turner and Hulme 1997: 126–9). The theory is that competitive tendering between providers will give greater value for public money. Other measures include setting up performance-based agencies with managerial autonomy but accountable for outputs and outcomes. Examples include tax-collection agencies in Ghana, Uganda, and Zambia. Performance indicators provide yardsticks for measuring the efficiency and effectiveness of such agencies.

The decentralization of political authority to territorial units of government can also contribute to the state's capacity for policy-making and implementation. Public policies can be made more responsive to local needs when politicians and bureaucrats are accountable to local communities. The efficiency with which resources are allocated will be improved if outcomes reflect the actual needs and preferences of citizens. Decentralization is intended to reflect unique sets of local circumstances in policy-making and implementation. For example, in Karnataka, India, local councils were given control over almost all development funds, enabling them to be unusually responsive to local needs (see Box 12.3). Under Ghana's Local Government Act 1993 district assemblies are responsible for a wide range of public services, including health, education, and social services, as well as development planning. However, despite relatively high levels of participation, local elected representatives are weaker than the central government in determining spending priorities (Crook and Manor 1998).

Of particular importance in the development of policy capacity is the ability of the state to tax more equitably and effectively. Tax revenues in low-income countries averaged only 12 per cent of GDP in 2003, compared with 25 per cent in high-income countries. When tax systems are poorly designed and administered the results are chronic fiscal deficits and inequity (the taxation of the rich in developing countries is notably weak and taxes are predominantly indirect and regressive). If existing tax legislation were implemented effectively in sub-Saharan Africa, for example, revenues would be increase by 30 per cent. Building an effective

BOX 12.3

Democratic Decentralization in Karnataka State, India

Between 1987 and 1991 local councils in the Indian State of Karnataka were given control over more than half the number of state public servants, and made responsible for a wide range of services including education, health and family welfare, and a range of economic development functions in agriculture, animal husbandry, fisheries, rural employment, and rural development generally. Roughly 40 per cent of the state budget was decentralized, representing 'a genuinely radical devolution of authority and resources'.

To allow politically weak groups a larger role in local government, 25 per cent of council seats were reserved for women, and 18 per cent for Scheduled Castes.

As a result, government became more responsive to local needs. The speed, quantity and quality of response improved. Most development projects implemented by councils corresponded to the expressed needs of local people. This was mainly because decentralization provided much better information on local problems and needs, but also because accountability and transparency in local decision-making were stronger. However, while territorial equity improved, decentralization 'did little to benefit vulnerable groups'.

When the Janata Party at state level lost control to the Congress Party in 1989, the powers and resources of decentralized institutions were severely curtailed. Politicians in the state government resented the loss of powers, patronage, and the opportunities created for wider participation and therefore political influence.

(Crook and Manor 1998)

---

tax administration entails tackling corruption and political interference in assessment and collection, as well as improving administrative procedures and personnel.

Influenced by Britain's adoption of the idea of executive agencies, a number of developing countries have set up revenue authorities detached from finance ministries in order to improve administration and increase revenues, albeit at the expense of accountability (Devas *et al*. 2001). An example is Uganda (see Box 12.4), where the creation in 1991 of a revenue authority was part of state-building following a combination of civil war, rapacious military government, and war with Tanzania, which left a legacy of decaying judicial institutions, unreliable law enforcement, a lack of political and financial accountability, a weak yet overstaffed civil service, systemic corruption, a shallow and insecure tax base, and ineffective public administration (Langseth 1995).

Numerous reforms have been advocated and tried to strengthen levels of competence among *public sector staff* including meritocratic recruitment and promotion and better pay. Singapore pays public servants the market rate for comparable private sector jobs—salaries that are very high by international standards. Salaries attractive to capable and qualified people might be funded by the elimination of surplus posts and 'ghost' workers (in 2006 a census of public servants in Cameroon revealed 45,000 ghost workers on the payroll, costing the country nearly US$5 million a month). Other savings might be had from the enforcement of retirement age limits, the freezing of recruitment in some departments, and the introduction of voluntary redundancy schemes.

Morale and *esprit de corps* can be improved by training, team-work, self-management, and the recognition of achievements as in Malaysia's Public Services Innovation Awards. Other incentives such as professionalization, job satisfaction, corporate mission, status, and working conditions—elements of organizational culture—can help to retain good staff and induce improved performance A comparative study of budgeting, agricultural extension, and health care in Bolivia, the Central African Republic, Morocco, Ghana, Sri Lanka, and Tanzania strongly suggested that effective public sector performance

BOX 12.4

The Uganda Revenue Authority

Established in 1991, the URA is a body corporate with its own board of directors and autonomy in personnel and financial management. Staff were transferred from the revenue departments of the Ministry of Finance (MOF) with salary increases in order to reduce corruption, increase morale and productivity, and so increase revenue. The Authority's chief executive is the Commissioner General (CG).

In the following 10 years revenue grew as a percentage of GDP from 7 to 12.1 per cent, although government targets were not met after 1996 despite having been lowered substantially. Total revenues increased from 181 billion Ugandan shillings to 1264 billion in 2001.

However, autonomy has constantly been threatened by political factors:

- MOF control of the URA's budget, and interference in its management

- Loss of the Authority's advisory role on tax policy in 1997
- Increased representation of MOF on the Board of URA
- Reduction of the Board's responsibilities
- Political interference in staffing matters
- Loss of Authority legitimacy because of the re-emergence of corruption, heavy-handedness when dealing with taxpayers, the recruitment of staff by clientelism rather than merit (including the CG), and the involvement of foreign donors in setting revenue targets
- Interventions by the President
- The untransparent role of the military in the URA's anti-smuggling activities.

(Therkildsen 2003)

---

is more dependent on organizational culture than on rules, regulations, and pay scales (Hilderbrand and Grindle 1997: 45–56).

Lessons from administrative reforms

Capacity-building for policy formulation has tended to concentrate on the supply side (government agencies and personnel) when greater benefits might be had by strengthening the demand side. One aim here would be to improve the policy advice and advocacy coming from civil society, especially NGOs, trade unions, political parties, research institutes, and pressure groups. Another would be to strengthen the capacity of user and client groups as well as other sectional interests to demand better public policies. However, inclusion of clients in policy-making is relatively rare and runs up against professional hostility in public bureaucracies. Decentralization also experiences hostility from bureaucrats in central government, and is frequently undermined by central government

controls, fiscal dependence, poorly qualified staff, administrative incapacity, and global forces which restrict the ability of local governments to respond to local needs.

Attempts to improve service delivery by contracts and competition risk weakening accountability and creating new opportunities for corruption. The private sector may be too weak to take on contracts, government agencies may lack the specialist skills to write them properly, and the rule of law may be too weak to enforce them. Competition may not work in certain cultures which socialize people into avoiding conflict. A 'one size fits all' approach to public sector management risks failure in highly variable cultural contexts.

Civil service reform programmes have often been too far-reaching, raising unattainable expectations. At the same time they have lost sight of ultimate objectives, such as service quality or accountability, concentrating on inputs such as training or downsizing. They have generally met with little lasting success. Retrenchment has been obstructed by senior officials or incurred huge costs—Ghana's downsizing exercises between 1987 and 1990 caused cumulative financial losses (Olowu 1999: 15).

Furthermore, the concept of attractive salaries does not fit easily into administrative systems where wage bills already crowd out other recurrent spending as well as essential capital expenditure, or where the IMF has imposed a wage freeze as part of a loan agreement. Other incentives also encounter obstacles. Kinship obligations, tribal networks, consensus-seeking, and the importance attached to secure employment, leisure, and celebrations, can militate against bureaucratic norms. State employees may also be highly risk-averse when jobs are scarce.

The politics of building policy capacity

Capacity-building efforts encounter powerful political obstacles. Domestic political support and commitment may be lacking if reforms are driven by foreign aid conditionalities. A sense of local 'ownership' is then missing. There are also vested interests in the public sector that are threatened by downsizing and meritocratic recruitment or promotion. Political leaders stand to lose powers of patronage: a politicized civil service suits ruling elites for whom public service employment is a form of patron–client linkage. Patronage strengthens electoral support, serves the business interests of politicians, and enables opponents to be punished by, for example, the withholding of import licences, foreign exchange permits, bank loans, tax exemptions, public utilities (water, power, and telephone), and even cargo space in ports and on aircraft, as in Kenya, for example. Local political and economic elites may have little interest in administrative reforms, particularly those aiming to strengthen policy implementation, because these are likely to threaten their domination and exploitation of subordinate social groups and classes. It is thus unlikely that new management techniques will have much impact on their own. Political reforms and stronger policy capacity must go hand in hand.

KEY POINTS

- Policy capacity includes both policy-making and implementation.

- The state's policy capacity has been undermined by both political and administrative problems.

- Prescriptions for reform have focused on policy analysis and coordination, service delivery, and the quality of the public service.

- Competition, performance-based agencies, and performance indicators have been advocated to improve the performance of public services.

- Pay and morale have been identified as crucial for personnel reforms.

- Change to the policy process needs to recognize the role and defects of politicians, aid donors, civil society, the private sector, senior bureaucrats, and local cultures.

- Building policy capacity poses threats to ruling elites and local power-holders.

Conclusion: State-Building and Democracy

Throughout the post-colonial era political science has been concerned with state-building in one sense or another. Political order has been resisted by strong societies with which states have had to make 'accommodations'. The idea that strong societies are able to weaken the state's effectiveness

246

has implications for theories of democratization which maintain that a vibrant civil society is a necessary condition for the consolidation of democracy. Democracy presupposes that strong states and strong societies are mutually supportive.

Debates about the unique characteristics of developmental states, and especially their early authoritarian tendencies, are equally relevant to contemporary interest in transitions from authoritarian to democratic regimes. Whether the developmental state can be democratic depends upon which understanding of democracy is being used. A more inclusive, participative, and egalitarian conception of democracy could possibly experience greater difficulties in adopting strategies, institutions, and policies favouring growth in investment, output, and incomes than a purely procedural one, with its emphasis on political rights and the constitutional rules of representative government.

Institutional capacity has implications not only for economic development but also for human rights, justice, and poverty alleviation. Institutions are important for democracy, especially the rule of law and impartial bureaucracy, which offer those who lack the political power associated with wealth and social status some guarantee that their rights will be respected whether as litigants before the courts, claimants before state officialdom, or participants in electoral competitions or policy-making. Institutions have the potential to empower people and make their citizenship effective. Policy capacity also has implications for democracy. It is by no means a purely technical or managerial matter. Democratic governments need the capacity to formulate good policies and have them implemented so that targets are hit. If social hardship is to be alleviated, it is necessary that sound policies are legally enforceable, and that resources reach the intended beneficiaries. The more public servants administer regulations according to statute rather than unfairly discriminating under the influence of bribes, kinship obligations, prejudices, or fear of local elites, the greater the fairness in bureaucratic allocations and the more meaningful the equality of citizens. This in effect brings the discussion back to the topic of state strength and the relationships with society which enable states effectively to achieve their policy aims.

QUESTIONS

1 What are the main tasks to be included in rebuilding failed and collapsed states?
2 Does the interdependence of state and society necessarily weaken the state?
3 What are the key requirements of a developmental state?
4 What have been the main causes of failures in policy-making and implementation in developing countries?
5 What obstacles are reforms to strengthen or build policy capacity likely to encounter?

GUIDE TO FURTHER READING

■ **Appelbaum, R., and Henderson, J. (eds.) (1992),** *States and Development in the Asian Pacific Rim* **(Newbury Park, Calif.: Sage).** Case studies of South Korea, Malaysia, Japan, Hong Kong, Singapore, and Taiwan show the importance of state interventions through both economic and social policy to the Asian 'miracle'.

■ Bilgin, P., and Morton, A. D. (2002), 'Historicising representations of "failed states": beyond the cold-war annexation of the social sciences', *Third World Quarterly*, 23/1: 55–80. Contemporary representations of post-colonial states as weak, failed, rogue and so on are criticised as being too unhistorical to explain adequately the political economy of insecurity.

■ Carment, D. (2003), 'Assessing state failure: implications for theory and policy', *Third World Quarterly*, 24/3: 407–27. Argues that understanding and responding to state failure requires a multifaceted, multilayered, and multi-actor methodology.

■ Clague, C. (ed.) (1997), *Institutions and Economic Development. Growth and Governance in Less-Developed and Post-Socialist Countries* (Baltimore, MD: Johns Hopkins University Press). Shows how economic performance is affected by property rights, democracy, and patterns of participation, while the rule of law and bureaucracy emerge as the most significant institutions supporting property rights and contract enforcement.

■ Evans, P. (1995), *Embedded Autonomy. States and Industrial Transformation* (Princeton, NJ: Princeton University Press). Using case studies of Brazil, India, and Korea during the 1970s and 1980s, this book advances our understanding of the developmental state.

■ Grindle, M. S. (1996), *Challenging the State. Crisis and Innovation in Latin America and Africa* (Cambridge: Cambridge University Press). Shows how states try to respond to crises by strengthening their institutional, technical, administrative, and political capacities, with particular reference to Mexico and Kenya.

■ Leftwich, A. (2000), *States of Development. On the Primacy of Politics in Development* (Cambridge: Polity Press). A comparative study showing that type of politics rather than regime (democratic or authoritarian) is important if a state is to become developmental.

■ Migdal, J. S. (1998), *Strong Societies and Weak States. State–Society Relations and State Capabilities in the Third World* (Princeton, NJ: Princeton University Press). Argues that states can be arranged along a continuum between 'strong' and 'weak' depending on the degree of fragmentation of social control, with particular reference to Sierra Leone, Egypt, and Palestine.

■ Polidano, C. (2001), 'Don't discard state autonomy: revisiting the East Asian experience of development', *Political Studies*, 49/3: 513–27. Argues that autonomy is an important element of the capacity of developmental states, in contrast to the institutionalists' claim that an effective state must be well connected to civil society.

■ Rotberg, R. I. (ed.) (2004), *When States Fail. Causes and Consequences* (Princeton NJ: Princeton University Press). Explores the nature of failure and collapse among nation-states in developing countries, methods of preventing state failure, and the reconstruction of failed states.

■ Turner, M., and Hulme, D. (1997), *Governance, Administration and Development. Making the State Work* (London: Macmillan). A critical analysis of different approaches to public policy and its management, and their applicability to developing countries, which challenges the orthodoxies of 'new public management' and the 'minimalist' state.

■ Zartman, W. (ed.) (2005), *Collapsed States. The Disintegration and Restoration of Legitimate Authority*, (London, Colo.: Lynne Rienner). Fourteen essays analysing the nature and correlates of state failure, methods of prevention, and strategies for rebuilding failed states. Strong, weak, failing, and collapsed states are defined and categorized.

WEB LINKS

● **www.crisisstates.com** The Crisis States Research Centre at the London School of Economics provides explanations of the causes of crisis and breakdowns in the developing world, asking whether globalization precipitates or assists in the avoidance of state fragility.

● **www.worldbank.org** The World Bank places institutional development at the centre of development efforts, and identifies policy capacity as an important area of reform. It also has a programme for Low Income Countries Under Stress (LICUS).

● **www.fundforpeace.org** The Fund for Peace is a Washington DC-based non-governmental research and educational body that publishes an annual Failed States Index, using twelve social, economic, and political/military indicators; and Country Profiles which measure the capacity of the state to cope with pressures exposed by the indicators.

● **www.undp.org/governance** The United Nations Development Programme supports capacity development, including institutional and social capital, and associates the democratic state with development, especially for the poor.

● **www.oecd.org/dac/fragilestates** The Fragile States Group of the OECD brings together experts on governance, conflict prevention, and reconstruction to identify ways of enhancing development effectiveness in fragile states. The Development Assistance Committee supports public sector reform and 'capacity development' through its Network on Governance.

ONLINE RESOURCE CENTRE

For additional material and resources, see the Online Resource Centre at:
www.oxfordtextbooks.co.uk/orc/burnell2e/

13 State Collapse, Civil Conflict, and External Intervention

MARTIN DOORNBOS

Chapter Contents

- Introduction
- Understanding State Collapse
- Dynamics of Civil Conflict and State Collapse
- State–Society Linkages Under Threat
- Diverse Trajectories
- Statelessness and the International Context
- External Actors and the Politics of Reconstruction
- Conclusions

Overview

In examining the incidence of **state collapse**, two central themes predominate, one concerned with the search for causalities and the other concerned with appropriate responses. There is often a misplaced tendency to look for single causes and explanations of state collapse, and similarly to propose single, ready-made solutions. Instead, a more nuanced scrutiny that differentiates the distinctive factors leading to collapse in specific instances offers most insights, and calls for a reconsideration of possible responses and approaches by external actors. Such analyses must be related to the broader discussion of dynamics of civil conflict, which at times has given rise to the collapse of state systems. This chapter introduces these themes. First, it considers the complex web of conditioning and facilitating factors that can instigate a chain reaction eventually leading to state collapse, examining the extent to which any emerging patterns can be identified. This requires proper conceptualization and identifying different patterns or trajectories of state–society relationships. Secondly, it looks more closely at the response side to incidences of state collapse, specifically by the international community. Whilst external actors, notably the 'donor community', are trying to better prepare themselves for the eventualities of crises of governance and state collapse in various countries, designing more effective strategies and instruments, it is not obvious they have yet discovered a perfect 'fit' between the determinants and dynamics of state collapse and the responses and solutions for restoration.

Introduction

Until little more than a decade ago, it would have seemed almost inconceivable, even to professional political analysts, that incidences of state collapse would be on the increase, that the prospect of short-lived or more enduring statelessness would become more common, and that discussion about these phenomena would grow rapidly. For a long time, states were accepted as normal in a very basic sense. An extensive literature in history, archaeology, anthropology, and political science developed on the dynamics of state *formation*—discussing and weighing variables that may give rise to it, such as conquest, trade routes, population pressure, and many other factors—but generally there was little writing on state *collapse*. Normatively, once states had come into existence they were expected to last—and, in recent decades, to help sustain the international system that had in turn come to be based on them.

Yet understanding the dynamics of state collapse may be no less important than appreciating those at work in state formation. Moreover, a better grasp of processes leading to collapse should offer additional insights into what makes states work, as well as what fails to work. Indeed, although they seem to be situated at opposite ends of a continuum, there are several key connections between the dynamics of state 'formation' and state 'collapse', which, on closer inspection, are not as far apart as they first appear. Ali Mazrui, referring to the contemporary drama, asked the cardinal question: 'Have Somalia, Rwanda, Liberia, Angola, Burundi been experiencing the death pangs of an old order dying and groaning for refuge? Or are we witnessing the birth pangs of a real but devastating birth of a genuinely post-colonial order?' (Mazrui 1995: 22). Depending on one's understanding of collapse and the political dynamics that give rise to it, it is conceivable to regard collapse as part of processes of state reconfiguration and formation. Certainly, a better

understanding of processes of collapse is crucial to determine how political reconstruction might best be approached.

If incidences of state collapse seem on the increase, then obviously answers are needed to a number of why and how questions. However, it is equally important to ask what we mean by state collapse and whether different understandings and definitions influence our assumptions about its incidence. What are the significant features of state collapse? How do we (how should we) define it? What triggers it? Are some state systems, or contexts, more prone to it than others, and if so, under what kind of conditions? What are the implications of collapse—both internally within the state system concerned, and externally with respect to the relations with the world outside? At another level, what does state collapse and the disappearance of the state mean for the idea of 'normalcy' and sovereignty of states, as now enshrined in the United Nations system? What is the international system's response to state collapse? What lies beyond collapse and how should we propose to handle the connections between state collapse and state formation or political reconstruction, in the contemporary era? These are the questions that this chapter seeks to address.

This chapter disentangles 'collapse'—a term that, unwittingly perhaps, has come to be used to describe quite a range of different things, which is not helpful for clarity of analysis. Then it addresses two related concerns.

First, even if we adhere to a strict definition of collapse as referring only to when 'the basic functions of the state are no longer performed', we are likely to find some quite distinct patterns of and different and contrasted trajectories, or paths leading to, collapse. It is thus important to investigate the complex web of conditioning and facilitating factors that may be responsible for a chain reaction eventually leading to state collapse. This will enable us to understand not only why certain dynamics, usually emanating from key social cleavages and civil conflict, might end in state collapse but also the extent to which we can identify any different patterns emerging.

The second concern to address is the response side—how the international community addresses these peculiar situations. In some degree external actors, notably the donor community, now see fit to intervene, although not always decisively or soon enough, as the Rwandan genocide in 1994 testifies. Their actions are generally guided by assumptions as to how state systems in the contemporary world should be structured and how they ought to function, and by what appears to be called for—in that light—in order to restore or establish effective government. The big question here is whether there will be a fit between the determinants and dynamics of state collapse in various situations and the responses and solutions for restoration offered. A key precondition for meaningful action here—but

not always observed in practice—must be a careful scrutiny of the background and dynamics leading up to the collapse.

KEY POINTS

- Until relatively recently the social science literature was strongly focused on state formation but paid little attention to the analysis of state collapse.

- Processes of state collapse and state formation are closely related in different ways.

- The increasing incidence of state collapse qualifies the normalcy of state systems in the international arena.

- Closer analysis shows different and contrasted trajectories leading to state collapse.

- External responses often take insufficient account of the specific conditions that have led to state collapse.

Understanding State Collapse

To understand better some of the key questions thrown up by the incidence of state collapse, we need to unpack the notion of state collapse and investigate the different understandings of the failure of state functions. One of the earlier authors on the subject, Zartman (1995: 5), submitted that 'collapse means that the basic functions of the state are no longer performed, as analysed in various theories of the state'. This seems straightforward. However, when further delineating the concept, Zartman (1995: 6) writes that '[s]tate collapse . . . is the breakdown of good governance, law and order'. This is more problematic, as it links the signalling of instances of state collapse to our understanding of good governance, which is essentially judgemental and potentially controversial (see Chapter 15 below). Moreover,

collapse in principle should be used to refer not only to the breakdown of good governance, but to that of any pattern of governance, good or bad. Otherwise we might find many more instances of collapse than is analytically meaningful—as indeed seems underscored by Zartman who refers to 'many' current instances of collapse. Moreover, employing such a normative notion could lead to endless quibbles and disputes as to whether particular instances of deterioration in good governance illustrate state collapse. Historically, there have been many examples of 'bad' governance where in true Machiavellian (or neutral Weberian) spirit it remained geared towards the implementation of the rulers' chosen and usually selfish objectives. In contrast, instances of complete collapse, in the sense of the decline and virtual disappearance of a once functioning state system, still seem rather exceptional. Somalia and Sierra Leone in recent years have provided the most clear-cut examples, closely followed by others like Liberia, the Democratic Republic of the Congo (DRC), Cambodia, and Afghanistan.

However, there are other important reasons to reappraise notions of breakdown of '(good) governance, law and order', in Zartman's term, as defining the essence of state collapse. For can we assume that when a state no longer functions a breakdown of order, or even of law and order, is necessarily implied? That would seem to imply viewing 'order' as state-given: take away the state, and order too will disappear. While possibly true for various situations as in Liberia, Sierra Leone, and DRC at different recent intervals, it might nonetheless be wrong to assume too readily such a one-to-one relationship. Early anthropologists contributed greatly to our understanding of these questions by pointing to the existence of stateless societies which had meaningful forms of government without state structures. The distinction then developed between states and stateless societies is worth revisiting in the light of the spread of uncertain political futures following cases of state collapse.

Now is an appropriate time to study political processes within stateless societies and the associated dilemmas. For ever since 1991 Somalia has done without the benefit of a state system, a situation which still largely obtains notwithstanding the fact that several attempts have been made to reintroduce a central government. Whatever this might eventually lead to, in several Somali regions people for more than a decade have managed to cope, and to cope relatively well and in relatively orderly ways, without a functioning state system—some might even say better than when the state system was still intact. This tells us that whatever useful functions states may have to offer, the presence of a state and of order cannot always be equated. By comparison it is worth recalling the opposite possibility, that of state terror coinciding with severe disorder—something that Somalia experienced at an earlier stage and which similarly had been the fate of Uganda under Idi Amin (1971–9), Ethiopia under Mengistu (1974–91), Cambodia under Pol Pot (1975–9) and in numerous other situations. For definitional clarity, therefore, it is helpful to limit the notion of state collapse to the kind of situation in which a functioning state system ceases to exist—whatever that situation may imply in terms of order. The term **state failure** is more appropriate for situations of less than complete collapse, although even this is not unproblematic. For example we can distinguish between the failure to deliver essential public welfare services, the failure to provide basic security (vis-à-vis internal as well as external threats), and the failure to act as a moderator of opposed interests. Finally, there is the possibility of state collapse turning into (or already resulting from) a situation of frightening anarchy.

Closely connected are some other important distinctions. Aside from instances of total collapse of state frameworks, there have been some recent cases of partial collapse, where some state functions persist as in the DRC—and of territorially restricted collapse due to ethnic or other conflict, like in Sudan (1973–present) and Sri Lanka (1983–2001). Then there is merely temporary versus enduring state collapse, as illustrated by the contrasting cases of Albania and Somalia, and the occurrence of twilight states—a presence of state authority during the day, and rebel authority during the night—although these probably also qualify as instances of state failure.

KEY POINTS

- Conceptual clarity requires distinguishing between the debate on what constitutes good governance and that concerned with the determinants of state collapse.

- 'Order' is not necessarily state given: conceivably order may coincide with statelessness while disorder may follow from state terror.

- The distinction made in anthropological analyses between states and stateless societies carries renewed relevance in the contemporary international arena.

- Aside from total state collapse, state failure in various forms and degrees may be distinguished.

Dynamics of Civil Conflict and State Collapse

The collapse of a state can hardly occur spontaneously, or all at once. If and where it happens, it is likely to have been preceded and initiated by complex and conflict-ridden processes of deterioration, decline, and erosion of state functions. Actual collapse is likely to constitute the final moment of such processes, and to occur when a certain point of no return has been passed. These processes have their own dynamics, which is not to say that they are strictly internal processes. Indeed, the precise ways in which external and internal determinants interact and coalesce in prompting processes leading to state collapse are extremely important for a better understanding of the phenomenon.

As processes, dynamics of decline are theoretically reversible. We can only speculate about the number of instances where timely intervention—from below or from above, from inside or outside—may have stopped a chain of events that could have culminated in state collapse. A trite yet relevant truism would be to say that proper performance and maintenance of state functions and institutions provides the best protection against state collapse. But the dynamic quality of the processes concerned also makes it difficult to identify with any certainty at what point in a spiral of potential collapse a state system may find itself. As with historical state formation processes, where one may recognize in retrospect that a state has emerged out of various formative processes, the root causes of state collapse will similarly have been at work well before any actual collapse manifests itself.

Just as generalizing about the meaning of state collapse can be hazardous, the same is true when it comes to identifying the causes and consequences. Although in a sense the end result may appear to be uniform, the trajectory—that is the pattern and dynamics leading to that condition—may differ greatly. Nor should this be surprising. The fragile Sierra Leonean situation around 2000, for example,

with its massive insecurity and violence at the hands of armed rebel groups enjoying significant external support (Reno 2000), appears qualitatively different from the fragmentation of the erstwhile Somali state system into different regional entities vying with each other for power (Doornbos 2002). Superficially, the common element in both cases seems to be the presence of warlords. But closer investigation shows there is much more to it than that and many differences between the two situations.

In the Somali case, it was the inability to accommodate conflicting interests, often articulated on a clan basis, and the instrumental use to which the state apparatus was put in the pursuit of this inter-clan violence, that brought about disintegration. For all its repressive qualities, the Somali state had a relatively 'thin' presence within the society, which meant that it could all the more easily collapse and be jettisoned when inter-clan conflict and repression came to a head. In Sierra Leone, it was the greed for profit from control over the lucrative illegal diamond trade that became a key factor fuelling the rebellion and by implication the progressive undermining of the state system. However, this still leaves open the question of why the rebellion started. Different explanations have been offered, most notably ethnic grievances spurred by unequal access to power and resources (Richards 1996). The Somali context in recent times has comprised several regions with ambitions for either far-reaching political autonomy (like Puntland) or full-fledged independence (namely Somaliland)—thus for statehood in one form or another.

Other examples also illustrate this differentiation of patterns. For instance, the complex dynamics that led to the crisis and collapse of the Cambodian state framework succeeded years of protracted and destructive struggle between the Pol Pot government and liberation forces. Eventually the UN led a complex effort to restructure a state system expected to be reasonably open to and representative of the various political strands. Other recent configurations of collapsing states have included the compound crises that occurred—and in several instances still continue in some measure—in Haiti, Liberia, DRC, and indeed Afghanistan. Each of these evidently requires its own explanation of what went wrong in terms of failing state systems no longer able to provide basic security, ending up in final collapse. In several cases, like Haiti or DRC, state power had for so long been personalized—resembling non-formal militias loyal only to the president—that the degeneration of the system caused the fragile state structure to become largely irrelevant and eventually to collapse. In Afghanistan, prolonged violent conflict started as a late cold war proxy war between the superpowers, in 1979, resulting in ongoing stalemate among the conflicting groups and pervasive social disorientation in the population at large. In the wake of this, and in the face of non-state forces with an entirely different cultural and ideological agenda—the Taleban—the former state largely became irrelevant. That saga was subsequently brought to completion with the externally induced collapse of the Taleban regime, which exposed the state system it had controlled to be in ruins.

Trying to better understand state collapse, therefore, must mean getting a better grip on the conditioning factors. That is what makes some political and economic contexts more vulnerable than others to dynamics leading to state collapse. Internally, as noted, there are various distinct factors to explore, such as a lack of meaningful linkages between state and society, greed for resources, excessive concentration of power, and gross institutional mismanagement. More generally still there is the nature and dynamics of social cleavages and civil conflict along class, ethnic, religious, or regional lines, or some combination of these.

Externally, again, several recurrent patterns seem to present themselves, working alone or in concert with others. One is the strategy of deliberate destabilization on the part of neighbouring powers, either for geopolitical reasons as in Lebanon or Cambodia (after 1979), or for economic gain as in DRC and Sierra Leone. Another is the general vulnerability of poor countries, especially African countries, vis-à-vis forces emanating from the world economy. With regard to the Rwandan genocide in 1994, though strictly speaking not a case of complete collapse there has been some debate about the role played by the preceding slump in international coffee prices together with IMF/World Bank-imposed austerity measures. Consumer prices and fees for health and education had indeed been rising in the context of austerity policies, adding to economic hardships. The recent Afghan case of the Taleban regime was special in its own way, with a state system that had by and large ceased functioning as a 'normal' state, though in the end receiving its *coup de grâce* with the American intervention (2001).

KEY POINTS

- State collapse occurs at the final end of complex and conflict-ridden processes of deterioration, decline, and erosion of state functions.

- Understanding state collapse requires sound analysis of the contextual and conditioning factors, including the interaction of internal and external variables.

- State collapse may result from significantly different tracks of civil conflict and the erosion of state functions.

State–Society Linkages Under Threat

Discussions about state collapse are closely related to discussion of the causes and consequences of civil conflict. However, the latter evidently represents a much broader field than that concerned with state collapse as such. If we keep strictly to a bottom-line definition of state collapse as referring to situations where all normal state functions have ceased to exist, then *most or all recent patterns of state collapse will have been preceded by sub-state conflict and violence of one kind or another*. An all-out civil war, for example, can seriously weaken the central state and eventually cause its collapse. Ethnic or religious strife and other forms of sub-national conflict (see Chapters 6 and 7) can severely affect the chances of survival of the state system as a whole. Again, as discussed in Chapter 5, widening socio-economic gaps within the population, induced or aggravated by factors emanating from the global economy, can fuel conflicts and eventually incapacitate the state system to handle them.

State collapse may itself constitute a moment in ongoing civil conflict, inaugurating new episodes in the strife, such as in Liberia. Again, as suggested earlier, state collapse in due course could open up processes of renewed state formation. But the relation between state collapse and civil conflict is not a chicken and egg one. If we reverse the equation, *it is by no means the case that all instances of civil conflict, no matter how severe, will lead to state collapse*. Historically, there have been numerous cases of prolonged or profound civil conflict which have not led to ultimate state collapse (see Box 13.1). If it

appears to have done so more frequently in recent times, this may be due to particular conditions resulting from the fragility of state systems within the current global context having come to play a larger role—a point returned to later.

In discussing dynamics that may lead to state collapse, Zartman (1995) points to a 'necessary' factor which is contained in the paradox of 'the effectiveness of the state before collapse, through repression and neglect, in destroying the regulative and regenerative capacities of society: the collapsing state contracts, isolates itself, retreats. As it implodes, it saps the vital functions of society' (Zartman 1995: 7). Thus state collapse is seen here as one side of a coin of which societal collapse is the other. Linking the (mal-)functioning of the state to that of societal processes and capacities touches on an important dimension.

Nonetheless, that kind of crisis can arguably occur more easily in some situations than in others, notably in those where the fabric of linkages and two-way mechanisms between state and society has not grown into a dense cluster of connections but has remained fairly thin and superficial. Indeed, collapse could be more readily anticipated in contexts where there has been a limited and somewhat artificial state presence 'in' society, Somalia or Chad, for example, than in others where the idea and reality of statehood has a long-standing background, as in Ethiopia and India. This would remain true even if ex-imperial Ethiopia, for example, fell apart at some point as a territorial entity. For the

---

BOX 13.1

Civil Conflict without State Collapse

Angola 1975–91	Nepal 1996–2006	Guatemala 1960–96
Sudan 1955–72	Sri Lanka 1983–present	Colombia 1949–58/armed conflict to the present

idea of 'state' and 'stateness' are likely to reassert themselves among several of the parts into which it might then fragment. Already, Eritrea's resurgence as a distinct political entity separate from Ethiopia after 1991 has taken a very 'statist' form. Generally speaking, as the incidence of state collapse in recent years has been stronger in Africa than in Asia and other world regions, it seems reasonable to assume that this is connected with the existence of weaker state–society linkages in Africa than elsewhere.

In this connection, Zartman argues there is insufficient evidence to say that collapse results from inadequate or inadequately functioning institutions, that is, mal-adapted and mal-functioning Western-style colonially derived state institutions. It is certainly true that some inconsistency between implanted institutions and their new contexts has been present in numerous situations, sometimes with major implications such as in India and South Asia generally. And indeed, maladapted as they have been, they have nonetheless often continued to 'function' and create new streams of interaction, resource management, and power structures. However, it may not so much be the mal-'functioning' of implanted institutions that has fuelled collapse but rather the extent of mismatch of novel institutions with their environment. This would have allowed only few meaningful linkages between state and society to develop, thus leaving the state structure as a fairly artificial body hanging over society. If in addition mal-functioning in such instances also means arbitrary rule, enhancing people's insecurity, and engendering gross inequities in the access to resources, then a process leading towards ultimate collapse can easily accelerate, as in the Somali case. But again, we should not generalize on the basis of only limited case-study material, as for instance Bayart *et al.* (1999) appear to do when they talk about the 'criminalization of African politics'. Even a demonstrable or increased incidence of criminalization in specific contexts cannot provide a valid basis for generalizations or for broadly depicting African politics in those terms. Nor can the occurrence of greed-driven and hence basically criminal, rebel activity, witnessed in Sierra Leone and Liberia, provide sufficient ground to equate all rebel action in Africa with criminal activity as Collier (1999) suggests. Again, there may be different layers of causality within one and the same context, requiring careful analysis that can reach below the surface. But while generalization about causal patterns is hazardous this is not to deny that factors identified in the general theories have played an important role in some particular cases.

KEY POINTS

- State collapse is usually preceded by civil conflict of one kind or another, but civil conflict does not necessarily lead to state collapse.

- State collapse can occur more easily in situations where the state framework has a relatively thin presence in society than in contexts where state and society are strongly interwoven.

- 'Greed versus grievance' is too dichotomous a representation of realities and allows insufficient recognition of mutations occurring in the course of conflict.

- Generalizing about the causes of state collapse stimulates debate but tends to obscure sound analysis.

Diverse Trajectories

Short of, or beyond, some mega explanation pointing to changed global (pre-)conditions that have prompted an increased incidence of state collapse, it is important to identify to what extent different political and economic constellations have prompted different trajectories of collapse.

There is no single recipe for collapse or single path or set of determinants. At the same time, what evolves clearly is not just random: recent examples suggest there are some recognizable and potentially recurrent patterns. Therefore it is reasonable to say that instances of state collapse, even if superficially similar, represent the provisional end result of different sets of dynamic processes, subject to different clusters of contextual variables and forces.

Yet it remains true that the present global context, where the major powers no longer have the same interest in maintaining inter-state balances of power, and by implication in maintaining states that they supported during the cold war—appears more prone to the incidence of state collapse than was previously the case, especially in Africa. Several years after September 11 the picture has not essentially changed in this regard, except that the chances of external intervention in existing state systems, possibly followed by their collapse, has evidently increased—witness the case of Iraq in 2003 and the anxieties generated by Israel's military invasion of southern Lebanon in 2006.

Generally, the rapidly changing global context, characterized by the drive towards economic liberalization and privatization, the pursuit of global market relations, the propagation of the rolling back of the state, the demanding role of the international financial institutions, and related features such as the global communications transformation, can certainly be viewed as offering a mega explanation of sorts. And the end of the cold war, together with the changed rationales of big power politics in the international arena and the new global conditions by which these have been accompanied, usually does figure as one general explanatory cluster of variables.

Notwithstanding the presence of such a major change of (pre-)conditions it remains true that a common cause does not necessarily trigger common results. The kind of pattern that ensues will depend on more distinctive factors such as the structuring of political forces, societal divisions, resource endowments, and so on. In facing the forces of post-cold war globalization, state systems with different fault lines in their social or economic structures exhibit contrasted patterns of fragmentation.

When trying to identify different chain reactions to collapse a number of distinct patterns suggest themselves (see Box 13.2). The first four are more basic in character, the last two conceivably more supplementary.

In addition to these specific variants, we could think of states in which institutional failures to provide basic security in one or more respects (physical security, health, nutrition) have gone beyond a point of repair—for whatever specific reasons—thus invoking a state bankruptcy of sorts. This more general variant could figure as both a manifestation and determinant of collapse, the latter as deteriorating conditions become a factor in their own right.

It should also be understood that the above categorization does not imply strictly separate tracks. Rather, several of these dynamics could be operative at the same time, reinforcing one another. In this connection, one of the most important, and most difficult, distinctions to be made arises from mutations that sometimes set in. Even where rebel activity was born out of grievances based on ethnic inequalities, as in the DRC and Sierra Leone, for example, in due course it can still become transformed into coercive systems of primitive accumulation. The resulting pattern of development is therefore not necessarily strictly linear or singular. And we can never be certain until it has happened that any of these tracks will result in collapse. A whole range of chance factors may in the end make all the difference between collapse and a state that simply lingers, or limps, on.

Mapping out different trajectories to collapse is important also for the choice of possible remedial or preventive action, and should take note of the mix of internal and external factors and actors involved. For instance, if the key problem in a given situation were identified as one of grossly malfunctioning institutions (as is often assumed), then presumably there could be a case for major institutional repair or overhaul. Of course that might leave unattended

BOX 13.2

Patterns of State Failure and State Collapse

- States in which the privatization of state assets and prerogatives of state rulers has become extreme, and in which there are deepening challenges to that rule from former associates as well as from various liberation fronts (Zaire/Congo under Mobutu, Haiti under Duvalier, Uganda under Amin, Somalia under Barre).

- States with a marked historical mismatch between the nature and orientation of state institutions and the socio-political processes and divisions within the society concerned (Somalia, Chad, Rwanda).

- States in which there are deepening fights over the control of strategic resources like diamonds, oil, and timber involving rebel groups and privatized armies, making state institutions irrelevant (Congo/DRC, Sierra Leone, Liberia, potentially Nigeria).

- States undergoing a major struggle over power and over the political and cultural orientation and organization of society (Cambodia, Afghanistan, potentially Sudan).

- States in which secession attempts escalate, potentially affecting the continuity of the state system as a whole (DRC, potentially Indonesia).

- Fragile states suddenly facing deteriorating economic conditions which seriously affect the livelihood of a large majority of the population, leading to a breakdown of state.

the real root causes of arbitrary rule, such as ethnic grievances or other conflicts responsible for the failing institutions in the first place. But if collapse has occurred or is threatening because of a state system's extreme vulnerability to changing, externally driven economic conditions, then obviously the focus for remedial action should reflect that. Again, if a basic mismatch between a country's state framework and societal structure lies at the root of collapse, then it may be more prudent to allow fresh departures to emerge out of that situation than expect the previous failing state structures to be reinstated. In other words, different routes for possible remedial or preventive action will be appropriate for different tracks leading to collapse. Mistakes in identifying the pattern of causality not only mean poor analysis but could give rise to unsuitable policy recommendations.

Unsurprisingly, several instances of collapse in recent years have been followed by international calls for restoration of order, sanctions, or even advocacy of some form of international trusteeship for certain situations. The latter was advocated for

Sierra Leone, for example, and in a de facto way was implemented for a short while with the British military intervention there.

More generally, however, the option of intervention and international trusteeship has been advanced as a possible form of international action for wider clusters of countries. There have even been proposals for a 'de-certification' of certain categories of countries, a measure meant to exclude them from normal privileges and reciprocities among UN members. Such generalized responses are problematic, because they do not distinguish the merits or demerits of specific situations or how they have come about. Rather, they seem to be based on an assumption that the order which had previously existed—such as that under the erstwhile Sierra Leone government—was in itself legitimate but was derailed and destroyed at the hands of unlawful elements. As a hypothesis, such a reading of the route to collapse emphasizes institutional failures as a root cause, while as a remedy it recommends redressing proper institutional mechanisms and procedures, thus putting the state back into place. This is not necessarily wrong, but that still does not make it right, or sufficient. For it begs the question how those institutional mechanisms (that is, state structures) came to be undermined, and at the hands of what forces? Furthermore, although collapse at one level looks synonymous with disorder, the most appropriate response may not be to try to restore the previous order. What is more, especially in the wake of September 11, external actors should beware of intervening prematurely and in ways that do not allow the country's own actors to play a central role in efforts at political reconstruction. Iraq post-Saddam is a striking example.

KEY POINTS

- The lifting of cold war hegemonic structures laid various states open and vulnerable to new very challenging economic and political conditions.

- The routes towards remedial or preventive action may need to be as different as the tracks leading to state collapse.

- External actors should refrain from massive interventions likely to create new internal-external dichotomies.

Statelessness and the International Context

Statelessness may follow for longer or shorter periods after state collapse. The situation will vary dramatically from one context to another, and there are some instances, like East Timor at the height of crises (2000 and 2006), where a forceful and timely international presence is essential. It is also hard to imagine Afghanistan now and in the foreseeable future without a strong international presence. Yet in the longer run it is important that Afghans themselves regain control over their own affairs, in ways which will be most consistent with their societal and political divisions.

The implications of collapse and statelessness vis-à-vis the external environment seem full of contradictions, as can be illustrated with the example of Somalia. Over a more than ten-year period, during which major parts of Somali society acted as if no useful purpose would be served by a return to the former unified Somali state, the UN and other international agencies, as well as foreign governments, have held on to the myth of the sovereignty of the former Somali state. They maintained working relations on the ground with a plurality of actors, while strenuously upholding the image of undivided Somali sovereignty. Meanwhile, Somaliland, the former British protectorate that had merged with Italian-controlled Somalia at independence in 1961, determined that it wanted to revert to its own, separate status at the collapse of the Somali state in 1991, thus (re-)declaring its independence. So far its calls for international recognition tabled with the UN have gone unheeded.

In explaining this there seems to be a sense of unease at the sight of blank spaces emerging on the world's maps. With the end of colonialism, all global territory was supposedly divided into states. This has become a bottom-line to the 'new world order', representing a new, prescriptive normalcy. There is now even an emerging, yet entirely unsubstantiated assumption that where there are no states, there might be terrorists.

More practically: the international system needs mailboxes and addressees for each entity within its orbit. In that light, no constituent unit should be allowed to disappear or to go underground. But also, there must be a natural fear for precedents: if one weak state collapses and is allowed to get away with it, others might follow. More serious, and more difficult to resolve, is the fact that all countries, even the poorest and most vulnerable, have become tied to a whole web of treaties and international obligations through the sheer fact of their independent status and membership in the international order. Last but not least, if a collapsing state has incurred huge debts, who is to be held responsible for those debts? The idea of debtor countries one by one disappearing, dissolving, leaving no address whatsoever, must be an international banker's nightmare.

Looking at these issues in terms of sovereignty, two points demand attention. Sovereignty supposedly embodies a nation's ultimate self-determining powers over its own future, which is entrusted in conditional custody by its people to the state. In the case of collapsed states, however, it now appears that the international system, specifically the United Nations Security Council, is advancing itself as an alternative custodian, empowered to withhold sovereignty and to grant it to successor rulers when it considers that the appropriate moment has come.

Second, with reference to many of Africa's postcolonial states it has been argued that their survival as independent states would have come to a halt had it not been for the international recognition of their sovereignty (and the big powers' interests in propping it up) (Jackson 1990). This thesis tended to disregard the role of international actors themselves in narrowing the room for manoeuvre and the sovereign scope for policy initiatives and policy coordination by the governments of many countries,

not just in Africa. Nevertheless, sovereignty in this perspective could be viewed as a saving grace for otherwise failing or collapsing states.

With collapse, therefore, new kinds of situations are arising: international recognition may no longer serve as a protective umbrella for weak regimes, but may become a potential stumbling block to fresh starts and rejuvenation by insisting on holding on to old territorial boundaries and political entities. This departs sharply from the idea of international recognition following the logic of internal evolution and paths of reconfiguration and state formation. Inevitably, therefore, this raises new questions about the scope for political restarts in situations where external recognition plays an increasingly decisive role.

If the incidence of state collapse and non-recognition of newly emerging entities were to increase, it is conceivable that earlier (pre-UN) patterns in international relations might be repeated once again, entailing recognition of states by some other (neighbouring or like-minded) partners, but not necessarily by the system as a whole. This would add to recent trends towards unilateral action on the international front in other respects, threatening the aspirations to universality for the United Nations and its institutions. The US invasion of Iraq, though strictly not belonging to the domain of state collapse, has brought this out dramatically. If the UN in the long run is to retain a central role in these matters, it needs to develop some degree of positive flexibility in this regard.

External Actors and the Politics of Reconstruction

Given the incidence of failing states and instances of state collapse and civil conflict, international actors have engaged in a variety of ways to restore order and in reconstruction programmes. A

complex field of action and discourse on the 'politics of reconstruction' has emerged, comprising multi-faceted strategizing among the donor community and involvement of foreign troops for peacekeeping operations of various kinds. On the donor front, several features deserve attention. Many aid agencies in recent years have set up programmes and divisions meant to respond to complex political emergencies. A common objective is to try to be prepared for rapid and effective action. There is a tendency to search for common strategies, in part as a corrective to situations in which different external agencies were all doing their own thing, resulting in confusion. Significantly, however, these developments acquire a dynamic of their own, which may ultimately lead away from, rather than towards, developing capacities to design approaches more specific to the individual circumstances.

Closely related is a tendency to work towards set recipes which can be deployed at once and in all situations, again in response to perceived urgencies and demands of effectiveness. Also, some authors and agencies are becoming less inhibited about suggesting the need to sideline the sovereignty of some of the affected countries, proposing to limit or temporarily abrogate it through a UN or some other mandate—as in Kosovo. Finally, there is a trend among leading multilateral agencies to see post-conflict contexts as a suitable ground, and moment, to install market-friendly frameworks.

All this creates a paradox of sorts. As external parties become increasingly prepared to intervene, with a view to re-creating political space in ways that promise accelerated political and economic liberalization, the chances of taking the distinctive features of specific situations into account or of leaving the initiative to internal actors will arguably diminish. However, the effectiveness of external interventions often remains limited, as policy recommendations and prescriptions are frequently ignored or may face distorted implementation. Also, the nature of external-internal policy interactions is likely to vary considerably from one context to another in the light of local cultural and power configurations.

Such actions generally take place in situations in which the state framework is supposedly recovering from collapse or is extremely weak and fragile due to other causes, calling for external intervention.

But while at one level such engagements, as indicated, may promote certain similarities in the shaping of external-internal political-institutional relationships, at other levels highly contrasted patterns must be expected as a result of different kinds of contexts. Such diversity becomes apparent particularly in situations where the severity of internal conflict has called for sending in foreign troops—one of the few last resort instruments available for external intervention in conflict-prone contexts. In any such situations a distinct interplay of forces and factors—internal divisions, external actors, other socio-structural features, and the occurrence or prospects of civil conflict—is likely to ensue, rendering different meanings to 'political reconstruction' and to prospects of the deepening or resolution of civil war. Some examples of such contemporary situations—a few of them supposedly post-conflict, others instigated as preventive action, yet others showing recurrent conflict cycles—may illustrate the complexity and diversity of external-internal relationships emerging in contexts marked by state collapse and civil conflict.

East Timor

East Timor, the newest new state in Asia and independent since 2002, in 2006 became a sobering case of a failing and collapsing state system whose government had to call in Australian-led foreign troops to restore basic order. Massive disorder and violence then erupted and inflamed regional and tribal social divisions throughout the small country following the prime minister's dismissal of some 600 soldiers (of a total of 1,400) who had gone on strike and mutiny after their demands for equal conditions had been refused. Conflicts within the military and police soon spread among corresponding ethnic and regional divisions within the Timorese population, especially but not only between the eastern (*lorosae*) and western (*loromunu*) parts, resulting in widespread chaos and virtual anarchy. This was in fact the second time that massive social unrest broke out. The first time had been in 1999–2000, when pro-Indonesian factions and military caused widespread violence, killing, and plunder following East Timor's overwhelming vote in favour of independence in a plebiscite (see Chapter 20a below). The referendum put an end to Indonesia's occupation, begun upon the termination of Portuguese colonial rule in 1975 but contested for decades in a bitter guerilla struggle waged by the Revolutionary Front for the Independence of East Timor (FRETILIN). Following Indonesia's abrupt departure, a special United Nations Transitional Administration in East Timor (UNTAET) was installed to help prepare the country for independence over what has been generally agreed was a much too short three-year time span. At that juncture there was no choice except for East Timor to become a UN sanctioned independent state within a world order that offered only the 'nation state model' for possible adoption. Its entry into the world of states became surrounded by high expectations as well as considerable scepticism (Chopra 2004).

Inevitably, perhaps, East Timor as a state has since hardly appeared viable and has been seriously failing in its essential functions. As one of the poorest countries in the world, with a population of under a million, an economy offering virtually no paid employment nor showing any signs of growth, it is beset by extremely complex social divisions and heterogeneity, and has virtually no shared politico-cultural structures to bind its diverse population groups together. The national government has not been able to overcome the deep-seated regional, tribal, and other sectarian divisions that had surfaced and itself carries primary responsibility for the triggering of the recent conflict within the armed forces. With its fate once again laid in the hands of the international community and the UN Secretary-General taking an active lead in exploring ways to mitigate the crisis, including the mobilization of a new United Nations Integrated Mission in Timor-Leste (UNMIT), external forces can do little more than temporarily carry out essential policing to calm down social unrest and try to lay a basis for renewed reconciliation amidst pervasive mutual distrust and hostility. With all the social, political, and economic ingredients for a resumption

of violence and disorder lingering on, reconstruction acquires a euphemistic connotation but must yet entail some crucial first steps in state-building 'from scratch' as well as offer some prospects for meaningful employment.

Congo

In terms of the extent and depth of human misery in the wake of state failure, with over 4 million dead in combination with unprecedented havoc and displacement, the Democratic Republic of Congo (DR Congo) since 1998 has provided the scene of one of the greatest humanitarian disasters worldwide since 1945. With great reserves of mineral resources and extremely weak post-colonial state structures unable to effectively govern the vast country, large sections of its population in recent years became the victim of numerous external and internal actors competing to forcefully capture and exploit its resource basis. Following the brutal regime of Joseph Mobutu from 1965 to 1997 and the political instability that arose in the void it left, rival rebel factions in conjunction with invading forces from neighbouring states—Angola, Namibia, Zimbabwe, Rwanda, Uganda—engaged in a prolonged and multi-layered civil war, also dubbed Africa's 'first world war'. At more than one point Congo's continued existence as a distinct state and territorial entity became uncertain, as de facto fragmentation had become a reality and several neighboring states were evidently interested in carving out a piece of the rich cake. Numerous efforts were made at UN and AU circuits to halt the violence and plunder, though more often than not resolutions to that effect were ignored or being undermined through clandestine external support to rebel groups—often in exchange for control over much-coveted minerals such as coltan, diamonds, and gold. At the international level, though, specifically that of the UN, it is noteworthy that a splitting up and departure from Congo's accepted ex-colonial and AU sanctioned boundaries was never entertained as an option.

Upon prolonged international efforts and diplomacy, a settlement was reached in 2003 to end the warfare and create a transitional regime in which the various, largely regionally based, rebel factions agreed to jointly participate. Large parts of the country nonetheless continued to be notoriously unsafe, with various militia leaders keen to retain control over their home territories and ready to resume fighting for it. As part of the international efforts towards reconstruction, elections were staged for parliament and a new president in July 2006, for which rebel groups were encouraged to put up their representative candidates. Much was at stake for them in taking this step, the elections from their perspective signifying the continuation of warfare by other means (Tull 2006). External involvement in this complex process not only entailed the monitoring of polling by thousands of election observers, but the stationing of close to 20,000 foreign troops (mainly from the UN but including 2000 European reinforcements, partly stationed in neighboring Gabon) to ensure orderly procedures. These multi-party elections, the first in forty years, were called in order to consolidate reconciliation between rival rebel factions and provide a legitimate governmental set-up while at the same time offering a valid exit strategy for the external presence. Still, one key concern was that, though constituting a step deemed necessary in the peace process, the election might trigger renewed conflict if aspirants to power felt their claims were poorly reflected in the popular vote, as initially happened. Hence the stationing of additional foreign troops was scheduled to last until at least the finalization of the re-constitutive process, to culminate in the installation of a new government and parliament.

Afghanistan

If in various contexts an external military presence is expressly meant to contain ethnic and other political rivalries, to come to some measure of orderly government and pave the way for reconstruction, the Afghan situation differs from these in several significant respects. Historically, Afghanistan did not have a strong central government but was characterized by pronounced urban–rural cleavages and a dichotomy between a weak central state versus relatively autonomous regional and tribal power-holders. The Afghan state had emerged as a tribal confederacy and developed into a buffer state, but had never managed to develop an extractive and economically stimulating relationship with its rural hinterland from which in turn it would draw its own strength. During most of the nineteenth and twentieth centuries, in fact, the Afghan state system was largely externally financed and upheld, consecutively from the UK, the US, and the USSR (Cramer and Goodhand 2004).

After the US-engineered removal in 2001 of the neo-fundamentalist Taleban regime which had emerged in wake of the defeat of Soviet-backed forces, the new government of President Karzai has been making efforts to get its presence accepted but faces powerful opposition from the side of various regional warlords, between which it attempts to manoeuvre with due circumspection. Current attempts to prop up an Afghan central state through external military support thus could easily come to fit within a historical pattern of limited state–society relationships. Moreover, as a strategy to defeat the Taleban it is likely to prove illusory, unless a strong and independent Afghan state would be built in the process. The Taleban, which had rested on a strong rural basis and for a while had seemed eclipsed, returned as a formidable guerilla force which can still count on a virtually unlimited supply of young rural recruits otherwise faced with chronic unemployment. A massive multi-national external presence which in recent years has been mobilized to restore law and order and contribute towards reconstruction, has increasingly found itself forced to engage instead in combat. If meaningful economic alternatives are not developed, a military victory and a return to normalcy may remain remote prospects.

Somalia

Within the domain of state formation and collapse Somalia in recent times has set a new record of sorts, namely as the country that has gone longest without an effective state framework—or a state system of whatever description for that matter. This has not meant there would not be a 'need' for a state, or that there would not have been parties prepared or keen to perform its functions. Though over the past fifteen years numerous Somalis have demonstrated that they can manage reasonably well—some even quite well—without the benefits of a state system, many or most would acknowledge that having a state is essential for various tasks that no form of privatization can fulfill: registration of property, issuance of licenses and visas, policing, coastal patrol, and many more.

However, the previous Somali state of Syad Barre had also shown another face, namely that of a brutal and capricious regime which made life risky and miserable to many of its citizens (see Box 12.1, p. 231). The various warlords that emerged in different regions have been vying for state power ever since, spending considerable energy in stopping rivals from attaining their goal while by and large themselves remaining unprepared to share power. Thus a classical Somali pattern of clan-based warfare among shifting coalitions of warlords has been a characteristic feature of the period from 1991 onwards. Significantly, however, the nature of the coalitions and the strategies for state reconstruction, in accordance also with various reconciliation efforts initiated by neighbouring states, shifted notably over time. For the first ten years or so of Somalia's stateless period, the overriding goal of most parties was reunification, implying the re-establishment of Somalia's central state system (with the inclusion of Somaliland that had seceded). Depending on which of Somalia's neighbours was trying to negotiate a settlement, one or another panel of coalition partners then stood a better chance of being prominently represented in a proposed government, while other factions would choose to stick to armed opposition. But when after many peace conferences a return to a centralized state seemed as remote as ever, the idea of creating mini state frameworks in different regions began to catch on, rationalized as the 'building-block' approach

that laid priority on 'putting one's own house in order first', and leaving the question of reunification for later. This laid the basis for the emergence of Puntland state, among others, which featured a full-fledged constitution and governmental set-up (Doornbos 2006: chapter 8), though this soon ran into internal conflicts. Subsequently a number of these regional, though mainly warlord-led, entities as of 2004 came together in a Transitional Federal Government (TFG), supported by Ethiopia and the US. However, the TFG remained powerless to enforce any decisions and for its own security stayed away from the capital of Mogadishu, confining itself to Baidoa in the south. New opposition emerged meanwhile from Islamist groups, consistent with an alternative unifying organizational principle in Somali culture and society and assuming the form of a Union of Islamic Courts (UIC), which in the course of 2006 rapidly spread its influence over most of the Somali territory and provided a rare sense of tranquillity as well as a fresh approach to solving security problems. As the US feared that the UIC might provide a haven for al-Qaeda operations, it stimulated and funded the setting up of an Alliance for the Restoration of Peace and Counter-Terrorism (ARPCT) based on a network of warlords, though without much avail. Since the disastrous end of the US-led United Nations operation in 1992–5, the US government had refrained from further direct intervention in Somalia. Its active support now to warlord factions, together with Ethiopia, entails the risk that the ongoing Somali crisis will become further internationalized, with dim prospects for reconstruction.

Iraq

If in various current crisis situations an external military presence has been called in or mobilized to contain severe internal civil conflict and create a climate of normalcy conducive to social reconstruction, the Iraq case is diametrically opposite to any such a scenario. Here the US–UK invasion, ostensibly intended to bring 'democracy' to Iraq and the larger Middle East region, not only has inflicted untold damage, disaster, and casualties upon the country, but has provoked internal civil strife of unprecedented magnitude which only officially is not recognized as civil war, leaving the Iraqi state in great disarray and disunity. The external military presence, in no way perceived by the population as a liberating force but as an occupation army, has shown itself incapable of halting the civil strife which it has ignited. The US strategies of state restructuring have resulted in sharp disunity between the Shi'ite and Kurdish communities and to further divisions within them, particularly among the Shiites (see Box 7.1, p. 136). Above all, it has left profound unresolved questions about their future mode of coexistence, potentially leaving the country fragmented and with a seriously weakened and vulnerable state structure. The 'politics of reconstruction' has a long and arduous road ahead in Iraq.

KEY POINTS

- The international system, theoretically based as it is on membership of all independent and sovereign states, has difficulty accepting the reality of statelessness. By insisting on the conservation of (former) state boundaries and the myth of enduring state sovereignty it blocks possible new departures in state formation.

- International reliance on the Westphalian state model lies at the root of various instances of state failure in which states are unable to comply with the model's presuppositions.

- International actors increasingly search for common strategies and set recipes in response to situations of state collapse and civil conflict. This leaves less chance for situation-specific approaches and priorities and for the social leaderships of affected countries to have a decisive influence over the processes of reconstruction.

- The 'politics of reconstruction' is emerging as a pivotal field of academic interest as well as of international engagement.

- The possibility of powerful new tensions between domestic and influential external actors is one possible outcome of international intervention in situations of civil conflict and state collapse.

Conclusions

State collapse can be understood in different ways and should be distinguished from state failure. The chapter has shown that in order to understand forms of state collapse, its causes and consequences, a tendency to excessive generalization should be avoided—a lesson applicable both to analysts and to external actors who are minded to get practically involved. Surely the routes to state failure and collapse are many and complex. But what lies beyond collapse, and what lessons can be drawn from past experiences? Historically speaking, one would expect a new political order to surface from amidst the ruins of the old, possibly building on elements that had been suppressed or ignored. Connections between old and new can be extremely important in understanding the emergence and evolution of new political forms. In European history, state formation processes often restarted in new directions and in new constellations following the demise of a previous order. Today in various developing world settings it is important to recognize that the internal social and political actors and dynamics should play a central role in recreating order and some kind of normalcy.

Fresh start moments, almost by definition, are delicate. They may be full of promise and expectations of brighter futures, distanced from the past. At the same time, they are extremely fragile, as the conflicts and violence that were inherent in the processes of breakdown and collapse will still be alive in the memory, and could conceivably be reignited. Fresh starts therefore need sound understanding of the circumstances that gave rise to them, and careful handling by all concerned. Although external actors have become increasingly if selectively involved and can make an important contribution they should be aware of the risks of complicating the process if they expect *their* designs for new political futures and structures to play a primary role. Powerful tensions between political actors inside the country and influential external parties can easily deepen and sharpen in the process, and novel forms of domination emerge around the introduction of new frameworks of political and economic accountability and control.

? QUESTIONS

1 How do state collapse and civil conflict relate to one another?

2 What kinds of developments may lead to the collapse of state structures?

3 Why has there appeared to be an increase of the incidence of state collapse in the post-cold war era?

4 What role do international actors and the international community tend to play vis-à-vis collapsed states?

5 What main factors determine the varying outcomes of armed external engagement in fragile state contexts?

6 Under what conditions can armed external presence be expected to contribute to 'state reconstruction'?

7 What are the pitfalls of generalizing about the causes of and external responses to instances of state collapse?

8 How should one assess the chances of external intervention of all kinds provoking or deepening rather than mitigating civil war?

GUIDE TO FURTHER READING

■ Addison, T. (ed.) (2003), *From Conflict to Recovery in Africa* (Oxford: Oxford University Press).

■ Bayart, J.-F., Ellis, S., and Hibou, B. H. (1999), *The Criminalization of the State in Africa* (Bloomington, Ind.: Indiana University Press/Oxford: James Currey).

■ Berdal, M., and Malone, D. (eds.) (2000), *Greed and Grievance: Economic Agendas in Civil Wars* (Boulder, Colo.: Lynne Rienner).

■ Chopra, J. (2004), 'Building State Failure in East Timor', in J. Milliken (ed.), *State Failure, Collapse and Reconstruction* (Oxford: Blackwell Publishing).

■ Collier, P., Elliott, L., Hegre, H., Hoeffler, A., Reynal-Querol, M., and Sambanis, N., (2003), *Breaking the Conflict Trap* (Washington DC: World Bank and Oxford University Press).

■ Cramer, C., and Goodhand J. (2004), 'Try Again, Fail Again, Fail Better? War, the State and the "Post-Conflict" Challenge in Afghanistan', in J. Milliken (ed.), *State Failure, Collapse and Reconstruction* (Oxford: Blackwell Publishing).

■ Doornbos, M. (2006), *Global Forces and State Restructuring: Dynamics of State Formation and Collapse* (Houndsmill: Palgrave Macmillan).

■ Jackson, R. H. (1990), *Quasi-States: Sovereignty, International Relations and the Third World* (Cambridge: Cambridge University Press).

■ Reno, W. (1998), *Warlord Politics and African States* (Boulder, Colo.: Lynne Rienner).

■ Zartman, I. W. (ed.) (1995), *Collapsed States: The Disintegration and Restoration of Legitimate Authority* (Boulder, Colo.: Lynne Rienner).

 WEB LINKS

● **www.colorado.edu/conflict** Comprehensive gateway to the website of the University of Colorado Conflict Resolution Consortium.

● **www.crisisgroup.org/home/index.cfm** The site of the International Crisis Group, an independent, non-profit, non-governmental organization engaging in conflict prevention and resolution.

● **www.prio.no** The site of the International Peace Research Institute, Oslo.

● **www.roape.org** The site of the *Review of African Political Economy*, which publishes many articles about state collapse, state failure, and political violence in Africa.

 ONLINE RESOURCE CENTRE

For additional material and resources, see the Online Resource Centre at:
www.oxfordtextbooks.co.uk/orc/burnell2e/

STATE COLLAPSE, CIVIL CONFLICT, EXTERNAL INTERVENTION

14 Democratization

PETER BURNELL

Chapter Contents

- Introduction
- Regime Transformation, Democracy, and Democratization
- Democratization as Process
- Explaining Democratization
- The International Politics of Democratization
- Conclusion

Overview

The late 1980s and early 1990s saw a wave of change embracing political liberalization and democratization in Africa, Asia, and other developing areas. The completion of an almost worldwide process of democratization that began earlier in the 1980s with the widespread return to elected civilian governments in Latin America seemed imminent. However, by the turn of the new millennium many doubts and reservations had begun to surface, and attention has turned most recently to the quality of democracy and authoritarian persistence. This chapter elucidates the idea of democratization and its relationship to democracy; summarizes recent trends; compares different understandings of democratic consolidation and explanations for successful transition. The relationship between democratization and development provides a central theme, not least because of worries that continuing social and economic problems could undermine at least some new democracies. The implications of **globalization** and international **democracy promotion** as well as of economic liberalization for democratic self-determination of developing countries are also raised.

Introduction

Democracy is an essentially contested concept. The long history of theorizing about its meaning provides few certainties about what 'democratization'—a relative newcomer to the vocabulary—really means. Clearly democratization refers to a process of change; but most writers conceive of it as a journey without end. Obviously it is not a new phenomenon. In a widely used metaphor Huntington characterized the extension of democracy beginning around 1974 as the third wave of democracy, the two earlier waves in 1828–1926 and 1943–62 each being followed by a reverse wave. Huntington's influential book *The Third Wave* (1991) pre-dated the large number of more recent democratic experiments in the developing world which now occupy the literature. Nevertheless we should not forget that recent trends have witnessed not so much democratization as attempts to redemocratize, following earlier democratic failure(s), such as Argentina returning to elected civilian rule in 1983, or Uruguay where military-controlled civilian government prevailed from 1973 to 1985 and many African examples too. Thus Ghana, which now carries many of the hallmarks of an established liberal democracy, only returned to democracy in 1992 after successive earlier attempts to re-establish rule by elected civilian politicians failed, the military holding power in 1966–9, 1972–9, and 1981–92.

Regime Transformation, Democracy, and Democratization

There is a temptation to present democratization as a unilinear movement from political authoritarianism to democracy, which implies a simple dichotomy of regime types. There are different kinds of authoritarian regime—absolute monarchs; personalist dictators; military-bureaucratic rule, *de jure* one-party states as in Zambia, 1973–91, and so on. That an authoritarian regime can enjoy a measure of legitimacy at least in the eyes of some of the citizenry should not be ignored. Collectively they draw on a variety of legitimating bases or combinations of such sources. These include religious belief, as in Iran and Saudi Arabia, nationalism, and a conviction that the status quo is better equipped to meeting popular desires of personal security and material well-being (functional legitimacy) than the uncertainties of political upheaval. This last claim draws extra strength where an invidious regional comparison can be made like, for example, the suffering experienced by Iraqis especially in Baghdad since the removal of Saddam. Of course the different regimes have distinctive vulnerabilities too; and some are more institutionalized than others (Ulfelder 2005).

Similarly there are a variety of possible outcomes of authoritarian breakdown. The collapse of an authoritarian regime could be followed by protracted civil war (as in Angola and Mozambique after gaining independence), or 'warlordism' and the disintegration of the state, as happened in Somalia in the 1990s. Alternatively it could lead to a different kind of authoritarian regime or a diminished sub-type, for instance semi-authoritarian or one of its variants, competitive authoritarianism. In competitive authoritarian regimes, 'formal democratic institutions are widely viewed as the principal means of obtaining and exercising political authority. However incumbents violate those rules so often and to such an extent that the regime fails to meet conventional minimum standards for democracy' (Levitsky and Way 2002: 52). Regime transformation could also lead to some other intermediate regime type or hybrid version of democracy—one of the many varieties Collier and Levitsky (1997) called 'democracy with adjectives', for instance proto, semi, quasi, limited, partial, pseudo, façade democracy, and so on. The term 'low-intensity democracy'—'not even an approximation to actual western liberal democracy or present forms of bourgeois rule' (Gills *et al.* 1993: 8)—has also caught on in the literature. In large countries, such as federal systems, regime variations and unevenness in democratization can occur across provinces or localities. But not unusually, although countries may be in transition from an authoritarian regime, there is no certainty about what they are in transition to.

Democracy, from the Greek for rule by the people, has been called an inherently debatable and changeable idea. Even so, ideas resembling the model of polyarchical democracy (polyarchy) advanced by the American political scientist Robert Dahl in the 1970s (see Box 14.1) have dominated much of the democratization discourse, although challenged by writers like Gills *et al.* (1993) who prefer a more 'participatory progressive' idea of democracy. Polyarchy centres on two main pillars: public contestation and the right to participate. Liberal democracy, which is akin to polyarchy, remains

the most commonly cited yardstick for judging the progress of democratization, and is generally believed to avoid the fallacy of electoralism. Diamond (1996), a prominent contributor to the literature, thus usefully distinguishes between liberal democracy, where there is extensive provision for political and civic pluralism as well as for individual and group freedoms, and mere 'electoral democracy' (even where elections appear free and fair). In the latter civil freedoms are less prized and minority rights are insecure.

How do we know which countries are democracies? Many people consult Freedom House ratings of freedom. Freedom House is a US non-profit organization that conducts annual evaluations of political rights and civil liberties almost everywhere in the world. It defines democracy, at minimum, as a political system in which people choose their authoritative leaders freely from among competing groups and individuals who are not chosen by the government. Freedom is the chance to act spontaneously in a variety of fields outside the control of government and other centres of potential domination. Democracies are judged either free or partly free, as measured along a seven-point scale (1–2.5 = free; 3–5 = partly free; 5.5–7 = not free).

Freedom House's approach has been criticized on a number of grounds. For example, the UNDP's *Governance Indicators: A User's Guide* while acknowledging that Freedom House usefully simplifies a complex subject into an easily understood rating, says it has been shown to exhibit an ideological bias against communist or former communist states. It also maintains that Freedom House's additive approach to scoring rights is contrary to the principles of international human rights norms,

BOX 14.1

Dahl on Democracy

Citizens must have unimpaired opportunities to formulate their preferences, signify them and have them weighted equally. This requires certain institutional guarantees: freedom to form and join organisations; freedom of expression; right to vote; eligibility for public office; right of leaders to compete for support; alternative sources of information; free and fair elections; institutions for making government policies depend on votes and other expressions of preference. **(Dahl 1971)**

and cautions that the assessments should not be treated as a reflection of the views of citizens within the countries. Nevertheless, Freedom House ratings are widely used for depicting global trends in democratization and making comparisons cross-nationally and over time. They are convenient and accessible; the alternatives are not flawless. For Diamond, Freedom House's 'free rating' is the best available indicator of liberal democracy.

Trends

The data indicate that following a dramatic initial expansion of democracy after the onset of Huntington's third wave, which increased both the number and proportion of all states that could be termed democratic, the number of liberal democracies levelled off in the early 1990s. Some countries like Vietnam and Libya were never caught up in the tide; others actually moved against it, like the Gambia, where a military coup in 1994 interrupted the democracy that dated from independence (1965). Many of the newer democracies soon began to show signs of democratic erosion or 'hollowing out', settling on the form but less so on the substance of electoral democracy, although usually retaining multi-partyism and elections. By the twenty-first century a trend towards pseudo-democracy is as striking as the earlier trend toward democracy (Diamond 2002).

Nevertheless the 2002 Freedom House survey claimed a new high-water mark in the number and proportion of democratically elected governments worldwide (121), while being able to identify only 86 free countries, with strong regional variations. And for 2005 the survey reported the following breakdown (Piano and Puddington 2006: 119–21):

- Sub-Saharan Africa (48 countries): 11 free; 23 partly free; 14 not free. Twenty-three countries were marked as electoral democracies or better.
- Asia-Pacific (39 countries): 16 free (several being small island states); 12 partly free; 11 not free. Seventeen countries were marked as electoral democracies or better.

- Americas (35 countries including many Caribbean island states): 24 free; 9 partly free; 2 (Cuba and Haiti) not free. Twenty-nine countries were marked as electoral democracies or better.
- Middle East (18 countries plus Occupied Territories of Palestine): 1 free (Israel); 7 partly free; 11 not free. Only Israel and Turkey were marked as electoral democracies or better.

In recent years there has been little overall change, notwithstanding some small improvements in the Middle East and North Africa, although by mid-2006 gains registered in the Lebanon, where in April 2005 an impressive demonstration of people power had caused Syria to withdraw its occupying forces, and the Palestinian Authority were looking precarious. In 2005 the Philippines, Nepal, Thailand, and Guyana all declined in status. Relevant to debates about the connections between politics and levels of development, the 2003 survey revealed that freedom levels are significantly lower among the countries with annual per capita Gross National Income of less than $1,500. In 2003 only three out of 29 countries having incomes below $300 were judged free. Yet among countries with an annual per capita GNI not exceeding $3,500, more than a quarter qualified as free.

KEY POINTS

- The dichotomy of authoritarian and democratic regimes is too simple: it ignores the variety of non/pre-democratic regime types and the different possible outcomes of political transition.

- As an idea democratization is beholden to the fact that the very meaning of democracy itself is contested.

- The recent progress of democratization in the developing world has been erratic and uneven; some regimes remain authoritarian and others are experiencing democratic decay.

- We should not exaggerate democratization's usefulness as an analytical framework for understanding the politics of all developing countries.

PETER BURNELL

Democratization as Process

Conceptual distinctions between political liberalization, democratic transition, and democratic consolidation are commonplace, but do not imply a necessary let alone inevitable sequence of events. As a prelude to 'political opening', authoritarian breakdown can happen in different ways—gradual or sudden, violent or peaceful—and may range from moderate to absolute. Political liberalization usually refers to a top-down process, made by political leaders aiming to maintain power for themselves and not willing to accept that institutionalized uncertainty over electoral outcomes should be the determining principle of who governs (and the possibility of alternation in office that implies). Liberalization advances political freedoms less than civil liberties. In contrast democratization introduces arrangements for genuinely competitive elections. Liberalization can become stalled or frozen rather than lead on to democratization, and may even go into reverse, as appears to have happened in Jordan. Conversely, largely free elections might be introduced without first establishing the rule of law, full executive accountability, and a flourishing civil society—or what has been called democratization backwards. It gives rise to what Zakaria (1997) called rather controversially 'illiberal democracy', citing Iran and President Fujimori's Peru as examples. But liberalization and democratic opening can also happen simultaneously, where authoritarian collapse is sudden and complete, as in South Africa's abolition of apartheid. Although rulers who at first allowed some liberalization without intending to embrace democracy may subsequently lose control of the momentum, and find themselves overtaken by demands for fuller democratic opening, this pattern has not happened in the Middle East. In Egypt for example the government has effectively deployed some measure of political liberalization as a way to prevent more significant movement towards democracy.

A related distinction some analysts make is that democratization 'comes from below', and involves political, though not necessarily violent, struggle. However this unnecessarily precludes cases of negotiated or pacted transition, including those where the elites set out with an intention of forestalling a groundswell of popular sentiment seeking more radical change. Much of the early analyses of democratic transition in Latin America focused on intra-elite divisions over the wisdom of democratic change and how the strength of pro-democratic alliances that cut across elements within the ruling elite and leading actors in civil society could make the difference between successful transition and failure.

Democratic consolidation

Just as there can be political transition without transition to democracy so there can be democratic transition without democratic consolidation—the situation typical in many 'emerging' democracies. Similarly democratic decline need not lead to full-blown autocracy. But how do we recognize democratic consolidation? Answers range from those which equate consolidation to longevity to answers that identify it with democratic 'deepening'. This refers to qualitative improvements, such as in the levels of participation or real political equality. Schedler (1998) recommends we restrict consolidation to two 'negative' notions: avoiding democratic breakdown and avoiding democratic erosion. Put differently, democratic consolidation refers to expectations of regime continuity—and to nothing else. A minimal definition like this maximizes the number of developing countries qualifying for democratic consolidation. More extravagant accounts that rest on democratic 'widening'—the incorporation of democratic principles in economic and social areas like the family—may impose criteria that not even the developed countries satisfy. One solution is to reserve such claims for some idea of 'post-consolidation'. Even so recent developments in the theoretical literature have attempted to decipher the quality of democracy, and specify what makes for 'good democracy' and its opposite, or 'defective democracy'. That the latter seems quite capable of offering a stable form of regime makes these exercises look especially relevant (see *Journal of Democracy* 15 April 2004).

More significant for democratic consolidation than a democracy's longevity may be its ability to survive threats and withstand shocks—generated at home or abroad, and inclusive of political (e.g. an attempted military coup) and financial or economic shocks like the East Asian crisis, 1997. One thesis is that resilience is strengthened by progress in respect of democratic deepening. However, we would not be able to know whether a democracy is consolidated—or that expectations of continuity are justified—until it has been so put to the test. Certainly a number of developing countries have persisted with (e.g. India) or have successfully reintroduced (e.g. Ghana) democracy against seemingly unfavourable odds. Yet to make that a criterion for consolidation seems biased against democracies privileged by more favourable circumstances. These include the international democracy support now available and which contrasts with the cold war period.

A more easily applied notion of consolidation is Huntington's (1991: 266–7) double turnover test. The test requires that a party that took office after a democratic election should relinquish office after losing a comparable election without seeking to resist or overturn the result. This would exclude Botswana, where the Botswana Democratic Party has yet to lose an election since the country gained independence (1966). A more persuasive view sees consolidation as being achieved once democracy has become the only game in town. This requires an appropriate attitudinal shift, not just a temporary behavioural accommodation. The military, then, however reluctantly no longer think it appropriate to meddle in government. On that basis Venezuela, after 1958 one of Latin America's longest

continuous democracies, appeared to fail the test in April 2002, when the army briefly deposed the elected president, Hugo Chávez. Ironically President Chávez's return and the way he has exercised power since then has made more critics doubt Venezuela's democratic credentials, partly because of Chávez's populist and left-leaning pretensions that trade on hostility to US imperialism.

Democrats regard legitimacy as one of democracy's most distinguished properties. For Diamond, democratic consolidation is legitimation. Legitimacy is like reinforcing glue, helping ensure survival in the face of crises and shocks. Indeed, we could say a democracy truly consolidates when it ceases to rely on 'performance legitimacy' (acceptance grounded on meeting society's wants or needs), and achieves 'intrinsic legitimacy'—grounded in acceptance of and respect for democracy's fundamental values and principles. Intrinsic legitimacy shelters democracy against such failings as poor developmental performance. In a settled democracy discontent with the performance of government is exacted on the government, by peacefully removing it from office at the polls. So far public support for many of Africa's new democracies appears to be withstanding economic hardship: Bratton, Mattes, and Gyimah-Boadi (2004: 353) find that 'even if political transition is not immediately followed by prosperity, democracy can still win popular legitimacy via the delivery of good governance'. In Latin America, however, there is a view that what most endangers democracy now is neither populist demagoguery nor the military but 'continuing mediocre performance—the inability of democratic governments to meet the most important needs and demands of their citizens'(Hakim 2003: 122). This becomes even more threatening when combined with popular disapproval of the poor quality of political representation.

The conceptual baggage of transition and consolidation can be criticized for presenting too rigid a framework for analysing what in reality are likely to be multifaceted, multi-dimensional and multi-directional processes of political change. As Schedler (1998) has argued, in practice the 'tip over' point between transition and consolidation and their outer boundaries are blurred; elements of the two movements could overlap. In consequence it could be more insightful to liken democratization to variable geometry: some of democracy's ingredients could be moving in one direction (possibly at different speeds), others moving in the opposite direction (again at different speeds), and yet others standing still, all contemporaneously. For example a competitive party system may strengthen even as civic activism decreases from the heights that successfully campaigned for the end of authoritarian rule. To require evidence of progress on all fronts may be too demanding. A more nuanced model of assessment then is offered by the concept of democratic audit pioneered by David Beetham and colleagues, in their *Handbook on Democracy Assessment* (2002) produced for the International Institute for Democracy and Electoral Assistance (IDEA). The framework groups issues under four headings: citizenship, law, and rights; representative and accountable government; civil society and

popular participation; and international dimensions. The authors claim the assessment can be used by the people of any country for assessing their own democracy. Several country-based assessments have since been published.

KEY POINTS

- A minority of developing countries qualifies as liberal democracies although many more approximate to electoral democracies, with marked regional variations.

- Democratic consolidation has been defined in different ways, with implications for which developing countries are thought to qualify. The quality of democracy is as important as its longevity.

- Democratization can be a slow and protracted affair whereas a democracy's deterioration or collapse may be swift.

- The idea of democracy assessment offers a potentially powerful tool of comparative analysis and self-assessment.

Explaining Democratization

Explaining how democratization occurs and why it takes particular forms generates considerable debate. Explanations of consolidation can be expected to diverge from democratic transition. Similarly, the reasons that illuminate deconsolidation and stalled transition might not explain a former democracy's complete collapse.

One approach to explaining different experiences with democratization emphasizes the impact of historical legacies (political, financial, economic) and path dependence. At its most elaborate path-dependence claims that the nature of the pre-existing regime and the mode used to change it influence the sequel and, ultimately, can determine a new democracy's chances of survival. This

confirms why it is important to distinguish between types of authoritarian regime as well as to establish if there were any previous, failed attempts to democratize. For example in Chile the democratic transition from the military dictatorship of General Pinochet in 1990 respected the privileged position of the armed forces that was constitutionally enshrined in 1981. Critics claim this has limited Chile's new democracy, which even today can seem rather lacklustre. Like much of the theorizing in the democratization literature, path dependence provides more valuable insights for some countries than for others (see Box 14.2).

One of the most widely accepted ideas is that national unity 'must precede all the other phases of

BOX 14.2

275

DEMOCRATIZATION

Rustow's Methodological Propositions

Although Rustow (1970: 346) advanced the following methodological propositions before Huntington's account of the third wave they help make sense of recent democratic experiments in developing countries:

- The factors that keep a democracy stable may not be the ones that brought it into existence: explanations of democracy must distinguish between function and genesis.

- Not all causal links run from beliefs and attitudes to action: the flow can be in both directions.

- The genesis of democracy need not be geographically uniform; there may be many roads to democracy.

- The genesis of democracy need not be temporally uniform: different factors may become crucial during successive phases.

- Correlation is not the same as causation: a genetic theory must concentrate on the latter.

- Not all causal links run from social and economic to political factors: the flow can be in both directions.

- The genesis of democracy need not be socially uniform: even in the same place and time the attitudes that promote it may not be the same for politicians and common citizens.

(Rustow 1970: 346)

democratization' (Rustow 1970: 351). By national unity Rustow meant 'the vast majority of citizens . . . must have no doubt or mental reservation as to which political community they belong to' (ibid.). Some developing countries seem to lack this very simple condition. They may even look to democracy as a means to manage or resolve inter-group conflicts peacefully. Yet democratic advance may itself on occasions be responsible for increasing (violent) conflict in a country, such as by encouraging demands for national self-determination by minorities or at least causing them to have fears about the tyranny of the majority. Sri Lanka's history has been one of both democracy and long-running civil war between the Sinhalese and Tamil separatists in the north.

More broadly, the literature explaining democratization can be distinguished into accounts emphasizing structure and accounts that dwell on agency. The first investigates the 'conditions' and even preconditions whereby democratic trends are variously enabled, facilitated, and actively promoted, or come to be frustrated. The second focuses on process, highlighting the role of actors and institutions. Institutions are so defined as to include rules, norms, expectations, and traditions, both formal and informal, and more concrete

organizations like parliaments and parties. The impact of actors may be greater at key turning points, such as democratic transitions or their timing, than over the long haul. All things considered, democratization is perhaps best understood as a complex interaction that links structural constraints and opportunities to the shaping of contingent choice (Karl 1990).

Socio-economic conditions

Following a seminal article by S. M. Lipset in the *American Political Science Review* (1959) on 'Some Social Requisites Of Democracy: Economic Development and Political Legitimacy' (revisited in Lipset 1994), one school of thought maintains a positive relationship exists between, on the one side, the persistence of stable democracy or the chances of democratic consolidation and the levels of socio-economic modernization. 'Requisites' are not *pre*requisites or *pre*conditions, that is to say these conditions need not be established in advance; authoritarian breakdown and democratic transition can take place amid poverty and economic backwardness. Overall, the idea that material progress even though not essential to democratic transition, enhances the chances of extending democratization and experiencing democratic longevity is strongly supported by developing world evidence, accumulated since Lipset's original inquiry.

Only relatively recently have social scientists begun to investigate seriously the possibility that development could be the dependent variable and treat democracy as the independent or 'causal' factor (see Democratization's significance for development p.284–5 below). The idea that certain sorts of freedoms, notably economic freedoms, are beneficial to wealth creation goes back a long way, to Adam Smith (1723–90). But for many years after 1945 the view that developing countries faced a cruel choice proved very persuasive. Either countries could do what was necessary to develop their economies, mainly by concentrating on saving and investing to expand the productive capital stock, or they could emulate the political systems of the West. The former probably requires government to take some unpopular decisions, like enforcing abstinence from current consumption. Authoritarian regimes that are well insulated from social pressures seemed best situated to this purpose. In contrast the structure of political incentives posed by competitive party politics appears biased towards raising popular expectations about public spending on welfare. Politicians running for office will promise 'jam today', at the expense of doing what is needful for 'jam tomorrow'. In the long run economic ruin beckons—seemingly the experience of Argentina for much of the second half of twentieth century, culminating in a spectacular financial crisis in December 2001.

The moral seemed to be that democracy is a luxury that poor countries can ill afford. After development, sustainable democracy becomes more viable—an option whose opportunity cost (the alternatives forgone) becomes more affordable. The term wealth theory of democracy captures the idea. The dramatic economic performance of East Asian tiger economies like Taiwan and South Korea which only later experienced successful democratic transition appear to bear out the general theory. Critics, however, point to examples of developing world democracies like Mauritius (since independence,

1968) and Costa Rica (a democracy since 1899 with only brief interruptions in 1917 and 1948) that have a generally good record of both economic and social development. Rather than being exceptional cases there are arguments that it is East Asia's undeniably successful deployment of the authoritarian model, which continues today with China and Vietnam, that provides the real exceptions (Halperin et al. 2004). India, for over fifty years 'the world's largest democracy' and where for much of the time economic growth barely kept pace with population increase, shows that democracy can be maintained even where socio-economic conditions look unpropitious. Moreover, rising prosperity does not guarantee that democracy will emerge. In rentier states the effective manipulation of rent-funded public spending by an authoritarian regime and only modest levels of taxation might postpone demands for democracy more or less indefinitely. The Gulf oil sheikhdoms seem to bear this out. However, this kind of 'resource curse' need not operate where democracy is already established, as Botswana, which is well blessed with revenue from diamonds and cattle, illustrates.

The significance of development for democratization

There is much statistical evidence that democracies can survive even in the poorest nations especially *if* they manage to generate development and reduce inequality while meeting certain other conditions (Przeworski et al. 1996). But what makes modernization and development significant for democratization? Is it primarily a matter of resources? Or is it more a case of transforming attitudes, values, and patterns of behaviour? Or of the changing class structure that comes with capitalist development in particular? Or is it something to do with the consequences of development's tendency to integrate society into global structures and norms? Different theories emerge from concentrating on different aspects of development:

- Democratic institutions require substantial financial and economic resources, demand high levels of organizational commitment and public involvement that an affluent and well-educated society can most easily provide. Technological and economic progress should improve the physical infrastructure of political communication.

- Social modernization erodes old values that inculcated deference to traditional authority and generates self-confidence; it inclines people to see themselves more as citizens than just subjects, so increasing demands for, and acceptance of, rational-legal authority. Pragmatic values sympathetic to the politics of compromise and consensus lying at the heart of the 'democratic way' supplant traditional non-negotiable values like exclusive ethnic loyalties that can frustrate national unity and produce violent disagreements. The attainment of material security for all is an opportunity for *homo politicus* to move centre stage. Closer integration into the global economy brings exposure to the liberal and democratic values already enjoyed in the outside world (demonstration effect).

- There is a well-known aphorism 'no bourgeois, no democracy'. Development breaks the exclusive power of feudal landlords. Capitalist development creates a plurality of potential centres of power and influence independent of the state. A property-owning middle class has a vested interest in checking the arbitrary use of executive power, and has the economic means and know-how to organize pressure for the redistribution of power. There is a caveat, however. Necessary conditions are not sufficient conditions. Economic growth can produce wide economic inequalities that sustain inequalities of power. Middle-class elements will defend an illiberal or undemocratic regime if they believe it serves their interests, for instance by providing stability. Thus, notwithstanding an average annual income per capita that is among the highest in the world Singapore is still only partly free in the Freedom House classification.

- Industrialization and urbanization make it possible for an organized working class to mobilize mass support to demand greater political rights and civil liberties for ordinary people, especially in response to the unequal distribution of the benefits of economic growth. Thus Rueschemeyer, Stephens, and Stephens (1992) reject the view that democracy is the creation of the bourgeoisie. They highlight the progressive role of the working class acting together with middle-class elements. Some larger developing countries have very sizeable manufacturing sectors. For example in Brazil the political base of President Luiz da Silva lies in the labour movement. But in many countries the industrial base is still small; and in some it has been weakened by economic liberalization. For example Zambia's mineworkers who pushed for the return of multi-party democracy in 1991 are now much fewer in number: they are politically emasculated. Organized labour is a major weakness of civil society in many developing countries compared to its leading role in democratizing Western European countries.

The ambivalent relationship of market economy and democratic polity

A frequent assumption is that the market constitutes a necessary but not sufficient condition of democracy: there have been authoritarian regimes with market economies but no examples of non-market democracies. In reality the relationship is more ambivalent. As Beetham (1997) explains, there are some negative effects associated with the virtues of the market, and even its positive points must be qualified (Box 14.3). This complex issue can be reformulated in terms of the effects on democracy's quality. Thus for example for Rueschemeyer (2004: 89) 'Even formal democracy is more than what its critics denigrate, because it is an opening for greater democratic quality. To deepen democracy in the direction of greater political equality requires systematic and strong policies promoting social and

---

BOX 14.3

Positive and Negative Connections between Democracy and the Market

Positive connections

- The more extensive the state, the more difficult it is to subject to public accountability or societal control.

- The more that is at stake in elections, the greater is the incentive for participants to compromise the process, or reject the outcome. Market freedoms and political freedoms are mutually supportive: both require the rule of law, and to ensure this for one is to ensure it for both.

- Sovereignty of consumer and voter both rest on same anti-paternalist principle.

- Market economy is necessary for long-term economic growth which assists durable democracy.

Negative connections

- Independence of the market from the state makes the economy difficult to subject to democratic control.

- Free market competition intensifies economic and social inequalities, which can translate into political inequality and so compromise democratic institutions.

- Market dispositions undermine the integrity of the democratic public sphere: market choices come to pre-empt political choices; the logic of private self-interest tends to colonize the public sphere.

(Beetham 1997)

---

economic equality. The quality of democracy, then, depends on social democracy, on long-sustained policies of social protection and solidarity'.

Political culture

Ideas about the significance of political culture date from G. Almond and S. Verba's *The Civic Culture: Political Attitudes and Democracy in Five Nations* (1965). Political culture embodies the attitudes, beliefs, and values that are said to underlie a political system. For Almond and Verba 'civic culture' supports democracy. After years during which some analysts argued the concept has no scientific validity, providing at best an explanation of last resort, sustainable democracy is now said to require a special set of values such as tolerance, mutual respect, a willingness to trust in fellow citizens together with a healthy scepticism towards persons in authority, in addition to possessing basic knowledge and understanding of democracy's mechanics. Analysts routinely pore over the public attitude surveys that are now regularly carried out by organizations like Afrobarometer and Latinobarometer, looking for significant trends in the newer democracies.

The principal constituents of a democratic political culture and the relationships among constituents, and their requisites, are all contested. For instance it was once thought that the Protestant ethic made famous by the German sociologist Max Weber was more closely adapted than Roman Catholicism or Confucianism to liberal democracy, yet evidence from many developing countries now makes that doubtful (see Chapter 7). An especially topical debate is over whether it is the Muslim world or instead the Arab world that should be regarded as inhospitable terrain for easy democratization, in the light of persistently poor scores for political and civil liberties in the Middle East. Although Hinnebusch's (2006) critical review of the competing theories reminds us not to neglect the international influences, cultural perspectives would point to a religious connection in particular, not least because of the seeming incompatibility of ideas of popular sovereignty and the sovereign power of God. However, democracies with large Islamic populations like Turkey, Bangladesh, Indonesia, and Malaysia seem to contradict that. Attitudes to female equality are quite critical here, for although a great deal of the democratization literature is gender blind the political advancement of women in practice is often neglected (see Chapter 8). Progress may depend as much on overcoming culturally and historically embedded forms of disadvantage as on more formal political concessions, such as female quotas in legislative representation (Cornwall and Goetz 2005).

If something like civic culture is essential to democracy, is it a prerequisite or can it be allowed to develop later and, if so, what will encourage that to happen? This introduces the idea of civic education, instruction in democracy that goes well beyond 'voter education' in the procedure of secret ballots. It also gives rise to further questions about whose culture is most important for democratic sustainability, particularly in the early stages of democratization—the culture of the elite or the mass? One argument is that the primary threat to new democracies comes from the people in power, especially 'old generation' politicians who have taken on democratic pretensions simply to stay in power rather than out of conviction. The existence of many examples from recent experience fits well with Bermeo's (2003) argument formed in the context of the Americas in the 1960s and 1970s as well as Europe, that it is not the ordinary people but instead small elite coalitions who bear the main responsibility for democratic collapse. Public attitude surveys in fact repeatedly report widespread attachment to the idea of democracy existing alongside dissatisfaction with the elected leaders and disenchantment with the performance of democratic institutions.

Institutional crafting

The design of political institutions can have important consequences not just for the distribution of political power but for how well the democratic process operates and the democracy's sustainability. The designs themselves are often the result of political activities oriented to particularist, self-regarding goals. On the one hand, formal organizational changes sometimes make little difference to the way things actually work, where inherited informal institutions or patterns of behaviour like patron-clientelism seem impervious to change. On the other hand institutional reforms can acquire a degree of permanence once new constellations of vested interests build around them and resist any changes they calculate will be to their disadvantage.

Designing democracy in problematic surroundings, such as a long history of social conflict or very weak state structures, should take account of the possibility that there will be unintended consequences—what Bastian and Luckham in their review of war-torn societies are tempted to call an 'iron law of the perverse consequences of institutional design' (Bastian and Luckham 2003: 314). In reality considerable tension sometimes exists between the imperative of state-(re)building or its requisites and democratization or its requisites. Where priority is given to the former, the consequences of path dependence may be unhelpful for democratic improvement later. Iraq shows how difficult democracy-building can be in the absence of a functioning state. But there is another belief that the early emphasis on recreating state capacity after the fall of the Taliban regime in Afghanistan took place at the expense of democratic design, and that strategy could now set back the development of democracy for years to come.

Two sets of institutional concerns that have attracted special attention in new democracies are, first, the balance of power and mutual oversight among the executive, legislature, judiciary, and other constituents of a 'self-restraining state'; secondly, elections and party systems. A self-restraining state embraces multiple institutional mechanisms for making government accountable (see Schedler, Diamond, and Plattner 1999). So, for instance, much effort has been devoted to comparing presidential systems with parliamentary and other more mixed systems. On balance the evidence appears to indicate that presidentialism is more likely to be unstable when combined with vigorous multi-partyism. However recent experience in South Korea and Indonesia also shows that presidential democracies can accommodate rapid political change without necessarily endangering democracy.

O'Donnell (1994) proposed the category delegative democracy, much cited in a Latin American context. It rests on the premise that whoever wins election to the presidency is thereby entitled to govern as they think fit—constrained only by the hard facts of existing power relations and a constitutionally limited term of office. The last is something many presidents have schemed to remove, although not always successfully, as the failed attempts by Argentina's President Menem and Malawi's President Muluzi for instance show. Electoral victors in delegative democracies may present themselves as being above political parties and organized interests; they aspire to be accountable to no one. Accountability has been called the linchpin of democratic control of government by the governed (Beetham *et al.* 2002: 45). O'Donnell makes the valuable distinction between vertical accountability, which makes government accountable to the ballot box and includes supervision by civil society as well as opposition parties, and horizontal accountability across a network of relatively autonomous institutions. The judiciary's power to enforce the rule of law—even, and especially, against democratically elected governments—is significant in this context, as are bodies like the Auditor General, Ombudsman, Truth and Reconciliation Commissions, and Human Rights Commissions, which have proliferated in developing countries. There comes a point at which democrats may be legitimately concerned about the power such unelected bodies wield. In practice governments often obstruct their operational effectiveness, by providing inadequate resources and exercising control over appointments. Anyway, horizontal accountability is usually weak in delegative democracies. Even an institution of direct democracy such as the referendum can operate in ways that reduce, not increase executive accountability, as shown in Breuer's (2007) study of Latin America. That compares unfavourable examples from Bolivia and Ecuador against Uruguay's more positive experience.

Elections and parties

A number of issues to do with how electoral systems and elections management structure political competition are especially relevant to new democracies. Pastor (1999: 7–8) noted that in developing countries the problem of conducting free and fair elections is 'compounded by the intensity of politicization at an early stage in the democratization process'. He found 41 per cent of elections in Africa in 1989–99 were flawed, compared with 21 per cent in Asia and only 6 per cent in Latin America and the Caribbean. Growing recognition of the importance of the competence and impartiality of independent Elections Commissions forms but a part of the more general consideration of how to assess election quality. Governments minded to rig the outcome usually take steps well before the formal campaign.

Although civil society has been credited with responsibility for bringing about authoritarian collapse in some countries, and theorists argue a vibrant civil society is essential to healthy democracy, there is a consensus that political parties are indispensable to liberal democracy and democratic consolidation. Certain vital functions cannot easily be replicated by other actors, although where parties are weak and the party system under-institutionalized some tasks may be carried out more effectively by civic associations, social movements, and other grass-roots organizations (see Chapters 9 and 10). A party system is defined by the number of parties and the relations between them, their relative size, and how much meaningful choice is presented to the electorate. At minimum an effective party system furnishes government; a competitive party system means there is some possibility of alternation in power. In many emerging democracies the development of viable parties and the establishment of reasonably competitive party systems is proving to be a major challenge, particularly in Africa where financial support is limited and neo-patrimonial and clientelistic patterns reduce the salience of parties' policies and programmatic performance (see Randall and Svåsand 2002). The design of the electoral system is only one of many influences on the party politics, but examples abound where inappropriate choices have had adverse consequences, such as by entrenching sectarian political competition in Iraq. In Afghanistan the single nontransferable vote system adopted in the 2005 parliamentary election 'decreased turnout by confusing voters, it created a fragmented legislature largely unrepresentative of the votes cast, and it diminished prospects for legislative-executive cooperation' (Reynolds 2006: 115–16). The funding of political parties and their activities between as well as during election campaigns is a particular conundrum that has echoes in the West. A majority of developing countries have opted for public funding, but in countries like Thailand and parts of Africa such traditional practices as gift-giving and even attempted vote-buying are still in evidence (Pinto-Duschinsky 2002).

> **KEY POINTS**
>
> - Different dimensions and phases of democratic change require their own explanation.
>
> - In the long run economic development may be one of the best guarantors of durable democracy especially if the benefits are widely distributed.
>
> - Different understandings of how and why socio-economic development advances the democratic prospect resonate differently in different countries.
>
> - The relationship of market-based or capitalist development to democratization is ambivalent.
>
> - 'New institutional' perspectives on the process of political change complement economistic explanations of democratization's successes and failures.

The International Politics of Democratization

A distinguishing feature of democratization in the last thirty years is the role played by external or international factors. The end of the cold war and collapse of Soviet power help explain the increased agitation for political reform in the developing world, although the return to democracy in Latin America was already well advanced. It is the interplay between internal and external factors that is often most significant.

External influence can work in various ways, such as by example, persuasion, and various kinds of direct involvement. The active engagement of some established Western democracies has been prominent, but even the United Nations has become a major actor, such as by assisting with the staging, monitoring and observing of elections particularly in new states like East Timor. The United Nations Development Programme has become a substantial funder of projects in democratic governance.

And in 2006 the UN got round to launching a Democracy Fund, to which India along with the US was the most generous of the first 26 sponsoring states.

The influence on democratic trends in developing countries that is exerted by developments in their neighbours and the surrounding region should not be ignored either. A number of regional organizations have undertaken to encourage the spread of democratic values, principles, and practices in their member states. They have instituted mechanisms to promote and defend democracy. In Latin America the Organization of American States (OAS) sets out to uphold the Inter-American Democratic Charter (see Box 14.4). The African Union's New Partnership for Africa's Development (NEPAD) established the African Peer Review Mechanism (APRM), with a view to advancing both economic and democratic governance among the continent's states (Box 14.5). Of the two the OAS can claim some of the most notable interventions. The first invocation of the OAS's Democratic Charter was in 2002, when the Permanent Council condemned the military coup that temporarily removed Venezuela's elected President Chávez from office. The OAS Secretary-General subsequently facilitated talks that produced agreement on an electoral referendum to seal the return to elected government. In Africa the expectation is that the burden of political governance peer review will lie with the African Union rather than NEPAD.

BOX 14.4

Key Issues for the Organization of American States

According to the Inter-American Democratic Charter of 2001 'The peoples of the Americas have a right to democracy and their governments have an obligation to promote and defend it.' The OAS says the Charter is significant because it:

- Reflects the political will and collective commitment of 34 democratic nations and defines what the OAS member countries agree are democracy's essential elements.

- Responds directly to a mandate from the region's heads of state and government, who stated at the 2001 Summit of the Americas that the hemisphere needed to enhance its ability to strengthen democracy and respond when it is under threat.

- Establishes procedures for when democracy has been ruptured, as in a coup, or is seriously altered and at risk.

- Points out ways in which democracy can and should be strengthened and promoted in the hemisphere.

The Inter-American Democratic Charter says 'essential elements' of representative democracy include respect for human rights and fundamental freedoms; the exercise of power in accordance with the rule of law; the pluralistic system of political parties; and the separation of powers and independence of the branches of government. Other elements include transparency; probity and responsible administration on the part of governments; respect for social rights; freedom of expression and citizen

Under the terms of the Charter, OAS member states may seek advisory services or assistance from the OAS to strengthen their electoral institutions and processes. And the OAS subscribes to the Declaration of Mar del Plata, Fourth Summit of the Americas (Mar del Plata, Argentina, November 2005) which states 'Increased participation by citizens, communities, and civil society will contribute to ensuring that the benefits of democracy are shared by society as whole'.

'Today, more than 170 non-governmental organisations are registered to take part in OAS activities. Guidelines for their participation are available at www.civil-society.oas.org'.

(Extracts from Organization of American States, *Key OAS Issues*, 2005)

BOX 14.5

NEPAD and Democracy

NEPAD's first stated *priority*: 'establishing the conditions for sustainable development by ensuring peace and security; democracy and good, political, economic and corporate governance; regional cooperation and integration; and capacity building.'

NEPAD's statement of *immediate desired outcomes*: 'Africa adopts and implements principles of democracy and good political economic governance, and the protection of human rights becomes further entrenched in every country'.

'We undertake to work with renewed determination to enforce: the rule of law; the equality of all citizens before the law and the liberty of the individual; individual and collective freedoms, including the right to form and join political parties and trade unions, in conformity with the constitution; equality of opportunity for all; the inalienable right of the individual to participate by means of free, credible and democratic political processes in periodically electing their leaders for a fixed term of office; and adherence to separation of powers, including the protection of the independence of the judiciary and of effective parliaments.'

'Women have a central role to play in Africa's efforts at democracy, good governance and economic reconstruction.'

'In support of democracy and the democratic process we will ensure that our respective national constitutions reflect the democratic ethos; promote political representation; enforce strict adherence to the position of the African Union on unconstitutional changes of government; strengthen and, where necessary, establish an appropriate electoral administration and oversight bodies in our respective countries and to provide the necessary resources and capacity to conduct elections which are free, fair and credible'.

(Extracts from *NEPAD in Brief* and *A Summary of NEPAD Action Plans: African Peer Review Mechanism*. Additional extracts on NEPAD on economic and corporate governance can be found in Box 15.2)

Nevertheless, much of the attention paid to the international promotion of democracy especially following the announcement of President George Bush's mission to advance freedom and democracy in the Middle East and elsewhere during his second term, has focused on the role of the West. Two approaches stand out. One attaches democratic, human rights, and governance conditionalities to offers of development aid and other concessions such as trade concessions. The other provides technical, financial, material, and symbolic support to democracy projects and programmes, namely democracy assistance (see Box 14.6). By and large democracy conditionalities have been found to be ineffective when faced by determined opposition, by the likes of Zimbabwe's President Mugabe and Myanmar's military rulers. Of course society pays a heavy price through the aid and other benefits forgone. Its most notable achievements have been in respect of European accession candidates to the European Union, which is not applicable to the developing world. Democracy assistance worldwide and from all sources has increased to between US$5 and 10 billion annually. However it too has a mixed record. While giving support to the holding of free and fair elections has long been considered insufficient, strengthening civil society on a sustainable basis has been found to be difficult. A more recent enthusiasm, which is helping to build political parties and party systems, is even more problematic (see Burnell 2006).

A third alternative, the imposition of democracy by force, has been largely discredited. Unlike post-war Germany and Japan, few developing world examples exist where it has been successful. In fact the conflating of democracy promotion with regime change understood as ousting the government, principally Saddam Hussein's toppling by US and British military intervention in Iraq, is now widely believed to have harmed the cause of democracy promotion. It has made it easier for authoritarian leaders to utilize anti-imperialist rhetoric and stir nationalist sentiment against interference in their country's politics. The ruling authorities in over 20 countries where external democracy initiatives have taken place now seem significantly less willing to allow or cooperate with such endeavours. All in all, the evidence suggests that linkage or the density of a country's ties to West, more so than Western leverage applied to vulnerable governments, makes the most difference in helping bring about real and sustainable democratization (Levitsky and Way 2005). Nevertheless, in the long run it is domestic rather than international factors that probably most determine the survival of a new democracy, even though some external forces, globalization in particular, may carry powerful negative effects.

The real motives behind international democracy promotion efforts are undoubtedly mixed. One notion that appeared after 9/11 is that democratization will help combat international terrorism. This draws on the belief that terrorism's roots lie in the repression and political exclusion practised by autocratic regimes, Saudi Arabia for instance. However many analysts view this as simplistic; a review of the evidence suggests it is invalid (Dalacoura 2006). A more widely respected if still fairly recent set of relevant ideas refers to the positive effects that democracy can have on development and living standards (see p. 381). Here then we need to reconsider the question of democratization's usefulness to development, raised earlier when discussing the socio-economic conditions of democratization.

Democratization's significance for development

The thinking behind the idea of a 'cruel choice' between democracy and development is no longer fashionable. Many examples show that authoritarian regimes—especially weak and fearful autocracies, as well as some rentier states—can be self-serving and will mismanage economic and financial resources precisely because they are not accountable and lack legitimacy. In contrast party-based government may offer a responsible approach to economic management in democracies: the parties judge that over the long run a reputation for being responsible will influence their electoral fortunes. Also, democratically elected governments possess the legitimacy to take tough but necessary economic decisions. Accountability makes the gross abuse of public resources less likely. Furthermore, the UNDP has argued that human development depends as much on whether poor people—assumed to be the majority—have political power as on their opportunities for economic progress. The UNDP's *Report* (2002: v) claims too that democracies are better adapted than authoritarian regimes to handle domestic conflict in ways that do not damage the economy. By arguing that sustained poverty reduction requires equitable growth but also requires that poor people have political power, the possibility of a virtuous circle is implied. Democratic opening improves the outlook for human development by empowering people to exert pressure for an expansion of social and economic opportunities. In other words, it furthers social justice and brings more social democracy. That in turn makes democratic sustainability and democratic deepening even more achievable.

Once again, however, a necessary condition is not a sufficient condition; thus the UNDP's *Report*

BOX 14.6

Democracy Assistance Objectives and Modalities

Sector	Sector Goal	Type of Aid
Electoral process	Free and fair elections	Electoral aid
	Strong national parties	Party building
State institutions	Democratic constitution	Constitutional assistance
	Independent, effective judiciary	Rule-of-law aid
	Competent, representative legislature	Legislative strengthening
	Responsive local government	Local government development
	Pro-democratic military	Civil–military relations
Civil society	Active advocacy bodies	Building civil society organizations
	Politically educated citizenry	Civic education
	Strong, independent media	Media strengthening
	Strong, independent unions	Union building

Source: Adapted from Carothers (1999: 88)

acknowledges there is insufficient evidence to claim democracy actually causes economic growth; it does not *guarantee* equitable social and economic development either. The great variety of political regimes makes generalization about their economic performance very risky. The developing world's established democracies do not stand out in terms of tackling poverty: deep and widespread poverty persists in India for example; and social inequalities have tended to widen in countries undergoing simultaneous market-based economic and political transition (see Box 14.7 for different views). Part of the reason for this is thought by many to lie in increasing globalization.

Globalization, democracy, and democratization

International influences exert both positive and negative effects on democratization. Western powers still extend support to some undemocratic or illiberal regimes where they judge it crucial to such interests as national security. Pakistan's President Musharraf is an example. In any case a plausible argument is that the West's unsystematic approach to promoting democracy, and the spotlight placed on democratic development in developing countries, are really a sideshow, because of globalization and its effects.

Globalization has been defined as 'processes whereby many social relations become relatively delinked from territorial geography, so that human lives are increasingly played out in the world as a single place' (Scholte 2001: 14–15). Globalization diminishes the value of conventional democratic models if it makes state-bound structures less tenable, and this is said to be particularly true for many developing countries. In a globalizing world the human forces that most influence people's lives are increasingly transnational and supraterritorial; in contrast democracy is historically rooted in and confined to the borders of the nation-state. Although globalization's impact on the state is explored in more detail in Chapter 15, the specific implications for democracy are mentioned here.

First, powerful agencies of global governance like the World Trade Organization are shrinking the space available for national political self-determination. These agencies are not themselves democratically accountable and possess specialized technical knowledge of complex global issues that small poor countries and micro-states can only envy. By devaluing democracy's credibility these developments threaten to induce political apathy among citizens.

Secondly, the political space where self-rule remains an option is penetrated more and more

---

BOX 14.7

Three Views on Democracy and Development

- Democracy is too conservative a system of power. It has a bias towards consensus and accommodation that cannot promote the radical change in the system of wealth that is essential to establishing developmental momentum, especially in late developing societies. A truly developmental state needs to be insulated from society and may not be a democracy (Leftwich 2002).

- Developing countries differ from the West in that democratic contestants do not have to compromise with capitalists; instead they aim to capture power for themselves. This rent-seeking behaviour

by politicians destroys the chances of development (Khan 2002).

- Powerlessness and poverty go together. Democratic models more expansive than the minimalist versions offer an emancipatory potential that would empower the poor and serve development, for example by attacking the corruption that benefits the privileged few (Grugel 2002).

Source: Adapted from 'Debate: Democracy and Development', in *New Political Economy*, 7/2 (2002)

by a variety of non-accountable external actors, who establish local branches or subsidiaries and form linkages and alliances that enable capture of the domestic policy and decision-making processes. Small and poor states with internal political weaknesses are the most vulnerable. Corporate bribery of politicians and officials by transnational enterprises is one example. In some places the Bretton Woods institutions may actually prefer democratically elected government because, unlike less legitimate and unpopular regimes they could possess the political strength to implement the sort of tough economic measures these institutions call for in return for offers of international financial support. Western assistance to ideological development by new political parties and civil society can help implant, or reinforce, the overall message of valuing private enterprise and free economic markets. Similarly it is argued that international democracy promotion seeks to control the reform process by limiting it to 'low intensity' democracy, thereby serving the interests of transnational capital.

However, there are several counter-arguments not least that globalization's progress need not be uniformly adverse to democratization over time. The threat it poses may be more to some specific forms of democracy, or to certain countries only, rather than to democracy as such.

First, the international spread of democratic values is itself a part of globalization—hence we can speak of globalizing democracy. This process is furthered by the increased mobility of people, knowledge, and ideas that comes from revolutions in information technology, international communications, and transportation—highly visible signs of globalization. Globalization forces political openness, which threatens authoritarian regimes. Many developing countries themselves now actively contribute directly or indirectly to the global spread of values central to democracy and human rights, both individually or like the OAS on a collective, regional basis. For example the personnel employed

in Commonwealth election observer missions are recruited from right across the membership, both rich and poor country democracies.

Second, if globalization can be made a more powerful force for economic progress and especially if development's benefits are shared more equitably, the prospects for stable democracy will increase.

Third, democracy is predicated on there being some measure of state capacity, if only to counter democracy's enemies at home and abroad. If the wealth generated by globalization helps finance state reconstruction and increased capacity to govern then weak or ineffective states in particular can become more responsive to societal demands. Voting for political leaders will then have some point.

Fourth, the UNDP *Report* (2002) calls for greater pluralism in respect of global decision-making, through enlarging the space for participation by non-state actors. The globalization of civil society (global civil society) is already under way, and could recapture influence for the people even where familiar state institutions and political parties seem incapable. Global networks give support to local civic actors in their struggles to open up political space at home; local actors draw support from regional and global coalitions when endeavouring to stand up to such powerful international institutions as the World Bank. The global justice movement (see Box 10.3) is illustrative.

Finally, there are projected schemes, some more visionary than others, pertaining to 'cosmopolitan democracy' (i.e. a democratic international order) and ideas for democratizing institutions of governance at levels reaching all the way from the local to the global and including the United Nations. When accompanied by measures to empower such institutions vis-à-vis market forces that affect people's livelihoods, such proposals could rescue democracy's purposes. However, for the time being they remain firmly tied to the realms of speculation.

KEY POINTS

- The jury is still out on the potency of democratization to bring about the very socio-economic conditions that could underpin emerging new democracy's survival.

- There are many different routes by which the international environment can influence democratization in developing countries: only some are supportive; some are unintentional, and their effects vary among countries.

- The West's capacity to determine sustainable democratic development through political

conditionalities or democracy assistance should not be overestimated.

- From a democratization perspective, globalization invites us to think not only about how to make the political space more democratic but how to restore power to the political as well.

- Globalization has helped undermine some authoritarian regimes but might pose a longer-term threat to democracy.

Conclusion

Key issues at the heart of debates about democratization in developing countries include: what is democratization and how much progress has there been? What explains democratic developments and the influence on future prospects? What are democratization's relationships to development? And how important are the international dimensions? This chapter has argued that democratization's meaning, like democracy itself, is contested. And while most developing countries have undergone political change over the last two decades or so, the number of stable, new liberal democracies is modest. In many countries competing analytical frameworks such as nation-building and state-building may offer more insights into their contemporary politics.

Attention has turned away from explaining democratic transition (transitology) and specifying the character and causes of democratic consolidation (consolidology) and towards: identifying democracies' hazard rates (the probability that they will decay or die); specifying the quality of

democracy; and explaining authoritarian persistence. Our typology of regimes has been enriched by the proliferation of different forms of diminished authoritarianism (authoritarianism with adjectives) and diminished democracy. There is a chicken and egg conundrum of how to sort out democratization's many apparent requisites from its possible consequences.

Thus it is important to establish how far economic circumstances and external forces over which governments might have little control determine democratization's fortunes, and how much is influenced by political choice and institutional initiatives. In the long run development appears to favour democracy, but there are reservations about the full effects of the market. Indeed, there is keen interest in whether disappointing social and economic conditions for the majority of the citizens could eventually erode their willingness to uphold democratic rule. Latin American countries are being studied closely for this very reason. Moreover, whereas in places like Zimbabwe democratic reform might be essential to achieving development it offers no guarantee anywhere, and in some places might even disrupt development. China is an example.

A comprehensive assessment of the possibilities for democratic self-rule and of progress to date should take account of the international involvement in developing countries and globalization and their consequences. Globalization can have significant consequences for the state and for public policy in developing countries, as is elaborated in Chapter 15. That also details the recent emergence of a global fascination with the topic of governance. Although closely connected with matters intrinsic to classifying different types of political regime, 'governance' embraces a large and overlapping penumbra of political issues that have recently come to the fore in the attention not just of international development experts but the governing elites of developing countries as well.

? QUESTIONS

1 Why are some developing countries democratizing more successfully than others?

2 What is democratic consolidation and how does it relate to ideas about the quality of democracy?

3 What does the evidence tell us about sustainable democracy's requirement that certain economic and socio-economic (pre-)conditions must be met?

4 What sort of trade-offs can be envisaged between building democracy and rebuilding political order in countries with failed states or a recent experience of civil war?

5 How can democratization promote development and in what circumstances might it be a hindrance to development?

6 When crafting democracy are the instruments of horizontal accountability more difficult to 'get right' than the institutions of vertical accountability?

7 What if anything should international actors like the United Nations and democracy foundations in the West do that will help pro-democratic forces bring change inside their own countries?

8 How can developing countries make globalization serve the aims of democratic development?

GUIDE TO FURTHER READING

■ Anderson, J. (2005), *Religion, Democracy and Democratization* (London: Routledge). All the main religions are represented in this collection.

■ Beetham, D., Bracking, S., Kearton, I., and Weir, S. (2002), *International IDEA Handbook on Democracy Assessment* (The Hague, London, New York: Kluwer Law International).

■ Burnell, P. (ed.) (2003/2006), *Democratization through the Looking-Glass* (Manchester: Manchester University Press and Somerset, New Jersey: Transaction Publisher). Introduces multi-disciplinary perspectives on democratization and comparative analysis from the regions.

■ Carothers, T. (1999), *Aiding Democracy Abroad* (Washington DC: Brookings Institution). Critically assesses US' democracy assistance.

■ Cornwall, A., and Goetz, A. M. (2005), 'Democratizing Democracy: Feminist Perspectives', *Democratization*, 12/5: 783–800. A critical review of the issues.

■ Diamond, L. (2002), 'Thinking about Hybrid Regimes', *Journal of Democracy*, 13/2: 21–35. Explores regime types that combine democratic and authoritarian elements.

■ Hagopian, F., and Mainwaring, S. (eds.) (2005), *The Third Wave of Democratization in Latin America: Advances and Setbacks* (Cambridge and New York: Cambridge University Press). A comprehensive overview.

■ Halperin, M. H., Siegle, J. T., and Weinstein, M. M. (2004), *The Democracy Advantage: How Democracies Promote Prosperity and Peace* (London and New York: Routledge).

■ 'The Quality of Democracy' (2004), *Journal of Democracy*, 15/4, Special issue.

■ Leftwich, A. (2002), 'Democracy and Development', *New Political Economy*, 7/2: 269–81. This sets out contending perspectives on the relationship between democracy and development.

■ Levitsky, S., and Way, L. (2005), 'International Linkage and Democratization', *Journal of Democracy*, 16/3: 20–34. Compares the effectiveness of international linkage and leverage.

■ Rustow, D. A. (1970), 'Transitions to Democracy', *Comparative Politics*, 2/3: 337–63.

■ Schedler, A. (ed.) (2006), *Electoral Authoritarianism* (Boulder, Colo.: Lynne Rienner).

■ United Nations Development Programme (2002), *UNDP Human Development Report 2002: Deepening Democracy in a Fragmented World* (New York and Oxford: Oxford University Press). Introduces a political dimension into human development.

■ *Democratization* (edited in the UK) and the *Journal of Democracy* (edited in the US) are two well-known journals. Each year of the latter includes a digest of the latest annual Freedom House Survey.

 WEB LINKS

- **http://democracy.stanford.edu** The comparative democratization project led by Larry Diamond among others.

- **www.freedomhouse.org** The site of the US-based Freedom House, and includes access to its annual comparative measures of freedom.

- **www.cdi.anu.edu.au** The site of the Centre for Democratic Institutions, Australian National University, useful for democracy developments in the Asia-Pacific region.

- **www.idea.int** The site of the multi-member International Institute for Democracy and Electoral Assistance (Stockholm) and its democracy research and promotion activities.

- **www.afrobarometer.org** The site for national public attitude surveys on democracy, markets, and civil society in Africa.

- **www.latinbarometer.org** The site for national public attitude surveys in Latin America.

- **www.ned.org** The site of the Washington-based, non-governmental, National Endowment for Democracy, which among other things houses the International Forum for Democratic Studies.

● **www.undp.org/governance** Presents the UNDP's work on democratic governance.

● **www.oas.org** The site of the Organization of American States, which contains statements of key OAS issues such as strengthening the democratic commitment, building healthy democratic issues, protecting human rights, observing elections, and civil society.

● **www.nepad.org** The official site of the New Partnership for Africa's Development, which includes documents representing the AU's formal commitment to democratization among member states.

 ONLINE RESOURCE CENTRE

For additional material and resources, see the Online Resource Centre at:
www.oxfordtextbooks.co.uk/orc/burnell2e/

Governance and Conditionality in a Globalizing World

PETER BURNELL

Overview

This chapter introduces debates about the implications of globalization for the state and public policy in developing countries. A prominent aspect for many developing countries has been the requirement to agree **conditionalities** concerning policy and institutional reform with major international financial institutions and other donors. The theory and practice of conditionalities and recent moves towards greater selectivity in lending to countries is explained. Several 'generations' of conditionality, and **process conditionality** which is connected with strategies for tackling poverty, are introduced. **Governance** is central to what conditionality and selectivity have now come to focus on. Difficulties in making notions of governance at the state level operational, and disagreements over how **good governance** can be achieved and the reforms that will make that possible, are noted, in addition to the significance of governance for development.

PETER BURNELL

Introduction

In the contemporary discourse on politics in the developing world at least three major trends are reflected: an increasing tendency to locate politics at the level of the individual country level within the international context; an erosion of disciplinary boundaries between politics and development studies; a meshing of the more theoretically oriented investigations and studies that are policy-related or carried out for their police relevance. Evidence of all three trends can be found in the debates on globalization, governance, and the influence of globalization on governance through such mechanisms as international aid conditionality—three topics that are strongly interrelated. A particular focus in the first section of this chapter is globalization's implications for the state in developing countries. The second section traces the evolution of aid conditionality through to its most recent connection with the agenda for reducing poverty. The third section shows that although ideas of governance generally and good governance specifically have gained considerably prominence internationally in policy debates, and are thought to be central to understanding the prospects for development, there is still considerable disagreement over what the concepts mean, their normative standing, and their relationships to more traditional themes in the study of politics.

Globalization and the State

Globalization has come to occupy a vast literature. The meaning of the term, the historical origins of the phenomenon, its significance for developing countries, and its desirability are all subjects of extensive debate. Here is not the place to offer a survey or review. Many excellent commentaries exist, for example Baylis and Smith (2005), where McGrew (2005: 20) informs us that globalization is a process that involves the widening, deepening, and speeding up and growing impact of worldwide interconnectedness.

Not all states are touched evenly by globalization or make an equal contribution to its momentum. And in so far as globalization entails both costs and benefits the nature and extent of these varies widely globally, among the countries of the developing world, and as between different social groups within developing countries. For example certain East Asian economies like South Korea and Singapore have successfully followed export-led strategies of development for decades, and India and China are now major engines of the current growth in international trade and investment activity (Chapter 3). They are among its main economic beneficiaries as well. In contrast much of Africa remains marginal to the growth in international trade and corporate investment flows. And in so far as some already fragile states incur certain costs of globalization, such as through depending on remote markets for their commodity exports, they may be made even more vulnerable as a result of disadvantageous trade deals engineered by powerful lobbies in the OECD countries.

Indeed, the opening of financial borders has contributed to a situation whereby capital exports (capital flight) from many low-income countries in Africa exceed their external public debts. This in turn has placed the governments at the mercy of discretionary offers of support by international financial institutions. In some places the quid pro quo for such support, namely economic policy conditionalities led to phenomena that came to be called 'IMF riots' and 'IMF coups'. And yet although on the one hand economic globalization has yet to significantly reduce poverty in Africa, on the other, many African countries have been caught up in the major international wave of democratization that characterised the early 1990s. The collapse of one-party rule in communist Eastern Europe galvanized demands for freedom of association and expression and helped bring competitive elections to countries like Zambia.

The most catholic interpretations of globalization go well beyond economic features and maintain it has political, social, and cultural dimensions too. We should investigate all of these and the interconnections. In the developing world there are some striking trends and differences in respect of the several different dimensions of globalization. Individual countries show some notable variations between their economic, political, and social globalization (Box 15.1 illustrates with figures from the CSGR Globalization Index. Appendix 2 provides figures for this book's case-study countries and explains how the index is constructed). Overall the findings show that a country's ranking can fluctuate quite markedly in a short time, not least because the indexes represent a growing numbers of countries over the years.

BOX 15.1

Globalization Rankings and Scores from the Developing World

Of all the regions of the world sub-Saharan Africa is the least globalised both *overall* and in terms of *political globalization*. The Middle East is the one region that is even less globalised in *economic* terms. Nevertheless even sub-Saharan Africa's absolute measure of globalization more than doubled between 1991 and 2001.

In terms of *globalization overall*, where country size appears to be a major determinant (in 2001 the three most globalised of the 96 countries worldwide were Belgium, Ireland and Switzerland), the highest ranking developing countries have consistently included Singapore and Malaysia (respectively 4th and 17th overall in 2001). Panama fell from 7th overall in 1983 to 52nd in 2001; Zimbabwe fell from 36th in 1985 to 80th in 2001.

In purely *economic* terms Guyana is consistently one of the most globalised of the 122 countries (being in third place overall for the first half of the 1990s). Botswana has gone from being 5th in 1987 to 43rd in 2001; Bolivia has fallen from 29th place in 1983 to 101st in 2001.

In terms of *political globalization*, Argentina, Egypt and India consistently feature in the top 20 of all 187 countries. Malaysia has risen from 70th place in 1982 to 20th in 2001. South Africa before it abolished apartheid in 1988 was a lowly 132rd, and then

climbed steadily to a high of 41st place in 1999. The absolute scores of countries show a wide range, from the low scores typical of small poor countries such as Bhutan's 0.055, through to the quite considerable scores attained by some modestly sized countries like Ghana's (0.492), to scores for sizeable countries like Nigeria, India and Pakistan that in 2001 were higher than for Japan and the Netherlands. For comparison the US and UK scores for political globalization were 0.865 and 0.827 respectively.

In terms of *social globalization* developing countries generally compare very poorly with most western countries, irrespective of size. Appendix 2 shows that in contrast to Mexico which has consistent scores across all three dimensions of globalization, India, Pakistan and Nigeria have rankings for *social globalization* out of 130 countries that are very much lower than their rankings for *political globalization* and for globalization *overall*. Zero for Myanmar, 0.001 for Ethiopia and 0.002 for Central African Republic offer striking contrasts with Australia's 0.625 and Canada's 0.716.

(Lockwood and Redoano 2005)

Note: additional data for countries in Part 5 of this book together with details of the CSGR index methodology can be found in Appendix 2.

The emergence of an increasingly integrated global economy with increased trade and investment flows and technology transfer is certainly a major aspect of globalization, powered by an almost universal tendency to adopt neo-liberal economic prescriptions and practices associated with the Washington consensus. But the appearance of a plurality of centres of governance, variously described as polycentrism and multilevel governance, at different levels above and below the national state are further prominent features of contemporary globalization. Both power and authority appear to be relocating to a large and disparate group of supranational and trans-territorial institutions. The emergence of global sites of regulation and decision-making together with growing political interconnectedness between supra, sub and non-state actors contribute to what Higgott and Ougaaard (2002: 1) call the 'globalization of political life'.

An additional aspect of globalization follows from the revolutions in global information technology and international transport and communications. These enable ideas, values, tastes, information, and even people to travel enormous distances in almost no time at all. As part of this opening up, political ideas to do with human rights and democracy travel around the world just as do the latest consumer fashions or sporting celebrities. Regional as well as global institutions such as the UN now take part in the global spreading of democracy. Against this background, the implications for the state and public policy are of particular interest.

State and policy

Our understanding of what globalization means for the state has evolved from sweeping claims that sovereignty is seriously threatened or that the state is just about finished as an influential economic actor, to more complex, nuanced, and even ambiguous perspectives. These perspectives distinguish among different states and dwell on how states are being transformed in a variety of ways, as they address the challenges posed by globalization. They also look at how states to varying degrees shape and harness the opportunities that globalization provides. Contrasting views on economic and welfare policies exemplify this shift in views. For some analysts the triumph of economic neo-liberalism and the increasingly competitive scramble to attract international capital and retain global market share, inevitably means that the state has less freedom to deviate from a narrow range of market-friendly economic polices.

At its most dramatic, there is the idea that socialism is no longer a viable option. Furthermore even the welfare state, never more than a distant prospect for many poor countries anyway, will have to go into retreat even in the richer countries especially if they are to remain competitive with the more dynamic of the emerging economies in the post-communist and developing worlds, India for instance. On this account electorates can look forward to diminishing scope for making meaningful choices between alternative programmes for economic management and welfare provision. The only credible political parties will be those that occupy a centre-ground in a context where the centre of gravity has itself moved to the right, towards less direct involvement by the state in economic affairs and an increasing reliance on market solutions to solve social problems.

However, other commentators disagree with these prognoses and suggest that the reality even in the developing world is not so straightforward. To illustrate, more scholars now draw attention to the difference that domestic political institutions and political agency can make, by mediating the impact of external linkages and events. Weiss (2005: 346) in the course of countering the 'myth' of the powerless state goes so far as to argue that rather than loss of state power there has been structural and political entwinement—a mutual reinforcement of contemporary global networks and the domestic structures of nation-states. Weiss argues that globalization is actually reinforcing and in some important respects augmenting the role of territorially-based institutions. Rather than the state overall incurring a net loss in its powers, it is the balance between the different institutions of state and government departments that is affected, with some gaining relative to others.

To illustrate, professional technocrats in the government bureaucracy may be empowered vis-à-vis elected politicians. Politicians with technocratic qualifications gain an advantage. Liberia's President Ellen Johnson-Sirleaf, Africa's first elected female head of state, is a US-educated economist who has worked for the World Bank and Citibank. She defeated a former football star in the 2005 presidential election. Central government executives gain in power relative to parliaments and municipal institutions, as a result of the growing importance of working with regional and global governance institutions. At the same time major international financiers including the World Bank and of course big transnational corporations now do deals directly with city and provincial administrations, circumventing the central government. Yet structures for local communities and their political representatives to take part in this are usually non-existent.

Within government, Finance Ministries and Central Banks become more powerful vis-à-vis spending ministries, as a consequence of requirements to agree terms and conditions of borrowing with external creditors. It is not just the additional patronage resources that government acquires but because the policy constraints that come from contacts with external organisations like the Bretton Woods institutions may increase state autonomy of society. Governments manipulate these relationships to their own advantage vis-à-vis their political opponents at home.

Overall, then, Phillips (2005: 102) observes that a 'mainstay of the globalization-state debate, in both orthodox and critical perspectives, is the contention that states are increasingly centralized, insulated and "technocratic", and accountable primarily to global market forces rather than national societies'. At the same time Phillips remarks that this framework of reference has limitations and should not be applied uniformly. This outlook sums up the transformationalist approach. It does not view states as subservient to global forces but rather argues they are undergoing variegated processes of adaptation

and transformation, and in some cases are critical to the 'authoring' and propulsion of globalization (Phillips 2005: 95).

The main burden of attention in the international political economy literature continues to be focused on the more developed countries. And it has to be admitted that contributors to that literature usually add that the freedom to adopt distinctive policy responses in the presence of globalization is probably more constrained in parts of the developing than in the developed world (Mosley 2005: 357; Phillips 2005: 107–8). For instance particular emphasis has been given to the power of international capital markets to influence currency values and monetary policy even in sizeable industrializing countries like South Africa and Brazil (Koelble and Li Puma 2006). Nevertheless, the transformationalist approach has not been confined solely to OECD countries. For example Mosley's (2005: 357) account of government autonomy and cross-national policy diversity notes the discrepancies in social policy between Chile and Mexico. She claims this stems from domestic political alliances, the degree of organisation of the poor in society and the competitiveness of the political party system. Kaufman and Segura-Ubiergo (2001) too found in Latin America that although globalization has had some negative social consequences this is primarily through reducing social security transfers; in contrast, investments in health care and education actually rose. At a time when Latin America was becoming more closely integrated into the global economy social spending as a whole increased. The authors hold electoral competition and political participation responsible.

So, as Phillips convincingly argues (2005: chapter 4), more significant than the degree of state intervention in markets that globalization brings about is the *type* of intervention and the nature of the strategies that states actually pursue. Notwithstanding the global hegemony of neo-liberal economics, the state as such and its economic governance remain central to the implementation and enforcement of appropriate regulatory frameworks. For developing countries, the state's role in economic governance is 'about how to incorporate societal actors in order to gain the capacity to formulate and implement efficient economic policies' (Kjaer 2004: 148).

In all of this, political features such as the neo-patrimonialism and clientelism found in much of Africa can make an enormous difference to the way the policies are implemented and to the outcomes, even where convergence towards adopting standard neo-liberal policies seems apparent. That said, the difficulties political parties in particular face in meeting the challenges of globalization, such as how to make government accountable for its conduct towards institutions of multilevel governance, and how to combat the feelings of powerlessness that citizens might have due to the impact of extra- and supra-national influences on their lives, are considerable. Burnell (2006) discusses this in the context of international support to parties in emerging democracies.

KEY POINTS

- There are some notable differences in political, economic and social globalization among developing countries.

- Globalization's consequences for states in the developing world warrant much greater theoretical reflection and empirical inquiry, if the competing claims that pitch arguments about state transformation against claims that the state is being eclipsed are to be resolved.

- Investigating the effects of different features of globalization, or the different aspects of economic globalization even, on different states and their policies could be more revealing than searching for uniform generalizations.

- Some empirical studies show that even in the developing world social and economic policy convergence is not absolute: the responses to globalization vary in accordance with domestic political circumstances.

From Aid Conditionality to Selectivity

For many developing countries especially those categorized as heavily indebted poor countries and many African countries in particular, their relationship with the Bretton Woods institutions is one feature of globalization that has special significance (see Chapter 3). It is relevant both to globalization understood as the growing power of global governance institutions and to economic integration driven by growing endorsement of neo-liberal economic analysis. For while the World Bank group and the International Monetary Fund (IMF) along with regional development banks, the European Union, and bilateral donors have been important sources of finance, it is the policy and institutional conditionalities associated with their assistance that consistently have proven controversial.

Conditioning financial support spells out steps that the recipient must agree to take. In theory,

non-compliance or failure to take those steps jeopardizes the support, which may then be withheld, or the offer may even be withdrawn. In terms of the actual conditions that have supplied the content of conditionality, at least three generations can be identified. Each successive generation has added to rather than supplanted its predecessors. The first phase, concentrated on economic and financial policy measures that reflected the so-called Washington consensus, was expressed in the structural and sectoral adjustment lending of the 1980s. The second generation beginning around 1989 introduced governance considerations. Many bilateral donors supplemented these with various combinations of explicitly political considerations embodying ideas of human rights and democratic political reform. Around a decade later a new or third generation of conditionality began to gain

the engagement of a more broadly based constituency that includes the poor and their authentic representatives could be needed if there is to be a sustainable shift towards anti-poverty development strategies. And for this to happen, Bräutigam (2004) argues on the basis of evidence from Brazil, Chile, Mauritius, Costa Rica, and even Ireland that the political organization of the poor in the form of political parties, and a greater involvement of legislatures in the PRSP, could be essential.

In the meantime, there is a sense that some donors risk undermining the intentions behind PRSP by continuing to fund poverty and related projects separately, instead of or outside the framework of general budgetary support. This perpetuates the external orientation that is said to be responsible for the past failures of so many aid initiatives and reform recommendations from the international institutions. Although pro-poor spending does now appear to be on the increase in many developing countries, a weak ability to implement policy will not be rectified by the PRSP alone and could yet frustrate the poverty objectives. Added to which there are the economic worries that heightened levels of social spending cannot be sustained in the long term unless the economy's productive capabilities are increased. And that may be less likely to happen where increased consumption by the poor is privileged over capital investment.

Post-conditionality

'Post-conditionality' has affinities with both selectivity and process conditionality. It refers to a state of affairs inside the machinery of government in developing countries, without involving heavy ex post conditionalities or threats of sanctions in the face of non-compliance.

Harrison (2001) described post-conditionality as being where donor involvement comes to be internalized in the state, following extreme financial or economic dependence and the external provision of advice and technical support for capacity-building. The external–national distinction breaks down in

these circumstances. Rather, donor power can be conceptualised as 'part of the state itself', not a 'strong external force to the state' (Harrison 2001: 669). A mutual but unequal dependence takes hold. The international financial institutions have invested so much capital and, more importantly, their credibility in achieving at least the appearance of a success story for their approach to development. They cannot break off relations lightly. But far from anticipating the kind of 'slippage' that Mosley, Harrigan, and Toye (1995) and Killick documented with conditionality (1998), post-conditionality embeds the recommendations for reform—and possibly even the thinking that underlies them—in the very form of the state not least through the kind of personnel who head the key offices. To Gould (2005: chapter 5) it seems as if the multilateral creditors now exercise relatively direct control over core politico-administrative functions in many poor states. There are exceptions but these rest on being less aid dependent, or having the residual strength of nationalist ideology as in Vietnam, or possessing bargaining chips that come from economic or other strategic interests of value to the West. Once again, the precise configuration taken by the leading political groups and forces will make a difference.

There is no teleological inevitability to post-conditionality; hence it should not be described as a stage. Harrison argues that it exists selectively: he cites Uganda and Tanzania. And it is not free of tensions and contradictions either, which means that it may not last indefinitely. Yet something like post-conditionality may come close to what the international financial institutions themselves hope to achieve through policy dialogue, through providing technical assistance rather than the overt manipulation of financial incentives or more coercive measures. And it is more in keeping with the changing global financial market that is emerging in the twenty-first century, where developing economies like Argentina and Brazil no longer feel captive to IMF or World Bank lending, and exploit alternative sources of finance such as direct inwards investment (Woods 2006). Some major oil exporting countries are in an analogous position, as they reap the financial harvest of substantial price increases for internationally traded oil. At the same time, however, state autonomy understood as the capacity to formulate and implement policy preferences separately and differently from the wishes of powerful global actors like the Bretton Woods institutions still remains questionable for countries like Uganda and Tanzania. In a sense, then, the essence of conditionality remains a 'central aspect of the donor–state relationship' (Harrison 2001: 668), so long as the international financial institutions not only dominate the supply of knowledge about how to mange development but can structure and shape the demand for such know-how as well. This point applies just as much to the theme of governance as to any other theme in development.

KEY POINTS

- For over twenty years developing countries have been exposed to the practice of attaching conditionalities to concessionary financial support.

- Conditionality's significance for the political autonomy of countries depends both on how we understand the nature of relationship and the individual circumstances of states involved in the relationship.

- The policy and institutional content of conditioned lending has diversified and multiplied over time, from economic to political and social conditions.

- Conditionalities are a very imperfect substitute for ownership and cannot of themselves create ownership. Conditionality's perceived ineffectiveness has led some major donors to pioneer more selective approaches to lending. This has not meant the complete abandonment of conditionality although in some cases it has brought a change of form, which has been called post-conditionality.

- Possible weaknesses of the process conditionality associated with PRSPs are that by having two or more objectives and by failing to concede much power to the poor it offers no certainty that it will reduce poverty.

Governance

According to Payne governance 'is probably second only to globalization in use and abuse' (2005: 55). Governance is not the same as government. Governance can take place in venues and at levels other than the formally constituted governing authorities of the state. Intergovernmental networks, transnational non-state actors, and state–society interactions more generally have all been loosely linked to ideas of governance. For example a major feature of the trend towards an 'emerging global polity' (Higgott and Ougaard 2002) is the development of an international institutional architecture for global governance, of which the World Trade Organization (see Chapter 4) is a leading example.

Global governance, according to McGrew (in Higgott and Ougaard 2002: 208), refers to the process by which governments, inter-governmental bodies, non-governmental organizations, and transnational forces come together to establish global rules, norms, and standards, or to resolve specific transborder problems, the global trade in illicit drugs for instance. Regional governance is exemplified most strikingly in the European Union: the developing world has no comparable examples but does have regional institutions that aspire to influence political matters internal to the member states. The Organization of American States and the African Union are instances. Among the rules, norms, and standards that have increasingly come to the fore in processes of dialogue and practical engagement between developing countries and institutions of global and regional governance, many concern the quality of governance in the developing countries' internal arrangements. Initially this was encapsulated in the good governance agenda of second generation conditionality, introduced at the end of the 1980s by the World Bank in particular. Although notions of good governance have become highly contested since then, there can be no doubt that governance per se, whether defined as a process or activity or both, is now a major *leitmotif* in the development discourse.

Governance is thought to matter for the investment climate and for the effectiveness of international development cooperation in particular. Ideas for improving governance and better governance are now central features of aid donor–recipient relations. This is in spite of the fact that institutions of global governance themselves, the International Monetary Fund especially, have been sharply criticized for being deficient in respect of some of the main features associated with good governance. Reservations about their openness and transparency, about the way power is distributed in their internal arrangements and their external accountability, all question the legitimacy of the way organizations like the IMF operate (Higgott and Ougaard 2002; Stiglitz 2003; Woods 2006). For instance according to Stiglitz (Chief Economist and Senior Vice-President of the World Bank, 1997–2000), the IMF is responsive to just a narrow community of finance ministers and central bankers who are accountable neither to the developing countries to whom the IMF lends nor to a broader set of interests in the richer world.

From good governance to governance indicators

The disappointing results of economic conditionality prompted the World Bank to identify poor governance in the developing countries rather than simply too much government, or statism, as a major culprit. The new thinking dates from a Bank report on *Sub-Saharan Africa: From Crisis to Sustainable Growth* (1989), and was elaborated further in the early 1990s. Demands by the Bretton Woods institutions for good governance quickly came to be woven into the fabric of conditionality. Later, governance criteria were carried over into selectivity, when the policy of selective aid allocation came to be seen as an improvement on traditional conditionality-based lending. An influence here has been the record of exacting governance conditionalities in return for making loans, which seems to have been barely more effective than the experience of economic conditionality that had come earlier (Doornbos 2006: chapter 4).

No less a figure than UN Secretary-General Kofi Annan has said that good governance is perhaps the single most important factor in eradicating poverty and promoting development. That its perceived importance has registered in the developing world too is evidenced in the formal adoption of commitments to 'Democracy and Good Political Governance', and to 'Economic and Corporate Governance', in the Action Plans of the New Partnership for Africa's Development (NEPAD) (see Box 15.2). The record so far suggests that the first of these two sets of commitments may not be taken as seriously as the second, in the self-monitoring mechanism and peer group pressure that the Organization of the African Union (now African Union) adopted in 2002 and enshrined in an African Peer Review Mechanism (APRM). Nevertheless, participation in the APRM takes place on a voluntary basis. At the point of formally acceding to the peer review process states should define a time-bound Programme of Action for implementing the mechanism's Declaration on Democracy, Political, Economic and Corporate Governance, which includes actual periodic reviews. The Commission for Africa also vested considerable hopes in these arrangements in its report *Our Common Interest* (2005) (see Box 15.3). A majority of the seventeen Commissioners were distinguished African figures drawn from Botswana, Ghana, Nigeria, and South Africa. They included Tanzania's President Mkapa and Ethiopia's Prime Minister Meles Zenawi too. At the time of the Commission's report twenty-four governments representing 75 per cent of Africa's population had signed up to the APRM initiative.

Initially the Bank's idea of good governance centred on such qualities as transparency, fiscal accountability, and sound management of the public sector, in other words, economic governance. Other actors such as foreign ministries and bilateral aid agencies in the West explored their much greater freedom to expand the agenda towards political

---

BOX 15.2

New Partnership for Africa's Development

The first of NEPAD's eight *principles* reads 'Good governance as a basic requirement for peace, security and sustainable economic development'.

Listed second in NEPAD's *priorities* for *establishing the conditions for sustainable development* is 'democracy and good, political, economic and corporate governance'.

'Good' *economic and corporate governance* including transparency in financial management 'are essential pre-requisites for promoting economic growth and reducing poverty. Mindful of this, we have approved eight prioritized codes and standards for achieving good economic and corporate governance'.

'These codes and standards have been developed by a number of international organisations through consultative processes that involved the active par-ticipation of and endorsement by African countries. Thus the codes and standards are genuinely global as they were endorsed by experts from a vast spectrum of economies with different structural characteristics'.

Codes of Good Practices on Transparency in Monetary and Financial Policies; Codes of Good Practices on Fiscal Transparency; Best Practices for Budget Transparency; Guidelines for Public Debt Management; Principles of Corporate Governance; International Accounting Standards; International Standards on Auditing; and the Core Principles for effective Banking Supervision.

(Extracts from *NEPAD In Brief* and *A Summary of NEPAD Action Plans. African Peer Review Mechanism.* For NEPAD statements *on democracy and political governance* see Box 14.5)

BOX 15.3

Commission for Africa Report: *Our Common Interest*

'One thing underlies all the difficulties caused by the interactions of Africa's history over the past 40 years. It is the weakness of governance and the absence of an effective state. By governance we mean the inability of government and the public services to create the right economic, social and legal frameworks which will encourage economic growth and allow poor people to participate in it'. (p. 28)

'The issue of good governance and capacity-building is what we believe lies at the core of all of Africa's problems. Until that is in place Africa will be doomed to continue its economic stagnation'. (p. 29)

'There is more to governance than how the government conducts itself. It is about the whole realm in which the state operates, including areas like parliament, the judiciary, the media and all the other organisations of society which remain in place when government changes. Next it is about the policies of government. But it is also about whether a government has the staff and organisational systems to design its policies and the ability to implement them with the participation of its citizens.

It has another crucial dimension: how well the government answers to its people for its policies and actions, whether it is "accountable" to its citizens. Democracy of some kind is an absolute fundamental here.' (p. 33)

'Good governance is about much more than sound policies. Governments have to be able to put those policies into effect.' (p. 33)

(Commission for Africa 2005)

governance, bringing in issues of human rights and democratic accountability, more specifically political pluralism, multi-party politics, and free and fair elections. Although for the Bretton Woods institutions governance offers the attraction of a certain technocratic and apolitical quality, which comports with the political restrictions imposed by their Articles of Agreement, there is little doubt, as Kjaer (2004: 174) argues, that this appearance is superficial. Even good governance programmes touch on sensitive issues to do with the distribution of power and resources in society, between state and society, and between states and external actors like the international financial institutions. And by 1994 the Bank had come to embrace the rule of law, a capable judiciary, and freedom from corruption among its governance objectives. In Harrison's telling phrase, when offered to weak or fragile states, the Bank's governance reforms have been 'as concerned with *constructing* the state as they have with *reforming* it (Harrison 2005: 250).

Inevitably the solutions for better governance must reflect an understanding of the origins of bad governance. Here too the explanations tend to have substantial political content of one sort or another. They vary from the legacy of colonial rule (see Chapters 2 and 11) to weaknesses in the domestic architecture of government and low democratic accountability (see Chapter 14). They range from certain distinguishing properties of a country's political culture, such as patron–clientelism and the privileging of informal practice over formal rules-based behaviour in public office specifically, and political life generally, to arguments about external dependence and the influence exercised by 'metropolitan countries'. On this last, Moore (2004) draws attention to the adverse consequences rentier states have for governance or 'political underdevelopment', where state elites substitute international support in the form of unearned income from trade, for example resource rents gained from duties imposed on commodity exports, or foreign aid (strategic rents), for firm roots in society.

Inevitably the different explanations issue in different prescriptions. Thus whereas for Kjaer (2005:

148) 'the starting point for developing economies is how to strengthen economic governance in a context of weak state institutions and economic dependency', in Moore's analysis the challenge would be to convert the external relations of states from a malign to a benign influence, while fundamentally redistributing political power at home. But Moore falls short of claiming that in rentier states a better governance 'dividend' must inevitably follow from having to impose higher taxation or from relying more on taxing the citizens: indeed, 'we do not have a good theory of the political economy of rentier states' (Moore 2004: 305).

Governance indicators

Although at first sight measuring governance quality might seem a largely technical exercise it is not a purely objective one and there are some significant disagreements over how to proceed. Many development economists and policy advisers refer to the pioneering work on governance indicators led by Daniel Kaufmann of the World Bank Institute, beginning in the late 1990s and represented in *Governance Matters IV: Governance Indicators for 1996–2004* (Kaufmann, Kray, and Mastruzzi, 2005). Kaufmann *et al.* take an all-encompassing approach to the concept of governance and its measurement. The *Governance Matters* research defines governance as the traditions and institutions that determine how authority is exercised in a country, which includes the process by which governments are selected, held accountable, monitored and replaced, and as well as the capacity to effectively formulate and implement sound policies, and the respect of citizens and the state for the institutions that govern economic and social interactions among them. The surveys presently cover 209 countries and territories for five time periods: 1996; 1998; 2000; 2002; 2004. They are based on several hundred individual variables measuring perceptions of governance, drawn from thirty-seven different data sources constructed by thirty-one different organizations.

As befits the World Bank's own internal structure as an organization of competing fiefdoms, the governance indicators here represent not one monolithic or unified concept. Indeed there are no les than six dimensions: (1) voice and accountability; (2) political instability and violence; (3) government effectiveness; (4) regulatory quality; (5) rule of law; (6) control of corruption. Kaufmann *et al.* claim a relatively high ability to identify significant changes in governance over time, which is one reason why the data they provide are used so widely. Unsurprisingly they find that good governance is correlated with better development. They claim there is a large causal effect running from improved governance to better development outcomes *and not the other way round.* Sub-Saharan Africa displays a particularly striking coincidence of governance and incomes that are both considerably inferior to the global average. On the whole *Governance Matters IV* could detect no really significant recent trends in the global averages for governance but did find significant fluctuations for some countries, such as the substantial declines in almost all indicators for Ivory Coast and Zimbabwe. (See Box 15.4)

There are countries where the different dimensions of governance have not all moved in the same direction over time. And corruption, to which international lenders pay exceptional attention—the World Bank Institute Governance Group currently operates anti-corruption initiatives in nearly thirty countries—appears to have got worse. But realistically the survey methodology freely acknowledges that even the best cross-country indicators of governance remain imprecise. They tell us little about the specific institutional failures that give rise to weak governance in a particular setting. Only detailed indepth country case studies can shed more light on that. In fact, rather than aiming to theorize the cause of bad governance as a whole it might be more productive to conduct the analysis at a more disaggregated level. That means trying to make sense of a country's record with respect to the different components of governance individually, especially if there appears to be no strong correlation or co-variance among them.

The *Governance Matters* project is of more than just academic interest. The US government's Millennium Challenge Account for instance consults

---

BOX 15.4

Governance Matters IV: Large Point Changes in Governance Score, 1996–2004

Voice and accountability (improvement)
Gambia; Ghana; Indonesia; Mexico; Nigeria; Peru; Sierra Leone

Voice and accountability (deterioration)
Central African Republic; Eritrea; Haiti; Ivory Coast; Nepal; Zimbabwe

Political stability (improvement)
Algeria; Angola; Libya; Sierra Leone

Political stability (deterioration)
Benin; Central African Republic; Haiti; Indonesia; Ivory Coast; Laos; Nepal; Philippines; Zimbabwe

Government effectiveness (improvement)
Tanzania

Government effectiveness (deterioration)
Argentina; Ivory Coast; Sierra Leone; Zimbabwe

Regulatory quality (improvement)
None

Regulatory quality (deterioration)
Argentina; Bolivia; Cuba; Indonesia; Myanmar; Paraguay; Venezuela; Zambia; Zimbabwe

Rule of law (improvement)
Barbados

Rule of law (deterioration)
Argentina; Indonesia; Ivory Coast; Paraguay; Philippines; Saudi Arabia; Swaziland; Thailand; Zimbabwe

Control of corruption (improvement)
Bahrain; United Arab Emirates

Control of corruption (deterioration)
China; Ivory Coast; Zimbabwe

(Kaufmann, Kray, and Mastruzzi 2005: 54–5)

it before determining which low income countries should be eligible for funds. Investment choices by the World Bank and other donors that support governance capacity-building efforts also take account of the evidence that governance indicators provide. However the *Governance Matters* project is not the *only* source of such information.

The United Nations Development Programme's (UNDP) Governance Centre in Oslo believes the World Bank's governance agenda is too narrow to bring about the UN's own MDGs. Accordingly the UNDP has not only developed a *User's Guide* to governance indicators but also aims to develop a dataset of its own—one that will be more sensitive to human development, placing greater emphasis on the entitlements and needs of women and the poor (www.undp.org/oslocentre/). The UNDP in the late 1990s defined governance as the exercise of economic, political, and administrative authority to manage a country's affairs at all levels. In contrast the conceptualisation that its own Governance Centre now advances prefers the idea of 'humane governance' to 'good governance': from a human development perspective, good governance really means democratic governance, which the UNDP claims is valuable in its own right as well as being a means to achieving progress towards the MDGs. This explains the UNDP's practical interest in helping to strengthen institutions of democratic accountability, like parliaments and judiciaries, support to decentralization and, even, political parties (at US$1.4 billion per annum expenditure in around 130 countries the UNDP claims to be the world's largest funder of democratic governance programmes). All this places its contribution at considerable remove from the emphasis on efficient and effective public sector management and financial accountability that characterized the earliest notions of good governance, even if it is the interpretation that first originated in World Bank discourse that 'will keep standing out as the core of "good governance" concerns for many donors' (Doornbos 2006: 89). The UNDP claims to support nationally owned processes for assessing and monitoring democratic governance. This is a critical accountability mechanism that local stakeholders can use as a tool for strengthening the responsiveness of institutions and processes to the needs of ordinary citizens, especially women and the poor. Such an approach places the UNDP's orientation closer to the account of governance that has been formulated by Hyden, Court, and Mease (2004), who also emphasize the political at the expense of economic notions of governance.

For Hyden, Court, and Mease (2004) governance refers to the formation and stewardship of the informal and formal rules that regulate the public realm, the arena in which the state as well as economic and societal actors interact to make decisions. They see governance as a matter of behavioural disposition, not technical capacities. The point is first to avoid chaining governance assessments too tightly to liberal democratic models of politics. Second it is to render both our understanding of governance and its measurements sensitive to the subjective opinions of 'local stakeholders' in the developing countries themselves: experts from the government, civil servants, legislators, lawyers, representatives of media and civil society organizations including trade unions, religious groups, business people, academics, and officials in international organizations. The methodology for data collection and the analytical framework, which includes six 'principles' of good governance (participation, fairness, decency, accountability, transparency, and efficiency) have been incorporated in a major project called the World Governance Assessment (WGA) (see www.odi.org.uk/wga_governance).

Among the more noteworthy empirical findings collected by Hyden *et al.* (2004) so far from sixteen countries (the set includes three from Latin America, six from Asia, two from Africa, and one from the Middle East) is that successful democratization tends to enhance the quality of governance, even though not all countries scoring high on governance are also the most democratic. In contrast increasing autocracy does not lead to improvement in governance quality. Chile, Thailand, India, Jordan, and Tanzania attained relatively high WGS governance scores, whereas Togo, Pakistan, and the Philippines were among the lowest. Although the authors do not see their findings supporting the idea of a unilinear causal connection between governance and development, there are implications nonetheless for arguments about which type of political system is most conducive to development (see Chapter 14).

In conclusion, international development agencies seem convinced that governance holds a key to development and the effective use of international financial and economic assistance. So much so that donor willingness to make disbursements for PRSPs has been held back in some countries by their concerns about political governance. It has led to 'the imposition of unpredictable, non-transparent "last minute" conditionality' (Driscoll with Evans 2005: 14). Yet there remains much scope to increase our understanding of how governance can be improved and the constructive impact that external actors could make. Capacity-building projects and programmes such as those that introduce professional accounting procedures into managing public sector organizations, support official anti-corruption commissions, and bolster the judiciary are popular

with some donors, the World Bank group especially. But the record seems very patchy, and barely more impressive than the experience of governance conditionalities. And while they address surface features they may still not get to grips with more fundamental limitations lying deep in the political structures that determine relations of influence and power within and between societies. A 'good enough' approach to improving governance, that concentrates on strengthening executive capacity, might seem appropriate in a weak or failing state. But by skirting round such essentially political issues as voice and accountability it could end up reinforcing executive autonomy of society. If political power continues to reside in the hands of an unrepresentative minority then the prospects for good governance and pro-poor development will probably both remain fragile and uncertain. In rentier states especially, a more diversified economic structure that brings increasing numbers of citizens into more direct contact with the financing of the public services could also be part of the solution, in the long term.

KEY POINTS

- Governance has such an open character and is used is so many different contexts that more closely specified accounts of 'good' or 'bad' governance and their properties offer more useful analytical purchase for examining the experience of developing countries.

- The negative developmental consequences of bad governance or misgovernance are probably better understood than the origins of good governance.

- Governance is not a purely technical or bureaucratic matter, although the term is hotly contested and its usage betrays varying political content.

- Indicators of governance reflect particular ideas about governance and the purposes to which those

who construct the indicators wish to put the information.

- The *Governance Matters* series and the UNDP's Governance Indicators project provide extensive data while acknowledging some measurement weaknesses. The second claims to be less tied to Western notions and more accommodating of local opinions about governance in the developing world.

- For developing countries the political and developmental returns from improving their governance may depend in part on reforming governance in the institutions of global governance and making those organizations more accountable, that is to say, a more democratic form of global governance.

Conclusions

Globalization is a multifaceted phenomenon that touches unevenly on different parts of the developing world. Nowhere does it make the state redundant. Conditionality as practised by the major international lenders of balance of payments support and development finance is a prominent and long-established but contentious feature of developing country participation in the global financial and economic system.

Although its effectiveness as an instrument has been strongly criticized conditionality has not disappeared. On the contrary, successive generations of conditionality, and selectivity, even, can be interpreted as extending its reach. There is an enduring tension between conditionality-based lending and country ownership of donor-inspired recommendations. The devolution of conditionality through regional arrangements to monitor institutional and policy performance like the African Peer Review Mechanism for example has yet to prove its full worth.

Over the last two decades the contribution that governments can make to helping economic markets work efficiently and effectively has acquired growing recognition. In line with this the quality of governance in developing countries too has come under the spotlight. The idea that governance is as a crucial determinant of developmental performance has acquired global status. It manifests globalization as an intellectual or ideological and cultural phenomenon with strong political content. Governance indicators are a current fascination.

There is a confusing number and array of governance perspectives to choose from. In pursuing the objectives of better governance in states, international organizations have taken initiatives ranging from incorporating governance conditions into conditionality-based lending, to ensuring that governance advisers become almost embedded in the machinery of government at the state level. However the authority of such organizations is diminished by, among other things, inadequate representation for developing country voices in their own governance arrangements—something that the Commission for Africa for instance was keen to point out. Furthermore governance initiatives to date have not aimed to transfer power directly to the mass of society and the grass-roots. Doubts persist about the chances that investment in strengthening governance capacity and adherence to recommendations spelled out in poverty reduction strategies will benefit the majority of poor people, the most needy in particular (see Chapter 16). The doubts are amplified where external linkages with powerful transnational and supranational actors or forces are seen to take precedence over full democratic accountability at home.

The theme of governance as well as the issue of conditionality in a globalizing age points us towards what governments do and how they do it. That in turn means their policy responses to the challenges and opportunities that are arising internally and issuing from the international environment, and that come from the growing intertwining of domestic and external and circumstances. The policy responses are elaborated in Part Four.

? QUESTIONS

1   In what ways is the state in developing countries affected most significantly by globalization?

2   What conditions influence the success of conditionality as an instrument that institutions of global governance use towards developing countries?

3 How significant are the differences among the three generations of conditionality and post-conditionality?

4 Is governance too vague and wide-ranging a concept to offer much insight into the particular political situation existing in developing countries?

5 How plausible is the claim made by the Commission for Africa's *Our Common Interest* that issues of good governance and capacity-building are at the core of all of Africa's problems?

6 Are contemporary ideas and explanations of good governance so rooted in the thinking and needs of Western-based institutions that they provide an unsuitable basis for advising developing countries on political reform?

7 What explains the presence and persistence of poor governance?

 GUIDE TO FURTHER READING

■ **Baylis, J., and Smith, S. (eds) (2005),** *The Globalization of World Politics*, **3rd edn. (Oxford: Oxford University Press).** Authoritative and wide-ranging text that is periodically updated.

■ *Development Policy Review* **(2003), 21/2.** A special issue of this journal devoted to the early experience of PRSPs in Africa.

■ **Doornbos, M. (2006),** *Global Forces and State Restructuring* **(Houndmills: Palgrave Macmillan).** Essays on issues relating to globalization, governance, and the state in developing countries.

■ **Gould, J. (2005),** *The New Conditionality: the Politics of Poverty Reduction Strategies* **(London: Zed Press).** A critical examination informed by a variety of case studies.

■ **Harrison, G. (2005), 'The World Bank, Governance and Theories of Political Action in Africa',** *British Journal of Politics and International Relations*, **7/2: 240–60.** A critical analysis of the World Bank's governance agenda and the prospects for reform in Africa.

■ **Hyden, G., Court, J., and Mease, K. (2004),** *Making Sense of Governance. Empirical Evidence from Sixteen Developing Countries* **(Boulder, Colo.: Lynne Rienner).** A comprehensive assessment informed by extensive evidence covering half the world's population.

■ **Kaufmann, D., Kray, A., and Mastruzzi, M. (2005),** *Governance Matters IV: Governance Indicators for 1996–2004* **(World Bank Policy Research Working Paper Series No. 3630).** Also available at http://papers.ssrn.com.

■ **Kjaer, M. (2004),** *Governance* **(Cambridge: Polity Press).** A good introduction to the wide-ranging usage of governance in contemporary discourse.

■ **Moore, M. (2004), 'Revenues, State Formation, and the Quality of Governance in Developing Countries',** *International Political Science Review*, **25/3: 297–319.** Explores the implications of fiscal sociology for governance in the developing world's rentier states.

■ **Mosley, L. (2005), 'Globalization and the State: Still Room to Move?',** *New Political Economy*, **10/3: 355–62.**

■ **Woods, N. (2006),** *The Globalizers: The IMF, the World Bank and Their Borrowers* **(Ithaca, NY: Cornell University Press).**

WEB LINKS

● **www.worldbank.org/wbi/governance** The World Bank Institute's site on governance and its activities in support of governance capacity-building.

● **www2.warwick.ac.uk/fac/soc/csgr** The CSGR Globalization Index compiled by Ben Lockwood and Michela Redoano.

● **http://commissionforafrica.org/** The report of the Commission for Africa (2005), *Our Common Interest*.

● **www.nepad.org** The official site of the New Partnership for Africa's Development (NEPAD).

● **www.undp.org/oslocentre/** Provides information on the UNDP's Governance Indicators project and its reports such as *Governance Indicators: A Users' Guide*.

● **www.odi.org.uk/wga_governance/About_WGA.html** Site of the World Governance Assessment, an ongoing project which aims to conduct the WGA globally and may eventually lead to a World Governance Report.

 ONLINE RESOURCE CENTRE

For additional material and resources, see the Online Resource Centre at:
www.oxfordtextbooks.co.uk/orc/burnell2e/

GOVERNANCE AND CONDITIONALITY IN A GLOBALIZING WORLD

PART 4

Policy Issues

In this part several major policy domains in development are examined. The themes do not concern developing countries only; but in all the developing regions they represent notable challenges to both state and non-state actors at the present time. Our concern is not with 'development' per se or as a universal concept, although the increasingly holistic way in which development tends to be understood these days inevitably has implications for the presentation here. Rather, this part again has two main aims.

First it aims to show how states like other major actors in the economy and society are confronted by certain key issues in development and face seemingly inescapable challenges. States in particular have to entertain large decisions that involve political risks and impose considerable administrative burdens, concerning such matters as economic development, welfare, the environment, and human rights. However as for instance the chapter on security amply illustrates, we cannot understand the precise nature of the issues simply by seeing them through the lens of concerned actors in the West. All the policy issues must be viewed against the background of the local context in the developing countries. This can differ dramatically from one country and social group to another.

If the first aim is to explore the issues, a *second* aim is to show the different ways in which governments and non-governmental actors and international bodies too determine their response, by comparing different strategies and their likely consequences. Here, the relevance of international influences to the way policy agendas are formed and, often to policy implementation is undeniable but nevertheless should be examined critically. The object of Part Four is to illuminate the policy process while necessarily being limited in how much detail it can convey about the policy substance. What choices really are open to developing countries, and just how much scope for exercising choice independently have they experienced to date? Does state action necessarily offer the most appropriate way forward? Does one size fit all, or does the evidence suggest that the political response can embody distinct national and sub-national frameworks for defining problems, devising solutions, and implementing a course of action? Readers are encouraged to read the introduction to Part Five and consult relevant case studies alongside the chapters in Part Four.

16

Development

TONY ADDISON

  Chapter Contents

- Introduction
- Defining Development Policy Objectives
- Markets and States
- Trade Policy as an Instrument for Development
- Capital Flows and Economic Reform
- Conclusions

  Overview

This chapter discusses development policy objectives, noting how these have changed over the years, with a more explicit focus on poverty reduction coming to the fore recently. It also examines the relationship between economic growth and poverty reduction. The chapter then discusses how to achieve economic growth and then moves on to the big question of the respective roles for the market mechanism and the state in allocating society's productive resources before discussing the relationship between trade and development. The chapter then discusses how economic reform has been implemented, and the political difficulties that arise. It concludes that getting development policy right has the potential to lift millions out of poverty. The issue of how to achieve economic growth and development in an environmentally sustainable way—the idea of environmentally sustainable development—is introduced in Chapter 17.

Introduction

There are over 1 billion people living in extreme poverty today, defined as having less than one US$ per day to survive on (see Table 16.1). The situation in sub-Saharan Africa is especially desperate; nearly half of the population is poor and poverty has increased over the last decade. Some 799 million people, or 17 per cent of the population in developing countries, are undernourished, and in sub-Saharan Africa one-third of the population is undernourished, the largest of any developing region, and a percentage that is rising (World Bank 2003c: 6). Yet, set against this grim picture there has also been considerable progress, notably in East Asia where the percentage of people living in extreme poverty has been cut in half (see Table 16.1). Even in South Asia, which has the largest numbers of poor people of all the main regions, the percentage of people in poverty has fallen substantially over the last decade.

Looking at economic growth (the rate of growth in Gross Domestic Product (GDP) often presented on a per capita basis), many East Asian countries have grown at rates that are historically unprecedented. Whereas it took the United Kingdom—the world's first industrial nation—fifty-four years to develop from a low per-capita income economy to a middle-income economy, it took Hong Kong, Singapore, and Taiwan (the 'tigers') only ten years to achieve middle-income status (estimates from Parente and Prescott 2000). China is presently growing at over 9 per cent a year, and India's growth has accelerated as well, and their demand for oil and other commodities has pushed up global commodity prices to the benefit of sub-Saharan Africa (which remains overwhelmingly dependent on commodity exports) as well as Latin America (where commodities still have a large export share). But while growth in sub-Saharan Africa has risen in recent years,

---

Table 16.1 Extreme Poverty, 1990–2002

	People living on less than $US1 a day (millions)		Share of people living on less than $US1 a day (%)	
	1990	2002	1990	2002
East Asia and Pacific	472	214	29.6	11.6
China	375	180	33.0	14.0
Europe and Central Asia	2	10	0.5	2.1
Latin America and Caribbean	49	47	11.3	8.9
Middle East and North Africa	6	5	2.3	1.6
South Asia	462	437	41.3	31.2
Sub-Saharan Africa	227	303	44.6	44.0
Total	1218	1015	27.9	19.0
Excluding China	844	835	26.1	21.1

Source: World Bank (2006a), http://devdata.worldbank.org/wdi2006/

Table 16.2 Economic Growth, 1990–2004 (Average Annual % Growth)

	1990–2000	2000–04
Low income	4.7	5.5
Middle income	3.8	4.7
Lower middle income	5.2	6.0
Upper middle income	2.1	2.7
Low and middle income	3.9	4.8
East Asia and Pacific	8.5	8.1
Europe and Central Asia	−0.8	5.0
Latin America and the Caribbean	3.3	1.6
Middle East and North Africa	3.9	3.8
South Asia	5.6	5.8
Sub-Saharan Africa	2.5	3.9
High income	2.7	2.0
Europe EMU	2.1	1.3

Source: World Bank (2006a), http://devdata.worldbank.org/wdi2006

Africa has performed very badly for much of the period since 1980 (with notable exceptions such as Botswana and Mauritius) and GDP per capita is lower than in 1960 in many countries that have experienced civil war (for example Angola, the Democratic Republic of the Congo, and Liberia). Latin America achieved steady if unspectacular growth in the period up to the late 1970s but then went into deep recession during the debt crisis of the 1980s (described by Latin Americans as the 'lost decade'). Latin America recovered in the 1990s, but then underwent another bout of turbulence (with a spectacular economic collapse in Argentina which was the star reformer of the early to mid-1990s) before strong commodity earnings once again pushed up growth (especially in Brazil and Chile). Lastly, oil wealth raised living standards in the Middle East and North Africa but this region has, with only a few exceptions, largely failed to achieve economic diversification and provide employment for a growing and young population. (See Table 16.2.)

In sum, the developing world today presents a very mixed picture: very fast growth and poverty reduction in much of Asia; hesitant growth after long-term decline in sub-Saharan Africa combined with high poverty; growth after considerable economic volatility in Latin America; and disappointing performance in North Africa and the Middle East, despite often abundant natural resources.

What role has development policy played in these different outcomes? What policies are most important for accelerating development? Is the development past a guide to the development future? What lessons can we transfer across countries? As Nobel Laureate Robert Lucas says, 'the consequences for human welfare involved in questions like these are simply staggering. Once one starts to think about them, it is hard to think about anything else' (Lucas 1988). And thinking about development policy has changed over time. On some issues there is now considerable agreement about what needs to be done. But many issues remain deeply controversial, with starkly contrasting viewpoints.

TONY ADDISON

KEY POINTS

- Over 1 billion people live in extreme poverty, about one-sixth of the world's population.

- Poverty is falling in Asia, but remains high in sub-Saharan Africa and widespread in Latin America.

- Asia is growing fast, but sub-Saharan Africa has performed very badly and Latin America tends to boom and bust.

Defining Development Policy Objectives

Much of today's debate is centred on poverty reduction as the primary objective for development policy (as can be seen when you look at the websites of the international agencies given at the end of this chapter). People differ as to how to define poverty: economists typically favour monetary measures, using data collected from household surveys of incomes and expenditures. If the household falls below a defined poverty line then it is classified as poor. However, not all countries have the data to define poverty in this way, so the US$1 per day measure is often used to calculate the global and regional aggregates.

Non-monetary measures of poverty are increasingly used—measures such as infant mortality, life expectancy, and literacy—and people vary in how well they are doing across these different dimensions. Some may have a rising income but remain illiterate, for example, and women often do worse than men, reflecting gender discrimination (in access to education and jobs, for example). People in chronic poverty suffer from multiple deprivations making it very difficult for them to ever escape, and poverty is passed down the generations; the children of the chronically poor generally remain poor when they become adults (CPRC 2005). The Millennium Development Goals (MDGs) which were adopted by the world's leaders in the UN Millennium Declaration of September 2000 as guiding principles for the international development community (see Box 16.1) reflect the multi-dimensional view of

poverty. The smaller, poorer, and conflict-affected countries (mostly in Africa) are unlikely, on present trends, to fully achieve all of the MDGs, but this is not to say that significant progress cannot be still made in areas such as child killers like malaria (where there are major initiatives and funding). The larger and faster growing economies such as Brazil (which has also stepped up its anti-poverty programmes) and China stand the best prospects for MDG success. You can check on progress in the MDGs by visiting www.un.org/millenniumgoals.

In the early days of development policy, during the era of decolonization from the late 1940s through to the 1960s, poverty reduction was often more implicit than explicit in development strategies. These tended to focus on raising GDP per capita (more loosely income per capita) by means of economic growth—it being assumed that poverty reduction would then follow, more or less, from growth. Early development thinkers emphasized raising output, in particular increasing overall labour productivity (output per person) by shifting labour from sectors where its productivity is low to sectors where it is high. This led to a concentration on industry (which was seen as the dynamic sector) while many policy-makers saw smallholder (peasant) agriculture as hopelessly backward and unproductive (it could therefore release large amounts of labour for industry). Crudely put, industrialization and urbanization became synonymous with development in the minds of many

BOX 16.1

The Millennium Development Goals

Goal 1: Eradicate extreme poverty and hunger
Target 1: Halve, between 1990 and 2015, the proportion of people whose income is less than US$1 a day
Target 2: Halve, between 1990 and 2015, the proportion of people who suffer from hunger

Goal 2: Achieve universal primary education
Target 3: Ensure that, by 2015, children everywhere, boys and girls alike, will be able to complete a full course of primary schooling

Goal 3: Promote gender equality and empower women
Target 4: Eliminate gender disparity in primary and secondary education, preferably by 2005 and in all levels of education no later than 2015

Goal 4: Reduce child mortality
Target 5: Reduce by two-thirds, between 1990 and 2015, the under-five mortality rate

Goal 5: Improve maternal health
Target 6: Reduce by three-quarters, between 1990 and 2015, the maternal mortality ratio

Goal 6: Combat HIV/AIDS, malaria, and other diseases
Target 7: Have halted by 2015 and begun to reverse the spread of HIV/AIDS
Target 8: Have halted by 2015 and begun to reverse the incidence of malaria and other major diseases

Goal 7: Ensure environmental sustainability
Target 9: Integrate the principles of sustainable development into country policies and programmes and reverse the loss of environmental resources
Target 10: Halve by 2015 the proportion of people without sustainable access to safe drinking water

Target 11: Have achieved by 2020 a significant improvement in the lives of at least 100 million slum-dwellers

Goal 8: Develop a global partnership for development
Target 12: Develop further an open, rule-based, predictable, non-discriminatory trading and financial system (includes a commitment to good governance, development, and poverty reduction—both nationally and internationally)
Target 13: Address the special needs of the least developed countries (includes tariffs- and quota-free access for exports, enhanced program of debt relief for and cancellation of official bilateral debt, and more generous official development assistance for countries committed to poverty reduction)
Target 14: Address the special needs of land-locked countries and small-island developing states (through the Program of Action for the Sustainable Development of Small Island Developing States and 22nd General Assembly Provisions)
Target 15: Deal comprehensively with the debt problems of developing countries through national and international measures in order to make debt sustainable in the long term
Target 16: In cooperation with developing countries, develop and implement strategies for decent and productive work for youth
Target 17: In cooperation with pharmaceutical companies, provide access to affordable essential drugs in developing countries
Target 18: In cooperation with the private sector, make available the benefits of new technologies, especially information and communication technologies.

(UNDP 2003: 1–3)

Table 16.3 Inequality in Selected Countries (Gini index: income or consumption, latest available year

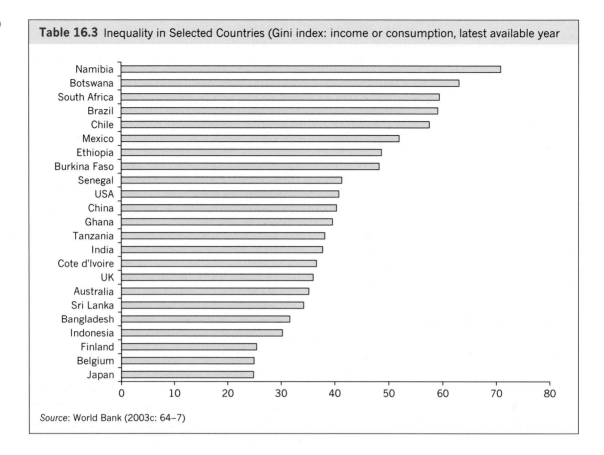

Source: World Bank (2003c: 64–7)

policy-makers from the 1940s to the 1960s. This was reinforced by what appeared, at the time, to be the successful example of the Soviet Union a country that achieved large-scale industrialization from the 1930s onwards. Aid donors enthusiastically supported big infrastructure projects, especially when these benefited the commercial interests of their own countries.

Income per capita is an *average* measure of a country's living standard, and there can be a wide *variation* around this mean. This variation—the inequality of income—exhibits substantial differences across countries (see Table 16.3), reflecting differences in the distribution of wealth (land, other property, and financial wealth) and **human capital** (peoples' skills and capabilities, which are partly a product of their education, and which make

them more productive). The differences in turn reflect country-specific histories of colonization, war, and policy decisions. South Africa's extreme inequality in income and wealth is a legacy of apartheid and Latin America's high inequality reflects the dispossession of indigenous communities by Portuguese and Spanish colonial elites, for instance.

Some people worry about inequality more than others (see Chapter 5). Quite apart from the ethical dimension (do the rich deserve their wealth?) and social stability (will resentment against the rich lead to violence and undermine development?), high inequality makes economic growth less effective in reducing poverty. A Latin American landowner with millions of hectares will benefit much more from agricultural export growth than a smallholder eking out a living on just a few hectares. Put differently, high-inequality societies need to grow a lot faster to achieve the same amount of annual poverty reduction as low-inequality societies.

So, countries need to protect and build the assets of the poor, particularly their human capital as well as the natural capital such as the soils, forests, and fisheries on which their livelihoods depend. Providing primary education, basic health care, water, and sanitation will not only raise the human development of poor people but will also raise their productivity. This will help them diversify their livelihoods in both self-employment (e.g. from dependence on subsistence agriculture and into cash crops and micro-enterprises) and wage-employment (the poor will earn more as skilled workers than as unskilled workers). Asset *redistribution* may also be necessary to build the assets of the poor. Often this applies particularly to land and its transfer from the rich to the rural poor. Asset redistribution is much more challenging politically, and large-scale redistributions tend to be associated with political revolutions. In these ways, economic growth will start to become more pro-poor, and each percentage point of growth will deliver more poverty reduction. This is not to say that all of the poor are in a position to benefit from growth; the chronically poor who suffer from multiple-deprivations may be elderly or so sick that they are unemployable, and the illiterate are the least attractive to employers even in a growing economy. Many of the chronically poor live in remote regions far from the main economic centres, and even strong economic growth can bypass them. For the chronically poor it is important to use the additional public revenues generated from growth (collected through the tax system) to finance more social protection (pensions, food-assistance, as well as education and health provision targeted to their needs). State-building is therefore vital to achieving poverty reduction through public programmes.

Awareness of what holds poor people back came to the fore in the 1970s, in part because of disillusion with the outcomes of the first development decades. The high hopes of decolonization proved to be largely illusory in Africa; and poverty persisted in Latin America notwithstanding growth. This led to a radicalization of the development debate with dependency theory much in vogue. In addition, by the 1970s there was much more evidence from academic research on the determinants of poverty and how poverty responds to economic and social change. This led to a reconsideration of the earlier view that smallholder agriculture was un-dynamic, and a new emphasis on the talents of poor people as farmers and micro-entrepreneurs. Development professionals began to see new ways of helping the poor to build their livelihoods, and for the first time the knowledge of the poor themselves came to be valued. The World Bank, under its then president, Robert McNamara, began to move away from its traditional emphasis on lending to physical infrastructure and towards poverty reduction, particularly through agricultural development, the principal livelihood of the world's poor.

Note that a direct focus on poverty reduction has a sharper political dimension than a focus on growth in a development strategy. For a start, the poor may be poor because they have very little, if any, political voice. This is true of many of the rural poor in sub-Saharan Africa, for instance, and is evident in the way that development strategies often ignored them or, perversely, taxed them (see Bates 1981). Politicians need to expend very little political capital when they talk about economic growth being 'like a tide that raises all boats'. But when it comes to spending public money, basic pro-poor services—especially those that serve the rural poor—are often left behind, after services that prioritize the needs of more vocal, and more effectively organized, non-poor groups (especially in urban political centres). A general bias against the rural areas and in favour of the urban areas (urban bias) was evident in much of post-independence Africa. Vocal and wealthy interests can effectively control the legislatures that determine the pattern of public spending and taxation (as in Central America) and the political power that accompanies wealth is another reason why many people worry about high inequality. When economic crisis strikes

TONY ADDISON

governments often let the burden of adjustment fall on the meagre services that actually benefit the poor. They protect presidential spending and make cuts in basic health care for example.

However, some governments do more for poor people than others, and there are substantial differences in outcomes for poverty and human development across countries at similar levels of per capita income as can be seen if you consult the UNDP's annual report on human development (available at www.undp.org). Vietnam is one such success story (Box 16.2). Moreover, within countries, different regions often spend very different amounts on pro-poor services, reflecting the operation of local political factors: for instance in India, the state of Kerala is an outstanding success.

KEY POINTS

- Poverty reduction has become a more explicit objective of development policy, and economic growth is now seen as more of a means to an end, rather than a final objective in itself.

- Growth is important to reducing poverty, but not all poor people benefit from growth, and the chronically poor often miss out.

- Effective states are necessary to achieve development objectives, particularly in providing pro-poor services and infrastructure.

BOX 16.2

The Vietnam Success Story

Vietnam, a country of 84 million people that suffered a devastating war from the 1950s to the 1970s, is Asia's best-performing economy after China; it grew by 7.8 per cent in 2006. Vietnam is also one of the world's success stories in poverty reduction. Poverty has fallen from 58 per cent of the population in 1993 to under 20 per cent in 2004.

The key to this success has been the construction of a vigorous export economy, the creation of more opportunities for small enterprises, and investment in agriculture. Exports have expanded rapidly enabling the economy to diversify, with considerable foreign investment especially following a 2000 bilateral trade deal with the United States which opened up the latter's market to Vietnamese exports (thereby encouraging US multinationals such as Disney and Nike to establish factories employing Vietnam's cheap and abundant labour). This trend is set to accelerate with Vietnam's accession to the World Trade Organization (WTO) in 2007.

Following the end of the war in 1975 and the country's unification, the Hanoi government extended Marxist central planning with its heavy restrictions on private enterprise to the country's capitalist south (which had, along with its ally the United States, lost the war). The economy performed badly under this system, with hyper-inflation and a sharp fall in living standards being the main results. Tentative reform

began in the 1980s with a move from collectivized agriculture to a market-orientated smallholder system and gathered pace with the adoption of the 'Doi Moi' (new changes) strategy in 1986. Reform intensified in the early 1990s as financial pressures grew with the drying up of aid from the Soviet Union, Vietnam's old cold war ally. The government restored macro-economic stability, liberalized restrictions on small private enterprises, and sought out foreign investment. However, the government is far from relinquishing all control over the economy, and there are still many state-owned enterprises; these account for 40 per cent of GDP in what is officially called a 'socialist-orientated market economy' (also the case in China which, like Vietnam, has pursued economic liberalization in the context of a one-party Marxist state).

Export manufacturing has led to more urban jobs, and urban poverty has fallen substantially. Vietnam has gone from a country of food shortages to become a leading exporter of rice and coffee, resulting in increased incomes and a diversification of livelihoods in rural areas. But poverty remains stubbornly high in less advantaged regions such as Vietnam's Central Highlands where many of Vietnam's ethnic minorities live. They constitute 15 per cent of the total population but 40 per cent of the poor. Vietnam's rapid economic growth is not therefore delivering enough benefits for these people and they need better education and health care and more investment in transport and communications infrastructure to improve their market access.

Vietnam is a success, but its economic growth has come from a very low level of per capita income, reflecting the impact of the long war and the economic crisis of the immediate post-war years. Its government administration is very bureaucratic, corruption is a growing problem, and the communist government's grip on power is threatened by the economy's opening-up and the accompanying increased flow of ideas and information from abroad. Vietnam therefore faces some tough challenges ahead in maintaining the momentum of its success.

Markets and States

Achieving growth is far from easy, especially in countries that are land-locked and distant from markets (Bolivia and Niger, for example), subject to tropical diseases (West Africa in particular), and with climates and terrain that make them vulnerable to floods and droughts (Bangladesh and Africa's Sahel zone). Some countries therefore start with more favourable prospects for growth than others. But the prospects for growth also very much depend upon the design of development strategy, and particularly on the state's role.

Most people agree that states have an important role to play in protecting property rights, enforcing contracts, and defending their citizens against external aggression. Economists have emphasized the importance of the first two of these in providing a favourable climate for investment and for reducing the transaction costs of market exchange, both of which facilitate growth.

However, beyond a core set of public goods such as law and order and defence, people start to disagree about how much economic and social infrastructure the state should provide (public versus private education and health care, for example). And people often have radically different views about how far (if at all) the state should intervene in market mechanisms to set prices, control quantities (to ration, for example), set standards, and regulate producers (or to act as a producer itself through public ownership). Much of the debate

about development strategy can be reduced to differences in views about what is the appropriate level of state provision and whether the state should mostly leave the market alone, or intervene extensively.

These different viewpoints partly arise from different perspectives on how markets work. Much disagreement centres on how well market mechanisms yield poverty reduction—or, indeed, whether markets sometimes work against poor people, making them poorer. Market optimists favour light regulation to let the market deliver the economic growth that best reduces poverty. Market pessimists favour state intervention, arguing that market outcomes reflect power and that this is often unfavourable to the poor (monopolies rather than competition might prevail in unregulated markets for example).

But people differ over the appropriate role for the state because they also hold different views over what constitutes the 'ideal society'. Thus nearly everyone is agreed that an ideal society must achieve absolute poverty reduction, but some people also favour state action to reduce overall income inequality as well. Others are vehemently opposed to such egalitarian ideas, citing individual freedom, including the right to accumulate wealth (this is reflected in the traditional political debates of social democracy versus conservatism). Also controversial are the ability of market mechanisms to yield economic growth, and whether a higher (or lower) growth rate will result from state intervention in the market mechanism (and how different types of intervention increase or decrease the prospects for growth). Similarly, there is much debate on how far 'market-led' or 'state-led' development is supportive of democratization and domestic political stability, as well as national sovereignty.

Market optimists will favour a minimal state: one that provides protection for property rights together with public goods that the market either does not supply or under-supplies (defence is one example, transport infrastructure is another). In contrast, people who are pessimistic about the market's ability to deliver their ideal society will favour a more active state, but their conceptualization of what the state should do can show a very wide range. At one extreme is central planning (practised by the former Soviet Union) where society's productive factors are allocated according to a plan without reference to market prices, and where state ownership of enterprises and property prevails (North Korea is one of the few examples left, and even it has partially liberalized the economy). The 'European model' is at the other end of the scale of active states; continental European states provide very high levels of public goods, regulate the market 'in the public interest', but otherwise encourage a very vigorous private sector (the Nordic countries being the most successful at implementing this model).

Views on state effectiveness have swung like a pendulum over the last fifty years. As countries came to independence, they built national planning apparatuses and wrote national plans. The Soviet Union's example was very influential in China, Cuba, and Vietnam and so was the state planning that even the capitalist economies introduced during the 1940s and many retained afterwards. However, by the late 1970s this confidence in the state's abilities was starting to erode as growth slowed down due to policy failure in many (but certainly not all) countries that pursued state-led development, together with the first (1974) and second (1979) oil price hikes, and the associated world recessions, which tested state capacities to breaking point.

The intellectual pendulum swung back (albeit with considerable resistance) towards the market mechanism in the 1980s and accelerated with the collapse of communism, and the start of the transition to market economies in Eastern Europe and the Soviet Union. This was reinforced by the IMF and the World Bank and their loan conditionality (often dubbed the Washington consensus on what constitutes good policy). Policy change was not always externally-induced. India undertook significant economic liberalization in the early 1990s, reflecting domestic criticism of the longstanding strategy of planning and state ownership

More recently a reaction against market liberalization and privatization has set in, and the intellectual pendulum has begun to swing back towards the state, owing to sharp increases in inequality, rising concern over liberalization's social effects, and the mismanagement of privatization. This is bound up in an intense debate about globalization and its effects (see Nayyar 2002). Latin America is experiencing especially intense criticism of liberalization, reflecting the very mixed outcome from reform programmes in the 1990s (see Box 16.3). Economists increasingly recognize the importance of institutions to making the market mechanism work well for development and poverty reduction. The World Bank has stepped back from its emphasis in the 1980s on the market alone and now gives more attention to institution-building, although its critics argue that Bank policy still fails to equip countries with the strategies that they need to cope with globalization.

Venezuela is an example of the political forces that are now playing out right across Latin America. Bolivia and Peru have similarly moved to extend state control over their mining and energy sectors (see Box 16.3). The commodity price boom is enabling governments to pay off their debts and the improved credit rating of the region's sovereign borrowers is reducing the influence of the IMF and the World Bank upon which Latin America relied for financing in times of economic crisis. The influence of the Washington consensus on domestic policy-making is therefore falling. Whether this leads to better development outcomes depends upon how governments use their new revenues, whether they can reduce political polarization to get agreement on effective development strategies, and whether they can build better states capable of helping the poor.

BOX 16.3

Venezuela: Reacting Against the Washington Consensus

Venezuela is the world's fifth largest oil producer. But nature's bounty has not delivered economic success; growth largely collapsed from 1980 to 2000. Inequality and poverty are both high; 48.5 per cent of Venezuelans were below the poverty line in 2000, and the richest 20 per cent of Venezuelans receive over half of all income.

Foreign oil companies began producing oil in the early twentieth century. The state increasingly intervened from the 1940s onwards as oil became the main source of government revenue (it now accounts for about half of total revenue) and the oil industry was fully nationalized in 1976. Global oil prices were driven up by OPEC (of which Venezuela was a founding member in 1960) and grand promises were made that within a few years Venezuela would be a developed country with no poverty. Between 1950 and 1980 Venezuela was one of Latin America's fastest growing economies. But the massive windfall eventually undermined the non-oil economy (a phenomenon often called 'Dutch Disease' after the problems the Netherlands faced in adjusting to an energy windfall). Venezuela became heavily indebted as it borrowed on the back of high oil prices in the late 1970s thereby exposing itself to the price collapse that came in the 1980s. Severe problems in debt-servicing resulted, growth collapsed and living standards fell precipitously with the country going through a succession of unstable governments in the 1990s each with its own unsuccessful economic recovery plan.

The present president, Hugo Chávez, a former military officer who first took office in the 1998 elections, attracts strong opinions: some see him as a heroic figure doing battle with the forces of global capitalism, a champion of Venezuela's national interests, and defender of the country's poor. Others see him as a demagogue intent on consolidating his personal power by changing the constitution and cracking down on media criticism after the 2007 presidential elections (which he won with a large majority). The president has become more radical in recent years, denouncing neo-liberalism and the Washington consensus (and he is also highly critical of the United States).

With a robust world economy and growing energy demand in China and India, oil prices are high once again and export earnings have filled the government coffers allowing it to massively expand public spending, including spending on programmes for the poor whose numbers appear to be falling. Political support for President Chávez is not surprisingly high among the poor.

President Chávez now proclaims the need for '21st century socialism' including the reversal of the privatization of Venezuela's telecommunications and electricity utilities so that public ownership is restored of the economy's 'strategic sectors'. This has frightened foreign investors who have invested large amounts in the country since the privatizations of the early 1990s. He is also further extending state control over Venezuela's oil sector by negotiating new agreements with the oil multinationals to capture more of the revenue for the Venezuelan state.

KEY POINTS

- The economic role of the state is one of the central issues dividing opinion on development strategy.

- An early emphasis on state-led development was eventually challenged by a market-liberal view, leading to widespread economic liberalization.

- Despite the roll-back of the state, it still has many roles to play in providing public goods as well as in regulating markets in the public interest.

Trade Policy as an Instrument for Development

For market liberals, developing countries that follow their comparative advantage will reap higher living standards by trading as much as possible with the developed countries and with each other (see Chapter 3). Their export earnings can then finance imports of products in which they have a comparative *disadvantage*. The market liberal story of trade is one of mutual gains from trade for both the developing and the developed worlds.

For market liberals comparative advantage also underpins their view of how trade contributes to economic growth, through outward-orientated development. Growth in developing countries' labour-intensive exports (their comparative advantage) will eventually bid up the price of labour (thereby contributing to poverty reduction) and encourage capital-for-labour substitution. The skill content of exports will also rise as educational investment builds human capital, allowing developing countries to start competitively producing what is presently made in the developed world. The state must assist this process through judicious public investment in infrastructure for example, but it is the market that drives it.

In the early years, many policy-makers felt that such outward-orientated development would not yield much growth. Instead, many saw the domestic market as the main growth driver, and they favoured inward-orientated development and import-substituting industrialization (see Chapter 3). Producers who would benefit from protected markets also lobbied for the policy and their influence increased over time as they used the economic rents associated with protection to fund sympathetic politicians and political parties, sometimes engaging in outright corruption. Critics of protection argue that rent-seeking comes to dominate the strategy, no matter how well-intentioned initially, and this view underpinned the World Bank's efforts to open up economies in the 1980s.

In practice the effects of lobbying and rent-seeking vary widely. They were at their worst in sub-Saharan Africa where weak states were easily captured by powerful rent-seekers, and where the smallness of domestic markets made import-substitution unviable without high tariffs and very tight import quotas (which encouraged massive evasion and smuggling). Criticism of India's 'license Raj' led to economic liberalization in the early 1990s but India's growth was respectable, if undramatic, prior to liberalization. And import substitution achieved some 'learning by doing', facilitated by India's enormous domestic market which gives domestic manufacturers larger economies of scale. South Korea's planning mechanism effectively contained rent-seeking and export subsidies offset the disincentive to export production inherent in import protection. Since South Korea is an outstanding development success, it is difficult to believe that it would have achieved even higher growth without import protection (see Chapters 3 and 23b).

The conduct of trade policy is also made more complex by the scale of protectionism that still exists in world trade despite the liberalization conducted under GATT and WTO auspices. Nowhere is this more apparent than in world agriculture. Rich countries pay large subsidies to their farmers, and restrict imports from developing countries (although some countries exporting to the European Union currently still get preferential access). This depresses the world prices of some major export earners for developing countries, notably cotton and sugar, thereby reducing the incomes of their farmers. Brazil has used the WTO to successfully challenge US protectionism, but the smaller and poorer countries lack the resources to defend their interests. They also find it difficult to access the markets of the larger developing countries such as India, which also protects its farmers from foreign competition (although the scale of this protection has been recently reduced). The developing countries do not always have common interests in world trade negotiations and they face powerful political bodies such as the European Union which are adept at protecting their interests. The doctrine of comparative advantage is therefore a useful guide to development policy but it offers only a start since world trade is far from being a completely free market. For this reason, many policymakers continue to favour a very interventionist policy when it comes to the role of trade in development, but much depends on the state's capacity to implement it successfully.

> **KEY POINTS**
>
> - Import-substitution works much better in countries with large domestic markets, and where policy encourages export production as well.
>
> - While the failure of many countries to achieve growth through import protection increased support for outward-orientated development, this too requires a well-designed strategy, particularly in creating new skills to sell in the global marketplace.

Capital Flows and Economic Reform

The world economic shocks of the 1970s and 1980s were a major catalyst for reform. But changes in the level and composition of international capital flows—foreign aid, commercial bank lending, and foreign direct investment—to developing countries have also been influential in inducing reform.

In the 1970s the non-oil-producing developing countries encountered serious macro-economic trouble with the first (1974) and second (1979) oil price shocks when the Organization of Petroleum Exporting Countries quadrupled the world price of oil. During this time the IMF became very important in providing balance of payments support. Several of the oil exporters also borrowed heavily using their oil revenues as collateral (for example Nigeria, Mexico, and Venezuela) and they suffered macro-economic crisis when the world oil price fell during the 1980s. All this brought about the debt crisis (see Chapter 4). In Asia, Malaysia, Singapore, South Korea, and Taiwan escaped largely unscathed and indeed maintained high growth during the 1980s and into the 1990s, until the Asian financial crisis of 1997–8. And although by the early 1980s South Korea was as highly indebted as some

Latin American countries, by then its strong export economy was able to generate the foreign exchange necessary to maintain debt service. This brought home an important lesson: countries neglect export markets at their peril. Chinese policy-makers quickly learned this lesson and China now has a significant share of global manufacturing exports. Some analysts believe China's success poses a problem for smaller developing countries also seeking to grow by increasing their share of world markets for relatively low-cost manufactured goods.

Structural adjustment

With so many of its client countries in deep distress, the World Bank was compelled to move beyond its traditional project lending and in the 1980s it started to provide balance of payments support through **structural adjustment loans** (SALs). These carried such policy conditionalities as currency devaluation (to stimulate the supply of exports); the conversion of import quotas into import tariffs to reduce rent-seeking (and then tariff reduction in order to place more competitive pressure on inefficient infant industries); the removal (liberalization) of market controls in agriculture (to provide more incentives for farmers); and the reform of public expenditures and taxation (to shift more spending towards development priorities and to mobilize more public revenues to finance spending). The IMF's policy conditionality also includes reducing the fiscal deficit to curb inflation (high inflation reduced export competitiveness and economic growth).

Although World Bank and IMF adjustment lending was intended to deal with the immediate macro-economic crises, it was also seen as a way of making poor economies more efficient and therefore more able to grow. For, according to the Washington consensus, that required a reduced role for the state in the productive sectors (hence the start of privatization in the 1980s) as well as reduced controls (liberalization) on the private sector. Irrespective of the merits or otherwise of reform, most countries had little alternative but to sign up to the conditionality, since private capital flows slowed dramatically with the onset of the debt crisis in the 1980s, and official development flows became one of the few sources of external finance. This was especially true for the low-income countries (see Chapter 15 on conditionality).

Yet market liberalization has had very mixed results. Take the market for food staples, for example. This market is vital, for it affects farmers, who produce a surplus to sell, farmers who produce too little themselves and must buy food, rural wage-labourers, and urban households. If the state withdraws (partially or wholly) from buying, storing, transporting, and selling food then it has to be replaced by private entrepreneurs willing to undertake these tasks and bear the risks. But there is more profit to be made in supplying food to major urban centres than in marketing in remote and poor rural areas. Similarly, market liberalization in the manufacturing sector has had mixed effects. The rapid removal of import protection led to factory closures and the loss of jobs in many reforming countries. New jobs may eventually be created once export activities grow, but the necessary investment takes time. In the meantime, unemployment may rise sharply.

Not surprisingly, liberalization has many opponents and it is risky for governments, who often procrastinate (thereby deepening the severity of the economic crisis). Moreover, reform's effects are never clear cut. Many people oppose reform (*ex ante*) fearing a loss, even if this is not the case (*ex post*). Conversely, some people may gain a lot (for example those producing exports) but the gains are not immediate. Sometimes a particular reform will benefit the majority of people but if each person's gain is small then they do not have much incentive to mobilize in support of reform, whereas the minority may stand to lose a lot and therefore has a much greater incentive to mobilize against reform. Reform can therefore stall even if, in aggregate, it benefits the majority. This is a good example of what Olson (2001) calls a collective action problem, which refers to the difficulties that arise in organizing a group of people to achieve a common objective.

Although it is highly controversial, liberalization is straightforward in its implementation because the state simply withdraws, partially or wholly, from the market. But some reforms require a strengthening of state capacity for their success (see Chapter 12). This is especially true of revenue and public expenditure reforms. The state's capacity to mobilize tax and customs revenues and to then spend these resources effectively on pro-poor services and development infrastructure requires a capable and well-motivated government administration, at both central and local levels (the latter being especially important to improving local education and health, for example). However, the quality of civil services, together with their motivation, was in steep decline before reform began in many countries, especially in Africa where inflation eroded real wages in the public sector. Governments were therefore attempting to implement demanding changes with very limited institutional and human resources, and in some cases IMF fiscal-conditionality weakened state capacities further. Reform breakdown and policy reversals are common. Zambia, for example, has gone through many donor-supported adjustment programmes that largely failed to achieve progress, notwithstanding there being greater political commitment by the government to this in the 1990s than in earlier years. There is also a fierce debate on whether economic reform contributed to the breakdown of states and societies in countries like Sierra Leone and Somalia (see Chapter 13).

So-called 'second generation' economic reforms (privatization and financial reform, in particular) have been taking place since the 1990s in countries such as Ghana, Uganda, and Tanzania that began their first-generation reforms (devaluation and trade liberalization) in the 1980s. Implementation of second-generation reforms has often been problematic. For instance privatization has been non-transparent in many cases, thereby transferring valuable assets to the politically connected. Financial reform has been especially difficult. Asia's financial crisis, and Africa's bank failures, both highlight the need to build capacity for prudential supervision and regulation in central banks before major liberalization of financial controls. Tax reform and the construction of better systems of public expenditure management (both essential to not just more investment in development infrastructure but pro-poor services specifically) have stalled in many cases. All this illustrates the importance of building effective state capacities and improving governance (Chapter 15), to regulate the (financial) market in the public interest, and to achieve improvements in the public goods essential to a well-functioning market economy as well as poverty reduction.

KEY POINTS

- Economic reform is driven by the failure of past development strategies, policy conditionality attached to development aid, and the need to attract private capital.

- Market liberalization is much easier to achieve than making states effective, which is often a long haul.

- Reform may be opposed because it has large social costs, or because the losers from reform often have more incentive, and find it easier to organize themselves politically, than the winners.

Conclusions

There are issues on which there is considerable consensus and issues where deep controversy remains. That development policy must have an explicit focus on poverty reduction is one of the main areas of consensus in today's development policy community. In contrast to the period up to the 1970s, when it was thought that economic growth would automatically deliver poverty reduction, it is now recognized that pro-poor policies are necessary to maximize growth's benefits for the poor. Moreover, it is widely agreed that poverty reduction does not just entail higher incomes, but also improving human development indicators: poverty is a multi-dimensional concept. This implies improving the delivery of pro-poor services, particularly in basic health care, safe water and sanitation, and primary education, with a particular emphasis on delivery to rural areas (which contain high levels of poverty) and to women (see Chapter 8). Relatedly, it is widely agreed that the formation of human capital through better health and education is not only good for poverty reduction, but also contributes to growth by enabling diversification into skill-intensive manufactures and services. In this way, poor economies can seek to benefit from globalization.

Compared with the early years of development there is now a greater recognition that the market is important to growth. This shift is somewhat grudging and reflects more the failure of state-led development in many (but certainly not all) countries rather than a large-scale intellectual conversion. Accompanying this has been a move away from heavy import protection and a greater awareness of the value of exporting. Yet, many of the poorer countries find it difficult to achieve export success, especially outside their traditional primary products. They are highly vocal critics of rich country protectionism, especially in agriculture. There is much less support for public ownership of factories and farms and a greater recognition of the private sector's strengths. However, there is much less consensus on whether utilities—power, water, transport infrastructure—should be in private or public ownership, although the fiscal crises of developing countries have driven many governments to privatize their state utilities nevertheless. Finally, countries are now keener to attract private capital flows especially when they bring new technologies but private flows remain concentrated on relatively few countries, and smaller and poorer economies are less attractive to private capital.

Getting development policy right has the potential to lift millions of people out of the misery of poverty. But making the right policy choices is not just a technical matter. It requires careful political judgment about how to promote economic and social change in ways that stand the most chance of success.

? QUESTIONS

1   How have the objectives of development changed over time, and how do differences in development strategy reflect different conceptions of the 'ideal society'?

2   Why does growth reduce poverty more in some countries than in others, and what policies do you recommend to increase growth's benefits, especially for the chronically poor?

3   Why does market-intervention work well in some countries but not in others, and what conclusions can be drawn for the politics of development strategy?

4   Why did East Asia achieve more success than Africa and Latin America in its development strategy, and what role did trade play in this success?

5   What determines the political chances of economic reform being implemented, and what can governments do to build coalitions of support for economic reform?

GUIDE TO FURTHER READING

■ Addison, T. (2003), 'Economics', in P. Burnell (ed.), *Democratization through the Looking Glass* (Manchester: Manchester University Press). Examines how democracy affects economic performance, and contrasts democracy to autocracy in its development effects.

■ Amsden, A. H. (2001), *The Rise of the 'Rest': Challenges to the West from Late-Industrializing Economies* (Oxford: Oxford University Press). A comprehensive discussion of the East Asian success, and the role of the state in guiding the growth process.

■ Chang, H.-J. (2002), *Kicking Away the Ladder: Development Strategy in Historical Perspective* (London: Anthem Press). Contrasts the historical experiences of today's developed countries, and challenges the conventional wisdom on how development institutions are created.

■ Chronic Poverty Research Centre (CPRC) (2005), *The Chronic Poverty Report 2004-05* (London: Chronic Poverty Research Centre). Discusses people who remain poor for much or all of their lives, and who benefit least from economic growth.

■ Kanbur R. (2001), 'Economic Policy, Distribution and Poverty: The Nature of Disagreements', *World Development*, 29/6: 1083–94. A clear and balanced view of the contemporary poverty debate, and why people differ over growth's effects on poverty. Includes very useful comparisons between the differing viewpoints of the World Bank and non-governmental organizations on poverty.

■ Kirkpatrick, C., Clarke, R., and Polidano, C. (eds.) (2002), *Handbook on Development Policy and Management* (Cheltenham: Edward Elgar). Provides summaries of the main economic and political issues in development policy, including further discussion of many of the topics of this chapter.

■ Rodrik, D. (2003), *In Search of Prosperity: Analytic Narratives on Economic Growth* (Princeton, NJ: Princeton University Press). A good place to start on the causes of the different development outcomes of countries, and the role of development strategy in determining success.

■ Wade, R. (1990), *Governing the Market: Economic Theory and the Role of Government in East Asian Industrialization* (Princeton, NJ: Princeton University Press, repr. 2003 with a new introduction by the author). An authoritative assessment of how East Asia achieved its economic success, which challenges the market liberal view and emphasizes the role of the state.

 WEB LINKS

www.developmentgateway.org An independent site that introduces the latest development research, with frequent updates of new research papers and breaking news in development.

www.chronicpoverty.org An international partnership of researchers and NGOs working on chronic poverty and its eradication in Africa, Asia, and Latin America.

www.eldis.org Very easy-to-use site, with downloadable research papers, reports, and many links to other sites. It has a very useful section on how to use the web for development research, and the issues facing web users in developing countries with slow band width.

www.imf.org The IMF posts reports on its member countries, and agreements with governments (such as 'Letters of Intent') which spell out in detail economic reforms. The IMF's annual reports on the state of the world economy are also widely read.

www.odi.org.uk The website of the Overseas Development Institute (UK), an independent think-tank on development issues. The ODI *Briefing Papers* provide authoritative insight into the latest development issues.

www.undp.org The website of the United Nations Development Programme (UNDP) which is leading the UN's work on the Millennium Development Goals. The UNDP's annual *Human Development Report* can also be viewed at this site.

www.unrisd.org The website of the United Nations Research Institute for Social Development (UNRISD). UNRISD focuses on the social dimensions of development, as well as development's political aspects.

www.wider.unu.edu The website of the United Nations University's World Institute for Development Economics Research (UNU-WIDER). WIDER's *Discussion Paper* series offers a wide range of viewpoints on economic development issues, particularly in the areas of measuring poverty and the development effects of violent conflict.

www.worldbank.org The website of the World Bank offers an enormous range of country material, particularly on poverty reduction, as well as many of the statistics (such as the *World Development Indicators*) used by the development community.

 ONLINE RESOURCE CENTRE

For additional material and resources, see the Online Resource Centre at:
www.oxfordtextbooks.co.uk/orc/burnell2e/

17 Environment

PETER NEWELL

Chapter Contents

- Introduction
- Global Context
- Environment and Development: An Uneasy Relationship
- Policy Processes
- New Policy Instruments for Environmental Protection
- Futures

Overview

This chapter explores how developing countries are managing the relationship between environment and development. Traditionally considered a threat to their economic development and prospects for growth, environmental issues have come to feature on policy agendas throughout the developing world. Driven by donors, public concern, and vocal environmental movements, responses to these issues have taken a number of different forms as they compete for 'policy space' with other pressing development concerns and are subject to changing thinking about the effectiveness of policy tools to tackle environmental problems. This chapter explores these issues, connecting global agendas to national policy processes, explaining differences and similarities between countries on these issues, and identifying patterns of continuity and change in the politics of environment in the developing world.

PETER NEWELL

Introduction

From an issue on the periphery of the policy agendas of most developing country governments, the environment has assumed an important and rising status on the national political agendas of states in Africa, Latin America, and Asia. This shift results from a combination of pressures from global institutions, donors, and active citizen movements, and has evolved alongside a growth in both scientific understanding of environmental problems and rising levels of public concern, often generated by environmental disasters.

Yet the status of the environment as an issue on developing country agendas is not secure. Environmental issues, in many areas of the world, are only loosely embedded within national policy processes, incoherently related to wider economic and social agendas and subject to displacement by issues which assume a greater priority for most countries. The theme of this chapter then is continuity and change. Most countries are operating in a radically different policy context in which an increasingly globalized economy impacts more directly than ever before on the relationship between environment and development concerns. At the same time, environmental issues have been grafted onto existing policy agendas, national priorities, and decision-making processes that, in many cases, are characterized by bureaucratic inertia, organized opposition to reform, and reluctance to realign priorities.

The chapter is organized into four sections. The first part sketches the increasingly important global context for debates about environment and development and the links between them. Such links have been institutionalized through the growth of global bodies and areas of international environmental law produced through a series of UN negotiations. The second looks at policy processes at the national level; how these global agendas have been responded to and addressed by individual governments. This means tackling questions about what is unique about policy processes in developing countries and what extra challenges are associated with tackling environmental problems in these settings. The third section looks at the range of tools and strategies that developing countries have adopted in order to combat environmental degradation. This includes discussion about the shifting roles of governments, market actors such as businesses and civil society in natural resource use management and protection. The final section explores probable future directions of environmental politics in the developing world, pulling together these patterns of continuity and change.

KEY POINTS

- The environment has assumed an important and rising status on the national political agendas of states in Africa, Latin America, and Asia.

- Yet the status of the environment as an issue on developing country agendas is not secure. It is often displaced by issues which assume a greater priority for most countries.

- We can observe a process of continuity and change, in which environmental challenges are handled within existing national policy frameworks but where globalization has changed the relationship between environment and development and among the actors charged with delivering sustainable development.

Global Context

There is little agreement about what we mean by the environment and particularly about which issues are most deserving of an effective policy response. It is often assumed that differences of opinion on this issue fall along North–South lines, where developed countries are more concerned with global problems such as climate change and ozone depletion and conservation issues such as whaling and forest protection, while developing countries attach greater priority to rural issues such as desertification and soil erosion and local environmental issues such as water pollution and air quality in cities. Even a cursory look at the politics of global negotiations on these issues suggests that these categorizations are at best only partially accurate.

First, we need to consider issues of causation and impact. Many of those people who contribute most to global environmental degradation are not those that will suffer its most adverse consequences. While climate change will have global impacts, wealthier countries are better placed to adapt to its adverse consequences. While the Netherlands can build sea defences against sea-level rise, Bangladesh will suffer serious flooding of low-lying agriculturally important areas. While Australians can use sun lotions to protect themselves from harmful UV rays that are stronger as a result of ozone depletion, many rural Chileans will not be able to afford the luxury.

Yet it is the developed world that contributes to global environmental problems to a proportionally much greater extent. For example, 80 per cent of the world's climate-changing carbon dioxide is produced by less that 25 per cent of the world's population. Despite increasing efforts to integrate developing countries into the ozone negotiations, the key deals leading to the conclusion of the landmark Montreal Protocol in 1987 were negotiated between developed countries, principally the US and EU. This reflected the fact that, at that time, these countries were the largest contributors to the

problem and were best placed technologically to find substitutes to ozone-depleting chemicals such as CFCs (chlorofluorocarbons).

Secondly, the economic importance of natural resources to a country's economic development is a significant determinant of its position on a particular environmental policy problem, making it difficult for developing countries to form common policy positions. Brazil has traditionally resisted calls to view the Amazonian rainforests as part of the common heritage of humankind because of their strategic importance to the country's economic development. Many other developing countries, however, have called for this principle of **global stewardship** to apply to a range of common pool resources such as Antarctica and the deep sea-bed on the basis that if those resources are to be exploited, it should be for the benefit of all and not just those that are in a position to exploit them. Similarly, while the Alliance of Small Island States (AOSIS), threatened by sea-level rise associated with global climate change, have strongly advocated controls on greenhouse gas emissions, the OPEC bloc whose economies are heavily dependent on the export of oil, have resisted such controls.

While some developing countries view environmental policy as an opportunity to secure additional aid and new forms of technology transfer, others feel threatened by agendas which appear to constrain their prospects for growth. While the G77 bloc of least-developed countries (formed at the UN after a meeting of UNCTAD in 1964, for the purpose of promoting the collective economic interest of Third World countries) has traditionally placed the responsibility for short-term action on climate change upon the North in the negotiations on the subject, many Latin American and Asian countries now see opportunities to earn much-needed revenue from participating in projects under the Clean Development Mechanism set up under the Kyoto

Protocol concluded in 1997. Such projects entitle Northern countries to claim credits for paying for carbon 'sink' (carbon-absorbing) projects in heavily forested areas of Central and Southern America, for example. The rapid growth of industrial powerhouses such as India, China, and Brazil has further fractured the unity of the G77 bloc. It is increasingly difficult, in light of their rising contribution to the problem of global warming, for these countries to refute the need for their own legally binding emissions reduction obligations. Countries such as the US have made their cooperation in further negotiations contingent on these countries accepting cuts in their own future emissions.

Third, aside from areas where core national economic interests may be at stake, global environmental institutions have played a key role in shaping the national environmental policy agendas of many developing countries. Box 17.1 summarizes the mandates and key activities of some of the more prominent global environmental institutions.

It is their access to financial resources and the mandate they have to oversee the implementation of key global environmental accords that allows these bodies to play this role. As Box 17.1 shows, the Global Environment Facility (GEF) has responsibility for overseeing the transfer of aid and technology transfer to developing countries in order to help meet their obligations under the Rio agreements, for example on climate change and biodiversity conservation. The provision of aid and technology to developing countries to meet these commitments recognizes that these countries require assistance in making a contribution to global efforts to tackle forms of environmental degradation to which most currently contribute very little. Concern was expressed at the time of the UN Conference on Environment and Development in Rio that aid for the implementation of these international environmental agreements should be 'additional' to that which developing countries receive for other development purposes.

BOX 17.1

Key Global Environmental Institutions

United Nations Environment Programme

- Created following Stockholm conference on the Human Environment in 1972
- Initially conceived as clearing-house of environmental data and research and to set up demonstration projects
- No statute or charter to describe its function and role
- Governing Council of fifty-eight members elected by UN General Assembly on regional formula for four-year terms
- The council is mandated to promote cooperation on environmental issues; recommend appropriate policies
- Budget of only US$10.5 million a year from regular UN budget.
- Depends on volunteer contributions from member countries for financing specific projects
- No structured system of dispute settlement
- Enforcement reliant on peer review and moral pressure

Commission on Sustainable Development

- Inter-governmental body; members selected from UN
- Composed of fifty-three members elected for three-year terms
- Meets annually
- Reports to ECOSOC (Economic and Social Council) of UN
- Purpose: to review progress at international, regional, and national level in implementation of Rio ('Earth summit') agreements such as Agenda 21, the Rio Declaration, and the Forest Principles
- Means: provide policy guidance; promote dialogue; build partnerships with major groups

Global Environment Facility	• Three implementing agencies: UNEP, UNDP, World Bank
• Key financing body for actions on climate change, biodiversity loss, ozone depletion, international waters, land degradation, persistent organic compounds (POPs); new and additional grant and concessional funding for incremental costs for global benefits	• World Bank administers facility on day-to-day basis and is trustee of the GEF trust fund
	• Decisions made by consensus; where dispute, decisions made on double majority basis

Increasingly, however, these institutions and the conventions they seek to enforce have sought to facilitate the integration of environmental and developmental concerns rather than see them as competing issues. There has been a clear shift towards addressing development concerns that can be traced from the Stockholm Conference on the Human Environment in 1972 onwards (see Box 17.2). This prepared the ground for the famous Brundtland Report *Our Common Future* (1987)—which first coined the phrase sustainable development, defined as 'Development which meets the needs of the current generation without compromising the ability of future generations to meet their own needs'. The title of the Rio conference that followed five years later encapsulated the rhetorical integration of environmental and developmental objectives, namely the United Nations Conference on Environment and Development. Ten years on, the language of sustainable development was placed centrally in the naming of the follow-up to Rio, the 'World Summit on Sustainable Development' in Johannesburg in 2002.

Despite this rhetorical shift, many developing countries and activists have been critical of the way in which certain issues have been actively kept off

---

BOX 17.2

Chronology of Environment and Development on the International Agenda

1972: Stockholm Conference on the Human Environment

• Created UNEP
• Established key principles of responsible global environmental stewardship
• Set in train global scientific cooperation

1980: Brandt Commission

• North–South: A Programme for Survival
• Addressing North–South elements more clearly: trade, debt, energy, food

1987: World Commission on Environment and Development

• *Our Common Future* (Brundtland Report)
• Birth of a concept: Sustainable Development

1992: UNCED

• United Nations Framework Convention on Climate Change
• Convention on Biological Diversity
• Rio declaration
• Statement of Forest Principles
• Agenda 21

2002: WSSD: Johannesburg

• Agreement on water and sanitation (to halve the number of people without access to basic sanitation by 2015)
• Agreement on fisheries (plan to restore world's depleted stocks by 2015; create marine areas around the world by 2012)

the agenda of these summits. The Rio conference attracted criticism for not addressing issues such as debt, terms of trade, or the regulation of multinational companies, issues which some developing countries have sought to advance since the early 1970s, initially through the platform of the New International Economic Order. The US delegation to the conference fought hard to remove references to unsustainable levels of consumption in the Rio documents and concerns were raised during the World Summit on Sustainable Development (WSSD) at attempts to thwart the negotiation of a new convention on corporate accountability.

Rather than viewing environmental issues as stand-alone concerns, it is becoming increasingly clear that it is necessary to 'mainstream' environmental concerns into the activities of leading development actors. While the World Bank continues to draw fire for the environmental impact of some of its lending operations, as far back as 1987 it set up an environmental department and now insists on detailed environmental impact assessments of all its lending programmes. Also largely as a result of a vocal lobbying by environmental groups, the World Trade Organization has created a Committee on Trade and Environment which first met in 1995 to look at the relationship between environmental standards and trade liberalization, though notably and controversially not the environmental impacts of trade. The emphasis has, therefore, been on defining the legitimate circumstances in which environmental and human health concerns can be invoked as exceptions to the normal obligations countries assume through membership of the WTO, rather than the ecological cost of transporting greater volumes of goods across ever larger distances, for example (see Box 17.3). The question is whether environmental considerations should be allowed to drive decisions about which types of trade are desirable and necessary from the point of view of sustainable development or whether all environmental measures which impact upon trade have to be compatible with WTO rules. For developing countries, one of the key concerns has been the growth in environmental standards that many fear will be used as barriers to trade and disguised forms of protectionism to protect Northern producers from competitive exports from the South. High-profile cases that have come before the WTO's Dispute Settlement Mechanism such as the notorious dolphin-tuna case have reflected this

---

BOX 17.3

The Ecological Footprint of Trade

Asparagus

To import 1 kg of asparagus from California to Europe requires four litres of fuel. If grown domestically the 'energy grab' from transport would be over 900 times less.

Kiwis

Kiwi fruit by freight carrier plane from New Zealand to Europe results in 5 kg of CO_2 being pumped into the atmosphere for every 1 kg of fruit carried.

Yogurt

Delivering glass cups of yogurt produced for the German market in the mid-1990s required journeys for the contents and finished product that added up to 8,000 km.

Cotton

Energy intensive transport of textile products is increasing with globalization. After the soil erosion and chemical typical of its growing stage, transport is, by a long way, the next highest environment cost of producing cotton.

(New Economics Foundation 2003)

fear. In this case, the US sought to ban yellow-fin tuna from Mexico on the grounds that the nets being used by the Mexican fishing industry to catch tuna fish were also killing dolphins.

This apparent integration of environmental issues into the policy practice of development actors has not just occurred at the inter-governmental level. One of the millennium development goals agreed by the Development Assistance Committee of the OECD is for all countries to have in place by the year 2005 a National Strategy for Sustainable Development (NSSD). Interestingly, country ownership is highlighted as a central component of an effective NSSD. Broad consultation to open up the debate and build consensus are seen as key for strategy formulation. This approach acknowledges that while sustainable development is a universal challenge, the practical response to it can only be defined nationally and locally according to different values and interests. An OECD report on the issue notes that a standardized blueprint approach should be avoided, and is at best irrelevant and at worst counter-productive (OECD 2001).

Instead, working with existing approaches and institutional arrangements according to individual countries' needs, priorities, and available resources is preferable.

KEY POINTS

- There is now a wide range of global environmental agreements which developing countries have signed and are in the process of implementing.

- Though development issues have gained a higher profile in global environmental summits and agreements, there is still some concern that Northern countries control the agenda.

- Countries' positions on these issues do not fall neatly along North–South lines, however, and key differences exist between developing countries on many high-profile global environmental issues.

- There has been a move towards mainstreaming environmental concerns into the lending practices of multilateral development agencies and into poverty reduction strategies.

Environment and Development: An Uneasy Relationship

The relationship between environment and development is not an easy one, and many conflicts are subsumed under the convenient banner of 'sustainable development' whose aims it is difficult for anyone to refute. The term has been used to describe all manner of projects and activities from large dams to controversial mining projects. Many have, therefore, questioned its value as an analytical concept, when it can be invoked so easily to justify 'business as usual' polluting activities. The term disguises conflicts over priorities between environment and development, gives few, if any, indications about which forms of development are sustainable, and is

inevitably interpreted by different actors in different contexts to mean different things. Fundamental conflicts over the causes and appropriate solutions to environmental degradation persist. These include the debate about the extent to which population growth is a cause of environmental degradation. Malthusian (after the eighteenth-century thinker the Reverend Thomas Malthus) analysis of resource degradation, popular in certain strands of 1970s environmental thinking (Ehrlich 1972), suggested that rapid increases in population were driving the planet towards ecological collapse. The influential 'limits of growth' report in 1972 of the Club of Rome suggested instead that unsustainable patterns of resource use would ultimately bring about ecological collapse because of the finite nature of the natural resource base upon which we all depend. Many developing countries and more radical environmental groups target over-consumption and affluence in Western societies, rather than population, as the key cause of the global environmental crisis.

Given this lack of consensus on the causes of environmental degradation, it is unsurprising that consensus eludes attempts to find appropriate solutions. Old conflicts in development over aid, trade, debt, and the role of technology get replayed through discussions about how to combat environmental degradation. Those believing that poverty leads people to use resources unsustainably have looked to ideas such as debt-for-nature swaps as a way out of this cycle. These swaps provide debt relief in exchange for commitments to preserve areas of forest. Critiques of the effects of aid and technology transfer on developing countries that circulated in development discourse for decades get rehearsed in environmental debates. It is claimed that the use of aid to extract environmental commitments amounts to eco-colonialism: the forced imposition of the North's values. Technologies that are transferred as part of global environmental agreements are often out of date and serve both as a subsidy to Northern producers of technologies for which markets no longer exist and to entrench the dependency of developing countries on the North. In environmental terms, it is also argued that technology is no substitute for tough action aimed at reducing unsustainable patterns of production and consumption and that developed countries often prefer to transfer technologies to developing countries rather than take measures to address the source of environmental degradation in their own countries.

This then is the global historical and contemporary context that shapes the ways in which developing countries have been seeking to tackle environmental issues at the national level. The next section looks in more detail at the commonalities and differences in the ways developing countries have responded to these global environmental agendas while grappling with their own unique environmental problems and development needs.

KEY POINTS

- The term sustainable development disguises key conflicts over priorities between environment and development.

- There is no consensus on the social causes of environmental degradation and the importance that should be attached to population growth in the South as opposed to unsustainable consumption in the North.

- Fundamental disagreements arise concerning the role of aid, trade and technology as appropriate solutions to environmental problems.

Policy Processes

Political diversity

It is impossible to make generalizations about environmental policy that would apply across the entire developing world. Though nearly all developing countries are involved in global negotiations on the issues raised above, the processes by which they translate those commitments into workable policies at the national level are very different. First, there is the issue of power. There is clearly a difference between a country like China or India with significant scope for independent action and power to assert their interests in global fora dealing with these issues and smaller and less powerful countries such as Uruguay or Zambia. This difference relates in part to the resources that can be committed to participating in global processes which can be highly time and resource intensive. Environmental negotiations often take place in Bonn, Geneva, or New York and to participate effectively in them requires a large delegation with access to scientific and legal expertise. Developing countries are often only able to send at most one or two government representatives to these negotiations which are often run with parallel meetings that a small delegation cannot attend.

But the difference is also a function of the degree of power that a country wields in global economic terms and the extent to which it is aid-dependent. Countries such as Mali and Ethiopia are highly dependent on aid. In Mali's case the overwhelming majority of that aid comes from its former colonizer, France. Research programmes and policy priorities are, therefore, strongly affected by such bilateral financial ties. Countries such as Brazil, on the other hand, have a larger degree of discretion in determining policy positions and they can draw on greater economic weight in trade and industrial terms to advance their preferences on environmental issues.

Secondly, but related, are issues of capacity for the enforcement of policy. Many countries, such as India, have some of the most impressive legislative acts on environmental issues in the world. But lack of resources, training, and corruption of local pollution control officials often conspire to delay implementation. Sometimes the nature of the problem and the size of the country are the key constraints. For example, regulating the cultivation and trade in genetically modified (GM) seeds is almost impossible in a country the size of China and many instances of illegal growing of non-authorized seeds have been reported. Managing the transborder movement of GM seeds, as is required by the Cartagena Protocol on Biosafety (2000), presents many problems for developing countries where seed markets are often poorly regulated and even basic equipment with which to test shipments of seeds across borders is unavailable. Where countries have a strong economic and developmental incentive to ensure active compliance, extra steps may

be taken. Kenya is keen to be seen as an attractive tourist location for wildlife safaris. Because tourism provides a large source of revenue, officials have gone to controversial lengths to tackle the problem of illegal poaching of elephants and rhinos for their ivory and horns, including shooting poachers and banning tribal groups from culling animals for food, even on their own ancestral lands.

Thirdly, the degree of importance that will be attached to environmental concerns, at the expense of broader development goals, will reflect the nature of democratic politics in the country. The strength of environmental groups in a country, pushing for new policy and acting as informal 'watchdogs' of compliance with environmental regulations will be determined by the degree of democratic space which exists within the country. Countries such as India and Mexico have strong traditions of active civil society engagement in environmental policy (see Chapters 21a and 22c). India, for instance, hosts such globally recognized institutions as the Centre for Science and Environment and its more research-oriented counterpart, TERI (The Energy and Resources Institute) which are active in global policy debates as well as domestic agenda-setting. In Singapore and China, by contrast, the avenues for policy engagement are few and tightly restricted. The scope and effectiveness of environmental policy will also be shaped by the extent to which the interests of leading industries are affected by proposed interventions. Where policy directly impinges on the interests of a particularly powerful industry, policy reform is often stalled or environmental concerns are kept off the agenda altogether. The close ties between logging companies and state officials that often have personal commercial stakes in the companies is an often-cited reason for the lack of progress to reverse unsustainable logging in South-East Asia (Dauvergne 1997).

The way governments formulate and implement policy also reflects the diversity in styles of environmental policy-making across the developing world. Each country has a unique history when it comes to its approach to regulation, the organization of its bureaucracy, and the extent to which public participation in policy is encouraged. The Chinese government is able to act decisively and in a 'command-and-control' fashion to sanction industries failing to comply with pollution control regulations. In India, the Supreme Court has played a decisive role in moving environmental policy forward, often in controversial circumstances, setting strict and sometimes unrealistic targets for the phasing out of non-CNG (compressed natural gas) vehicles in Delhi, for example, or instructing the eviction of thousands of small industries from the outskirts of Delhi because of the pollution their activities were generating. Other countries have a more reactive policy style, influenced by popular politics. In Argentina, the government had consistently failed to take action to protect a forest in the north of the country until football legend Maradona joined Greenpeace's campaign to protect the forest, prompting immediate government action.

Approaches to environmental policy also reflect the different ways in which knowledge, especially scientific knowledge, informs policy. Keeley and Scoones (2003: 5) show how, in the case of soils policy: 'By shaping the way development problems are thought about, science influences the nature of networks and relationships between states, within and across bureaucracies and in relation to how alternative expertise is thought about'. Scientific knowledge does not provide a neutral and value-free guide to which environmental problems are the most serious or how they should be addressed. It is employed strategically by government officials to support their position within the bureaucracy, but can also change political practice and priorities by highlighting some areas of concern while ignoring others. The power of expert communities in this regard explains why developing countries have sought greater representation of Southern-based scientists in international environmental bodies providing advice to policy-makers such as Cartagena Protocol on Biosafety's 'Roster of experts'.

Given these factors, there is sometimes also a mismatch between the expectations contained in multilateral environmental agreements about the way in which commitments should be implemented and the realities of what is possible in many developing country settings. There is the problem of capacity where the resources and skills to oversee micro-level implementation of environmental regulations emanating from central government to meet global commitments are often lacking. In addition, many agreements, including the Cartagena Protocol on Biosafety, specify the process by which national environmental frameworks should be designed, for example to involve active public consultation and participation. While some developing countries have recently engaged with the policy process requirements of the World Bank/IMF Poverty Reduction Strategy, many are poorly placed to meaningfully set up elaborate participatory processes for deliberative and inclusive decision-making across a wide range of issues, involving a cross-section of their societies. Democratic values are weakly embedded in many societies, and publics in many places remain sceptical of interaction with official bodies such that good global intentions may not translate well into local practice.

Common challenges

Despite these differences in the policy positions and policy styles that developing countries have adopted, it is worth highlighting some common challenges that nearly all developing, and of course many developed, countries face in the design and execution of environmental policy. First, there is the scale of resources required to tackle environmental problems. Undertaking scientific research and monitoring the enforcement of pollution control places large resource demands on developing countries in particular. International environmental agreements create new demands of governments for more regulation, more monitoring, and an efficient and effective bureaucracy to oversee these, often across multiple levels of governance right down to the local level. Despite the availability of global funds to support some of these activities (see Box 17.1), it remains difficult even for larger developing countries to meet these expectations for many of the reasons mentioned above.

Secondly, in spite of the efforts of active environmental movements within developing countries, as well as globally, it remains true that political constituencies with a strong preference for more effective environmental policy are often very weak. The issue is not only that the beneficiaries of environmental policies are not present in policy debates (future generations) or not adequately represented (indigenous peoples for example), but that political parties with strong commitments to environmental issues are not well developed in most parts of Asia, Africa, and Latin America. Conversely, the presence in Europe of Green parties has served to keep environmental issues on the agendas of the main parties.

This issue is not just one of party politics, but also of class. It has traditionally been the case in the North that wealthier social groups, predominantly the middle classes, are the strongest advocates of environmental protection measures and those most likely to belong to environmental interest groups such as World Wide Fund for Nature (WWF). While there is evidence that urban middle classes in larger developing countries such as China and India are demanding consumer rights and have sought, for example, to get labelling for foods containing GMOs, in many developing countries rural environmental issues are often closely related to more controversial and intractable issues of land reform and rural livelihoods. Campesino (peasant-based) movements in Latin America often incorporate environmental issues into broader campaigning platforms for land redistribution and greater levels of compensation for the appropriation of their resources (Newell 2007). Struggles to protect biological resources in India often get caught up in broader debates about access to genetic resources and whether foreign multinationals should be able to patent living organisms that derive from India. Explicitly framing their campaign in anti-colonial terms, activists opposed to biotechnology called on the company Monsanto to 'Quit India!' Movements for environmental justice which oppose the

location of often hazardous and highly polluting industries in poorer communities often frustrate the development ambitions of policy elites. The ability of movements to use environmental issues to advance broader political agendas serves to entrench the suspicion that many governments have of environmental agendas. Occasionally, however, governments see in environmental issues an opportunity to gain political capital on an issue of national concern. The Argentine government is locked in conflict with neighbouring Uruguay over pulp mills set up there which it is alleged are contaminating the Uruguay river the two countries share. Argentina even initiated proceedings at the International Court of Justice in The Hague over the issue.

Thirdly, we have to recognize the global economic pressures which all countries face but which developing countries face more acutely. Crushing debt burdens and the conditions attached to structural adjustment programmes often create incentives for economic activities that are highly destructive of the environment. Export-led growth patterns which often require intensive use of land with heavy applications of chemical fertilizers, and the creation of export-processing zones whose aim is to attract foreign capital to areas where labour is cheap and environmental standards are lower, provide examples. Deteriorating terms of trade for timber, minerals, and agricultural produce also drive developing country economies, dependent on single commodities, to exploit that resource unsustainably. In the aftermath of the financial crisis in South-East Asia in the late 1990s, for example, timber producers increased exports to unsustainable levels to compensate for the losses they incurred from depreciating national currencies.

The broader issue is what has been termed the 'race to the bottom' in environmental standards as developing countries compete to lower environmental regulations in order to attract increasingly mobile investors. The evidence for this is mixed. Some argue that increased patterns of trade interdependence have the effect of raising standards as developing country exporters seek access to lucrative Western markets that require higher environmental standards (Vogel 1997). However, there are many examples of regulatory reforms not being introduced or not implemented for fear of deterring investors. For example, in response to pressure from soybean exporters in the US, the Chinese government delayed plans to introduce a series of biosafety measures which exporters considered overly restrictive. In other cases, lack of environmental regulation has been used as a comparative advantage to attract environmentally hazardous production of substances such as toxic wastes and asbestos that have been banned in the North. The desperation of many developing countries to attract investment on any terms clearly, therefore, both affects their ability to prioritize action on the environment and in certain situations will lead them to lower standards in order to attract mobile capital.

It is also the case that many developing countries have abundant natural resources which make them key locations for extractive industries. For years activists have berated the mining industry for its environmental pollution, human rights violations, and displacement of indigenous peoples. The oil industry too has been accused of double standards when it operates in developing countries. The activities of firms such as Shell in Nigeria's Niger Delta and Texaco in Ecuador have attracted global attention as a result of activist exposure and high-profile legal actions against the companies. It is often the case that foreign companies get caught up in local disputes over access to land and conflicts between particular tribal groups or regions and the central government. This adds costs and heightens the risks associated with their operations as instances of sabotage of pipe lines and recent abductions of oil company staff in the Niger delta make clear. In most cases, however, the strategic importance of the minerals and resources found in those countries means that companies are willing to endure the controversy and bad publicity, preferring instead to launch public relations campaigns defending their actions, as well as invoking arguments about using their economic clout to press for social and

environmental reforms in the country where they are operating.

It is also important, however, to differentiate between countries regarding the extent to which the 'greening' of business has taken place. It is now commonplace for larger companies based in the North to claim that their companies adopt the principles of sustainable development in their investment decision-making. Among globally connected industry associations in the developing world, such as the Makati Business Club in the Philippines or the Confederation of Indian Industry, this discourse is being picked up. However, it remains the case that many of the drivers of corporate environmental responsibility, including government incentives, civil society watchdogs, and consumer and investor pressure are currently underdeveloped in many parts of the developing world. It is almost certainly the case that firms within countries with strong trading ties to overseas markets where compliance with tougher environmental regulations is expected will have higher standards than firms in parts of sub-Saharan Africa, for example, that are more isolated from such global pressures.

Ironically, when developing countries have sought to implement high levels of environmental protection, they have faced criticism. There are many instances of developing countries being subject to intense pressure when their environmental regulations impinge upon exports from powerful developed countries. For example, on many recent occasions the US has shown itself willing to use threats to withdraw aid or bring a case at the WTO against countries whose regulations on GMOs are alleged to be incompatible with their obligations under the trade body. Despite bringing a case against the EU's GMO regulations before the WTO in 2003, the US has not yet brought such a case against a developing country. Instead, candidates like Sri Lanka and Croatia, fearful of the economic consequences of not succumbing to the US's demands, have backed down. These sorts of pressures clearly serve to restrict the menu of policy options that developing countries can realistically chose from when deciding what course of action to take.

Fourthly, the underdevelopment of the scientific expertise that underpins environmental policy is a characteristic common to many developing countries. While there are many international scientific research programmes on environmental issues and many international environmental agreements have panels or rosters of experts associated with their activities, the representation of scientists from developing countries is often low. There have been initiatives from UNEP to try and address this problem by ensuring, for example, that a percentage of scientists on such bodies are from developing countries. But the problem endures, and the implication is that the policy and scientific agendas of Northern researchers and their policy networks attract greater attention and resources than issues and concerns that are more pertinent to the developing world. This criticism has been levelled at the work of GEF, for instance, for being more responsive to the agendas of Northern donors upon which it is dependent for funding than to the recipients of its capacity-building measures in the South. The World Bank

(2000: 14) itself has conceded that its 'preference for big loans can easily distract regulators from confronting their communities' most critical pollution problems'.

KEY POINTS

- Despite facing similar international pressures to integrate environmental issues into development policy, the willingness and ability of developing countries to address environmental challenges is highly uneven.

- There are some important differences in priorities, power and policy autonomy, resources and capacity, policy styles, and the role of environmental and business groups in policy formulation and implementation across the developing world.

- There are, however, many common challenges that developing countries face when it comes to environmental policy: weaknesses in enforcement capacity; economic vulnerability, which means trade and aid leverage can be used to change policy; and an underdeveloped knowledge base from which to develop environmental policy.

New Policy Instruments for Environmental Protection

We have already noted the different policy styles that developing countries around the world have employed in the design and implementation of environmental policy. It is also the case, however, that they have been affected by shifts in prevailing thinking about the most efficient and effective way to provide environmental goods without jeopardizing development progress. Strong developmental states are still willing and able to intervene forcibly to close down polluting industry; the important role of legal systems in driving environmental policy reform and

in protecting the rights of citizens against their own government has also been noted.

Courts have been a key site for poorer groups to seek compensation for socially and environmentally destructive investments that have undermined their livelihoods. They have provided a venue to draw attention to grievances that have not been recognized elsewhere and, where successful, legal cases can uphold key rights to environmental information, to have environmental impact assessments undertaken in advance of large industrial projects or to contest the forced displacement that is associated with infrastructural projects such as dams. Cases have been brought in Brazil and India over the legality of the process by which the governments authorized the growing of GM crops, for example. In Nigeria numerous cases have been brought against the oil giant Shell, amongst others, seeking compensation for damage to land caused by oil spillages from the company's pipelines in the Niger Delta. Companies exploiting lower health and environmental standards in developing countries, providing their workers with less protection than counterparts in the North, have ended up paying large out-of-court settlements to victims of industrial hazards. More positively and proactively, poorer groups have also been able to use legal remedies to realize their rights to key resources such as water, which is a constitutional right in South Africa, or to claim livelihood rights to health, housing, and decent working conditions (Newell and Wheeler 2006) (see Box 17.4).

Relying on legal remedies to tackle environmental problems is often inadequate, however. Often people resort to the law only after the pollution has occurred. There are also limits to how poorer groups can use the law to their benefit. Poorer communities that are often the frontline

victims of industrial pollution frequently lack the financial resources to bring a case and lack the 'legal literacy' necessary to understand their rights under the law and how they can be realized. These problems of access are often compounded by long backlogs of cases, distrust in the independence of the legal system, and the many legal barriers to successfully demonstrating cause and effect between a polluting activity and evidence of damage to human health or the environment.

State-based environmental regulation, in general, however, has been subject to sustained criticism from key development actors such as the World Bank on the grounds that it is excessively inflexible, inefficient, and often ineffective at delivering the change in behaviour that it intends. Increasingly, the preference is for the use of the market as a tool for incentivizing positive action and deterring polluting activities. Examples of pollution charging in China, Colombia, and the Philippines show that pollution from factories has been successfully reduced when steep, regular payments for emissions have been enforced. Familiar problems of tax collection and corruption may yet undermine the effectiveness of some such initiatives, but there can be little doubt that their increasing use indicates a shift in policy direction. Market tools such as

---

BOX 17.4

The Right to Water in South Africa

- South Africa is the only country that recognizes the human right to water at the constitutional and policy level through its Free Basic Water policy.

- The Water Services Act of 1997 provides for a basic level of water for those that cannot pay. People are entitled to 25 free litres of water per day for personal and domestic use.

- There is nevertheless uneven access to water. Problems of capacity of local authorities to deliver on the commitment and financial constraints have led to undersupply and people being cut-off. This has led some people to get water from unprotected sources leading to health problems.

- The government is also under immense pressure to introduce user-fees and cost recovery in line with market-based approaches to water provision.

- Many people are also unaware of their constitutional right to water and therefore when their rights are violated.

- Though some legal cases have secured interim relief from disconnections by invoking the right to water, the onus on proving inability to pay rests with the water user and depends on their access to legal representation.

(Mehta 2006)

labelling have also been accepted in many developing countries as a means by which to assure global buyers of the environmentally responsible way in which the product has been produced as well as to facilitate consumer choice. For example certification has been used in the forestry sector where the popular FSC scheme (Forestry Stewardship Council) is based in Oaxaca, Mexico.

Another general trend in environmental policy that is catching on in the developing world is the popularity of voluntary measures by industry. Codes of conduct among leading companies are now commonplace in the North and many of those firms investing overseas are insisting that their suppliers and partners adopt the same principles. The trend comes on the back of a rejection of the efficiency and effectiveness of central government 'command and control' policy measures imposed from above. But it also reflects the preference of firms to set their own standards appropriate to their own circumstances in a way which avoids or pre-empts state intervention. In the environmental context, environmental management systems such as ISO 14001 created by the International Organization for Standardization (ISO) are increasingly popular. While traditionally such standards have tended only to apply to larger firms that can afford the compliance costs and those seeking access to developed country markets, there is some evidence from countries like Mexico that even small and medium-sized enterprises are seeking ISO certification in order to serve as subcontractors for ISO-certified enterprises.

There are also sector-specific programmes such as 'Responsible Care' in the case of the chemical industry, which set up a programme to deflect criticism away from its track record in the US and which has been adopted in countries like Mexico and Brazil. Garcia-Johnson (2000) describes this as 'exporting environmentalism'. It is clear then that global market pressures from buyers and consumers increasingly exercise as significant an influence on environmental policy practice in many parts of the developing world as the international agreements which governments sign up to.

As a reaction to the limitations of market-based and voluntary mechanisms, there has also been a growth in what has been termed civil regulation (Newell 2001): civil society based forms of business regulation. The increasing use of such tools as shareholder activism and boycotts, and the growth of watchdog groups such as OilWatch based in Ecuador, are illustrative of the trend. New forms of engagement in constructing codes of conduct and building partnerships also come under the umbrella of civil regulation. While concern has been expressed that many of these tools are only available to well-resourced groups with good access to the media and in societies with strong traditions of free speech, there does seem to be evidence of these strategies being employed on an increasing scale in most parts of the global South. Strategies of resistance and exposure of corporate wrongdoing date from colonial times, but there has also been a notable proliferation in groups across the entire spectrum, ranging from confrontation to collaboration. Many of these groups are also increasingly globally well connected, so that companies engaging in environmentally controversial activities in the developing world can also expect to face shareholder resolutions and embarrassing media publicity in their home countries. The Canadian company Tiomin, for example, has faced considerable pressure from activists in Canada over its proposed mining operations on Kenya's coast, working with local groups such as CoastWatch in Kenya.

It is unclear at this stage what the net effect of these forms of civil regulation will be on the environmental performance of investors in developing countries. The hope is that groups with the expertise and capabilities to plug gaps and weaknesses in systems of government pollution control and monitoring can play an important complementary role as informal regulators. O'Rourke's study of community-based regulation in Vietnam shows how this has been possible when 'the energies and actions of average community members and the responses of front-line environmental agencies' were brought together (2004: xvii). Their very presence may encourage firms to respect the environmental standards of the countries in which they operate to a greater degree than if they were not there, and so help deter the exploitation of double standards by firms when they operate in developing countries. The extent to which groups will be allowed to perform this role will depend on the strength of civil society in a given setting and the extent to which its activities are tolerated or encouraged by the state.

Issues of whom the groups represent and to whom they are accountable will also have to be faced if they are to be seen as legitimate actors in environmental policy. It will be important that such groups are not seen to deter much-needed investment, but instead seek to attract investors that are more socially and environmentally responsible, and therefore more likely to bring long-term development gains to countries.

KEY POINTS

- Many countries continue to use central government controlled 'command and control' environmental policy measures.

- Despite their limitations, poorer groups have sought to use legal remedies to claim rights to resources, contest planning processes, and seek compensation for loss of livelihood.

- There has been a shift, however, in thinking about how best to tackle environmental pollution towards the use of market instruments and voluntary approaches and away from state-based approaches.

- Many companies in developing countries are seeking certification for their products in order to get access to Northern markets.

- In recent years there has been a trend towards informal industry regulation by civil society groups. The long-term impact of this form of civil-society-based regulation will vary by country and the extent to which such groups are able to address issues of their own accountability and representation.

Futures

Attempting to predict the likely future of environmental policy in the developing or developed world with any degree of accuracy and precision is a fruitless endeavour. It is, however, possible to identify certain patterns of continuity and change. We have seen how many developing countries face common challenges in terms of how to reconcile pressing development needs with longer-term environmental goals. While countries have inevitably responded in different ways which reflect, among other things, their political systems, the nature of their economies, and the level of civil society engagement, we have seen similar problems of enforcement at the national level, constraints that arise from economic

relationships of trade, aid, and debt, and conflicts between global, often Northern-determined, environmental priorities and more pressing issues at the local level.

Through global processes of negotiation, increasingly integrated supply chains, and globally interdependent trading patterns, we have seen how pressures come to be exerted on developing countries to design and implement environmental policies in ways which reflect the priorities of others. Shifts in thinking about environmental policy and what makes it more effective and efficient are transmitted through donor lending and the global reach of transnational companies. These are the sorts of pressures that bring about conformity and harmonization in environmental politics in the developing world.

But there is much that is subject to change, such is the fragile and often ephemeral status of environmental issues on the policy agendas of countries the world over. The status of such issues is as vulnerable to the state of the world economy as it is to the health of the planet. Government spending on environmental programmes notoriously goes down in times of recession, when other issues assume a higher profile. In recent times issues of regional and global security have risen rapidly on the agendas of many developing countries in the wake of the events of September 11 and the ongoing violence in Iraq. Resources are often both a cause and a manifestation of these geo-political conflicts, especially oil and water. While access to water has long been a source of tension for Jordan and its neighbours, access to oil drives Western interest in the affairs of the Middle East. The continued dependence of many Western economies on profligate supplies of fossil fuels inevitably embroils those countries in conflict-torn regions of the world. The human and ecological costs of such a destructive dependence may yet prompt a more serious search for alternative sources of energy such as renewables. However, rising energy demand makes a short-term transition unlikely.

Priorities shift according to global events as much as they reflect changes in domestic politics following changes of government. A realignment of donor priorities in the wake of these shifts may have a significant impact on resource allocations for environmental projects, or the extent to which some regions of the developing world come to be favoured over others on the basis of their strategic value to Western interests. Nevertheless, with or without donor support, developing countries face many environmental challenges of their own, including water pollution and urban air quality. It is often the human impact of these problems that attracts attention and acts as the driver for change. In developmental terms, the increasingly high human cost of environmental degradation exacts an economic price; costs to health systems increase, levels of disease increase, and an unhealthy workforce is an unproductive workforce. Despite increasing acknowledgement of the human and developmental case for tackling environmental degradation, stark trade-offs between environmentally damaging investment and no investment at all continue to force governments to put profit above people and planet. Global economic pressures from highly mobile companies and global economic institutions further load the dice towards investment and exports over the imperatives of sustainable development.

Sometimes, of course, environmental problems draw attention to themselves, and demand action from governments. Floods in Mozambique, droughts in Ethiopia, tsunamis in South-East Asia, the intensity of which will increase as our climate changes, and other such crises prompt short-term emergency measures. Rarely, however, do they initiate deeper reflection about the causes of the crisis. Calls upon President George W. Bush to change his government's opposition to tougher action on climate change in light of the devastating hurricanes and floods that reaped such destruction in the poorest states of his own country in 2005, appear to have fallen on deaf ears. Nevertheless, the increased incidence of such human-induced yet seemingly 'natural' events may, more than any other single factor, serve to focus the world's attention on the environmental consequences of current patterns of development and act as a catalyst to more radical action aimed at combating environmental degradation.

PETER NEWELL

 QUESTIONS

1   Why has the relationship between environment and development been so uneasy in the past?

2   Is the environment still primarily a 'Northern' issue?

3   Does the concept of sustainable development have any practical or analytical value?

4   Why do developing countries attach such different degrees of importance to environmental issues?

5   Is there still a basis for G77 unity on global environmental issues?

6   How much evidence is there that environmental issues have been effectively integrated within national development strategies?

7   How far is poverty the cause as opposed to the result of environmental degradation?

8   How effective are market-based policy tools at tackling environmental degradation?

9   What is the nature and consequence of the relationship between environment and national and international security?

10 Under what circumstances might environment and development issues be reconciled more effectively in the future?

 GUIDE TO FURTHER READING

■ **Adams, W. M. (2001),** *Green Development: Environment and Sustainability in the Third World,* **2nd edn. (London: Routledge).** Provides a detailed history of the concept of sustainable development and the different ways in which it has been interpreted and applied in the mainstream and by its critics.

■ **Barry, J., and Frankland, E. G. (2002),** *International Encyclopedia of Environmental Politics* **(London and New York: Routledge).** This encyclopedia provides short summaries and guides to further reading on key issues from 'African environmental issues' to 'Water pollution' and just about everything in between.

■ **Bryant, R. L., and Bailey, S. (1997),** *Third World Political Ecology* **(London: Routledge).** Provides a useful actor-based introduction to the key forces shaping environmental politics in the developing world from business and multilateral institutions to NGOs and the role of the state.

■ **Elliott, L. (1998),** *The Global Politics of the Environment* **(London: Macmillan).** Wide-ranging textbook that covers not only the global environmental agenda but also issues of trade, debt, and aid which bring together environmental and development agendas.

■ **Keeley, J., and Scoones, I. (2003),** *Understanding Environmental Policy Processes: Cases from Africa* **(London: Earthscan).** Drawing on research in Ethiopia, Mali, and Zimbabwe, this book examines the links between knowledge, power, and politics in understanding how environmental issues come to be framed and the consequences of this for how they are acted upon.

■ **Newell, P., and Wheeler, J. (eds.) (2006),** *Rights, Resources and the Politics of Accountability* **(London: Zed Books).** Drawing on cases of struggles over resources such as water and oil as well as for livelihood rights such as health, housing, and work, in countries as diverse as Bangladesh, Nigeria, and the US, this book provides an analysis of how poorer groups mobilize to claim resources from state and private actors.

■ **Peets, R., and Watts, M. (eds.) (1996),** *Liberation Ecologies: Environment, Development and Social Movements* **(London: Routledge).** Explores the theoretical implications of the relationship between development, social movements, and the environment in the South. Draws this out through case studies on a range of environmental issues from countries including China, India, Zimbabwe, Ecuador, and Gambia.

WEB LINKS

● **www.steps-centre.org** (Institute of Development Studies and Science Policy Research Unit, University of Sussex, UK) This research centre on social, technological, and environmental pathways to sustainability produces research on a range of environmental and development issues. The IDS site also provides access to the Eldis gateway from where searches for information and studies on particular environmental issues in specific developing countries can be undertaken.

● **www.iied.org** (International Institute of Environment and Development, London, UK) This contains details on latest research and publications produced by the institute on a range of environment and development issues.

● **www.iisd.org** (The International Institute for Sustainable Development, Winnipeg Canada) Among other useful databanks this site gives access to the 'Earth Negotiations Bulletin', which provides updates on all the leading international environmental negotiations.

● **www.cseindia.org** (Centre for Science and Environment, Delhi, India) Contains reports and details of campaigns on key environmental challenges facing India, though maintains a global focus too.

● **www.twnside.org.sg** (Third World Network, Kuala Lumpur, Malaysia) Contains position papers, reports, and information updates from the network's members on issues such as trade, biotechnology, and climate change.

● **www.itdg.org** (Practical Action, UK (formerly known as Intermediate Technology and Development Group)) Contains details on the organization, its project and research work, and reports and publications.

● **www.acts.or.ke** (African Centre for Technology Studies, Nairobi, Kenya) Provides useful studies, resources, and news items on issues such as agriculture and food security, climate change, and biotechnology.

● **www.unep.org** (United Nations Environment Programme, Nairobi, Kenya) A mine of information about global environmental issues and the negotiations aimed at tackling them.

 ONLINE RESOURCE CENTRE

For additional material and resources, see the Online Resource Centre at:
www.oxfordtextbooks.co.uk/orc/burnell2e/

18 Human Rights

MICHAEL FREEMAN

Chapter Contents

- Introduction
- The Concept of Human Rights
- Human Rights Regimes
- 'Human Rights Begin at Breakfast'
- Universalism and Cultural Diversity
- The New Political Economy of Human Rights
- Conclusion

Overview

The language of **human rights** is a pervasive feature of contemporary international politics, but it is not well understood. This chapter offers an analysis of the concept, a brief account of its history and a description of the **international human rights regime**. It proceeds to examine two persistent problems that arise in applying the concept to developing countries: the relations between human rights and development; the relations between the claim that the concept is universally valid and the realities of cultural difference around the world. The idea of human rights derives from historical problems of the West. It is necessary to consider its applicability to the problems of developing countries in a world constituted by great inequalities of political power and wealth.

MICHAEL FREEMAN

Introduction

The concept of human rights derives primarily from the United Nations Charter, which was adopted in 1945 immediately after the Second World War. The preamble to the Charter declares that the UN was determined to 'reaffirm faith in fundamental human rights, in the dignity and worth of the human person, in the equal rights of men and women, and of nations large and small'. In 1948, the General Assembly of the UN adopted the Universal Declaration of Human Rights, which sets out a list of human rights 'as a common standard of achievement for all peoples'. The list includes such civil and political rights as those to freedom from slavery, torture, arbitrary arrest, and detention, freedom of religion, expression, and association, and a number of economic and social rights, such as the rights to education and an adequate standard of living. These rights were intended to protect everyone from tyrannical governments like that of Nazi Germany, and from the economic misery that was thought to have facilitated the rise of fascism.

Although the countries of Latin America, Asia, and Africa formed the majority of those that produced the Declaration, many of the world's people lived at that time under colonial rule, and were thus excluded from this process. The concept of human rights was derived from a Western philosophical tradition, and was shaped mainly by European historical experience. Colonialism was itself condemned for its human rights violations, and, when worldwide decolonization brought many new states to the UN, the post-colonial states accepted human rights in principle, although their priorities differed from those of the West, emphasizing self-determination, development, economic and social rather than civil and political rights, and anti-racism.

Disagreements about which human rights should be legally binding led to the adoption of two UN human rights covenants in 1966: the International Covenant on Civil and Political Rights and the International Covenant on Economic, Social and Cultural Rights. The UN's World Conference on Human Rights, held in Vienna in 1993, declared all human rights to be 'indivisible and interdependent'. Now, each covenant has been ratified by more than 80 per cent of the UN's member states.

The UN has adopted several more specialized conventions (see Box 18.1). There are also regional human rights conventions, although these do not cover the whole world, especially the Middle East

---

BOX 18.1

Universal and Regional Human Rights Regimes

Universal Declaration of Human Rights 1948

European Convention on Human Rights 1950

International Covenant on Civil and Political Rights 1966

International Covenant on Economic, Social and Cultural Rights 1966

[International Convention on the Elimination of Racial Discrimination 1966]

American Convention on Human Rights 1969

Convention on the Elimination of Discrimination against Women 1979

African Charter on Human and Peoples' Rights 1981

Convention against Torture 1984

Convention on the Rights of the Child 1989

International Convention on the Protection of Migrant Workers 1990

and Asia. The European Convention on Human Rights was adopted in 1950; the American Convention on Human Rights in 1969; and the African Charter on Human and Peoples' Rights in 1981.

Many developing countries have poor human rights records. There are internal and external explanations of this. The internal explanations include poverty, ethnic tensions, and authoritarian government. Some of the internal problems of developing countries are legacies of colonialism. The external explanations include support for dictatorships by the great powers, especially during the cold war, and the global economic system, which many believe is biased against developing countries, and thereby hinders their capacity to develop the institutions necessary to protect human rights. Since the end of the cold war, and the discrediting of the Soviet, state socialist model of development, neo-liberalism—the ideology of free markets—has dominated global economics. Whether neo-liberalism promotes respect for, or violation of human rights is highly controversial. The Universal Declaration's conception of human rights, however, presupposed effective states, and neo-liberalism tends to weaken states, and especially their capacity to protect social and economic rights, such as those to health, education, and freedom from poverty. The harmful effects of such policies disproportionately affect women and children.

Developing countries have been vulnerable both to military coups and to ethnic conflict. Both are attributable to legacies of colonialism, and both lead to serious human rights violations. While the dominant human rights discourse is highly *legalistic*, and emphasizes legal solutions to human rights problems, social scientists have recently revived the concept of civil society (see Chapter 9) as a barrier to tyranny. Developing countries vary considerably in the strength of their civil societies, but some observers see civil society as the best hope both for development and the improvement of human rights protection. Human rights seem to require a balance between effective states and strong civil societies, which is difficult to achieve when resources are scarce.

In 1979 the authoritarian, Westernizing regime of the Shah was overthrown in Iran, and an Islamic republic established. This stimulated challenges to dominant conceptions of human rights from the perspectives of Islam and other non-Western cultures. In the mid-1990s government representatives and intellectuals from the economically successful countries of South-East and East Asia argued that human rights should be reinterpreted according to 'Asian values' in their societies. The critique of human rights from the standpoint of cultural diversity was thereby added to, and sometimes confused with, the critique from the standpoint of economic inequality. Following the financial crisis of 1997, talk of 'Asian values' diminished. Debates about Islam and human rights, however, increased, and became more intense after the terrorist attacks on the USA on 11 September 2001.

KEY POINTS

- The concept of human rights derives from the determination of the United Nations after the Second World War to oppose dictatorship and the social conditions that gave rise to dictatorship. It was embodied in the UN Charter (1945) and the Universal Declaration of Human Rights (1948).

- At that time many of the world's people lived under colonial rule, and were thus excluded from participating in the formulation of the UN's human rights concept. After decolonization, the new, postcolonial states accepted human rights in principle, but gave higher priority to development-related rights.

- In the decades after 1948 the UN developed a large body of international human rights law.

- Many developing countries have poor human rights records. This can be explained by internal factors, such as poverty, ethnic divisions, and authoritarian governments, and external factors, such as great-power rivalries and the effects of the global economy.

- Developing societies have been vulnerable to military coups and ethnic conflicts, both of which lead to serious human rights violations. Some see hope in the development of civil society, but this is difficult where resources are scarce.

- Many developing countries have challenged dominant interpretations of human rights by appealing to their own cultural traditions.

The Concept of Human Rights

Human rights are rights of a special kind. The concept of 'rights' is derived from that of 'right'. Right is distinguished from wrong, and all societies have standards of right and wrong. 'Right' is sometimes called 'objective', because it refers to a supposedly objective standard. Many people would say that the prohibition of murder is objectively right. Rights are sometimes called 'subjective' because they 'belong' to individuals or groups who are the 'subjects' of rights. Thus subjective rights are entitlements, and differ from objective concepts such as 'right' by emphasizing the just claims of the rights-holder. The idea of subjective rights is often said to be distinctively Western and relatively modern.

Human rights are commonly defined as the rights that everyone has simply because they are human. Philosophically, this is problematic, because it is not clear why anyone has rights because they are human. A theory of rights is needed to justify this belief. Legally, it is also problematic, because some human rights are denied to some humans: for example, the right to liberty is denied to those who have committed serious crimes. Politically, human rights are those rights that have generally been recognized by governments. The Universal Declaration provides us with an authoritative list of human rights, but it is difficult to distinguish precisely between human

rights, other rights, and other social values. It may, however, be important to do so, because people increasingly claim as their human rights what may not be human rights, or may not be rights at all, but social benefits or merely what people happen to want.

The two 1966 covenants distinguish between two categories of human rights: civil and political rights, on the one hand, and economic, social and cultural rights, on the other. Western governments tend to give priority to the first type, while developing countries tend to give priority to the second. The distinction itself is, however, controversial: the right to property, for example, is often regarded as a civil rather than an economic right, which seems absurd. The Vienna Declaration (1993) sought to overcome the distinction by proclaiming that all human rights are 'indivisible'. This idea has become increasingly influential as the United Nations, its member governments, and international institutions, such as the World Bank, have come to recognize that neglect of human rights is at least sometimes a barrier to development. It is now also often said that there are three generations of rights: the two types already mentioned constitute the first and second generations, while there is a third generation, consisting of 'solidarity' rights, such as the right to development. These distinctions are also controversial, both because the reference to generations misrepresents the history of human rights, and because the meaning and value of third-generation human rights are questionable.

A brief history

Some say that the concept of human rights is ancient, and found in all or most of the world's cultures. This claim usually confuses subjective rights with objective right. Notions such as justice or human dignity are found in many cultures. The idea of individual, subjective rights is more unusual and, consequently, more controversial.

Some scholars have argued that individual rights cannot be found before the late Middle Ages, and did not become politically important until the seventeenth century in England. The concept of *citizens' rights* is, however, found in ancient Greek and Roman thought. The modern concept of human rights derives from that of natural rights, which was developed in Europe in the late Middle Ages, and featured prominently in the political struggles of seventeenth-century England. Natural rights were derived from natural law, and were known by reason. This idea burst onto the stage of world politics with the American and French revolutions in the late eighteenth century. In the nineteenth century it fell out of favour, because it was thought to be unscientific and subversive of social order. The concept of human rights evokes that of natural rights, but differs from it in at least two important ways. First, it does without the controversial philosophy of natural law; and secondly, it sees rights as social rather than natural.

Contemporary conceptions

The dominant conception of human rights today derives from its origins in Western liberalism, the philosophy that gives priority to individual freedom. Human rights are the rights of individuals, and the individualism of the concept (its isolation of the human individual and the special value placed on that individual) is often said to be alien to non-Western cultures. It is not certain, however, that all human rights are individual rights. Both the 1966 covenants recognize that *peoples* have the right to self-determination. The right to development may be an individual or a collective right, or both. Western countries have a strongly individualistic conception of human rights, whereas developing countries have a more collectivistic conception.

KEY POINTS

- Human rights are rights of a special kind. Rights are entitlements of individuals or groups, and differ from ideas of justice or human dignity. Human rights are either the rights everyone has because they are human or those generally recognized as such by governments or in international law.

- Distinctions are often made between civil and political rights, on the one hand, and economic, social, and cultural rights, on the other hand, and also among three generations of human rights. Theorists have criticized these distinctions as confused.

- Citizens' rights were recognized in ancient Greece and Rome, but human rights are modern, deriving from the late mediaeval idea of natural rights. This idea fell out of favour after the French Revolution because it was believed to be unscientific and subversive. It was revived by the UN as the concept of human rights.

- The dominant conception of human rights is controversial in developing countries because it is thought to express the Western philosophy of individualism.

Human Rights Regimes

MICHAEL FREEMAN

A regime is a set of rules and practices that regulate the conduct of actors in a specified field. Human rights regimes exist at international, regional, and national levels.

The UN system

The international human rights regime consists of a large body of international law and a complex set of institutions to implement it. Chief among these institutions was the UN Commission on Human Rights, established 1945–7. Its members represented governments, and it was criticized for political bias. In 2006 the UN replaced the Commission with the Human Rights Council in an attempt to improve its human rights performance. Independent experts work in various parts of the system. The Commission employed them as members of working groups or as rapporteurs on specific themes (such as torture) and countries. The members of the Sub-commission on the Promotion and Protection of Human Rights and of the committees that monitor the various treaties are also independent experts. **Non-governmental organizations (NGOs)**—consisting of citizen activists and experts—play an important role in providing information. It is difficult to evaluate the effectiveness of the international regime, but the consensus of scholars is that it is rather weak. The future of the regime after the creation of the Human Rights Council remains to be seen.

Regional and national regimes

There are regional human rights regimes in Europe, the Americas, and Africa. The European is the most effective, and the African the least effective. Many scholars believe that the most important location for the protection of human rights is that of national law. The international regime is fairly effective in *promoting* human rights, but relatively ineffective in *implementing* them. Regional regimes are generally effective only if they are supervising relatively effective national regimes.

Legal regimes and power politics

Developing countries frequently complain that the international human rights regime is a smokescreen behind which the powerful states of the West pursue their interests at the expense of the poorer states. There is undoubtedly truth in this charge, but many governments of developing countries have terrible human rights records, and this has in most cases probably hindered rather than promoted development. The powerful states of the West, and the UN itself, have been criticized both for not intervening to prevent human rights violations, as in the Rwandan genocide of 1994, and for intervening too forcefully or for dubious motives, as in Iraq in 2003.

KEY POINTS

- The human rights conduct of states is regulated, with varying degrees of effectiveness, by legal and political regimes at international, regional, and national levels.

- The international human rights regime is a fairly effective promotional regime but a relatively ineffective implementation regime.

- Of the three regional regimes in Europe, the Americas, and Africa, the European is the most effective.

- Human rights can be promoted and fine-tuned at international and regional levels, but are best protected by national laws.

- The international human rights regimes are predominantly legal, and, behind them, international power politics dominates the human rights agenda, which for developing countries makes them matters of intense controversy.

'Human Rights Begin at Breakfast'

There is a widely held view that developing countries must give development priority over human rights. The fundamental intuition underlying this view is that starving people cannot benefit from, say, the right to free speech, and that, without development, human rights are not possible, and perhaps not even desirable. 'Human rights begin at breakfast', Léopold Senghor, the former President of Senegal, is supposed to have said. Various arguments support this position. It is claimed, for example, that human rights—especially economic and social rights—are simply too expensive for poor countries. It is also maintained that, especially in less developed countries with problematic ethnic divisions, human rights subvert social order and thus hinder development : the government of Singapore, for example, has often made this argument. Even if this is not so, free societies tend to divert resources from savings and investment to consumption, and this slows down long-term development. Empirically, the so-called Asian tigers—South Korea, Taiwan, Malaysia, and Singapore, in particular—and, more recently, China, are cited as examples of successful economic development under authoritarian rule. The idea that human rights are *necessary* for development—an idea commonly promoted by the West—is thereby falsified. Most Western countries developed their economies and human rights over long periods of time, and generally recognized human rights only when they had sufficiently developed economies to support them. Developing countries are less favourably placed in the world economy, and there is a view that only authoritarian government can deliver rapid economic progress.

Conceptions of development

'Development' is often assumed to mean economic development, and economic development has often been measured by per capita income. Recently, however, development has been reconceptualized as 'human development', with emphasis on the quality of life. The economic development of states is compatible with the misery of many people. The new conception of development sees human rights and development as *conceptually* overlapping. There is, for example, a human right to an adequate standard of living. If development is defined in terms of the standard of living, then human rights and development are positively correlated *by definition*. The new conceptualization has had practical implications: the UN Development Programme, for example, has recently included the protection of human rights in its policies.

Are human rights and development interdependent?

The Vienna Declaration asserted that human rights and development are 'interdependent'. Is this true?

The arguments that restrictions of human rights are either *necessary* or *sufficient* for development are not well supported by the evidence. The arguments often rely on very selective use of case studies, especially from East Asia. South Korea and Taiwan achieved rapid economic development under authoritarian governments, but both developed into liberal democracies. Singapore has also been economically successful with a so-called 'soft authoritarian' regime, which does not appear to be liberalizing. Other cases are ambiguous. Some Latin American countries—such as Pinochet's Chile—had some economic growth, but also some economic setbacks, under authoritarian rule, while China has achieved rapid economic growth combined with serious human rights violations in recent years. Authoritarian regimes can sometimes achieve rapid economic development. Most repressive regimes, however, have failed to deliver development. This suggests that violating human rights as such does not explain economic development. The causal connection between human rights violations and development has never been established. Some countries that have combined economic development with restrictions of civil and political rights—such as South Korea, Singapore, and China—have relatively good records with respect to economic and social rights, such as education and health. Some development economists believe that investment in education is conducive to success in development.

The relations between development and human rights may well be mediated by other factors, including the economic strategies adopted by governmental elites and the country's security situation. Taiwan, South Korea, and Singapore all faced external and/or internal security threats that made authoritarian government more likely, if not strictly necessary, and all were able to locate themselves favourably within the global economic system.

Respect for human rights is, therefore, not generally *necessary* for economic development, and violation of human rights is certainly not *sufficient* for economic development. *Most countries that have persistently and seriously violated human rights have been unsuccessful in developing their economies.* The increasing political repression in Zimbabwe, for example, has been accompanied by economic collapse, and the former is certainly a cause of the latter. It is very difficult to generalize about the relations between development and human rights, however, and we should be very cautious about inferring policies for particular countries from generalizations, and, *a fortiori*, from the experience of selected countries. It does not follow from the fact that Singapore developed its economy with a fairly authoritarian government that Burkina Faso should follow its lead.

The relation between human rights and development is very complex and almost certainly strongly influenced by other factors specific to the individual countries. Attempts to establish statistical relations between human rights and development in large numbers of countries have produced inconclusive and sometimes apparently contradictory results.

The famous Indian economist, Amartya Sen, has argued that the evidence suggests little correlation, positive or negative, between respect for civil and political rights and economic growth, and that the violation of such rights is not *necessary* to economic development. He reminds us that human rights have a value that is independent of development, in so far as we believe in 'the dignity and worth of the human person', and argues consequently that the available evidence is no barrier to the policy of pursuing development-with-human-rights (Sen 1999b). But if the relation between human rights and development is unclear, and developed states have far from perfect records in respecting human rights, then the most grave human-rights disasters of recent years—such as the tyranny of Idi Amin in Uganda (1972–8), the mass killings by the Khmer Rouge in Cambodia (1975–9), the terror regime of Saddam Hussein in Iraq (1979–2003), and the genocide in Rwanda (1994)—have taken place in developing countries. Why is this?

Developing countries are mostly poor, and are economically vulnerable to the power of rich states. This makes economic development difficult. Without economic development, the resources for implementing human rights are scarce. Paradoxically, where resources are not scarce (as in oil-producing countries, such as Nigeria, Saudi Arabia, Iraq, and Iran), the temptations of corruption and authoritarianism may also be great.

The achievement of independence from colonial rule, the ethos of the United Nations and world culture, and the spread of information and images through modern media of communication have raised expectations of economic progress among the peoples of the developing countries. The combination of these rising expectations and the persistent inability of governments to meet them have created widespread and intense social frustration, active opposition to governments, and consequent repression.

These problems are aggravated in many developing countries by ethnic divisions. Ethnic diversity does not necessarily lead to conflict and human rights violations. Colonial rulers often created the potential for conflict where it did not exist before: for example, the genocidal conflict between Hutus and Tutsis in Rwanda had significant colonial origins. In situations of scarcity and high expectations, however, ethnic divisions are difficult to manage, because ethnicity is a potent source of competition, and they can therefore lead to serious human rights violations.

Developing countries should not be seen simply as dependent victims of domination by rich states, international institutions, multinational corporations, or global capitalism. They have some autonomy, however limited, as the success of the Asian tigers demonstrates. Corrupt and incompetent government has contributed to the economic failures of many developing countries, and human rights violations are partly explained by the desire of powerful and corrupt rulers to remain in power. China, Indonesia, Iraq, Saudi Arabia, Nigeria, and Zimbabwe are only some of the developing countries in which power has been corrupting, and corruption is among the causes of human rights violations.

Most developing countries lack traditions of human rights (see Box 18.2). They may have traditional cultures with morally admirable features, such as mutual solidarity, and they may also have active human rights organizations—which are found throughout much of Asia, Africa, and Latin America—and even individual 'human rights heroes' (such as Aung San Suu Kyi in Myanmar/Burma). But, in contrast with Europe, the value of human rights may not be deeply embedded in the public culture of the society. Even where the government has ratified international human rights treaties, and human rights are written into national constitutions, human rights may not be a strong feature of the political culture. It has been suggested, for example, that the military was able to mount successful coups and maintain repressive regimes in Latin America in the 1970s and 1980s partly because both the political right and the left

had 'solidaristic' ideologies that allowed little place for individual rights (Roniger and Sznajder 1999). Some developing countries have rulers whose ideologies are considered extremist in the West: Iran and Sudan are examples.

The Vienna Declaration maintained that democracy, development, and human rights were interdependent. The relations between democracy and development are complex in ways that are similar to those between human rights and development. The relations between democracy and human rights are, however, less straightforward than they are often assumed to be. Democracy may be compatible with human rights partly by definition, because democracy may be defined in terms of such rights as those to freedom of expression, association, and political participation. There is also empirical evidence that democracies generally respect human rights better than authoritarian regimes do. Nevertheless, democracies can violate human rights in serious ways. The transition from authoritarian rule to democracy in several Latin American countries (for example, Brazil) has not diminished all kinds of human rights violations, and may have increased some kinds. The protection of human rights by legal institutions may run counter to the democratic will of the people. The human rights of suspected criminals, refugees, and ethnic and political minorities are particularly vulnerable to democratic violations, in developed and developing countries. Finally, in developing countries with ethnic divisions and weak human rights traditions, the process of democratization itself may lead to serious human rights violations. Democratization played a role in ethnic conflict and genocide in Rwanda, for example. In both the Philippines and Indonesia, democratization has led to new forms of human rights violations, as space is made for ethnic demands that are met by repressive responses. The war on terrorism has led to human rights violations in some democracies as well in some authoritarian countries.

MICHAEL FREEMAN

BOX 18.2

Barriers to Human Rights Implementation by Developing Countries

- Most developing countries are poor and cannot afford the full implementation of human rights.

- Most developing countries have little power in the global economic system, and are consequently vulnerable to the policies of powerful states and non-state actors that are often unfriendly to human rights.

- In the conditions of contemporary global culture and media of mass communication, where the expectations of many people in developing countries for economic progress are high, the inability of governments to meet those expectations stimulates protest and repression.

- Most developing countries have ethnic divisions that predispose them to conflict in conditions of scarcity, and consequently to repression.

- Corrupt and incompetent government has been common in developing countries, and human rights are explained in part by the desire of corrupt rulers to remain in power.

- Many developing countries have had traditional cultures, wherein human rights enjoyed little place, and have developed a modern human rights culture only in a weak form.

KEY POINTS

- It is commonly argued that development should have priority over human rights, and that some restriction of human rights is necessary for development.

- Development may be defined as per capita income or alternatively as quality of life which makes development and human rights overlapping concepts.

- Some repressive regimes have produced rapid economic development, but most have not.

- No one has shown that violating human rights is necessary for economic development. It is likely that other factors are the major causes of economic development.

- Although the empirical relationship between human rights and development is not well understood, the available evidence suggests that it is weak. There are independent reasons for valuing human rights.

- Democracies generally respect human rights better than authoritarian regimes do, but democracies sometimes violate human rights, and human rights are intended to protect individuals from abuse of power by democratic, as well as non-democratic governments. The US war on terrorism has led to human rights violations by both democratic and authoritarian governments.

Universalism and Cultural Diversity

The Preamble to the Universal Declaration of Human Rights refers to 'the equal and inalienable rights of all members of the human family', and the Declaration proclaims itself to be 'a common standard of achievement for all peoples'. Article 1 states that all human beings 'are born free and equal in dignity and rights'. The Vienna Declaration reaffirmed the universality of human rights (the belief that human rights belong to all human beings simply because they are human beings).

This universalism of human rights beliefs derives from the liberal Enlightenment doctrine of eighteenth-century Europe that the 'Rights of Man', as human rights were then called, were the rights of everyone, everywhere, at all times. This doctrine derived in turn from Christian teaching that there was only one God, and that the divine law applied to everyone, equally, everywhere, and at all times. One source of Christian philosophy was the Greco-Roman theory of natural law, which taught that all human beings formed a single moral community, governed by a common law that was known to human reason. The philosophical school of the Stoics was the proponent of pre-Christian, natural-law philosophy. The natural-law philosophical tradition that runs from the Stoics through medieval Christianity to Enlightenment liberalism and the contemporary concept of human rights forms a powerful, though controversial, component of Western, and to some extent global, culture.

Cultural imperialism and cultural relativism

The belief that human rights are universal appears to conflict with the obvious cultural diversity of the world. Moral and political ideas, many people say, derive from culture, and different societies have different cultures. To impose human rights on everyone in the world is therefore intolerant, imperialistic, and unjustified. This moral logic may be supported by the *historical* claims that: (1) the concept of human rights is a Western concept; and (2) the West has a history of political, economic, and cultural imperialism that is not yet over. Some non-Western critics of human rights argue, not only that human rights is a concept alien to non-Western cultures, but its use by the West is part of a project of global political and economic domination. The 2003 war in Iraq might be cited as an example of the use of human rights to legitimate political expansionism.

In the 1990s a number of governments and intellectuals from East and South-East Asian countries that had achieved considerable economic success called into question the dominant interpretation of human rights by appealing to what they claimed were distinctively Asian values. This claim was somewhat puzzling, as the cultures of East Asia are extremely diverse, ranging from officially atheist China to predominantly Muslim Malaysia. One of the leading proponents of 'Asian values'—Dr Mahathir Mohamad, then Prime Minister of Malaysia—acknowledged that Asian values were similar to *conservative* Western values: order, harmony, respect for authority. The Asian values argument was partially acknowledged by the Vienna Declaration, which reaffirmed the universality of human rights, but conceded that 'the significance of national and regional particularities and various historical, cultural and religious backgrounds should be borne in mind'. Read literally, this statement is uncontroversial, for it would be foolish to interpret and implement human rights without bearing in mind the significance of these cultural differences. However, many Asian non-governmental organizations continued to affirm the universalist orthodoxy without qualifications. Thus two different Asian approaches to human rights were produced during this controversy. Some human rights scholars and activists saw the appeal to Asian values as an ideological attempt to justify authoritarian government, but it did provoke a debate about how the universal values of human rights should be reconciled with the world's cultural traditions.

This issue requires careful analysis. Much of the *moral* critique of human rights derives from the claim that it constitutes cultural imperialism, and relies on the intuition that imperialism is obviously wrong. If we ask *why* imperialism is wrong, however, we may say that it violates the rights of those who are its victims. If we next ask *which* rights of the victims are violated by imperialism, the most common answer is the right to self-determination. At this point, the objection to moral universalism depends on a universal principle (the right to self-determination) and is therefore self-contradictory.

If there is at least one universal right (the right to self-determination), there may also be others. It is difficult to argue that the right to self-determination is a universal right without accepting that the right not to be enslaved is also a universal right. This appeal to universalism does not necessarily justify the full list of rights in the Universal Declaration, but it does refute one common line of argument against universalism.

Another approach would be to reject all forms of universalism, and rely on the claim that all moral principles derive from *particular* cultures, particular cultures are *diverse*, some cultures reject at least some human rights principles (gender equality is a common example), and human rights are valid only within the culture of the modern West. On this view, there is a human rights culture. But it is only one culture among many, and, because it derives from Western (secular) liberalism, it is not particularly appealing, still less *obligatory*, for those who, perhaps on the basis of their religious beliefs, subscribe to non-liberal moral and political codes. This argument has been proposed by some (but not all) Muslims, who believe that Islam requires submission to the will of God, and this must have priority over any secular obligations, such as those of human rights.

This argument avoids the self-contradiction of the anti-imperialist approach, but at a considerable cost. The first difficulty is that the argument that all actual moral principles are justified by the cultures of which they form a part is another universal principle that cannot be used against universalism as such without self-contradiction. The next difficulty is that, if all principles are justified by their cultures, then imperialism would be justified by imperialistic cultures—a view which is anathema to critics of human rights universalism. They could argue that, according to the criteria of their culture, imperialism is wrong, but not show would-be imperialists why they should act according to these criteria. In practice, most critics of human rights universalism accept that racism is universally wrong, and cannot be justified by racist cultures like that of apartheid South Africa. A further difficulty with the

'culturalist' conception of morality is that actual cultures are complex, contested, and overlapping. There are, for examples, many schools of Islamic thought, there are disputes about the requirements of the religion, and Islamic ideas have mixed with other ideas in different ways in different societies. The idea of a homogeneous culture that justifies particular moral ideas is a myth. The world is full of a great diversity of complex moral ideas, some of which cohere in different ways, with different degrees of uniformity and solidarity, into patterns which are themselves subject to change, in part as the result of interaction with other cultures.

These arguments do not themselves provide a justification of human rights. Only a justificatory theory of human rights could do that, and any such theory is likely to be controversial, not just between the West and the rest, but within Western thought, and even among human rights supporters. They also imply no disrespect for culture as such. Culture provides meaning, value, and guidance to human life, and there is a human right to participate in the cultural life of one's community. They do show that cultures are not self-justifying, and that we commit no logical or moral error in subjecting actual cultures to critical scrutiny.

Islam, human rights, and the war on terrorism

The rise in oil prices in the early 1970s, the Islamic Revolution of Iran (1979), the persistence of corrupt, authoritarian governments and extreme poverty in many Muslim countries, and the continuing Israel–Palestine conflict contributed to the development of fundamentalist Islamic parties and movements.

As Soviet troops withdrew from Afghanistan in 1988, Osama bin Laden, son of a rich Saudi businessman, who had recruited non-Afghans to support the Afghan resistance to the Soviet occupiers, formed al-Qaeda to continue a *jihad* (holy war) against the perceived enemies of Islam. In 1991 the forces of the secular Iraqi regime of Saddam Hussein invaded Kuwait, whose population is almost wholly

Muslim. A US-led force, acting with UN authority, and based in Saudi Arabia, expelled the Iraqi invaders from Kuwait. Following this war, several attacks on US and other targets were attributed to al-Qaeda, culminating in the attacks on the USA on 11 September 2001. The USA responded by invading Afghanistan, whose extreme Islamic government, the Taleban, were believed to have protected al-Qaeda. President Bush declared a war on terrorism. The USA set up a detention camp in Guantanamo Bay, Cuba, where it held several hundred suspected terrorists without due process of law. Many countries introduced new anti-terrorists laws, which were criticized by non-governmental organizations for their neglect of human rights protections. After the USA and some of its allies invaded Iraq, in 2003, many allegations of human rights violations by US troops became common. Allegations of torture by US forces in Afghanistan, Iraq, and at Guantanamo Bay, and charges of the 'rendition' (transportation) of suspects to other countries where torture was common, are commonplace and are usually denied by the US government. However, pictures of the mistreatment of Iraqi prisoners in the Abu Ghraib prison in Baghdad created an international scandal.

These events changed the context of the global human rights struggle because the USA had become the only superpower; administration officials had, both in internal memoranda and public pronouncements, shown contempt for the UN, international law, and human rights. Many governments have used the war on terrorism as an excuse for increasing human rights violations. Although most Muslims oppose terrorism, the use of Islam by al-Qaeda to justify its actions; the widespread targeting of Muslims as suspected terrorists; the election of the Islamist terrorist group, Hamas, as the government of the Palestinians; the election of a hard-line Islamist President of Iran; and the publication of cartoons highly offensive to Muslims in a Danish newspaper all contributed to a crisis in the relations between Islam and the West. Human rights activists had to come to terms both with the war on terrorism and their own relations with Islam. There are many schools of thought within Islam, some incompatible with human rights in important respects (especially relating to the rights of women), while others seek reconciliation between Islam and human rights. Some experts believe that the question of Islam and human rights is not fundamentally one of religion, but of the political and economic problems of the Middle East. These problems derive in part, but by no means wholly, from the history of Western imperialist intrusions into the Middle East.

365

BOX 18.3

Islam and the War on Terrorism

" For more than seven years the United States has been occupying the lands of Islam in the holiest of places, the Arabian Peninsula, plundering its riches, dictating to its rulers, humiliating its people, terrorizing its neighbours and turning its bases in the peninsula into a spearhead through which to fight the neighbouring Muslim peoples.... These crimes and sins committed by the Americans are a clear declaration of war on God, his messenger and Muslims. And ulema [Muslim scholars] have throughout Islamic history unanimously agreed that the jihad is an individual duty if the enemy destroys the Muslim countries. On that basis, and in compliance with God's order, we issue the following fatwa [decree] to all Muslims: The ruling is to kill the Americans and their allies is an individual duty for every Muslim who can do it, in order to liberate the Al Aqsa mosque [in Jerusalem] and the Holy Mosque [in Mecca]... "

(al-Qaeda, February 1998)

> " I also want to speak tonight directly to Muslims throughout the world. We respect your faith.... Its teachings are good and peaceful, and those who commit evil in the name of Allah blaspheme the name of Allah. The terrorists are traitors to their own faith, trying, in effect, to hijack Islam itself. The enemy is not our many Muslim friends. It is not our many Arab friends. Our enemy is a radical network of terrorists and every government that supports them. Our war on terror begins with al Qaeda, but it does not end there. It will not end until every terrorist group of global reach has been found, stopped and defeated. "

(President George W. Bush, 20 September 2001)

> " The Muslim Council of Britain utterly condemns today's indiscriminate acts of terror in London.... We must and will be united in common determination that terror cannot succeed... "

(Muslim Council of Britain, 7 July 2005, the day on which 52 people were killed by terrorists bombs on the London transport system)

> " Each day brings more information about the appalling abuses inflicted upon men and women held by the United States in Iraq, Afghanistan, and elsewhere around the world. U.S. forces have used interrogation techniques including hooding, stripping detainees naked, subjecting them to extremes of heat, cold, noise and light, and depriving them of sleep.... This apparently routine infliction of pain, discomfort, and humiliation has expanded in all too many cases into vicious beatings, sexual degradation, sodomy, near drowning, and near asphyxiation. Detainees have died under questionable circumstances while incarcerated.... In the course of 2005, it became indisputable that U.S. mistreatment of detainees reflected not a failure of training, discipline, or oversight, but a deliberate policy choice. The problem could not be reduced to a few bad apples at the bottom of the barrel. "

(Human Rights Watch)

KEY POINTS

- Human rights are supposed to be universal. In view of the cultural diversity in the world, some say that they are Western, and that attempts to universalize them are imperialistic.

- The anti-imperialistic argument presupposes the universal right to self-determination and therefore fails as a critique of universal rights.

- The argument that all values are relative to culture is unconvincing because cultures are not self-justifying, and hardly anyone believes that anything done in the name of culture is justified.

- The concept of human rights includes the right to practise one's culture, and thus human rights and culture may be compatible. Some cultural practices may, however, violate human rights standards.

- The rise of political Islam and the US war on terrorism have raised new challenges for the human rights movement.

The New Political Economy of Human Rights

Marxists have traditionally argued that human rights conceal real inequalities of wealth and power. The inclusion of economic and social rights in the list of human rights has been intended to meet this criticism, but its success has been very problematic. First, economic and social rights have been relatively neglected in international politics compared with civil and political rights. Secondly, great inequalities of wealth and power persist worldwide. Nevertheless, some attempts have been made recently to integrate human rights with development, and to improve poverty-reduction strategies.

Globalization

Globalization is a contested concept in social science. Global trade is ancient, and there is a dispute as to how it may have changed in recent times. However, whatever economic historians may say about global trends, it is obvious that we live in a dynamic, interrelated world that is changing rapidly in certain important respects. What is the impact of globalization on human rights?

Globalization has been opposed by a worldwide protest movement expressing diverse concerns, including world poverty, environmental degradation, and human rights. This has replaced, to a considerable extent, the earlier socialist movement opposing capitalism. The targets of this movement are primarily rich states, associations of rich states (such as the so-called G8), and multinational corporations (MNCs). The human rights movement has recently increased its concern about the role of MNCs in human rights violations, either directly (for example, by the employment of child labour) or in collaboration with repressive governments. Issues of globalization, development, the environment, and human rights have often come together as MNCs seek to develop natural resources in ways that damage the environment (see Chapter 17) and local ways of life, and popular protests (see Chapter 10) are sometimes met by governmental repression.

The relations between human rights and globalization are complex, however. The idea of human rights claims to be universal, and the human rights movement seeks global reach, and achieves it to some extent by global means of communication (email, internet, mobile phones). Meyer (1998) has conducted an empirical investigation into the impact of MNCs on human rights in developing countries, and concluded that there is a positive correlation between MNC investment in developing countries and human rights. He does not deny that some MNCs are involved in human rights violations in these countries. Other scholars, using different methods, have reached different conclusions (Smith, Bolyard, and Ippolito 1999). Globalizing, some say, increases inequality, drives the vulnerable to the margins of survival, and thereby feeds religious and nationalist extremism. After the financial crisis in South-East Asia at the end of the 1990s, for example, the International Monetary Fund imposed strict conditions on Indonesia that led to ethnic and religious riots. On the other hand, it has been argued that neo-liberal globalization has tended to undermine the caste system in India, thereby emancipating the untouchables and advancing the cause of human rights (Sikand 2003: 112).

Global capitalism is a dynamic process that probably has positive and negative consequences for human rights. There is also a global economic regime—consisting of organizations such as the G8, the European Union, the North American Free Trade Agreement (NAFTA), the World Bank, the International Monetary Fund (IMF), and the World Trade Organization (WTO)—that regulates global capitalism and the economies of the developing countries. The World Bank and the IMF are powerful actors in the international economy, and have traditionally been unconcerned with human rights. Critics have alleged that their policies have often been very harmful to human rights, especially economic and social rights. The World Bank has recently opened up a dialogue with NGOs and independent experts on human rights, but it remains to be seen whether this will change its policies significantly. The WTO is also accused of working to the disadvantage of the developing countries (Pogge 2002: 17–19). The UN conception of human rights is a statist, social democratic idea, whereas the global economy, and the international financial institutions that are supposed to regulate it, are based on a neo-liberal ideology that prefers vibrant markets and weak states.

A new approach to globalization and human rights is based on the concept of human security.

This idea grew out of the UN Millennium Summit which focused on freedom from fear and freedom from want. An independent Commission on Human Security was established, and its report was presented to the UN Secretary-General on 1 May 2003. It invites us to consider the security of individuals as well as that of states. It invites us also to consider, not only threats of violence from both political and criminal actors, but also the insecurity arising from extreme poverty, disease, and lack of access to food. The special vulnerability of women and children to the effects of conflict and poverty are often emphasized. The concept of 'human security' seeks to investigate in an integrated, interdisciplinary way the connections between human rights, poverty, conflict, global crime and terrorism, and development (see Box 18.4). The protection of human rights is central to the idea of human security, but the new concept may throw light on important connections that traditional approaches to human rights have ignored (see Chapter 19 for further discussion).

BOX 18.4

Human Security: The Case of Darfur

" It took three months for Fatouma Moussa to collect enough firewood to justify a trip to sell it in the market town of Shangil Tobayi, half a day's drive by truck from here. It took just a few moments on Thursday for janjaweed militiamen, making a mockery of the new cease-fire, to steal the $40 she had earned on the trip and rape her. Speaking barely in a whisper, Ms. Moussa, who is 18, gave a spare account of her ordeal. 'We found janjaweed at Amer Jadid,' she said, naming a village just a few miles north of her own. 'One woman was killed. I was raped.' Officially, the cease-fire in Darfur went into effect last Monday. But the reality was on grim display in this crossroads town, where Ms. Moussa and other villagers were attacked Thursday as they rode home in a bus from Shangil Tobayi. The Arab militiamen who attacked them killed 1 woman, wounded 6 villagers and raped 15 women, witnesses and victims said. "

(*New York Times* correspondent, Lydia Polgreen, 12 May 2006)

Darfur is a region of western Sudan, about the size of France, with a population of approximately six million. After a long and brutal civil war between the Sudanese government and the Muslim north against the Christian south, a peace agreement was signed in January 2005. Darfur, composed of many ethnic groups, all Muslim, has suffered from extreme economic and social neglect since colonial times. The relative stability of Darfur was undermined by increased competition for diminishing land resources as a result of desertification, the emergence of a racist Arab ideology in Sudan, expansionist policies by Libya's Colonel Gaddafi in neighbouring Chad, and the intrusion of southern Sudanese rebels into Darfur. Darfurian self-defence organizations developed into a number of rebel forces. The Sudanese Government sought to repress these rebellions by a savage counter-insurgency, called by some, including the US government, a 'genocide', employing Arab militias known as the *Janjaweed* (evil horsemen). A peace agreement was signed in Abuja, Nigeria, on 5 May 2006 by the Sudanese government and the largest rebel group, but not by other rebels. Estimates of those killed in the period 2003-6 range from 200,000 to 500,000, those displaced more than two million, and those suffering deprivation nearly four million. The UN Secretary-General, Kofi Annan, compared Darfur to the Rwandan genocide of 1994. Two months after the signing of the peace agreement, the Sudanese government was showing no sign of implementing it and had refused to replace the small African Union force with a larger and more effective UN force that the international community was calling for. UN representatives and humanitarian agencies were predicting a further humanitarian catastrophe. By July 2006 the UN and the European Union had passed various resolutions, a few rich countries had supplied some, but insufficient, humanitarian aid, and the peace agreement remained empty words.

Conclusion

The concept of human rights became important in world politics only with the adoption of the United Nations Charter in 1945. Although it was derived from Western moral, legal, and political philosophy, it was declared to be universal. On the foundation of the UN Universal Declaration of Human Rights (1948) a large body of international human rights law has been elaborated. Most of this is legally binding on most states, and the principles of the Declaration have been reaffirmed by all UN members. Nevertheless, international procedures for implementing human rights are weak, human rights violations are common, and the concept of human rights is not universally accepted as culturally legitimate.

The main question raised by human rights in the developing countries is the relationship between development and human rights. This is a complex issue. There is more than one definition of 'development', and some definitions include human rights. There is, however, a widespread view that some restriction of human rights is a precondition of development, and that development should take priority over human rights. There is no doubt that

some countries have achieved rapid rates of economic development while violating civil and political rights. However, most rights-violating countries have poor records of development. The relations between human rights and development are still not well understood, but the evidence suggests that, generally, factors other than human rights are more important in promoting or obstructing development. The case for violating human rights for the sake of development is therefore much weaker than it has often been thought to be. The view that human rights are necessary for economic development is, however, not well supported by the evidence. There are also strong reasons for respecting human rights independently of their relation to development. Recently, international efforts have been made to integrate human rights and development.

Developing countries are generally poor, which makes it difficult to fund the implementation of human rights. They may not want to do so because their governments are corrupt and unconcerned with human rights. They may not be able to because external agents—for example, donor governments and/or international financial institutions—limit

MICHAEL FREEMAN

their capacity to do so by insisting on the reduction of state budgets.

The United Nations is right in seeing development and human rights as interdependent, not in the sense that each always helps the other, but in so far as improvements in each makes the achievement of the other easier. Crises of development are often accompanied by crises of human rights, as countries like Somalia, the Democratic Republic of Congo, and Liberia show. Development success is good news for human rights—as South Korea and Taiwan illustrate—although the interests of elites and local cultures may limit human rights achievements, as in Singapore. Rwanda and Zimbabwe show that apparent initial success in development accompanied by human rights violations may lead to disaster for both human rights and development.

The process of globalization has been associated with the assertion of cultural difference. This has meant that the claim that human rights are universal, although reaffirmed by UN member states in 1993, is constantly challenged. Some of these challenges express the interests of the powerful, who are reluctant to allow a voice to dissenters. Others raise difficult questions about legitimating universal principles in a culturally diverse world. Debates about Asian values in the 1990s have been succeeded by debates about Islam and terrorism, but the underlying problems may be political and economic, rather than cultural or religious.

Arguments that the concept of human rights expresses the interests of the West or the rich are generally not convincing. Taking human rights seriously would benefit most the poorest and most oppressed. There is a danger, however, that Western states may discredit the concept by associating it with their own foreign policies motivated by their own interests. The cause of human rights will be damaged if it is, or is perceived to be, a new form of imperialism. Although human rights are now well established in great power politics, it may be that the best hope for their future lies with the increasing number of grass-roots movements in the developing countries.

? QUESTIONS

1   Is there now a global consensus on human rights?

2   What are the best arguments for human rights?

3   What are the prospects for the success of the UN Human Rights Council?

4   What are the main problems raised by the idea of the rights-based approach to development?

5   Can Islam be reconciled with human rights?

6   What are the implications of human rights for global poverty-reduction strategies?

7   Can poor countries afford human rights?

GUIDE TO FURTHER READING

■ Alston, P. and Robinson, M. (eds.) (2005), *Human Rights and Development: Towards Mutual Reinforcement* (Oxford: Oxford University Press). A useful collection of essays on the integration of human rights and development.

■ Brownlie, I., and Goodwin-Gill, G. S. (eds.) (2002), *Basic Documents on Human Rights*, 4th edn. (Oxford: Oxford University Press). An authoritative collection of international legal texts.

■ Donnelly, J. (2003), *Universal Human Rights in Theory and Practice*, 2nd edn. (Ithaca, NY: Cornell University Press). An excellent introduction to the international conception of human rights and the principal issues of human rights implementation.

■ Forsythe, D. P. (2006), *Human Rights in International Relations*, 2nd edn. (Cambridge: Cambridge University Press). An authoritative introduction to the topic.

■ Freeman, M. A. (2002), *Human Rights: An Interdisciplinary Perspective* (Cambridge: Polity Press). A comprehensive introduction for social science students and law students who want a non-legal approach.

■ Human Security Centre (2006), *Human Security Report: War and Peace in the 21st Century* (New York: Oxford University Press). An important attempt to develop the concept of 'human security' in a rigorous, interdisciplinary way.

■ Office of the United Nations High Commissioner for Human Rights (2004), *Human Rights and Poverty Reduction* (New York and Geneva: United Nations). An influential analysis of the relations between human rights and development.

■ Pogge, T. (2002), *World Poverty and Human Rights* (Cambridge: Polity Press). A collection of philosophical essays on various aspects of development and human rights.

■ Sen, A. (1999), *Development as Freedom* (Oxford: Oxford University Press). A thought-provoking argument for the mutual relations between development and freedom.

■ Uvin, P. (2004), *Human Rights and Development* (Bloomfield, CT: Kumarian Press). A provocative critique of various attempt to integrate human rights and development.

WEB LINKS

● www.ohchr.org The website of the Office of the UN High Commissioner for Human Rights, which is the best way into the UN human rights system.

● www.hri.ca Excellent website for communication about, and among, human rights activists.

● www.amnesty.org Amnesty International.

● www.hrw.org Human Rights Watch.

● www.humanrightsfirst.org/index.asp Human Rights First, a leading advocacy organization.

● www.umn.edu/humanrts Important resource centre at the University of Minnesota.

● www.phrusa.org Physicians for Human Rights—an important NGO.

● www.crisisgroup.org An important NGO dealing with conflict resolution with significant human rights implications.

● http://cesr.org Center for Economic and Social Rights.

● www.chrcr.org Center for Human Rights and Conflict Resolution.

● www.hrea.org Human Rights Education Associates—an NGO.

● www.unglobalcompact.org Website of UN Global Compact, which coordinates international efforts for global corporate social responsibility, including human rights protection.

MICHAEL FREEMAN

● **www.freedomhouse.org** US NGO for democracy and freedom, commonly used source for human rights data.

● **www.humanrightsdata.com** Data source for quantitative analysis.

● **www.benetech.org** Organization dedicated to using science and technology for humanitarian purposes, including human rights protection.

● **www.genodynamics.com** Organization that brings a quantitative approach to the study of genocide.

● **www.humansecurity-chs.org** Information about the Commission on Human Security.

● **www.humansecuritycentre.org** Useful source for the academic study of human security.

 ONLINE RESOURCE CENTRE

For additional material and resources, see the Online Resource Centre at:
www.oxfordtextbooks.co.uk/orc/burnell2e/

19 Security

NICOLE JACKSON

Chapter Contents

- Introduction
- Scholarly Debates about Security
- Violent Conflict: War and Terrorism in the Developing World
- International Organized Crime
- Infectious Disease
- Conclusions

Overview

This chapter examines the contested concept of security and its application to issues in the developing world. The study of security today has widened to include far more than an examination of military issues and threats to states. It now includes a range of real and perceived threats to peoples, societies, regions, networks, and the global community. The topic generates scholarly debates about the definition of security and the impact of globalization on security issues. Three key security issues which concern us here are violent conflict (including state and non-state); international organized crime; and infectious disease. To varying degrees, these issues pose threats to much of the developing world and have provoked a wide range of local, regional, and Western policy responses. The challenge for both the developed and developing worlds is to adopt a more holistic approach to security policy, one that bridges the increasingly artificial divide between traditional security and development studies.

Introduction

Security is a highly contested term and there is considerable debate over its definition. The study of security has traditionally taken place within International Relations (IR), and especially in its subfield 'security studies'. Only more recently has it been considered within Development Studies (DS). In its more traditional form, the discipline of security studies examines military issues and the interplay among 'great powers'. It has therefore been criticized for being Western-centric and dismissing or marginalizing the weaker developing world and the so-called real threats to its people and societies.

The term security is derived from the Latin *se* (without) and *cura* (care), suggesting the absence of a threat. Security is the absence of threat—to the stability of states, regions, the global community, networks, and/or human lives. For a nuanced understanding of security, issues must be considered at different levels of analysis. There are many security issues in the developing world which threaten to various degrees, peoples, societies, and states. They include violent conflict (state and non-state), international organized crime (trafficking in persons, narcotics and small arms), and disease (AIDS, SARS). How these issues are perceived and acted upon form the subject of this chapter. These three issues are chosen for examination here because they pose immediate and pervasive security concerns across the developed and developing worlds.

The chapter begins with an overview of major scholarly debates about security. It identifies key Western-defined security concepts which are applicable or useful to understanding the developing world. It then examines the impact of globalization on security issues. Today, many issues in one area of the world increasingly affect security in another. Globalization also allows the West to have a major influence on how security issues around the world are perceived and challenged. The rest of the chapter is divided into three parts to examine the following key security issues in the developing world: violent conflict; international organized crime; and infectious disease. Each section asks what is the geographical distribution of the so-called threat, who or what is threatened, and explores variations in perceptions and key policy responses.

> **KEY POINTS**
>
> ● Security is a contested term.
>
> ● Security is the absence of threat—to the stability of states, regions, the global community, networks, and/or human lives.

Scholarly Debates about Security

Realists or traditionalists, who dominated International Relations from 1940–90, define security as 'national security'. Stephen M. Walt: (1991: 212) says 'security studies may be defined as the study of the threat, use and control of military force'. The emphasis is on military threats to the state, and inter-state conflict. The traditional understandings of security have thus emphasized states and their competition for power in the international system. Today, this approach continues to be popular and is generally termed strategic studies.

After the cold war, new approaches in security studies proliferated with the aim of challenging traditional and realist theories. This debate began in response to the claim that the security agenda must be broadened to examine threats beyond state and military security. For example, in 1983 Buzan (1991) defined security as including military, social, economic, political and environmental 'sectors' or dimensions.

Today, other threats to the security of states are termed non-traditional issues or non-traditional security threats (that is, non-military). These issues include environmental problems (ozone depletion and global warming); threats from nationalism; migration, international crime (narcotic trafficking, human trafficking), and disease, such as AIDS and Severe Acute Respiratory Syndrome (SARS). This expansion of the concept of security does not undermine the realist logic of traditional security studies as the main focus is still on the state system. Nevertheless, many traditionalists argue that this widening makes the concept redundant, and dilutes the important task of analyzing military threats and inter-state conflict. Other scholars within IR ask *whose* security is threatened. And the reply is that it is not just states that are threatened.

These 'new security' scholars deepen the concept to include global, network, regional, societal, and individual security. There are many issues, such as wars, terrorism, crime, and health epidemics, each of which can affect security at many different levels. Threats also change over time; they vary depending on context, and the perceptions of peoples and states. Perceptions themselves may even be undefined or ambiguous. Security issues defined by the peoples and states in the developing world are often different than those defined by peoples and states in the developed world.

Concepts of security and the developing world

Security Studies as a discipline is mostly Western-oriented and defined by Western theories (see Box 19.1). Although its practitioners increasingly note unique political and cultural conditions, they rarely draw on the rich variety of other philosophical traditions, such as Islamic thought, Indian or Chinese philosophy. In the developing world, academic work on specific security issues tends to occur within traditional policy-oriented circles that are often dominated by strategic studies. However, this is changing as more scholars and practitioners recognize a misfit between wider IR theory and developing world realities. Traditional security thinking, with its focus on sovereignty, inter-state

---

BOX 19.1

Approaches to Security Studies

Realism: Classical realists define security as national security. These traditionalists emphasize military threats to the state and inter-state conflict.

Modified realism: These scholars continue to emphasize the state, however some broaden the focus away from military threats while others move the focus away from the 'great powers' towards the developing world.

Constructivism: Mainstream constructivists examine the role of ideas, identity and other cultural factors in our understanding or 'construction' of security. Generally, the state remains the key actor.

The Copenhagen School: The Copenhagen School broadens the security agenda to five 'sectors': military, political, economic, societal, and ecological. The state remains the referent object.

The Aberystwyth School: These scholars conceptualize security not in terms of its relation with the state but with its people. Scholars attempt to identify victims of social exclusion and to evaluate strategies for their emancipation.

war and abstract theory, is increasingly confronted by the reality of interlinked political, economic, and social systems, and internal and transnational conflicts, particularly seen in the developing world.

Critical security studies, in its broadest sense, is a collection of approaches all united by dissatisfaction with so-called traditional security studies and in particular its state and military centrism. Critical approaches range from conventional constructivists, through the Copenhagen and Aberystwyth schools to feminist and more radical post-modern positions.

Recent Western concepts about security may be more applicable to the developing world. For example, the Aberystwyth School of critical security studies differs from traditional security studies in its focus on the lives of people and in its concept of emancipation or freedom (of people from threats) and may be understood as particularly relevant to the developing world where the states themselves are often the source of the threat. Realists, however, counter that the focus should remain on the state and that critical security studies imposes 'a model of contemporary Western polities ... that are far removed from Third World realities' (Ayoob 1995: 97).

The human security perspective, with its focus on individuals and the protection of lives from critical and pervasive threats, also attempts to move the focus away from realist, state-centred concerns to those which are more salient to the peoples of the developing world. The concept of human security is increasingly being considered by scholars in Asia and Africa, and even adopted in some regional security arrangements, for example the Association of South-East Asian Nations (ASEAN). Generally, however, the difficulty with putting the human security concept into practice is that its focus on individuals and human rights appears threatening to many authoritarian leaders, and is contrary to the emphasis many societies place on community and the state. Most states in the developing world are the providers of security whose power is predicated on the concepts of absolute sovereignty and non-interference in domestic affairs.

Another Western-defined concept which has applicability to the developing world is securitization, defined as 'the move that takes politics beyond the established rules of the game and frames the issue either as a special kind of politics or as above politics' (Buzan, Waever, de Wilde 1998: 23). The securitization framework highlights how language is used to construct threats. Although it is a helpful descriptive and explanatory tool, particularly in understanding how states elevate particular threats, again there are difficulties with putting this concept into practice. There are fears that securitization arguments (that is, the labelling of an issue as a security threat) could be misused by rulers for domestic purposes. For example, in Latin America there is a widespread consciousness about how security rhetoric has been used by military governments in the past against their own people, and there is therefore distrust about how it may be applied.

Finally, within the developing world, new (and non-Western) thinking about security is being developed and put into practice. For example, China's multilateral cooperation and dialogue through the Shanghai Cooperation Organization (SCO) on a range of new security issues (such as terrorism and trafficking) demonstrates a unique type of cross-regional cooperative thinking and action on non-traditional security issues.

Globalization of security

The study of security has evolved largely in tandem with globalization. Globalization, understood as a state of interdependence, accelerated by advances in technology, trade, political relationships, transboundary communication, and movement of peoples, goods, and services, has created new channels for exercising power outside the state. The state is not about to disappear but is confronted by new global forces, transborder flows (financial, population, environmental, viral), international regimes, and complex networks (media, criminal, terrorist). Thus, globalization has heightened new security priorities such as terrorism, organized crime, narcotic trafficking, and disease.

Globalization can turn essentially local problems into regional or global security challenges. It allows issues and events in the developing world to reach the developed world, and vice versa.

This process should not be overstated however. The interrelatedness of the world is not new, the degree is simply greater. There is also a real danger that globalization is facilitating new forms of interaction (or power) which increasingly allow the West to dominate the security agenda and to structure the way security issues around the world are perceived and challenged. This is of particular concern for the developing world and is reflected in the partial merging of security and development policy agendas.

The merging of security and development agendas?

There has been an increasingly vigorous debate among scholars and practitioners over efforts to link development and security agendas, most recently over the controversial link of development aid to the war on terror. A serious concern is that development goals based on humanitarian principles, poverty reduction for instance, could be increasingly subordinated to Western foreign and security policy objectives. Some countries well known for human rights abuses have been offered US aid to take a supportive position on the war on terror. Examples include Pakistan and Uzbekistan. From the perspective of many development studies scholars, development concerns should not be subordinated to international security issues, and the securitization of aid does not address real development issues.

Of course, the merging of security and development agendas is not new. During the cold war, development aid was linked with the geopolitical power struggles of the US and the Soviet Union. Today, economic prosperity and growth are generally viewed as co-dependent on security, and linked as policy issues by many Western governments. Underdevelopment is often viewed more in terms of the potential threat it poses to the security of powerful countries than in terms of the well-being of affected populations. Underdevelopment is thus considered by Western governments and organizations as threatening national and global security, for example by fuelling illicit drug-trafficking, or supporting the spread of terrorism. The World Bank report, *Breaking the Conflict Trap* (2003d), for example, describes conflict and its associated security problems as a failure of development.

Realists would argue that Western governments have always linked their aid policies to their strategic interests, relatively neglecting countries of lesser economic or political interest to them. Countries deemed to be of direct interest, like Afghanistan, Iraq, Kosovo, Israel, and East Timor, receive ongoing consideration. However, there currently seems to be a movement towards a more overt and instrumental securitization of the development agenda.

KEY POINTS

- Security cannot be fully understood through a single level of analysis. Security issues may include threats to individuals, societies, states, networks and/or the global community.

- Approaches to security studies are predominantly Western-defined and include realist, constructivist, feminist, critical, and post-modern interpretations.

- Concepts from wider security studies such as emancipation, human security, and securitization have some benefits for understanding the developing world, as well as some limits in their practical application.

- Globalization and the increased inter-relatedness of the world, mean that local issues can affect any combination of national, regional, and global security.

- Development goals based on humanitarian principles are increasingly subordinated to Western-defined security objectives. This is particularly the case with the link of development aid to the war on terror.

NICOLE JACKSON

Violent Conflict: War and Terrorism in the Developing World

One of the key security issues in the developing world is violent conflict. Most of the world's poorest countries are suffering, or have recently suffered, from large-scale, violent conflict. Traditionally, security analyses of the developing world focused on inter-state wars, with a particular focus on the role of the colonizers or superpowers in fuelling the conflicts. However, since the end of the cold war, there has been an acknowledgement in the discipline that much of the violence in the world actually occurs within states, and that civilians have been the victims of violence perpetrated by both state and non-state groups.

Therefore, the previously dominant state-level of analysis is increasingly being supplemented by other levels—individual, regional, network, or global. The following section outlines the geographical distribution of the wide variety of violent state and non-state conflicts to be found throughout the developing world. It then examines how the Western belief in a link between weak states and terrorism is structuring global priorities and actions. Of all the types of violent conflict, terrorism is currently considered by most Western states as the greatest threat to global security, even though it kills significantly fewer people than genocide, interstate, or civil wars (for data see Human Security Centre 2005).

Traditional and non-traditional violent conflict

Traditional security studies examine violence between states. However, since the end of the cold war, the number of inter-state wars around the world has declined. Even in the region with the greatest number of ongoing inter-state wars, Central and West Africa, many of these interstate tensions and conflicts, have arisen from spillovers of interethnic conflict and civil war, and are therefore different from traditional wars between states. For example, in Congo from 1998–2003 approximately three million people died in a civil war which ended up involving nine other countries: Angola, Zimbabwe, Namibia, Chad, Sudan, Uganda, Burundi, Rwanda, and Tanzania.

Scholars of traditional security studies quantify military power. The developing world spends a comparatively high proportion of its gross domestic product (GDP) on defence. Of course, military power is a double-edged sword. It may undermine rather than enhance a country's security. Arms expenditures divert resources and often have an enormous economic as well as human drain on a country. Moreover, when states become trapped in arms races that consume a great percentage of their resources, war may become more likely. In 2005, conventional arms sales to the developing world were US$30.2 billion, up from US$26.4 billion in 2004 (Grimmett 2006). Russia, for the first time since the collapse of the Soviet Union, surpassed the United States in terms of military deals with the developing world (US$7 billion). France was second (US$6.3 billion) and the US third (US$6.2 billion). The leading developing world buyers of these weapons in 2005 were India, Saudi Arabia, and China.

Increasingly, much of the developing world is also confronted with the traditional threat of the use of nuclear weapons. In October 2006, North Korea alarmed its regional neighbours and the great powers when it joined India, Pakistan, China, Israel, Russia, the US, Britain, and France in the nuclear club. Other potential members, who in the past have shown interest in developing a nuclear programme or who are suspected of pursuing nuclear ambitions, include South Africa, Brazil, Iran, and Venezuela.

While traditional wars between states have been declining, intra (within)-state conflict is common, particularly in the developing world. Internal security problems are pervasive in many areas of Asia, the Middle East, Latin America, and especially Africa where interethnic conflicts, insurgencies, and civil wars have been endemic and prolonged (see Chapter 13). In contrast to the traditional approach, the human security approach is helpful in stressing internal dynamics and the human costs of war. This includes issues such as child soldiers and landmines, which pose considerable threats to the lives of peoples of the developing world. The use of children in war is not new but is believed to be rapidly growing. Children fight in almost 75 per cent of today's armed conflicts (Human Security Centre 2005: 35). They have been used in terrorist operations in Northern Ireland, Columbia, and Sri Lanka.

The human security approach also highlights that the greatest human costs of war are not the battle-deaths but the 'indirect' deaths caused by disease, lack of access to food, clean water, and heath care services. The lives of refugees, who commonly result from wars, are often at great risk—for example the 1.5 million refugees who fled the Rwandan genocide of 1994 into neighbouring Zaire (the Democratic Republic of Congo), Tanzania, and Burundi.

Distribution of the conflicts and Western response

Overall, the number of active major armed conflicts went down from 31 in 1991 to 17 in 2005 (SIPRI Yearbook 2006). However, many small wars have erupted as others have died down, and currently many groups are rearming. Most violent conflicts in Asia, the Middle East, Africa, and Latin America are geographically separate and often unrelated. However, linkages within regions are common, as are ties with the developed world, particularly because of the involvement of great powers. In just one of many examples, the US and North Atlantic Treaty Organization (NATO) are currently (September 2007) engaged in robust peacekeeping in Afghanistan. This allows them much more leeway to make peace as opposed to keeping and monitoring it.

The UN currently has approx. 92,200 personnel serving in eighteen UN-led peacekeeping operations across four continents, and numbers will soon rise with the newly established mission in East Timor and the recently expanded UN operations in South Lebanon and in Sudan. All but three of these eighteen UN Department of Peacekeeping Operations (DPKO)-led missions are in the developing world. The exceptions are Cyprus (since 1964), Kosovo (since 1999), and Georgia (since 1993).

Increasingly, the international community perceives the need for a unified global agenda, rather than unilateral approaches, to resolve these conflicts. However, international action continues to be mostly limited and very selectively applied. Western approaches have ranged from outright neglect via preventative measures to (unilateral and multilateral) military intervention. From the perspective of most developing countries, international involvement, and in particular military intervention, is highly problematic and contrary to their state sovereignty. Increasingly, the developed world is perceived as posing security threats to the developing world, in particular through the threat of military intervention, and the projection of Western or Northern power through the process of globalization.

In this spirit, the Non-Aligned Movement (NAM), originally developed to combat colonialism and avoid competing superpower alliances, is becoming increasingly influential. NAM is now made up of 116 developing countries which are increasingly concerned with reasserting their influence in a world dominated by the United States, as well as with specific issues like globalization, AIDS, and international crime. The current challenge for NAM is to move beyond anti-Western rhetoric and to gain world attention in order to effectively promote the interests of the developing world.

Asia and Oceania

Since the end of the Vietnam War, security problems in South-East Asia have arisen primarily from internal sources—ranging from demands for territorial secession and the threat of state disintegration through insurgency and terrorism. Examples include the separation of the former Portuguese colony of East Timor from Indonesia in 1999 (see Chapter 20a); and recent clashes and violent insurgencies in the Philippines, Burma, and Nepal. South Asia has also suffered ongoing inter-state violence, for example between India and Pakistan, and violent secessionist movements, for example, the Tamils in Sri Lanka. The oldest conflict dates to 1948 and is the separatist struggle of the Karen people in Myanmar. In Asia many internal and transnational security problems are inter-related. For example, in India insurgency and terrorism by resident Muslim extremists are often aided by other non-state actors from across borders. International involvement in the region continues, since 2001 most dramatically with the US and NATO operation in Afghanistan. Current UN military observer groups exist in India and Pakistan (since 1949) and a new UN mission is being developed in East Timor (2006).

Middle East

The Middle East has seen considerable inter-state violence, for example between Israel and the Arab countries and Iran and Iraq, as well as violent secessionist movements such as the Kurds in Iraq and Turkey. Today, violence continues between Israel and the Palestinian territories, and between Israel and Lebanon (2006). The deadliest current war is the US-led military intervention in Iraq (since 2003). Current UN DPKO-led missions in the Middle East exist in Israel (since 1948), Syria (since 1974), and Lebanon (since 1978).

Africa

Violent conflicts in Africa are often characterized by widespread ethnotribal conflicts, famines caused by droughts and civil wars, and criminalization of state activity. Africa differs from the other continents in that it has suffered significantly more deaths yet has received relatively little world attention. Following the colonization of Africa, many states have been continually on brink of collapse. State collapse weakens political society making it difficult for new groups to restore the state, often leading to internal conflict (see Chapter 13). Many states lack the ability to control their territory, and are unable to care for their populations.

Since the end of the cold war, violence in Africa has occurred largely unimpeded by the West. In addition, the three million people who died from the fighting and starvation that stemmed from the 1998–2003 civil war in the Democratic Republic of Congo and an estimated one million people died in the Rwanda genocide in 1994. International neglect of major tragedies and humanitarian crises continues to date, for example towards the civil war and genocide in Sudan's Darfur province. There, over the past three years, 200,000 people (some estimates are up to 500,000) have been killed, with two million more driven from their homes by Sudanese troops and their proxy Arab militias (see Box 18.4).

However, despite the continuation today of violent conflict, there have been some recent positive developments (as in Rwanda and Algeria). Major African conflicts dropped from eleven in 1998 to three in 2005: Sudan, Burundi, and Uganda (SIPRI Yearbook 2006). Africans are increasingly coming up with their own solutions to these pervasive conflicts, for example the African Union now provides African peacekeepers to African conflicts, as in Sudan. The difficulty is that the African Union's finances and power are very limited. There are some positive signs that the world community, in some cases, has been more willing to act. UN DPKO-led missions in Africa include Sudan (established 2005), Burundi (2004), Côte d'Ivoire (2004) Liberia (2003), the Democratic Republic of Congo (1999), Ethiopia-Eritrea (2000), and Western Sahara (1991). In mid- 2006 Sudan's president was blocking the UN Security Council from sending

20,000 peacekeepers to Darfur, saying that it would violate state sovereignty.

Latin America and the Caribbean

Violent conflict in Latin America has generally involved narcoterrorism and international organized crime, or insurgencies including indigenous movements seeking some kind of autonomy. Internal conflicts in the region have seen guerrilla movements in Colombia, Peru, Guatemala, and Mexico; frequent coups; military interventions in the civilian sphere; and the regional implications of the drug-related insurgency in Colombia. As in Africa, Asia, and the Middle East, external great powers have also been involved. For example, in the 1980s, the US was involved in military operations in Nicaragua, Colombia, and Peru. Today, the US is not directly militarily involved but major armed conflict continues in Columbia and Peru. Other serious violence includes anti-police violence in Brazilian slums which verges on the definition of armed political conflict. The only current UN DPKO-led operation is in Haiti (since 2004).

The securitization of terrorism in the developing world

Despite the variety of ongoing violence in much of the developing world, there has been a recent shift of Western attention towards global terrorism in that part of the world. Terrorism is an asymmetrical strategy available to weak actors seeking to level the strategic playing field. It is a tactic designed to achieve an objective (usually political) by using violence against innocent civilians to generate fear. Terrorism has been widely used in both the developed and developing world.

Since 2001 and the beginning of the war on terror, the West has focused particularly on transnational terrorist violence rather than other types of internal or inter-state conflict. The declining capacity of some states to meet basic human needs and enforce the rule of law is increasingly perceived to provide fertile conditions or training areas for global terrorist sympathizers. For example, in Afghanistan, some areas of Pakistan and Somalia and other very weak or collapsed states, groups with links to al-Qaeda are commonly understood to have developed, posing transnational or global threats. Western security focus has therefore increasingly shifted to organizations and groups at the network and global levels which are considered to require networked and global responses.

While a causal relationship between poverty and terrorism has not been established, it is clear that non-state armed groups are able to exploit the dehumanising conditions that result from poverty. The militarization of society and the context of violent occupation and war, which characterize many developing states, can be used by terrorists to gather sympathy for violent acts against perceived oppressors and their supporters. Globalization has also provided them new means to finance, carry out and publicize attacks, as well as to forge alliances or networks with other groups around the world. Nevertheless, most terrorist actions remain localized. Non-state groups view terrorism as cheap and effective, and thus a weapon of choice for their wars against oppressive states. For example, since the 1970s the Liberation Tigers of Tamil Eelam (LTTE) has fought the Sri Lankan government army with a well-organized terror campaign, with objectives ranging from greater autonomy to complete secession. Of the 186 terrorist attacks world wide between 1980 and 2001, the LTTE accounted for 75 (Kay 2006: 233)

When the war on terror became the West's first global priority in 2001, states with large Muslim populations and insurgency movements became priorities for US assistance. Washington substantially increased its foreign aid to Pakistan, India, the Philippines, Indonesia, and Uzbekistan as part of its anti-terrorism efforts. US military and security aid to Africa have also increased. The post-9/11 war on terror, by its very definition, took a primarily military approach consistent with traditional security. However, unless social, economic, and political contexts are addressed, and other tactics such as diplomacy and intelligence are deployed, problems will not disappear and global terrorism could escalate.

The West's abuse of power and neglect of certain issues is also felt strongly in the developing world. Examples of Western hypocrisy include when the West acted to protect the abuse of Kurds in Iraq, but not Kurds in Turkey; and the US and UK provided military support for regimes with very poor human rights records (as in Uzbekistan), while preaching the need for democracy and human rights. Ironically, such hypocrisy creates fertile ground for organizations in the developing world that advocate terror and the rejection of the West and its agenda of **good governance** and democracy (see Chapters 14 and 15).

> **KEY POINTS**
>
> - Today, violence between states, the traditional subject of security studies, is less common than intra-state violence.
>
> - Human security focuses on individual lives and the human costs of war.
>
> - Violent conflict in the developed world is diverse and specific to regions and particular states and localities.
>
> - Western involvement in conflicts ranges from neglect to outright military intervention.
>
> - Western hypocrisy and focus on the military approach to counter global terrorism creates fertile ground for a growing anti-Western approach in the developing world.

International Organized Crime

International organized crime (IOC), a significant threat to peoples, societies, and states, is often overlooked when examining the developing world. However, the movement of illicit goods across borders is not new, and around the world organized crime has always presented a variety of threats. What is new today is the scale of the problem and the growing power and capability of organized crime. IOC includes activities such as trafficking in narcotics, small arms, nuclear materials, and people, smuggling of illegal aliens, and money laundering. Few of these activities are confined to specific areas of the globe, rather they have taken on a transnational character. The global aspect of the drug trade, for example, mirrors the global divisions of labour found in other economic realms, where production in the developing areas has risen largely to meet the demand in advanced industrial states.

Criminals have benefited significantly from globalization—that is from the rise of information technology, the development of stronger political and economic linkages, and the shrinking importance of global distance. Globalization has expanded illegal markets and increased the size and resources of criminal networks. Some IOC groups operate within strategic alliances like firms; some work in globally-coordinated networks; others have looser and more ad hoc affiliations. Global criminal organizations vary in terms of their cohesion, longevity, degree of hierarchical control, degree of penetration, and acceptance within society. IOC groups based in the developing world include, for example, the Triad gangs of Hong Kong, China and various overseas ports, and the Colombian cocaine cartels.

Securitization of crime

Traditionally crime has been categorized as an economic activity, a 'low politics' topic best suited to disciplines such as economics or criminology. However, increasingly, it has become obvious that crime may threaten individual, societal, state, regional, and even global security. The network level is particularly relevant here because while criminals often act in interconnected groups across borders, there is similarly a need for international cooperation (or networks) to counter them.

As described above, the determination by governments that an issue constitutes a security problem is generally driven more by realist, state-centred calculations than by humanitarianism. Drugs and arms are thus considered by states to be security issues in part because of their connection to violence. From a traditional standpoint, they may threaten the stability of governments. However, IOC also impacts on human security directly at the individual level in specific national, regional or local contexts.

IOC poses a considerable challenge to states in the developed and developing world. At its most extreme, it can control territory, extract rents, provide services for local populations, and even wage war, as in Colombia and Afghanistan. It can also pose long-term structural damage such as the erosion of rule of law. The direct threat to state control is exacerbated by the relative weakness or low levels of political institutionalization of the state (as in Nigeria, Laos, and Tajikistan). IOC also erodes faith in democratic institutions depending on the degree to which criminality pervades the political, institutional, and financial infrastructure of the state, a significant problem in the post-Soviet states. Finally, IOC can undermine the state by destroying trust relations between people and state, eroding tax basis and diverting resources.

IOC poses specific problems for developing countries. Crime is perceived as a sign of social instability which may drive away foreign investment, foreign aid, and business. For example, in some African states, investment levels are low partly because of the perception that the rule of law does not prevail. IOC can also undermine the ability of a state to promote development. Finally, crime can harm social and human capital and is associated with increased violence. It can have a far greater impact on human lives in countries where the state is less able to intervene to protect individuals, for example in Brazil and South Africa.

Three key types of IOC which, to varying extent, impact on security at all levels of analysis are trafficking in persons, narcotics and small arms.

Trafficking in persons

Trafficking in persons is a highly complex phenomenon which includes recruitment, movement, and exploitation. It is a threat to human security because, in its many forms, it violates human rights by depriving people of basic human dignity and jeopardizing individual and public health. Human rights violations include the lack of freedom of movement, and physical, sexual, or mental abuse. Trafficking in persons may also be perceived as a threat to global security because it is often part of a larger phenomenon of illegal migration and transnational organized crime.

There are many types of human trafficking: forced labour including that of children (e.g. in South Asia where people are forced to work in sweat shops), slavery (Sudan), selling of organs (Latin America and Asia), selling of orphans (for example, following the Tsunami disaster in south Asia, December 2004). However, the most common and most lucrative is sex trafficking. Sex trafficking is global in scope, but particularly affects peoples in the developing world, from Ukraine to Tajikistan, and Nigeria to Thailand.

Narcotic trafficking

Narcotic trafficking similarly affects, to varying extents, the security of peoples and states around the world. Traditionally, Asia and Latin America have been key source regions, while Europe and North America have been key regions of demand. However, overall narcotic consumption is increasing around the world. There is also evidence that transit states eventually become consumer and distributor states, as is currently happening in much of the post-Soviet Union and Africa.

Narcotic trafficking activity in places like Colombia and Afghanistan damages economies, corrupts institutions, and affects regional stability and security. Colombia epitomizes the security threats posed by crime. There, drug trafficking represents a direct security threat to people, while criminal organizations, as well as violent political organizations such as the Revolutionary Armed Forces of Colombia (FARC) and National Liberation Army (ELN) in Colombia, have undermined the capacity of the government to rule the country.

Narcotic trafficking affects human security because individuals suffer the negative health effects of drugs such cocaine and heroin, and the spread of HIV/AIDS associated with intravenous drug use. The total number of drug users in the world is now estimated at some 200 million people, or about 5 per cent of the global population age 15–64. (UNODC 2006: 9). Narcotic trafficking also tends to be associated with other types of crime. For example, in Colombia, murder and kidnapping are among the highest in the world, with two out of six million people being displaced by guerrillas or kidnappers. Throughout Latin America drug trafficking undermines civil society through pervasive corruption and intimidation of politicians, and through the breakdown of law and order.

Small arms trafficking

The third IOC security issue is small arms trafficking. At the end of the cold war, there was a surplus of weapons which become ready stockpiles for legal and illicit markets. Today, over two-thirds of the world's legitimate arms sales (and likely more of the illegal sales) are directed towards developing states. This both reflects and contributes to violence in the developing world. Worldwide, small arms and light weapons are responsible for between 60 and 90 per cent of direct conflict deaths (Small Arms Survey 2005: 6). The new conflicts which characterized the post-cold war world tend to be fought using small arms and light weapons,

and not conventional weapons or the threat of weapons of mass destruction which characterized the cold war.

The widespread availability of small arms has been a factor in facilitating and sustaining wars and violence. It is thus a concern to human and state security. In the developing world, small arms are inexpensive and widely available, which makes them very difficult to regulate. Their small size and the fact that they are relatively easy to use, make them ideal for untrained combatants and children. They have thus contributed to the tragic growth in numbers of child soldiers, particularly in Africa.

The ability of developing countries to obtain an abundance of weapons has often been facilitated by great power struggles, through direct or illegal sales. During the cold war, rival powers armed regional antagonists, as in. India and Pakistan, Iran and Iraq, Israel and Syria, Ethiopia and Somalia. However, increasingly, producers of arms are selling them simply for commercial profit in many conflicts throughout the developing world and especially in Africa.

International policies

In the past, illicit trades and trafficking were most often perceived to be the responsibility of the state harbouring the clandestine transnational activities (CTAs). Today, there is a broad consensus among the international community that these are global security threats and that the international community must be actively engaged to counter them. Criminal (and terrorist) networks are believed to increasingly pose distributed and mobile threats. There is often no obvious source which is easy to target and thus international cooperation is required to effectively counter them.

Some developing states are perceived by international organizations as having become transhipment regions for organized crime activities and there is a fear that they are becoming safe havens for them. Overall, governments in developed and developing countries have obsolete tools, inadequate

BOX 19.2

United Nations Conventions on Organized Crime

Year	Convention title
2000	UN Convention against Transnational Organized Crime
2000	UN Convention against Transnational Organized Crime: Protocol against the Smuggling of Migrants by Land, Sea and Air
2000	UN Convention against Transnational Organized Crime: Protocol to Prevent, Suppress and Punish Trafficking in Persons, Especially Women and Children
2001	UN Convention against Transnational Organized Crime: Protocol against the Illicit Manufacturing of and Trafficking in Firearms, Their Parts and Components and Ammunition
2003	UN Convention against Corruption

laws, ineffective bureaucratic arrangements and ineffective strategies to deal with IOC. However, the situation in many developing countries is comparatively worse. There, power generally rests in the hands of a small group of elites who have ambiguous attitudes towards crime.

In this context, international organizations are currently taking steps to securitize (defined as push to the top of the political agenda) these activities. UN Conventions have been signed, however difficulties in implementation remain (see Box 19.2). Another major challenge is that in many regions of the world, criminal groups are either tolerated, or more directly supported, by governments. IOC may pose **security dichotomies** for peoples and states. As well as the negative effects on individual and state security, trafficking activities may provide work for people when the state can not help them, and may contribute to a state's economy, especially in times of crisis or transition.

The effectiveness of many of the policies initiated by the international community against IOC is questionable. The securitization of crime has meant that several specific strategies—in particular border management and law enforcement—have been adopted. These strategies are important but limited. The most extreme examples of securitization include the use of special military forces in the 1990s by the UK and USA in tackling South American drug cartels, and the use of NATO today to counter trafficking in Afghanistan. The increasing flow of cocaine and heroin shows the limitations of such traditional security approaches.

Finally, once again Western governments are generally not interested in the root causes or the effects of crime on individuals (the human security approach), but rather in the effects of transnational or global effects on Western states and peoples. Western states are therefore often viewed as hypocritical by the developing world for lecturing them, for example, to do more to decrease narcotic trade, when the trade is mostly driven by Western demand.

KEY POINTS

- IOC groups pose a variety of levels of threat to peoples, states, and regions in the developing world, as well as to the global community.

- IOC operates in transnational groups, demands transnational responses, and thus can be usefully considered at the network or global level of analysis.

- While trafficking in persons is predominantly a human security threat, narcotic and arms trafficking pose threats to individuals, societies, and states. All three types of trafficking are increasingly perceived by the international community as global security threats because of their real and perceived negative effects on Western peoples and states.

- IOC poses security dichotomies for developing states, in that their activities may be perceived, by states and peoples, positively and negatively.

Infectious Disease

Health and disease have traditionally not been understood as security issues. Most often, they have been viewed within the framework of development studies and human rights, with health and freedom from disease being key goals of local and state socio-economic development efforts. However, recently, health is also being examined as one of many factors that contribute to human security, while the dangers to health are perceived as new threats to state security. At the global level, health security is increasingly framed within foreign and security policy concerns, for example the transnational threat of HIV/AIDS, SARS, and bioterrorism.

In the course of history the threat posed by disease to human security and well-being has been at least comparable to the effects of war. In just one example, the Spanish Flu in 1918–19 killed between 40 and 50 million people worldwide, compared to approximately 15 million people killed during the Second World War. Today, throughout the world, infectious diseases kill more people than all other causes combined (Kassalow 2001: 6). Compounding the tragedy is the fact that each year, millions of people die from preventable, curable, and treatable diseases. Most of these deaths occur in the developing world, where there is a lack of vaccines and basic sanitation.

The securitization of transnational diseases

The increasingly high-level attention given to global health since mid 1990s is largely due to the recognition that there is a strong relationship between health and development. People in the developing world suffer greater ill health and shorter life expectancy, partly as a result of higher than average child and maternal mortality, as well as inequitable access to health care and social protection. However, more recently, health has also come to be linked to the security agenda, both in the traditional state sense, and with the human security agenda and its focus on individuals.

Although modern medicine has made great advances, it has achieved only limited success in halting the spread of infectious diseases. Across the world, cures for some of the older diseases are even at risk of being reversed, for example tuberculosis, cholera, and malaria. Meanwhile, new diseases have emerged, such as HIV/AIDS, Ebola virus, hepatitis C, SARS, and avian flu. The increase in globalization, particularly the ease of travel, has made it more difficult to prevent deadly pathogens from spreading across borders.

These diseases are therefore currently perceived by many world leaders, and many international organizations, as threats to global security. For example, the avian influenza virus (H5N1) broke out in 1997 in Hong Kong, killing six of the eighteen people infected with it. As of October 2006, H5NI has spread across ten countries with 148 reported deaths (WHO 2006). Currently there is no vaccine for the virus and the World Health Organization (WHO) has warned that the flu virus could unleash a pandemic that could kill up to a million people. In other cases, vaccines have been successfully developed. For example, in 2002, SARS was first identified in southern China. During the next two years 9,000 cases were identified and 900 people died, mostly in Asia but also Canada. Apart from its threat to human lives, it negatively affected the economies of those states. Most recently, in September 2006, the WHO warned of a deadly new strain of tuberculosis, untreatable with drugs, spreading across the globe and possibly putting to an end any attempts to contain the AIDS pandemic.

Of course, even localized diseases can spread fear around the world, such as the outbreak in 2000 of the Ebola hemorrhagic fever in Uganda, which remained relatively contained, but caused panic due to the rapid spread of the disease and its horrific symptoms. Finally, particularly since the events of September 2001, there has been a heightened concern that terrorist or other groups could use diseases such as plague, anthrax, and smallpox to raise attention for their cause, by creating panic and instilling fear. This particular concern, has most greatly contributed to the recent Western attempts to securitize some infectious diseases.

HIV/AIDS

HIV/AIDS is an example of a disease no longer seen as just a health or public policy issue. Increasingly, it is perceived as a security issue at many levels. It challenges human security, the political, economic, and social stability of states and regions, and the broader global security.

HIV/AIDS directly threatens the lives and health of individuals and communities around the world.

Between 1981 and 2005, approximately 23 million people worldwide died of the disease and almost 39 million were infected (UNAIDS 2006). Ninety-five per cent of those infected with HIV are in the developing world. Africa is the epicentre of the pandemic with approximately 30 million infected in sub-Saharan Africa. UNAIDS estimates that by 2010 as many as 25 million African children will have lost one or both parents to AIDS, thereby creating an entire generation of orphans. This is related to other human security issues, in that orphans have an increased risk of being recruited into trafficking rings or as child soldiers. Overall, the decline of life expectancy throughout Africa has been directly related to the spread of AIDS.

Beyond Africa, the rest of the developing world has witnessed a dramatic increase in HIV infection across Asia, and throughout the former Soviet States, Central Asia, and Latin America. Nevertheless, globally, the HIV incidence rate is now believed to have peaked in the late 1990s. Treatment access has dramatically expanded over the past five years in developing countries, notably in Botswana, Kenya, South Africa, Uganda, and Zambia. However, antiretroviral coverage varies considerably within regions. In sub-Saharan Africa, treatment coverage ranges from 3 per cent in the Central African Republic to 85 per cent in Botswana. While more than 80 per cent of affected people in Argentina, Brazil, and Venezuela are receiving treatment, only 29 per cent have access to it in Paraguay and 37 per cent in Bolivia. In India coverage was only 7 per cent and in Russia only 5 per cent in 2005 (UNAIDS 2006). Thus, while medical advances can halt or slow the spread of the disease, in developing countries, only 12 per cent of people who would benefit from drug treatments receive them.

As well as the horrific toll on human lives, HIV/AIDS also weakens social and state security. It can affect family, community and social cohesion. It often harms the productive members of society, including teachers and healthcare workers. HIV/AIDS is a risk to human capital, natural resource development, and business investment, and thus an economic liability to national economies.

HIV/AIDS may also be perceived as a traditional military security threat. Singer (2002) and Elbe (2002) have analyzed the high rate of AIDS in the military forces, as well as its relation to conflicts in Africa. The average rate of infection for African militaries is 30 per cent and AIDS is a primary cause of death in many African armies. The weakening of militaries can make states more vulnerable to attack, and make it more difficult for them to keep stability or order. HIV/AIDS has also been used as a weapon of war, for example, in the Rwandan genocide, between 200,000 and 500,000 women and children were raped, increasing the risk of the spread of diseases.

One of the many difficulties in responding effectively to the HIV/AIDS crisis in the developing world is concern that it may draw resources away from other health challenges or infectious diseases, such as malaria which still kills more than one million Africans a year, or tuberculosis, which is the leading cause of death of AIDS victims. There is an ongoing debate within the global health community about whether health investment should be targeted at trying to improve the entire health system, or on specific programmes aimed at improvement in particular areas, like AIDS. Another grave difficulty is the great diversity in response to HIV by different countries and the unwillingness of certain state leaders to acknowledge the seriousness of the issue. For example, South African President Mbeki has questioned the scientific conclusion that HIV causes AIDS and until recently refused to sanction public funding of antiretroviral drugs.

Around the world, there are some success stories in countering AIDS, for example Uganda, while other countries such as Cameroon or India have not yet responded to the severity of the problem. As it is, more than 70 million people worldwide will die from AIDS by 2020 (WHO 2005).

International policy responses

Globalization may be a cause of global health concerns, but it also offers opportunities to enhance health security through the dissemination of medical knowledge, and to empower organizations such as the World Health Organization to coordinate policy. In 2000, the UN Security Council adopted a resolution calling on UN agencies to collaborate in response to the HIV/AIDS pandemic which if unchecked may pose a threat to stability and security.

World leaders are increasingly recognizing that global health and global security are intertwined. In 2000, the US formally identified HIV/AIDS as a security threat by, controversially, linking it to violence and state failure. According to the US National Intelligence Council (NIC), dramatic declines in life expectancy due to this disease are strong risk factors for revolutionary wars, ethnic wars, genocides, and disruptive regime transitions in the developing world. The social consequences of HIV/AIDS have particularly strong correlations with the likelihood of state failure in partial democracies (NIC 2000).

Health issues thus have become linked with traditional security agendas and human security. From the perspective of the development community, closer linking of aid with traditional security policy shifts the referent object away from the most vulnerable/those with greatest need, to individuals or populations that pose the greatest perceived threat to the strategic interests of selected states. Some fear that health is becoming a tool of foreign and security policy. Meanwhile, security sector adherents fear that broadening the definition of security means that they are, or will be, forced to deal with issues best left to state social policy.

The human security approach supports broadening the responsibility for health security. It shifts responsibility down from the national level to communities, civil organizations and individuals; and upwards to international institutions and networks. In 2002, the Global Fund to Fight HIV/AIDS, Tuberculosis and Malaria was created to fulfil commitments by G8 countries to improve the health of populations in low-income countries. Three of eight **Millennium Development Goals** (MDG) call for specific health improvements by

2015: reducing child deaths, reducing maternal mortality, and slowing the spread of HIV/AIDS, malaria and tuberculosis. US President Bush established a Millennium Challenge Account (MCA) beginning in 2004 that would give foreign assistance, including in the health sector, to low income countries that are ruling justly, investing in their people and encouraging economic freedom. Unfortunately, since then, the allocation to health funding has been reduced. The US programme, expected to save some nine million lives, is up for renewal in 2007.

A serious cause of concern is that Western and international focus on health issues in the developing world is primarily focused on transnational diseases and not those specific to developing countries. In this regard, a recent positive step is that the WHO has set up new guidelines to launch a preventative and treatment programme to tackle specific diseases which affect hundreds of millions of people in the developing world such as river blindness and bilharzia (a disease caused by parasitic worms). This will be the first large-scale attempt to use drugs on healthy (as well

as infected) people to offer quasi-immunization in an attempt to eliminate the diseases. At the same time, the WHO along with funds from USAID and the Bill and Melinda Gates Foundations will support preventative chemotherapy in six countries—Tanzania, Uganda, Burkina Faso, Mali, Niger, and Ghana. These are significant, if still small, steps in global cooperation on health in the developing world.

> **KEY POINTS**
>
> ● Infectious diseases pose a variety of different threats to human, state, and global security.
>
> ● Africa is the epicentre of an HIV/AIDS pandemic. 95 per cent of those infected with HIV/AIDS are in the developing world.
>
> ● Globalization, especially the ease of travel, has made it more difficult to prevent the spread of diseases across borders. However, it also offers opportunities to share knowledge and to coordinate policy.

Conclusions

Key issues in current debates about security and the developing world include: What is security? Are Western-defined concepts and approaches about security applicable to the developing world? What have been the ramifications of globalization on security issues? Are development goals based on humanitarianism increasingly subordinated to Western foreign and security policy objectives?

Security is a contested concept and this chapter argues that security must be examined through different levels of analyses. Today, the discipline of security studies increasingly includes not only

state-centred analyses and the study of military threats and inter-state conflict, but also intra-state conflicts and direct threats to individual lives. Critical security studies, including feminist, normative, and post-structuralist approaches, all question the concept of security and critique of the realist/traditionalist approach. This chapter adopts a comprehensive definition of security, to be examined at the individual, state, regional, network, and global level.

Many security issues impact strongly on developing states. The three key issues examined in this chapter—violent conflict, international organized crime, and disease—all affect security at many levels of analysis. Security threats are perceived differently in the developed and developing worlds. They change over time, depend on context and the perceptions of peoples and states. The developing world, similar to the developed world, is not monolithic and different issues affect different countries, areas, and regions.

Western states and organizations have structured global priorities according to their own, generally traditionally defined, security interests. Those interests are mostly focused on the transnational effects of so-called threats to Western peoples and states, rather than on the issues which directly threaten developing states and their peoples. For example, the current preoccupation with global terrorism has diverted attention and funding from many development issues (even though there is some evidence that development issues may be related to terrorism), and terrorism pales in comparison to the scope of other global security challenges.

From the perspective of many developing countries, the developed world itself poses many security threats, in particular the threat of military intervention, and the projection of Western or Northern power through the process of globalization. Developing countries have limited means available to make their voices heard and little bargaining power. In the absence of a conventional military balance, developing states with sufficient economic and technical capacity have sought WMD to level the playing field. Less well-off state and non-state actors have increasingly turned to terrorism as a potential equalizer, others engage in 'bandwagoning' with the dominant power, or join regional organizations and the Non-Aligned Movement to pool resources and project a unified response. The current question for the developing world is how to move beyond violence and anti-Western rhetoric and promote their interests effectively in a world where few listen to their voices. The challenge for both worlds is to adopt a more holistic approach to security policy, one that bridges the increasingly artificial divide between traditional security and development studies.

QUESTIONS

1 What is security?

2 What is the impact of globalization on security issues in the developing world?

3 What is the human security approach towards violent conflict?

4 Does the West's 'securitization' of terrorism have any specific implications for improving security in the developing world?

5 How does international organized crime affect the security of peoples and states in the developing world?

6 Is disease a security threat? What are the dangers in securitizing health?

7 To what extent are Western governments responding appropriately to security challenges in the developing world?

GUIDE TO FURTHER READING

■ **United Nations (2005),** *A More Secure World: Our Shared Responsibility, Report of the UN Secretary General's High Level Panel on Threats, Challenges and Change* **(London: Stationery Office).** This UN-commissioned report outlines the key security challenges facing the world today and gives proposals for their resolution.

■ **Ayoob, M. (1995),** *The Third World Security Predicaments: State Making, Regional Conflict and the International System* **(Boulder, Colo.: Lynne Rienner).** An important book examining security in the developing world from a state-centric perspective.

■ **Chen, L., Fukuda-Parr, S., and Seidenbsticker, E. (eds.) (2003),** *Human Insecurity in a Global World* **(Cambridge, MA: Global Equity Initiative, Asia Center, Harvard University).** Examines global issues from the human security perspective.

■ **Friman, R. and Andreas P. (eds.) (1999),** *The Illicit Global Economy and State Power* **(New York: Rowman and Littlefield).** Offers a solid introduction to the subject of transnational organized crime.

■ **Human Security Centre (2005),** *Human Security Report 2005; War and Peace in the 21st Century* **(Oxford: Oxford University Press, 2005).** A groundbreaking report that defines human security as freedom from violence. It provides data and analysis about the effects of violence on peoples around the world.

■ **Kay, S. (2006),** *Global Security in the Twenty-First Century: the quest for power and the search for peace* **(Oxford: Rowman and Littlefield).** An excellent introduction to global security and to the liberal and realist perspectives.

■ **Kegley, C. W. Jr. (ed.) (2003),** *The New Global Terrorism: Characteristics, Causes, Controls* **(New Jersey: Pearson Education).** An excellent edited volume of major academic articles on non-state violence.

■ **Pettiford, L. and Curley, M. (1999),** *Changing Security Agendas and the Third World* **(London and New York: Pinter).** This thought-provoking book examines security from a developing world perspective, countering traditional international relations theory.

■ **Tickner, J. A. (1992),** *Gender in International Relations: Feminist Perspectives on Achieving Global Security* **(New York: Columbia University Press).** A ground-breaking book introducing feminist perspectives on global security.

WEB LINKS

● **www.humansecuritygateway.info/** The Human Security Gateway, an excellent research and information database on human security issues.

● **www.crisisweb.org** Site of the International Crisis Group (ICG), a non-profit NGO which provides high quality reports and briefs on deadly conflicts around the world.

● **www.isn.ethz.ch/** The site of the International Relations and Security Network, which shares specialized information among international relations and security professionals worldwide.

● **http://first.sipri.org/index.php** Facts on International Relations and Security Trends (FIRST) gives access to a large number of databases on traditional and non-traditional security issues.

- **www.unodc.org** The website of the United Nations Office on Drugs and Crime (UNODC).

- **www.who.int/en/** The website of the World Health Organization (WHO).

 ONLINE RESOURCE CENTRE

For additional material and resources, see the Online Resource Centre at:
www.oxfordtextbooks.co.uk/orc/burnell2e/

PART 5

Case Studies: Experiences Compared

In this part we deploy a range of case studies to add 'thick description' to the 'thin description' provided by the wide selections of examples that have been cited in the discussions in the earlier parts. There are two main aims. *First*, to illustrate in depth many of the larger themes that have been introduced and discussed in the earlier parts, by reference to countries carefully chosen as cases for their capacity to reveal the complexity of the issues involved. Our *second* aim is to demonstrate the great diversity of experience through a combination of cases drawn from the main developing regions, with some countries showing what might be considered positive developments or genuine achievements and others displaying more troublesome features. The intention to illustrate good news as well as less attractive features was a primary criterion in the selection process. Basic data for socio-economic and political indicators for all the countries and their globalization rankings too can be found in Appendix 1 and Appendix 2.

The country cases themselves each tell their own story but the pairings, or in one case group of three, supply evidence of some contrasting experiences. At the same time the evidence shows that often we must be qualified in our judgement. Indeed, what counts as for instance good news is to some extent in the eye of the beholder: the country analysts were encouraged to bring their own views to bear and apply their own interpretation of the evidence. Moreover, the political dynamics of developing countries are such that the way and extent to which a country illustrates a particular politics, for example state-building or conversely state collapse, can change significantly over time, in some instances no less rapidly than the time it takes for a book to move from a first to a second edition. Put differently, the country cases do illustrate specific themes from Part 1 through to Part 4 but no one should expect them to do so in straightforward black-and-white fashion.

Thus for example Indonesia, with its far flung archipelago and mixture of peoples might seem like a country where increasing fragmentation is only to be expected, given the decay of political authoritarianism that followed the fall of President Soeharto. And it is true that some secessionist tendencies have been in evidence, most dramatically in the acquisition of independence by East Timor in 2002. There, increasing political instability rather than an easy path to state construction has been apparent in this new state that was formerly administered as part of Indonesia. And yet the account of Indonesia given in Chapter 20 while documenting the tensions inside Indonesia also presents a more complex and nuanced picture of the forces of both disintegration and reintegration.

In contrast South Africa's recent past is suggestive of a more unambiguously positive experience in nation-building, coming as it did after the forecasts of political disintegration on the attainment of black majority rule—predictions that we now know were unfounded. Even so, the remarkable story of national reconciliation and racial harmony in South Africa since the end of apartheid does not dispel all doubts about the future. Class based inequalities could come to pose a greater challenge or at minimum bring about serious divisions among organized political forces, possibly reshaping the party system and lessening the political dominance currently exercised by the African National Congress. Indonesia and South Africa together illustrate the possibilities as well as pitfalls of state reshaping and nation-building in countries where European imperial expansion and the colonial legacy inevitably left behind a major impact.

In Chapter 21 the complexities of civil society and its political implications are brought out in the cases of India and Saudi Arabia. At first glance Indian society might be considered both heterogeneous and vibrant, with the citizenry of Saudi Arabia offering a clear contrast in both respects. In reality we find civil society is not passive in either country. Furthermore in both India and Saudia Arabia there are elements of civil society that pose a significant source of political tension: even in India there seems to be no unequivocal and universal accommodation to liberal democratic norms. Nevertheless India is and seems likely to remain the world's largest democracy; in contrast Saudi Arabia continues to enjoy an unfavourable reputation for civil liberties and political rights. In the West both countries are widely perceived to be of very considerable importance. India is featured not least because of its growing contribution to cultural and economic expressions of globalization, and because it is viewed as a major key to security in the South Asia region. Saudi Arabia of course is home to the world's largest known national reserve of that most precious commodity, oil. At the same time it is linked to the origins of al-Qaeda. Readers must judge for themselves whether Indian society really does provide shining evidence of democracy's oft-proclaimed ability to sustain freedom and stability, and whether Saudi Arabia exemplifies more the belief that political repression, and unequal rights for women in particular, might ultimately create the conditions for regime collapse.

In Chapter 22 three countries illustrate contrasting versions of a global contest between the different overarching principles of political organization that have occupied much of the developing world over the last fifty years or more. It is a contest where not only have different countries exhibited diverse trajectories but in many cases the precise positioning of countries in relation to the different models of authoritarian and democratic rule even now is uncertain or remains in flux. Pakistan, a country that seems crucial to international efforts to combat terrorism by radical Islamic groups, seems unable to relinquish rule by the armed forces. The chapter explains why this is the case. It conveys the consequences for Pakistan's own development. However while it is tempting to say that Pakistan is stuck in the past this would be simplistic, and the contributions that the military must make to Pakistan's own public security and to governance in the future should not be overlooked.

Nigeria appears to provide a contrast. Although like Pakistan it has a history of military intervention, since 1999 it has sustained a return to elected civilian rule. But how precarious is this development? Nigeria is a multiethnic society that has known civil war. Regional and religious differences are strongly felt; and Nigeria's political leaders continue to be criticized both at home and abroad for not doing enough to end corruption and for failing to face up to difficult but major policy decisions. And yet by virtue of its size, oil wealth and political traditions Nigeria is one of Africa's most powerful countries. Nigeria is not just pivotal to prospects in West Africa but, along with South Africa and a handful of other states it is central to African initiatives to promote objectives like peace and better governance across the continent as a whole.

Mexico is an example of yet a third political path, in this case from dominant one party rule to political pluralism, or in Schedler's words from 'electoral authoritarianism' to 'democratization by elections'. And yet Mexico shows that even where there may be no reason to think the military would intervene in politics the process of democratic political change is not necessarily smooth or bereft of surprises. The disputed result of the presidential election in 2006 is a particularly vivid illustration.

In the final chapter holistic approaches to development and underdevelopment that treat each as an interacting bundle of social, economic, and political characteristics—in short as a system—are illustrated by two countries from contrasting ends of the spectrum. Guatemala is a good example of how difficult it can be to break away from the structural cycle of underdevelopment, even where political agency-led reforms appear on one level to have introduced some meaningful change. In particular Guatemala illustrates well the connections between organised crime and politics, raised earlier on in the chapter on security (Chapter 19). There is also a continuing high level of human rights abuse notwithstanding Guatemala's having an elected civilian government. South Korea, by contrast is a success story not simply in terms of its strong record of economic and social development but also because of the political transition it has made to stable democracy. Not only has development proceeded on all fronts, then, but the country may be examined for guidance over what makes such an achievement possible, for instance over issues of right sequencing of the various initiatives concerning political and economic change. Yet South Korea also illustrates that the political challenges of development are never completely resolved—any more so than are the economic challenges which rocked the country in the late 1990s. And like Mexico too the country also shows that even movement towards western-style liberal democracy does not signal an end to all forms of political conflict. On the contrary, discord over issues like probity in public office, the distributive consequences of economic growth, and foreign relations then seem more likely to come to the fore, providing new focal points around which political mobilization can take place. While taken as a whole Guatemala in Central America and South Korea in East Asia represent the extremes of underdevelopment and development, the perhaps more typical experience of the many countries that lie somewhere between these two extremes can be can be found illustrated on the Online Resource Centre to this book, in the form of Zambia.

All told, the chapters in this final part demonstrate that to understand politics in the developing world a detailed historical knowledge acquired on a case-by-case basis forms an indispensable complement to the larger theorizing. This part should help us to decide which theoretical approaches offer the most insight into this or that particular case. These case studies are brought together here and can be read on a free-standing basis. But all readers are also recommended to consult the case study or studies that are most relevant to a big issue or theme immediately after studying the relevant chapter or chapters on that issue or theme in the earlier parts. The brief introduction to the cases here is offered as a guide to matching up the different parts of the book in this way.

To round off the country studies the Online Resource Centre also includes specially commissioned material on China. Readers should access the site with a view to considering what features China most has in common with the developing world and which distinguishing features most set it apart. Does China have anything to learn from the developing world? Is there something in particular that countries in the developing world should learn from China? These are intriguing and important questions, although they take us well beyond the limits of what could be encompassed in this book.

20 | Disintegration or Nation-Building?

20a | Indonesia: Coping with Fragmentation

EDWARD ASPINALL

Chapter Contents

- Introduction
- Making Indonesia
- Democratization and National Disintegration
- Toward Reintegration?
- Conclusion

Overview

This chapter focuses on the crisis of 'national disintegration' (as it was sometimes known) in Indonesia in the years following the collapse of President Suharto's authoritarian regime in 1998. After decades of militaristic and centralized rule, there was a sudden eruption of fragmentary and contentious politics based around ethnic, regional, and religious identities. Civil disturbances, inter-communal warfare, and separatist insurgencies occurred in several regions. Government leaders feared that decades of nation-building efforts were unravelling. This chapter surveys the historical experiences which led to this outcome and outlines the main dimensions of the crisis. It also discusses alternative explanations for it. The chapter notes a divergence between those who point to the intractable nature of Indonesia's problems, ultimately deriving from the heterogeneity of the population and the 'artificiality' of the country's colonial origins, and those who instead emphasize the role of the post-colonial state, especially during authoritarianism, in generating ethnic tensions and violence.

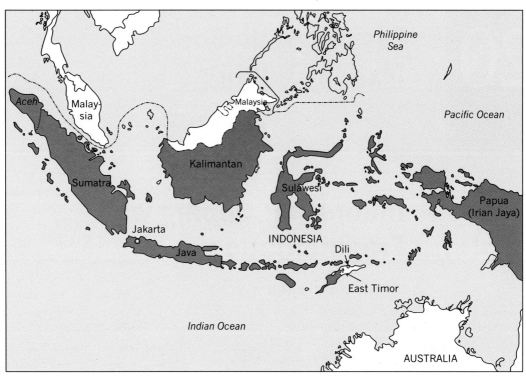

INDONESIA

BOX 20a.1

Key Dates in Indonesia's History

1942	Japanese military occupies the Netherlands East Indies.
1945	Nationalist leaders proclaim Indonesian independence.
1945–9	Independence revolution: armed conflict and negotiations with the Dutch.
1955	Indonesia's first parliamentary elections produce a fractured political map.
1959	President Sukarno dissolves parliament and establishes 'guided democracy'.
1965	Failed coup attempt in Jakarta, army begins massacre of communists.
1966	Suharto's 'New Order' regime begins.
1997	Asian financial crisis.
1998	Nation wide student protests force resignation of President Suharto.
	Suharto's vice-president, B. J. Habibie, takes over and initiates political reform.
1999	Indonesia's second democratic elections.
	East Timor votes to become independent.
	Major violence in Maluku and Aceh.
2003	President Megawati Soekarnoputri declares martial law to eradicate separatist insurgency in Aceh.
2004	Second post-Suharto democratic elections proceed peacefully and successfully.
2005	Helsinki peace agreement signed by Acehnese rebel leaders and government representatives.

Introduction

When President Suharto's military-based regime collapsed in 1998, hopes were high in Indonesia that the country was entering a new democratic era. However, democratization was accompanied by a surge of mobilization along ethnic and religious lines. In the worst instances, communal conflicts caused thousands of deaths. In three provinces, long-standing separatist movements re-emerged, leading to the independence of one province, East Timor, which became an internationally recognized sovereign state in May 2002. Many Indonesians began to fear that their country was about to break up.

Indonesia's political trajectory over recent decades mirrors broad trends in the developing world. The country has faced nation-building challenges similar to those experienced by other post-colonial states, and it has experimented with solutions resembling those tried elsewhere. In the post-independence years of the 1950s, Indonesia adopted a political format (parliamentary democracy) and a development strategy (economic nationalism and state-led industrialization) similar to those of many other African and Asian post-colonies. Also as in many other newly independent states, democratic rule did not long survive the divisions unleashed by independence, social transformation, and the cold war. From the late 1960s, Indonesia approximated more to the model of authoritarian development-alism pioneered by states in East Asia such as South Korea and Taiwan. Even the communal mobilization and fragmentation from 1998 mirrors developments elsewhere over the last two decades (India is one example).

As well as outlining the main trends, this chapter surveys the alternative explanations for recent fragmentary pressures. With some simplification, it can be seen that there are two basic schools of thought. On the one hand are those who see fragmentation as virtually an inevitable product of Indonesia's great ethnic and religious heterogeneity. In this view, the post-1998 violence was merely the latest explosion of tensions which first surfaced in the early post-independence years. President Suharto's authoritarian rule kept the lid on centrifugal forces, but once repressive constraints were removed, these forces reasserted themselves. A second set of explanations takes a less pessimistic view of Indonesian society, instead pointing to the disruptive effects of the state's own political and economic policies as causes of fragmentation. Broadly speaking, this debate mirrors larger ones in the fields of political science, history, and sociology, about whether contemporary ethnic and national political identities and conflicts arise naturally from deep-seated social divisions ('primordialism'), or whether they are produced by modern phenomena, such as economic development, state formation, the impacts of post-colonial states, and communication technologies ('modernism') (Smith 1998). This chapter evaluates these explanations for Indonesia's post-1998 crises, and finds the second set more convincing.

Making Indonesia

A starting point for understanding Indonesia's post-1998 fragmentation is noting the great ethnic and religious diversity of the country. Indonesia consists of approximately 17,000 islands, about 6,000 of which are populated. There are over 700 languages, and perhaps 1,000 ethnic or subethnic groups (depending on how they are defined). By far the largest ethnic group is the Javanese, at about 42 per cent of the population. Approximately 88 per cent of Indonesians are Muslims, alongside significant Christian, Hindu, and Buddhist minorities. While almost all Indonesian Muslims are *sunni*, they are themselves divided, notably between 'traditionalists', who are followers of *ulama* (religious scholars) in rural areas, and the more urban 'modernists'. Like many post-colonial states, Indonesia is not heir to any long-standing pre-colonial polity (indeed, the word 'Indonesia' was not coined until the nineteenth century and became popular only in the early twentieth century). Instead, it was the Dutch colonialists who united the diverse societies of what is now thought of as Indonesia into a single colony, the Netherlands East Indies. The boundaries of this colonial entity were not coterminous with any indigenous ethnic group or state. Instead, they simply marked the reach of Holland's imperial conquests and the treaties it made with other European imperialist powers. Indonesia inherited the borders of this colonial precursor.

For scholars who argue that durable nations arise out of ethnic affinity or belief in common descent (e.g. Connor 1994: 90–100), it would follow logically that Indonesia is not a true nation-state. In fact, the Indonesian experience demonstrates the historical processes by which a sense of nationhood may come into being and, over time, strike deep roots in a population. In Indonesia, this process has taken several generations and arguably has not ended today.

Before the twentieth century, resistance to the Dutch was led by the aristocratic and religious leaders of the old states and societies which were being subsumed into the Dutch empire. In the early twentieth century, such resistance was ending and a new Indonesian nationalist movement emerged, led by Western-educated elites. The novel idea of Indonesia itself arose out of their shared colonial experience. As a result, the early nationalist leaders stressed the need for unity among the diverse peoples of the archipelago. For example, they re-labelled the Malay language (already a *lingua franca*

in colonial times) as Indonesian, the 'language of unity'. Experiences of struggle and sacrifice during the early nationalist movement (c. 1912–42) and independence revolution (1945–9) popularized the ideas of Indonesian unity and independence and sanctified them in blood. In the early years of independence, nation-building became the theme *par excellence* of the country's leaders, especially its first president, Sukarno.

Despite the emphasis on unity, the transition to independence was fractious. Elections in 1955 produced a parliament divided between secular-nationalists, communists, traditionalist Muslims, and modernist Muslims. Cabinets rose and fell in quick succession. Tensions between Muslims and secularists over whether the state should oblige Muslims to observe Islamic law caused deadlock in a constituent assembly. Armed revolts in several regions expressed regionalist, Islamic, and anti-communist urges. Rapid growth of the communist party seemed to endanger the entire socio-political order.

President Sukarno tried to overcome these divisions by a system of left-populist but authoritarian rule which he labelled 'Guided Democracy' (1959–65). However, this system did not prevent polarization between the massive communist party on the left and the military and its allies on the right. The military was ultimately victorious, cementing its triumph with the massacre of approximately 500,000 leftists in 1965–6, an event that was enthusiastically welcomed by the United States and its allies. Under Suharto's leadership the military then established an authoritarian regime, the 'New Order', which lasted from 1966 to 1998.

The New Order still focused on nation-building, but whereas Sukarno had tried to unify Indonesia by mobilizing and channelling popular passions, Suharto and the military tried to suppress them. They proclaimed that they aimed at 'accelerated modernization' which would gradually eliminate 'primordial' divisions. They believed they had to limit political mobilization in order to create a stable environment for economic development. Indonesia experienced almost three decades of rapid

BOX 20a.2

Indonesia's economic transformation

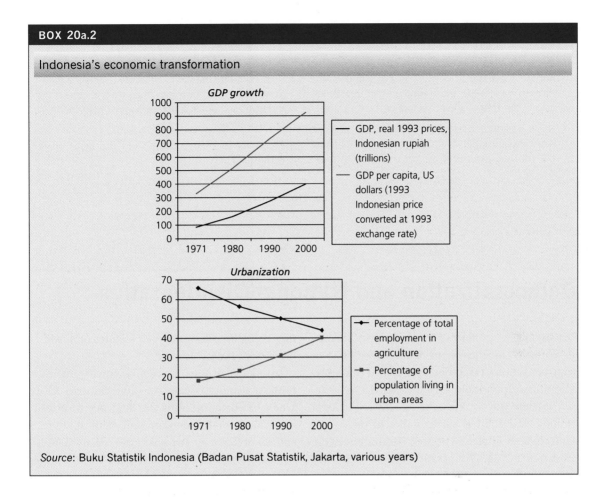

Source: Buku Statistik Indonesia (Badan Pusat Statistik, Jakarta, various years)

growth, producing substantial urbanization, a tiny but wealthy capitalist class, a larger middle class, and gradually rising living standards for even many of the poor (see Box 20a.2). The regime also encouraged national cohesion by pursuing economic integration and propagating unifying national symbols and cultural habits. For example, it developed a **Pancasila** ideology, to which all citizens were expected to adhere, and expanded uniform national education for school students (Drake 1989).

Rapid economic and social change was not matched by political evolution. Suharto remained in power, ageing and inflexible. His regime still aimed to constrain, control, and repress popular pressures rather than accommodate them. Political strains increased in the early 1990s, as speculation

grew about presidential succession and rising social forces became more assertive. The collapse of the regime, however, was triggered not by economic growth, but by economic crisis. When the Asian financial collapse of 1997 hit Indonesia, it triggered student-led protests which, in May 1998, forced Suharto to resign.

At this point, Indonesia did not seem to be facing elemental crisis. There had been separatist unrest in some provinces, but it had been militarily suppressed. Some communal violence accompanied rising anti-Suharto sentiment, but it was of secondary importance to the anti-Suharto protests, whose leaders wanted to solve the country's national problems by introducing political reform (*reformasi*). Overall, their mood was optimistic.

EDWARD ASPINALL

Democratization and National Disintegration

Responding to popular discontent, post-Suharto governments pursued rapid democratization. Defying predictions, this process proceeded smoothly. The military, politically central under the New Order, lost the will to intervene directly in national politics. New political parties and civil society organizations multiplied. The press became one of the most free in Asia. Democratic elections were held in 1999 and again in 2004 (see Box 20a.3).

But democratization was accompanied by fragmentation and, in some areas, violence. At the national level, parliamentary elections produced a fractured political map (in 2004, the seven largest political parties shared about 80 per cent of the vote, the largest gained only 22 per cent). More important for present purposes was the new political prominence of regional, ethnic, and religious identities. It was hard for regional and ethnic identities to be formally represented in the party system, for reasons which are discussed below, but parties based on Islamic identities became politically important. Such parties won 35 per cent overall, including about 14 per cent for pluralist Islamic parties, which were linked to mass-based Islamic organizations but proclaimed their loyalty to the state's inclusive Pancasila philosophy, and 21 per cent for parties that might broadly be defined as Islamist, in so far that

they recognized Islam in their statutes or aimed to implement Islamic law.

In many regions, anti-government *reformasi* protests seamlessly gave way after Suharto fell to a new localism, meaning the tendency to prioritize local cultural, economic, and political interests and identities over national ones. Many demonstrators wanted to replace discredited local officials and voiced long-suppressed local grievances. Often, their protests were framed in terms of reassertion of local cultural identities. In some regions, there were demands that only *putra daerah* (sons of the region) should obtain political posts, government contracts, or civil service employment. This process accelerated after the government of President Habibie (1998–9) introduced regional autonomy legislation which devolved wide-ranging political powers and financial responsibility to several hundred district governments (Aspinall and Fealy 2003). In one of the world's most radical experiments in decentralization, political and economic power shifted massively to the local level.

In some places, localism took violent form. There were two main categories of violence. First, was conflict *within* local societies, between rival religious or ethnic communities. Sometimes this involved one-sided attacks on largely defenceless

Fragmentation: Indonesia's Party System

Major vote winners in the 1999 and 2004 legislative elections.

	1999 (%)	2004 (%)
Secular nationalist parties		
Golkar, the ruling party under Suharto's New Order regime.	22	22
PDI-P, Indonesia Democracy Party—Struggle, led by Megawati Soekarnoputri and heir to Soekarnoist nationalist traditions.	34	19
PD, Democrat Party, personal vehicle for president Susilo Bambang Yudhoyono.	—	7
PDS, Prosperous Peace Party, Christian party.	—	2
PKP (later PKPI), Justice and Unity Party, Golkar splinter.	1	1
PKPB, Care for the Nation Functional Party, Suharto nostalgia party.	—	2
Pluralist Islamic parties		
PKB, National Awakening Party, aligned with the main traditionalist Islamic organization, Nadhatul Ulama.	13	11
PAN, National Mandate Party, aligned with the main modernist Islamic organization, Muhammadiyah.	7	6
Islamist parties		
PPP, United Development Party, Islamic party first formed under the New Order.	11	8
PKS, Justice and Welfare Party, party of puritanical, urban intellectuals.	1	7
PBB, Moon and Star Party, hard-line, sharia-oriented party.	2	3
PBR, Star Reform Party, splinter from PPP.	—	2

Source: Author's calculations taken from Komisi Pemilihan Umum, General Elections Commission: www.kpu.go.id

minority groups. A series of mob attacks against ethnic Chinese (a group which makes up about 2 per cent of the population—the figure is disputed—but which is prominent in trade) coincided with the fall of Suharto (Purdey 2006). Violence in Kalimantan (Borneo) was directed largely against migrants from the island of Madura. Some hostile communities were more evenly matched. The worst inter-communal violence occurred in Maluku (the Moluccas), where the population was almost equally divided between Muslims and Christians, resulting in virtual civil war and approximately 5,000–6,000 deaths.

A second category of violence involved local communities confronting state authority. These conflicts mostly involved separatist movements fighting with (or being repressed by) security forces. The best-known case internationally was East Timor, which had long been a site of conflict and source of diplomatic difficulties for Indonesia. President Habibie unexpectedly allowed a UN-supervised vote on independence there in 1999, prompting the military to organize militias to terrorize the population. They caused approximately 1,500 deaths during a wave of destruction after 78.5 per cent of the population voted for independence. Violence was worse in Aceh, in northern Sumatra, where a long-running insurgency reignited after Suharto fell. For a time, the guerrillas of GAM (Free Aceh Movement) controlled much of the countryside. Between 1999 and 2005, approximately 7,200 persons were killed in the ensuing conflict and counter-insurgency operations. In Papua, the western half of the island of New Guinea, support for independence was also great among the indigenous Melanesian population, although here most independence supporters used non-violent means (Chauvel 2003).

Observers have offered many different explanations for post-Suharto disintegrative tendencies and violence. Given the variety of the processes involved and the complexity of the analyses and debates, it is possible to give only a schematic overview here. In general terms, the debates mirrored broader ones between advocates of primordialist and modernist interpretations of ethnic and nationalist conflicts.

First, some argued that violence reflected deep-seated, primordial, and even ancient identities and enmities. This view was mostly discredited among scholars (Mote and Rutherford 2001). However, it was popular among some journalists and commentators, who sometimes used the metaphor of the 'seething cauldron' to describe Indonesia. Western journalists were often fascinated with seemingly exotic or pre-modern manifestations of violence (such as head-hunting by Dayak fighters in Kalimantan: Parry 2005). A few foreign analysts suggested that these conflicts were occurring because (as one anonymous Western diplomat explained to a journalist) Indonesia was 'an artificial country held together by artificial means' during the Suharto years (Gaouette 1999). Suharto's exit had taken the lid off the cauldron.

Similar views were also held, at least implicitly, by many actors directly or indirectly involved in violence. Participants in ethnic or separatist violence invariably described their enemies in absolutist and essentialist terms. For example, Hasan Tiro, the founder of GAM, claimed that Indonesia was a fabrication designed to cover Javanese dominance and that Indonesians were a 'non-existent human species' (Tiro 1984: 68). GAM leaders believed that Indonesia's old ethnic groups were beginning to reassert themselves and that the country would inevitably disintegrate. Ironically, some in the military and national government agreed that Indonesia was fragile (though they obviously did not think it

was inherently flawed) and might collapse if they loosened political controls too much.

The second set of arguments, more dominant in the scholarly literature, held that post-Suharto violence did not result from immutable enmities or from Indonesia's 'artificiality', but stemmed instead from recent processes of economic development, social change, state formation, and repression. In particular, most analysts stressed the legacies of Suharto's authoritarian rule. For example, they argued that popular support for independence in Aceh resulted from inequitable resource exploitation in the province under Suharto (Aceh had major natural gas reserves and had been a big contributor to national income) and from the military violence used to eliminate what had initially been a tiny separatist movement there (Robinson 1998). Analysts of violence in Maluku pointed to the accumulation of tensions in that province under Suharto, caused by migration and competition between Muslims and Christians for bureaucratic positions and economic resources, in conditions in which such tensions could not be resolved by democratic means (Bertrand 2002).

Such analyses did not see Indonesia as inherently flawed, but rather looked for specific causes of violence in each case. It was invariably possible to identify grievances that had developed or accumulated under authoritarian rule. Such analyses thus viewed the Suharto regime not as having held Indonesia together in the face of intrinsic disintegrative pressures, but rather as having generated latent grievances that erupted once authoritarian rule was relaxed.

Examination of the extent and variety of post-Suharto violence makes this second group of explanations more convincing, and does not justify the 'seething cauldron' image. Overall, the death toll in post-Suharto violence (approximately 20,000 in an overall population of 200 million), while very great, was far less than in many other recent internal conflicts in the developing world. Amidst the media's concentration on places where violence was worst, it tended to be overlooked that most regions remained peaceful. The image of a country on the verge of disintegration also loses force if we remember that it was in only three provinces (out of a total of 27 in 1998) that there was significant support for independence. In some other provinces (notably Riau, Bali, and Maluku) a few intellectuals argued for independence but failed to rally popular enthusiasm.

Analysis of the three 'separatist provinces' (Aceh, Papua, and East Timor), however, requires us to qualify the view that disintegrative pressures arose only because of Suharto's authoritarianism. It is certainly true that repression under Suharto increased support for independence in each place. Narratives of local suffering at the hands of the military became central to separatist ideologies. But repression in these provinces was also a *response* to popular resistance as much as being a cause of it. Aceh, for example, was not notably more militarized than other provinces prior to the establishment of GAM in 1976. Understanding the origins of separatism requires us to extend our historical inquiry to before Suharto's rule, back to the colonial origins of Indonesia.

One distinguishing feature of each separatist province was that its mode of incorporation into the Indonesian nation-state produced a strong regional identity at least partly defined against Indonesia. East Timor was the obvious example: it had never been part of the Netherlands East Indies but was instead a Portuguese colony. Against a backdrop of cold war tensions, Suharto's army violently invaded the territory in 1975, causing great loss of life. Many East Timorese never accepted the Indonesian presence, viewing it instead as an occupying power. Papua had been ruled by the Dutch, but it also had a distinct history. The Indonesian nationalist movement had not struck deep roots there in the early twentieth century. Crucially, when Indonesia became independent in 1949, Holland retained control over Papua and began to groom a layer of local leaders for independence. Following US pressure on Holland, Papua was incorporated into Indonesia in the 1960s, but by then most politically conscious Papuans already imagined a future separate to Indonesia. Incorporation itself involved Indonesian military action and intimidation, causing lasting resentment. Aceh was different again: its population enthusiastically supported the Indonesian independence struggle in 1945–9, so much so that Aceh was the only part of their former colony which the Dutch did not dare to try to re-conquer. As a result, Aceh's leaders had unfettered control over local affairs during that period. When Indonesia became independent, they lost much of that autonomy, causing bitterness and gradual evolution of a distinct identity. GAM built on this underlying resentment when it called for Aceh's independence.

Exploring how recent separatist conflicts originated in processes of colonization and decolonization does not validate primordialist arguments that Indonesia, as a post-colonial state containing diverse ethnic groups, was congenitally flawed. On the contrary, ethnic differences alone did not motivate these conflicts. For example, the East Timorese are very similar ethno-linguistically to their neighbours in Indonesian West Timor. Rather than arising out of the mere fact of ethnic difference, separatism arose out of interactions between local populations and processes of state formation. Where those interactions gave rise to identities that were defined in opposition to what was elsewhere an over-arching Indonesian identity, they later became bases for separatist mobilization.

KEY POINTS

- Democratization unleashed fragmentation pressures, including communal conflicts and revived separatist movements in some regions.

- One set of explanations for this unrest stresses the artificiality of Indonesia due to its social heterogeneity, its colonial origins, and consequent inevitability of violence in the absence of authoritarian constraints.

- A second group of arguments blames violence on state actions, especially during Suharto's rule.

It views this period of authoritarianism not as having saved Indonesia from disintegrative pressures, but as having generated them.

- The second set of arguments is more convincing. Communal and other violence did not occur in most areas of Indonesia. In places where it did occur, it was always possible to identify specific societal grievances, usually generated by recent state behaviour.

- The roots of recent violence in the three main separatist provinces can also be traced to experiences of colonization and decolonization.

Toward Reintegration?

By about 2003, Indonesia no longer appeared to be on the verge of disintegration. The worst violence was passing: for instance, leaders of the warring communities in Maluku reached a peace agreement in February 2002. Even in Aceh, GAM leaders agreed to give up their independence goal and signed an accord with the government in August 2005.

In part, the crisis ended because violence had simply exhausted itself. But the state's own response also contributed. The crisis had prompted two contradictory policy approaches from national elites. First, it had triggered toughening of views and a return to hard-line, even militaristic, policies in some instances. This reflected the view in some elite circles, especially in the military, that Indonesian unity was fragile and should be maintained with constant vigilance. After the 'loss' of East Timor and experimentation with tolerating separatists elsewhere, from about 2001 post-Suharto governments once again suppressed separatist movements. In Papua, security forces harassed, arrested, and (in one case) assassinated pro-independence leaders, while in Aceh a full-scale military assault on rebels was launched in May 2003. Military and government leaders were adamant that such steps were needed to stop a domino effect whereby the separatist contagion would spread to other provinces. Critics argued that violent methods would fan separatist sentiment in the long run, as they had in the past. Yet the return to military solutions in the short

term ended the sense of possibility that had arisen in separatist provinces after Suharto fell. In Aceh, for example, GAM rebels abandoned independence partly because they realized their guerrilla campaign had reached an impasse. As in many countries, in Indonesia, state violence and warfare still plays a role in state-making and nation-building. Indeed, President Megawati Soekarnoputri (1999–2004), while addressing an audience in Washington, DC in late 2001, defended her approach in Aceh by comparing it to America's own civil war: 'as did Lincoln in the United States, we will defend the integrity of Indonesia no matter how long it will take' (Soekarnoputri 2001).

The return to hard-line policies was not the dominant response, however, and it does not provide the main explanation for how the crisis ended. Most of Indonesia's new leaders knew that Suharto's old centralized and authoritarian system could not be revived, and they blamed it for the crisis. Instead, they saw democratization and decentralization as the means to ensure national survival, believing such policies would empower local communities to redress their own grievances. Even in Papua and Aceh therefore, alongside military operations, the government offered concessions in the form of Special Autonomy laws (Box 20a.4). In most regions of Indonesia, democratization and the nation wide decentralization laws had the desired effect. Most local leaders

BOX 20a.4

Special Autonomy in Aceh and Papua

Key Points of the Papua Special Autonomy Law (2001) and the Government of Aceh Law (2006)

- Wide-ranging grant of powers, covering everything except foreign affairs, defence, security, judiciary, monetary and fiscal matters, and religion, which are retained by the central government.

- Both provinces retain a larger share of natural resource revenues than other provinces, including from oil and gas (80 per cent for Papua; 70 per cent for Aceh).

- Both provinces may have their own symbols, including a flag and an anthem.

- Human Rights Courts and Truth and Reconciliation Commissions.

Papua	*Aceh*
• Establishment of a Papuan People's Council, consisting of representatives of women, traditional communities, and religious groups; charged with ensuring indigenous rights are upheld.	• Application of Islamic law (*Sharia*) to Muslims in Aceh; establishes a *Sharia* court with authority over both civil and criminal matters.
• Indigenous Papuans granted certain special rights. For instance, only an indigenous Papuan may become governor.	• Establishment of a council of *ulama* (religious scholars) with special advisory powers.
• Provincial government charged with protecting customary law, land rights, and local culture.	• Independent candidates (that is, those not nominated by political parties) can run in elections for governor and district heads; formation of local political parties, to run in local elections from 2009.

Source: Author's compilation

---

no longer concerned themselves with challenging Jakarta, but instead busied themselves with local affairs.

This change does not mean that Indonesia experienced a sudden and miraculous transition to **good governance**, as some of the international agencies promoting decentralization had hoped. On the contrary, old elites adapted to the new system. In most regions **corruption** proliferated, as local leaders used state funds to enrich themselves and their supporters. But the transformation did mean that the axis of political contention, including struggles to control economic resources, shifted from the national level to the regions. Localism still flourished,

but not in ways that directly undermined the idea of Indonesia.

Although the crisis of the post-Suharto years has passed, the new dispensation raises other possibilities: not of sudden disintegration, but rather of gradual decline in national cohesion. Whatever ordinary citizens thought about the former regimes of Presidents Sukarno and Suharto, they could see that each articulated a clear set of national goals and had concrete ideas about how to achieve them. Evidence of nation-building was visible everywhere: ubiquitous mass mobilization under Sukarno; economic development, infrastructure projects, and ideological indoctrination under Suharto. A uniform national political culture seemed to be developing. Even today, there are still factors creating a sense of commonality (such as the national electronic media, especially television). But in a new era of decentralized politics, for the first time for fifty years there are also strong countervailing pressures. Indonesia seems to be becoming a patchwork of regions, in which local interests and dynamics predominate over national ones.

An example is the contest over the political role of Islam. In the 1950s, division over whether the constitution should require Muslims to observe Islamic law rent the body politic at the national level. After the fall of Suharto, Islamic parties made only token efforts to revive the national constitutional debate. Instead, by late 2006, several dozen local administrations had begun to introduce regulations that included elements of Islamic law (for example, making the Islamic dress code mandatory for women) piecemeal. Secular-oriented groups tried to oppose such initiatives nationally, but failed to gain much traction in the regions concerned.

An additional factor leading to diminution of shared national purpose is the new international economic context. In the first decades after independence, there was a strong view in Indonesia, as in many developing countries, that the state should play a major role in marshalling the country's resources to achieve national goals. State-led industrialization was the order of the day, leading to nationalization and protection of strategic industries. From the 1980s onwards, a neo-liberal orthodoxy became increasingly influential. Instead of using the state to direct and protect national economic development, governments have increasingly tried to roll back its influence and deregulate markets. Whatever the wisdom of this approach, it has been harder for national leaders to generate the national purpose and enthusiasm evoked by earlier nation-builders in the post-Suharto era. Instead,

many policies (such as removing state subsidies for fuel and other commodities, or decentralizing economic decision-making to the regions) have either generated discontent or weakened the role of the national state in the economy.

And yet, it would be rash to pass a negative judgement on the future of Indonesia's national project. For many Indonesians, the new diversity produced by democratic politics and regional autonomy does not signify loss of national cohesion, but simply readjusts a political formula that had been tilted too far in favour of uniformity. Although localism is vigorous, many factors still underpin national unity, including widely shared pride in national history and symbols. Belief that diversity is integral to Indonesian identity is itself a core element in Indonesian nationalism. Finally, certain safeguards have been built into Indonesia's new institutional framework to constrain disintegrative tendencies (for instance, to register for elections, political parties must prove that they have a broad national presence).

KEY POINTS

- The extreme post-Suharto fragmentary pressures and violence lasted for a brief period (approximately five years). Indonesia is currently undergoing reconsolidation.

- State violence played a role in overcoming this crisis, especially in ending (at least for a time) separatist challenges.

- More significant were decentralization and democratization. These policies assuaged local grievances and provided incentives to regional elites to engage in local political processes rather than challenge the central state.

- The major challenge facing Indonesia today, therefore, is not dramatic disintegration but rather gradual decline of cohesion.

Conclusion

This chapter has surveyed the crisis of national dis-integration experienced by Indonesia from the late 1990s, and discussed two sets of explanations for the crisis: those which locate the source of these problems in the country's multi-ethnic makeup and its origins as heir to an artificial colonial state, and those which instead focus on grievances caused by state action, especially under the authoritarian Suharto regime. The brief survey of the evidence in the chapter suggests that the second group of explanations is more convincing.

Indeed, it should be stressed that while the country has great ethnic and linguistic diversity, Indonesia is no more artificial than any post-colonial, or indeed any other, modern state. Modern nation-states did not arise seamlessly from pre-existing ethnic communities, but were instead produced by long processes of state- and nation-building. In most cases, these processes involved force, as well as gradual construction over generations of polit-ical institutions, standardized education, and other mechanisms for generating national cohesion.

The fragmentation pressures experienced by In-donesia from the late 1990s were similar to those experienced in many developing countries over the last two decades. For instance, ethnic and religious identity politics have in many places stepped into the vacuum created by declining popular enthusi-asm for early post-independence nation-building policies. The suddenness and scale of the crisis in Indonesia resulted from the steady build-up of social tensions during Suharto's authoritarian rule, and their sudden release with democratiza-tion. Indonesia was not inherently flawed. Instead, authoritarianism was an unsustainable method of managing the country's diversity.

GUIDE TO FURTHER READING

■ **Aspinall, E., and Fealy G. (eds.) (2003),** *Local Power and Politics in Indonesia: Democrat-ization and Decentralization* **(Singapore: Institute of Southeast Asian Affairs).** An early survey of the flowering of local politics prompted by regional autonomy.

■ Bertrand, J. (2004), *Nationalism and Ethnic Conflict in Indonesia* **(Cambridge: Cambridge University Press).** Overview of the ethnic conflicts which accompanied and followed the fall of Suharto. The author explains the grievances which motivated each conflict and links them to the broader institutional shifts associated with democratization.

■ Bresnan, J. (ed.) (2005), *Indonesia: The Great Transition.* **(Lanham, MD: Rowman & Littlefield Publishers).** A comprehensive, and generally positive, evaluation of democratization.

■ Robison, R., and Hadiz, V. R. (2004), *Reorganizing Power in Indonesia: The Politics of Oligarchy in an Age of Markets* **(London and New York: Routledge).** An account of the democratic transition, emphasizing political economy and the preservation of elite authority and privilege.

■ Tiro, H, M. (1984), *The Price of Freedom (The Unfinished Diary)* **(Information Department, National Liberation Front Acheh Sumatra, Norsborg, Sweden).**

■ Van Klinken, G. (2007), *Communal Violence and Democratization in Indonesia: Small Town Wars* **(London: Routledge).** Uses a sociological approach to explain six key episodes of post-Suharto communal violence.

WEB LINKS

● **www.insideindonesia.org** Australia-based quarterly magazine which focuses on human rights and political and environmental issues.

● **www.thejakartapost.com** Indonesia's premier daily English-language newspaper, complete with a useful search engine and archives.

● **http://cip.cornell.edu/Indonesia** Produced by Cornell University, *Indonesia* has since the late 1960s been the premier academic journal on Indonesian affairs.

ONLINE RESOURCE CENTRE

For additional material and resources, see the Online Resource Centre at:
www.oxfordtextbooks.co.uk/orc/burnell2e/

20b South Africa: From Divided Society to New Nation

ROBERT A. SCHRIRE

 Chapter Contents

- Introduction: The Historical Legacy
- Negotiations
- The New Order: From Apartheid to the Rainbow Nation
- Political Transformation and Nation-Building
- Leadership, National Identities, and the Future
- Conclusion

 Overview

If ever a country's history made it seem predestined to fail, South Africa would be such a country. From its creation in 1910 to the first democratic elections in 1994, South Africa was ruled by a white minority determined to maintain power and privileges irrespective of the costs to nation-building or other social groups. The interests of this minority were placed above those of over a dozen other ethnic and racial groups. Many discriminatory economic and political policies were implemented over several decades. In time the white regime began to meet the growing black challenge with increased ruthlessness, which frequently transcended even **apartheid** legality. Authoritarian white rule in turn created a powerful black response, increasing from the 1970s onwards. Few observers prior to 1990, then, believed in the possibility of relatively peaceful deracialization. Even fewer would have predicted that an African National Congress-controlled South Africa would be able to manage peacefully the massive historical cleavages, based upon class, ethnic, and racial interests. Yet with stunning speed, power was transferred from white to black hands. And far from collapsing, South Africa, a genuine democracy since 1994, has experienced uninterrupted economic growth and relative internal peace. This chapter explains this paradoxical outcome by exploring the historical legacy of apartheid, the nature of the armed struggle, the negotiation process, the complex question of identity, and the significant role of leadership in shaping nation-building in South Africa.

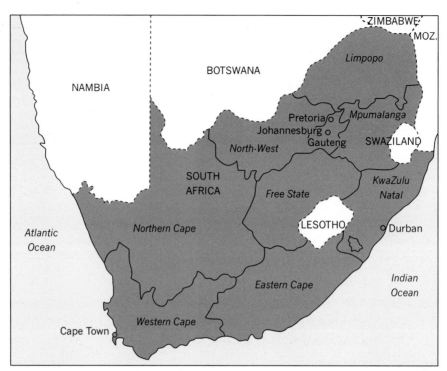

SOUTH AFRICA

Introduction: The Historical Legacy

The Union of South Africa, established in 1910, faced many problems, none more important than the issues of nationality and political rights. The Union constitution reflected a compromise between the different 'native' policies of the former colonies and in general represented a reduction in the limited black political rights exercised previously. English- and Afrikaans-speaking whites competed fiercely for power up to the decisive victory of Afrikaner nationalism in 1948. The English, as a demographic minority, tended to advocate the politics of white unity, while many Afrikaner leaders advocated the politics of exclusive Afrikaner nationalism. After 1948, the National Party (NP) representing Afrikaner nationalism was able to consolidate its political dominance, as white unity took precedence in response to growing

pressures, from both the outside world and black South Africans, accelerating after the establishment of a republic in 1961. The key dilemma—never resolved—was to create a morally acceptable political framework which did not endanger the Afrikaner's grasp of power. Meeting the political aspirations of the African majority was an intractable problem. The government's answer was the policy of grand apartheid, which constituted the African population as ten ethnic nations, each entitled to sovereign independence. Every African, irrespective of culture, birthplace, residence, or personal preferences, was assumed to be an immutable member of one of these ethnic communities. The ostensible aim of the policy was to create ten independent African nations, in which the Africans would have full citizenship rights. However, most of the

BOX 20b.1

Key Dates in South Africa's History

1652	Dutch settlement under Jan van Riebeck at the Cape.	1991	Congress for a Democratic South Africa (CODESA) begins.
1795	First British occupation at the Cape.	1992	De Klerk wins a whites-only referendum to approve negotiations with the ANC.
1836	Beginning of the Great Trek by Afrikaners into the interior.	1992	(May) CODESA 2 convenes, then breaks down over deadlock in negotiations.
1910	Union of South Africa founded, with merging of conquered Boer Republics of Transvaal and Orange Free State and the British Colonies of the Cape of Good Hope and Natal.	1993	(March) A new negotiating council convenes (November). National Council adopts Interim Constitution.
1912	African National Congress founded to resist Native Land Act.	1994	(April) South Africa's first democratic election, ANC wins large majority.
1948	Nationalist-Afrikaner Party coalition wins election on apartheid platform.		(May) Nelson Mandela inaugurated President Government of National Unity takes (GNU) office.
1960	Sharpeville massacre. State of emergency declared. ANC and PAC banned.	1995	Truth and Reconciliation Commission formed.
1976	Soweto student uprisings.	1996	(May) Constitutional Assembly adopts final SA Constitution.
1982	Period of tentative informal negotiations between the Apartheid government and ANC leaders, first in exile and then in prison, begins.	1997	National Party under F. W. De Klerk withdraws from GNU.
1984	Mass black township uprisings begin. Government declares state of emergency.	1999	South Africa's second democratic election. ANC again wins a large majority.
1989	F. W. De Klerk becomes leader of National Party.	2004	ANC wins a two-thirds majority in the third democratic election.
1990	(2 February) Nelson Mandela released from prison.	2005	New National Party disbands and many of its leaders join the ANC; Deputy President Jacob Zuma dismissed from his office under a corruption cloud.
1990	ANC and NP leaders meet to sign historic Groote Schuur Accord charting the way to negotiations.	2006	COSATU and the SACP threaten to leave the ANC tripartite alliance.

ROBERT A. SCHRIRE

homeland leaders, most notably KwaZulu's Mangosuthu Buthelezi, rejected the proposals, in part because of their normative vision of an undivided South Africa under democratic control, although some traditional leaders did accept the separatist paradigm, leading to the creation of four independent homelands.

The struggle

The African National Congress (ANC) was founded in 1912 to oppose the land acts, which were designed to ensure that most of South Africa's land resources remained permanently in white hands. Until the 1950s it was marginal to the great dramas taking place in white politics. Its strategy of seeking allies in the white, coloured, and Indian communities and especially from the ranks of the South African Communist Party (SACP) had mixed results, and caused the government to view it increasingly as an enemy of the state; repression escalated, polarizing national politics even further. The Pan Africanist Congress (PAC) split from the ANC in 1958 and fierce competition for African support ensued, including mass protests, the burning of passes that restricted movement, and attempts to force the police to engage in mass arrests, culminating in 1960 in the Sharpeville 'massacre'. Both the ANC and PAC were banned (the SACP had already been proscribed) and went underground and began to plan an armed insurrection. Nelson Mandela was chosen by the ANC to organize an armed struggle. That said, the commitment to violence was taken only with great reluctance by a largely Christian leadership, and by the early 1960s the insurrection was smashed, and Mandela and other leaders either imprisoned or in exile. Peace returned to South Africa for another decade, but the illusion was shattered in 1976 by another massacre, at Soweto, sparked in part by educational grievances. Violence and protests spread rapidly throughout the country, forcing the government to declare yet another state of emergency, which this time proved to be less effective.

In 1983 new constitutional proposals by the government unexpectedly brought massively increased politicization and anger, leading the National Party to embark on modest reform initiatives for urban Africans, coloureds, and Indians. Widely resented by the black population, the proposals nevertheless opened up political space for public debate and greater participation. The United Democratic Front (UDF), formed in August 1983 to oppose the government's constitutional proposals, was a highly significant development for several reasons. It brought together a wide range of civil society groups into the political arena, supported by the ANC in exile. Its membership and leadership were drawn from all segments of the population: white, African, coloureds, and Indian, rural and urban, middle class and poor. The UDF was an important and successful experiment in non-racial political cooperation. The new tricameral system failed to gain legitimacy despite gaining the support of a whites-only referendum.

KEY POINTS

- With the establishment of the Union of South Africa, Africans were formally excluded from access to political institutions, and Afrikaner nationalism became the dominant political force.

- The normative ideal of a democratic and non-racial South Africa remained overwhelmingly powerful to the majority of Africans.

- Armed struggle increasingly seemed inevitable, as Africans' political aspirations were continuously

thwarted by apartheid and the creation of the homeland system.

- The clear rejection of African interests by the NP government brought about a new and significant degree of cooperation between moderate and conservative African leaders.

- The NP government increasingly had to react to protests through the use of state-sponsored violence, indicative in the handling of the 1976 student uprisings.

- Growing resentment and politicization throughout the 1980s, encapsulated by the creation of UDF, created the possibility of future non-racial cooperation.

Negotiations

The factors favouring a negotiated outcome included national economic decline, white divisions, sanctions, and other global pressures, which had seriously dented growth and prosperity, increasing both unemployment and the tax burden especially on the white community. Three additional factors are of pivotal importance in understanding the transition. First, the government failed to restore 'normality' to South African society after the unrest resumed in the early 1980s. The country was far from being ungovernable, but there seemed no end in sight to the turmoil in black areas, the industrial unrest, and the implosion in black education: a genuine stalemate existed. Secondly, once the negotiations began, there were very strong forces at work, which would make a failure to reach an accommodation very costly because it would destroy the leaderships in both parties. White politics would at best have seen a move to the ultra-reactionary right and at worst a military takeover. In the ANC, failure would have ensured that the moderate leadership of Mandela and Mbeki would have been discredited. The country would have been plunged into escalating violence—consequences 'too dreadful to contemplate' in the words of former Prime Minister Vorster.

Finally and perhaps paradoxically, the negotiations, once initiated, did not take the form of white versus black. Although there were racially exclusive splinter groups, including the fragmented Afrikaner right, the key players—the ANC and the NP—fielded multiracial delegations. The ANC, in partnership with the UDF and SACP, had a significant and influential non-African component including communist leader Joe Slovo. Similarly, the NP led a heterogeneous grouping, which included conservative coloureds and African tribal leaders. Although the core of the historical conflict was the issue of political power and the consequent struggle between Afrikaner and African nationalism, the negotiations themselves involved teams of multiracial delegates seeking to determine the broad principles, which would regulate a post-apartheid South Africa.

The informal discussions initiated by the Convention for a Democratic South Africa (CODESA) began in 1991. The following year, De Klerk won a whites-only referendum on the reform policy which he interpreted as a mandate for legitimizing the final proposals. The alienation of the conservative Zulu Inkatha Freedom Party (IFP) and its leader Buthelezi, who threatened violence and the boycott of elections, was not easily defused. Despite challenges and setbacks along the way, in 1994 broad agreement was reached around the principles embodied in an interim constitution. After ad hoc arrangements were in place to ensure that the ruling NP did not use the advantages of incumbency to advance its cause, including an independent electoral commission, elections were held. All major groups and interests, including the white right and Zulu traditionalists, took part in the election. The newly elected parliament, acting as a constituent assembly, drew up a final constitution based upon the principles agreed to in the interim constitution, and in 1996 the final constitution was ratified both by the legislature and the Constitutional Court. The country's second general election in 1999 was thus the first election held in terms of the new constitution and the results followed closely those of 1994.

KEY POINTS

- Although not yet ungovernable, entrenched structural weaknesses in the South African economy, growing internal unrest, the changed regional context, and the hardening of international attitudes towards South Africa by her traditional allies resulted in a genuine stalemate.

- There was realization by the leadership on both sides that failure to reach a negotiated compromise would ensure that South Africa would face a devastatingly violent future.

- Negotiations culminated in the multi-party elections of 1994 that included participation by groups on the margin of the political spectrum, the white right, and Zulu traditionalists.

The New Order: From Apartheid to the Rainbow Nation

The emergence of a non-racial and democratic South Africa constituted a dramatic reversal of centuries of history which few had imagined possible. Perhaps the real South African miracle was not the successful negotiations but the transformation of the political discourse away from race and ethnicity. Both the dominant ANC and the NP espoused a vision for South Africa that transcended their historical race/ethnic constituencies. Although the core of ANC support came from the African population, the party was greatly influenced by the minority of coloureds and Indians and a few notable whites. Yet it is still surprising how rapidly the ideal of a non-racial and non-ethnic society captured the reform process. The initial leanings of the NP and the largely Zulu-based Inkatha Freedom Party towards a society in which ascriptive group rights were to be constitutionally entrenched were soon thrust aside. The negotiations produced, in Mandela's words, a 'normal democracy'. And Africanist proponents of an African-only state exercised even less influence on the deliberations.

South Africa is constitutionally a non-racial democracy but it has based itself upon a very liberal notion of nationality. The so-called rainbow nation has been built upon a rejection of the model of a nation conceptualized as a people united around one identity, language, and set of national symbols. To give institutional content to this vision, new institutions had to be created profoundly different from those existing in the former centralized and monocultural state. The foundation of a stable order has thus been based upon recognition both of a common nationality and of important diversities. Indeed, the motto under the National Coat of Arms is 'Diverse People Unite'. The national anthem is composed of a combination of the old Afrikaner (South African) national anthem and a traditional African unity anthem. To give expression to the demographic diversity, the country has been divided into nine provinces, which reflect the historical continuities of history and ethnicity, which although not genuinely federal, does create a power structure outside the centre. Each province is headed by a premier and may draw up its own constitution. The divisive issue of the allocation of resources between provinces has been taken out of the political arena with the creation of a technocratic Financial and Fiscal Commission, which makes decisions on the basis of fixed criteria such as population and poverty levels. The country has eleven official languages, with English the language of record. Each province may determine which languages will be used officially. The national parliament has two chambers—the popularly elected National Assembly, constituted on the basis of strict proportional representation, and the ninety-member National Council of Provinces in which each province has ten members, including *ex officio* the premiers of all the provinces or their representatives.

A critical problem has been the issue of dealing with the past. Would perpetrators of human rights abuses face legal retribution? Would victims receive reparations? The political solution devised was to pass the Promotion of National Unity and Reconciliation Act, which created the Truth and Reconciliation Commission (TRC) to deal with these issues. However, its attempts to be even-handed managed to antagonize almost all key parties including the ANC and NP. In that sense it may have succeeded by creating a consensus in favour of ignoring many of its findings! One could argue that this has liberated the polity to focus on issues of contemporary public policies. The resolution of amnesty and other contentious issues made it possible

to adopt the interim constitution which mandated a government of national unity (GNU) to include the majority party and all other parties which received at least 10 per cent of the vote. In 1994, the GNU under President Mandela worked quite harmoniously for two years until De Klerk led a divided NP out of the coalition. After the 1999 elections, in which the ANC effectively won a two-thirds majority, it kept its coalition partner the IFP in the cabinet and indeed offered its leader the deputy presidency—which was declined. For elections, the strict system of proportional representation with no threshold ensures that even minor interests that can mobilize some support can be represented in parliament. The official language policy and the various associated statutory bodies dilute the implications of the reality of English-language dominance.

KEY POINTS

- The 'real miracle' of South African transition is transformation of the political discourse from one based on race and ethnicity to one founded on a common national identity based on important diversities.

- An institutional framework was created to reflect the principle of inclusiveness, by creating a quasi-federal system, proportional representation, formal and informal power-sharing, all designed to ensure significant space and legitimacy for cultural and political minorities.

Political Transformation and Nation-Building

Had South Africa disintegrated into ethnic and racial conflicts, analysts would have had many explanations: the legacy of white domination, traditional ethnic animosities, high levels of inequality, and many others. So, why has South Africa thus far confounded so many of the critics? In multi-ethnic societies, several types of conflicts may threaten to

destroy the state. The most serious by far is directly related to the central issue of nation-building: whose country is it? What symbols and values should dominate? Indeed, who is a citizen of the state? Today the issue seems to have been decisively resolved in favour of a broad South Africanism. The two threats from Zulu and Afrikaner nationalists have been decisively defeated. There is no **clash of civilizations** in South Africa; most of the population is predominantly Christian and Western-oriented in core value systems. Politics, then, revolves largely around issues of who gets what, when, and how. The issue of citizenship is illustrative. South Africa has been an independent state for almost a century, and even before Union in 1910 many of the provinces had lengthy experiences of centralized administration, producing a large measure of acceptance of an identity that transcended in part traditional ethnicities. The vast majority of Africans and coloureds became converts to Christianity. The emergence of a capitalist economy too created powerful integrating forces. All who resided legally in the country were accepted as South Africans—at least until the social engineering of the 1960s.

Then the NP policy of apartheid and ethnic mobilization created a powerful reaction in black politics against race and ethnicity and helped legitimize the demand for a non-ethnic and non-racial South Africa. The manipulation of ethnicity by whites produced exactly the outcome it was designed to prevent—an African leadership committed to the ideals of one nation. White racism did not create black racism and the only major black party with a race-based policy, the PAC, has been all but eliminated as both an electoral and political force. The racial/ethnic composition of the ANC leadership reflects its normative commitment to a united South Africa, and the vital importance of utilizing the skills of all sectors of the population in grappling with often intractable problems. Thus following the 1994 elections, the ANC's parliamentary delegation included 170 Africans, 40 whites, 23 Indians, and 19 coloureds. After the 1999 elections, the composition was 193 Africans, 31 whites, 27 coloureds, and 15 Indians. Racial minorities are strongly represented in executive positions in the party, parliament, and the government.

A second set of factors contributing to national unity and a decline in the politics of ethnic mobilization is the political arithmetic of race and ethnicity. If the salient divisions are seen to be African (79 per cent), white (9 per cent), coloured (8.8 per cent),

and Indian (2.5 per cent), then the dominance of the African population makes it unnecessary for an African-oriented party to emphasize race for political ends. Similarly, parties with traditional support bases in the white, coloured, and Indian communities have a strong incentive to try to attract African support if they wish to play a major role in national politics. If, however, language and ethnicity are seen as constituting the prime elements of political identity, as the old NP used proudly to proclaim when it described South Africa as a nation of minorities, then the political arithmetic also contributes to nation-building. No political party with national aspirations can build a powerful constituency by mobilizing ethnicity, as the statistics in Table 20b.1 confirm.

The dynamics of the political economy reinforce the demographic implications. The core of South Africa's industrial wealth lies in the Gauteng Province, which includes Johannesburg, the largest city, and Pretoria, the executive capital. This area has the largest concentration of wealth and second largest population, and is the most ethnically mixed. The rise of large urban centres from the late

Table 20b.1 South African linguistic groups, 2001

	Number (m.)	%
Zulu	10.7	23.8
Xhosa	7.9	17.6
Afrikaans[a]	6.0	13.6
Sepedi	4.2	9.4
English	3.7	8.2
Tswana	3.7	8.2
Sesotho	3.6	7.4
Tsonga	2.0	4.4
Swazi	1.2	2.7
Venda	1.0	2.3
Ndebele	0.7	1.6

[a]The most important components are 2.9 m coloured people and 2.6 m whites.

nineteenth century weakened the ethnic allegiances of the new urban migrants and for the first time created a significant non-ethnic community. The economic heart of the country is thus national and has played an important role in integrating the country, not least through channelling revenues to the other provinces, especially the impoverished rural homelands. The Western Cape, the second wealthiest region, similarly has no dominant ethnic community, with large populations of whites, coloureds, and Xhosas.

Race and inequality

Although the most important aspect of nation-building is the presence or absence of competing nationalisms in a single territory, the relationship between ascriptive groups is also significant. Historically, race and class coincided to a significant degree and, of course, this was no accident but reflected deliberate colonial and white policies over many centuries. The claim that South Africa was divided into two nations—a poor black and an affluent white nation—rang true up to the end of the 1980s. However, this historical relationship is now being undermined through public policy especially, as ANC leaders recognized the urgent need to move away from a racialized economy. Labour legislation, increased social expenditures, the deracialization of educational institutions, affirmative action especially in the public sector, and black empowerment policies have all contributed. As a consequence, there are now three nations: a wealthy white, a wealthy black, and an impoverished black nation. Although the poor constitute about half of the total, what is politically important is that the size of the wealthy black and white groups are about equal and trends confirm that black wealth will in time overtake white wealth. Race and class are becoming delinked.

However, the critical problem of a large black underclass remains, which the upward mobility of privileged blacks does not resolve. Indeed, inequality within the black community, including African,

has increased dramatically. For example, whereas in 1975 the top 20 per cent of African households income was eight times higher than the bottom 40 per cent, this had increased to thirty-one times higher in 1996, and today may be forty times as great. Meanwhile, vast inequalities between whites and Africans continue to exist: in 1995 whites earned more than seven times African incomes and five times coloured incomes, a reality which is unlikely to have changed significantly. A major cause of inequality is unemployment: at the beginning of 2003, 37 per cent of Africans, 22 per cent of coloureds, and only 7 per cent of whites were officially unemployed.

These inequalities produce two sets of political problems. Policy measures such as affirmative action and black empowerment risk alienating whites and provoking emigration and the export of capital. Given the inevitably slow rate of change, black frustration could express itself in mass protests, violence, and the growth of support for populist and radical parties and movements.

KEY POINTS

- The history of the South African state, the political arithmetic of race and ethnicity, and the structure of South Africa's political economy all help explain why there is neither a public demand for separate nationalities nor a set of elite-driven political strategies based upon ethnic/race mobilization.

- Historically, race and class have coincided in South Africa, dividing it into two nations. The emergence today of a rapidly expanding black middle class undermines this conception and is delinking race and inequality.

- Strategies to address historical inequalities have the potential to frustrate both blacks and whites and could ultimately threaten nation-building and political stability.

- A powerful ANC is a force for reconciliation and nationhood, yet this very power constitutes a potential threat to a genuine democratic order should its power be threatened.

ROBERT A. SCHRIRE

Leadership, National Identities, and the Future

South Africa has developed a remarkable tradition since 1989 of resolving apparently intractable problems through often tough negotiations. Part of the explanation lies in a mix of both history and personalities, which produced such remarkable leaders as Mandela, Oliver Tambo, and De Klerk.

Mandela took office with the recognition that his advanced years made a one-term presidency probable. He made as his central mission the reconciliation between the former oppressors and the newly liberated. His larger-than-life personality and his message of one nation with many cultures gave the new democracy an encouraging beginning.

Mandela's successor, Thabo Mbeki, has faced a more difficult task. If symbolism could inspire the first democratic government, the second administration had to deliver. Mbeki himself, and the ANC in general, remain wedded to the Mandela paradigm of the rainbow nation and Mbeki has repeatedly maintained that all who live in South Africa have a claim to being Africans. The ruling party remains wedded to the ideal of inclusivity. Personalities alone cannot explain the quality of leadership. Mandela and Mbeki came into power at a very favourable historical juncture. The implosion of Marxism and the failures of grand apartheid heralded the final discrediting of social engineering and macro planning. The lesson from elsewhere in post-colonial Africa was that ambitious state-led projects to create nations by destroying indigenous customs and traditions were doomed to failure. Key ANC leaders spent many years in exile and personally witnessed such failures.

BOX 20b.2

The Zuma Saga

1997	Elected Deputy President of the ANC.
1999	Appointed by President Mbeki to the post of Deputy President of South Africa.
2001	Investigated by the state for possible corrupt involvement in a major arms deal.
2005	Financial adviser and close friend Schabir Shaik found guilty of 'a generally corrupt relationship' with Zuma. Mbeki fires Zuma from his government but not party position. Zuma charged with corruption. Turmoil in the ANC over the issue of presidential succession, with the ANC Youth League and COSATU strongly supporting Zuma for the presidency.
2006	Zuma charged with rape but found not guilty. Charges of corruption dropped after a judge rejects the state's request for a postponement of the trial. The Supreme Court of Appeal unanimously upholds Shaik's conviction on all key counts. Growing polarization within the ANC, with many Zulu traditionalists joining with the left to claim that Zuma is a victim of a plot. State to decide whether to recharge Zuma.

In addition, the magnitude of the challenges of poverty, inequality, and HIV/AIDS was almost overwhelming. In a world of financial globalization and Western dominance, the new rules of the economic game are dominated by the imperative to encourage multinational corporations to invest in South Africa. South Africa's elites recognized very quickly that the absence of rapid economic development would doom the country to poverty and social unrest. Government leaders have thus frequently been forced to repress their own personal prejudices and racial/ethnic attitudes in order not to alienate important domestic and foreign economic players.

On almost every major issue with cultural implications, the government has compromised rather than asserted its authority, in areas from minority rights of Afrikaners to traditional authorities and ethnic symbols. Of course, an ANC that is not threatened from the left or from Africanist forces can afford to be magnanimous. It has had the political space to adopt nation-building policies. It is impossible to predict how it would react to a genuine threat to its power base.

It is not inevitable that the South African miracle will continue. But the historical factors discussed above have created a common web of identities in which a transcendent South African identity is prominent. Survey research confirms that although most South Africans have multiple identities, more than nine out of ten Africans are nonetheless proud to be called South Africans.

KEY POINTS

- Individual leadership has played a significant role in shaping the conception of a non-racial and democratic South Africa.

- The process of nation-building is ongoing.

Conclusion

In contemporary South Africa, no important political party is asking the critically destructive question 'whose country is this?' The struggle cry 'one settler, one bullet' has disappeared from the debate. Historically the two major threats to nation-building have come from the Afrikaner right and Zulu traditionalists. The former has almost totally disintegrated despite occasional posturing by a few. Zulu alienation could yet pose a problem.

Class and nationality conflicts are not the same. There is clearly a possibility of a black populist party emerging from the poorest sections of the population. But although it might contain anti-white elements, it would be unlikely to challenge the core identity of the South African nation. However, most observers believe that the future challenge to the ANC will come from the class-oriented trade union movement under the banner of the Congress of Trade Unions (COSATU) and the SACP.

The existing opposition parties are widely viewed as historically tainted by their history under apartheid. The Democratic Alliance, the official parliamentary opposition, is perceived to be a 'white' party despite its significant coloured support. The IFP is seen as a party of Zulu traditionalists. Both parties have found it difficult to reinvent themselves in order to win black support. New parties such as the Independent Democrats have found it difficult to access resources and create an attractive image as a viable alternative to the ANC.

However, politics is always dynamic as interests and leaders change. The broad church which is the ANC is already under increased pressure as class and ethnic tensions grow. A new ANC leader may

ROBERT A. SCHRIRE

be able to reduce these tensions which have been aggravated by the leadership succession race. However, it is inevitable that the alliance will fragment, and this may happen sooner than most analysts predict.

South Africa's political leadership reflects the sophistication of the country's large First World economic and administrative systems. A recognition of the mutual dependency of all ethnic and racial communities and its importance is perhaps the most powerful factor shaping elite policies and attitudes. But South Africa continues to face major problems of race and class. Indeed, almost all problems—from HIV to job creation—are exacerbated by high levels of inequality. The high levels of unemployment have also produced an explosion in crime, especially violent crimes such as armed robbery. This threatens all sectors of society, especially the poor. These unresolved issues could yet destroy growth prospects by discouraging investment. The lack of a strong parliamentary opposition poses a real danger to the quality of democracy and creates both the temptation and the opportunity for corruption and authoritarianism in the ruling party. This danger has been compounded by the centralizing tendencies of the Mbeki presidency where to an increasing extent policy and personnel decisions are now concentrated. Many of the conflicts over former deputy president Zuma and the future ANC leadership are a direct consequence of this centralization (see Box 20b.2). A weak parliamentary opposition contributes to the critical importance of policy conflicts and leadership choices within the ruling party. However, it could be argued that nation-building and democracy remain fragile and robust politics could tear the nation apart. As Mandela frequently claimed, popular black opinion was frequently a good deal less moderate on economic and racial issues than the more broad-based ANC leadership. However, these challenges should not be confused with the issue of nation-building. Whatever other problems South Africa faces, there is little debate over the definition of citizenship. The future debate will be over how this citizenship is to be given meaning.

? QUESTIONS

1 How important is the distinction between class and nationality conflicts with regards to nation-building in South Africa?

2 What key realities forced the ANC and the NP to begin the negotiation process?

3 What factors contributed to the decline of black versus white conflict during the transition to a non-racial democracy in South Africa?

4 How important in relative terms were internal and external factors in contributing to the end of apartheid in South Africa?

5 What are the key features of nation-building in South Africa?

6 How does the nature of the democratic system in post-apartheid South Africa relate to the principles of nation-building?

7 What are the implications of class and race coinciding in South Africa for the future of nation-building?

8 Name the key factors that have ensured that ethnic identity has not been the primary tool for mobilizing popular support in post-apartheid South Africa.

9 Discuss how South Africa's handling of the vexed question of national identity has implications for other entrenched conflicts, such as those in the Middle East.

10   Is the alliance between the ruling ANC and its partners COSATU and the SACP an obstacle to the consolidation of democracy?

11   Can the struggle for power between individuals such as Xhosa-speaking Thabo Mbeki and Zulu-speaking Jacob Zuma ignite broader ethnic conflicts?

12   What are the prospects for the emergence of a strong non-racial opposition party?

13   Can South African democracy continue to survive in a region dominated by turmoil, conflict, and poverty?

 ## GUIDE TO FURTHER READING

■ Butler, A. (2004), *Contemporary South African Politics* (Basingstoke: Palgrave). An introduction to emerging patterns of economic, social, and political life in South Africa with reference also to its place in the regional and wider environment.

■ Daniel, J., Southall, R., and Lutchman, J. (eds.) (2005), *State of the Nation: South Africa 2004–5* (Cape Town: HSRC Press).

■ Giliomee, H., and Schlemmer, L. (1989), *From Apartheid to Nation Building* (Cape Town: Oxford University Press). Analysis of the roots of apartheid and of the possibilities for conflict-resolution in South Africa as seen from the vantage point of the late 1980s, before the system reached the point of collapse.

■ Ishikawa, K. (1999), *Nation Building and Development Assistance in Africa: Different but Equal?* (New York: St Martin's Press).

■ Lodge, T. (2003), *Politics in South Africa: From Mandela to Mbeki* (Cape Town: David Philip, 2002 and Bloomington, Ind.: Indiana University Press). Thirteen detailed essays on contemporary politics starting with the Mandela presidency.

■ Simkins, C. (1988), *The Prisoners of Tradition and the Politics of Nation Building* (Johannesburg: South African Institute of Race Relations).

■ Southall, R. (ed.) (2001), *Opposition and Democracy in South Africa* (London: Frank Cass). A substantial collection on the political parties and party system—past, present, and future prospects.

■ Terreblanche, S. (2004), *A History of Inequality in South Africa 1652–2002* (Pietermaritzburg: University of Natal Press). Historical examination of the economic exploitation of the indigenous peoples by settler groups. Argues that society in South Africa is more unequal now than ever, with social democracy offering a more appropriate solution than 'neo-liberal democratic capitalism'.

■ Venter, A., and Landsberg, C. (2006), *Government and Politics in the New South Africa* (Pretoria: Van Schaik).

 ## WEB LINKS

● www.anc.org.za   The website of the African National Congress.

● www.elections.org.za   The website of the South African Independent Electoral Commission.

- **www.gov.za** The official website of the South African government.

- **www.hsrc.ac.za** The site of the Human Sciences Research Council, Pretoria.

- **www.idasa.org.za** The Institute for Democracy in South Africa (Cape Town), an independent, non-profit, public interest organization.

- **www.iol.co.za** Independent Online, a South African news website.

- **www.mg.co.za** The *Mail* and *Guardian* online.

- **www.nedlac.org.za** The National Economic Development and Labour Council—'South Africa's primary institute for social dialogue'.

- **www.parliament.gov.za** The site of the Parliament of South Africa.

- **www.polity.org.za** Policy and Law Online News.

 ONLINE RESOURCE CENTRE

For additional material and resources, see the Online Resource Centre at:
www.oxfordtextbooks.co.uk/orc/burnell2e/

21 Civil Society: Active or Passive?

21a India: Associational Life and its Discontents

ROB JENKINS

 Chapter Contents

- Introduction
- Size and Composition of India's Civil Society
- State Fostering of Civil Society
- Civil Society and the Promotion of Better Governance
- Conclusion

Overview

This chapter examines civil society in the 'world's largest democracy'. Unlike most developing countries, India has maintained a democratic political system since emerging from colonial rule—a feat often attributed to the vibrancy of its civil society. After outlining some of the salient features of India's recent political history, this chapter examines: (1) controversies surrounding the size and composition of India's civil society; (2) issues relating to regional variations in the nature of associational life; (3) the question of whether states can help to spur the development of civil society; and (4) problems in understanding the contribution of civil society to improved governance, including consideration of civil society's darker side.

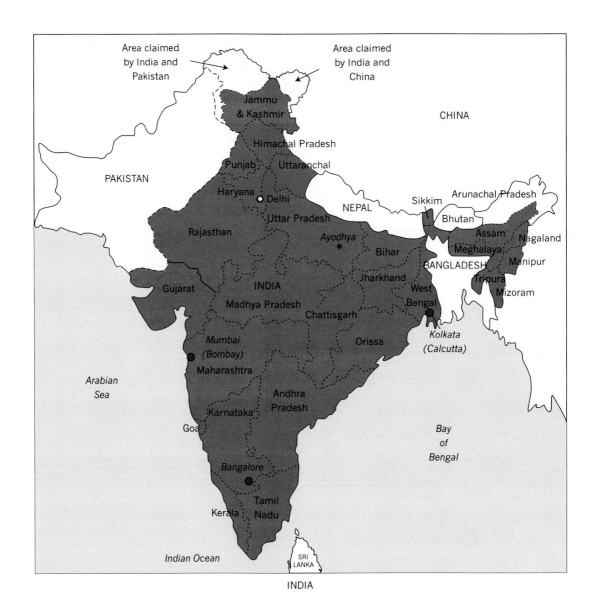

INDIA

Introduction

The Indian National Congress, which led the struggle for independence from British rule, was formed in 1885 by a group of English-educated lawyers and professionals. It was in the 1920s, under the leadership of Mohandas K. Gandhi, that 'Congress' became a mass movement capable of pressing the colonial authorities for greater self-rule. This was also the period when, largely through Congress-related efforts, India's **civil society** began to flourish. The process was aided by the mobilizing efforts associated with the pre-independence elections to legislative councils. India's constitution of 1950 outlined the functions of its political institutions, including the division of powers between the central and provincial tiers of its federal system. The constitution contained the usual liberal protections that make civil society possible (freedom of speech, of assembly, and so forth). But India's civil society was also shaped by other legal provisions, such as the 'reservation' of roughly one-fifth of parliamentary constituencies for members of the so-called Scheduled Castes and Scheduled Tribes. Within the Hindu caste system, a complex and ancient, though evolving, system of social stratification in which people's caste status is determined at birth, Scheduled Castes (now often referred to as Dalits) were marginalized and regarded as almost subhuman 'untouchables'. The mainly forest-dwelling Scheduled Tribes were similarly regarded as beyond the pale of civilized life.

BOX 21a.1

Key Dates in the History of Independent India

1947	'Partition' of colonial India creates two independent states, India and Pakistan; more than a million people killed in accompanying Hindu–Muslim riots; Jawaharlal Nehru (of the Indian National Congress) becomes first Prime Minister.	1984	Mrs Gandhi assassinated by Sikh bodyguards; her son, Rajiv, becomes Prime Minister.
		1991	Rajiv Gandhi assassinated by Sri Lankan Tamil separatists; new Congress government of P. V. Narasimha Rao initiates economic liberalization programme.
1950	Constitution ratified, confirming India as federal, democratic, secular, and committed to social justice.		
1967	Fourth General Election: under Prime Minister Indira Gandhi Congress loses power in several states.	1992	Destruction of Babri Mosque by Hindu nationalist militants.
1975–9	Mrs Gandhi's national 'Emergency' (1975–7); widespread protest action leads to electoral defeat for Mrs Gandhi (1977) and India's first non-Congress central government (1977–9).	1998	BJP assumes national power (in coalition); following year, BJP receives fresh electoral mandate (also in coalition).
		2002–3	After a train carrying Hindus is burned, thousands of Muslims are killed in Gujarat, with suspected state complicity.
		2004	Voters replace BJP-led coalition government with coalition headed by Congress.

Congress dominated the first twenty years of post-Independence politics. Its stranglehold over state-level (i.e. provincial) power was broken only at the 1967 general elections. Another decade elapsed before Congress first lost power at the national level in the 1977 general elections. By the late 1980s, not only was unchallenged Congress dominance a thing of the past; so was control over electoral politics by the richer, more powerful, and better-educated groups in the Hindu social order—the so-called upper castes. Increasingly, parties appealed to members of the lower castes, particularly those just above the Scheduled Castes in the hierarchy, often recruiting a greater number of candidates from these communities. Parties constructed around lower-caste identity also emerged. From the late 1980s, regional parties—those confined mainly to a single state—began increasing their share of the vote.

To these trends, the 1990s added two others of great significance. First was the ascendancy of the Hindu nationalist Bharatiya Janata Party (BJP). The BJP's primary pledges were to tear down the Babri Mosque in the north Indian town of Ayodhya (accomplished by BJP-affiliated militants in 1992), and to bring religious minorities under a uniform civil code. The BJP began the 1990s as a pariah party with which almost no other mainstream grouping would ally; by 1998 it was leading the national coalition government (although a Congress-dominated alliance replaced it in 2004). The BJP was aided by the 'regionalization' of party politics, through which single-state parties emerged as significant electoral players. In several states, regional parties were happy to ally with the BJP in order to defeat their long-time local rival—the Congress. The BJP—which polling data have consistently shown as more popular among richer and higher-caste voters—also benefited from a backlash against the political assertiveness of traditionally subordinated lower-caste groups.

Second was the shift from a state-dominated economic policy framework to one giving greater scope to market signals. The programme of economic liberalization undertaken by a Congress government in 1991, but continued by successive governments from the left and the right, has unfolded much more gradually than similar reforms in other developing countries. But while much controversy remains concerning the impact of India's reforms, particularly on the poor, by the twenty-first century India's role in the world economy (and in international economic diplomacy) had clearly increased.

KEY POINTS

- India's civil society first emerged with nationalist and electoral mobilization by Congress.

- Congress dominance was increasingly challenged from the late 1960s.

- The BJP's rise during the 1990s coincided with the regionalization of party politics.

- Since 1991 there has been significant economic liberalization.

Size and Composition of India's Civil Society

Whatever its shortcomings, India's democratic system is well known as a site of lively political contestation, with all manner of civic groups endlessly aligning and realigning with one another on every conceivable issue—from affirmative action provisions to nuclear policy. Even during periods of democratic institutional decay, observers (within and outside India) have always trusted India's vast and varied civil society to take up some of the slack (Kothari 1984).

It may therefore seem surprising that considerable controversy has recently surfaced over whether India's civil society is so impressively diverse and prolific after all. In *Democracy Without Associations*, Chhibber (1999) up-ended conventional wisdom, arguing that India's civil society was actually small and insubstantial. The dearth of civic associations, Chhibber maintained, caused India's political parties to mobilize people on the basis of caste, sect, ethnicity, or linguistic group. In a vicious circle, politicization of these ascriptive identities—groupings to which people belong by birth, rather than by choice—further shrank the space available for non-partisan civil society.

The role of ascriptive identity

These claims drew intense criticism. Particularly targeted was Chhibber's apparent insistence that 'informal' associations—those without office-bearers or codified rules—did not qualify for inclusion within a narrow definition of civil society. There is a long-standing argument over whether ethnicity-based organizations—such as caste associations, religious brotherhoods, and groups that seek to politicize linguistic identity—should be considered part of Indian civil society. But Chhibber's critics felt he had gone too far in the restrictive direction. One otherwise positive reviewer asked: 'is focusing on formal associations a reasonable indicator of the presence of solidarities between the family and the state?' (Sethi 1999: 94). In another review, the co-author of a key 1960s text that challenged the assumption that organizations had to be either modern or traditional (Rudolph and Rudolph 1967), argued that Chhibber was defining civil society too narrowly: 'Caste associations are anomalous; they are intentional associations, hybrids that combine voluntary with ascriptive characteristics' (Rudolph 2003).

These associations exemplify 'the modernity of tradition': in order to advance the interests of traditional caste groups, they sought access to modern means of social mobility and political influence.

In north India, caste associations representing Jat community groups did so by establishing scholarship programmes and student hostels, promoting internal reforms of the community's social practices (particularly around gender relations), and demanding representation in government service. Jat and other caste associations sometimes endorse candidates or parties at election time. But even when they do not, they are engaged in modern politics. In fact, contesting elections can alter the structure and meaning of caste itself—modernizing it, one could say. For instance, the geographical and social boundaries of a caste often broaden considerably as associations seek to increase their numbers, the currency of electoral democracy. Divisions within the Maratha 'caste cluster' in western India are papered over to create a more encompassing political identity (Lele 1990).

Rudolph's main point, however, concerned the broader characterization of India's civil society: '[i]f caste associations, demand groups, issue and movement politics, and nongovernment organisations are taken into account, India could be "read" as having a pervasive and extraordinarily active associational life, perhaps one of the most participatory in the world' (Rudolph 2003). Even if Chhibber's critics are largely right on the question of civil society's vibrancy—their case looks extremely strong on certain methodological points—Chhibber has still usefully indicated places where civil society's size or importance has been overstated, or it is looking frayed around the edges. Foreigners encountering elements of India's civil society tend to be impressed by the absolute numbers of associations, and the amount of noise they generate in English-language media, forgetting how unimpressive these numbers are given India's huge population. Take the trade union sector. Organized labour only exists in the outermost layer of Indian economic activity. Three per cent is commonly cited as the proportion of the population that belongs to a union. And yet, even here caution is warranted. Many labour organizations are unregistered, and though this means they are less capable of obtaining full legal recognition, it also means that there may be more associational activity taking place in various hidden parts of India's vast hinterland than the statistics indicate.

As for civil society's frayed edges, Varshney (2004), among others, observes that, whatever its merits, India's civil society may be living on borrowed time. Many associations exist in theory, but are shells of their former selves, lacking organizational substance. In some regions, the better part of local civil society consists of associations founded during the movement for independence. This is an institutional inheritance from an earlier era of organization-building. It consists of many functional organizations affiliated with the Congress movement—women's leagues, student federations, and so forth, not to mention cooperatives of various sorts, many of which are highly compromised by government interference.

On the other hand, civic associations representing social groups that have traditionally been discriminated against have continued to proliferate. For instance, organizations representing India's so-called tribal communities—traditionally forest-dwelling or nomadic groups—exist throughout India, and in some cases have been crucial in creating a sense of shared identity among people that are widely dispersed or who share certain social attributes but otherwise have not been inclined to join together in pursuit of common aims. One reason why tribals have recently become more organized is that many have been targeted by Hindu nationalist groups, who see tribals as susceptible to conversion by Christian missionaries. The extent of tribal conversion has been wildly overstated by Hindu nationalist groups—and the notion of converting tribals 'back' to a Hindu identity that they probably never possessed originally has made this question even more controversial. The point here, however, is that the civic organizing by one identity group (Hindu nationalists) has generated a substantial organizational response of another such group (tribals seeking to resist political exploitation). This is a prominent dynamic throughout India, helping to account for the almost continuous reinvention of the civic associational realm.

Civic associations based on other subaltern, or low-status, identities also regularly emerge. This is largely due to the constantly changing rules governing the affirmative-action programmes mentioned earlier. These programmes not only reserve seats in India's legislatures (federal and state-level), but also provide quotas in public-sector employment and educational activities to groups officially designated by government bodies as having been severely disadvantaged by traditional social attitudes. These include not only tribals and scheduled castes, but also members of the so-called Other Backward Classes, or OBCs, Hindu groups less deprived than the Scheduled Castes but still deemed deserving of state action. The issue of affirmative action has raised many intractable questions. Which caste categories are deserving enough to qualify for special treatment? Which localized groups actually can be included within these administratively defined caste categories? Which kinds of benefits should they be accorded—just government jobs, or should all publicly aided educational institutions be covered? How large should the overall quota for disadvantaged communities be? And should the more prosperous among the OBCs be excluded? Because these questions inevitably generate enormous political controversy, social entrepreneurs from potentially affected communities seek to increase their influence by forming new associations, often based around novel identities, covering a wider (or narrower) geographic area. Accordingly, the civil society landscape is constantly shifting as new groups emerge to either take advantage of new administrative provisions, or demand that the social constituencies they purport to represent be recognized and permitted similar benefits.

Regional variations in civil society

In addition, both the strength and effectiveness of civil society vary by state. The southern state of Kerala, for instance, is a land of civic bounty: there one can find reading clubs, cinema clubs, drama clubs, alongside more familiar actors such as trade unions (Kerala's strong Marxist political tradition has ensured this), business associations, and such. In the eastern state of Orissa, conversely, civil society is extremely weak, in some areas non-existent.

The memberships (and conceptual horizons) of most associations rarely extend beyond state borders. Katzenstein *et al.* (2001: 245) argue that 'issue-based Indian social movements have remained substantially limited to the regions within which they operate ... even when the issues and interests they represent are national in their relevance'. There are good reasons for even functional associations (let alone 'movement' groups) to confine their work within the boundaries of their 'home' state. First, the sheer size of most states—in population terms alone—usually suffices to occupy the efforts of civic groups that deal intensively with public authorities. Second, in India's federal system states form a powerful tier of government. State governments make many important policy decisions, particularly in the era of economic liberalization. Third, most Indian parties are geared to the state level: they would prefer control over a state government to even the most senior national cabinet position, short of the prime ministership. Fourth, since India's federal system is organized along linguistic lines, there are natural barriers to the spread of many associational forms. Kerala's literature societies, for instance, find it hard to break out of their provincial boundaries. Associated cultural differences between states (not least the existence of distinct regional caste systems) further reinforce the federally segmented nature of associational life. Despite all these constraints, civil society's largely state-specific nature is undergoing profound change: the proliferation of national and international media (including the internet) has made national organizing possible for an increasing number of associations.

The difficulty of pinning down the implications of these trends for the development of civil society is exemplified by the ambiguous impact of the regionalization of Indian politics. Because political contestation is increasingly between single-state parties, one might expect a corresponding regionalization of civil society. There is some evidence of this: state-level units of national trade union federations are increasingly going their own way—or at least acting more autonomously (vis-à-vis their national leaderships) than previously. However, over the past decade, these same regional parties have joined with national parties of left and right to form coalition governments in New Delhi. This makes them key actors on the national political stage. Again, it would not be surprising to find civil society mirroring this crucial political trend, with national-level ministers from, say, Andhra Pradesh's Telugu Desam Party providing a much-needed point of access to central government agencies for Andhra Pradesh-based civic groups. Some anecdotal evidence supports this claim, but it requires systematic empirical study. If true, such a trend would represent a major shift from past practice. The state-wise organization of India's civil society has often impeded the emergence of effective national lobbies on controversial policy matters—notably agriculture. In the 1980s, an alliance formed among farmers' organizations from Karnataka, Maharashtra, and Uttar Pradesh collapsed when each group became focused on events in its respective home state.

KEY POINTS

- The reputed vibrancy of India's civil society has recently been questioned.

- One issue is whether associations based on ascriptive identity should count as part of civil society.

- Many of the civil society organizations formed during the independence movement are moribund.

- India's federal system means that the nature and effectiveness of civil society varies between states, which also tends to impede activism across state boundaries.

State Fostering of Civil Society

While state-wise variations in the texture of civil society clearly exist, the *reasons* for these differences are much debated. For instance, while some attribute Kerala's diversified civil society to its high literacy rate, the nature of the Keralan state's interaction with civil society can also be seen to breed further civic associationalism. The People's Plan Campaign (PPC), a radical programme of democratic decentralization, was established by the state's Left Democratic Front coalition in the mid-1990s. This new system of political representation (and development planning) did not just create more state bureaucracy; it also catalysed a burgeoning of civil society. Whether entities such as user committees, women's groups, and neighbourhood groups—voluntary associations that under the People's Plan *had* to be formed in order to obtain certain state benefits—qualify as bona fide manifestations of civil society is another longstanding debate. Clearly, many such associations do spring up merely to obtain a specific benefit, and have no substantive influence over state functioning. Indeed, many get 'captured' by syndicates of 'contractors', the politically connected people—sometimes politicians themselves—who obtain contracts for development works. But evidently at least some of Kerala's state-fostered associations have sought improvements in systems of governance (Isaac 2000).

Readers may be surprised that it is considered legitimate in India for state policy to be explicitly geared towards creating civil society groups; the two sides of the state–civic divide are usually conceived of as autonomous and separate. But two considerations make this less unusual. First, as noted, India's nationalist movement was a hothouse of association-forming activism. This introduced into India's liberal political culture the idea that civil society need not spring up organically but could be fostered, whether by parties or state (Congress, institutionally speaking, straddled the two). Second is the influence of aid agencies, accustomed, from working in countries where the public sphere is less fertile than in India, to funding programmes deliberately designed to create civil society organizations that could improve accountability (Jenkins 2001).

> **KEY POINTS**
>
> - One reason for variation between states is the role of state governments in fostering civil society.
>
> - Opinions differ on whether state-fostered associations should qualify for inclusion within civil society.

Civil Society and the Promotion of Better Governance

Despite these hopes, the Indian case demonstrates that civil society's role in promoting better governance is ambiguous at best, as demonstrated by considering civil society groups opposed to corruption and communal violence.

Chandhoke (2003: 184) argues that 'legal and bureaucratic languages ... even as they penetrate civil society, are embedded in the power of the state'. The language, and indeed practice, of legal-bureaucratic rationality has been increasingly taken up by certain civil-society actors in India. It has long been the operating idiom of the professionalized sector of civil society—for instance, NGOs and policy advocates in obscure areas of technical competence—but only during the past decade has it been embraced by the 'mass movement' sector of civil society.

The rise of public-interest litigation in India has arguably triggered an interest by social movements in adopting, almost mimicking, legal processes. This has taken the form of procedurally complex public hearings—the approach taken by Mazdoor Kisan Shakti Sangathan (MKSS), detailed below, is but one version. People's hearings are held where voluntary groups feel compelled to substitute for authorities that fail to provide information or consult with citizens, especially on controversial infrastructure projects deemed likely to have damaging environmental impacts, such as the Enron power project in Maharashtra. The logistics of collecting evidence, both for one-off civil society-led hearings and for the researching of *faux*-official 'status reports' on incidents of police violence, are formidable. They represent a 'legalization' of social action. Instead of demanding an inquiry, these civic groups conduct inquiries themselves, and if sufficiently successful in conveying their evidence to a larger constituency, can be in a strong position to demand inclusion in state investigations.

Civil society activism geared towards combating corruption tends to produce organizational hybrids, in so far as they expand beyond their conventional roles. Thus, rather than merely mobilizing voters *during* elections, and pressing governments to live up to their campaign promises *between* elections—that is, providing vertical accountability—many civic associations have insinuated themselves into horizontal channels of accountability, which traditionally involve state agencies (auditors, ombudsmen, judiciaries) monitoring other

branches of the state (executive ministries, parastatal organizations) (Goetz and Jenkins 2004).

Based in the state of Rajasthan, the MKSS, or Workers' and Farmers' Power Organization, embodies this trend. The MKSS immediately presents the question of categorization. Is it a movement, as its leaders claim? Ironically, this claim is both bolstered and undermined by the MKSS's participation in the National Alliance of People's Movements (NAPM)—a 'movement' group, as its name suggests, but also an increasingly organized force in mainstream, institutionalized Indian politics. Is the MKSS a union? The 'Worker' part refers to day labourers on employment-creation schemes, so it qualifies in one sense, but does not engage in the kind of collective bargaining conventionally recognized as trade unionism. Is it a party? Not really, but it has run, sometimes successfully, a few candidates in village elections.

However it is classified, the MKSS's great innovation has been to use financial information from government documents as the catalyst for a participatory auditing exercise. This involves ordinary villagers cross-checking information from official files against what has actually been constructed by public works programmes on the ground. Workers on employment schemes are asked how much they were actually paid, a sum almost always less than what official financial records show. By exposing these discrepancies, in public, and based on people's own energies and testimonies, some corrupt officials and local notables have been forced to apologize and return stolen funds—major, if isolated, victories. A minor local deterrent effect has been felt (Jenkins and Goetz 1999).

But the odds against long-term impact are huge. This may be partly why the MKSS has branched out into at least two other areas of work. First, it has made use of new rules requiring candidates to declare their financial assets and whether they have criminal records. During state-level elections in 2003, this information was publicized in a form accessible to voters (Khera 2004). Second, the MKSS has participated in public-interest litigation against government agencies that have failed to use public grain stocks to alleviate famine in various parts of India. This has involved monitoring activities in coordination with commissioners appointed by the Supreme Court to obtain evidence of government compliance and non-compliance. Such state–civil society partnerships are often criticized for neutralizing civil society. But in this case there appears to be a genuine difference in the *quality* of the partnership: the litigants, MKSS among them, are engaged as active demanders of accountability, rather than as subcontractors delivering public services.

Communal relations is another area where lines between traditional and modern, and between state and civil society, are blurred. It also invokes the distinction between civil and uncivil forms of associationalism. On the one hand, civil society organizations and the state seem—sometimes—excessively intertwined. In 2002–3, the state of Gujarat suffered India's worst communal rioting since partition. Thousands of Muslims lost their lives; tens of thousands their homes. A pivotal player in these events was the 'voluntary sector' organization, the Rashtriya Swayamsevak Sangh (RSS), or National Volunteers' Association, which is the ideological core of the Hindu nationalist movement, the then ruling BJP being its political expression. The RSS's presence within organs of the state administration—among elite civil servants, the police, paramilitary units—crucially influenced the grisly outcome.

On the other hand, one of the few apparently effective mechanisms for combating communal violence is something very similar, in terms of breaching the state–civil society divide. Varshney (2004: 206) argues that under certain circumstances, to prevent communal violence, 'Civil society organizations, for all practical purposes, become the ears and arms of the state.' Rather than sinister, this is a positive version of state–civil society partnership with a proven ability to tackle small, localized communal flare-ups before they escalate.

Varshney's study of civil society and communal violence in Kerala and Uttar Pradesh (UP) asks why UP suffered so much Hindu–Muslim violence, compared to Kerala, which during the early part of the twentieth century had been a communal tinderbox. Conventional wisdom has interpreted the statistical correlation between state-wide levels of illiteracy and the propensity towards communal rioting as implying a causal relationship: fewer illiterates in Kerala mean fewer chances to manipulate communal passions. Varshney suggests that states are the *wrong unit of analysis* here. Communal violence is a local (primarily urban) phenomenon, and when data on development and communal violence are aggregated at the city or town (instead of state) level, the literacy-communal violence correlation disappears. What does correlate, inversely, with lower levels of communal violence is the extent of *inter*-communal associations, spanning the Hindu–Muslim divide, that can act as an unofficial institution for defusing disputes and preventing further escalation.

Great hopes have been placed in the ability of India's rising middle class to help catalyse improvements in governance. Theories of democracy (notably Moore 1966) have long emphasized the middle class's importance as a stabilizing force. In terms of combating corruption, increasingly prosperous middle-class groups can, in theory, come to possess a political voice sufficiently powerful to demand a cleaner, more transparent public administration. And in many of India's urban centres, such groups have indeed made a difference. One example is a New Delhi-based association, Parivartan. While Parivartan may at times have focused on issues of middle-class concern—one campaign dealt with corruption in the income-tax bureaucracy, in a city where only the comparatively well-off pay income tax at all—it has also sought to address problems of slum-dwellers and other deprived groups. A key question is whether India's middle class, despite its clearly rising prosperity, is large enough in electoral terms to force fundamental changes in the way government operates. Even if 200-million strong, at less than a fifth of India's population, the middle class forms a minority of voters. Feelings of electoral impotence are indeed widespread among India's middle classes. As a result, many such people opt out of whatever public services they can, reducing their incentive to work towards reducing corruption in such key public services as health and education.

India's middle classes, moreover, are divided, in terms not only of social background, but also of their professional profiles. As Sridharan (2004) points out, this affects their attitudes towards other key aspects of government policy, beyond merely curbing corruption. In particular, while India's middle classes are usually seen as supporters of economic liberalization, their attitude is more ambivalent. Most notably, a large percentage of them is still employed by the public sector, or relies on public sector procurement in the private industries in which they are employed. Many benefit from public subsidies for access to tertiary education, cheap electricity, or other things that allow them to remain within a broadly defined middle class. Whereas most analyses of the political difficulties facing the Congress-led coalition government of Prime Minister Manmohan Singh focus on the potential for discontent among the poor to undermine popular support for economic reform, there is at least as much concern among leading politicians about the rising expectations among India's middle classes, who want access to private markets without sacrificing the public subsidies to which they have grown accustomed.

> **KEY POINTS**
>
> - Evidence that civil society organizations improve governance is ambiguous.
> - The MKSS's efforts to combat corruption provide a good illustration.
> - Some civil society organizations foment communal violence but other cross-communal organizations may contain it.

Conclusion

The complex nature of India's associational life has spurred debates about its size and composition, its regional variations, its relations with the state, and its capacity to improve governance. The difficulty of resolving these issues demonstrates both the protean nature of India's civil society in particular, and the ambiguity of concepts used to analyse civil society more generally. Indian civil society challenges conventional analytical categories separating modern and traditional identities, civil and uncivil expressions of the associational impulse, and vertical and horizontal forms of accountability. India's civil society tends to revise and reconstitute itself with remarkable frequency. Though the exact nature of the impact is unclear, it is hard to deny that this process is being affected by globalization. Many Indian civic organizations have received a boost from their connections abroad—largely through transnational social networks connecting members of the Indian diaspora. In some cases, such linkages illustrate other trends discussed in this chapter. For instance, the reportedly large role played by overseas Indians in fund-raising for the Vishwa Hindu Parishad (or World Hindu Council), another RSS-linked group, suggests not only that India has not bucked the worldwide trend towards mobilizing so-called traditional identities through modern means, but also that its civic associations are unafraid of deploying *un*civil methods to obtain their objectives.

? QUESTIONS

1 What can India's civil society teach us about the relationship between traditional and modern forms of politics?

2 What measures could be used to assess the *health* of India's civil society?

3 Do all federal systems give rise to state-wise variations in the texture of civil society to the degree found in India?

4 Under what conditions might state–civil society partnership be likely to result in improved governance, and under what conditions might it make matters worse?

5 What might be some of the constraints on civil society's capacity to curb corruption?

6 How can the aspirations of the rising middle class and the problems of the rural poor be reconciled at the same time that India is undergoing a profound economic transformation?

7 With particular reference to the Indian case, what arguments could be deployed to make the case that political parties should be included within a working definition of civil society?

8 Is a group that represents the interests of public-sector employees from a particular caste group a union? Or is it an ascriptive association?

≋ GUIDE TO FURTHER READING

■ **Chandhoke, N. (2003),** *The Conceits of Civil Society* **(Delhi: Oxford University Press).** Uses the case of India to advance theoretically informed arguments about the way in which the idea of civil society has been deployed in much contemporary scholarship.

■ **Jaffrelot, C. (2003),** *India's Silent Revolution: The Rise of the Lower Castes in North India* **(London: Hurst and Co.).** Sensitively analyses the emergence of socially marginalized groups into the mainstream of party politics, a process both reflecting and profoundly influencing the nature and development of India's civil society.

■ **Jeffrey, R. (2000),** *India's Newspaper Revolution: Capitalism, Politics and the Indian-Language Press, 1977–99* **(Delhi: Oxford University Press).** Charts, in fascinating detail, both encouraging and disturbing trends in the development of one of the key elements of any functioning civil society—the press.

■ **Mahajan, G. (1999), 'Civil Society and Its Avatars: What Happened to Freedom and Democracy?',** *Economic and Political Weekly,* **15–21 May (available at www.epw.org.in).** Excellent account of the relationship between thinking about civil society in the West and in India.

■ **Sainath, P. (1996),** *Everybody Loves a Good Drought: Stories from India's Poorest Districts* **(New Delhi: Penguin).** An excellent collection of reportage on the plight of India's most vulnerable citizens, showing both their need for strong associations to represent their interests and how sometimes oppressive forms of civil society contribute to the problem.

■ **Varshney, A. (2002),** *Ethnic Conflict and Civic Life: Hindus and Muslims in India* **(New Haven, CT: Yale University Press).** Combines statistical sophistication and conceptual rigour to examine the role of *some* forms of civil society in defusing communal conflict.

WEB LINKS

www.pucl.org The site of the People's Union for Civil Liberties, an Indian civil society organization that campaigns for human rights.

http://sarn.ssrc.org The site of the South Asia Research Network set up by the South Asia programme of the independent, international Social Science Research Council based in Washington, DC, United States.

www.indiastat.com An extensive site of social, economic, and political data on India.

http://parliamentofindia.nic.in The site of India's parliament.

www.hinduonline.com The online version of *The Hindu*, a leading English-language daily newspaper.

www.focusweb.org/india The India site of Focus on the Global South, a worldwide association of civic groups seeking great social justice.

www.ncasindia.org The National Centre for Advocacy Studies, a social change resource centre for activists, scholars, and journalists.

www.epw.org.in The site of *Economic and Political Weekly*, a venerable and excellent source of scholarship, opinion, and news about Indian civil society and other topics.

www.pria.org The site of the Society for Participatory Research in Asia, a leading centre of research on civic advocacy in India.

ONLINE RESOURCE CENTRE

For additional material and resources, see the Online Resource Centre at:
www.oxfordtextbooks.co.uk/orc/burnell2e/

21b — Saudi Arabia: Between Tradition and Modernity

ORIGINAL CHAPTER BY DAVID POOL. UPDATED AND AMENDED BY PETER BURNELL AND VICKY RANDALL.

Chapter Contents

- Introduction
- The Historical Context of State-Building
- Opposition, the Rentier State, and Islam
- Foreign Policy and Dissent
- Conclusion

Overview

This chapter examines the emergence of the Saudi state from a tribally based stateless society to a kingdom with rulers drawn from the Saud family. The twin pillars of dynastic legitimacy are Islam and oil. Both pillars have consequences for the limited character of civil society. Since the late 1970s, there have been stirrings of civil society and political opposition. Two political tendencies have emerged: liberal reformist and conservative Islamist. Underpinning these new dynamics have been increasing diversification of Saudi society, a decline in oil revenues in the 1980s followed by a rebound in the last few years, and reactions to Saudi Arabia's alignment with the USA. Buffeted by these competing pressures, the ruling family has pursued policies balancing between them with uneven results for the evolution of civil society.

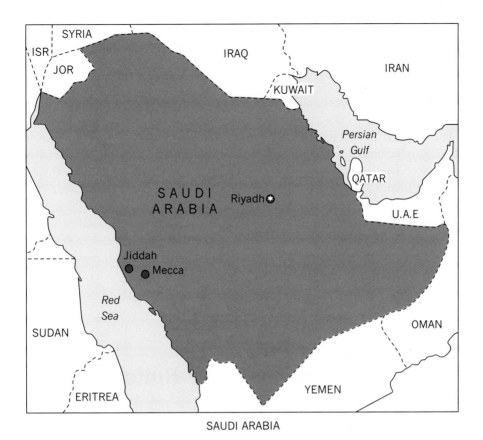

SAUDI ARABIA

BOX 21b.1

Key Dates in Saudi Arabia's History

1774	Oath of Dhiriyya between Saud and Muhammad Abd al-Wahhab.	1974	Oil revenues quadruple.
		1975	Khalid succeeds.
1902	Abd al-Aziz ibn Saud took Riyadh.	1979	Seizure of Holy Mosque in Mecca.
1926	Abd al-Aziz proclaimed king of Hijaz and Sultan of Najd.	1982	Fahd succeeds.
1932	Establishment of kingdom of Saudi Arabia.	1985	Abdullah effective ruler as crown prince following Fahd's stroke.
1938	Beginning of exploitation of oil.	1990–1	War over Iraqi occupation of Kuwait.
1953	Saud son of Abd al-Aziz succeeds.	1993	Consultative Council established.
1964	Saud deposed. Faisal succeeds.	2005	Elections for half the seats in each of 178 Municipal Councils. Abdullah ascends to the throne.

Introduction

Civil society and civil society organizations have played a limited role in Saudi Arabia's political development. The character of civil society has been shaped by the interrelationship between dynastic rule of the House of Saud and the twin pillars of dynastic legitimacy: Islam and oil. Whereas the link between the ruling Saud family and a strict version of Islam pre-date the establishment of the state, the impact of oil on Saudi society and politics is more recent. In the contemporary period there has been a complicated interplay between state, govern-ment, Islamic politics, and the economic and social impact of oil revenues. These multiple factors are layered into the relationship between Saudi Arabia and the United States and have resulted in indica-tions of a more active civil society, albeit a mix of the clandestine and unstructured. The emergence of two different tendencies (liberal-reformist and Islamic orthodox) have resulted in the monarchy attempting to balance between the two with uneven consequences for the emergence of an active civil society.

The Historical Context of State-Building

From stateless society to the subordination of society

Saudi Arabia is exceptional among developing countries in that it was never colonized. External control was limited to military garrisons of the Ottoman Empire during the nineteenth century. It was not geared to the extraction of natural resources and did not generate the phenomena usually asso-ciated with colonialism: a colonial bureaucracy, the expansion of education, and a modern educated class to staff the indigenous institutions of colonial rule. There was no anti-colonial nationalist move-ment built on the social strata usually involved in nationalist activity: students, the intelligentsia, and merchants.

Prior to the establishment of the state, Saudi Arabian society had two main forms of social organ-ization: pastoral tribes located in the desert interior and the settled population of the oases and coastal areas. There was no central authority and inter- and intra-tribal disputes, changing tribal alliances and conflicts with enclaves of the settled population, were endemic. It was not through consensus on Is-lam nor through acceptance of the rule of the Saud family that Saudi Arabia was unified but through force and conquest.

Islamic legitimation for the House of Saud ori-ginated with the alliance of Muhammad bin Saud, a local ruler from the interior village of Dhiriyya, and Muhammad bin Abd al-Wahhab, an Islamic preacher. It was symbolized by the oath to return to true Islam sworn between the two in 1744 and cemented by marriages between the two families that have continued until today. The alliance ad-ded a new Islamic dimension to conflicts as some tribes and tribal segments were incorporated into the *ikhwan* (the brethren)—the followers of Abd al-Wahhab. Tribal conflicts and the waxing and waning of tribal ascendancies continued for more than a hundred years until, at the beginning of the twentieth century, Abd al-Aziz bin Saud (known as Ibn Saud) began extending his conquests through war and Wahhabi doctrines. The *ikhwan* were sent among the tribes and tribal settlements were established based on common Islamic practice rather than kinship solidarity. The combination of Saud warrior leadership and the brethren's religious passion provided the dynamic for the establishment of the kingdom of Saudi Arabia in 1932.

With a new central power in the peninsular, marked by naming the state after the conquering family, and a Sunni Islamic ideology focused on enforcing religious conformity, segmentary tribal conflicts were contained as tribal leaders and tribes became subordinated to or associated with the centre. One means to achieve this was the practice of marrying Saud males to the daughters of prominent tribal families. The main opposition to the emergent state was a rebellion by a segment of the *ikhwan*. The growth of oil revenues through the 1950s presented the ruling family with the material means to reinforce its power and authority and provide patronage as a means of incorporating dissident tribes and the conquered peripheries under Saud rule and Wahhabi principles. Oil revenues also permitted the gradual establishment of a state bureaucracy, increasing numbers of salaried officials and the growth of budgetary allocations for socio-economic development and educational expansion. These changes, however, took place in the context of strictly enforced conformity to Wahhabi principles. As a result, other than a network of chambers of commerce, social and economic development did not generate an organized civil society.

Islam

The grounding of authority and legitimacy in Saudi Arabia in a conservative version of Sunni Islam has provided both constraints on civil society organizations and justification for them. Contradictorily, it was in the fuzzy interstices between state and religion that Islam provided some justification for organizations with a degree of independence from the state. One institution difficult to categorize as either a civil society or state organization is the *ulema*. It is a body consisting of those educated in Islam and *Sharia* (Islamic law) with the function of ensuring the implementation of Islamic precepts and thus has some characteristics of a corporate non-state organization linking together the local mosque preacher and the highest legal authority. However, given the role of Islamic law as state law there is a fusion between state and religion at the highest level of *ulema* positions.

The Wahhabi message was based on the unity of God and opposed to the idolatrous accretions of saint worship found among mystical Islamic orders, the practices of the minority Shia community and general lax behaviour. With the establishment of the kingdom, Islam became the basis of the state, state institutions, and law. Saudi publications stress that the holy Koran is the constitution and *Sharia* the determinant of personal and public behaviour. The judicial system was unified under the Hanbali school of law, the strictest of the four Islamic legal schools. The duty of the ruler, and basis of his legitimacy, was to ensure implementation of Islamic principles. There was no space for political parties or mechanism for expressing group interests outside of Islam. The *ulema* had a critical voice in decision-making given the absence of a formal constitution and a secular legal system. Clergy dominated key institutions—the Council of Higher Ulema, the High Judicial Council, and the Council of Grievances. The Committee for the Condemnation of Vice and Recommendation of Virtue policed moral conduct, ensuring proper Islamic behaviour, including female modesty. There was, then, an officially prescribed set of principles for both social and political values and behaviour.

Civil society in Saudi Arabia is constrained by a framework that stresses the promotion of the fulfilment of Islamic duties. In so far as civil society is understood to grow from a diverse range of social interests formulated in associations autonomous from the state, this Islamic framework provides limited scope for organized civil society based on factors other than religion. Although Islam in Saudi Arabia lacks anything like the structure of a church, in some respects the *ulema* are the only institution with a degree of autonomy from the state and accepted as a channel between society, government, and state. The centrality of Islam also provides scope for Islamic charitable organizations.

The House of Saud

The Saud family played an important role in the tribal politics of the Najd interior from the eighteenth century onwards. After thirty years of expansion and conquest, Ibn Saud took control of the Hijaz, with its holy towns of Mecca and Medina, in 1925, declared himself King of Hijaz and Sultan of Najd and its Dependencies in 1926, and in 1932 proclaimed himself as first king of Saudi Arabia.

Since founding the state, the Saud family has embedded itself in government and administration, invariably holding key positions like defence, foreign affairs, security, and provincial governorships. Other members are spread through important ambassadorships, the military and security establishment, and government commissions. Ibn Saud had scores of wives and descendants, and when collateral family branches are added it is estimated that male family members number around ten thousand, all recipients of government stipends. It is an extended family of such proportion that recruitment from it into official positions is not difficult.

Reinforcing the official view of Islamic legitimacy, there is an additional emphasis on two concepts: *shura* and *majlis*. *Shura* refers to consultation between the people and the ruler, although the more traditional practice is consultation with the *ulema*. *Majlis*, traditionally the tribal forum for male elders, has evolved into an institution for consultation between ruler and ruled. In practice, it functions as a forum for airing grievances and the delivery of petitions. The latter process has been undermined by the growth of bureaucracy.

The framework of Islamic principles in Saudi Arabia and the family's pivotal historic role did not necessarily ensure legitimacy for family-dominated government and administration and its key role in the economy. An index of the symbiotic relationship between power and wealth are the land grants by Ibn Saud and his successors to Saud family members and advisers that became a source of enrichment with the massive increase in property prices after 1974 during the construction boom. The presence of such large numbers in important public positions, the allocation to them of stipends from public funds, and, in the 1970s, the increasing number involved in influence peddling and brokering state contracts illustrate the tension between family political power and the autonomy of governmental institutions.

Of particular significance was the involvement of princes in the racket of commissions for state contracts and weapons procurement. In so far as the role of the family was legitimated by Islam, the extravagant palaces, reports and rumours of corruption, and un-Islamic behaviour in the fleshpots and casinos of Europe by some family members reflected badly on the Islamic pillar of legitimacy. Though the population of Saudi Arabia generally benefited from the oil boom, members of the House of Saud were the major beneficiaries and particularly well placed to profit through kinship connections to those members of the family in key decision-making positions. As recently as 2007, a fraud probe by British authorities into British arms contracts with the Saudi regime that date from the 1980s was called off, in the context of a new arms deal worth around £6 billion, on the pretext that the Saudis were threatening to withdraw intelligence cooperation

---

BOX 21b.2

Saudi Arabian Oil Revenues ($, Unadjusted for Inflation)

1965	655m	1979	70bn
1973	4bn	1985	20bn
1974	23bn	2000	70bn
		2006	180bn+

vital to Britain's national security interests if the investigation went ahead.

Oil and the rentier state

Saudi Arabia possesses around a quarter of the world's known oil reserves. And the role of oil revenues provides another competing and parallel explanation to that of Islam for Saud autocracy, the relative stability of dynastic power, and the weakness of civil society. The theory of the **rentier state** defines a state like Saudi Arabia and accounts for a particular pattern of politics and social organization. In brief, a rentier state exists where the bulk of its revenues derive from external sources, akin to renting oil fields in return for income. In 1973–4 oil revenues quadrupled and have provided between 70 and 90 per cent of government revenues ever since. Several political and social consequences are seen to follow from oil rent.

First, external rent accrues to the state and provides it with a high degree of autonomy from society. The major function of the state is the allocation of revenues to society. This allocative process is distinct from a state whose citizens are involved in producing goods and resources generated from taxing production. Secondly, citizens of a rentier state develop a 'rentier mentality'. Bureaucratic employment, welfare, medical care, and education are all provided through the state's allocation of oil revenues. Very few citizens are involved in the production of oil and taxation is minimal. In so far as the state does not tax its citizens, they make no claims on the state. Those involved in most of the productive work are non-citizen migrant workers on short-term work contracts, dependent on Saudi citizen employers for their residence permits and are marginal members of Saudi society. In fact, there are around 5.5 million foreigners resident in Saudi Arabia's current population of around 27 million people. The political implications of rentier state theory are that civil society is relatively passive; it lacks any imperative to challenge the authorities allocating the oil revenues; and opposition movements and demands for democratic reform

and governmental accountability are unlikely to emerge. These implications have been concretized by the official prohibition against political parties and forms of social organization like trade unions and women's movements that might develop as a consequence of social diversification.

Saudi Arabian society, however, has not been totally passive. Demonstrations and protests have occurred sporadically, show a degree of civil organization, and reflect a disquiet at the lack of political and social change. These occurrences suggest the existence of a skeletal and clandestine civil society. Calls for reform and the emergence of clandestine groups using violent means are indicative of a polarization in Saudi society along two axes: liberal reform and a return to Wahhabi orthodoxy. That these political trends have emerged while Saudi Arabia has remained *by definition* a rentier state, albeit one where revenues have fluctuated widely, raises questions about the limits of rentier state theory for explaining state–society relations. This is especially so in Saudi Arabia, where religious leaders continue to have very considerable influence among the people.

Dependence on oil revenues makes Saudi Arabia vulnerable to changes in the demand for and price of oil. The collapse of oil prices in the 1980s resulted in declining oil revenues, leading to cuts in government spending, pressure on the private sector to expand its employment of school and university graduates, and encouragement to family firms to become public companies. The rise of a more activist civil society was probably connected with these trends. Whether the recent return to greater prosperity as a result of dramatic increases in the oil price, which is evident in the return to large public budget surpluses, will now stifle further development of civil society remains to be seen. Saudi Arabia's ability to stay insulated from the increasing political flux in the wider Middle East region and the grassroots radicalization linked to Islamist causes there cannot be assured, especially as the kingdom continues to be home to around a quarter of a million Palestinian refugees.

KEY POINTS

- The Saud family is at the apex of politics and the king at the apex of the family.

- Islam provides legitimacy for the monarchy and provides constraints against the development of civil society.

- Saudi Arabia is a rentier state: oil revenues strengthen the state and limit the development of civil society.

- Allocation of oil revenues legitimates the ruling family but results in a more diversified society.

- By definition, Saudi Arabia has remained a rentier state, but the political opposition that emerged as oil revenues and per capita income declined is unlikely to evaporate now that revenues have increased.

Opposition, the Rentier State, and Islam

One political implication of the rentier state is that civil society and opposition to government are unlikely to emerge given the material well-being of those who have all the privileges of citizenship. An analysis of the occurrence and character of opposition, therefore, is a means of assessing the utility of the rentier state explanation of Saudi society and state–society relations. Given the secret nature of Saudi politics the analysis of opposition must necessarily be somewhat interpretative. It is, however, possible to link sporadic eruptions of protest to broad social and political trends. In the case of Saudi Arabia, it is becoming clear that stirrings of civil society activism are a consequence of the role of ideas in mobilizing civil society even if the initial catalysts were declining oil revenues and shrinking per capita income, on the one hand, and Saudi foreign policy, on the other.

Liberalization protests

From the early 1990s, there have been increasing calls for liberalization of the political system. In January 2003, formal reform proposals were presented to Crown Prince Abdallah in 'A Strategic Vision for the Present and Future' (Dekmejian 2003). While accepting the monarchy and invoking Islamic precepts, the document called for the separation of powers, introduction of popular representation and participation, and a framework for establishing civil society organizations. The signatories, educated, professional middle class, and male, reflected the social change of the previous three decades. They signed as individuals and there was no organizational imprimatur, indicative of the loose and limited nature of civil society. It was followed by a National Forum for Dialogue attended by liberal and moderate Islamist reformers and sanctioned by the Saud family. Popular support for reform

BOX 21b.3

Shura Response to Civil Society Demands

❝ Passing over the demands of civil society could lead to our falling into the abyss ... The Saudi citizen needs to have his basic rights and freedom of expression guaranteed ... and his role in social and political participation strengthened, so he can feel part of an inclusive order. ❞

(Mohammad Ibrahim al-Helwa, Member of the Consultative Council, December 2003)

was signalled later in the year with an unprecedented public demonstration demanding freedom of expression. In recognition of pressures for liberal reform, the government introduced a *Shura* (Consultative) Council. In 2005, elections were held for half the seats in each of the 178 Municipal Councils, the other half being chosen by appointment. The Councils have only advisory status. Moreover, political parties were, and still are, banned. And women were allowed neither to stand as candidates nor to exercise the vote. Overall, candidates who had been endorsed by popular religious leaders came out on top, at the expense of candidates with more 'liberal' leanings and business connections or those who had the backing of tribal elders.

The case of women

An examination of the role and position of women provides a useful case study. Female rates of economic participation are low, and officially sanctioned prohibitions against women range from dress codes to driving cars. Justifications for this are that Islam determines the obligations of women, gives priority to their role within the family (Al-Farsy 1990: 135), and demands modest behaviour. Priority is given to the strict Islamic principle rather than economic imperatives. However, there is a tension between the women's low participation in the workforce and the need to import foreign labour with its perceived potential to undermine the traditional Islamic values.

One aspect of social change has been the expansion of educational opportunities of which women have been significant beneficiaries. Educational development also provides an index of the growth of the educated middle class, the usual candidates for civil society organizers. Total enrolment in secondary education in 1969 was 16,000. Of these, 2,000 were girls. By 1986, there were almost 200,000 secondary-school students including 85,000 girls, and 15,000 university graduates, half of whom were female. By the mid-1980s, female participation rates in employment showed an increase among the younger generation: about 9 per cent for women in their twenties and 3 per cent for those in their forties. The issue of women's role in society and participation in the economy is controversial, linked to questions of liberalization and equality. The issue dramatically surfaced into politics in 1991 when a large group of educated women, defying the prohibition against women drivers, got behind the wheels of their cars and drove into the centre of Riyadh to the horror of the religious authorities. The women were publicly vilified as akin to prostitutes. The incident was indicative not only of the growing demands of educated Saudi women for equality and liberalization but also of an informal organizational network of women who were willing to take significant political action. In order to placate conservative Islamic circles, the government introduced restrictions on women's travel abroad.

Islamic protests and opposition

Contrasting with liberalization protests have been protests within a Wahhabi and neo-Wahhabi Islamist tradition. They have ranged from the takeover of the Holy Mosque of Mecca in 1979, to mosque sermons opposed to the US presence in Saudi Arabia in 1990 and terrorist bombings in Riyadh in 2003, to violence targeted against foreigners more recently, and apparently linked to al-Qaeda. While Islam has provided legitimacy for the House of Saud, it has also provided a basis for opposition. This contradiction places the *ulema* in a difficult and ambiguous position: is it an organization that reflects the Islamic values of important segments of civil society, an institution subordinated to the state authorities, or a corporate social group independent of both state authorities and society?

The first serious Islamist eruption occurred in 1979 when Juhayman Utaibi, a religious studies student, and hundreds of followers, seized the Mecca mosque, one of the holiest of Islamic sites. His opposition to the ruling family was grounded in religious principles and Saudi history. He rejected the ruling family's legitimacy on the grounds that they did not follow the Koran and the Sunna. He was also critical of Ibn Saud's subordination of the *ikhwan* and called for the *ulema* to oppose the House of Saud. His letters also included attacks on the alliance with the Christians, a clear reference to the West. Juhayman and his group and supporters represented a modern return to past principles and early Saudi Muslim society. The higher *ulema* rejected Juhayman's appeal to oppose the Saud family and supported the authorities with a *fatwa* (religious edict) permitting use of force to expel the rebels from the mosque. In doing so the *ulema* aligned itself with the state authorities rather than with a protest movement rooted in old Saudi society.

When the Iraqi army invaded and occupied Kuwait in 1990, Saudi Arabia was placed in a dilemma over whether to accede to US requests for a military presence to free Kuwait of Iraqi forces or to oppose a Western military intervention against a Muslim state. Consequent on the arrival of US forces a vigorous campaign against the foreign military presence was conducted by mosque preachers who distributed their sermons through cassettes.

Following the high *ulema* sanctioning the presence of foreign forces in Saudi Arabia, a 'Memorandum of Advice' was issued in September 1992 signed by 107 *ulema*, an indication of the existence of an autonomous section of the *ulema*. Among other things, the Memorandum called for greater supervision over the state and government policy by a religious review body, a religious supreme court, and the invalidation of laws contradictory to *Sharia*. A starker challenge to the ruling family was the anti-monarchy citation of chapter 27, verse 43 of the Koran. Making an implicit link between corruption and the ruling family, it also called for those who had gained wealth illegally, regardless of rank, to be punished (Cordesman 2002). Indicative of the need for Islamic legitimacy, the authorities purged those who did not denounce the Memorandum from the Supreme Council of Senior Ulema. An additional response was the restriction on charitable

---

BOX 21b.4

Koran Excerpt

> When kings enter a city, they cause it to be corrupt, turning its honourable people into a humiliated people.

(Koran, chapter 27, verse 43; cited in the Memorandum of Advice, September 1992)

---

fund-raising without government authorization, a measure weakly enforced within Saudi Arabia and impossible to enforce on groups outside.

In so far as church groups and church leaders in the West can be considered a part of civil society, so too could the Saudi *ulema*. Though fragmented with regard to their relationship to the state authorities, *ulema* networks could be viewed as informally organized expressions of civil society. The compliance of some of the leading *ulema* with state policy has brought forth non-*ulema* groups inspired by Islam like the Committee for the Defence of Legitimate Rights. That was established by the physicist Muhammad al-Masari in 1993 and fused together religious demands with democratic positions. Its adherents were subsequently arrested or fled into exile.

KEY POINTS

- Two poles of reformism opposition have emerged in Saudi Arabia despite its rentier character.
- Both are suggestive of the growth of civil society even if it is not formally organized.
- Liberal reformists advocate reform of the political system but maintenance of monarchy.
- Islamists and members of the *ulema* have called for strengthening the role of Islam and the *ulema*.
- The Saud family attempts to balance between the two poles of opposition.

Foreign Policy and Dissent

Saudi foreign policy, and especially the US–Saudi relationship, has been a catalyst for Islamist opposition. Saudi Arabia's long-standing informal alliance with the USA has been reflected in both its foreign policy and its oil supply and pricing policies. Most arms purchased by Saudi Arabia were from the USA, and accompanying them was a significant growth in American military personnel as advisers and technicians. There have, however, been persistent tensions arising from its ties to the USA and the latter's policies in the Middle East, particularly support for Israel and Israel's occupation of Palestine. The cold war mitigated the tensions in that Saudi Arabia's alignment with the West was against the atheistic communist East.

There were serious domestic repercussions of Saudi Arabia's foreign policy following the Iranian Revolution of 1978–9, the Soviet invasion of Afghanistan in 1980, and the Iraqi invasion of Kuwait in 1990. The establishment of the Shii Iranian Islamic Republic brought demonstrations by the downtrodden Saudi Shii community, possibly inspired seizure of the Mecca mosque, and tacitly challenged the Islamic legitimacy of monarchy in Saudi Arabia. The Soviet presence in Afghanistan, an Islamic country, resulted in organized Islamic resistance within Saudi Arabia providing money and arms, and, more importantly, encouraging Saudi citizens to enlist. In the longer term, Saudi Arabia's involvement in Afghanistan lay behind the subsequent emergence of the most violent and organized opposition to the Saudi regime. Osama bin Laden, from a prominent Saudi family and key recruiter of young Saudis to the Afghan resistance, built the al-Qaeda movement and radicalized its members against the West, in their language the Jews and Christians. Ultimately,

the Saudi monarchy became a target because of its ties to the West, dramatically symbolized by its permission for the Western military presence in the kingdom for the offensive against the Iraqi army occupying Kuwait. Although organized abroad, the appeal of al-Qaeda has domestic roots in Saudi Arabia and could be considered the tip of a politicized network of clandestine civil society groups. Concerted attacks against US interests in Saudi Arabia and the wider region culminated in the 9/11 attacks. Most of those involved were Saudi citizens and subsequent investigation has made clear that funding from Saudi charities had played a significant role in the growth of al-Qaeda and its political and military activities. Islamic charitable organizations were the only civil society organizations permitted by the state. Since then the government has expanded its supervisory and regulatory role over charities after strong US pressure. Extremist Islamist supporters of al-Qaeda consider these developments a mark of the subordination of Saudi Arabia to US interests. The US and British invasion of Iraq and subsequent occupation in 2003 have only added further incitement to the extremists.

KEY POINTS

- The US–Saudi relationship has generated internal opposition.

- Saudi state support for Afghan resistance and participation of Saudis gave rise to a clandestine and violent internal opposition linked to al-Qaeda.

- In reaction Saudi government has extended state control over charitable organizations, the only active civil society organizations.

Conclusion

The development of civil society in Saudi Arabia has been a faltering process. The establishment of the Saudi state resulted in the subordination of autonomous tribal units to an autocratic monarchy drawn from the Saud family, whose members were politically, socially, and economically highly privileged. The monarchical system was underpinned by a moral and religious legitimacy provided by the centrality given to Islam and the *ulema*. In addition, massive increase in oil revenues and the family's control over their allocation have buttressed the power of both state and dynasty over society. As a consequence, civil society and civil society organizations have played a limited role in Saudi Arabia's political development until recent decades.

Concurrent with declining state and personal income, the increasing differentiation of society and regional developments in the Middle East, the traditional position of the ruling family has been challenged. Caught in a vortex of social change and political challenges, the monarchy has sought to balance new forces represented by the emergence of a liberal reformist trend, and older forces represented by the *ulema* and civilian movements inspired by an anti-Western Islam. In the past, elements of emergent civil society like the inchoate women's protest movement have been curtailed in the name of balance. On the other hand, emergence of a violent and clandestine Islamist movement linked to al-Qaeda benefited the forces of change. However, the balance of opinion is that the municipal elections in 2005 should not be interpreted as but the first step in an inevitable process of further political opening and democratization. Moreover, that step itself was an extremely conservative affair. While recent vastly increased oil revenues continue to help bolster the regime, it is difficult to believe that wider regional developments including the likely advance of Iranian Shi'ite and Syrian influence in Iraq and, once more, in Lebanon, and violence between groups in Palestine, will not have some impact on Saudi Arabia. However, the precise implications for political stability there are hard to foretell. So although the future of civil society might seem brighter than before, it will remain vulnerable to government strategies to balance competing domestic forces, fluctuations in oil income, and regional political events.

? **QUESTIONS**

1 How does the character of Islam in Saudi Arabia shape civil society and constrain the emergence of civil society organizations?

2 Does the theory of the rentier state account for the weakness of civil society?

3 Can the *ulema* be considered a part of civil society?

4 How well do feminist political theories and concerns help us make sense of the position women occupy in Saudi society and politics?

5 Why and how does the Saud king seek a balance between Islamic and liberal reformist protests?

6 What has been the impact of Saudi foreign policy on domestic politics?

7 Are domestic politics in Saudi Arabia held hostage to political developments in the wider Middle East and to US government policies towards the region?

8 Do any of the leading theories purporting to explain democratization help us to gauge the future prospects for political reform in Saudi Arabia?

GUIDE TO FURTHER READING

■ **Al-Farsy, F. (1990),** *Modernity and Tradition: The Saudi Equation* **(London: Kegan Paul International).** Reflects the official view of Saudi society and politics.

■ **Cordesman, A. H. (2002),** *Saudi Arabia Enters the 21st Century* **(Washington DC: Center for Strategic and International Studies).** Clear analysis of opposition, Islam, and Saudi government reaction to 9/11.

■ **Dekmejian, R. (1998), 'Saudi Arabia's Consultative Council',** *Middle East Journal,* **52/2: 204–18.** Discussion of the origins, membership, and functions of the Consultative Council.

■ ——**(2003), The Liberal Impulse in Saudi Arabia',** *Middle East Journal,* **57/3: 400–13.** Interesting synthesis of the liberalizing tendency.

■ **Luciani, G. (1992), 'Allocation vs. Production States: A Theoretical Statement', in G. Luciani (ed.),** *The Arab State* **(Los Angeles, Calif.: UCLA Press), 65–84.** Clear statement of rentier state theory.

■ **McLoughlin, L. (1993),** *Ibn Saud: Founder of a Kingdom* **(Basingstoke: Macmillan).** Good introduction to the founder of the modern dynasty and the process of state formation.

■ **Niblock, T. (2006),** *Saudi Arabia* **(London: Routledge).** An excellent up-to-date analysis of the development of the Saudi state since the earliest days with chapters on religion, oil, international relations, and the impact of 9/11 and the 2003 war in Iraq.

■ **Yamani, M. (2000),** *Changed Identities: The Challenge of the New Generation in Saudi Arabia* **(London: Royal Institute of International Affairs).** Overview of attitudes of young Saudis; extensive illustrative quotes span the political and social spectrum.

WEB LINKS

● **www.saudinf.com** Website of the Saudi Ministry of Culture and Information.

● **www.eia.doe.gov/emeu/cabs/saudi.html** Detailed update of the country's oil industry.

● **www.iad.org** The religion of Islam home page.

● **http://lcweb2.loc.gov/frd/cs/satoc.html** Saudi Arabia profile by US Library of Congress Federal Research Division offers wealth of social, economic, and political data.

ONLINE RESOURCE CENTRE

For additional material and resources, see the Online Resource Centre at:
www.oxfordtextbooks.co.uk/orc/burnell2e/

22 Military in Politics Versus Democratic Advance

22a Pakistan: The Military as a Political Fixture

DAVID TAYLOR

→ **Chapter Contents**

- Introduction: From Independence to State Breakup in 1971
- Unstable Government: 1971–99
- General Musharraf's Rule Since 1999
- Conclusion

✔ **Overview**

Since its creation in 1947, Pakistan has struggled to develop a system of sustainable democratic government, and for more than half its history the country has been under either military or quasi-military rule. From 1999 onwards, the country has been ruled by General Pervez Musharraf. This is in stark contrast to India, despite sharing the same colonial background. Ironically, the reintroduction of military rule has usually been welcomed in Pakistan as a relief from the factional disputes among the civilian political leaders and accompanying high levels of **corruption**. This chapter explains how and why the military continues to be central to the political process in Pakistan.

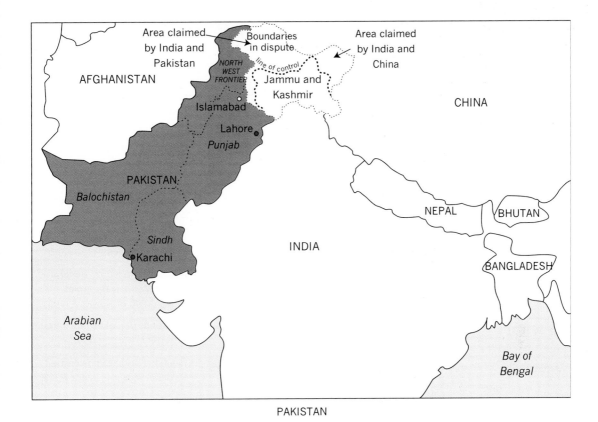

PAKISTAN

Introduction: From Independence to State Breakup in 1971

Pakistan's military forces (principally the army, which numerically and politically has always been the key player) have dominated the country for most of its history since independence. This has meant not only political power but the pre-emption of a substantial share of economic resources. According to the 2006–7 Federal Budget defence expenditure is 2.8 per cent of GDP, a figure which has been declining in the past few years, but most analysts suggest the real figure is significantly higher. Defence consumes as much as the total federal expenditure on social and economic development. The army is 550,000 strong, and many more depend

on the army directly or indirectly for employment. Internationally, the image of Pakistan as a garrison state, although acceptable at times to the USA, has often created difficulties, for example the country's suspension from the Commonwealth after the 1999 military coup until 2004. A garrison state is a state maintained by military power and, in some definitions, is a state organized to secure primarily its own need for military security.

The dominance of the military in Pakistan has been explained in different ways. Some note the way Pakistan inherited a strong army from the colonial state; others see it as an aspect of a social order

BOX 22a.1

Key Dates in Pakistan's History

14 August 1947	Pakistan independence
11 September 1948	Independence leader Mohammad Jinnah dies.
February 1954	Pakistan joins a US-led military alliance (also known as the Baghdad Pact and later as CENTO).
March 1956	First constitution passed (but never fully implemented).
October 1958	General Ayub Khan carries out first military coup.
February 1960	Ayub Khan elected president through indirect election.
March 1961	Muslim Family Laws Ordinance.
March 1962	New constitution passed.
September 1965	Indecisive war with India.
March 1969	Military coup led by General Yahya Khan deposes Ayub Khan.
December 1970	Elections give absolute majority to East Pakistan-based Awami League.
December 1971	Indian intervention brings about defeat of Pakistan army and separation of Bangladesh.
	agitation claiming the results were rigged.
January 1972	Zulfikar Ali Bhutto becomes president (later prime minister).
April 1977	General election returns Bhutto to power but opposition launches.
December 1984	Referendum gives Zia the basis to become president.
February/ November 1985	Elections held, sweeping constitutional amendments strengthen Zia's discretionary power.
August 1988	Zia killed when his plane is blown up.
November 1988	Elections return Benazir Bhutto to power.
October 1999	Military coup led by General Pervez Musharraf topples government of Nawaz Sharif.
April 2002	Referendum makes Musharraf president.
October 2002	Elections bring to power the Pakistan Muslim League (Q), a party sympathetic to Musharraf.
July 1977	Military coup led by General Zia-ul Haq.
April 1979	Bhutto executed.
December 2003	Political deal between Musharraf and opposition elements leads to parliamentary approval for constitutional changes.
January 2004	Pakistan resumes political dialogue with India over Kashmir.

still dominated by landowning groups. The two arguments come together in the fact that the army is recruited very heavily from the Punjab—the most populous of the country's four provinces and with a strong representation of landlord politicians, although the officer corps is increasingly coming from more middle-class families. The army thus tends to share a strong sense of Pakistan as a unitary state. Regional and international factors are also important, with Pakistan's long-running conflict with India over Kashmir and the cold war both influential. While Pakistan's efforts to define its identity as a Muslim state may not be directly linked to the dominance of the military, there is undoubtedly a connection. General Zia, in particular, who held power for much of the 1980s, tried to merge the role of the army chief with that of a legitimate ruler of a Muslim country.

Pakistan inherited its state structures from the colonial period. At that time, the army was kept in reserve for use in emergencies (as, for example, in Amritsar in 1919 when an army commander perpetrated the Jallianwala Bagh massacre). Except for the North-West Frontier, where constant skirmishing took place between specially assigned and trained army units and local tribesmen, national security was hardly an issue, until the Second World War brought Japanese forces to the frontiers of India. On the other hand, Indian troops were regularly used outside India in pursuit of imperial objectives. The Indian army was a distinct entity from the British army, and most of its recruits came from a limited number of districts in the Punjab and the North-West Frontier Province. British colonial policy was designed to encourage this recruitment and maintain the soldiers' loyalty to the state, for example by generous treatment in the allocation of land and through the racially based classification of Indians into martial and non-martial groups.

When British India became independent in 1947, and was simultaneously divided into the two successor states of India and Pakistan, the armed forces were similarly divided. Pakistan got more than its proportionate share of soldiers. It also inherited a social structure in which control of land and of the people who worked the land was the single most important basis of political power. This was challenged by the arrival of large numbers of refugees from India. Those who were not Punjabi for the most part moved to Karachi, the initial capital, where they formed the core of the new state bureaucracy and the professions.

At first the unchallenged authority wielded by Muhammad Ali Jinnah, who had led the Pakistan movement from its inception, kept tensions between provinces and between locals and newcomers in check. However, after his death in 1948, the country lacked political leadership of national standing. While popular leaders emerged in the eastern wing of the country (now Bangladesh), in the west (from where the army was recruited), provincial politicians battled for local control with little regard to national issues.

At the same time as Pakistan was facing difficulties in establishing stable structures of government, there was a belief that India's leaders had agreed to the partition of British India grudgingly and would miss no opportunity to sabotage its new neighbour. The distrust soon found a focus in the conflict over the princely state of Jammu and Kashmir. As a Hindu ruler with a powerful Hindu minority dominating the upper ranks of the bureaucracy, but with an overall Muslim majority, the Maharaja, Hari Singh, prevaricated over which new state to affiliate to. A 'tribal invasion' from the Pakistan side triggered an ultimatum from India that help to repel the invaders would only be forthcoming if he signed an instrument of accession to India. War ensued between India and Pakistan, until a truce under United Nations auspices was negotiated in August 1948. These events consolidated the army's position at the forefront of Pakistani society.

The weakness of Pakistan's political institutions and perceived need for security against a more powerful India meant the army as an institution became increasingly important in Pakistan's public life and took on a prominent political role. The first Pakistani Commander-in-Chief of the army, General Ayub Khan, became minister of defence for a period in 1954 and played a key role in bringing Pakistan into the US-led military alliance system that was constructed in Asia in the early 1950s. A complementary development was the assertion of the role of the bureaucracy as a guardian of the state in the absence of strong national leadership and in the face of challenges to the dominance of the established social order, in particular of the Punjab. While not identical, the social base of the army and the bureaucracy overlapped, and their perceptions of Pakistan were similar.

Under the constitution that had been adopted in 1956, Pakistan's first parliamentary elections were due in 1958. To avoid the accession to power of an East Bengal based politician, H. S. Suhrawardy, the then president, declared martial law. Shortly after, Ayub Khan assumed political control. Ayub Khan was anxious to ensure his own formal legitimacy in terms of Pakistan's legal institutions, and was able to obtain a judgment from the Supreme Court authorizing his rule. He also conducted a campaign against the political leaders he had displaced. Hundreds of politicians were disqualified from further political activity, on the grounds of corruption. This was complemented by an analysis of the situation which seemed to draw both on colonial assumptions and on some of the contemporary thinking in the USA about economic and political development. Pakistan was seen as a society which needed leadership and guidance from the top if it was to move along a trajectory towards healthy national development. With considerable help and advice from the USA, with whom Pakistan now engaged in military alliance, the government initiated a programme of industrialization.

Building on this analysis, Ayub Khan initiated what was called the Basic Democracies system which brought around 80,000 local leaders into politics on a non-party basis. As well as electing a National Assembly, they also formed an electoral college for the presidency, and in 1960 Ayub Khan was duly elected president. This enabled him to dispense with

martial law and to formulate a new constitution for the country—duly brought into effect in 1962. This defined Pakistan as a progressive Muslim state, pursuing policies that reflected a dynamic interpretation of religious values. In line with this, Ayub Khan's government in 1961 issued the Family Laws Ordinance which introduced reforms in the area of marriage and divorce, significantly improving the rights of women. Although Ayub Khan eventually permitted the re-establishment of political parties in order to provide a safety valve, and in fact placed himself at the head of one of them so as to attract many of the local leaders who had dominated rural politics in the past, he was unable to cope with the increasing alienation of East Bengal, and in basic democrat and presidential elections held in 1964–5 he was unable to gain a majority there.

Following Indian Prime Minister Nehru's death in 1964, Ayub Khan launched an audacious plan to seize control of Kashmir. The plan backfired and led to all-out war with India in September 1965. Although a ceasefire was quickly arranged through the UN, growing discontent paved the way for the then army chief, General Yahya Khan, to displace Ayub Khan in March 1969 and declare a fresh period of martial rule. He promised direct parliamentary elections but also announced that when the new National Assembly met to frame a new constitution it would have to work within a certain set of assumptions embodied in what was called the Legal Framework Order. These emphasized the integrity of Pakistan and were clearly designed to head off East Pakistan's demands for autonomy. However, East Pakistan's demographic majority was reflected in the distribution of seats; the province voted overwhelmingly for the Awami League, led by Sheikh Mujibur Rahman. Zulfikar Ali Bhutto, a former protégé of Ayub Khan who had established his own Pakistan People's Party (PPP) in 1967, won convincingly in the west but on a smaller scale. Sheikh Mujibur Rahman's insistence on his right to the prime ministership and on his power to write a constitution which would give full autonomy to the east was rejected by the army and

West Pakistan's politicians, and in March 1971 the army deployed force to assert the authority of the (West) Pakistan state. Indian intervention led to a decisive military defeat for Pakistan, providing the circumstances for Bhutto to take over in the west.

KEY POINTS

- Pakistan has been dominated by the army since its creation in 1947. Social and political factors, as well as the cold war context, have contributed to this situation.

- Pakistan's state structures derive from the colonial period; the colonial army was recruited heavily from the areas of British India that became Pakistan in 1947.

- Because conflict with India, especially over Kashmir, has fostered insecurity, the army has been able to place its needs and requirements at the centre of political life.

- Ayub Khan, Pakistan's first military ruler following the 1958 coup, attempted to develop an alternative political structure based on mobilization of rural leadership.

- The unsuccessful 1965 war with India ultimately led to Ayub Khan's downfall. The failure of his successor, General Yahya Khan, over Bangladesh led to his displacement by Zulfikar Ali Bhutto.

Unstable Government: 1971–99

The Bhutto era represented an attempt at a politics of **populism**, but by using the apparatus of the state to achieve his ends, Bhutto remained caught within its folds. The army as an institution remained a central actor, being used in 1974 to put down an internal rising in the province of Balochistan. The personalization of power by Bhutto alienated many army officers. In 1977, he faced a political crisis largely of his own making when he was accused by the opposition parties of rigging elections. Following three months of continuous agitation in the main cities, the army, headed by General Zia-ul Haq (whom Bhutto had promoted ahead of more senior generals in the belief that he had no political ambitions) intervened and called for fresh elections.

But Bhutto's evident popularity among his supporters persuaded General Zia to have him re-arrested and the elections postponed. Bhutto was arraigned on murder charges and executed in April 1979, although the judicial decision was not unanimous. At the same time, Zia began to take steps to reconstruct Pakistan's institutions in a generally Islamic direction, with the support of a growing number of officers who were taking a prominent role in helping those Afghan forces that were fighting against the Soviet-backed government in Kabul during the 1980s. Other officers too held the civilian politicians in general, and the PPP in particular, in contempt, and had no difficulty with the continuation of military rule.

During the early 1980s, Zia pressed ahead with the Islamization of the country's institutions on several fronts, for example changes to the banking system to eliminate the payment of interest. In practice this also meant strengthening his own role as president. In 1985 he felt strong enough to end the period of direct martial rule, reintroducing a heavily modified constitution which gave the president sweeping discretionary powers, including the right to dismiss the prime minister and dissolve the

National Assembly. This had been preceded by a referendum which was widely regarded as bogus but which enabled him to claim a five-year term as president. Elections held under the new constitution on a non-party basis then allowed the choice of a traditional landlord politician, Mohammad Khan Junejo, as the prime minister. Nearly three years later, Zia exercised his power to dismiss the prime minister, claiming that Islamization was proceeding too slowly. Zia seemed set to continue to rule through a civilian façade but with strong presidential powers retained by himself, until in August 1988 he was killed by a bomb planted on his plane.

After Zia's death the elections brought back to power the PPP under Bhutto's daughter Benazir, and she alternated in office with the other major civilian political leader, Nawaz Sharif, whose power base lay in the Punjab. In eleven years there were four elections but throughout effective power was in fact shared between the political leadership, the army, and sections of the civilian bureaucracy. This uneasy arrangement produced constant difficulty. In 1993, a deadlock between the president, Ghulam Ishaq Khan, a former senior civil servant who had been close to Zia, and the then prime minister Nawaz Sharif, was eventually resolved through the intervention of the army chief, who insisted that both resign prior to new elections under a neutral, caretaker prime minister. Nawaz Sharif returned to power in 1997, and succeeded in amending the constitution to restrict the powers of the president, which had been abused by both Ghulam Ishaq Khan and his successor. He also appeared to be asserting his authority over the army, and forced General

Jehangir Karamat, the army chief, to resign in 1998. He appointed as his successor General Pervez Musharraf, who was born in India and came to Pakistan as a refugee at independence. Musharraf reasserted the right of the army to take part in policy-making, by unilaterally embarking on a military adventure in the Kargil district of Kashmir in 1999. The fighting—the most intense since 1971—was brought to an end through US diplomatic pressure and without any gains by Pakistan. This left the army and the government deeply suspicious of each other. In October, General Musharraf launched a military coup to prevent his own dismissal.

KEY POINTS

- Bhutto's failed attempt at populist politics, bypassing the military, triggered a coup by General Zia-ul Haq in 1977 and his own execution in 1979.

- Zia's political strategy relied heavily on presenting himself and the army as the guardians of Pakistan's Islamic goals: he retained sweeping powers as head of state but in 1985 introduced changes to the Constitution enabling restoration of the political process.

- Following Zia's assassination, the period 1988 to 1999 saw unstable civilian governments alternating between the PPP and Pakistan Muslim League, with the army and the bureaucracy continuing to exercise power behind the scenes.

- A failed military adventure over Kashmir in 1999 ultimately generated a further military coup led by General Pervez Musharraf.

General Musharraf's Rule Since 1999

Coming after a period of instability, Musharraf began with substantial popular support. He promised action against the more notoriously corrupt politicians and bureaucrats and seemed in tune with the aspirations of many of Pakistan's urban population for a more liberal lifestyle. The question he had to resolve, however, was how quickly to return to civilian rule while maintaining his own and the army's decisive power to intervene in areas that were deemed critical to national interests.

Musharraf's initial political move was to hold a referendum to make himself president, but the exercise was seen as manipulated and lacking legitimacy. In another echo of previous military rulers' strategies, Musharraf also increased devolution of administration to the local level and matched it with non-party elections to local councils. Elections later in 2002 were fought on a party basis, but the leaders of the two main parties, who were both abroad, were unable to participate directly and strong official backing was given to a faction of the Muslim League that broke away from Nawaz Sharif's party. In advance of the elections, Musharraf introduced the Legal Framework Order (LFO) (echoing Yahya Khan's innovation), which strengthened the power of the president and sought to establish a National Security Council, where the military chiefs would have representation. The constitutional status of the LFO was unclear, and for the whole of 2003 the opposition brought the National Assembly to an effective halt over the issue, questioning Musharraf's entitlement to remain as army chief while also posing as a civilian president. At the beginning of 2004 a deal was struck with the main Islamist parties to allow an amended LFO to be adopted, but, given Musharraf's own liberal leanings, this was a tactical deal (for the Islamists the *quid pro quo* was a clear run for their government in the North-West Frontier Province) and served only to heighten the contradictions in his efforts to remain above civilian politics.

According to the 2004 agreement, Musharraf promised to relinquish one of his two offices by the time of the elections that were due in 2007. However, as the date approached he appeared to be backtracking and laying the ground for a continuation of the status quo. This meant, however, that he became increasingly dependent on the 'time-servers' and local political bosses who were responsible in the past for blocking progressive and consistent policies of social and political reform. He also had constantly to consider the risk of pushing the religious parties into outright opposition to the regime, and therefore moved only with extreme caution on social reform, for example the protracted attempt in 2006 to reform the law on sexual offences. There were persistent rumours, reaching a new intensity in 2007, that he might eventually strike a deal with Benazir Bhutto and the PPP, which would exclude Nawaz Sharif from any chance of returning to power.

Externally, Musharraf has enjoyed the political and financial support of the USA, although the latter clearly sees India as an emerging major power. In return, he has continued to support US actions in Afghanistan, included incursions into Pakistani territory along the frontier, where the Taliban and other groups enjoy significant local support. While he constantly faces pressure to do more, substantial sections of public opinion resent the subordination to a US agenda that is widely perceived as anti-Muslim. In the second half of 2006, after a lengthy and unsuccessful attempt to use armed force to establish control over the area of Northern Waziristan, where many Taliban had taken refuge, there was a reversal of policy and an agreement was made, ostensibly with local tribal elders, by which the army withdrew from the region. The agreement came under severe criticism from the US, who regarded it as a dangerous step but was popular domestically.

While initially staunch in his support for Pakistan's longstanding positions on Kashmir, at the beginning of 2004 Musharraf set in motion fresh talks with India over Kashmir, partly in response to pressure from the international community, and perhaps partly in the hope that a breakthrough would win back much of the civilian electorate. However, these talks and negotiations have moved very slowly, in large part because of India's reluctance to make matching concessions. If a deal is eventually agreed, perhaps on the basis of soft borders between Kashmir and its neighbours while the former remained formally part of India, Musharraf would have to use all his political skills to sell it both to the armed forces and to the mainstream political parties.

An important factor in Musharraf's ability to mobilize at least some support for his regime was the continuing relatively strong performance of the economy, buoyed by increased inflows of funds both from official donors, following Pakistan's strategic importance in the wake of 9/11, and from diaspora Pakistanis. Inflation was brought under control and industrial production picked up, so that significant real growth in the economy became evident. However, poverty levels remained stubbornly high, and Pakistan failed to match the economic transformation taking place in India. By 2006, the trade gap was widening alarmingly, and poor growth in the agricultural sector was holding back the rest of the economy.

> **KEY POINTS**
>
> - Musharraf enjoyed substantial support for his coup, seen as promising relief from corrupt and incompetent civilian governments.
>
> - Musharraf responded to 9/11 by giving full support to the USA, although this was unpopular with some sections of the population.
>
> - Like his predecessors, Musharraf sought to discredit existing political leaders and build a party loyal to himself; he amended the constitution to increase his discretionary powers as president.
>
> - Musharraf enjoys less popular support than in 1999, and has had to resort to political manoeuvring that brings short-term benefits at the cost of long-term stability for the country.

Conclusion

Zia was in power for eleven years; Ayub Khan for over ten. Musharraf seems intent on a similarly extended stretch in power. The three military rulers differed in social background and personal agenda, yet each turned out to follow similar strategies to stay in power. Rather than trying to rule in a wholly despotic and arbitrary manner, they have all sought to ground themselves in Pakistan's history and institutions.

A discourse on politics has developed which is shared not just by the military but to some degree by other sections of society. Politics as it has been practised is envisaged as an aspect of the 'feudal' phase of Pakistani history. To break its hold and to usher in a new phase (the precise lineaments of which have been specific to each leader), the army may need to intervene to help the process along. The 'ordinary' Pakistani is a key figure in this discourse, and is brought into politics through carefully tailored institutions from which party politics are excluded, at

least on the surface. At the same time, politicians are seen as people who may for their own selfish reasons betray Pakistan's key national interests, particularly over Kashmir.

While the army leadership projects itself as the guardian of the national interest, it is often seen by others as just concerned with its own interests. Army officers are often appointed to senior administrative positions after retirement and are given preferential treatment in many different areas, most significantly perhaps the allocation of prime rural and urban land. Nothing has changed in this respect in recent years. A further issue is the extent to which the army is committed to preserving the existing social structure. The officer corps has been drawn by and large from the social elite and there has been little desire to challenge the status quo, either in terms of property ownership or the power of the central government versus the provinces. This may, however, be changing in respect to religious issues.

Partly in consequence of the Zia period, Islamist ideas appeal to some sections of the army, and with recent world developments post 9/11 and post the invasion of Iraq these are likely to have gained greater resonance. The possibility of a coup within the army (as against the pattern to date where all four coups have been carried out by the army as an institution) cannot be ruled out.

Repeated cycles of military intervention have led both the army and many civilians to a belief that Pakistan cannot sustain a political system that does not give a major role to the armed forces. Turkey is often cited as a parallel example. The weakness of civil society and of the civilian political process and the special security needs not only of Pakistan itself but of the Muslim world more generally are seen as justifications for this view. This point of view is held particularly strongly in the Punjab, while in the other three provinces, especially Sindh and Balochistan, there is less willingness to accept a permanent role for the army. However, until there has been a lengthy spell of civilian rule under a prime minister who has the skills to wean the army away from its current set of assumptions without provoking a backlash, the present situation is likely to continue.

At the beginning of October 2007, Pakistan's political situation appeared to be at a crossroads. A pact had been struck in September between President Musharraf and Benazir Bhutto (see above, p. 459), and the former had achieved his initial goal of winning the presidential election held on 6 October, with a promise that he would shortly stand down as army chief. But a great deal depended on the intervention of the Supreme Court, which announced that it would rule on the validity of Musharraf's candidature at a later date. Several scenarios seemed plausible: martial law, declared either by Musharraf or his successor as army chief, or the implementation of a partnership between Musharraf, as a civilian president, and Benazir Bhutto as prime minister.

QUESTIONS

1   What policies did the colonial state pursue that prepared the way for recurrent military intervention in politics after independence?

2   To what extent was the cold war a factor in facilitating the dominance of the army in Pakistan?

3   What analysis do army leaders make of Pakistan's politics, and how do they see their own role within it?

4   Compare and contrast the political strategies of Generals Ayub Khan, Zia-ul Haq, and Pervez Musharraf.

5   What have been the consequences for Pakistani society of prolonged periods of military dominance?

6   What has been the impact of military rule on Pakistan's relations with India, especially in the light of the dispute over Kashmir?

7   How helpful is the idea of a 'garrison state' in understanding the place the military occupies within Pakistan's political and social structures?

8   Explore the contribution Pakistan makes to our understanding of the relation between military rule and social change.

GUIDE TO FURTHER READING

■ Ali, T. (1983), *Can Pakistan Survive? The Death of a State* (Harmondsworth: Penguin Books). Highly critical analysis by a leading journalist and political activist.

■ **Cloughley, B. (2000),** *A History of the Pakistan Army—Wars and Insurrections* **(Karachi: Oxford University Press Pakistan).** A history of the army that details its role at various stages of Pakistan's history. The author has known many of the key personalities involved.

■ **Cohen, S. P. (2002),** *The Pakistan Army* **(Karachi: Oxford University Press).** Based on extensive interactions with the Pakistan army's leadership, this carefully documented analysis of the history and development of the army is coupled with a discussion of its political attitudes.

■ **Dewey, C. (1999), 'The Rural Roots of Pakistani Militarism', in D. A. Low (ed.),** *The Political Inheritance of Pakistan* **(Basingstoke: Macmillan) 255–83.** The author is a historian of the Punjab, and relates the persistence of military influence to the army's embeddedness in the structures of power in rural soceity.

■ **Jaffrelot, C. (ed.) (2002),** *A History of Pakistan and its Origins* **(London: Anthem Press).** An up-to-date collection on different aspects of Pakistan's history and social structure. The contributions by the editor are especially valuable.

■ **Jalal, A. (1990),** *State of Martial Rule: The Origins of Pakistan's Political Economy of Defence* **(Cambridge: Cambridge University Press).** A detailed study of the process by which the Pakistan army became central to the Pakistan state. The author locates internal processes within the general cold war context.

■ **Musharraf, P. (2006),** *In the Line of Fire* **(London: Simon and Schuster).** General Musharraf's own (ghostwritten) account of his life and times.

■ **Rizvi, H-A. (1986),** *The Military and Politics in Pakistan* **(Lahore: Progressive Publishers).** Detailed study of civil–military relations by a leading Pakistani scholar.

■ **Siddiq, A (2007),** *Military Inc.: Inside Pakistan's Military Economy* **(London: Pluto Press).** This work by a Pakistani political scientist caused a huge stir in the country when first published. It documents and analyses the extent of the Pakistan army's involvement in the civilian economy.

■ **Talbot, I. (1998),** *Pakistan: A Modern History* **(London: Christopher Hurst).** The most reliable of recent histories of the country. Talbot has a strong sense of the provincial roots of contemporary Pakistan.

 WEB LINKS

● **http://countrystudies.us/Pakistan** A detailed US-based compilation of information on the history, economy, society, and politics of Pakistan.

● **www.sacw.net** The South Asia Citizens Web is an independent space that provides exchanges of information between and about citizen initiatives in South Asia.

● **www.pakistaniforces.com** A Pakistan-based website which is devoted to all types of information about the Pakistan armed forces, and which hosts extensive discussions on military issues.

 ONLINE RESOURCE CENTRE

For additional material and resources, see the Online Resource Centre at:
www.oxfordtextbooks.co.uk/orc/burnell2e/

22b Nigeria: Building Political Stability with Democracy

STEPHEN WRIGHT

 Chapter Contents

 Overview

Since independence from Britain in 1960, Nigeria has struggled to maintain stability in the face of significant ethnic, regional, and religious divisions. Military governments have ruled the country for almost thirty years, but there is hope that the civilian government of President Olusegun Obasanjo, elected to office in 1999 and again in 2003, has consolidated democracy in the country. Obasanjo was defeated by the Senate in 2006 in his efforts to amend the constitution to allow him to contest a third term in office in the presidential election scheduled for April 2007. This outcome is perhaps evidence of a growing political maturity in the country, but barely conceals intense regional and religious divisions, and disillusionment over the inability to control corruption. Despite this ongoing instability, Nigeria has continued to promote a forceful foreign policy. This strong external policy has been shaped by Nigeria's demographic size as Africa's largest country, as well as by its very significant petroleum exports, but probably its influence cannot be maintained without a strengthening of democracy internally.

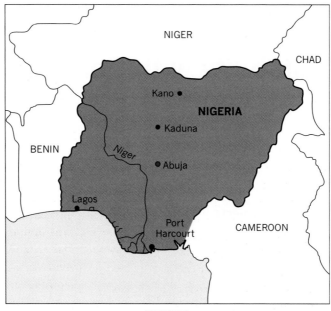

NIGERIA

BOX 22b.1

Key Dates in Nigeria's History

1914	Britain pulls together various territories into the colony of Nigeria.	1985	Ibrahim Babangida takes over in palace coup, and postpones multiple attempts to return to civilian government.
1960	Independence from Britain.	1993	Moshood Abiola wins the presidency, but elections annulled by Babangida; later that year Sani Abacha seizes power in a coup.
1966	Two military coups end the first civilian republic.		
1967	The start of the three-year civil war over Biafran secession.	1999	Following the death of Abacha in 1998, a new transition is undertaken which elects Obasanjo to the presidency, and a new civilian republic begins.
1976	Murtala Muhammed assassinated, and Olusegun Obasanjo takes over as military head of state, supervising a transition to civilian rule.		
		2003	Obasanjo re-elected for a further term amid allegations of electoral irregularities.
1979	Second civilian republic inaugurated, under President Shehu Shagari.	2007	Obasanjo's bid to stand for a third term defeated by the Senate.
1983	Military coup on New Year's Eve ushers in sixteen years of military rule.		

Introduction

The West African state of Nigeria offers an interesting case study of a country that has struggled since its independence with chronic political instability, resulting in the longest period of unbroken civilian rule being the most recent since 1999. Prior to colonial rule, the territory that was to become Nigeria consisted of numerous empires, and these were gradually absorbed into three administrative regions by the British. In turn, these regions were amalgamated into the colony of Nigeria in 1914, though each maintained a strong degree of identity and separation. Tensions between the three regions deepened in the 1950s, as ethnicity became a critical political issue in the jostling for power in a post-independent Nigeria. The inability to manage ethnic tensions has been a constant feature and has significantly contributed to the country's instability.

Instability

The British installed a parliamentary democracy in Nigeria prior to their departure in 1960, but the system could not function effectively in the highly combative political environment. The first of many military *coups d'état* took place in January 1966, sweeping the civilians from office. A second coup later in the year slid the country towards a brutal civil war between 1967 and 1970, and civilian government was not allowed to return again until 1979. Despite efforts to ease ethnic and religious tensions, notably by breaking up the three powerful administrative regions into smaller units—eventually ending up with thirty-six internal states—instability remained high. The civilian government installed in 1979 barely lasted four years before the military swept back, and a despotic era of military rule lasted until 1999, when the civilian government of President Olusegun Obasanjo (himself a former military head of state) was elected to office. His re-election in 2003 was considered a hopeful sign of a maturing democratic system, but this has not fully

materialized. All this is indicative of the challenge of building democracy in a severely fractured state.

Regional influence

Nigeria's regional prominence stems largely from two key factors: population and petroleum. Ethnicity politicizes the census process and makes an accurate headcount problematic, but the population is estimated to be around 140 million, a fraction under one-sixth of the continent's total population, and places the country as the world's tenth largest. Geological good fortune enabled Nigeria to be a prominent producer and exporter of oil and gas, making Nigeria's the largest economy in the region, and one of the largest in Africa. Currently, Nigeria stands as the world's fourteenth largest producer of oil, and the seventh largest in the Organization of Petroleum Exporting Countries (OPEC), almost on a par with Kuwait. Since its founding in 1975, Nigeria has been the leading member of the Economic Community of West African States (ECOWAS), and has often taken up leadership causes on behalf of the continent as a whole. Its demographic and economic prowess has assured close foreign policy linkages with countries outside Africa, notably the United States, Britain, and the European Union, with China also becoming an important oil trading partner since 2005.

KEY POINTS

- British colonization created a 'new' country of Nigeria, whose people had lived separately prior to colonial rule.

- Nigeria's population is the largest in Africa.

- Nigeria is the leading country in the fifteen-member Economic Community of West African States (ECOWAS), and its influence is based on population size and oil revenues.

STEPHEN WRIGHT

The Political Economy of Oil

Transformation of the economy

At independence in 1960, agriculture dominated the economy. Climatic conditions had led the British to oversee the export production of single crops for each region—groundnuts in the north, palm oil in the south-east, and cocoa in the south-west. Oil production, focused in south-eastern Nigeria, began in earnest in the 1960s and proved to be a contributing factor in the country's civil war. Once peace was attained, oil production accelerated rapidly, contributing to an economic boom in the 1970s, helped significantly by soaring prices after 1973. Agriculture quickly lost its prominence as oil revenues contributed more than 90 per cent of export revenues, a figure which has remained fairly constant ever since. Massive development schemes were started, including dams, roads, airports, universities, and hospitals, but some of these projects were of more political significance than economic benefit.

The combination of oil wealth and a large consumer population led to considerable foreign investment. By the end of the 1970s, Nigeria was widely touted as the champion of Africa, both in diplomatic and economic terms, and utilized this status to pursue important foreign policy initiatives, notably working for the 'liberation' of Zimbabwe and South Africa, and attempting to represent the views of developing countries in their call for a transformed global political economy.

Elusive development

The hopes and ambitions of the 1970s were undermined after 1980 by a series of events. The most important of these was the glut of oil in world markets, which contributed to the collapse of Nigerian revenues. An economy distorted by the oil bonanza was in turn further dislocated by the rapid bust of the market. Development projects quickly became expensive white elephants, and import dependence racked up large national debt. Oil revenues had not only been squandered, but had been siphoned off to corrupt civilian and military elites, taking billions of dollars out of the development process. The governments of the 1980s, civilian and military, were forced to relinquish their outspoken role in world politics and take up the very different challenge of seeking structural adjustment funding and debt support from the World Bank and International Monetary Fund.

The 1990s was arguably the most difficult decade in Nigeria's political and economic development. Continuing low oil revenues served to debilitate social and human development, and indicators such as infant mortality (78 deaths per 1,000 births) and life expectancy (average of 52 years) worsened as the new millennium opened. Infrastructure and transport crumbled, despite efforts at privatization and liberalization of critical sectors. External debt rose to its current level of US$34 billion, the largest in Africa. Compounding the problem was the country's military leader between 1993 and 1998, General Sani Abacha, whose brutal rule led to Nigeria's ostracism from most international bodies.

The election of Obasanjo in 1999 helped to stabilize the economic environment. His attempt to crack down on corruption brought some limited success. Obasanjo was able to engage the international financial community, and gained agreements on debt-rescheduling as well as helping to facilitate large investment inflows into the oil and gas sectors. As global demand for oil picks up, Nigeria is aiming to increase oil production from its current 2.1 million barrels a day (b/d) to 4 million b/d by 2010, with new reserves being found regularly. If the country is successful, then this revenue will provide another opportunity to promote economic and social development, hopefully with better results than previously.

Political economy challenges

Many challenges remain to promote a more balanced, stable, and equitable political economy. Diversification away from a dependence upon oil has not occurred. The thorny problem of revenue allocation within Nigeria still pits communities against the federal government, most notably in the oil-producing areas of the delta region, where ethnic groups feel cheated out of a greater share of resources. Despite some efforts by the Obasanjo administration, corruption continues to occur on a massive scale, where lucrative contracts are still in the hands of patrimonial elites. The more the country explores democracy—or the more it teeters on the brink of implosion—the more intense the forces of corruption are, as elites seek to take advantage while they can.

Social Change, Democracy, and Instability

Social fabric

Nigeria is made up of a complex mosaic of ethnic, regional, and religious identities, all of which have served at some time or other to undermine the country's stability. British colonialism forged together a country of disparate people, and also helped to create a heightened sense of ethnic identity and competition. The three regions—north, west, and east—of colonial Nigeria contained a single dominant ethnic group in each—Hausa, Yoruba, and Igbo respectively—who increasingly viewed politics as a battle for resources between the ethnic groups. The fledgling federal state at independence could not contain this animosity, and the early experiment was brought to a close in the 1966 military coup. Tensions between three powerful ethnic groups, while still a valid factor in the country's instability, form only a part of the story. Minority ethnic groups, particularly from the centre

of the country, who form an important element of the armed forces, and from the country's oil belt have increasingly become a major factor in politics. Superimposed upon this ethnic tension is religion. Again, a rough division sees the country divided into a Muslim north and a Christian south, although the reality is much more complex. Religious differences have become increasingly politicized since the 1980s, and the establishment of *Sharia* (or Islamic) law in twelve northern states, has exacerbated an already tense situation. Religious riots killing hundreds at a time are now commonplace, and provide a problem that no Nigerian government has been able to puzzle out.

It is probably fair to say that Nigeria's political elites, both civilian and military, have failed the country. Politics is based upon patrimonial inclinations, where access to political office normally translates into corrupt access to the nation's wealth. Even though the country is one of the continent's wealthiest countries, social development has remained poor, as money often does not make its way into productive usage. The most obvious example of this skewed development can be seen in the oil-producing areas of the Niger River delta. Potentially the wealthiest of all the regions, the people inhabiting the delta, such as the Ogoni and Ijaw peoples, have the lowest indicators of social development, and the environmental degradation of the region is staggering. This has led to massive social protests over the past decade, but these have consistently been met with brutal force from the federal government, often with the connivance of the oil corporations.

Institutions and parties

Since 1960, Nigeria has had just under thirty years of military government, four different constitutions and republics, both parliamentary and presidential forms of government, at least eight governments overthrown by the military, and numerous different sets of political parties. The internal federal structure has evolved from three regions to thirty-six states in an effort to undermine the strength of regional and ethnic politics (and to offer more politicians the opportunity to extract wealth). In this environment of experimentation and instability, it is little surprise that democratic institutions and structures of government have been unable to establish themselves.

At independence, Nigeria was bestowed the Westminster model of government. This failed to contain the conflicts between government and 'opposition', which were themselves exacerbated by the power struggle between fledgling federal government and established ethnically driven regional governments. With hindsight, this system perhaps only effectively operated for two or three years, but it lingered until the 1966 military coup. Military governments ruled for all but four years between 1966 and 1999, and ranged considerably in capability and probity. Political parties were proscribed during much of military rule, and little progress

was made in solving the social, ethnic, and religious problems facing the country. The civilian Second Republic (1979–83) was, like the first, dominated by northern power groups, and fizzled out in extreme corruption, ethnic bias, and electoral fraud before being swept from office on New Year's Eve 1983. This republic was very much fashioned upon the American presidential model, with an executive president, a Senate, and a House of Representatives. This political model is perhaps better suited to Nigerian political life, and was adopted for the Fourth Republic in 1999.

The 1990s proved to be the darkest period of political development, as the federal government became the personal plaything of one leader, Sani Abacha. In elections for the Third Republic in 1993, results pointed to a win by Chief Moshood Abiola, a Yoruba Muslim businessman. Alarmed at the possible consequences, the military government under Ibrahim Babangida—perhaps prompted by Abacha as the powerful minister of defence—annulled the elections and transferred power to a military and civilian coalition that lasted a few months before being overthrown by Abacha. When Abiola returned from exile in 1994, he was detained by Abacha, and eventually died in prison. Plans for a return to civilian government were repeatedly postponed, as civilian political leaders were hand-picked and dropped by Abacha. By 1998, Abacha had manipulated the political process to the extent that he was the sole presidential candidate of all five parties allowed by his regime. Upon his surprise death (assassination?), yet another political transition was started, and again a new slate of political parties created. The success of Obasanjo, a former military head of state, indicates the residual power of military leaders in the political process. In 2003, the presidential election was contested by two former military leaders, Obasanjo and Muhammadu Buhari, with a third, Babangida, biding his time for the 2007 elections. Elections have always been manipulated by incumbents, and the 2003 elections were no exception.

The April 2007 presidential election offered the first-ever transfer of power from one civilian government to another, but with little guarantee of political stability. Tensions within the ruling People's Democratic Party (PDP) were rife during Obasanjo's second term, with the president and vice president Atiku Abubakar trading barbs and, by 2006, each calling for the other's resignation. Also, the vice president faced court charges of corruption. Abubakar accepted the presidential nomination from the opposition Action Congress in December 2006, sparking further conflict. The PDP selected a relatively unknown governor from the northern state of Katsina, Umaru Yar'Adua, to be its presidential candidate. Obasanjo is to remain as chairman of the PDP, and likely to be the power behind the throne. This public debacle reflected severe tensions on religious and ethnic grounds. In the event, the 2007 elections were marred by widespread fraud and some violence.

Civil society

Despite long periods of oppressive rule, civil society groups have remained active and strong. The media have been outspoken during even the darkest times, and have helped to maintain a healthy dialogue about national and local policies. The universities have also played a strong role in voicing opinions about governments and policies, and student protests are a common feature. Similarly trade unions have been relatively well organized and not afraid to take action when their interests were threatened, and judges strove to maintain their independence. During the Abacha administration, repression of these groups was at its maximum, but many of them fought back against the regime,

often from exile. Human rights and democracy organizations flourished, and worked with external groups to maintain pressure upon the regime. Unfortunately, these groups were often divided upon ethnic lines, but nevertheless were an important indication of the strength and vitality of civilian society, resisting blatant oppression. Prominent Nigerian writers such as Chinua Achebe, Ken Saro-Wiwa, and Wole Soyinka, were also important in maintaining pressure upon the corrupt regimes.

With such a vibrant civil society, one perhaps might expect significant advances in the political arena in terms of **good governance** and accountability. Unfortunately, to date, this has not transpired.

KEY POINTS

- The military has played a dominant role in the political history of Nigeria.

- Significant political experimentation with institutions and structures of government has occurred, but little has proved effective in containing societal strains brought about by ethnic, regional, and religious cleavages.

- Civil society groups have maintained a consistently strong role in Nigerian political life, despite many years of military rule.

- The re-election of Obasanjo in 2003 gave hope to the idea that the cycle of military rule has been broken, though Obasanjo's government soon came under fire for delivering very little to the average Nigerian and for not ending corruption. His bid to change the constitution to enable a third term was defeated in 2006.

Regional Influence in Foreign Policy

Although opinions differ over the extent of Nigeria's influence in the international arena, it is evident that the country exerts considerable influence in

the West African region, and has an important role to play in many African issues, often representing the views of the continent on the world stage. The factors shaping this role are fairly evident. Nigeria's population size, market potential, military capability, oil and gas revenues, and OPEC membership provide important resources for the projection of influence. Conversely, most of its neighbours are very small and lack the demographic and economic resources to be all but reactive and relatively passive in the foreign policy arena.

West Africa has been the most important focus of foreign policy, although this has often been an unsympathetic arena for Nigerian endeavours. All of its neighbours are former French colonies, and the residual linkages of la francophonie have at times undermined Nigerian initiatives. Many neighbours, along with France, were supportive of Biafran secession during the civil war, and these divisions were only slowly healed through Nigerian largesse. In 1975, Nigeria's lead in diplomacy with Benin brought about ECOWAS as an attempt to check French influence in the region. During its thirty or more years, ECOWAS has attempted to improve trade and movement of people within the region. Official trade figures remain low, as vital trade partners are in Europe, but unofficial (illegal) trade has flourished, with the porosity of the Nigerian borders being an important contributory factor. The role of Nigeria in the region's trade is important, either way.

Nigerian governments have often taken on the role of African champion, promoting causes on behalf of the continent. During the 1960s and 1970s, these focused upon non-alignment, African independence, liberation in southern Africa, and economic rights. In 1973, for example, the administration of General Gowon was a leader of the New International Economic Order as well as in negotiations leading to the agreement signed in 1975 between the European Union and the African, Caribbean, and Pacific (ACP) States, which issued in the first of four Lomé Conventions. After 1980, as economic problems weakened Nigerian leverage, the country's global impact was less certain.

During the 1990s, Nigeria's position as Africa's proclaimed champion was undermined by several factors. First, the achievement of majority rule by South Africa meant that Nigeria's somewhat unchallenged 'leadership' of the continent was now rivalled by a stronger economic power, whose GDP is three times larger than Nigeria's. Second, whereas Nelson Mandela was, and remains, an icon to the world, the despotic military leaders in Nigeria left the country increasingly isolated in the world. Nigeria's isolation peaked during the mid-1990s, when minor sanctions were imposed by the West, and Nigeria was suspended from the Commonwealth. Third, the failure to democratize until 1999 and the obvious frailty of democracy in the country, served to undermine the legitimacy of the country to lead.

The new era opened up by the election of Obasanjo in 1999 helped to restore some credibility, and also repaired frayed relations with the United States, the European Union, and the international financial institutions. Investment in the oil and gas sectors increased considerably although they had not been affected much during the 1990s. The Obasanjo government helped to restore the country's battered image. Nigeria played an important role in helping to establish the New Economic Partnership for Africa's Development (NEPAD) in the early 2000s, a major development initiative for the continent in partnership with the UN and industrialized countries. Nigeria also benefited from the US's strategy to lessen its dependence upon Middle Eastern oil, and by 2006 some 40 per cent of Nigeria's oil exports went to the US.

KEY POINTS

- Nigerian governments in the 1970s were extremely active in promoting foreign policy objectives on behalf of the African continent.

- Nigeria championed the African, Caribbean, and Pacific (ACP) group of countries during negotiations leading to the Lomé Convention in 1975.

- In recent years, Nigeria's attempts to lead African opinion have been somewhat undermined by South Africa, with which some tensions have been witnessed.

Conclusion

Probably the best way to describe Nigeria is as a country of unfulfilled promise. Despite its demographic size and economic potential, the country has been dogged by numerous political and social problems, although it has scored some modest foreign policy successes. So how should we view Nigeria? In terms of a positive outlook, Nigeria still remains a strong state with viable potential. Unlike some of its neighbours, the federal government exerts considerable power internally, and the country's borders remain relatively secure. The re-election of Obasanjo in 2003, and the elections of April 2007, provide optimism that the country has finally turned away from military government, and may be moving closer to some resolution of its political development problems. A buoyant oil economy, and continuing large flows of foreign investment into this sector, indicate that the economic profile can remain strong.

Conversely, it is possible to pull together a number of negative factors that create a more pessimistic forecast. Instability and corruption remain endemic, with fraud being an important element of both the 2003 and 2007 elections. Ethnic and religious intolerance and violence is on the increase, with the government showing little capability to change that course. Talk of secession by different groups also increasingly fills the political airwaves. Continuing violence and labour unrest in the critical oilfields spell serious problems for Western oil companies. Democracy's quality is flawed and its future not yet secure.

Which Nigeria do we see? On the one hand, many of these problems are not new, and Nigeria has weathered them quite effectively to date. On the other hand, there appears to be little if any progress over more than four decades in solving these endemic issues. Nigeria is often seen as a bellwether for other countries across the continent, and so how it develops over the coming years is of vital importance to the West African region if not the continent as a whole.

? QUESTIONS

1 Was the breakdown of the new Nigerian state inevitable in the 1960s?

2 What key factors tend to hamper the development of a true national consciousness in Nigeria?

3 How important is oil to the economics and politics of Nigeria?

4 What factors help to explain the continuing prevalence of corruption in Nigeria?

5 Is democracy entrenched today in Nigeria, or not?

6 To what extent has Nigeria's international influence been undermined by its domestic political difficulties?

GUIDE TO FURTHER READING

 Falola, T. (1999), *The History of Nigeria* (Westport, Conn.: Greenwood Press). An overview of the historical development of Nigeria, and the legacies of history faced today.

STEPHEN WRIGHT

■ ——and Oyabude, A. (2002), *The Transformation of Nigeria: Essays in Honor of Toyin Falola* (Trenton, NJ: Africa World Press). Explores various issues in Nigeria's political development.

■ Ihonvbere, J. (1998), and Shaw, T., *Illusions of Power: Nigeria in Transition* (Trenton, NJ: Africa World Press). A political economy account of Nigerian development, offering a critique of more traditional perspectives on Nigeria.

■ King, M. (1996), *Basic Currents of Nigerian Foreign Policy* (Washington DC: Howard University Press). Offers an overview of the main themes of foreign policy, along with an account of major activities and policies.

■ Maier, K. (2000), *This House Has Fallen: Midnight in Nigeria* (New York: Public Affairs). A more informal account of the political and social demise of Nigeria during the 1990s.

■ Osaghae, E. (1998), *Crippled Giant: Nigeria since Independence* (Bloomington, Ind.: Indiana University Press). An overview of Nigerian political and economic development since independence.

■ Smith, D. J. (2007), *A Culture of Corruption: Everyday Deception and Popular Discontent in Nigeria* (Princeton, NJ: Princeton University Press). An examination of the methods and impact of corruption in Nigeria.

■ Soyinka, W. (1996), *The Open Sore of a Continent: A Personal Narrative of the Nigerian Crisis* (New York: Oxford University Press). The Nobel laureate's bitter account of the failings of the Abacha regime.

■ Wright, S. (1998), *Nigeria: Struggle for Stability and Status* (Boulder, Colo.: Westview Press). An analysis of Nigeria since independence, focusing upon domestic instability and efforts to promote a strong external policy.

WEB LINKS

- www.nigeriainfonet.com
- www.nigeria.com
- www.ngrguardiannews.com *Guardian* (Lagos) newspaper.
- www.vanguardngr.com The site of Vanguard news media (Nigeria).
- www.nigeriaworld.com

ONLINE RESOURCE CENTRE

For additional material and resources, see the Online Resource Centre at:
www.oxfordtextbooks.co.uk/orc/burnell2e/

22c Mexico: Democratic Transition and Beyond

ANDREAS SCHEDLER

Chapter Contents

- Introduction: From Independence to Revolution
- The Foundations of Electoral Authoritarianism
- The Structural Bases of Regime Change
- Democratization by Elections
- After Transition
- Conclusion

Overview

With a population close to 100 million, a vast and heterogeneous territory, an extended common border with the United States, and an enormously rich cultural heritage, Mexico is too important to be ignored. Traditionally classified as part of Mesoamerica, Mexico was formally admitted into North America following the enactment of the North American Free Trade Agreement with the USA and Canada in 1994. In 2000, the victory of conservative opposition candidate Vicente Fox in Mexico's presidential election sealed the end of more than seven decades of uninterrupted single-party rule. For most of the twentieth century, the country was ruled by a broadly inclusive hegemonic party seeking to ratify its monopoly hold on power through controlled, non-competitive elections at all levels. In contrast to much of the literature, this chapter presents Mexico's post-revolutionary political system not as a regime *sui generis*—a unique, idiosyncratic form of authoritarianism—but rather as a prototypical case of 'electoral authoritarianism' (see Box 22c.2). Similarly, it interprets the country's recent trajectory of regime change not as a transition *sui generis*—as a unique, idiosyncratic path to democracy—but instead as a prototypical case of 'democratization by elections'.

MEXICO

BOX 22c.1

Key Dates in Mexico's History

1810–21	War of Independence against Spain.
1846–8	War between Mexico and the United States.
1857	New republican constitution.
1876–1910	Presidency of Porfirio Díaz.
1910–20	Mexican Revolution.
1917	New constitution (still in force).
1929	Foundation of the National Revolutionary Party, later changed to PRI, that was to rule Mexico for seven decades.
1934–40	Land redistribution, social reforms, and oil nationalization under President Lázaro Cárdenas.
1982	Debt crisis.
1988	'Earthquake election': unprecedented competitiveness at a presidential election. The PRI candidate obtains a bare majority of valid votes; the opposition charges fraud.
1990	Foundation of the Federal Electoral Institute (IFE).
1994	North American Free Trade Agreement; Zapatista rebellion.
1996	The 'definitive' electoral reform.
1997	In mid-term election, PRI loses its absolute majority in the Chamber of Deputies; inauguration of divided government.
2000	Conservative opposition candidate Vicente Fox wins the presidency
2006	In a close and contested election, Felipe Calderón from the conservative PAN wins the presidency. Left-wing candidate López Obrador rejects the election as fraudulent.

Introduction: From Independence to Revolution

As Mexico reached independence from Spain after a decade of war in 1821, it faced the triple challenge of redefining its political regime, constructing a modern state, and laying the foundations of a capitalist economy. Failure in establishing a regime—in institutionalizing accepted rules of access to power and exercise of power—precluded success in building a state and developing a market. In its first thirty years of political independence, the country fell prey to the vicissitudes of *caudillismo*. Between 1821 and 1850, the country was (nominally) ruled by fifty different governments, most of them delivered by military rebellions. Internal instability was matched by external vulnerability. In the war against the United States (1846–8), Mexico lost around half its territory. At home, civilian politics was increasingly driven by the major cleavage common to most of nineteenth-century Latin America: conflict between conservatives and liberals. Conservatives sought to protect the inherited political, economic, and cultural power of the Catholic Church. Liberals strove to limit it and to create an autonomous sphere of secular politics.

The developmental dictatorship under Porfirio Díaz (1876–1910), while harshly repressive, brought an unprecedented measure of stability and institutional modernization. Having taken power by a coup, General Díaz proceeded to set up an early variant of **electoral authoritarianism**. Regular (indirect) presidential elections confirmed his continuity in power by acclamation. Regular legislative contests between extremely personalized and fragmented political parties produced mostly weak, even if nominally representative, legislatures. At the same time, something like a modern state started to take shape, with a central government, a national military, and a professional bureaucracy extending its reach to the country's periphery. In addition, foreign investment aided by public

BOX 22c.2

Electoral Authoritarianism

Electoral autocracies display a nominal adherence to the principle of democratic rule, while denying democracy in practice. Particularly, they hold regular multi-party elections, yet constrain and subvert them so deeply as to render them instruments not of democracy, but of authoritarian rule. Modern examples are the presidencies of Fujimori (Peru), Mugabe (Zimbabwe), and Soeharto (Indonesia).

infrastructure (railroads) enabled some incipient, dependent industrialization through the development of an extractive enclave economy.

The Mexican Revolution (1910–20) is customarily explained as a response to the growing impoverishment of the rural masses. Its first impulse, however, was entirely political. After three decades of developmental dictatorship, liberal reformer Francisco I. Madero demanded democratic elections (*sufragio efectivo*) and alternation in power (*no-reelección*). In the 1911 (indirect) elections, he won the presidency with 99.3 per cent of total votes. He was murdered two years later in a military coup. The ensuing civil war is commonly described as the first social revolution of the twentieth century, and about 1.4 million people out of a total population of 15.2 million lost their lives.

The revolutionary Constitution, enacted in 1917 and still in force today, enshrined a mixture of political liberalism and social reformism. It copied almost the full set of political institutions from the US Constitution: presidential government, federalism, bicameralism, and plurality elections at all levels. In addition, it limited the scope of the market economy by reserving 'strategic sectors' to the state while stipulating extensive social rights for peasants and workers. Ironically, under the one-party hegemony that emerged after the revolution, the constitution proved ineffective in its procedural as well as in its substantive aspects. It worked neither as an effective institutional constraint on politics nor as an effective policy programme.

KEY POINTS

- During much of the nineteenth century, Mexico's difficulties in institutionalizing a political regime frustrated its efforts at state-building and economic development.

- The revolutionary 1917 Constitution established (on paper) a liberal division of power, while locking in substantive policies in the fields of public education, labour rights, and control over national resources.

The Foundations of Electoral Authoritarianism

Post-revolutionary politics continued to be disorderly and violent. The bullet, alongside the ballot, enjoyed acceptance as a valid currency for gaining and losing public office. Violent protest, military rebellion, and the physical elimination of adversaries remained common. But regular elections took place at all levels, though nothing resembling a structured party system existed. Political parties were ephemeral collections of followers around local notables or military leaders. Politics remained a game of elite competition mediated by force, not by formal institutions.

The crisis of presidential succession in 1928 marked a turning point. After the assassination of president elect Alvaro Obregón in July, outgoing president Plutarco Elías Calles (1924–8) announced his intention to institutionalize the revolutionary government. In spring 1929, he founded the National Revolutionary Party (PRN) as an umbrella organization of all revolutionary leaders, factions, and parties.

Twin institutionalization

The PRN was to pacify electoral disputes by providing a transparent mechanism of electoral coordination: it would select winning candidates from among the 'revolutionary family', reward their followers, and crush their opponents. By the mid-1930s, the PRN was able to centralize candidate selection by dissolving local parties and prohibiting the immediate re-election of deputies. Within a few years, what was initially a loose alliance of local factions established itself as a centralized hegemonic party that was to rule Mexico for the rest of the century.

Before quitting power peacefully in the 2000 presidential elections, the successor party of the PRN, the Institutional Revolutionary Party (PRI), was the longest-reigning political party in the world. It had clearly excelled in fulfilling its original mission of pacifying and stabilizing the country. How did the PRI achieve this extraordinary success in party and regime institutionalization? Like all institutions, it had to accomplish two basic objectives: 'stability' and 'value' (Huntington 1968). The former is a matter of expectations, the latter one of evaluations. People had to know that the PRI was there to stay; that the revolutionary game it played was 'the only game in town'. But they had to value it, too. One-party hegemony had to appear as a fact of life as well as moral achievement.

The institutional infrastructure

Over seven decades, the PRI sustained a regime that looked as exceptional as its longevity. Scholars commonly described it as a civilian, inclusive, corporatist, and hyper-presidential authoritarian regime held together by a pragmatic, patronage-based state party. In essence, Mexico's 'authoritarianism with adjectives' rested upon three institutional pillars: a hierarchical state party, state corporatism, and electoral gatekeeping.

On the first, the hegemonic party operated as a big 'linkage mechanism' that turned the Mexican state into a unitary hierarchical organization. By controlling all branches and levels of government, the hegemonic party effectively cancelled the constitutional distribution of state power. It annulled the horizontal division of power between the executive, legislative, and judicial branches as well as the vertical division of power between central government, federal states, and municipalities. No political opposition, no checks and balances. The fusion between state and party granted almost unlimited meta-constitutional powers to the president. He acted as the supreme patron who sat at the peak of an immense clientelist pyramid that was the Mexican state.

The state in turn controlled civil society, not so much through repression as by coopting and corrupting potential dissidents and opponents. After all, it was supposed to be an inclusive, integrative enterprise, an institutional roof large enough to accommodate the whole revolutionary family. The party patronized, and at the same time domesticated, labour unions, peasant organizations, and popular movements by incorporating them into tightly controlled corporatist arrangements. It kept business people content with subsidies, market protection, and informal access to power. Through a mixture of material incentives and political constraints it kept the mass media quiet. Finally, the Catholic Church was persuaded to observe its constitutional mandate of keeping out of politics by reminders of the possible alternative: oppression by the state of religious institutions, as in the 1920s.

The state also controlled elections, which were held frequently. Unlike other electoral autocracies such as Taiwan until the 1980s, the PRI regime did not allow intra-party competition (within the ruling party) in the electoral arena. Instead, it admitted organized competition by opposition parties, albeit under (adverse) conditions not of their own making. Electoral autocracies like the PRI regime reproduce and legitimate themselves on the basis of periodic elections that show some measure of pluralism but fall short of minimum democratic standards. In such regimes, multi-party elections are not embedded in the 'surrounding freedoms' essential to liberal democracy. Instead, they are constrained through a variety of authoritarian controls. The violations of liberal-democratic norms may be manifold (see Schedler 2002b), and post-revolutionary Mexico had nearly all of them in place: limitations of civil and political liberties, restrictions on party and candidate registration, discriminatory rules of representation, electoral fraud, corruption, and coercion, as well as an uneven playing field, with the incumbent enjoying close to monopolistic access to media and campaign resources.

The ideological infrastructure

Following Sartori (1976), scholars commonly portray Mexico's post-revolutionary regime as 'pragmatic' authoritarianism. True, the PRI did not institute a mobilizational dictatorship that tried to coerce its subjects into ideological uniformity. It accepted some measure of economic and civil liberties, including religious freedom, encouraged political opposition parties to its left and right (as long as they remained harmless), and accommodated considerable programmatic diversity within the party. The relative tolerance of pluralism, however, should not be mistaken for the absence of ideology. Its revolutionary nationalism was not a mere echo chamber.

Actually, the PRI was remarkably successful in creating what Antonio Gramsci called cultural 'hegemony'. The state party defined the lasting coordinates of national identity—the national history, national foes and heroes, national symbols and rituals, and, last but not least, the promise of progress and justice. The official party effectively managed to turn its ideology—a combination of liberalism, nationalism, and the corporative defence of the welfare state—into the foundations of national political correctness. Even today, the language and ideology of revolutionary nationalism continues to constrain Mexican politics. It still sets the terms of public debate in numerous policy spheres, such as the management of natural resources, public education, and foreign policy.

KEY POINTS

- Post-revolutionary Mexico developed an electoral authoritarian regime held together by a hegemonic party, the PRI.

- The party commandeered the state as well as civil society. Through its centralized control of elections, it acted as the sole gatekeeper to public office.

- The PRI did not exercise its power 'naked' but draped in national-revolutionary ideology. Non-democratic rule lived off popular legitimacy.

The Structural Bases of Regime Change

The relationship between economic development and political democracy has been subject to intense debate (see Chapter 14). But although for long a democratic under-achiever, Mexico seems to confirm the elective affinity between socio-economic and political modernization.

Societal transformation

Not unlike Porfirio Díaz—even if less personalistic, repressive, and exclusionary—the PRI established its own version of developmental dictatorship. Especially during the 'Mexican miracle' between 1940 and 1970, it achieved steady rates of economic growth and expanding public services. Notwithstanding the economic crises that irrupted at each presidential succession from 1976 to 1994, seven decades of modernizing authoritarian rule by the PRI produced profound societal transformations. Mexico at the end of the revolution was a country dramatically different from Mexico at the turn of the century. In 1930, Mexico's population stood at 16.5 million, the annual per capita income stood

at US$166 (in 1960 terms), 70.2 per cent of the workforce was employed in agriculture, 68.8 per cent of Mexicans lived in villages with fewer than 2.500 inhabitants, and the illiteracy rate among the population of age 10 and higher was 61.5 per cent. In 1995, by contrast, the population had jumped to 93.7 million, annual per capita income reached US$2,790 (current), primary sector employment was only 22.3 per cent, urbanization 74 per cent, and illiteracy down to 10.6 per cent (figures from Banco de México, Instituto Nacional de Estadística, Geografía e Informática, and World Bank). Although about half of the population still counts as poor, and the country displays one of the most unequal income distributions in the world, similar to South Africa under apartheid, the structural transformation from poor and rural to middle-income and urban was bound to create strong pressures for democratization. The widening gap between socio-economic and political modernization was difficult to sustain. Societal pluralism could not be contained within the confinements of a single party. In addition, the structural dissociation between a hegemonic party and a complex society was deepened by economic mismanagement and crisis.

Economic crises

After 1970, a mixture of structural disequilibria and performance failure pushed Mexico into periodic economic recessions. Each presidential succession from 1976 to 1994 was marked by economic crisis. The oil boom and external debt first postponed, and then aggravated, the big crash of 1982. In 1983, per capita GDP fell 4.2 per cent, annual inflation reached 80.5 per cent, and real minimum wages plummeted by 25.2 per cent (Banco de México). Popular discontent sky-rocketed.

In retrospect, the debt crisis of the early 1980s was the starting point of democratization. There was nothing inevitable about it, however. Neither structural incongruence nor cyclical stress translate smoothly and automatically into democratizing progress. During the 1970s and 1980s, the talk of the day was about *crisis*—a situation of change and anxiety, without any clear sense of where the country was heading. Anything seemed possible, including a return to the violence of the past. It was only in the late 1980s that this diffuse sense of alarm receded. Actors and analysts started talking about democratic *transition*. And they started playing the game of transition—the game of peaceful, incremental political democratization.

> **KEY POINTS**
>
> - Socio-economic modernization created multiple pressures for democratization.
> - Cycles of economic crisis sapped the regime's legitimacy.

Democratization by Elections

Under electoral autocracies like the PRI regime, elections are not 'instruments of democracy' (Powell 2000) but battlefields of democratization. Unlike democratic elections, manipulated elections unfold as two-level games in which parties compete for votes at the same time as they struggle over basic rules. Electoral competition goes hand in hand with institutional conflict. Democratization 'by elections' ensues when opposition parties succeed at both levels, when they manage to undermine both pillars of authoritarian rule: its popular support as well as its anti-democratic institutions (Schedler 2002a). Mexico's emergent opposition parties—the right-wing National Action Party (PAN), a tenacious regime opponent since the late 1940s, and the left-wing Party of the Democratic Revolution (PRD), founded in 1989—were able to start just such a self-reinforcing spiral of rising competitiveness and democratic reform. As they turned into serious contenders, they were able to remove successive layers of authoritarian control, in five negotiated electoral reforms following 1987.

Electoral competition

Historic turnout figures indicate the hegemonic party's capacity for electoral mobilization was modest. Its official election results, by contrast, were impressive. Until 1982, all Mexican revolutionary and post-revolutionary presidents were elected by acclamation (except for 1946 and 1952 when they faced relatively popular splinter candidates). Plurality elections prevented opposition parties from winning legislative seats until the early 1960s. In 1963, the PRI introduced some element of proportional representation to keep the PAN in the electoral game, yet without jeopardizing its two-thirds majority—a condition to enact constitutional changes.

In the wake of the 1982 debt crisis, however, the governing party's hegemony began to crumble. First, the PAN started to win, and to defend its victories, in a series of post-electoral confrontations, at the municipal and state level in northern Mexico. Then, in the 1988 presidential election, the performance of PRI dissident Cuauhtémoc Cárdenas shattered the image of PRI invincibility at the national level. His followers continue to think he had actually won the contest, only being denied victory by blatant electoral fraud. Afterwards, opposition parties conquered more and more sites of subnational power, at the same time as they strengthened their presence in the bicameral national legislature.

Until the early 1980s, opposition parties succeeded in winning only occasional municipal elections; by the year 2000, opposition mayors governed more than half of Mexico's total population. Until 1989, opposition forces had not won any gubernatorial contests; by mid-2000 they controlled eleven of the thirty-one federal states. In 1988, the official party was stripped of its comfortable two-thirds majority in the Chamber of Deputies. In 1997, it lost its absolute majority, too, inaugurating an unprecedented period of divided government. Until 1988, no opposition candidate was elected to the Senate. In the 1997 senatorial elections, the PRI lost its two-thirds majority there, and in 2000 it fell below the 50 per cent threshold. Finally, in 2000 PAN candidate Vicente Fox won the real big prize in Mexican politics—the presidency.

Electoral reform

The rising competitiveness of the party system made possible (and was made possible by) profound changes in the institutions of electoral governance. Today, vote-rigging and the state control of elections belong to the past. Within less than a decade, Mexico effectively remodelled its electoral institutions. The electoral reforms, negotiated under

the pressure of hundreds of local post-electoral conflicts, and enacted in 1990, 1993, 1994, and culminating in 1996, added up to a veritable institutional revolution within the (self-denominated) regime of the institutional revolution.

The new electoral system rested upon three institutional columns: a new independent election body, the judicialization of conflict resolution, and comprehensive oversight by parties. Consonant with an international trend, Mexican parties decided to delegate the organization of elections to a permanent and independent election management body, the Federal Electoral Institute (IFE), founded in 1990. Electoral reformers have also set up a new system for the judicial resolution of election disputes: the Electoral Tribunal of the Judicial Power of the Federation (TEPJF) now has the last say in all electoral disputes, national as well as subnational. Finally, parties have institutionalized a 'panoptic regime' of surveillance that allows them to monitor closely the entire electoral process step by step.

Outside the electoral arena

While political parties are the lead actors in democratization by elections, they have to be responsive to shocks and actors outside the electoral arena. Given the civilian nature of the Mexican regime, political actors have not had to worry much about the military, but nevertheless faced a complex configuration of other domestic and international players.

Business people—for long supportive of electoral authoritarianism—began to disown the PRI after 1982. Economic crisis and nationalization of the banks taught them authoritarian discretion was bad for business. Democratic checks and balances promised more secure property rights and sound macro-economic management. By contrast, organized labour remained bound to the PRI even as individual workers and dissident unions grew autonomous. Until recently, the party could count as well on the green vote of the rural poor. The 1994 uprising by the Zapatistas in the southern state of

Chiapas opened the door for the entry of indigenous people into the arena of politics. Initially, as it forced political parties to resume reform negotiations (in early 1994), it played out a recurrent irony of history: the threat of violence acting as a midwife of democratizing consensus. (Later on, the Zapatista rebellion gradually faded from the national political agenda, even though the underlying structural problems remained unresolved.)

Undoubtedly, international factors carried weight as well. Historically, the United States, much like the Mexican middle class, has been more interested in Mexican stability than democracy. It started to distance itself from the PRI to the extent that the party lost its ability to guarantee the country's political and economic stability. The North American Free Trade Agreement (NAFTA), in force since 1994, did little to promote democracy directly. But by locking in liberal market reforms it made Mexican economic policies essentially immune to democratic alternation in power. Democracy, rendered conservative in this way, stopped frightening economic liberals in Washington as well as in Mexico City.

KEY POINTS

- Mexico's democratic advance resulted from the interplay between democratizing reform and increasing inter-party competition.

- The North American Free Trade Agreement constrains the macro-economic policies of future democratic governments.

After Transition

Often, after the excitement of transition, political boredom and disenchantment set in. With the 2000 alternation in power, Mexico has turned into a 'normal' Latin American democracy operating in the context of a weak state and an unequal society. Mexican elites and citizens now face the twin challenge of democratic consolidation and deepening (concepts discussed in Chapter 14).

Democratic deepening

In 2000, for the first time ever, Freedom House classified Mexico as an 'electoral democracy'. This could be misleading if it implies that democratizing progress had been limited to the electoral arena. True enough, struggles for democratization have revolved around the conduct of elections. Yet, as political actors were rebuilding the electoral arena they transformed other spheres of politics as well. Constructing new rules of *access* to power as well as new realities of inter-party competition had profound implications for the *exercise* of power as well.

The mere introduction of opposition at all levels changed the political system without the need to change its constitutional underpinnings. The rise of opposition parties to multiple sites of state power reinvigorated constitutional checks and balances that had lain dormant. Thanks to the new pluralism of the party system, the constitutional division of power, once a formality, is now meaningful reality. Today both the legislature and the judiciary impose tangible limits on the executive, and federalism is no longer hollow. Both state and municipal governments are real sites of power. A host of autonomous administrative, regulatory, and jurisprudential bodies complement the classic division of power, for instance, the Federal Electoral Institute, the National Commission for Human Rights, and the Federal Institute for Access to Public Information. Contemporary Mexico may not be a fully liberal democracy, but it is not a purely minimal democracy either. Given the dense web of formal and political constraints officeholders face, the country cannot be described as an illiberal or delegative democracy.

That said, there is considerable scope for democratic deepening. The rule of law is incomplete and fragile, much closer to the tyranny of bureaucracy than to formal justice. Above all, the realm of criminal law continues to form a theatre of tragic corruption and injustice, procedural as well as substantive, a persistent threat to the integrity of private life. The extractive capacities of the state are weak, its claim to a monopoly of physical violence contested. Crime has been soaring and drug-related violence is getting close to levels otherwise seen in civil wars. Mexico's multiple free-trade agreements have allowed a sustained expansion of exports, while they have contributed little to alleviate the plight of the rural poor. Persistent widespread poverty and socio-economic inequality betray the democratic promise of equal participation in public life. Powerful private monopolies and unaccountable public-sector unions perpetuate wasteful systems of rent-seeking. The prohibition of immediate re-election of legislators and mayors renders electoral accountability ineffective. Corruption is widespread and to the average politician austerity in office and republican self-restraint seem to be alien ideas. Citizen participation is shallow, discontent runs deep. Political incompetence, partisan infighting, and the constitutional fragmentation of power block urgent policy reforms.

All this remains true even after six years of president Fox's self-proclaimed 'government of change'. Lacking a sense of priorities, avoiding confrontation with the corporate survivors of the old regime, and resigning himself to the political limits of divided government, Fox followed a politics of incremental change in small, often imperceptible, steps. By and large, he seemed to content himself with the cheerful administration of the status quo. Of course, democracy never is the solution to all problems. It is an institutional framework for seeking solutions and resolving conflicts in a peaceful way. Yet democratizing democracy is clearly one of the big assignments of Mexico's fledgling democratic regime.

Democratic consolidation

Alternation in power in 2000 marked the symbolic end of the democratic transition. It also seemed to mark the instantaneous accomplishment of democratic consolidation. Clearly, it seemed, democracy had come to stay, recognized and practised by all relevant actors as 'the only game in town' (Linz and Stepan 1996). The contested 2006 presidential election did not shatter expectations of democratic stability entirely. Yet it did introduce serious question marks.

Left-wing candidate Andrés Manuel López Obrador lost by 233,831 votes, barely 0.58 per cent of valid votes, against the conservative Felipe Calderón. He revived the dramatic rhetoric of past democratizing struggles, claimed fraud, and took his followers to the streets. As the federal electoral tribunal denied his demand of a full vote recount, he accused a 'rapacious minority' of 'white-collar criminals and corrupt politicians' of having stolen the election to maintain the prevailing 'regime of corruption and privilege'. He sent existing political institutions 'to the devil' and had a crowd of followers proclaim him 'legitimate president' of Mexico. Overall, the election could be considered clean, fair, and democratic. Still, several coinciding factors allowed the losing candidate to mobilize institutional distrust: a defective system of ballot accounting, logical inconsistencies in the electoral tribunal's final ruling, the memory of past electoral fraud, the general context of weak legality, his firm expectation of victory, as well as the longstanding fear that his adversaries were willing to transgress democratic rules in order to keep him out of the presidential office (see Schedler 2007).

Many observers dismiss López Obrador's parallel presidency as a 'clownesque' manoeuvre not to be taken seriously by committed democrats. However, at the time of writing, the losing candidate and his followers remain seemingly determined to provoke a premature termination of Calderón's presidency. Even if unlikely, the extra-constitutional removal of the president through street pressure, as has happened in the various interrupted presidencies of contemporary Latin America, appears as a real possibility, perhaps only to be avoided if taken seriously. This implies that Mexico has lost one of its most precious historical achievements: the clockwise certainty of its electoral calendar. The contested elections of 2006 have blurred this valuable hallmark of democratic consolidation.

KEY POINTS

- Mexican democracy faces the twin challenge of socio-economic development and democratic deepening.

- With the 2000 alternation in power, with no extremist parties threatening the democratic system, Mexican democracy seemed to have achieved instantaneous consolidation.

- The close and contested presidential election of 2006, however, involved various threats to Mexico's democratic advances. The losing candidate did not concede defeat, a third of citizens believe the election was fraudulent, and the new president faces well-organized adversaries determined to force his resignation under the pressure of street mobilization.

Conclusion

At the turn of the twenty-first century, after traumatic experiences of instability and violence, followed by seven decades of authoritarian stability, Mexico finally seemed to have found a way of reconciling political stability and democracy. After the tranquil alternation in power of the year 2000, few things seemed to be capable of upsetting the new-found equilibrium of democratic politics. A close outcome in presidential elections was one of them. On the eve of the 2006 presidential elections, election authorities as well as independent observers feared one worst-case scenario: a close defeat of the left-wing opposition candidate. The worst scenario came true, and it involved a true test for Mexico's fledgling democracy. In the post-electoral phase, the system proved resilient to its strategic assault by a losing candidate who skilfully activated existing reservoirs of distrust through an aggressive anti-political and anti-institutional discourse. However, the only way of guaranteeing democracy is by not taking it for granted. If Mexican democracy is to be saved from a frustrating period of stagnation and disorder, it may only be through an audacious program of democratizing democracy. The constitutionalization of censorship in the most recent round of electoral reform in 2007 augurs badly for the health of Mexico's democracy. To secure the democratic advances of the past, politicians as well as citizens, rather than ceding to illiberal impulses, will have to push for further democratic advances .

? **QUESTIONS**

1   Compare and contrast the central political and economic challenges of post-independence Mexico.

2 How do you account for the institutional and ideological foundations of Mexico's post-revolutionary authoritarianism?

3 Did Mexico's socio-economic modernization in the twentieth century trigger political democrat-ization? Give reasons for your answer.

4 Identify the core features of 'democratization by elections' and assess their ability to persist over time.

5 What are the main democratic deficiencies of Mexican democracy today?

6 What are the implications of the close and highly contested outcome of Mexico's 2006 presidential election for the country's democratic consolidation?

 GUIDE TO FURTHER READING

■ Bruhn, K. et al. (2007), 'The 2006 Election and its Aftermath', *PS Political Science and Politics* **1/40 (January).** Symposium on parties and voters in the 2006 elections.

■ Casar, M. A., and I. Marván (eds.) (2002), *Gobernar sin Mayoría: México 1867–1997* **(Mexico City: Taurus and CIDE).** An insightful series of studies on historical and sub-national experiences of divided government.

■ Eisenstadt, T. (2003), *Courting Democracy in Mexico: Party Strategies and Electoral Institutions* **(Cambridge: Cambridge University Press).** A comprehensive study of the judicialization of post-electoral conflicts in the 1990s.

■ Elizondo, C., and Nacif, B. (eds.) (2003), *Lecturas sobre el cambio político en México* **(Mexico City: Fondo de Cultura Económica).** A fine collection of essays on political change in Mexico.

■ Forment, C. A. (2003), *Democracy in Latin America, 1760–1900: Civic Selfhood and Public Life in Mexico and Peru* **(Chicago: University of Chicago Press).** An in-depth study of civil society in pre-revolutionary Mexico.

■ Garrido, L. J. (1982), *El Partido de la Revolución Institucionalizada: La formación del nuevo Estado (1928–45)* **(Mexico City: Siglo XXI).** A detailed history of the hegemonic party.

■ Lawson, C. H. (2002), *Building the Fourth Estate: Democratization and the Rise of a Free Press in Mexico* **(Berkeley, Calif.: University of California Press).** A systematic study of media opening and democratization.

■ Levy, D. C., and Bruhn K., with Zebadúa E. (2001), *Mexico: The Struggle for Democratic Development* **(Berkeley, Calif.: University of California Press).** Broad introduction to Mexican politics.

■ Lujambio, A. (2000), *El poder compartido: Un ensayo sobre la democratización mexicana* **(Mexico City: Oceano).** A concise reconstruction of opposition advances at all levels of state power in the 1990s.

■ Magaloni, B. (2006), *Voting for Autocracy: Hegemonic Party Survival and its Demise in Mexico* **(New York: Cambridge University Press).** A theoritical and empirical analysis of voting behaviour in the last two decades of PRI rule.

■ Schedler, A. (2004), 'From Electoral Authoritarianism to Democratic Consolidation', in R. Crandall, G. Paz, and R. Roett (eds.), *Mexico's Democracy at Work: Political and Economic Dynamics* (Boulder, Colo. and London: Lynne Rienner), 9–37. An overview of democratic transition and consolidation with a synthesis of electoral reforms 1977–96.

■ —— (2007), 'Mexican Standoff: The Mobilization of Distrust', *Journal of Democracy*, 18/1: 88–102. A resumé and critical analysis of the 2006 post-electoral conflict.

■ Weldon, J. A. (1997), 'The Political Sources of Presidencialismo in Mexico', in S. Mainwaring and M. S. Shugart (eds.), *Presidentialism and Democracy in Latin America* (Cambridge: Cambridge University Press), 225–58. Much-cited analysis of the partisan foundations of Mexico's 'hyperpresidentialism'.

WEB LINKS

● **http://directorio.gob.mx** Web directory of the Mexican government, includes links to ministries, legislatures, courts, sub-national governments, embassies, media, and universities.

● **www.gob.mx** Citizen portal of the Federal Government contains legal and other information across a wide range of policy fields.

● **www.ife.org.mx** Federal Electoral Institute (IFE).

● **www.trife.gob.mx** Federal Electoral Tribunal (TEPJF).

● **www.ifai.org.mx** Federal Institute for Access to Public Information (IFAI).

● **www.unam.mx** National Autonomous University (UNAM).

● **www.banxico.org.mx** Banco de México (Central Bank).

● **www.laneta.apc.org** LaNeta—'alternative' civil society information.

ONLINE RESOURCE CENTRE

For additional material and resources, see the Online Resource Centre at:
www.oxfordtextbooks.co.uk/orc/burnell2e/

23 Underdevelopment and Development

23a Guatemala: Enduring Underdevelopment

RACHEL SIEDER

Chapter Contents

- Introduction: Guatemala's Poverty and Multiple Inequalities
- Patterns of State Formation
- The Peace Accords: A Turning Point?
- Conclusions

Overview

This study examines Guatemala as a persistent case of underdevelopment, defining development in terms of social, economic, cultural, and political rights. The principal features of underdevelopment in contemporary Guatemala are described. The account analyses historical patterns of state formation and economic development before examining the attempts to reverse historical trends and 'engineer development' represented by the 1996 peace agreement. The final section signals the main contemporary causes of the country's persistent underdevelopment: a **patrimonialist** and **predatory state** linked in turn to the strength and conservatism of the private sector, the weakness of the party system, the continuing influence of the armed forces, and extremely high levels of crime and impunity.

GUATEMALA

Introduction: Guatemala's Poverty and Multiple Inequalities

The influence of rights-based approaches to development (see also Chapter 18) in recent years has ensured that our understanding of 'development' and 'underdevelopment' has become more holistic. Where previously development was measured simply in terms of economic variables, today assessments tend to include composite measures of the socio-economic, cultural, and political rights enjoyed by its inhabitants, and the extent to which their inclusion and well-being is secured. Thinking on development policy has evolved accordingly (see Chapter 16).

Guatemala can be characterized as a country with persistent underdevelopment. Rates of poverty and inequality are amongst the highest in Latin America and the Caribbean. It ranks worst in the region—and amongst the worst in the world—for malnutrition (World Bank 2003b). Gini indices (see Chapter 5) for consumption and income for Guatemala are 48 and 57 respectively, making Guatemala one of the most unequal countries in Latin America, itself the most unequal region in the world. In other words, the population is characterized by a large, poor, low-income majority and a small, high-income minority. The percentage of Guatemala's population living in poverty (that is, on less than US$2 a day) stood at 56 per cent (some 6.4 million people) in 2000, with some 16 per cent of the population living in extreme poverty—that is, with income insufficient to meet their minimum daily calorific requirements (World Bank 2003b).

BOX 23a.1

Key Dates in Guatemala's History

1944	Forced labour abolished, universal male suffrage introduced.	1994–6	UN mediates peace process. Agreements reached on human rights, indigenous rights and identity, resettlement of displaced populations, clarification of human rights violations, agricultural modernization, and reform of the military and the state.
1952	Agrarian reform law approved.		
1954	Democratically elected government of Jacobo Arbenz overthrown in CIA-backed coup.		
1960	First guerrilla insurgency.	1996	Final peace settlement signed.
1978–83	Height of counter-insurgency war. 100,000 civilians killed or disappeared 1981–3.	1999	United Nations Truth Commission finds Guatemalan state guilty of acts of genocide during armed conflict. Recommends prosecutions.
1984–5	Military oversee guided transition to elected, civilian government.	1999	Frente Repúblicano Guatemalteco (FRG), led by former dictator Rios Montt, wins presidential elections.
1990	Oslo Accord between government and URNG establishes framework for national peace negotiations.		
1993	Attempted executive coup by President Serrano fails.		

Ethnic, regional, and gender inequality

Economic differences between different regions of the country and ethnic groups are huge. According to World Bank figures for 2000, while Guatemala's twenty-three indigenous groups represented 43 per cent of the population (a conservative estimate), they accounted for 58 per cent of the poor and 72 per cent of the extreme poor. Almost three-quarters of indigenous people live in poverty, as compared with 41 per cent for non-indigenous. The predominantly rural indigenous areas of the country have the worst conditions of poverty, health, education, and land shortages. Government spending on welfare provision is lower in rural areas. The rate of rural poverty in 1998 was nearly three times that of the urban areas (77 per cent to 29 per cent) and four times that of the capital, Guatemala City. The rural rate of extreme poverty (40 per cent) was nearly six times the urban rate (7 per cent). Poverty also disproportionately affects children—in 2000, some 68 per cent of children under 6 (about 1.7 million) and 63 per cent of young people under 18 (about 3.8 million) were poor (World Bank 2003b).

Guatemala is classified as a middle-income country, but has a long history of low social spending. This is partly accounted for by historically low rates of tax collection: Guatemala's tax coefficient of 7.7 per cent of GDP in 1998—the lowest in Latin America—contrasts with 18.3 per cent in Chile. Total public spending on education and health in 2000 was only 3.6 per cent of GDP, even though social spending improved somewhat during the late 1990s. Guatemala's rate of illiteracy (31 per cent in 2000) is third only to Haiti and Nicaragua in the

Table 23a.1 Population of Guatemala Living on less than US$1 a Day (2004)

Urban non-indigenous	6.1%
Urban indigenous	17.1%
Total	21.9%
Rural non-indigenous	26.3%
Rural indigenous	38%

Source: UNDP *Human Development Report* 2005: 109

entire region. The legacy of gender and ethnic discrimination is evident in literacy statistics: in 1989 a staggering 82 per cent of indigenous women were illiterate. By 2000, it was 62 per cent, but indigenous women still lagged far behind their non-indigenous counterparts: overall female illiteracy rates stood at 39 per cent (World Bank 2003b).

Health, education, and employment

Poverty and low educational achievement are directly correlated—very few poor children continue education through to secondary level. Child labour is a main cause of absenteeism and high school drop-out rates. Rural school drop-out rates are over twice as high as urban rates and girls attend school at lower rates than boys. Health spending per capita in 1998 put Guatemala at $155, ahead only of Haiti and well below Nicaragua ($266) and Honduras ($210)—both poorer than Guatemala. This is reflected in life expectancy—Guatemalans live an average of 65 years, compared with 70 for Latin America and the Caribbean.

For much of its recent history, Guatemala has enjoyed relative macro-economic stability and reasonable growth—an annual average of 3.9 per cent from the 1950s through the 1990s. Nonetheless, with one of the highest population growth rates in the region (around 2.6 per cent per annum) per capita growth rates were significantly lower (and even negative during the 1980s), averaging 1.3 per cent annually over the past fifty years.

Economic development has not generated sufficient low-skilled jobs to absorb the poor. Consequently between 700,000 and one million Guatemalans are forced to migrate for seasonal harvest work. Working conditions for migrant workers are extremely tough; they are often paid less than the minimum wage and have little or no access to health and educational facilities. In recent years the structural crisis of coffee and sugar markets (two of Guatemala's main agro-exports) has drastically reduced national and regional employment opportunities for migrant workers and the numbers of those attempting to reach the USA as illegal migrants increased. Poor families increasingly rely on dollar remittances from family members working in the USA. According to the Inter-American Development Bank, remittances from the USA to Guatemala tripled between 2001 and 2004, at $2681 million representing around 10 per cent of overall GDP. In 2004, remittances were twenty-one times greater than foreign direct investment and thirty times greater than official development assistance (cited in Migration Information Source 2006).

Democratic disenchantment

Like most of Latin America, Guatemala is now formally a democracy. However, while respect for political and human rights has undoubtedly improved compared to the 1980s these rights are still far from secure and democracy remains fragile. Since restoration of electoral rule in 1986 elections have become freer and fairer and an increasingly broad spectrum of political opinion has been represented at the polls, particularly following the successful conclusion of a negotiated settlement to the armed conflict in December 1996. During the 1990s, decentralization and electoral reforms increased opportunities for citizen participation in municipal government.

Yet Guatemalans' levels of political participation and faith in the institutions of government are low compared to other countries in the region. Voter turnout is comparatively poor and regional public opinion surveys such as the Latinobarometer regularly find that Guatemalans have some of the lowest regard for democratic norms in the region. One explanation could be corruption, endemic both at national and local level. Another is chronic impunity and citizen insecurity: Guatemala has one of the highest homicide rates in the region and extremely high levels of so-called common, especially violent, crime. Crime and gender-based violence are a common occurrence for many citizens, particularly the poor. The judicial system is weak, impunity is routine, and those responsible for criminal acts are rarely prosecuted. Respect for indigenous peoples' rights was a cornerstone of the peace accords (see below) but despite some advances, progress has been extremely slow. For most Guatemalans democracy clearly has yet to deliver.

KEY POINTS

- Guatemala has among the highest rates of poverty and inequality in Latin American and Caribbean.

- In 2001, 56 per cent of the population lacked sufficient income to meet their minimum subsistence requirements.

- Indigenous people, rural inhabitants, women, and children are amongst the poorest and most disadvantaged sectors of the population.

- Despite relative macro-economic stability, tax collection and social spending rates over the last three decades have been low.

- A return to electoral democracy occurred in 1986, but citizen disenchantment with democratic performance is high.

Patterns of State Formation

Guatemala's economic fortunes were built on agro-exports and based on a highly exploitative form of rural capitalism, which in turn was reflected in authoritarian and exclusive forms of politics and development. The dispossession of indigenous people from their historic lands began with colonization in the sixteenth century and accelerated during the late nineteenth-century coffee boom. New laws were introduced to stimulate coffee production and agro-exports, and inequality of access to land grew rapidly. Colonial forms of labour coercion were replaced by such mechanisms as forced indebtedness and vagrancy laws, which remained on the statute books until the mid-twentieth century. The capitalist planter class in Guatemala relied on forced wage-labour, becoming increasingly dependent on the coercive power of the central state, dominated by the armed forces, to ensure its supply of workers. Economic downturns necessitated repression by the military to quell wage demands and ensure

profitability margins. Ruling elites did not view the poor and particularly the indigenous as citizens, but rather as subjects to be disciplined, controlled, and 'civilized'. The richest families traced their descent to European settlers and viewed themselves as 'white'; indeed in the early twentieth century many still held *certificados de raza*—documents that supposedly proved they had no Indian blood. Race and class discrimination were mutually reinforcing and underpinned the economic system.

The cold war: reform reversed

Between 1944 and 1954, reformist governments were elected, following a coup by junior military officers. The administration of Juan José Arévalo (1944–51) introduced universal male suffrage, abolished forced labour and indentured servitude, and sponsored progressive labour and social security legislation. The more radical government of Jacobo

Arbenz (1952–4) introduced an agrarian reform law in an effort to stimulate agricultural production and address rural poverty. However, the expropriation of large, under-utilized estates and their distribution to landless peasants angered both rich landowners and the US-based United Fruit Company, one of the largest landowners in Guatemala. United Fruit conspired with US President Eisenhower's administration and elements of Guatemala's armed forces to overthrow the reformers, accusing the Arbenz government of communist sympathies. In 1954, Guatemala gained the dubious distinction of being the second country subject to a CIA-sponsored 'cold war coup' (Iran being the first in 1953).

Following the overthrow of Arbenz the agrarian reform was reversed and peasant organizers persecuted. The Guatemalan armed forces received significant support from the USA within the regional framework of counter-insurgency training. The state became increasingly dominated by the military, who by the 1970s had become powerful economic actors in their own right. Espousing a virulent anti-communism, the private sector relied on the army to repress workers' demands for improved wages or better working conditions. Delegating the business of government to the military, they nonetheless exercised a permanent veto on social reform. Regular elections took place but the spectrum was confined to transient centre-right and right-wing parties who invariably fielded military officers as presidential candidates. Participation was low and levels of political violence and intimidation high.

Insurgency, counter-insurgency, and genocide

Such acute socio-economic and political exclusion contributed to the emergence of a guerrilla insurgency in the 1960s. This was brutally repressed by the army. State violence increased throughout the 1970s targeting trade unionists, social activists, and reformist politicians, reaching a peak in the early 1980s when de facto military regimes fought an all-out war against the civilian population to stamp out a second guerrilla insurgency. This involved hundreds of army-led massacres, 'scorched earth' measures, forced displacement of thousands of Guatemalans, mandatory paramilitary 'civil patrols' for all indigenous men in the countryside, and the militarization of the entire state apparatus; it constituted one of the most extreme cases of state repression in twentieth-century Latin America. In total during thirty-six years of armed conflict, some 200,000 people were killed (2 per cent of the 1980 population), nearly a quarter of whom 'disappeared'. Another million were displaced, either internally or into Mexico. In 1999, the United Nations found that the Guatemalan state was responsible for over 90 per cent of gross human rights violations documented throughout the armed conflict and was guilty of acts of genocide against the indigenous population between 1981 and 1983. This massive destruction of human and social capital had significant negative consequences for Guatemala's development prospects.

Electoral democracy and peace negotiations

In the mid-1980s, the military returned the country to civilian rule in a 'guided transition' to democracy designed to improve the country's standing before the international community, while perpetuating effective control by the armed forces over national affairs. The return to elected government, encouraged by US President Reagan's administration, permitted restoration of US military aid—suspended since 1978 by US President Carter in protest at human rights violations. Presidential elections held in 1985 were won by the centre-right Christian Democrat party; a new constitution was adopted in 1986. Yet political parties remained weak and fragmented, the influence of the military was undiminished, and state-perpetrated political repression of political opponents and trade union and human rights activists continued. In 1993, gridlock between executive and congress led

President Jorge Serrano to attempt a 'self-coup', closing down congress and dismissing the Supreme Court. Serrano was thwarted by a combination of popular mobilization and opposition from the domestic private sector, the international community, and sectors of the armed forces, representing an important step in the strengthening of Guatemala's weak democracy.

The armed conflict was not resolved until December 1996, when the pro-business sector government of President Alvaro Arzú signed a definitive peace settlement with the insurgent Unidad Revolucionaria Nacional Guatemalteca (URNG), bringing nine years of stop-start peace talks to a successful conclusion. The international community exerted considerable pressure to secure a settlement: the final phase of the negotiations was overseen by the United Nations, and after 1994 an on-site UN mission (Misión de las Naciones Unidas en Guatemala, MINUGUA) was charged with verification and supervision of the peace accords. Through its sponsorship of the peace settlement the international community became highly involved in attempts to kick-start development in Guatemala.

> **KEY POINTS**
>
> - Guatemala's republican history is characterized by authoritarian rule, coercive rural capitalism, and racist discrimination.
>
> - A reformist democratic regime was overthrown in 1954 at the height of the cold war by a US-backed military coup.
>
> - In response to guerrilla challenges, the armed forces militarized the state and used extreme violence against the civilian population.
>
> - The country returned to elected civilian government in 1986, but the military continued to dominate politics and repress opponents.
>
> - Thirty-six years of civil war finally ended with a UN-sponsored negotiated settlement in 1996.

The Peace Accords: A Turning Point?

The peace accords aimed not only to formally end the armed conflict, but also to reverse the country's historically exclusionary pattern of development. They comprised thirteen separate accords, involving four main areas:

- Resettlement of displaced populations, reincorporation of former guerrillas, and reconciliation regarding past violations of human rights.
- An integrated programme for human development, which mandated a 50 per cent increase over five years in health and education spending.
- Goals for productive and sustainable development, including market-led reform of the agricultural sector.
- Modernization of the democratic state, including reduction in the role of the armed forces, strengthening the rule of law and increasing civil society participation, particularly in implementing the accords themselves.

Three cross-cutting elements were emphasized: the rights of indigenous communities, commitments regarding the rights and position of women, and greater social participation. The international community pledged more than $3.2 billion in aid—over 60 per cent as grants to implement the accords. The agreements also contained a commitment to reform taxation and increase revenues from 8 per cent to 12 per cent of GDP by 2000.

Lack of domestic commitment

The peace accords constituted important achievements in their own right, but implementation was slow and uneven. Given the country's violent past and history of socio-economic and ethnic and gender exclusion, meeting the comprehensive goals of the peace settlement was bound to be challenging. However, lack of commitment by key domestic actors further constrained prospects for success. While the international community and civil society organizations backed the agreements, the commitment of the main political parties, the military, and the private sector to the settlement was weak. The powerful and conservative private sector staunchly defended its privileges, despite the more progressive stance of certain reformist elements within the business community. During the negotiating process, the private sector association CACIF (Comité de Asociaciones Agricolas, Comerciales, Industriales y Financieras)—dominated by large landowners—steadfastly vetoed attempts at land reform, insisting on the sanctity of private property. In the wake of the settlement, CACIF successfully blocked far-reaching fiscal reform or tax reforms, especially any increase in direct taxes.

Implementation: a mixed record

Other aspects of the peace settlement were more successful. The guerrillas (all but decimated as a military force by the violence of the early 1980s) were reincorporated into civilian life—the ceasefire was not breached and the URNG became a political party. Displaced and returned refugee populations were resettled, though many complained of being allocated poor land and of insufficient access to credit. A UN-led truth commission was completed in 1999, a major achievement that signalled army responsibility for gross violations of human rights and recommended legal prosecutions. Yet, despite the efforts of human rights organizations to secure justice, impunity remains the norm. Attacks have occurred against human rights organizations and indigenous communities trying to secure exhumations of mass graves and bring perpetrators to trial. Spending on health and education did increase and a number of important structural reforms were

implemented, particularly in education. However, this has not yet had an appreciable impact on social indicators. Social spending was supposed to be redirected towards the poorer regions, but the record has been mixed. The global economic downturn in 2000–1 combined with the global fall in agro-export prices severely hampered even the limited development plans for the rural sector set out in the peace accords. The rural poor continue to lack access to land. In some cases large landowners made a healthy profit from the peace funds provided by the international community by selling unproductive lands at inflated prices to the national peace fund. Landless peasants settled on these lands found they were unable to feed themselves and saddled with debt repayment obligations they could not meet.

A patrimonialist state and weak party system

In addition to private sector intransigence, the failure to modernize the state and the weakness of democratic institutions provide clues to Guatemala's continuing underdevelopment. The internationally prescribed formula of institutional strengthening and 'civil society strengthening' contained in the peace accords failed to transform an exclusive, patrimonialist state into a developmental state. This reflects the balance of political forces and inherent difficulty of changing historically entrenched patterns. The nature of Guatemala's party system is both cause and effect of the patrimonialist state.

During the 1960s and 1970s, Guatemalan political parties were highly dependent on the armed forces; elections regularly took place but most presidential candidates were military officers from different factions backed by one or another group of private sector interests. During the transition to democracy in the 1980s, the Christian Democrat party rose to national prominence and enjoyed mass support, but its fortunes subsequently declined due to corruption and intra-party factionalism. A core nucleus of political parties on the right and centre-right of the political spectrum contested elections throughout the 1990s signalling a degree of stability of the party system, but these parties continued to be dominated by personalist politics within the private sector. Some centre-left parties, including the former guerrilla URNG, gained ground after 1995, but their share of the vote remains limited and the parties themselves far from consolidated.

In general, Guatemalan political parties tend to be dominated by powerful individuals who campaign on the strength of their personal, clientelist networks, rather than by programmatic coherence or the representation of different groups in society. They are subject to continuous division and fragmentation; indeed, many are little more than electoral alliances of convenience formed to support the interests of one or another economic sector. Traditions of coalition government and inter-party cooperation within congress are weak. In the absence of congressional majorities, governments are forced to rely on opportunistic coalitions between the different parties in congress. Party discipline is extremely lax, elected deputies often switching their allegiance during their term of office, and clientelism is rife.

In November 1999, the right-wing populist Frente Republicano Guatemalteco (FRG), led by former military dictator Ríos Montt, won national elections, fielding Alfonso Portillo as their presidential candidate. The FRG's electoral victory represented the displacement of the Guatemalan private sector from control of government for the first time since the return to democracy in 1986 and signalled the rise to power of a new economic elite linked to the military and organized crime. While in government, the FRG manipulated state institutions for its own political and economic advantage: accusations of government corruption, kickbacks, and clientelism mounted, and confrontation between government and civil society groups increased. Rios Montt himself was indicted by the UN truth commission for crimes of genocide; Guatemalan human rights organizations continue to seek his prosecution before the Spanish and Guatemalan courts. Following the return of traditional private sector interests to government with the election of Oscar Berger in 2003, some members of the former administration were imprisoned on charges of corruption. Portillo was stripped of his parliamentary immunity and fled the country following indictment for embezzlement of state funds. Prospects for improvement following general elections in 2007 are limited.

Military power, weak civil society, and continued human rights abuses

The Guatemalan armed forces largely retained their power following the peace settlement. In contrast to neighbouring El Salvador, the armed challenge from the guerrilla forces in Guatemala was negligible and the leverage of the USA over the armed forces limited. Troop numbers were reduced during the late 1990s, but the military budget increased, directly contravening the peace accords. Commitments to reform military intelligence services remain unfulfilled. While efforts to consolidate a civilian police force have advanced, the police remains weak, corrupt, and under-funded, and the army has again been employed in public security functions, once more in contravention of the peace settlement.

In addition to the slowness of institutional reform of the armed forces, more sinister manifestations of military power are evident. Serving and former military officers form part of a network of so-called 'parallel powers' which has influence within the highest spheres of government. These mafia-style networks are implicated in corruption scandals, organized crime, and maintaining impunity for those guilty of gross violations of human rights. Police and army units are implicated in extra-judicial executions of suspected gang members and in so-called social cleansing operations, including one notorious massacre of prison inmates in 2006. A United Nations Commission to investigate abuses by clandestine groups operating in the country was finally approved in late 2006, in part in response to consistent failure of the Guatemalan state to effectively tackle this problem.

Civil society organizations have become more vocal advocates of government transparency and accountability in recent years, but face adverse conditions. Violence and intimidation against rights activists continue and popular awareness of the historically high costs of dissent means that Guatemalan civil society remains comparatively weak. Indigenous Mayan organizations gained a national presence after the early 1990s and have advanced important national and local development initiatives, but their influence has recently declined. According to the framework for peace negotiations, all reforms to the constitution had to be approved by congress and then passed by a majority in a national referendum. A poll held in May 1999 (with a turnout of less than 20 per cent) rejected a package of constitutional reforms which included the official recognition of Guatemala as a multicultural and multi-ethnic nation-state. Elements of the private sector campaigned vociferously against recognition of indigenous peoples' rights, arguing it would lead to 'reverse discrimination' and balkanization of the country. Unlike other Latin American countries with large indigenous populations—for example, Bolivia or Ecuador—multicultural reforms of the Guatemalan state have been relatively limited to date. Guatemala has ratified the International Labour Organization's Convention 169 on the rights of indigenous and tribal peoples, but has largely failed to honour its international commitments to respect indigenous rights.

Despite some decentralization and greater involvement of non-governmental organizations (NGOs) in delivery of public services during the 1990s, state–civil society relations remain conflictive. Whilst in some cases more participatory local government has been strengthened, in others local administration is characterized by corruption and clientelism. Instead of working with the state, civil society organizations often go *around* the state in an effort to secure their demands. For example, echoing what has been called the 'boomerang effect', human rights organizations work through transnational networks to persuade foreign governments and donors to put pressure on the Guatemalan state to meet its human rights obligations.

In spite of the end of the armed conflict, the human rights situation in Guatemala remains extremely bleak. High levels of violent crime, continued impunity, and the ineffectiveness of the police and the judiciary mean weak civil rights protection. The growth of rival armed gangs linked to drug-trafficking during the 1990s worsened the security situation for ordinary Guatemalans, many of whom live in marginal urban settlements controlled by drug barons. Male homicide rates are amongst the highest in Latin America and the Caribbean; violent murders of women also increased in the 2000s, leading some Guatemalan human rights campaigners to talk about 'femicide'. More than 5,000 murders a year are committed in Guatemala, more than during the final years of the armed conflict; most are never investigated. United Nations officials have accused the Guatemalan government of fostering a culture of impunity.

KEY POINTS

- The 1996 peace accords set out a programme aiming to reverse exclusionary development and improve social participation, especially of women and indigenous peoples.

- The accords were backed by the international community and civil society groups, but the commitment of the armed forces, private sector, and political parties to the settlement was low.

- Some progress on implementation has been made, but targets have not been met. Private sector resistance to raising fiscal revenues remains high.

- Key factors impeding emergence of a developmental state include opportunist, clientelist, and fragmented political parties, a powerful and autonomous military and relatively weak civil society.

- Confrontational party politics and the rise of organized crime and 'parallel powers' pose serious threats to Guatemalan democracy and obstacles to development.

Conclusions

Guatemala is a predatory state rather than a developmental state. The US-supported derailing of the reformist administration of Jacobo Arbenz produced one of the most violent and authoritarian regimes in the region. The state lacked autonomy and was effectively colonized by powerful private interests to the detriment of the majority of the population. During the cold war, it was supported by the regional superpower under the aegis of anti-communism. Despite transition to electoral rule two decades ago, such predatory tendencies have not disappeared—indeed, many now point to the increasingly mafia-style operation of the Guatemalan state.

The peace process of the 1990s provided an important space for reorienting historically exclusionary patterns of development. However, without the political commitment of the most powerful domestic actors, international pressure and the support of civil society organizations were unable to secure such a shift. Guatemala today is a weak and illiberal democracy—the population may enjoy suffrage or political rights, but civil rights are not enforced and the rule of law is routinely flouted by powerful actors within and outside government.

Historical patterns of ethnic and economic exclusion combined with the legacy of extreme levels of state violence against the civilian population mean that citizen participation is relatively weak. The strength and conservatism of the private sector, its historic reliance on the armed forces, and the systematic persecution of the left and centre-left has engendered a particularly weak and venal political class and party system constituting another impediment to development. More progressive elements secured a foothold during the 1990s, but they face powerful opposition and have yet to consolidate effective parties capable of winning elections.

Finally, long-term structural factors have not favoured the Guatemalan economy. Historically reliant on a particularly exploitative form of rural capitalism, the private sector has largely failed to adapt to new global conditions despite the relative decline of traditional agro-exports. The historic lack of investment in human capital is a serious impediment to future economic development. And as in most of Latin America, adherence to neo-liberal orthodoxies of the international financial institutions has proved singularly incapable of generating greater development and equality.

? QUESTIONS

1　Critically examine Guatemala's performance in terms of right-based measures of development.

2　What impact did the end of armed conflict have on development prospects?

3　Can international intervention address the historical causes of underdevelopment, and if so, how?

4　What is the relationship between the patrimonialist state and underdevelopment in a country like Guatemala?

5　Are the main causes of underdevelopment in Guatemala largely economic or mainly political?

GUIDE TO FURTHER READING

■ **Jonas, S. (2000),** *Of Centaurs and Doves: Guatemala's Peace Process* **(Boulder, Colo., and London: Westview Press).** A comprehensive overview of the peace process and of contemporary Guatemalan politics.

■ **REMHI (1999),** *Guatemala: Never Again! Recovery of Historical Memory Project. The Official Report of the Human Rights Office, Archdiocese of Guatemala* **(London: Catholic Institute of International Relations/Latin American Bureau).** Based on testimonies from thousands of victims of Guatemala's dirty war.

■ **Sieder, R. (ed.) (1998),** *Guatemala After the Peace Accords* **(London: Institute of Latin American Studies).** Academics and practitioners consider the challenges following the peace agreements.

■ **——,Thomas, M., Vickers, J., and Spence, J. (2002),** *Who Governs? Guatemala Five Years after the Peace Accords* **(Washington DC: Hemisphere Initiatives/Washington Office on Latin America).** Reports on the progress of the peace settlement after five years.

WEB LINKS

● **www.desarrollohumano.org.gt** United Nations Human Development Report for Guatemala 2005.

● **http://lnweb18.worldbank.org** World Bank Guatemala Poverty Assessment (GUAPA) 2003.

● **www.migrationinformation.org/Feature/display.cfm?id=393** Migration Information Source, 2006 'Remittance Trends in Central America'.

ONLINE RESOURCE CENTRE

For additional material and resources, see the Online Resource Centre at:
www.oxfordtextbooks.co.uk/orc/burnell2e/

23b South Korea: From Development to New Challenges

PETER FERDINAND

Chapter Contents

- Introduction
- Historical Legacies
- Institutions of Development
- Development Policies
- The Consolidation of Democracy
- Conclusion: Emerging Problems

Overview

This chapter concentrates on the role of the state in directing and leading development in the Republic of Korea since the end of the Korean war in 1953. It falls into five parts, beginning with four legacies from recent Korean history that favoured success. The second part identifies key institutions of Korea's developmental state, most notably the Economic Planning Board and a bureaucracy with 'embedded autonomy' from societal pressures. The third part assesses the success of Korea's development policies: land reform, industrialization that from the mid-1960s was increasingly export-led, and investment in education. The fourth part examines the transition to democracy since 1987. The final part identifies new challenges for South Korea in a world of increasing globalization, especially the need to transcend the previously successful developmental state model, increasing pressures on the state to provide welfare services, and problems of corruption and democratic consolidation.

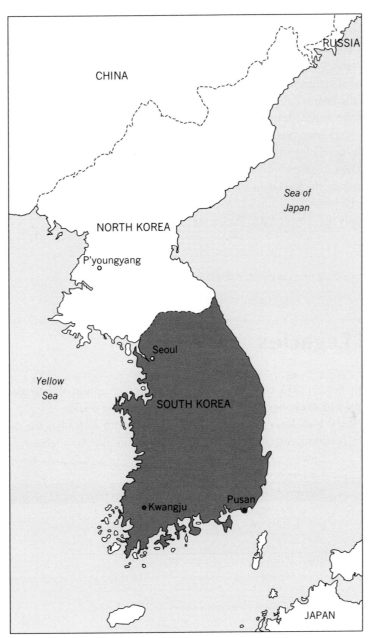

SOUTH KOREA

Introduction

In 1945 the Korean peninsula was freed from Japanese colonial rule by the USA and the Soviet Union. It was divided into two states—one communist in the north and one capitalist in the south. In 1950, North Korea (the Democratic People's Republic of Korea, or DPRK) invaded the south (Republic of Korea, or ROK). In three years over one million people died as a result of the conflict, and it left per capita income in the south, approximately US$67 per year (in 1996 dollars), among the lowest in the world. By 2001, that figure had risen to around US$9,400. In 1995, it became only the second Asian state after Japan and the second former colony after Mexico to be admitted to the Organisation for Economic Co-operation and Development (OECD). By 2005, too, according to the International Telecommunications Union, South Korea had the second highest figure for broadband penetration, after Iceland.

> **KEY POINTS**
>
> ● On all conventional measures, South Korea's record of development since the early 1950s is highly impressive.

Historical Legacies

Three legacies from before 1953 contributed to the drive for national economic development, especially after 1961: social traditions; the impact of Japanese colonialism, partition, and civil war; South Koreans' perception of their place in the East Asian region and the world.

First, South Korea has the distinct advantage of being ethnically homogeneous. The *ius sanguinis*

BOX 23b.1

Key Dates in Modern Korea's History

1910	Colonized by Japan.
1945	Creation of two separate independent Korean states in the north and the south.
1950–3	Korean war.
1961	General Park Chung Hee seizes power in South Korea.
1980	Kwangju massacre.
1987	Democracy re-emerges as President Roh Tae Woo allies with former oppositionist Kim Young Sam to form the Democratic Liberal Party and rule through it.
1992	Kim Young Sam becomes the first civilian president since 1961.
1997	Asian financial crisis and Kim Dae Jung is elected president.
2002	Roh Moo Hyun's election as president marks rise of new political generation.

determines Korean nationality and until 1997 this could only be transmitted from a Korean father, not a Korean mother, other than in exceptional circumstances. The only unresolved business was: which Korean state should represent the whole of the Korean nation?

Also, over the centuries Confucianism became the dominant ideology of social organization. Large numbers of Koreans are Buddhists or Christians, but principles of Confucian social organization are deeply embedded in Korean society. These respect a hierarchy of relationships within the family, where everyone knows their obligations towards everyone else, as the basis for a well-ordered society. The patriarchal head of the family was entitled to absolute respect. So too was the emperor or ruler. Filial piety—the devotion of the son to the father—was the core relationship.

Second, colonialism launched Korean modernization and development. Until the twentieth century, the Korean peninsula—the 'hermit kingdom'—was a poor backwater, largely ignored by its neighbours. After 1910, Japanese colonialism introduced a wider set of regional relations and industrialization in the north, but in consequence the Japanese occupied all the important managerial and administrative posts. The resentment over colonial experiences generated a very powerful sense of patriotism among Koreans, both in the north and the south.

Third, a hunger to remake the country after the civil war underlay the development drive in both north and south, where both were conscious of the immense size of their near neighbours and wary of their respective superpower protectors.

KEY POINTS

- A unique combination of three distinct historical legacies has exercised a powerful influence on South Korea's distinctive developmental success over the last fifty years.

Institutions of Development

South Korea's government was determined to pursue industrialization vigorously, for security's sake as much as prosperity.

Politics in South Korea was dominated by the military up until the 1990s. Rhee Syngman (Korean family names come first), its first president, was a civilian, but widely perceived to be corrupt. Following his downfall, General Park Chung Hee staged a coup in 1961, and from then until 1992 generals dominated government, presenting themselves as guardians of the nation and order, committed to making the nation 'rich and strong'. General Park declared, 'The Asian peoples want to obtain economic equality first and build a more equitable political machinery afterward' (in Jones and Il 1980: 43).

General Park laid the basis for what has subsequently been termed a developmental state. Its main features have been described as: (a) a nationalist agenda; (b) state direction of finance for priority development projects; (c) an effective and technocratic bureaucracy; (d) the state and business are partners; (e) authoritarianism; (f) favourable international circumstances (Woo-Cummings 1999: 1–31). The major development decisions were formulated by the Economic Planning Board (EPB), founded in 1961. For the next fifteen years the economy grew faster than 'planned'.

Table 23b.1 South Korea's Average Annual Growth of Gross Domestic Product (%)

1950–9	1960–9	1970–9	1980–9	1990–2000
5	8.5	9.5	9.4	5.7

Source: World Bank, *World Development Report* (various years)

A key factor was the state's embedded autonomy (Evans 1995): aimed at developing capitalist enterprises, the state was insulated from excessive pressure of those interests. The military's political domination helped. During the 1960s and 1970s, a solid, merit-based bureaucracy was created, replacing the political appointees of the 1950s. Military backing required and enforced firm decision-making. Favoured businessmen were allowed to build empires, the most successful putting together *chaebols*—business groups or conglomerates. These were family-based companies with cross-holdings of shares in subsidiaries. They benefited from government favouritism; financing remained the preserve of state banks, though this limited their experience of genuine commercial risks. Cartels were encouraged but they did compete among themselves. Individual *chaebols* were compensated for government-induced financial losses (Lee 1997). A few families grew exceedingly rich and were also widely resented (Eckert 1990). The government also tightly controlled the labour unions; calling up memories of the civil war and military service, and fear of communist infiltration (Janelli 1993).

Korea followed Japan in concentrating upon full employment policies to raise welfare, rather than introduce a welfare state for which there was no popular demand, in part because of the Confucian tradition of family obligations. Large construction and infrastructure policies rather than welfare programmes were used to stimulate economic activity when the business cycle turned downwards.

According to the World Bank, average annual per capital GNI growth between 1960 and 1995 was around 7.5 per cent (see Table 23b.1).

KEY POINTS

- An intensive period of economic development and industrialization between 1961 and 1979 created a powerful business sector but also solidified business dependence upon the state. Later the state became more dependent upon big business.

Development Policies

In 1953, the economy was still overwhelmingly agricultural. The first task was land reform, to introduce greater fairness into the size of landholdings and free up capital and workers for industrialization. The second priority was rebuilding the country—a nationalist project, whose execution created rents for businessmen who supported the government.

The government also strongly encouraged large-scale savings, by imposing punitive taxes on expensive consumer imports, and periodically mobilized the media to urge people to be patriotic in their

Table 23b.2 Gross Domestic Savings as a Percentage of South Korea's Growing GDP

1960	1970	1980	1990	2000	2004
2	16.2	20.8	36.1	33	34.6

Source: World Bank, *World Development Report* (various years)

spending. The results were impressive (see Table 23b.2), and the savings were channelled towards government-determined investment priorities.

Initially the government pursued import-substitution industrialization, as much for reasons of national security as for the prevailing orthodoxy of development economics. After 1965, however, the government was forced to change strategy and concentrate more upon exports. The selective targeting of industries for national development succeeded handsomely, though a later policy to develop heavy and chemical industries (HCI) brought only mixed results. But Japan's revaluation of the yen, in 1985, created new export opportunities, leading to a doubling of exports to the USA between 1985 and 1988. Also, Korean corporations were now able to tap international financial markets for investments, which allowed them to resist government demands when it suited.

The government's commitment to education had considerable long-term economic significance. Literacy was virtually eliminated by 1963; by 1978 the proportion of secondary-school-age pupils actually in school was higher than in Singapore, Argentina, Mexico, Turkey, or India. By the 1990s, the proportion of students in higher education was higher than in Japan. Amsden (1989: 219) remarked, 'Korea, therefore, is both a general case of a well-educated late industrializing country and a special case of an exceptionally well-educated one.'

South Korea's achievements stand in stark contrast with those of the North or Myanmar. Like North Korea, which before the civil war was more industrialized than South Korea, Burma (Myanmar) was traumatized by violent conflict during the Second World War. In 1950, Burma's population approximated to South Korea's and enjoyed a comparable level of development. Since 1962, the military leadership's 'Burmese road to socialism' has minimized contact with the world economy. South Korea's economic performance has been vastly superior. According to the Asian Development Bank, in 2004 per capita GNI was $220 in Myanmar and $14,000 in South Korea. While Burma remains predominantly an agricultural society with the structure of the labour force still very similar to that of South Korea in 1960, and whilst North Korea is predominantly an industrial country, the distribution of South Korea's workforce now more closely resembles the post-industrial societies of the West. But perhaps the most striking feature of South Korea's development has been its high degree of income equality. The Gini coefficient for income inequality was 0.312 in 1985 and fell as low as 0.283 in 1997 on the verge of the Asian financial crisis. That crisis led to increased inequality and by summer 2003 it had risen to 0.329—still low by international standards, though it still causes public anguish.

KEY POINTS

- South Korea's adoption of a state-led strategy for development has been outstandingly successful, especially by comparison with others in the region who pursued more socialist and inward-looking policies.

The Consolidation of Democracy

During the 1990s, Korea turned into a functioning multi-party democracy, which withstood the Asian financial crisis of 1997–8 without any attempt by the military to regain control. In elections in 1997 power changed hands from one party to another for the first time, and peacefully, allowing Kim Dae Jung, a veteran oppositionist to the military's rule, to become president.

Thus Korea's growing prosperity was followed by democratization, seeming to bear out theories that suggest a sequential link between the two. The political reform can be attributed in part to pressure from the labour movement and students, followed by white-collar workers, in part to increased pressure from the US, and in part to a greater willingness of later military leaders to make compromises.

Such was the country's economic development in the 1980s that in 1988 GDP exceeded US$3,000 per capita—the threshold beyond which for Huntington (1996b: 7–8) military coups rarely succeed. There was, however, still no permanently active civil society counterposed to the state. The owners of *chaebols* were becoming restive about state control and they no longer automatically deferred to government direction. Yet the main catalysts for change were elsewhere: workers and students. The labour unions saw democracy as essential to asserting their members' interests, after decades of repression. And although students benefited from the massive expansion of the education system, they were less deferential to their elders than previous generations. There were also now 1.4 million of them. When riot police repressed them, this antagonized parents, especially middle-class ones. And organized religion became a more potent factor in democratization. By the mid-1980s, roughly a quarter of the population had converted to Christianity. Both Protestant and Catholic churches openly challenged the military leaders and became a key forum for political protest.

The first crisis came in 1980. Students in Kwangju city took to the streets to show solidarity with striking industrial workers. The riot police reacted with force, leading to at least 240 deaths. The regime survived the crisis, but as the eyes of the world fixed on Korea and its preparations to host the 1988 Olympic Games, a new crisis emerged. For in 1987 General Park Chung Hee provoked widespread public anger and street protests by nominating General Roh Tae Woo as the next president. White-collar workers also joined in. The decision needed ratification by general election, but the regime failed to win an overall majority, and the opposition was divided. Although the precedent of direct presidential rule was an option, the regime wanted more sympathetic treatment from the international media, especially in the USA. President Reagan specifically telephoned President Park to warn against bloodletting. So the authorities embarked upon protracted secret negotiations, at the end of which Roh Tae Woo agreed with the leader of the largest opposition party, Kim Young Sam, to form a new party with the understanding that Kim would become the next president after Roh.

The 1990s saw democratic consolidation. The military did withdraw from politics. Kim Young Sam became president as planned and launched an anti-corruption campaign, which then ensnared the two preceding presidents, Chun Doo Hwan and Roh Tae Woo. Both were sentenced to long prison terms.

In 1995, Kim led Korea into the OECD, which many pro-democracy activists had long advocated as a means to strengthen the democratic basis of politics, as well as entrench a more market-oriented approach to economic management. Nevertheless, Kim's term of office ended in ignominy; the hopes of creating a hegemonic ruling party were dashed, and Kim Dae Jung replaced Kim Young Sam. He in turn promised to deepen democracy and root out corruption.

Kim Dae Jung was able to negotiate a national response to the financial crisis in part because of his long-established reputation for sympathy for workers and the disadvantaged. He set up a quasi-corporatist Tripartite Commission that gave equal voices to representatives of business and labour, though the more militant Korean Confederation of Trade Unions was still excluded. Nevertheless this helped to persuade the unions to agree to heavy sacrifices for their members, especially as there was a very confrontational relationship between the government and the *chaebols*. But his term of office also ended ignominiously with two sons arrested on charges of corruption.

By 2003, Korean politics was beginning to undergo a generational transformation, as leaders who had dominated the opposition movement for thirty years left the scene. The new president, Roh Moo Hyun, also from Kim Dae Jung's Millennium Democratic Party (MDP), was in his fifties and offered electors a fresh start. He appointed other newcomers to national office. Many came from the so-called '386 generation', that is, those who were in their thirties in the 1990s, attended college in the 1980s, and were born in the 1960s. But within nine months of his election he had resigned from the MDP after his plans for reform were obstructed. He was followed by most deputies from the MDP who set up the new Uri ('ours') Party. Then when he mildly indicated his support for them in elections to the National Assembly in 2004, he was impeached by the opposition Grand National Party (GNP) for allegedly contravening the constitutional principle of a politically impartial president. They were supported by the rump of the MDP. However this backfired. It was seen as an attempt to prejudice the elections. Uri won a narrow overall majority, and over 60 per cent of the deputies were elected for the first time. The Constitutional Court later cautiously vindicated the president.

The main parties are still dominated by individual leaders, but now much more briefly, and they re-form frequently. The electoral system was changed in 2004 to combine 243 first-past-the-post single-seat districts with 56 regional ones elected through list PR. This was intended to provide a more representative parliament, yet in 2004 it actually worked to the advantage of the two main parties, Uri and the GNP. For the first time since 1988, the leading party (Uri) won an overall, if bare, majority (Kim and Kim 2004). Yet soon the turbulence re-emerged. Within months, Uri lost its majority as a few deputies defected to other parties. And as the term of office of Roh Moo Hyun was drawing to an end along with his powers of patronage, Uri was beset by intense factional disputes as rivals looked beyond 2007. Some openly advocated realigning the party with either the GNP or the much smaller Democratic Party, even though both of these parties had recently voted to impeach Roh. None of these manoeuvrings encouraged public trust.

Party instability is exacerbated by the constitution in two ways. First, it allows the president only one term of office of five years. In practice this limits his effective control over the political system to at best three to four years, before would-be successors begin to assert themselves. The fact that there is no vice-president exacerbates this problem. Frustrated by infighting towards the end of 2006, Roh Moo Hyun floated the idea of constitutional reform that would allow a president two four-year terms. Secondly, the constitution lays down different electoral cycles for the presidency and the National Assembly, which regularly leads to cohabitation, with different parties controlling the two institutions. This is difficult for even France to handle with its more robust political parties. In Korea it undermines the already fragile party structures and favours policy gridlock..

The 2004 elections to the National Assembly also saw limited success for the Democratic Labour Party. Exploiting the lingering resentment of those who had suffered most from the 1997 financial crisis, it adopted a more explicitly left-wing ideological stance. This suggested that Korean politics might be taking a more identifiably ideological turn. However, it remains to be seen whether this is a long-term trend because the party fared disastrously in subsequent by-elections. And Roh Moo Hyun has also attracted a lot of support from trade unions.

One other political development needs to be noted. Korea is now one of the most 'wired' societies. More Koreans have access to broadband than US citizens. This also has an impact on its politics. Roh Moo Hyun claimed that he owed his election in large measure to the Internet for mobilizing support. And this has also affected the media's reporting of politics. Whilst most of the main national newspapers are conservative, the online *Ohmynews* has attracted a wide following because of the alternative coverage that it offers. It relies upon large numbers of 'citizen reporters' to file stories. Political groups have set up their own web sites to popularize their policies, though it has also been alleged that they have become political ghettoes (Chang 2005).

The Asia Barometer survey of 2003 showed that 88 per cent of respondents believed that democracy was 'fairly good' or 'very good' for Korea. On the other hand only 11 per cent had confidence in parliament, the lowest figure for any public institution and much less than the 59 per cent who had confidence in the army (Shin 2006: 280, 299). Respect for parties is even lower than for parliament. The 2004 Korea Democracy Barometer showed that respondents rated the current democratic system on a ten-point scale at a mean of 6.3 and expected it to rise to 7.5 in the next five years. On the other hand, the 2004 figure was scarcely larger than the figure for 1997 (6.2) and had dipped lower in the intervening years. The democratic system may have withstood the strains of the financial crisis, but it had not increased its credibility. And in 2004, 56 per cent responded that the current system works for neither the will of the people nor their welfare (Shin and Lee 2006).

A major factor in this is persistent political corruption (Ferdinand 2003). During the 1990s, there was a widespread perception that democracy had actually exacerbated the problem, by multiplying the number of decision-makers who needed to be 'squared'. According to the surveys of Transparency International, South Korea was ranked twenty-seventh out of forty-one countries in 1995, and forty-second out of 163 countries in 2006 (first place being least corrupt), with almost identical raw scores. It is not just that parties need funds to win elections. The issue involves Koreans' sense of family-based identity, which is threatened by globalization too. As long as Korean politicians are expected to perform social roles of giving gifts on constituents' family occasions when their official salaries are insufficient, this problem will persist.

> ### KEY POINTS
>
> - Economic development reconfigured social forces and gradually constrained military rule. Then a changing external environment acted as a key catalyst in South Korea's transition to democracy.
>
> - Democracy emerged as a pact between elites and above all key leaders.
>
> - Widespread acceptance of democracy in general persists, though it was shaken by the financial crisis.
>
> - There was continuing party instability.
>
> - Democratic consolidation has yet to witness a marked decrease in high-level corruption.

Conclusion: Emerging Problems

South Korea has come a long way since 1953. It is now a moderately prosperous and economically developed country with an apparently consolidated democracy. The new Confucian ethic has incorporated dimensions that promote patriotism and prosperity; whilst assimilating Western values such as individualism, material success, and pragmatism. Thus while traditional values continue to shape society, they are themselves reshaped by development. Korea is now qualitatively different from both the Korea of 1945 and much of the developing world. Yet the country does face substantial new challenges. Most of them stem from globalization.

The most significant economic challenge concerns the reform of the developmental state model that served Korea so well until 1997. Korea is moving towards a more market-based system of economic management, where the state will become increasingly a regulator rather than director of economic activity. Already in 1994 the Economic Planning Board was merged with the Ministry of Finance. In the aftermath of the 1997 financial crisis some of the regulatory functions were transferred from the Ministry of Finance and Economy to the Bank of Korea. The Fair Trade Commission has been given much greater powers to encourage competition. There will also be strengthened property rights. This does not mean, however, at least for a long time, that Korea will have anything like an Anglo-American liberal type of macro-economic management. Instead, it will be closer to the 'coordinated market economy' found in parts of Western Europe, where the state will still be needed to play a key active role. Change on this scale will take time. The Ministry of Commerce, Industry and Energy now actually employs 25 per cent more officials than it did in 1998 (Kim and Kim 2005: 61). In addition the state has had to restructure the main banks' capital reserves or allow them to be taken over by foreign banks. According to the OECD, this cost the state the equivalent of 16 per cent of GDP (Pirie 2005: 362). Average state ownership of the top ten banks fell from 37 per cent in 1997 to 6 per cent in 2004, whilst average foreign ownership of them rose from 12 to 21 per cent. Without the pressure arising from the Asian financial crisis of 1997–8, it is questionable whether the Korean state would have had the resolution to pursue reform.

A second economic challenge is to restructure the *chaebols*. Some have been allowed to go bankrupt. Others have undergone major restructuring. The complex cross-shareholdings between companies within the same group have been unwound. Between 1997 and 2004, the mean and median debt-equity ratios in Korean companies fell by around three-quarters. Popular opinion in Korea is very reluctant to see their prime economic assets sold to foreigners. Yet compared to most other countries in the region Korea now has the reputation of a greater willingness to tolerate foreign capital. A new, outward-looking generation of political and business leaders, many of them educated abroad, are coming forward. A few *chaebols* such as Samsung have acquired global reputations for advanced technology.

A third challenge concerns the provision of welfare, where until 1997 the Korean state spent relatively little. It thought that supporting industrial and agricultural production would generate the income to support the needy, and relied upon the family for distribution. The financial crisis has changed all that. This is no longer politically sustainable. Korean officials are looking to Europe for ideas on ways of combining state welfare provision with economic regeneration.

Then there are expressly political challenges. Collective action remains a problem. Civil society is still relatively underdeveloped. Political parties lack deep grassroots commitment.

Lastly, there is the challenge of relations with the US. Until the 1980s, Koreans had a very positive image of the US. This was based upon intervention in the Korean War and subsequent US aid. That has changed significantly. Many increasingly regard China as a more important economic partner. Younger people now feel closer to North Korea than before. Now the US is blamed for allegedly conniving in the 1980 Kwangju massacre, and for intransigence towards the North, and for exploiting Korean economic woes in the 1997 financial crisis. Accidents to Korean nationals caused by American military personnel spark large public protests.

Roh Moo Hyun has attempted to distance himself from the US, although he did still send troops to Iraq. Since the GNP remains staunchly pro-American, there is the possibility of relations with the US becoming one of the major divides in Korean politics, as it was in Japan in the 1950s.

PETER FERDINAND

? QUESTIONS

1 How far has Korea's traditional political culture adapted to democracy?

2 Is Korea's developmental state no longer viable? If so, why?

3 Why is civil society still so weak?

4 Why is political leadership still so personalized?

5 How far have Korean political parties developed coherent ideologies?

6 How far do globalization and external relations impact on domestic South Korean politics?

7 Did the 2007 presidential election bring any major changes to the political system? How would you explain this?

GUIDE TO FURTHER READING

■ **Amsden, Alice H. (1989),** *Asia's Next Giant: South Korea and Late Industrialization* **(Oxford: Oxford University Press).** Examines how and why Korea got prices 'wrong' and yet achieved dramatic economic growth.

■ **Chang, Woo-young (2005), 'The Internet, Alternative Public Sphere and Political Dynamism: Korea's** *non-gaek* **(polemic) websites',** *Pacific Review,* **18/3: 393–415.**

■ **Eckert, Carter J. (1990), 'The South Korean Bourgeoisie: A Class in Search of Hegemony',** *Journal of Korean Studies,* **7: 115–48.** Outlines the rise of the families owning *chaebols.*

■ **Evans, P. (1995),** *Embedded Autonomy: States and Industrial Transformation* **(Princeton, NJ: Princeton University Press).** Focuses on a key element of the developmental state.

■ **Janelli, R. L. (1993),** *Making Capitalism* **(Stanford, Calif.: Stanford University Press).** The internal life of a Korean *chaebol* based on extended fieldwork.

■ **Jones, Leroy P., and SaKong II(1980),** *Government, Business and Entrepreneurship in Economic Development: The Korean Case* **(Cambridge, MA: Harvard University Press).** A revealing early account of the key role of government in Korean development.

■ **Lee, Yeon-ho (1997),** *The State, Society and Big Business in South Korea* **(London and New York: Routledge).** A very good account of this key relationship.

■ **Pirie, I. (2005), 'Better by Design: Korea's Neoliberal Economy',** *Pacific Review,* **18/3: 355–74.** A good and provocative summary of the changes in Korean political economy since 1997.

■ **Shin, Doh C. (1999),** *Mass Politics and Culture in Democratizing Korea* **(Cambridge: Cambridge University Press).** The best single account of the emergence of Korea's democracy.

■ ——and Lee, Jaechul (2006), *The Korea Democracy Barometer Surveys 1997–2004: Unraveling the Cultural and Institutional Dynamics of Democratization* (Aberdeen: Centre for the Study of Public Policy, University of Aberdeen). An interesting comparison of various political opinion surveys.

■ Woo-Cummings, M. (ed.) (1999), *The Developmental State* (Ithaca, NY, and London: Cornell University Press). Outlines the basic principles and their realization in various countries around the world.

WEB LINKS

● **www.korea.net**   The South Korean government's official homepage.

● **www.kdi.re.kr**   Korean Development Institute.

● **www.ohmynews.com**   A purely online news service that relies upon citizen journalists for material, but the English-language version is only a pale shadow of the Korean.

● **http://english.yna.co.kr**   (The Yonhap news service) Much fuller coverage in English.

● **www.uparty.or.kr/g_english/index.html**   Website of the Uri Party.

● **http://uri-party-news.newslib.com**   A website of newspaper articles about the Uri Party.

● **www.hannara.or.kr/**   Website of the Grand National Party (but only in Korean).

● **www.nec.go.kr/english/**   National Election Commission.

● **www.kicac.go.kr/PORTAL/Eng/index.jsp**   Korean Independent Commission Against Corruption.

ONLINE RESOURCE CENTRE

For additional material and resources, see the Online Resource Centre at:
www.oxfordtextbooks.co.uk/orc/burnell2e/

Appendix 1
Case Study Countries: Basic Indicators

	Population million 2005	Average annual population growth 2000–2005, %	GNI 2005, $ billion, PPP	GNI per capita 2005, $ PPP	GDP: average annual % growth 2004–2005	% of population on less than $1 a day, PPP	GINI index	HDI (value), 2004	Political rights 2005	Civil liberties 2005
Guatemala	13.0	2.4	56	4410	0.8	13.5	55.1	0.673	4	4
India	1095	1.5	3787	3460	7.1	34.7	32.5	0.611	2	3
Indonesia	221	1.3	820	3720	4.2	7.5	34.3	0.711	2	3
Mexico	103	1.0	1034	10030	1.9	4.5	49.5	0.821	2	2
Nigeria	132	2.3	137	1040	4.7	70.8	43.7	0.448	4	4
Pakistan	156	2.4	366	2350	5.2	17.0	30.6	0.539	6	5
Saudi Arabia	25	2.7	362	14740	3.9	N/A	N/A	0.777	7	6
South Africa	45	0.5	548	12120	5.6	10.7	57.8	0.653	1	2
South Korea	48	0.5	1055	21850	3.5	under 2	31.6	0.912	1	2

Notes: GDP (Gross Domestic Product); GNI (Gross National Income); PPP (purchasing power parity); GINI index (income/expenditure inequality–0 = perfect equality and 100 = perfect inequality); HDI (Human Development Index—a composite of education, longevity, and GDP per capita); N/A (not available); political rights and civil liberties on scale 1 (most free)–7 (least free).

Comment: The most striking difference from the figures for earlier years published in this book's first edition is a marked general decline in population growth rates with a few exceptions, although the reasons differ among countries (South Africa's total population appears to have fallen not least because of AIDS). The economic data show mixed fortunes, with improvements particularly marked for oil exporters (Mexico is an exception). The freedom indicators show few changes, although Indonesia is now rated as more free on both counts. Guatemala stands out as a country where most of the indicators are either deteriorating or not improving, so bearing out the book's original choice of Guatemala as an example of continuing underdevelopment.

Sources: United Nations Development Programme (2006), *Human Development Report 2006* (columns 7, 8); World Bank (2007), *World Development Report 2007* (columns 1–6); Freedom House (2006), *Annual Freedom House Survey* (columns 9, 10)

Appendix 2

Case Study Countries: Globalization Rankings and Scores, 2001

	Overall globalization ranking	Economic globalization ranking	Political globalization ranking	Social globalization ranking	Political globalization index (score)
Guatemala	89	103	100	94	0.218
India	33	49	19	108	0.582
Indonesia	37	34	31	104	0.514
Mexico	51	52	54	58	0.363
Nigeria	28	28	21	119	0.578
Pakistan	35	71	17	120	0.586
Saudi Arabia	n/a	n/a	58	89	0.335
South Africa	59	47	76	62	0.266
South Korea	21	41	37	23	0.479

Note: The CSGR Globalization Index, which presents data from 1982 to 2001, is explicitly designed to be comparable across countries and time. It measures economic globalization as a function of trade (exports plus imports), foreign direct investment (inflows plus outflows), portfolio investment (inflows plus outflows), and international income flows (payments to non-resident workers and investment income from assets owned by non-residents). All these are measured as a proportion of Gross Domestic Product (GDP). Social globalization is assessed mainly in terms of the movement of people across borders including worker remittances and tourist arrivals and departures, together with the flow of ideas via telephone and internet usage, films, and book imports and exports. The volume of international mail per capita is also taken into account. The index obtains its measurements for political globalization from the number of foreign embassies in a country, its participation in United Nations peacekeeping operations and membership of international organizations. The total number of countries for which the index is *currently* available is 96 for overall globalization, and for economic 122; political 186; and social 130. N/A means not available.

Source: Lockwood and Redoano (2005).

Appendix 3
Regional Inter-Governmental Organizations in the Developing World

Different institutional forms and structures are represented among the more noteworthy regional inter-governmental organizations in the developing world. The organizations each have their own individual aims and objectives. And while progress towards realizing the stated purposes has varied considerably, the further development of regional cooperation and integration is the kind of initiative that the developing countries themselves can make. It is increasingly seen as an appropriate response to globalization.

Africa

African Union (2002, formerly Organization of African Unity, 1963): originally to promote the unity and solidarity of the African states.

Economic Community of West African States (ECOWAS) (1975): the largest regional economic community in West Africa, aims to promote co-operation and integration leading to a common market and monetary union.

Central African Customs and Economic Union (1966): to promote the establishment of a regional common market.

Common Market for Eastern and Southern Africa (COMESA) replaced the African Preferential Trade Area for Eastern and Southern Africa (established by treaty in 1981) in 1994, with the aim initially of finalizing a free trade area. The largest regional economic community in Africa.

Monetary and Economic Community of Central Africa: formerly the Central African Customs and Economic Union established in 1964, aims to promote a common market.

Southern African Customs Union; negotiated in 1969 but with its origins in the nineteenth century this union of South Africa, Botswana, Lesotho, Swaziland, and Namibia shares customs revenue in line with a negotiated formula.

Southern African Development Community (formerly Southern African Development Co-ordination Conference, 1980) (SADC): to promote economic integration and strengthen regional solidarity, peace, and security. Includes a SADC Parliamentary Forum with a focus on issues in democracy and governance and an HIV/AIDS programme.

Americas

Andean Community of Nations (formerly Andean Pact, 1969): to promote balanced, harmonious development through economic integration.

Association of Caribbean States (ACS) (1994): to promote economic integration.

Caribbean Community (and Common Market) (CARICOM) (1973): to promote economic integration and development.

Central American Common Market (CACM) (1960, collapsed 1969 and reinstated 1991): to establish a common market.

Free Trade Area of the Americas (FTAA): dating from 1994 Summit of the Americas, aims to establish a free trade area including all the countries lying between Alaska and Cape Horn with the exception of Cuba. Civil society participation in the negotiations has been a distinctive feature. Seven of the eleven candidate sites for the Secretariat are US cities.

Latin American Economic System (SELA) (1975): to promote intraregional cooperation on economic and social matters.

North American Free Trade Agreement (NAFTA) (launched 1994): to create a free trade and economic integration zone comprising Mexico, the United States, and Canada.

Organization of American States (OAS) (1948, with origins in 1890 as the International Union of American Republics): to promote an order of peace, justice, and solidarity among the American states; includes Canada and the United States, but Cuba excluded since 1962. 2001 saw the adoption of an Inter-American Democratic Charter: strengthening democratic commitment is styled a 'key OAS issue'.

Organization of Eastern Caribbean States (OECS) (1981): to increase cooperation in foreign relations and promote measures leading to deeper sub-regional integration.

Southern Common Market (MERCOSUR) (1991): to establish a regional common market in the southern cone but becoming more broadly based with the full accession of Venezuela in 2006 and Bolivia as prospective associate member.

Asia

Asia-Pacific Economic Cooperation (APEC) (1989): to provide a forum for discussion on a broad range of economic issues and to promote multilateral cooperation including freer and more open trade and investment within the region. Operates on the basis of non-binding commitments (i.e. no treaty obligations). Membership includes US, China, Japan, and Russia and claims around 40 per cent of world's population and half the world's trade and Gross Domestic Product.

Association of Southeast Asian Nations (ASEAN) (1967): to accelerate development through trade liberalization in the region and promote collaboration and mutual assistance in industrial development. Has adopted cooperative peace as well as shared prosperity as 'fundamental goal',

and expressly enshrines the principles of national sovereignty and non-interference in one another's internal affairs.

South Asian Association for Regional Cooperation (SAARC) (1985): to promote economic, social, and cultural cooperation.

Middle East

Arab Maghreb Union (1989): to promote political coordination, cooperation, and complementarity across various fields.

Cooperation Council for the Arab States of the Gulf (Gulf Cooperation Council) (1981): to strengthen cooperation and unity including on military and security issues.

League of Arab States (the Arab League) (1945): to strengthen relations among member states by coordinating policies and mediating disputes.

Other

Africa-Caribbean-Pacific (ACP) grouping of 79 states in a special development cooperation relationship with the European Union, dating from Yaoundé Convention (1969) and its successor the Lomé Conventions. Secretariat based in Brussels. 2005 saw the signing of a charter to create an ACP Consultative (Parliamentary) Assembly.

The Commonwealth (a voluntary association stemming from Britain's imperial past, formalized in 1931): 53 developing and developed nations claiming around 30 per cent of the world's people, to promote respect, encourage equal trust and friendship, and common prosperity. Includes the Commonwealth Foundation whose mandate is to strengthen civil society.

Non-Aligned Movement (NAM) (1961): originally formed to counter imperialism and promote independence of the competing superpowers and their blocs, NAM has had to change focus since the end of the cold war and tune in more to social and economic issues. The fourteenth summit, held in Cuba in September 2006, assembled over

50 leaders from the 118 members, some of them such as those from Venezuela and Iran using the occasion to criticise US imperialism. China and UN Secretary-General Kofi Annan attended as observers.

Organization of Arab Petroleum Exporting Countries (1968): to promote cooperation in the petroleum industry.

Organization of the Islamic Conference (OIC) (1969): organization of 56 Islamic states, to promote Islamic solidarity and cooperation in economic, social, cultural, and political affairs.

Organization of the Petroleum Exporting Countries (OPEC) (1960): to coordinate and unify petroleum policies of member countries and determine the best means of safeguarding their interests.

The developed world's oil producers, Russia and Mexico, are not members.

United Nations Conference on Trade and Development (UNCTAD) (1964): inclusive of all UN members, formed to promote trade for the economic benefit of developing countries. Presents itself as an 'authoritative knowledge-based institution' that works to shape policy debate and thinking on development. Office of Secretary-General based in Geneva.

World Community of Democracies (2000) a loose intergovernmental 'caucus' of over 100 countries at the United Nations claiming a commitment to the promotion of democratic governance everywhere, by using UN forums. Has no permanent secretariat but is accompanied by a civil society forum.

Glossary

aid selectivity determining aid allocations between countries on the basis of demonstrable commitment to pro-developmental policies and institutions rather than on the basis of future promises or conditionalities

apartheid an Afrikaans word meaning separateness, in South Africa expressed as the official government policy of racial segregation, between 1948 and 1989

ascriptive identities groupings to which people belong by birth rather than by choice

autonomy of politics/political autonomy the extent to which politics as a level or sphere of social life is determined by economic and/or social/cultural dimensions of society or is able independently to impact on those dimensions

balkanization referring to the breaking up of a region or country into small territorial units, often as a means to 'divide and rule'

caste a system of social stratification characterized by hereditary status, endogamy, and social barriers sanctioned by custom or law.

caste associations organizations to represent the interests of a caste group or cluster of closely related caste groups, largely confined to India

caudillismo historically referring to the organization of political life in parts of Latin America by local 'strongmen' (*caudillos*) competing for power and its spoils

chaebols the family-based business groups or conglomerates, many of them with cross-ownership, that have been South Korea's primary source of capital accumulation

Christian democracy the application of Christian precepts to electoral politics

civic national identities involving unity among citizens of an autonomous state

civil regulation in the environmental arena referring to a range of activities undertaken by civil society actors aimed at creating new frameworks of expectation and obligation for companies

civil society a term highly contested, and concerning the realm of voluntary citizen associations that exists between the family and the state, enjoying independence of the latter, and seeking to influence public policy without aspirations to public office. Modern civil society comprises formal, professionalized non-governmental organizations typical of the late twentieth century; traditional civil society is organized more informally, and may follow patterns with deep and enduring roots in history and society

clash of civilizations referring to Samuel P. Huntington's prediction that after the end of the cold war international conflicts would increasingly have cultural characteristics, most notably setting the Christian 'West' against the mostly Muslim, mostly Arab 'East'

clientelism referring to the exchange of specific services or resources (usually publicly funded) between individuals in return for political support such as votes, and essentially a relationship between unequals

collapsed state *see* state collapse

commodification the transformation of something into a commodity to be bought and sold on the market

comparative advantage the economic theory that countries should specialize in the production and export of those goods and services that they have a *relative* cost advantage in producing compared to other countries

competitive authoritarianism a kind of 'illiberal democracy' where formal democratic institutions are widely viewed as the principal source of political authority but rulers violate the rules so strikingly that the regime fails to meet conventional minimum standards of democracy

conditionality referring to the attachment of policy and/or other conditions to offers of financial and other assistance, with the possibility of aid sanctions for non-compliance

constructive programmes challenge systemic and structural violence by finding and applying solutions at the local level and in everyday life; they restructure power relations so that the oppressed are no longer dependent upon the oppressors but instead become self-reliant and autonomous from exploitive state or market relations

corruption involving the private use of public office and resources and generally considered illegal

cross-conditionality exists where one lender makes its aid offers conditional on the recipient meeting conditions laid down by one or more other lenders

critical security studies refers to approaches united by dissatisfaction with the so called 'traditional' security studies and in particular its state and military centrism

cruel choice Jagdish Bhagwati's term for the dilemma he believed faced developing countries: either concentrate on economic development, or emulate the political systems of the West

cultural imperialism the domination of vulnerable peoples by the culture of economically and politically powerful societies

decentralized despotism a pattern of colonial and post-colonial government identified by Mahmood Mamdani (1996) as arising from the colonial practice of indirect rule

delegative democracy according to Guillermo O'Donnell, resting on the premise that whoever wins election to the presidency is thereby entitled to govern as they think fit, constrained only by the hard facts of existing power relations and a constitutionally limited term of office

democracy assistance comprises largely consensual and concessionary international support to democratic reform chiefly by way of specific projects and programmes, for instance civil society capacity-building endeavours

democracy promotion encompasses a wide range of approaches including not only democracy assistance but also diplomatic pressure and in some accounts much more coercive forms of intervention where democratization is the stated goal

democratic peace theory the claim that democracies do not go to war with one another

democratization backwards describing situations where largely free elections are introduced in advance of such basic institutions of the modern state as the rule of law, full executive accountability, and a flourishing civil society

dependency theory an argument that the weak structural position of developing countries in the international capitalist system influences important variables in their political life as well as explains their failure to achieve stronger development

deprivation according to Fraser (1997) 'being denied an adequate material standard of living'

despotic power the power to control and suppress (as Michael Mann has called it), as opposed to infrastructural power, the power to penetrate and transform society

developing world a term conventionally referring to the predominantly post-colonial regions of Africa, Asia, Latin America and the Caribbean, and the Middle East, perceived to be poorer, less economically advanced, and less 'modern' than the developed world

development administration a field of study aimed at providing an understanding of administrative performance in the specific economic and cultural contexts of poor, non-Western societies

developmental state according to Adrian Leftwich, concentrating sufficient power, autonomy, and capacity at the centre to bring about explicit developmental objectives, whether by encouraging the conditions and direction of economic growth or by organizing it directly. The hallmarks include a competent bureaucracy and the insulation of state institutions from special interests in society, in other words, the state enjoys embedded autonomy. While there are significant differences among the cases commonly cited as examples of the development state, the most successful examples in East Asia have tended to be authoritarian

direct democracy exists where citizens can vote directly on public policy and decide what is to be done on other important political issues, such as through devices like referenda

discourse theory an interpretative approach closely associated with Michel Foucault that analyses power in terms of the dominant discourses, or chains of meaning, which shape understanding and behaviour

eco-colonialism an argument that the imposition of environmental conditions on financial and economic support for developing countries restricts their development

economic growth the rate of growth in a country's national output or income, usually measured by its Gross Domestic Product (GDP) or Gross National Product (GNP) and often presented on a per capita basis

economic marginalization 'being confined to undesirable or poorly paid work' (Fraser 1997)

economic rents incomes derived from the possession of a valuable licence or permit, particularly for the import of foreign goods

electoral authoritarianism/autocracy where elections are an instrument of authoritarian rule, an alternative to both democracy and naked repression

emancipation in IR theory comes from the Aberystwyth school of critical security studies that defines security in terms of 'emancipation' or freedom of people from threats

embedded autonomy according to Peter Evans characterized by the relative facility of the developmental state to transcend sectional interests in society, providing a sound basis for pursuing national industrial transformation

entitlements justified rights or claims belonging to individuals or groups

equality of outcome an approach that aims to make people equal whatever their original differences

ethnic identities socially constructed identities that follow when people self-consciously distinguish themselves from others on the basis of perceived common descent and/or shared culture. Many but not all such identities are politicized

ethnic morphology refers to the form and structure of groups

ethnonational identities defining the nation in ethnic terms, attaining unity through the merger of ethnic and national identities, and demanding autonomy for ethnic nations

ethnopolitical identities those ethnic identities that have been politicized, that is, made politically relevant

evaluation research research into the outcomes of programme intervention or policy change

evangelical Christianity usually refers to conservative, nearly always Protestant, Christian religious practices and traditions that emphasize evangelism, a personal experience of conversion, faith rooted in the Holy Bible, and a belief in the relevance of Christian faith to cultural issues

exploitation in Fraser's (1997) words, 'having the fruits of one's labour appropriated for the benefit of others'

extents of freedom in Sen's terminology, the capabilities or the *freedom* to achieve whatever functionings an individual happens to value

extractive state the idea that the extraction of the nation's (natural resource) wealth for the benefit of its ruler(s) become the primary goal of the ruler(s)

extraversion a theory of African political behaviour developed by Jean-François Bayart (1993) that argues that, historically, the relatively weak development of the continent's productive forces and its internal social struggles made African political actors more disposed to mobilize resources from their relationship with the external environment

failing state a state that is failing in respect of some or all of its functions without yet having reached the stage of 'collapse'

fallacy of electoralism privileging electoral contestation as if that were a sufficient condition for democracy to exist

fatwa a religious edict issued by an Islamic leader

feminism comprising recognition and action on women's common bonds and inequalities between men and women

garrison state is a state maintained by military power and in some definitions means a state organized to secure primarily its own need for military security

gatekeeper state a term coined by the African historian Frederick Cooper (2002) to denote a form of state focused on controlling the intersection of the territory with the outside world, collecting and distributing the resources that that control brought

gender referring to ideas about male and female and the relations between them as social constructions rather than the product of biological determinants only

genocide referring to deliberate extermination of a social group selected on grounds of culture, ethnicity, or race

Gini coefficient A commonly used measure of inequality (household income or consumption)—the higher the figure, the more unequal the distribution

global justice movement a loose, increasingly transnational network of non-governmental and social movement organizations opposed to neo-liberal economic globalization, violence, and North-South inequalities; they support participatory democracy, equality, and sustainable development

global stewardship referring to resources that are said to be part of the common heritage of humankind and should be managed for the benefit of all

globalization a highly contested term, defined in different ways that range from increasing global economic integration, in particular international trade, to processes whereby many social relations become relatively delinked from territorial geography and human lives are increasingly played out in the world as a single place

globalization theory focusing on a process of accelerated communication and economic integration which transcends national boundaries and increasingly incorporates all parts of the world into a single social system

good governance originated in World Bank discourse to mean the sound management of public affairs with a bias towards neo-liberal conceptions of the state's role in the economy, but went on to acquire broader connotations sharing many of the ideas and institutions associated with democracy, and hence democratic governance

governance An omnibus term with a variety of meanings that reflects its usage in diverse disciplines and practices ranging from new public management to international development cooperation, and spanning institutions at both the local and the global level. Best defined contextually, and best understood with reference to both the objective and normative purposes of the definer, as exemplified in, for instance, the similarly wide-ranging but nevertheless contrasting accounts offered by the Governance Matters Project of the World Bank and the World Governance Assessment, which lies closer to the thinking of the UNDP

Heavily Indebted Poor Countries Initiative (HIPC) arranged by the World Bank and International Monetary Fund has the objective of bringing the countries' debt burden to sustainable levels, subject to satisfactory policy performance, so as to ensure that adjustment and reform efforts are not put at risk by continued high debt and debt service burdens

Hindu caste system a complex and ancient, though evolving, system of social stratification in which people's caste status is determined at birth

HIV/AIDS refers to Human Immunodeficiency Virus, a retrovirus that infects cells of the human immune system. It is widely accepted that infection with HIV causes AIDS (Acquired Immunodeficiency Syndrome), a disease characterized by the destruction of the immune system

human capital referring to the knowledge, skills, and capabilities of individuals

human development according to the United Nations Development Programme, about freedom, well-being, and dignity of people everywhere; the UNDP's human development index measures longevity, educational attainment, and standard of living

human rights either the rights everyone has because they are human or those generally recognized as such by governments or in international law

human security is an emerging paradigm that links development studies and national security and is defined as the protection of human lives from critical and pervasive threats. A wide-ranging version claims human security is 'freedom from want': extreme poverty precludes real security. More narrowly, human security is 'freedom from fear': the emphasis is on safety from violence including wars and violent crime

Ikhwan The brethren, religious followers of *Wahhabism*

illiberal democracy Fareed Zakaria's term for polities where governments are elected but have little respect for constitutional liberalism—the rule of law, separation of powers, and such basic liberties as speech, assembly, religion, and property

import-substitution industrialization (ISI) referring to the economic strategy of protecting the growth of manufacturing industry by reserving the home market for domestic producers ('infant industries'), through introducing barriers to imports

indirect rule a mode of rule developed especially, though not only, by Britain under which the colonial power allowed native rulers and chiefs to exercise limited authority

informal economy referring to employment and wealth creation that is not captured by the official data, offering opportunities for people who are unable to participate in the formal economy; governments find it difficult to regulate and tax the informal sector

informal institutions are rules and procedures that are created, communicated, and enforced outside the officially sanctioned channels. They may undermine, reinforce, or even override the formal institutions

institutions collections of (broadly) agreed norms, rules, procedures, practices, and routines, either formally established or written down and embodied in organizations or as informal understandings embedded in culture

international community is a loose term denoting the main Western powers and the international organizations in and over which they exert considerable influence, for example in the United Nations

international human rights regime a large body of international law and a complex set of institutions to implement it

la francophonie is the international organization of French-speaking communities, given a formal institutional basis in 1970

legitimacy a psychological relationship between the governed and their governors, which engenders a belief that the state's leaders and institutions have a right to exercise political authority over the rest of society

liberal democracy embodying a combination of political rights and civil liberties which go beyond electoral democracy's more limited attachment to civil freedoms and minority rights

liberal imperialism the idea that powerful advanced Western states should intervene, if necessary by force, in other countries to spread good government and liberal democratic values.

liberalism a political philosophy that gives priority to individual freedom

liberation theology a school of theological thought with widespread influence in Latin America beginning in the 1960s, which explores the relation between Christian theology and political activism in the areas of poverty, social justice, and human rights

localism is the tendency to prioritize local cultural, economic, and political interests and identities over national ones

mainstreaming in the context of gender and environment, infusing public policies with a gender or environmental focus

majlis a traditional tribal forum for male elders and has evolved into an institution for consultation between ruler and ruled (Saudi Arabia)

microcredit the provision of small loans to poor people who cannot obtain normal commercial credit for entrepreneurial activities

Millennium Development Goals (MDGs) established by the United Nations Millennium Declaration (September 2000) in the following eight areas: eradicate extreme poverty and hunger; achieve universal primary education; promote gender equality and empower women; reduce child mortality; improve maternal health; combat HIV/AIDS, malaria, and other diseases; ensure environmental sustainability; develop a global partnership for development

modernization referring to a complex set of changes in culture, society, and economy characterized by urbanization, industrialization, and in some cases secularization, although one response to it may be religious revival

modernization revisionism a critique of modernization theory, centred on its oversimplified notions of tradition, modernity, and their interrelationship

multi-ethnic or multicultural national identities defining the nation in terms of several ethnic or cultural identities contained within citizenship, political interaction, and an overarching national identity in an autonomous state

national identities inherently political, emphasizing the autonomy and unity of the nation as an actual or potential political unit

nation-building referring to building a sense of national belonging and unity

natural capital comprising nature's free goods and services

neo-liberalism stressing the role of the market in resource allocation and a correspondingly reduced role for the state, together with integration into the global economy. Aspects of the neo-liberal agenda are exhibited in the Washington consensus associated with the Bretton Woods institutions

neo-patrimonialism combining patrimonialism and legal-rational bureaucratic rule, which gives formal recognition to the distinction between the public and the private

new institutional economics (NIE) an approach that focuses on the way society's institutions affect economic performance

New International Economic Order comprising a set of reform proposals for the international financial and trading systems, to help the economic development of the developing countries, first proposed at a summit meeting of the Non-Aligned Movement (1973) and incorporated in a Declaration of the UN General Assembly in 1974

new protectionism referring to the measures of developed countries to reserve their domestic markets for home producers by means of non-tariff barriers such as imposing environmental standards

newly (or new) industrialized(izing) countries (NICs) referring to those developing countries primarily but not exclusively in East Asia (also sometimes called 'dragon' or 'tiger' economies) that experienced dramatic industrialization soonest after 1945

non-governmental organizations (NGOs) organizations that operate in civil society and are not part of government or the state (although sometimes dependent, in part, on government for funding)

non-traditional security threats are non-military issues such as environmental problems, threats from migration, international organized crime, and disease

nonviolent action refers to methods of political action that do not involve violence or the threat of violence against living beings. Instead, they involve an active process of bringing political, economic, social, emotional, or moral pressure to bear in the wielding of power in contentious interactions between collective actors, through methods such as protest demonstrations, marches, civil disobedience, and land occupations

official development assistance (ODA) comprising resources transferred on concessional terms with the promotion of the economic development and welfare of the developing countries as the main objective

only game in town when applied to a perception that democratic elections are a permanent institution, often said to mark out democratic consolidation

ontological equality the assumption that all people are born equal

Orientalism referring to Edward Said's influential account (1978) of Western dominance of the East and how images of the Orient (the 'other') helped define the West as its contrasting image

outward-oriented development looking to the global economy as a driving force for economic growth, through the creation of a favourable policy environment for exports

overpopulation referring to birth rates that exceed death rates, producing growth that is difficult to sustain with the given resource base

pacted transition where transition to democracy comes about by agreement among political elites integral to the precursor regime

Pancasila the official ideology of Soeharto's Indonesia, enjoining belief in a supreme being, humanitarianism, national unity, consensus democracy, and social justice

path dependence claiming that where you come from, the method of change, and choices made or not made along the way significantly influence the outcome and final destination

patriarchy referring to the ideology and institutions of male rule, male domination, and female subordination

patrimonialism treating the state as the personal patrimony or property of the ruler (hence patrrimonialist state), and all power relations between ruler and ruled are personal relations

patronage the politically motivated distribution of favours, intended to create and maintain political support among groups

patron–client relations connecting patronage and clientelism

people power movements comprise popular civilian-based challenges to oppression and injustice that depend primarily on methods of nonviolent action rather than on armed methods

political culture embracing the attitudes, beliefs, and values that are said to underlie a political system

political development understood in the 1960s as a process of political change associated with increasing equality, political system capability, and differentiation of political roles and structures

political Islam refers to a political movement with often diverse characteristics that at various times has included elements of many other political movements, while simultaneously adapting the religious views of Islamic fundamentalism or Islamism

politicide referring to extermination of political enemies

politics on a narrow understanding, a kind of activity associated with the process of government, and in modern settings also linked with the 'public' sphere. On a broader understanding, it is about 'power' relations and struggles not necessarily confined to the process of government or restricted to the public domain

politics of order a critique of political development theory which focused on the need for strong government and political order

polyarchy Robert Dahl's influential idea of democracy that rests on the two pillars of public contestation and the right to participate

populism a political ideology or approach that claims to be in the interests of 'the people'

post-colonial state a state that came into being as a consequence of the dissolution of the European colonial empires

post-structuralism sometimes also referred to as post-modernism, a broad philosophical approach that questions the epistemological foundations of 'rational' enlightenment thinking

predatory state close to the idea of an extractive state, one that exploits the people for the benefit of the rulers and holds back development

privatization the transformation of something that is communally or publicly owned to private property

process conditionality refers to the requirement of the poverty reduction strategy process that a government formulates (pro-poor) development policy itself through the consultation of local stakeholders, civil society in particular, so as to secure 'local ownership', in principle thereby avoiding the failings of conditionality

pronatalism/pronatalist referring to policies or values that motivate high birth rates

proxy wars conflicts carried out on behalf of, and supported by, the great powers, as was often the case in developing areas during the cold war era

pseudo-democracy existing where there is not a sufficiently fair arena of electoral contestation to allow the ruling party to be turned out of power

public goods goods like defence that if supplied to anybody are necessarily supplied to everybody, and in consequence the market is unlikely to provide them in sufficient quantity

rational choice theory a deductive approach that argues from the premise that in making choices individual political actors behave rationally in terms of the objectives they pursue. The quest for individual utility maximization is assumed to be paramount

realists in IR theory include classical realists who define security as national security. They emphasize military threats to the state and inter-state conflict

regime a set of rules and practices that regulate the conduct of actors in a specified field (as distinct from political regime understood as a system of government)

regime change came to be applied to the practice of removing a government by external force, as in the military invasion of Afghanistan and Iraq to topple the Taliban and Saddam Hussein's government respectively, and whose purpose some opponents of international intervention in developing countries choose to identify with the aspirations behind democracy promotion and democracy assistance from the West

religio-politics political activity with religious dimensions

religious fundamentalism a disputed term applied most often to groups of Islamic, Hindu, and Christian worshippers who place strong emphasis on a return to their faith's fundamentals and resistance to secularization, often through political means

rentier state a state whose income takes the form primarily of rents from a resource like oil, or from foreign aid, rather than from taxing the subjects, which gives it high autonomy from society and may restrain citizens from demanding democratically accountable government

rent-seeking referring to the pursuit of gains (economic rents) to be derived from control over scarce goods or services—a scarcity that might be artificially created for the purpose

right to self-determination the claimed right of a distinct group of people to determine their own political, economic, and cultural destinies

robust peacekeeping is used by NATO to define the new type of peacekeeping its troops in Afghanistan are engaged in. There they have more leeway to make peace as well as keeping and monitoring functions

rule of law is the idea that all citizens including the lawmakers and all other government officials are bound by the law and no-one is above the law

scramble for Africa a name given to the late nineteenth-century territorial expansion of European powers in Africa, leading to the Congress of Berlin (1845) which formally adopted the division of the new colonies and protectorates

secularization the gradual diminution of the influence of religion on public affairs. Liberal secularism advocates separation of church and state, with the second power being dominant and no one religion having official priority

securitization occurs when an issue is presented as posing an existential threat to a designated object, traditionally but not necessarily the state. The designation of the threat in this way is used to justify the use of extraordinary measures in response

security dichotomies refer to a duality of perceptions, a division into two contradictory understandings of a security issue, one negative and one positive

Sharia law or Islamic religious law, incorporated to varying degrees in the legal systems of states with large Islamic populations

shura an Islamic term used for consultation between the people and the ruler

social capital referring to social networks, norms, and trust, that enable participants to function more effectively in pursuing a common goal. Arguably high levels are valuable both for political and economic cooperation

social movements loose networks of informal organizations that come about in response to an issue, crisis, or concern and seek to influence social and other public policy, such as environmental policy, often through using direct action, which may or may not employ violence

societal collapse occurring where the fabric of linkages and feedback mechanisms between state and society and within society are irreparably ruptured

soft state Gunnar Myrdal's term for states with low enforcement capacity such as those with lax bureaucracy and corruption

state collapse occurring where a functioning state system ceases to exist

state failure indicating a less than complete collapse of the state system

state–church relations the interactions in a country between the state and the leading religious organization(s)

stateless societies societies which do not have a state but may still enjoy a measure of social and economic order

status a quality of social honour or a lack of it, which is mainly conditioned as well as expressed through a specific style of life

structural adjustment programmes (SAPs) designed to shift economic policy and management in the direction of the Washington consensus, sometimes leading to more narrowly focused sectoral adjustment programmes, and often associated with structural adjustment loans (SALs) from the Bretton Woods institutions and other aid donors

subsistence economy referring to activity outside the cash economy for barter or home use

sustainable development a disputed term, which was defined by the Brundtland Report (1987) as development which meets the needs of the present without compromising the ability of future generations to meet their own needs; environmental degradation is minimized while ecological sustainability is maximized

terrorism is a tactic designed to achieve an objective (usually political) by using violence against innocent civilians to generate fear

third wave of democracy Samuel P. Huntington's term for democratization in the late twentieth century

transaction costs the costs of doing business in a market economy, including the cost of finding market information as well as the costs incurred when parties to a contract do not keep to their agreement

ulema islamic clergy or body consisting of those educated in Islam and *Sharia* (Islamic law) with the function of ensuring the implementation of Islamic precepts

underdevelopment or lack of development, according to dependency theory, which is a consequence of capitalist development elsewhere

unequal exchange the idea that international trade between developed and developing countries is an instrument whereby the former exploit the latter and capture the greater part of the benefits

unsecularization meaning a global religious revitalization

urban bias bias in public policy and spending against the rural areas in favour of urban areas or urban-based interests, due to their greater political influence

war on terror is the term given by the USA and its allies to an ongoing campaign with the stated goal of ending global terrorism. It was launched in response to the 11 September 2001 terrorist attacks on the USA

warlords powerful regional figures possessing coercive powers, inside a country

Washington consensus the term applied (by John Williamson, in 1989) to a package of liberalizing economic and financial policy reforms deemed essential if Latin America (and subsequently other parts of the developing world) are to escape debt and rejuvenate their economic performance. The term quickly became attached to the policy approach in the 1990s of the Bretton Woods Institutions especially, namely the International Monetary Fund and World Bank. The central elements are fiscal discipline, reorientation of public expenditures, tax reform, financial liberalization, openness to foreign direct investment, privatization, deregulation, and secure property rights (see Williamson 2003)

weak states according to Joel Migdal, states lacking the capability to penetrate society fully, regulate social relations, extract and distribute resources, or implement policies and plans

wealth theory of democracy claiming that the prospects for stable democracy are significantly influenced by economic and socio-economic development

Westminster model referring to the institutional arrangement of parliamentary government bequeathed by Britain to many of its former colonies

women's policy interests referring to official decisions or practices in which women have a special stake because of need, discrimination, or lack of equality

women's policy machinery units within government such as women's bureaux, commissions of women, ministries of women, and women's desks

References

Acharya, A. (1999), 'Developing Countries and the Emerging World Order', in L. Fawcett and Y. Sayigh (eds.), *The Third World Beyond the Cold War* (Oxford: Oxford University Press), 78–98.

Adam, H. M. (1995), 'Somalia: A Terrible Beauty Being Born?', in I. W. Zartman (ed.), *Collapsed States. The Disintegration of Legitimate Authority* (London: Lynne Rienner).

Adelman, I., and Morris, C. (1973), *Economic Growth and Equity in Developing Countries* (Stanford, Calif.: Stanford University Press).

Adeney, K., and Wyatt, A. (2004), 'Democracy in South Asia: Getting beyond the Structure-Agency Dichotomy', *Political Studies*, 52/1: 1–18.

Ahluwalia, P. (2001), *Politics and Post-Colonial Theory. African Inflections* (London: Routledge).

Ake, C. (2000), *The Feasibility of Democracy in Africa* (Senegal: CODESRIA).

Alavi, H. (1979), 'The State in Post-Colonial Societies', in H. Goulbourne (ed.), *Politics and the State in the Third World* (London: Macmillan), 38–69.

—— (1988), 'Pakistan and Islam: Ethnicity and Ideology', in F. Halliday and H. Alavi (eds.), *State and Ideology in the Middle East and Pakistan* (New York: Monthly Review Press), 64–111.

Al-Farsy, F. (1990), *Modernity and Tradition: The Saudi Equation* (London: Kegan Paul International).

Allison, R., and Williams, P. (1990), *Superpower Competition and Crisis Prevention in the Third World* (Cambridge: Cambridge University Press).

Almond, G. (1987), 'The Development of Political Development', in M. Weiner and S. P. Huntington (eds.), *Understanding Political Development* (New York: Harper Collins), 437–90.

——, and Verba S. (eds.) (1965), *The Civic Culture: Political Attitudes and Democracy in Five Nations* (Newbury Park, Calif.: Sage Publications).

Amsden, A. H. (1989), *Asia's Next Giant: South Korea and Late Industrialization* (Oxford: Oxford University Press).

Anderson, B. (1991), *Imagined Communities: Reflections on the Origin and Spread of Nationalism*, rev. edn. (London: Verso).

Aspinall, E., and Fealy G. (eds.) (2003), *Local Power and Politics in Indonesia: Democratization and Decentralization* (Singapore: Institute of Southeast Asian Affairs).

Ayoob, M. (1995), *The Third World Security Predicament: State Making, Regional Conflict and the International System* (Boulder, Colo.: Lynne Rienner).

Baker, C. (2003), 'Thailand's Assembly of the Poor: Background, Drama, Reaction', *South East Asia Research*, 8/1: 5–29.

Barnes, H., and Bigham, A. (2006), *Understanding Iran: People, Politics and Power* (London: The Foreign Policy Centre).

Barton, J. R. (1997), *A Political Geography of Latin America* (London: Routledge).

Bastian, S., and Luckham, R. (eds.) (2003), *Can Democracy Be Designed? The Politics of Institutional Choice in Conflict-Torn Societies* (London: Zed).

Bastos, S. and Camus, M. (2003), Entre el Mecapal y el Cielo: Desarrollo del Movimento Maya en Guatemala (Guatemala: FLASCO).

Bates, R. H. (1981), *States and Markets in Tropical Africa: The Political Basis of Agricultural Policy* (Berkeley, Calif.: University of California Press).

—— (2001), *Prosperity and Violence. The Political Economy of Development* (New York: W. W. Norton).

Bauer, P. T. (1981), *Equality, the Third World and Economic Delusion* (London: Methuen).

Bayart, J.-F. (1993), *The State in Africa. The Politics of the Belly* (London: Longman).

—— Ellis, S., and Hibou, B. (1999), *The Criminalization of the State in Africa* (Bloomington, Ind.: Indiana University Press/Oxford: James Currey).

Baylis, J., and Smith, S. (eds.) (2001), *The Globalization of World Politics*, 2nd edn. (Oxford: Oxford University Press).

—— and —— (eds.) (2005), *The Globalization of World Politics*, 3rd edn. (Oxford: Oxford University Press).

Bayly, S. (1999), *The New Cambridge History of India, IV.3. Caste, Society and Politics in India from the Eighteenth Century to the Modern Age* (Cambridge: Cambridge University Press).

Beetham, D. (1997), 'Market Economy and Democratic Polity', *Democratization*, 4/1: 76–93.

—— Bracking, S., Kearton, I., and Weir, S. (2002), *International IDEA Handbook on Democracy Assessment* (The Hague, London, New York: Kluwer Law International).

Berger, M. (1994), 'The End of the "Third World"?', *Third World Quarterly*, 15/2: 257–75.

—— (ed.) (2004), 'After the Third World?', special issue of *Third World Quarterly*, 25/1.

Berman, B. (1998), 'Ethnicity, Patronage and the African State: The Politics of Uncivil Nationalism', *African Affairs*, 97/388: 35–341.

530

Bermeo, N. (2003), *Ordinary People in Extraordinary Times: The Citizenry and the Breakdown of Democracy* (Princeton, NJ: Princeton University Press).

Bertrand, J. (2002), 'Legacies of the Authoritarian Past: Religious Violence in Indonesia's Moluccan Islands', *Pacific Affairs*, 75: 57–85.

Béteille, A. (ed.) (1969), *Social Inequality* (Harmondsworth: Penguin).

Beynon, J., and Dunkerley, D. (eds.) (2000), *Globalization: The Reader* (London: Athlone Press).

Bhalla, S. S. (2002), *Imagine There's No Country: Poverty, Inequality and Growth in the Era of Globalization* (Washington DC: Institute for International Economics).

Bilgin, P., and Morton, A. D. (2002), 'Historicising representations of "failed states": beyond the cold-war annexation of the social sciences', *Third World Quarterly*, 23/1: 55–80.

Billig, M. (1995), *Banal Nationalism* (London: Sage).

Birmingham, D. (1995), *The Decolonization of Africa* (London: UCL Press).

BIS (2005), *Triennial Central Bank Survey: Foreign Exchange and Derivatives Market Activities in 2004* (Basle: Bank of International Settlements).

Boserup, E. (1989), *Women's Role in Economic Development*, revised edn. (London: Earthscan).

BP (2003), *BP Statistical Review of World Energy 2003*, available at www.bp.com.

Branford, S., and Rocha, J. (2002), *Cutting the Wire: The Story of the Landless Movement in Brazil* (London: Latin America Bureau).

Bratton, M., and Van de Walle, N. (1997), *Democratic Experiments in Africa* (Cambridge: Cambridge University Press).

——, Mattes, R., and Gyimah-Boadi, E. (2004), *Public Opinion, Democracy and Market Reform in Africa* (Cambridge: Cambridge University Press).

Bräutigam, D. (1996), 'State Capacity and Effective Governance', in B. Ndulu and N. van de Walle (eds.), *Agenda for Africa's Economic Renewal* (Oxford: Transaction Publishers), 81–108.

—— (2004), 'The People's Budget? Politics, Participation and Pro-Poor Policy', *Development Policy Review*, 22/6: 653–68.

Breuer, A. (2007), 'Institutions of Direct Democracy and Accountability in Latin America's Presidential Democracies', *Democratization*, 14/4, 554–79.

BRIDGE Development–Gender (2003), *Gender and Budgets* (Brighton: Institute of Deveopment Studies, University of Sussex).

Brinkerhoff, D. W. (2005), 'Rebuilding Governance in Failed States and Post-Conflict Societies: Core Concepts and Cross-Cutting Themes', *Public Administration and Development*, 25/1: 3–14.

Brown, J. (1985), *Modern India. The Origins of an Asian Democracy* (Oxford: Oxford University Press).

Brundtland, G. (ed.) (1987), *Our Common Future: The World Commission on Environment and Development* (Oxford: Oxford University Press) (The Brundtland Report).

Burnell, P. (ed.) (2006), *Globalising Democracy: Party Politics in Emerging Democracies* (Milton Park: Routledge).

—— and Calvert, P. (eds.) (1999), *The Resilience of Democracy. Persistent Practice, Durable Idea* (London: Frank Cass).

Buzan, B. (1991), *People, States and Fear: an Agenda for International Security Studies in the Post-Cold War Era* (Boulder, Colo: Lynne Rienner).

—— Wæver, O., and de Wilde, J. (1998), *Security: A New Framework for analysis* (Boulder, Colo: Lynne Reinner).

Calvert, P., and Calvert, S. (2001), *Politics and Society in the Third World*, 2nd edn. (Harlow: Pearson Education).

Cammack, P. (1997), *Capitalism and Democracy in the Third World: The Doctrine for Political Development* (Leicester: Leicester University Press).

—— Pool, D., and Tordoff, W. (1993), *Third World Politics. A Comparative Introduction* (Basingstoke: Macmillan).

Cardoso, F. H. (1973), 'Associated Dependent Development: Theoretical and Practical Implications', in A. Stepan (ed.), *Authoritarian Brazil* (New Haven, Conn.: Yale University Press), 142–76.

—— and Faletto, E. (1979), *Dependency and Development in Latin America* (Berkeley, Calif.: University of California Press).

Carment, D. (2003), 'Assessing State Failure: Implications for Theory and Policy', *Third World Quarterly*, 24/3: 407–27.

Carothers, T. (1999), *Aiding Democracy Abroad* (Washington DC: Brookings Institution).

Casanova, J. (1994), *Public Religions in the Modern World* (Chicago and London: University of Chicago Press).

Cavanaugh, J., and Mander, J. (eds.) (2004), *Alternatives to Economic Globalization: A Better World is Possible*, 2nd edn. (San Francisco: Berrett-Koehler Publishers).

Chakrabarty, D. (2003), 'Postcoloniality and the Artifice of History. Who Speaks for "Indian" Pasts?' in J. D. LeSueur (ed.), *The Decolonization Reader* (London: Routledge), 428–48.

Chandhoke, N. (2003), *The Conceits of Civil Society* (Delhi: Oxford University Press).

Chandra, B., Mukherjee, M., and Mukherjee, A. (1999), *India after Independence* (New Delhi: Viking Penguin India).

Chaney, E. M., and Castro, M. G. (eds.) (1989), *Muchachas No More: Household Workers in Latin America and the Caribbean* (Philadelphia, Pa.: Temple University Press).

Chang, H. (2002), *Kicking Away the Ladder* (London: Anthem Press).

Chang, Woo-young (2005), 'The Internet, Alternative Public Sphere and Political Dynamism: Korea's *non-gaek* (polemist) websites', *Pacific Review*, 18/3: 393–415.

Chatterjee, P. (1986), *Nationalist Thought and the Colonial World: A Derivative Discourse?* (London: Zed Books).

——(1993), *The Nation and Its Fragments. Colonial and Postcolonial Histories* (Princeton, NJ: Princeton University Press).

Chauvel, R. (2003), 'Papua and Indonesia: Where Contending Nationalisms Meet', in D. Kingsbury and H. Aveling (eds.), *Autonomy and Disintegration in Indonesia* (London: RoutledgeCurzon), 115–27.

Chenery, H., *et al.* (1974), *Redistribution with Growth* (New York: Oxford University Press).

Chhibber, P. (1999), *Democracy without Associations: Transformation of the Party System and Social Cleavages in India* (Ann Arbor, Mich.: University of Michigan Press).

Chibber, V. (2005), 'The Good Empire. Should We Pick Up Where the British Left Off?', *Boston Review*, 30/1 (http://bostonreview.net/BR30.1/chibber.html).

Chiriyankandath, J. (1992), '"Democracy" Under the Raj: Elections and Separate Representation in British India', *The Journal of Commonwealth and Comparative Politics*, 30/1: 39–63.

Chopra, J. (2004), 'Building State Failure in East Timor', in J. Milliken (ed.), *State Failure, Collapse and Reconstruction* (Oxford: Blackwell Publishing).

Chronic Poverty Research Centre (CPRC) (2005), *The Chronic Poverty Report 2004–5* (London: Chronic Poverty Research Centre).

Clapham, C. (2000), 'Failed States and Non-States in the Modern International Order', paper presented at 'Failed States III: Globalization and the Failed State', Florence, Italy, 7–10 April (www.comm.ucsb.edu/Research/mstohl/failed_states/2000/papers/clapham.html).

——(2002), 'The Challenge to the State in a Globalized World'. *Development and Change*, 33/5: 775–95.

Cohn, B. S. (1996), *Colonialism and Its Forms of Knowledge. The British in India* (Princeton, NJ: Princeton University Press).

Collier, D., and Levitsky, S. (1997), 'Democracy with Adjectives', *World Politics*, 49: 430–51.

Collier, P. (1999), 'Doing Well out of War', Working Paper, World Bank (Washington DC: World Bank).

Commission for Africa (2005), *Our Common Interest* (London: Penguin).

Connor, W. (1994), *Ethnonationalism: The Quest for Understanding* (Princeton, NJ: Princeton University Press).

Cooper, F. (2002), *Africa since 1940. The Past of the Present* (Cambridge: Cambridge University Press).

——(2003), 'Conflict and Connection. Rethinking Colonial African History', in LeSueur (2003), 23–44.

——(2005), *Colonialism in Question. Theory, Knowledge, History* (Berkeley, Calif.: University of California Press).

Cooper, R. (2004), *The Breaking of Nations: Order and Chaos in the Twenty-First Century* (London: Atlantic).

Cordesman, A. H. (2002), *Saudi Arabia Enters the Twentieth Century* (Washington: Center for Strategic and International Studies).

Cornia, G. A. and Court, J. (2001), *Inequality, Growth and Poverty in the Era of Liberalization and Globalization*. UNU Policy Brief No. 4 (Helsinki: UNU/WIDER).

Cornwall, A., and Goetz, A. M. (2005), 'Democratizing Democracy: Feminist Perspectives', *Democratization*, 12/5: 783–800.

Coulon, C. (1983), *Les Musulmans et le Pouvoir en Afrique Noire* (Paris: Karthala).

Craig, A. L., and Cornelius, W. A. (1995), 'Mexico', in A. Mainwaring and T. R. Scully (eds.), *Building Democratic Institutions* (Stanford, Calif.: University of California Press), 249–97.

Cramer, C., and Goodhand, J. (2004), 'Try Again, Fail Again, Fail Better? War, the State and the "Post-Conflict" Challenge in Afghanistan', in J. Milliken (ed.), *State Failure, Collapse and Reconstruction* (Oxford: Blackwell Publishing).

Crook, R. C. (2005), 'The Role of Traditional Institutions in Political Change and Underdevelopment', Center for Democratic Development/Overseas Development Institute Policy Brief No. 4 (Accra: Ghana Center for Democratic Development).

Crook, R. C., and Manor, J. (1998), *Democracy and Decentralisation in South Asia and West Africa* (Cambridge: Cambridge University Press).

Croucher, S. L. (2003), 'Perpetual Imagining: Nationhood in a Global Era', *International Studies Review*, 5: 1–24.

Dahl, R. (1971), *Polyarchy: Participation and Opposition* (New Haven, Conn. and London: Yale University Press).

Dalacoura, K. (2006), 'Islamist Terrorism and the Middle East Democratic Deficit: Political Exclusion, Repression and the Causes of Extremism', *Democratization*, 13/3: 508–25.

Dauvergne, P. (1997), *Shadows in the Forest: Japan and the Politics of Timber in South East Asia* (Cambridge, Mass.: MIT Press).

Davidson, B. (1992), *The Black Man's Burden. Africa and the Curse of the Nation-State* (New York: Times Books).

Davis, M. (2001), *Late Victorian Holocausts. El Nino Famines and the Making of the Third World* (London: Verso).

De Tocqueville, A. (2000), *Democracy in America* (Chicago and London: University of Chicago Press).

Dekmejian, R. (2003), 'The Liberal Impulse in Saudi Arabia', *Middle East Journal*, 57/3: 400–13.

Devas, N., Delay, S., and Hubbard, M. (2001), 'Revenue Authorities: Are They the Right Vehicle for Improved Tax Administration?', *Public Administration and Development*, 21/3: 211–22.

532

Diamond, L. (ed.) (1996), 'Is the Third Wave Over?', *Journal of Democracy*, 7/3: 20–37.

—— (2002), 'Thinking About Hybrid Regimes', *Journal of Democracy* 13/2: 21–35.

Dicken, P. (2003), *Global Shift: Reshaping the Global Economic Map in the 21st Century* (London: Sage).

Dickson, A. K. (1997), *Development and International Relations: A Critical Introduction* (Cambridge: Polity).

Dirks, N. (2001), *Castes of Mind: Colonialism and the Making of Modern India* (Princeton, NJ: Princeton University Press).

Dirks, N. (2004), 'Colonial and Postcolonial Histories: Comparative Reflections on the Legacies of Empire', Global Background Paper for United Nations Development Programme, Human Development Report, *Cultural Liberty in Today's Diverse World*.

Dodge, T. (2003), *Inventing Iraq* (London: Hurst).

Dollar, D., and Burnside, C. (1998), *Assessing Aid. What Works, What Doesn't and Why* (Washington DC: World Bank).

Doornbos, M. (2002), 'Somalia: Alternative Scenarios for Political Reconstruction', *African Affairs*, 101: 93–107.

—— (2006), *Global Forces and State Restructuring: Dynamics of State Formation and Collapse* (Houndsmill: Palgrave Macmillan).

Dorr, S. (1993), 'Democratization in the Middle East', in R. Slater, B. Schutz, and S. Dorr (eds.), *Global Transformation and the Third World* (Boulder, Colo.: Lynne Rienner), 131–57.

Drake, C. (1989), *National Integration in Indonesia: Patterns and Policies* (Honolulu: University of Hawaii Press).

Driscoll, R., with Evans, A. (2005), 'Second-Generation Poverty Reduction Strategies: New Opportunities and Emerging Issues', *Development Policy Review*, 23/1: 5–25.

Duffield, M. (2006), 'Racism, Migration and Development: The Foundations of Planetary Order', *Progress in Development Studies*, 6/1: 68–79.

Dunn, R. M., and Mutti, J. H. (2000), *International Economics*, 5th edn. (London: Routledge).

—— (2004), *International Economics*, 6th edn. (London: Routledge).

Easton, D. (1965), *A Systems Analysis of Political Life* (New York: Wiley).

Eckert, C. J. (1990), 'The South Korean Bourgeoisie: A Class in Search of Hegemony', *Journal of Korean Studies*, 7: 115–48.

Edison, H. (2003), 'Testing the Links. How Strong Are the Links between Institutional Quality and Economic Performance?', *Finance and Development*, 40/2: 35–7.

Ehrlich, P. (1972), *The Population Bomb* (London: Pan/Ballantine).

Elbe, S. (2002), 'HIV/AIDS and the Changing Landscape of War in Africa', *International Security*, 27/2: 157–77.

Elliot, L. (1993), 'Fundamentalists Prepare for Holy War in Nigeria', *Guardian*, 14 April.

Eriksen, T. H. (1993), *Ethnicity and Nationalism: Anthropological Perspectives* (London: Pluto Press).

Escobar, A. (1995), *Encountering Development: The Making and Unmaking of the Third World* (Princeton, NJ: Princeton University Press).

Evans, P. (1995), *Embedded Autonomy: States and Industrial Transformation* (Princeton, NJ: Princeton University Press).

Fanon, F. (1967), *The Wretched of the Earth* (Harmondsworth: Penguin).

Fawcett, L., and Sayigh, Y. (eds.) (1999), *The Third World Beyond the Cold War: Continuity and Change* (Oxford: Oxford University Press).

Fearon, J. D. (2003), 'Ethnic and Cultural Diversity by Country', *Journal of Economic Growth*, 8: 195–222.

Ferdinand, P. (2003), 'Party Funding and Political Corruption in East Asia: The Cases of Japan, South Korea and Taiwan', in International IDEA, *Funding of Political Parties and Election Campaigns* (Stockholm: International Institute for Democracy and Electoral Assistance), 55–69.

Ferguson, J. (1997), *The Anti-Politics Machine* (Minneapolis, Minn.: University of Minnesota Press).

Ferguson, N. (2004), *Colossus: The Rise and Fall of the American Empire* (London: Allen Lane).

Fields, G. S. (1980), *Poverty, Inequality and Development* (Cambridge: Cambridge University Press).

Flavin, C., and Gardner, G. (2006), 'China, India and the New World Order', in World Watch Institute, *State of the World 2006* (New York: W.W. Norton), 3–23.

Foster-Carter, A. (1978), 'The Modes of Production Controversy', *New Left Review*, 177: 47–77.

Frank, A. G. (1969), *Capitalism and Underdevelopment in Latin America: Historical Studies of Chile and Brazil* (New York: Monthly Review Press).

—— (1971), *The Sociology of Development and the Underdevelopment of Sociology* (London: Pluto Press).

Fraser, N. (1997), *Justice Interruptus, Critical Reflections on the 'Postsocialist' Condition* (London: Routledge).

Freedom House (2006), *Annual Freedom House Survey* (Boston, Mass.: Freedom House).

Freston, P. (2004), *Protestant Political Parties. A Global Survey* (Aldershot: Ashgate).

Friedman, T. L. (2006), 'The First Law of Petropolitics', *Foreign Policy*, 154: 28–36.

Fukuyama, F. (1992), *The End of History and the Last Man* (Harmondsworth: Penguin).

Gaouette, N. (1999), 'Indonesian Togetherness at Stake', *Christian Science Monitor*, 18 May.

Garcia-Johnson, R. (2000), *Exporting Environmentalism: US Chemical Corporations in Brazil and Mexico* (Cambridge, Mass.: MIT Press).

Garnett, H., Koenen-Grant, J., and Reilly, C. (1997), 'Managing Policy Formulation and Implementation in Zambia's Democratic Transition', *Public Administration and Development*, 17/1: 77–91.

Ghosh, A. (2002), *The Imam and the Indian* (New Delhi: Ravi Dayal & Permanent Black).

Gill, S. (2003), *Power and Resistance in the New World Order* (Basingstoke: Palgrave).

Gills, B., Rocamora, J., and Wilson, R. (1993), 'Low Intensity Democracy', in B. Gills, J. Rocamora, and R. Wilson (eds.), *Low Intensity Democracy. Political Power in the New World Order* (London and Boulder, Colo.: Pluto Press), 3–34.

Gilmartin, D. (2003), 'Democracy, Nationalism and the Public. A Speculation on Colonial Muslim Politics', in LeSueur (2003): 191–203.

Go, J. (2003), 'Global Perspectives on the US Colonial State in the Philippines', in J. Go and A. L. Foster (eds.), *The American Colonial State in the Philippines. Global Perspectives* (Durham, NC: Duke University Press), 1–42.

Goetz, A. M., and Jenkins, R. (2004), *Reinventing Accountability: Making Democracy Work for the Poor* (Basingstoke: Palgrave/Macmillan).

Goodin, R. E., and Klingemann, H.-D. (2000), 'Political Science: The Discipline', in Goodin and Klingemann (eds.), *A New Handbook of Political Science* (Oxford: Oxford University Press).

Gopin, M. (2000), *Between Eden and Armageddon: The Future of World Religions, Violence and Peacemaking* (New York and London: Oxford University Press).

——(2005), 'World Religions, Violence, and Myths of Peace in International Relations', in G. Ter Haar and J. Busutill (eds.), *Bridge or Barrier? Religion, Violence and Visions for Peace* (Leiden: Brill), 35–56.

Gould, J. (2005), *The New Conditionality: the Politics of Poverty Reduction Strategies* (London: Zed Press).

Gramsci, A. (1992), *Prison Notebooks* (New York: Columbia University Press).

Gray, J. (2003), *Al Qaeda and What it Means to be Modern* (London: Faber & Faber).

Green, E. D. (2005), 'Understanding Ethnicity and Nationhood in Pre-Colonial Africa: The Case of Buganda' (London: Development Studies Institute, London School of Economics), http://personal.lse.ac.uk/greened/Ethnicity%20and%20Nationhood%20in%20Pre-Colonial%20Africa.pdf.

Grimmett, R. F. (2006), *Conventional Arms Transfers to Developing Nations, 1998–2005* (Washington DC: Congressional Research Service, US Library of Congress).

Guha, R. (1989), 'Dominance without Hegemony and its Historiography', in R. Guha (ed.), *Subaltern Studies VI. Writings on South Asian History and Society* (New Delhi: Oxford University Press).

Gurr, T. R. (1993), *Minorities at Risk: A Global View of Ethno-political Conflicts* (Washington DC: United States Institute of Peace Press).

——(2000), *Peoples Versus States: Minorities at Risk in the New Century* (Washington DC: United States Institute of Peace Press).

Hakim, P. (2003), 'Latin America's Lost Illusions. Dispirited Politics', *Journal of Democracy*, 14/2: 108–22.

Hall, S. (1996), 'When Was "The Post-Colonial"? Thinking at the Limit', in I. Chambers and L. Carti (eds.), *The Post-Colonial Question. Common Skies, Divided Horizons* (London: Routledge), 242–60.

Hallencreutz, C., and Westerlund, D. (1996), 'Anti-Secularist Policies of Religion', in D. Westerlund (ed.), *Questioning the Secular State. The Worldwide Resurgence of Religion in Politics* (London: Hurst).

Halliday, F. (1989), *Cold War, Third World: An Essay on Soviet-US Relations* (London: Hutchinson).

——(1993), 'Orientalism and its Critics', *British Journal of Middle Eastern Studies*, 20/2: 145–63.

——(2002), *Two Hours that Shook the World: September 11, 2001, Causes and Consequences* (London: Saqi).

Halperin, M. H., Siegle, J. T., and Weinstein, M. M. (2004), *The Democracy Advantage: How Democracies Promote Prosperity and Peace* (London and New York: Routledge).

Harff, B. (2003), 'No Lessons Learned from the Holocaust? Assessing Risks of Genocide and Political Mass Murder since 1955', *American Political Science Review*, 97/1: 57–73.

Harrison, G. (2001), 'Post-Conditionality Politics and Administrative Reform: Reflections on the Cases of Uganda and Tanzania', *Development and Change*, 32/4: 657–79.

——(2004), 'Sub-Saharan Africa', in A. Payne (ed.), *The New Regional Politics* (Basingstoke: Palgrave), 218–47.

——(2005), 'The World Bank, Governance and Theories of Political Action in Africa', *British Journal of Politics and International Relations*, 7/2: 240–60.

Harvey, D. (2003), *The New Imperialism* (Oxford: Oxford University Press).

Haynes, J. (1993), *Religion in Third World Politics* (Buckingham: Open University Press).

——(1996), *Religion and Politics in Africa* (London: Zed Books).

——(2007), *Introduction to Religion and International Relations* (Harlow: Pearson Education).

Hegel, G. W. F. (1942), *Philosophy of Right*, trans. with notes by T. M. Knox (Oxford: Clarendon Press).

Held, D., McGrew, A., Goldblatt, D., and Perraton, J. (1999), *Global Transformations* (Cambridge: Polity Press).

Hellman, J. S., Jones, G., and Kaufmann, D. (2000), ' "Seize the State, Seize the Day", State Capture, Corruption and Influence in Transition', World Bank Policy Research Working Paper 2444 (Washington DC: World Bank Institute, World Bank).

534

Herbst, J. (2000), *States and Power in Africa* (Princeton, NJ: Princeton University Press).

Herring, R. J. (1979), 'Zulfikar Ali Bhutto and the "Eradication of Feudalism" in Pakistan', *Comparative Studies in Society and History*, 21/4: 519–57.

Higgott, R. A. (1983), *Political Development Theory* (London and Canberra: Croom Helm).

—— and Ougaard, M. (eds.) (2002), *Towards a Global Polity* (London: Routledge).

Hilderbrand, M. E., and Grindle, M. S. (1997), 'Building Sustainable Capacity in the Public Sector. What Can Be Done?', in M. S. Grindle (ed.), *Getting Good Government. Capacity Building in the Public Sectors of Developing Countries* (Cambridge, Mass.: Harvard Institute for International Development).

Hinnebusch, R. (2006), 'Authoritarian Persistence, Democratization Theory and the Middle East: An Overview and Critique', *Democratization*, 13/3: 373–95.

Hirst, P. and Thompson, G. (1999), *Globalization in Question: The International Economy and the Possibilities of Governance* (Cambridge: Polity Press).

Hoogvelt, A. (1997), *Globalization and the Postcolonial World* (Baltimore, MD: John Hopkins University Press).

Horowitz, D. (1985), *Ethnic Groups in Conflict* (Berkeley, Calif.: University of California Press).

Human Security Centre (2005), *War and Peace in the 21st Century* (New York/Oxford: Oxford University Press).

Huntington, S. P. (1968), *Political Order in Changing Societies* (New Haven, Conn.: Yale University Press).

—— (1971), 'The Change to Change', *Comparative Politics*, 3/3: 283–332.

—— (1991), *The Third Wave. Democratization in the Late Twentieth Century* (Norman, Okla., and London: University of Oklahoma Press).

—— (1993), 'The Clash of Civilizations?', *Foreign Affairs*, 72/3: 22–49.

—— (1996a), *The Clash of Civilizations and the Remaking of World Order* (New York: Simon and Schuster).

—— (1996b), 'Democracy for the Long Haul', *Journal of Democracy*, 7/2: 3–14.

Hutchinson, J., and Smith, A. D. (eds.) (1994), *Nationalism* (Oxford: Oxford University Press).

Hyden, G., Court, J., and Mease, K. (2004), *Making Sense of Governance. Empirical Evidence from Sixteen Developing Countries* (Boulder, Colo.: Lynne Rienner).

Ibrahim, Y. (1992), 'Islamic Plans for Algeria on Display'. *New York Times*, 7 January.

International Energy Agency (2003), *Key World Energy Statistics 2003*, available at www.iea.org.

Isaac, T. M. T., with Franke, R. W. (2000), *Local Democracy and Development: People's Campaign for Decentralized Planning in Kerala* (New Delhi: LeftWord Books).

Isaak, R. A. (2005), *The Globalization Gap: How the Rich Get Richer and the Poor Get Left Further Behind* (London: FT Prentice Hall).

Jackson, R. H. (1990), *Quasi-States: Sovereignty, International Relations and the Third World* (Cambridge: Cambridge University Press).

Jalal, A. (1995), *Democracy and Authoritarianism in South Asia. A Comparative and Historical Perspective* (Cambridge: Cambridge University Press).

James, C. L. R. (1977), *Nkrumah and the Ghana Revolution* (London: Allison and Busby).

Janelli, R. L. (1993), *Making Capitalism* (Stanford, Calif.: Stanford University Press).

Jawara, F., and Kwa, A. (2004), *Behind the Scenes at the WTO: The Real World of International Trade Negotiations* (London: Verso).

Jenkins, R. (2001), 'Mistaking Governance for Politics: Foreign Aid, Democracy and the Construction of Civil Society', in Sudipta Kaviraj and Sunil Khilnani (eds.), *Civil Society: History and Possibilities* (Cambridge: Cambridge University Press), 250–68.

—— and Goetz, A. M. (1999), 'Accounts and Accountability: Theoretical Implications of the Right-to-Information Movement in India', *Third World Quarterly*, 20/3: 603–22.

Jones, Leroy P., and Il, Sakong (1980), *Government, Business and Entrepreneurship in Economic Development: The Korean Case* (Cambridge, Mass.: Harvard University Press).

Karatnycky, A. (2003), 'The 30th Anniversary Freedom House Survey', *Journal of Democracy*, 14/1: 100–13.

Karl, T. L. (1990), 'Dilemmas of Democratization in Latin America', *Comparative Politics*, 23/1: 1–21.

Kashyap, S. C. (1989), *Our Parliament. An Introduction to the Parliament of India* (New Delhi: National Book Trust).

Kassalow, J. S. (2001), *Why Health is Important to US Foreign Policy* (New York: Council on Foreign Relations).

Katzenstein, M., Kothari, S., and Mehta, U. (2001), 'Social Movement Politics in India: Institutions, Interests and Identities', in A. Kohli (ed.), *The Success of India's Democracy* (Cambridge: Cambridge University Press), 242–69.

Kaufman, R., and Segura-Ubiergo, A. (2001), 'Globalization, Domestic Politics, and Social Spending in Latin America', *World Politics*, 53/4: 553–87.

Kaufmann, D., Kray, A., and Mastruzzi, M. (2005), *Governance Matters IV: Governance Indicators for 1996–2004* (World Bank Policy Research Working Paper Series No. 3630). Available at http://papers.ssrn.com.

Kay, S. (2006), *Global Security in the Twenty-First Century: the quest for power and the search for peace* (Oxford: Rowman and Littlefield).

Keeley, J., and Scoones, I. (2003), *Understanding Environmental Policy Processes: Cases from Africa* (London: Earthscan).

Khera, R. (2004), 'Monitoring Disclosures', *Seminar* 534 (February): 51–8.

Killick, T., with Gunatilaka, R. and Marr, A. (1998), *Aid and the Political Economy of Policy Change* (London and New York: Routledge).

Kim, Eunmee, and Kim, Jiyoung (2005), 'Developmental State vs. Globalization: South Korea's Developmental State in the Aftermath of the Asian Financial Crisis of 1997–98', *Korean Social Science Journal*, 32/2: 43–70.

Kim, Hyung Joon, and Kim Dohjong (2004), 'Analysis of the 17th National Assembly Election Outcomes in Korea', *Korea Observer*, 35/4: 617–38.

Kipling, R. (1987), 'Tods' Amendment', in *Plain Tales from the Hills* (London: Penguin (first pub. 1890)), 179–84.

Kjaer, M. (2004), *Governance* (Cambridge: Polity Press).

Klemp, L. (2006), 'Difficult co-operation with fragile states', *Development and Co-operation*, 33/5: 208–9.

Koelble, T., and LiPuma, E. (2006), 'The Effects of Circulatory Capitalism on Democratization: Observations from South Africa and Brazil', *Democratization*, 13/4: 605–31.

Kohli, A. (2004), *State-Directed Development. Political Power and Industrialization in the Global Periphery* (Cambridge: Cambridge University Press).

Kothari, R. (1984), 'The Non-Party Political Process', *Economic and Political Weekly* (Mumbai) 4 February: 216–24.

Kuznets, S. (1955), 'Economic Growth and Income Inequality', *American Economic Review*, 45: 1–28.

Kynge, J. (2006), *China Shakes the World: The Rise of a Hungry Nation* (London: Weidenfeld & Nicolson).

Lal, D. (2004), *In Praise of Empires. Globalization and Order* (Basingstoke: Palgrave).

Landman, T. (2003), *Issues and Methods in Comparative Politics*, 2nd edn. (London: Routledge).

Langseth, P. (1995), 'Civil Service Reform in Uganda: Lessons Learned', *Public Administration and Development*, 15/4: 365–90.

Lee, Yeon-ho (1997), *The State, Society and Big Business in South Korea* (London and New York: Routledge).

Leftwich, A. (1993), 'Governance, Democracy and Development in the Third World', *Third World Quarterly*, 14/3: 603–24.

—— (1995), 'Bringing Politics Back In: Towards a Model of the Developmental State', *Journal of Development Studies*, 31/3: 400–27.

—— (2000), *States of Development. On the Primacy of Politics in Development* (Cambridge: Polity Press).

Lele, J. (1990), 'Caste, Class and Dominance: Political Mobilization in Maharashtra', in F. Frankel and M. S. A. Rao (eds.), *Dominance and State Power in Modern India: Decline of a Social Order*, vol. ii (Delhi: Oxford University Press, 115–211).

Le Sueur, J. D. (ed.) (2003), *The Decolonization Reader* (London: Routledge).

Levitsky, S., and Way, L. A. (2002), 'The Rise of Competitive Authoritarianism', *Journal of Democracy*, 13/2: 51–65.

—— and —— (2005), 'International Linkage and Democratization', *Journal of Democracy*, 16/3: 20–34.

Linz, J. J. and A. Stepan (1996), *Problems of Democratic Transition and Consolidation: Southern Europe, South America, and Post-Communist Europe* (Baltimore: Johns Hopkins University Press).

Lipset, S. M. (1994), 'The Social Requisites of Democracy Revisited', *American Sociological Review*, 53/1: 1–22.

Lister, S., and Wilder, A. (2005), 'Strengthening Subnational Administration in Afghanistan: Technical Reform or State-Building?', *Public Administration and Development*, 25/1: 39–48.

Lowndes, V. (2002), 'Institutionalism', in D. Marsh and G. Stoker (eds.), *Theory and Methods in Political Science*, 2nd edn. (London: Palgrave).

Lucas, R. E., Jr. (1988), 'On the Mechanics of Economic Development', *Journal of Monetary Economics*, 22/1: 3–42.

Lugard, Lord (1965), *The Dual Mandate in British Tropical Africa* (London: Frank Cass (first pub. 1922)).

McGrew, A. (1992), 'A Global Society?', in S. Hall, D. Held, and A. McGrew (eds.), *Modernity and Its Future* (Cambridge: Polity Press), 62–102.

—— (2005), 'Globalization and Global Politics', in J. Baylis and S. Smith (eds.), *The Globalization of World Politics* (Oxford: Oxford University Press), 19–40.

McMichael, P. (2000), *Development and Social Change: A Global Perspective*, 2nd edn. (London: Sage).

McMichael, P. (2004), *Development and Social Change: A Global Perspective*, 3rd edn. (Thousand Oaks, Calif.: Pine Forge Press).

Mair, P. (1996), 'Comparative Politics: An Overview', in R. E. Goodin and H. Klingemann, *A New Handbook of Political Science* (Oxford: Oxford University Press), 309–35.

Malek, C. (2004), 'International Conflict, the Conflict Resolution Information Service'. Available at: http://v4.crinfo.org/CK_Essays/ck_international_conflict.jsp.

Mamdani, M. (1996), *Citizen and Subject. Contemporary Africa and the Legacy of Late Colonialism*, (London: James Currey).

Mann, M. (1986), *The Sources of Social Power*, Vol. i (Cambridge: Cambridge University Press).

Manor, J. (ed.) (1991), *Rethinking Third World Politics* (London: Longman).

March, J., and Olsen, J. (1984), 'The New Institutionalism: Organisational Factors in Political Life', *American Political Science Review*, 78/3: 734–49.

—— (1989), *Rediscovering Institutions. The Organizational Basis of Politics* (New York and London: Free Press).

Martin, B. (2001), *Nonviolence versus Capitalism* (London: War Resisters' International).

—— (2006), 'Paths to Social Change: Conventional Politics, Violence and Nonviolence', in R. Summy (ed.), *Nonviolent Alternatives for Social Change*. In the *Encyclopedia of Life Support Systems* (Oxford: Eolss Publishers).

Marty, M. E., and Appleby, R. S. (1993), 'Introduction', in M. and S. Appleby (eds.), *Fundamentalism and the State. Remaking Polities, Economies, and Militance* (Chicago: University of Chicago Press).

Marx, K. (1970), *The German Ideology* (London: Lawrence and Wishart).

Mayall, J., and Payne, A. (eds.) (1991), *The Fallacies of Hope. The Post-Colonial Record of the Commonwealth Third World* (Manchester: Manchester University Press).

Mazrui, A. (1986), *The Africans. A Triple Heritage* (London: BBC Publications).

Mazrui, A. (1995), 'The African State as a Political Refugee: Institutional Collapse and Human Displacement', *International Journal of Refugee Law*, 7: 21–36.

Mehta, L. (2006), 'Do Human Rights Make a Difference to Poor and Vulnerable People? Accountability for the Right to Water in South Africa', in P. Newell and J. Wheeler (eds.), *Rights, Resources and the Politics of Accountability* (London: Zed Books), 63–79.

Merrill, D. (1994), 'The United States and the Rise of the Third World', in G. Martel (ed.), *American Foreign Relations Reconsidered, 1890–1993* (London: Routledge), 166–86.

Mesbahi, M. (ed.) (1994), *Russia and the Third World in the Post-Soviet Era* (Gainesville, Fla.: University Press of Florida).

Meyer, W. H. (1998), *Human Rights and International Political Economy in Third World Nations* (Westport, Conn.: Praeger).

Migdal, J. S. (1988a), 'Strong States, Weak States: Power and Accommodation', in M. Weiner and S. P. Huntington (eds.), *Understanding Political Development* (Boston: Little, Brown), 391–429.

——(1988b), *Strong Societies and Weak States. State–Society Relations and State Capabilities in the Third World* (Princeton, NJ: Princeton University Press).

——(1994), 'The State in Society: An Approach to Struggles for Domination', in J. S. Migdal, A. Kohli, and V. Shue (eds.), *State Power and Social Forces. Domination and Transformation in the Third World* (Cambridge: Cambridge University Press), 7–34.

——(1996), 'Integration and Disintegration: An Approach to Society Formation', in L. van de Goor, K. Rupesinghe, and P. Scarione (eds.), *Between Development and Destruction. An Enquiry into the Causes of Conflict in Post-Colonial States* (London: Macmillan), 91–106.

Mill, J. S. (1888), *A System of Logic* (New York: Harper and Row).

Milliken, J., and Krause, K. (2002), 'State Failure, State Collapse, and State Reconstruction: Concepts, Lessons and Strategies', *Development and Change*, 33/5: 753–74.

Missingham, B. D. (2003), *The Assembly of the Poor in Thailand: From Local Struggles to National Protest Movement* (Chiang Mai: Silkworm Books).

Moore, B., (1966), *Social Origins of Dictatorship and Democracy: Lord and Peasant in the Making of the Modern World* (Boston, Mass.: Beacon Press).

Moore, M. (2004), 'Revenues, State Formation, and the Quality of Governance in Developing Countries', *International Political Science Review*, 25/3: 297–329.

Morris-Jones, W. H. (1987), *The Government and Politics of India* (Huntingdon: Eothen Press).

Mosley, L. (2005), 'Globalization and the State: Still Room to Move?', *New Political Economy*, 10/3: 355–62.

Mosley, P., Harrigan, J., and Toye, J. (1995), *Aid and Power. The World Bank and Policy-Based Lending*, 2nd edn. (London: Routledge).

Mote, O., and Rutherford, D. (2001), 'From Irian Jaya to Papua: The Limits of Primordialism in Indonesia's Troubled East', *Indonesia*, 72: 115–40.

Mozaffar, S. (1995), 'The Institutional Logic of Ethnic Politics: A Prolegomenon', in H. Glickman (ed.), *Ethnic Conflict and Democratization in Africa* (Atlanta, Ga.: African Studies Association Press), 34–69.

——Scarritt, J. R., and Galaich, G. (2003), 'Electoral Institutions, Ethnopolitical Cleavages, and Party Systems in Africa's Emerging Democracies', *American Political Science Review*, 97/3: 379–90.

Myrdal, G. (1971), *The Challenge of World Poverty* (Harmondsworth: Penguin).

National Intelligence Council (USA) (2000), 'The Global Infectious Disease Threat and its Implications for the United States', NIE 99–17D, www.fas.org/irp/threat/nie99-17d.htm.

Nayyar, D. (ed.) (2002), *Governing Globalization: Issues and Institutions* (Oxford: Oxford University Press for UNU-WIDER).

Nehru, J. (1942), *An Autobiography* (London: The Bodley Head).

——(1961), *The Discovery of India* (Bombay: Asia Publishing House).

Nelson, J. (1979), *Access to Power: Politics and the Urban Poor in Developing Nations* (Princeton, NJ: Princeton University Press).

Neuman S. G. (ed.) (1998), *International Relations Theory and the Third World* (Basingstoke: Macmillan).

New Economics Foundation (2003), *Collision Course: Free Trade's Free Ride on the Global Climate* (London: New Economics Foundation).

Newell, P. (2001), 'Environmental NGOs, TNCs and the Question of Governance', in D. Stevis and V. Assetto (eds.), *The International Political Economy of the Environment: Critical Perspectives* (Boulder, Colo.: Lynne Rienner), 85–107.

——(2007), 'Trade and Environmental Justice in Latin America', *New Political Economy*, 12/2, 237–59.

——and Wheeler, J. (2006), *Rights, Resources and the Politics of Accountability* (London: Zed Books).

Ngũgĩ wa Thiong'o (1986), *Decolonising the Mind. The Politics of Language in African Literature* (London: James Currey).

Nkrumah, K. (1965), *Neo-Colonialism. The Last Stage of Imperialism* (London: Panaf Books).

Nolutshungu, S. C. (1991), 'Fragments of a Democracy: Reflections on Class and Politics in Nigeria', in J. Mayall and A. Payne (eds.), *The Fallacies of Hope* (Manchester: Manchester University Press), 72–105.

North, D. C. (1990), *Institutions, Institutional Change and Economic Performance* (Cambridge: Cambridge University Press).

Norval, Aletta (1996), *Deconstructing Apartheid Discourse* (London: Verso).

Nozick, R. (1974), *Anarchy, State and Utopia* (Oxford: Blackwell).

Nzomo, M., and Staudt, K. (1994), 'Man-Made Political Machinery in Kenya: Political Space for Women?', in B. J. Nelson and N. Chowdhury (eds.), *Women and Politics Worldwide* (New Haven, Conn.: Yale University Press), 415–35.

O'Brien, R., Goetz, A. M., Scholte, J. A., and Williams, M. (2000), *Contesting Global Governance: Multilateral Economic Institutions and Global Social Movements* (New York and Cambridge: Cambridge University Press).

—— and Williams, M. (2004), *Global Political Economy: Evolution and Dynamics* (Basingstoke: Palgrave Macmillan).

O'Donnell, G. (1994), 'Delegative Democracy', *Journal of Democracy*, 5/1: 55–69.

Olowu, B. (1999), Redesigning African Civil Service Reforms', *Journal of Modern African Studies*, 37/1: 1–23.

Olson, M. (2001), *Power and Prosperity: Outgrowing Communist and Capitalist Dictatorships* (New York: Basic Books).

Organisation for Economic Co-operation and Development (2001), *Strategies for Sustainable Development: Practical Guidance for Development Cooperation* (Paris: OECD).

O'Rourke, D. (2004), *Community-Based Regulation: Balancing Environment and Development in Vietnam* (Cambridge, Mass.: MIT Press).

Ottaway, M. (2003), *Democracy Challenged. The Rise of Semi-Authoritarianism* (Washington DC: Carnegie Endowment for International Peace).

—— and Carothers, T. (2000), *Funding Virtue: Civil Society Aid and Democracy Promotion* (Washington DC: Carnegie Endowment for International Peace).

—— and Chung, T. (1999), 'Debating Democracy Assistance: Toward a New Paradigm', *Journal of Democracy*, 10/4: 99–113.

Oxfam (2001), *Eight Broken Promises: Why the WTO isn't Working for the World's Poor* (Oxford: Oxfam Briefing Paper 9).

Parente, S. L., and Prescott, E. C. (2000), *Barriers to Riches* (Cambridge, Mass.: MIT Press).

Parry, J. H. (1966), *The Spanish Seaborne Empire* (London: Hutchinson).

Parry, R. L., (2005), *In the Time of Madness: Indonesia on the Edge of Chaos* (London: Jonathan Cape).

Parsons, T. (1960), *Structure and Process in Modern Societies* (Glencoe: Free Press).

Pastor, R. (1999), 'The Role of Electoral Administration in Democratic Transitions: Implications for Policy and Research', *Democratization*, 6/4: 1–27.

Payne, A. (2004), 'Rethinking Development Inside International Political Economy', in A. Payne (ed.), *The New Regional Politics of Development* (Basingstoke: Palgrave), 1–28.

—— (2005), 'The Study of Governance in a Global Political Economy', in N. Phillips, (ed.), *Globalizing International Political Economy* (Houndmills: Palgrave Macmillan), 55–81.

Perham, M. (1963), *The Colonial Reckoning. The Reith Lectures: 1961* (London: Fontana).

Phillips, A. (1999), *Which Equalities Matter?* (Cambridge: Polity Press).

Phillips, N. (ed.) (2005), *Globalizing International Political Economy* (Houndmills: Palgrave Macmillan).

Piano, A., and Puddington, A. (2006), 'The 2005 Freedom House Survey', *Journal of Democracy*, 17/1: 119–24.

Pieterse, J. N. (1992), 'Christianity, Politics and Gramscism of the Right: Introduction', in J. Pieterse (ed.), *Christianity and Hegemony. Religion and Politics on the Frontiers of Social Change* (Oxford: Berg), 1–31.

—— (2000), 'After Post-Development', *Third World Quarterly*, 21/2: 75–91.

Pinto-Duschinsky, M. (2002), 'Financing Politics: A Global View', *Journal of Democracy*, 13/4: 69–86.

Pirie, I. (2005), 'Better by Design: Korea's Neoliberal Economy', *Pacific Review*, 18/3: 355–74.

Pogge, T. (2002), *World Poverty and Human Rights* (Cambridge: Polity Press).

Porter, B. (1996), *The Lion's Share: A Short History of British Imperialism 1850–1995*, 3rd edn. (London: Longman).

Powell, G. B. (2000), *Elections as Instruments of Democracy: Majoritarian and Proportional Visions* (New Haven, Conn.: Yale University Press).

Prakash, G. (1999), *Another Reason. Science and the Imagination of Modern India* (Princeton, NJ: Princeton University Press).

Przeworski, A., Alvarez, M., Cheibub, J., and Limongi, F. (1996), 'What Makes Democracies Endure?', *Journal of Democracy*, 7/1: 39–55.

——, Alvarez, M. E., Cheibub, J. A., and Limongi, F. (2000), *Democracy and Development: Political Institutions and Well-Being in the World, 1950–1990* (Cambridge: Cambridge University Press).

Purdey, J. (2006), *Anti-Chinese Violence in Indonesia, 1996–1999* (Singapore: Singapore University Press).

Putnam, R. (1993), *Making Democracy Work: Civic Traditions in Modern Italy* (Princeton, NJ: Princeton University Press).

Pye, L. W. (1966), *Aspects of Political Development* (Boston: Little, Brown).

Rai, S. M. (ed.) (2003), *Mainstreaming Gender, Democratizing the State? Institutional Mechanisms for the Advancement of Women* (Manchester and New York: Manchester University Press).

Rakner, L. (1995), 'Is Rational Choice Institutionalism Useful for Development Studies?', *Forum for Development Studies*, No 1: 77–94.

Ramagundam, R. (2001), *Defeated Innocence: Adivasi Assertion, Land Rights and The Ekta Parishad Movement* (New Delhi: Grassroots India Publishers).

Ram-Prasad, C. (1993), 'Hindutva Ideology Extracting the Fundamentals', *Contemporary South Asia*, 2/3: 285–309.

Randall, V. (2004), 'Using and Abusing the Concept of the Third World: Geopolitics and the Comparative Study of Development and Underdevelopment', *Third World Quarterly*, 25/1: 41–53.

—— and Svåsand, L. (2002), 'Political Parties and Democratic Consolidation in Africa', *Democratization*, 9/3: 30–52.

Ravallion, M. (2001), 'Growth, Inequality and Poverty: Looking Beyond Averages', *World Development*, 29/11: 1803–15.

Rawls, J. (1971), *A Theory of Justice* (Oxford: Oxford University Press).

Reno, W. (2000), 'Shadow States and the Political Economy of Civil Wars', in M. Berdal and D. Malone (eds.), *Greed and Grievance. Economic Agendas in Civil Wars* (Boulder, Colo.: Lynne Rienner), 43–68.

Reynolds, A. (2006), 'The Curious Case of Afghanistan', *Journal of Democracy*, 17/2: 104–17.

Richards, P. (1996), *Fighting for the Rainforest: War, Youth and Resources in Sierra Leone* (Oxford: James Currey).

Robinson, G. (1998), 'Rawan Is as Rawan Does: The Origins of Disorder in New Order Aceh', *Indonesia*, 66: 127–56.

Robinson, W. I. (1996), *Promoting Polyarchy: Globalization, US Intervention, and Hegemony* (New York and Cambridge: Cambridge University Press).

Rondinelli, D. A., and Montgomery, J. D. (2005), 'Regime Change and Nation Building: Can Donors Restore Governance in Post-Conflict States?', *Public Administration and Development*, 25/1: 15–24.

Roniger, L., and Sznajder, M. (1999), *The Legacy of Human-Rights Violations in the Southern Cone: Argentina, Chile, and Uruguay* (Oxford: Oxford University Press).

Ross, M. (1999), 'The Political Economy of the Resource Curse', *World Politics*, 51/2: 297–322.

Rotberg, R. I. (ed.) (2004), *When States Fail* (Princeton, NJ: Princeton University Press).

Rousseau, J.J. (1755), *Discourse on Equality* (London: Everyman/Dent).

Rudolph, L. I. (2003), Review of Pradeep Chhibber, Democracy without Associations, *Comparative Political Studies*, 36/9: 1115–9.

—— and Rudolph, S. H. (1967), *The Modernity of Tradition: Political Development in India* (Chicago: University of Chicago Press).

Rueschemeyer, D. (2004), 'Addressing Inequality', *Journal of Democracy*, 15/4: 76–90.

——, Stephens, E. H., and Stephens, J. D. (1992), *Capitalist Democracy and Development* (Cambridge: Polity Press).

Rustow, D. (1970), 'Transitions to Democracy: Toward a Dynamic Model', *Comparative Politics*, 2/3: 337–63.

Said, E. W. (1993), *Culture and Imperialism* (London: Chatto & Windus).

—— (1995), *Orientalism* (Harmondsworth: Penguin (first pub. 1978)).

Samatar, A. I. (1999), *An African Miracle. State and Class Leadership and Colonial Legacy in Botswana's Development* (Portsmouth, NH: Heinemann).

Sartori, G. (1976), *Parties and Party Systems: A Framework for Analysis* (Cambridge: Cambridge University Press).

Scarritt, J. R., and Mozaffar, S. (1999), 'The Specification of Ethnic Cleavages and Ethnopolitical Groups for the Analysis of Democratic Competition in Contemporary Africa', *Nationalism and Ethnic Politics*, 5/1: 82–117.

—— (2003), 'Why Do Multi-Ethnic Parties Predominate in Africa and Ethnic Parties Do Not?'. Unpublished paper.

Schedler, A. (1998), 'What Is Democratic Consolidation?', *Journal of Democracy*, 9/2: 91–107.

—— (2002a), 'The Nested Game of Democratization by Elections', *International Political Science Review*, 23/1: 103–22.

—— (2002b), 'Elections Without Democracy: The Menu of Manipulation', *Journal of Democracy*, 13/2: 36–50.

—— Diamond, L., and Plattner, M. (eds.) (1999), *The Self-Restraining State* (Boulder, Colo.: Lynne Reinner).

Scheper-Hughes, N. (1992), *Death Without Weeping. The Violence of Everyday Life in Brazil* (Berkeley, Calif.: University of California Press).

Schneider, B. R. (1999), 'The *Desarrollista* State in Brazil and Mexico', in M. Woo-Cummings (ed.), *The Developmental State* (Ithaca, NY, and London: Cornell University Press) 276–305.

Schock, K. (1999), 'People Power and Political Opportunities: Social Movement Mobilization and Outcomes in the Philippines and Burma', *Social Problems*, 46/3: 355–75.

—— (2005), *Unarmed Insurrections: People Power Movements in Nondemocracies* (Minneapolis and London: Uiniversity of Minnesota Press).

—— (2006a), 'Defending and Reclaiming the Commons through Nonviolent Struggle', in R. Summy (ed.), *Nonviolent Alternatives for Social Change*. In the *Encyclopedia of Life Support Systems* (Oxford: Eolss Publishers).

—— (2006b), 'Nonviolent Social Movements', in G. Ritzer (ed.), *The Blackwell Encyclopedia of Sociology*, (Boston and London: Blackwell Publishing), 4458–4463.

Scholte, J. A. (2001), 'The Globalization of World Politics', in J. Baylis and S. Smith (eds.), *The Globalization of World Politics*, 2nd edn. (Oxford and New York: Oxford University Press) 13–32.

—— (2005), *Globalization: A Critical Introduction* (Basingstoke: Palgrave).

Scott, James C. (1998), *Seeing Like a State* (New Haven, Conn.: Yale University Press).

Sen, A. (1992), *Inequality Re-examined* (Oxford: Oxford University Press).

—— (1999a), *Development as Freedom* (Oxford: Oxford University Press).

—— (1999b), 'Human Rights and Economic Achievements', in J. R. Bauer and D. A. Bell (eds.), *The East Asian Challenge for Human Rights* (Cambridge: Cambridge University Press), 88–99.

—— (2006), *Identity and Violence. The Illusion of Destiny* (London: Allen Lane).

Sethi, H. (1999), *Review of Pradeep Chhibber, Democracy Without Associations*, Seminar 480 (August): 90–4.

Sharkey, H. (2003), *Living with Colonialism. Nationalism and Culture in the Anglo-Egyptian Sudan* (Berkeley, Calif.: University of California Press).

Shin, Doh C., and Lee, Jaechul (2006), *The Korea Democracy Barometer Surveys 1997–2004: Unravelling the Cultural and Institutional Dynamics of Democratization* (Aberdeen: Centre for the Study of Public Policy, University of Aberdeen).

Shin, Myungsoon (2006), 'Confidence in Public Institutions and Democracy in South Korea', *Korea Observer*, 37/2: 277–304.

Shiva, V. (1997), *Biopiracy: The Plunder of Nature and Society* (Cambridge, Mass.: South End Press).

—— (2005), *Earth Democracy: Justice, Sustainability, and Peace* (Cambridge, Mass.: South End Press).

Sikand, Y. (2003), 'Response to Shiva', in M. J. Gibney (ed.), *Globalizing Rights* (Oxford: Oxford University Press) 109–14.

Silverman, S. F. (1977), 'Patronage and Community–Nation Relationships in Central Italy', in S. Schmidt, J. C. Scott, C. Landé, and L. Guasti (eds.), *Friends, Followers and Factions* (Berkeley, Calif.: University of California Press), 293–304.

Singer, P. (2002), 'AIDS and International Security', *Survival*, 44/1: 45–158.

SIPRI (2006), *Yearbook 2006: Armaments, Disarmament and International Security* (Stockholm: Oxford University Press).

Sklair, L. (1991), *Sociology of the Global System* (London: Prentice-Hall).

Slater, D. (2004), *Geopolitics and the Postcolonial: Rethinking North-South Relations* (Oxford: Blackwell).

—— (2006), *Geopolitics and the Postcolonial: Rethinking North-South Relations*, 2nd edn. (Oxford: Blackwell).

Small Arms Survey (2005), *Weapons at War* (New York: Oxford University Press).

Smith, A. D. (1991), *National Identity* (Harmondsworth: Penguin).

—— (1995), *Nations and Nationalism in a Global Era* (Cambridge: Polity Press).

—— (1998), *Nationalism and Modernism: A Critical Survey of Recent Theories of Nations and Nationalism* (London: Routledge).

Smith, D. (1990), 'Limits of Religious Resurgence', in E. Sahliyeh (ed.), *Religious Resurgence and Politics in the Contemporary World* (Albany, NY: State University of New York Press).

Smith, J., Bolyard, M., and Ippolito, A. (1999), 'Human Rights and the Global Economy: A Response to Meyer', *Human Rights Quarterly*, 21/1: 207–19.

Smith, T. (1979), 'The Underdevelopment of Development Literature: The Case of Dependency Theory', *World Politics*, 31/2: 247–88.

Snyder, J. (2000), *From Voting to Violence: Democratization and Nationalist Conflict* (New York: W.W. Norton).

Soekanoputri, M. (2001), *Address by H. E. Megawati Soekarnoputri, President Republic of Indonesia at Usindo Gala Dinner* (Washington DC, 19 September (transcript)).

Sridharan, E. (2004), 'The Growth and Sectoral Composition of India's Middle Class: Its Impact on the Politics of Economic Liberalisation', *India Review*, 3/4: 405–28.

Staudt, K. (1997), *Women, International Development and Politics: The Bureaucratic Mire*, 2nd edn. (Philadelphia: Temple University Press).

—— (1998), *Policy, Politics and Gender: Women Gaining Ground* (West Hartford, Conn.: Kumarian Press).

—— and Coronado, I. (2002), *Fronteras No Más: Toward Social Justice at the US–Mexico Border*, (New York: Palgrave USA).

Stiglitz, J. (2002), *Globalization and its Discontents* (London: Allen Lane).

—— (2003), 'Democratizing the IMF and the World Bank: Governance and Accountability', *Governance*, 16/1: 111–39.

Strange, S. (1998), *Mad Money* (Manchester: Manchester University Press).

Sutton, P. (1991), 'Constancy, Change and Accommodation: The Distinct Tradition of the Commonwealth Caribbean', in J. Mayall and A. Payne (1991),106–17.

Swatuk, L. A., and Shaw, T. M. (1994), *The South at the End of the Twentieth Century* (New York: St Martin's Press).

Tarrow, S. (1998), *Power in Movement. Social Movements and Contentious Politics*, 2nd edn. (Cambridge: Cambridge University Press).

Tawney, R. H. (1952), *Inequality* (London: Allen and Unwin).

Ter Haar, G., and Busutill J. (eds.) (2005), *Bridge or Barrier? Religion, Violence and Visions for Peace* (Leiden: Brill).

Thomas, C. (2000), *Global Governance, Development and Human Security: The Challenge of Poverty and Inequality* (London: Pluto).

—— and Wilkin, P. (2004), 'Still Waiting After All These Years: The Third World on the Periphery of International Relations', *British Journal of Politics and International Relations*, 6/2: 241–58.

Tilly, C. (1999), *Durable Inequality* (London: University of California Press).

Tomlinson, B. R. (1993), *The New Cambridge History of India, III.3. The Economy of Modern India, 1860–1970* (Cambridge: Cambridge University Press).

Tordoff, W. (1997), *Government and Politics in Africa* (London: Macmillan).

Toye, J. (1987), *Dilemmas of Development* (Oxford: Blackwell).

Tull, D. M. (2006), 'Die Demokratische Republik Kongo vor den Wahlen: Chancen und Risiken für den Friedensprozess', *SWP-Aktuell 12* (Berlin: Stiftung Wissenschaft und Politik).

Turner, M., and Hulme, D. (1997), *Governance, Administration and Development. Making the State Work* (London: Macmillan).

Ulfelder, J. (2005), 'Contentious Collective Action and the Breakdown of Authoritarian Regimes', *International Political Science Review*, 26/3: 311–34.

UNAIDS (2006), *Report on the Global AIDS Epidemic* (Geneva: UNAIDS).

UNCTAD (2001), *World Investment Report 2001* (New York and Geneva: United Nations).

—— (2003), *Economic Development in Africa. Trade Performance and Commodity Dependence* (New York and Geneva: United Nations).

—— (2005a), *Handbook of Statistics 2005* (Geneva: United Nations).

—— (2005b), *World Investment Report 2004* (Geneva: United Nations).

UNESCO (1999), *UNESCO Statistical Yearbook* (Paris: UNESCO).

United Nations Development Programme (1995), *Human Development Report* (New York: Oxford University Press).

—— (2002), *UNDP Human Development Report 2002. Deepening Democracy in a Fragmented World* (New York and Oxford: Oxford University Press).

—— (2003), *Human Development Report 2003* (New York and Oxford: Oxford University Press).

—— (2005), *Human Development Report 2005, International Cooperation at a Crossroads: Aid, Trade and Security in an Unequal World* (New York: United Nations Development Programme).

—— (2006), *UNDP Human Development Report 2006* (New York and Oxford: Oxford University Press).

UNODC (2006), *Trafficking in Human Beings: Global Patterns* (Vienna: UNODC), August.

Valdez, S. (2003), *An Introduction to Global Financial Markets*, 4th edn. (Basingstoke: Palgrave).

Van Cott, D. L. (2005), 'Building Inclusive Democracies: Indigenous Peoples and Ethnic Minorities in Latin America, *Democratization*, 12/5: 820–37.

Varshney, A. (2004), 'States or Cities? Studying Hindu-Muslim Violence', in R. Jenkins (ed.), *Regional Reflections: Comparing Politics Across India's States* (Delhi: Oxford University Press), 177–218.

Viswanathan, G. (1990), *Masks of Conquest. Literary Study and British Rule in India* (London: Faber & Faber).

Vogel, D. (1997), *Trading Up: Consumer and Environmental Regulation in the Global Economy*, 2nd edn. (Cambridge, Mass.: Harvard University Press).

Waldron, A. (2005), 'The Rise of China: Military and Political Implications', *Review of International Studies*, 31/4: 715–33.

Wallerstein, I. (1979), 'The Rise and Future Demise of the World Capitalist System: Concepts for Comparative Analysis', in I. Wallerstein, *The Capitalist World-Economy* (Cambridge: Cambridge University Press), 1–36.

—— (2003), *The Decline of American Power* (New York: The New Press).

Walt, S. M. (1991), 'The Renaissance of Security Studies', *International Studies Quarterly*, 35/2: 211–39.

Weber, M. (1964), *The Theory of Social and Economic Organization*, ed. by Talcott Parsons (New York: Free Press).

—— (1970), *From Max Weber: Essays in Sociology*, ed. H. H. Gerth and C. Wright Mills (London: Routledge).

Weiss, J. (2002), *Industrialisation and Globalisation: Theory and Evidence from Developing Countries* (London: Routledge).

Weiss, L. (2005), 'The State-Augmenting Effects of Globalization', *New Political Economy*, 10/3: 345–53.

—— and Hobson, J. M. (1995), *States and Economic Development* (Cambridge: Polity Press).

Weldon, S. L. (2002), *Protest, Policy, and the Problem of Violence Against Women: A Cross-National Comparison* (Pittsburgh: University of Pittsburgh Press).

Westad, O. A. (2005), *The Global Cold War: Third World Interventions and the Making of Our Times* (Cambridge: Cambridge University Press).

White, G. (1984), 'Developmental States and Socialist Industrialization in the Third World', *Journal of Development Studies*, 21/1: 97–120.

—— (1998), 'Constructing a Democratic, Developmental State', in M. Robinson and G. White (eds.), *The Democratic Developmental State. Politics and Institutional Design* (Oxford: Oxford University Press), 17–51.

Wickham, C. R. (2002), *Mobilizing Islam: Religion, Activism, and Political Change in Egypt* (New York: Columbia University Press).

Wickramasinghe, N. (2006), *Sri Lanka in the Modern Age* (London: Hurst).

Wolf-Phillips, L. (1979), 'Why Third World?', *Third World Quarterly*, 1/1: 105–13.

Woo-Cummings, M. (ed.) (1999), *The Developmental State* (Ithaca, NY, and London: Cornell University Press).

Woodhead, L., and Heelas, P. (eds.) (2000), *Religions in Modern Times* (Oxford: Blackwell).

Woods, N. (2006), *The Globalizers: The IMF, the World Bank and their Borrowers* (Ithaca, NY: Cornell University Press).

World Bank (1989), *Sub-Saharan Africa: From Crisis to Sustainable Growth* (Washington DC: World Bank).

—— (1990), *World Development Report 1990* (Washington DC: World Bank).

—— (1997), *World Development Report 1997. The State in a Changing World* (New York: Oxford University Press).

—— (1999), *World Development Report 1999/2000: Entering the 21st Century* (Oxford: Oxford University Press), and available at www.econ.worldbank.org.

—— (2000), *Greening Industry: New Roles for Communities, Markets and Governments* (Washington DC: World Bank).

—— (2001), *World Development Report 2001* (Washington DC: World Bank).

—— (2002), *World Development Indicators 2002* (Washington DC: World Bank).

—— (2003a). *Global Development Finance 2003*, available at www.worldbank.org/prospects/gdf2003.

—— (2003b), *Guapa: Guatemala Poverty Assessment* (Washington DC: World Bank).

—— (2003c), *World Development Indicators 2003* (Washington: World Bank).

—— (2003d), *Breaking the Conflict Trap: Civil War and Development Policy* (Washington/Oxford: World Bank and Oxford University Press).

—— (2006a), *World Development Indicators 2006* (Washington: World Bank).

—— (2006b), *World Bank Development Report. Equity and Development* (New York: World Bank and Oxford University Press).

—— (2007), *World Bank Development Report* (Washington DC: World Bank).

World Health Organization (2005), *Ten Things You Need to Know about Pandemic Influenza*, 14 October.

—— (2006), *Confirmed Human Cases of Avian Influenza A (H5N1)*. Epidemic and Pandemic Alert and Response, www.who.int/csr/disease/avian_influenza/country/en/.

World Trade Organization (2005), *World Trade Statistics 2005* (Geneva: World Trade Organization).

Wright, A., and Wolford, W. (2003), *To Inherit the Earth: The Landless Movement and the Struggle for a New Brazil* (Oakland, Calif.: Food First Books).

Yadav, Y. (1996), 'Reconfiguration in Indian Politics. State Assembly Elections, 1993–95', *Economic and Political Weekly*, 13–20 January: 95–104.

Young, C. (1976), *The Politics of Cultural Pluralism* (Madison, Wis.: University of Wisconsin Press).

—— (1994), *The African Colonial State in Comparative Perspective* (New Haven, Conn.: Yale University Press).

—— (1998), 'Country Report. The African Colonial State Revisited', *Governance: An International Journal of Policy and Administration*, 11/1: 101–20.

—— (2001), 'Nationalism and Ethnic Conflict in Africa', in M. Guibernau and J. Hutchinson (eds.), *Understanding Nationalism* (Cambridge: Polity Press), 164–81.

—— (2004), 'The End of the Post-Colonial State in Africa? Reflections on Changing African Political Dynamics', *African Affairs*, 103: 23–49.

Zakaria, F. (1997), 'The Rise of Illiberal Democracy', *Foreign Affairs*, 76/6: 22–43.

Zartman, I. William (ed.) (1995), *Collapsed States: The Disintegration and Restoration of Legitimate Authority* (Boulder, Colo.: Lynne Rienner).

Index

in Africa 117, 124 (Asia) 116–17 (Caribbean) 116 (Latin America) 116
civic 112, 115, 116, 125, 519
Mexico's revolutionary nationalism 477–8
multi-ethnic nationalism 116, 125
national identities 115–7, 126–7, 140, 524
and religion 133
see also ethnopolitics
nation-building 524
in Indonesia 402, 404, 407, 409, 410, 411
in South Africa 418–24
see also nationalism
natural capital 321, 524
Nawaz Sharif, Prime Minister 458
Ne Win, General 191, 192, 193
neo-colonialism, *see* colonialism
neo-liberalism, *see* economic liberalization
neo- Marxist approaches 21–3, 26
see also dependency theory
neo-patrimonialism, *see* patrimonial authority
New International Economic Order (NIEO) 78, 99, 338, 524
newly industrialized countries (NICs) 56–7, 524
new institutionalism, *see* institutionalism
New Partnership for Africa's Development (NEPAD) 281, 282, 470
on democracy 282–3
on governance 303, 304
see also African Union, African Peer Review Mechanism
Nicaragua 74, 102, 133
Nigeria 4, 79, 190, 361
basic indicators 293, 511, 513
civil society 174, 469
colonial legacy 45
conflict 138, 465, 470
corruption 467
elected governments 464, 465, 468
environmental issues 346
and globalization 513–4
key dates 464
map 462
military rule 45, 463, 464, 465, 466, 467, 468
oil's importance 327, 344, 465, 466
regional role 465, 466, 469–70
religion in 130, 137–9
Nkrumah, President Kwame 47, 49
Nolutshungu, Sam 45

Non-Aligned Movement 4, 74, 85, 379, 516, 524
non-governmental organizations (NGOs) 109, 170, 172, 176, 177, 178, 179, 180, 181, 203, 358, 524
community-based organizations 169
see also civil society; global justice movement
non-violent action, *see* conflict; reform movements; people power movements; social movements
North American Free Trade Agreement (NAFTA) 481, 516
North Atlantic Treaty Organization (NATO) 379, 526
North, Douglass C. 215
North Korea, *see* Korea, Democratic People's Republic
Nyerere, President Julius 100

O

Obasango, President Olusegun 464, 465, 466, 469
Obrador, Andrés Manuel López 482
O'Donnell, Guillermo 27, 280, 520
official development assistance, *see* aid
oil 61
importance to Nigeria 327, 344, 465, 466–7
importance to Saudi Arabia 444–6, 450
see also Organization of the Petroleum Exporting Countries; Saudi Arabia, oil's impact
Olsen, J. 6
Organization of American States (OAS) 281, 282, 286, 302, 516
Inter-American Democratic Charter 281, 282
Organization of Arab Petroleum Exporting Countries 517
Organization of Eastern Caribbean States 516
Organization of the Islamic Conference 517
Organization of Petroleum Exporting Countries (OPEC) 61, 327, 335, 517
Organisation for Economic Co-operation and Development (OECD) 339
Development Assistance Committee (DAC) 2, 339
and environment
'Orientalism' 31, 32, 524
Ougaard, M. 294
overpopulation 153, 339, 525

'ownership' (of reforms) 299, 300, 302, 309, 339

P

Pakistan 48, 80, 131, 154, 307, 381, 396
basic indicators 293, 511, 513
Benazir Bhutto's rule 458
colonial legacy 43, 45, 219, 455
East Pakistan 455, 456
General Ayub Khan's rule 456, 457
General Musharraf's rule 458–60
General Yahya Khan's rule 456
General Zia-ul Haq's rule 457–8, 461
and globalization 513
Kashmir issue 454, 455, 456, 457, 458, 459
key dates 454
Legal Framework Order 459
map 453
military domination explained 452, 453, 455, 457, 461
Muslim state 133, 456
Nawaz Sharif's rule 458
Pakistan People's Party 456, 457, 458
and Taliban 459
US relations 459
Zulfikar Ali Bhutto's rule 224, 456, 457, 458
Palestine 130, 365, 380
Park, President Chung Hee 501, 504
Parsons, Talcott 18
Pastor, Robert 280
path dependence 37, 38, 274, 525
patriarchy 149, 150, 201, 525
patrimonial authority 213, 214, 222, 225, 493
neo-patrimonialism 20, 234, 280, 296, 524
patron–client relations 5, 20, 174, 221, 222, 279, 525
patronage 97, 99, 221, 225, 245
Payne, Anthony 37, 302
people power 188–207
and democratization 190–4
and development 194–201
movements 4, 186, 187–9, 194, 205, 525
weaknesses 202–3
see also global justice movement; social movements
Perham, Margery 36, 49
Peru 324
Sendero Luminoso 214
Philippines 40, 157, 180, 190–1, 193, 194, 203, 361